REAL
ESTATE
FINANCE

Jerome Dasso
University of Oregon

Gerald Kuhn
Northern Illinois University

REAL ESTATE FINANCE

PRENTICE-HALL, INC., ENGLEWOOD CLIFFS, NEW JERSEY 07632

Library of Congress Cataloging in Publication Data

Dasso, Jerome J.
  Real estate finance,

  (Prentice-Hall series in real estate)
  Bibliography: p.
  Includes index.
  1. Housing—United States—Finance. 2. Mortgages—
United States. 3. Real property—United States.
4. Real estate business—United States. I. Kuhn,
Gerald. II. Title. III. Series.
HD7293.Z9D37 1983   332.7′2′0973   82-20482
ISBN 0-13-762757-2

Editorial/production supervision and interior design by Margaret Rizzi
Cover design by Zimmerman/Foyster Design
Manufacturing buyer: Ed O'Dougherty

PRENTICE-HALL SERIES IN REAL ESTATE

Printed in the United States of America

10 9 8 7 6 5 4 3 2 1

ISBN 0-13-762757-2

Prentice-Hall International, Inc., *London*
Prentice-Hall of Australia Pty. Limited, *Sydney*
Editora Prentice-Hall do Brasil, Ltda., *Rio de Janeiro*
Prentice-Hall Canada Inc., *Toronto*
Prentice-Hall of India Private Limited, *New Delhi*
Prentice-Hall of Japan, Inc., *Tokyo*
Prentice-Hall of Southeast Asia Pte. Ltd., *Singapore*
Whitehall Books Limited, *Wellington, New Zealand*

Contents

three

Mortgage Types, 30

four

Mortgage Clauses, 56

five

Mortgage Default and Its Implications, 81

six

Trust Deed Financing, 102

appendix to chapter fourteen, 252

fifteen

Property Analysis, 260

sixteen

Lender Considerations and Analysis, 273

seventeen

Borrower Considerations and Analyses, 289

eighteen

Loan Repayment Patterns, 303

nineteen

Loan Negotiation Calculations, 321

twenty

Financing Residential Income Property, 341

twenty-one

Creative Financing, 361

PART 4   SECONDARY INSTITUTIONS
AND SOURCES OF FUNDS

twenty-two

Calculations for Buying
and Selling Existing Loans, 384

twenty-three

Federal Credit Agencies
and Mortgage-Backed Securities
in the Secondary
Mortgage Market, 399

APPENDICES

appendix a

Glossary, 419

appendix b

Time Value of Money Tables, 451

appendix c

Bibliography, 471

appendix d

Answers to Questions
and Problems, 475

appendix e

Index, 504

Preface

Real Estate Finance contains a basic knowledge of finance for anyone interested in real estate investing, brokerage, financing, developing, or counseling. Successful completion of a general course in real estate by the reader is assumed. Thus, a number of basic terms and concepts are only briefly reviewed in Chapter 1.

The subject matter of real estate finance is divided into four major sections in this work: (1) law and instruments, (2) primary institutions and sources of funds, (3) arranging and negotiating financing, and (4) secondary institutions and sources of funds. Basic concepts, terminology, and institutions are emphasized in the first two sections. Financial and economic analyses for making decisions and policies are increasingly emphasized in the last two sections.

Law and instruments are taken up first for a number of reasons. Basic knowledge, arrangements, and concepts are involved, which are seldom modified to any extent by negotiation between individual borrowers and lenders. The uniform instruments developed by the Federal National Mortgage Association and the Federal Home Loan Mortgage Corporation provide the focus of the discussion.

Primary lenders, the originators of new loans, are taken up next. These institutions are the mortgage market for most investor-borrowers.

Consequently, a knowledge of these institutions and their modes of operation is basic to an understanding of real estate finance.

In Part Three, loan negotiation and processing are discussed. Financial calculations and loan patterns are a crucial part of this discussion. The negotiations concerning amount borrowed, the interest rate, the term, and the debt service (the financial terms of the loan contract) between lenders and borrowers are also covered.

Finally, in Part Four, attention is focused on secondary lenders, including governmental agencies. These lenders and agencies provide liquidity to the mortgage markets and tie the markets to the national economy. A knowledge of these secondary institutions and how they function is extremely important to the long-run success of investors, brokers, lenders, builders, and developers, although the institutions themselves are removed from the immediate loan negotiations.

The pattern of our approach is to cover basic and more familiar material before going on to more complex financial calculations and loan negotiations. The intent is to gradually build from basic concepts to reality in the realm of real estate finance.

The viewpoint used herein is neutral, rather than biased toward either the lender or borrower. In this sense, the viewpoint is unique in that most books emphasize either the lenders' or borrowers' position.

The authors wish to thank Les Rouzaut and Jan Clayton for their patience in typing and retyping this manuscript. Appreciation is also extended to the editors at Prentice-Hall, John M. Connolly and Margaret Rizzi, who assisted in the preparation of this material, and finally, appreciation is expressed to our reviewers for their insightful reviews and helpful comments on the manuscript during its preparation.

Comments for improvement of this work would be greatly appreciated and may be sent to us in care of Prentice-Hall. We hope you find *Real Estate Finance* useful.

Jerome Dasso
University of Oregon

Gerald Kuhn
Northern Illinois University

one

Introduction and Overview

One definition of finance is "the science of managing money or wealth" of a person, an organization, or a nation. In speaking of real estate finance, it follows that we mean managing money or wealth as it affects or pertains to real property; and real estate involves huge wealth. According to Table 777 of the 100th edition of the *U.S. Statistical Abstract,* real estate accounts for over two-thirds of our tangible or nonhuman wealth. Real estate debt is currently greater than our gross federal debt. In turn, real estate finance is a significant part of our national economic activity. Indeed, it has been said that money is the life blood of real estate.

But what might real estate finance mean to us on an individual basis? Why should we study it?

We all wish to maximize our self interests, whether it be our wealth, free time, social status, power, or just the pure joy of living. Understanding real estate finance can help us to obtain the best type of housing for ourselves and our loved ones in a given situation. And, if we are investors, with a sound knowledge of real estate finance, we are likely to better manage and maximize our wealth while keeping risks of loss under control. We may learn to buy property on better terms, operate more effectively, and make the property more salable on disposition. We will also be able to negotiate more effectively with lenders. Indeed, knowledge of real estate finance may even enable us to obtain a job as a loan officer with a lending institution.

Real estate practitioners, or aspiring practitioners, may also benefit from a thorough knowledge of real estate finance. Greater recognition for competence may be received from clients and, in turn, higher fees or commissions may be realized. Difficult situations may be dealt with more readily. In short, a higher level of service may be rendered.

In this, our opening chapter, the intent is to provide basic background for the study of real estate finance and to provide an overview of material to be covered. We begin with a brief history of real estate finance and a short discussion of the real estate ownership cycle. We follow up with the organizational rationale of the book. And we conclude with a review of basic concepts.

BRIEF HISTORY

The practice of borrowing to help finance the ownership of real property dates back to the beginnings of civilization. By tradition and circumstances, real assets have inevitably been pledged as security for debts. Beyond this pledging, the history of real estate finance consists of hundreds of years of constant maneuvering for advantage between lenders and borrowers. In England, from which most of our real estate law comes, two principles of such financing eventually became generally recognized and accepted. First, the borrower was permitted to remain in possession of the property even though it was pledged. Second, the borrower had to repay the debt by an agreed date, termed the *law day,* or lose the property to the lender. These two principles continue to be accepted practice today, though almost every other aspect of the loan is subject to specific negotiation.

Financial institutions and governmental agencies entered the picture in the eighteenth and nineteenth centuries. The first life insurance company in America was chartered in 1759. In the late 1700s, commercial banks were first organized in the then new United States of America. In 1831, the first savings and loan association—the Oxford Provident Building Association—was established in Frankford, Pennsylvania. The federal government took exclusive control of the right to print money in 1863; previously individual banks issued their own notes which served as currency. Establishment of the Federal Reserve Banking System in 1913 greatly expanded the government's role in financial matters.

The federal government extended its influence into housing finance in the 1930s because of the Great Depression. The creation of the Federal Housing Administration (FHA) was undoubtedly the greatest single step in this direction. Amortizing loans and insured low downpayment loans were both ushered in by the FHA at this time. Government guarantees of VA loans against loss following World War II continued the emphasis on low down-payment loans to promote homeownership. As a result, homeownership increased from 44 percent in 1940 to 65 percent in 1975. During the quarter century from 1950 to 1975, mortgage debt grew by 1,015 percent, faster than any other major segment of public or private debt. See Fig. 1–1.

Beginning in 1966, periodic "credit crunches" and inflation made homeownership and real estate financing in general even more difficult. Interest rates on home loans increased to approximately 18 percent by late 1981. Construction costs nearly tripled in this period. The credit crunches, and the wildly fluctuating interest rates that resulted, have forced the development of new lending arrangements. Thus, today, in addition to fixed-rate mortgage loans, we see graduated payment, variable-rate, and renegotiable-rate loans. It appears that more things are happening faster in real estate finance, which is consistent with the theme of Alvin Toeffler's *Future Shock*. Anyone aspiring to a career in real estate as an investor or a practitioner needs a sound knowledge of real estate finance, as stated above. A sound knowledge will make it much easier to put and hold deals together and to adjust to change. As of this writing, unless a practitioner or investor understands and engages in "creative financing," nothing happens. Trends, economic conditions, and recent legislation all point to even greater importance being attached to creative financing. In addition, the steadily rising interest rates have resulted in many financial institutions paying higher rates on deposits than what is earned on mortgage loans in their investment portfolio. As a result, many of these institutions totter on the edge of insolvency.

FIGURE 1–1 Net Public and Private Debt[1]

(Billions of dollars, end of selected years, 1950–1975)

YEAR	PUBLIC			PRIVATE				TOTAL PUBLIC AND PRIVATE
	Gross Federal	State Local	Total	Corporate	Nonfarm Mortgage	Consumer and Other	Total	
1950	$256	$ 22	$278	$ 142	$ 55	$ 49	$ 246	$ 524
1960	284	65	349	303	151	112	566	915
1970	370	145	515	797	345	255	1,397	1,912
1975	533	223	756	1,287	613	387	2,281	3,037
PERCENT INCREASE 1950–1975	108	914	172	806	1,015	690	827	480

[1]1975 is the last year for which complete data are reported for all of these categories. Gross federal debt amounted to $971.2 billion in July 1981, whereas total mortgage debt outstanding jumped to $1,474.9 billion in the first quarter of 1981, according to Tables 1.41 and 1.55 of the August 1981 *Federal Reserve Bulletin*.

SOURCE: *Statistical Abstract of the United States,* 99th edition, Washington, D.C., U.S. Government Printing Office 1978. Table 881. Federal debt adjusted to gross to put on par with other types of debt.

The ownership cycle of real estate may be divided into three distinct phases insofar as the types of decisions made. The three phases are (1) acquisition, (2) ownership administration, and (3) disposition. Numerous decisions must be faced in the acquisition phase relative to investor goals and constraints, the investment climate, judgments about the specific property under consideration and its value, negotiation to purchase, and financing negotiations. These decisions must often be made in a matter of days or weeks.

Once ownership is acquired, relatively few decisions are necessary even though the period may last several years. Many of the decisions of acquisition must be made again during disposition, only from the seller's viewpoint. Again, the time span in which these decisions must be made is relatively short.

Much has been written about the management of financial institutions and how they may best maximize their assets or wealth. Relatively little has been written, however, about how an individual who is aspiring to real estate ownership or investment might best maximize his or her position in the passage through the ownership cycle.[1] In this text we are mainly interested in the financing aspects of the cycle. However, a brief review of the decision-making and administrative processes, as they apply in real estate, seems to be in order.

The Decision-making Process

The decision-making process is a series of orderly steps that encourages logical thinking and that is aimed toward solving a problem. The steps that might be taken in handling a real estate financing problem are listed below.

1. *Recognition of decision or problem situation.* Based on personal objectives or experience, the need to make a choice or to take some action becomes evident. For example, a couple wants money to buy a duplex as an investment. The problem is to obtain the money for a down payment at the least cost and with the least risk.

2. *Data collection.* Collect all pertinent data or facts within reasonable limits based on the importance of the problem and the time available to make a decision. The investors in our example investigate selling

---

[1]Alfred A. Ring and Jerome Dasso, *Real Estate Principles and Practices,* 9th ed. (Englewood Cliffs, N.J.: Prentice-Hall, Inc., 1981), chap. 1. See for a longer discussion of the real estate investment cycle.

stocks, taking money out of savings, selling one car, increasing the loan against their house, or borrowing on a short-term note.

3. *Problem identification.* The collected information is studied and key issues or subproblems are identified. Our investors decide they want a balanced investment program and that they need the quick liquidity provided by savings for possible emergencies. One car is inadequate for their transportation needs. A short-term loan seems a poor way to finance a long-term investment. However, their lender–mortgagee will advance additional monies against their house without any substantial change in terms.

4. *Comparison of alternatives.* Our investors now have several ways to raise money for their venture. They also have the choice to act now or to not make the investment. The time for a decision has arrived.

5. *Decision making.* The entire situation is reviewed, and the action most likely to give the desired result is chosen. In our example, the couple decides to borrow on a long-term loan against their personal residence to finance a long-term investment. Thus, they maintain their liquidity, mobility, and balanced investment program while keeping risk at a minimum.

In practice, the decision-making process is usually not quite this clean or clear-cut. Much discussion and going back and forth between the steps is likely. Thus, except for the last step, the sequence may not be exactly as indicated here. The important considerations are that facts be collected and studied and alternatives be identified and considered prior to making a decision. The steps ultimately boil down to answering three questions: (1) What problem is to be solved? (2) What are the alternative solutions? and (3) Which of the alternative solutions is the best?

THE ADMINISTRATIVE PROCESS

Making a decision to act is the first step in the administrative process. In this process, the emphasis is more on action than on analysis, and the action usually involves working with and through people. Five steps are involved.

1. *Deciding to achieve an objective.* For our purposes, our investors have decided to obtain the down payment on the duplex by refinancing their house.

2. *Organizing resources.* Money and people must be mobilized to accomplish an objective. In our example, the investors must plan more specifically how they will accomplish their objectives. The terms of borrowing are double checked on the refinancing and on the duplex. The cash requirements to carry both loans and the time requirements to manage and maintain the duplex must be determined and provided for. In effect, it must be determined that resources are adequate to cover the proposed venture.

3. *Exerting leadership.* Action is sparked to put the plan into action. The purchase of the duplex is negotiated and the residence refinanced.

4. *Controlling operations.* The new situation is monitored to assure that the plan is working as expected. Satisfactory tenants are found; cash flows are within expected tolerances. Soon, the new situation is accepted as the status quo.

5. *Periodic reevaluation.* On a longer term basis, the status quo must be occasionally reviewed to determine if changes or adjustments are needed. In one sense, this is fine tuning; in another sense, it is preparation for the next major decision or action.

CONTINUING THE CYCLE

An investor goes through the ownership cycle with each property. Thus, an owner may be negotiating for one property and disposing of another, while at the same time managing and maintaining several others. In every phase of the cycle, financial considerations are important. So let us return to our main topic, real estate finance.

ORGANIZATIONAL RATIONALE

The overall purpose of this book is to provide a basic knowledge of real estate finance for anyone interested in or aspiring to enter the field of real estate. The emphasis is on the financing of residential real estate.

The viewpoint of an investor acting in his or her own self-interest is maintained throughout the text, and the content of our discussion goes from the specific to the general. Anyone mastering the content of this book will have all the financial knowledge and tools necessary to successfully maneuver in real estate, financially speaking. The content is also appropriate for anyone interested in a career as a salesperson, broker, appraiser, builder, counselor, lender, manager, or escrow agent. Mastery will enable him or her to render a very competent level of services to clients, to convey a professional image to clients, and, in turn, to earn higher fees or commissions from clients. Understanding the investor-client's viewpoint and needs is of great help to any practitioner.

The organizational rationale for the book involves dividing the content into four major divisions or sections.

1. Law and Instruments of Real Estate Finance
2. Primary Institutions and Sources of Funds
3. Arranging and Negotiating Financing
4. Secondary Institutions and Sources of Funds

These four sections make up the broad framework of what an investor-buyer needs to know to finance the purchase of a property. The first three sections represent the three sides of the financing triangle: (1) the alternative techniques, ways, or instruments of financing, (2) the immediate sources of the funds, usually institutions, and (3) negotiations and calculations leading to the financing contract or agreement. The content in the first two sections is highly descriptive, of necessity. In sections three and four analyses of decisions and policy are increasingly emphasized. Secondary institutions and sources of funds—the topics of the fourth section—are of considerable importance to the experienced and sophisticated investor, and are therefore taken up following completion of the basic topics.

LAW AND INSTRUMENTS OF REAL ESTATE FINANCE

The basic techniques or instruments of financing real estate and the implied legal considerations of each are taken up in the first section. Thus, the many alternative ways of arranging financing, their uses, and their implications are taken up as a group. The most basic technique, of course, is the mortgage; thus several chapters are devoted to this instrument. Considerations are then given to alternative techniques, mainly the deed of trust, the land contract, and the lease. Many concepts carry over from mortgages to these other instruments or techniques.

Specific chapter numbers and titles in this section are as follows:

2. Mortgage Basics
3. Mortgage Types
4. Mortgage Clauses
5. Mortgage Default and Its Implications
6. Trust Deed Financing
7. Land Contract and Option Financing
8. Lease Financing

PRIMARY INSTITUTIONS AND SOURCES OF FUNDS

The nature and characteristics of the main sources of funds for debt financing are taken up next. Coverage of financial institutions is necessary because most funds for debt financing of real estate are provided through them. Each has its own lending motivations, procedures, and policies. The mortgage market is discussed before the institutions are discussed in detail in order to provide an integrated setting or background for the discussion. Specific chapter numbers and titles in this section are as follows:

9. Mortgage Market Overview
10. Private Depository Lenders
11. Private Nondepository Lenders
12. Government and Related Agencies

Private depository lenders include savings and loan associations, commercial banks, mutual savings banks, and credit unions. Nondepository lenders would include life insurance companies, pension funds, real estate investment trusts, mortgage companies, and private individuals.

Arranging and Negotiating Financing

The many considerations involved in arranging financing, including calculations, are taken up in Part Three. We open with a look at various ways to arrange investor or equity financing and at loan application and settlement procedures. We then consider the lender, the borrower, and the property as each pertains to the negotiations and pending loan arrangements. Next, we take up financial calculations and loan repayment patterns as they enter into the negotiations. The terms and the cost of borrowing are crucial to successful leveraging. We even look at creative or innovative financing as it might be used in times when money is tight or unavailable. A one-family residence is used in most of our discussions, although one chapter is devoted entirely to the financing of residential income properties. Chapter numbers and titles are as follows:

13. Equity Planning and Funding
14. Loan Underwriting and Settlement Procedures
15. Property Analysis
16. Lender Considerations and Analysis
17. Borrower Considerations and Analysis
18. Loan Repayment Patterns
19. Loan Negotiation Calculations
20. Financing Residential Income Property
21. Creative Financing

Secondary Institutions and Sources of Funds

A sophisticated investor or practitioner knows that an understanding of secondary institutions and sources of funds is important to his or her eventual success. We therefore move into a discussion of institutions that operate behind the scenes, including governmental agencies. These institutions tie mortgage markets to the financial markets of our country. Chapters in this section are as follows:

22. Calculations for Buying and Selling Existing Loans
23. Federal Credit Agencies and Mortgage-Backed Securities in the Secondary Mortgage Market

APPENDICES

A glossary of terms and phrases and a Bibliography are included in the Appendices along with Time Value of Money (TVM) Tables. Answers to the questions and problems at the end of the chapters are also included as Appendix D to aid the reader in his or her study of this material.

BASIC CONCEPTS REVIEWED

Every field has its own jargon or words of passage. Real estate finance is no exception in this respect. Accepted terminology greatly facilitates communication of those within the field. A review of the basic terminology for real estate finance therefore seems in order. We need these basic terms to quickly, effectively, and freely discuss real estate finance in more depth throughout the remainder of this book. Real estate finance as a course is usually taken after a general course in real estate in which real estate terminology is defined and discussed, so the review here is brief. The term *financial leverage* is discussed in more depth because of its great importance in both real estate finance and investment.

FINANCING INSTRUMENTS OR TECHNIQUES

Any property is financed in its entirety at all times. An owner may finance the entire amount without borrowing, which is termed *100 percent equity financing. Equity,* of course, means the owner's interest in the property. Alternatively, an owner may pledge the property to secure a loan, as with mortgage, trust deed, or land contract financing. From an owner's viewpoint, borrowing against a property is termed *debt financing;* and from a lender's point of view, making a loan to help finance a property is termed *credit financing.* When money is borrowed against a property, the total of the equity position and the loan equals the value of the property. Leasing provides another way to control a property, though a loan may not be specifically involved. Let us review these alternative techniques.

Mortgage. The traditional instrument in pledging a property to secure a debt is a *mortgage*. A mortgage is a written legal document. To be valid and enforceable, it must be accompanied by a promissory note or bond evidencing the debt. The owner-borrower is the *mortgagor*. The lender is the *mortgagee*.

Trust Deed. The property is pledged in a significantly different way in a trust deed financing arrangement. Three parties, rather than two, are involved: an owner-borrower, a trustee, and a lender-beneficiary. The trustee typically holds title to the pledged property during the life of the loan, with the *power of sale* on default. Upon repayment of the loan, the trustee returns title to the owner-borrower by a deed of reconveyance.

Land Sale Contract. A written agreement between a buyer and seller for the sale of a property, with payment stretched out over an extended period is a land sale contract. The seller provides the financing and retains title to secure the loan. The buyer usually gets immediate occupancy and use. Title is conveyed to the buyer when all terms have been met and the full purchase price paid. A land sale contract is also known as a land contract, a contract for deed, an installment land contract, and a real estate contract.

Lease. Real estate may be controlled through the use of a lease rather than through ownership. No debt is incurred by the user, although a personal obligation to pay rent is taken on. The owner becomes a *landlord* or a *lessor;* the user becomes a *tenant* or *lessee.* Lease arrangements, including sale and leaseback contracts, are widely used by businesses to control real estate and at the same time to raise or to conserve working capital. The working capital is assumed to be used more advantageously in the business itself. In a similar sense, a month-to-month lease for an apartment is a financing device for the tenant.

LOAN TERMINOLOGY

In negotiationg a loan, lenders and borrowers have found common terminology substantially helps to keep communications clear. That is, some terms or concepts relate to the loan and not to the legal instrument. Therefore, they remain the same whether the loan is secured by a mortgage, trust deed, or land contract. Key terms of loan negotiation are:

1. Loan-to-value ratio
2. Loan amount or principal
3. Interest rate
4. Loan duration or term
5. Loan amortization provisions
6. Debt service

An $80,000 loan on a $100,000 residence is used to illustrate our review of these concepts.

Loan-to-Value Ratio (LVR). The proportion of a property's market value financed by a loan is termed a loan-to-value ratio (LVR). The ratio is usually expressed as a percentage. In our illustration, the ratio is 80 percent.

$$LVR = \frac{Loan}{Market\ Value} = \frac{\$\ 80,000}{\$100,000} = 80\%$$

The lower the loan-to-value ratio allowed by a lender, the greater the amount of down payment required of a given borrower. Also, the lower the ratio, the lower the risk of loss to a lender in case of borrower default. The balance of the purchase price or market value is provided by the buyer-investor as a cash down payment of owner's equity.

Loan Amount or Principal. The number of dollars actually borrowed or the remaining balance of a loan is termed the loan *principal*. The principal directly affects the dollar debt service required of a borrower. The greater the amount borrowed, the greater must be the income of the borrower to meet the debt service requirements. In our example, $80,000 is the loan principal.

Interest Rate. *Interest* is the rent or price paid for the use of money. An interest rate is therefore the amount paid to borrow money, usually stated and calculated as a certain percent per year of the amount borrowed. The higher the interest rate, the higher the price to borrow money and therefore the higher the payments for principal repayment and interest over the life of the loan. For example, at 8 percent annual interest, our $80,000 loan would require yearly interest payments of $6,400. At 10 percent, yearly interest would equal $8,000, and at 12 percent, $9,600. It follows that lowering the interest rate serves to reduce the size of payments required on a loan.

Loan Duration or Term. *Duration* or *term* is the period of time allowed for the borrower to repay the loan. The maturity date in the note or loan agreement determines the duration. A loan duration of from 20 to 30 years is typical for residential properties. Extending the term of a loan acts to lower required debt service or loan payments.

Loan Amortization Provision. Periodic repayment of the principal amount of borrowed money is termed *amortization*. The amount for repayment is usually made at the same time interest payments are made. Amortization may not be required at all, as with a straight-term loan. With a straight-term loan, interest payments must only be made periodically, with repayment of the principal in full at the end of the loan contract. Repayment is usually by refinancing. The loan agreement may also call for partial amortization only.

Debt Service. The periodic payment required on a loan for interest and usually for principal reduction is termed *debt service.* If amortization or principal reduction is not required, debt service may consist of interest only. Debt service reflects the principal amount, the interest rate, the duration, and the amortization provisions of the loan. The larger the principal amount, the greater is the required debt service. The higher the interest rate, the greater is the debt service. And the shorter the duration, the higher is the required debt service. Debt service is sometimes considered to include payments for taxes and hazard insurance; actually these amounts are held in reserve accounts to meet the indicated charges and do not pertain specifically to the debt.

LEVERAGE

Real estate investors borrow money out of necessity or for leverage. Typically, about 20 to 30 percent of personal income goes for housing. At the same time, most buyers have savings equal to only 10 to 25 percent of the purchase price of a home. Therefore, the buyer must borrow the balance, which requires periodic debt service. Thus, most home buyers are borrowers of necessity. The alternative is to make rental payments. Home buyers, as well as other borrowers of necessity, frequently benefit from leverage without explicitly intending to do so, as has happened in recent years with the sharp increases in the values of housing units and other real estate.

Leverage is borrowing money at an agreed cost or interest rate to acquire an investment that hopefully earns at a higher rate. That is, funds are borrowed to purchase an investment, with the expectation that the acquired property will yield a return greater than the cost of borrowing the money. The investor therefore expects to earn a return on the borrowed money as well as on his or her own money. The net effect is to give a higher rate of return on the investor's money. The term *leverage* is an economic analogy to the use of a lever to gain mechanical advantage, as using a pole and fulcrum to move a large boulder. The saying "the deeper in debt one can get, the better off one becomes" is based on the assumption of *positive leverage.*

If the property does not earn at a rate equal to or higher than the cost of borrowed money, the result is *negative leverage.* With negative leverage, the investor's rate of return is reduced, sometimes sharply.

Understanding and using leverage is the key to successful real estate investing. Another term for leverage is "operating on OPM—other people's money." Two examples will serve to illustrate more specifically how leverage works. One involves increased return due to an increase in

FIGURE 1–2 Leverage Through Value Increase

Property Interests	Initial Financing	Financing after Property Value Increases
Market value	$100,000	$120,000
Less debt (fixed)	− 80,000	− 80,000
Owner's equity	$ 20,000	$ 40,000

property value; the second is due to an increase in earnings. Negative leverage is also illustrated.

Assume an investor owns a $100,000 residence with an $80,000 mortgage loan against it. The investor's equity in the property is therefore $20,000. An increase of $20,000 in the market value of the residence, to $120,000, goes entirely to the investor. Thus the value of the investor's position doubles from $20,000 to $40,000. The debt, at $80,000, remains unchanged. The change and the effect are shown in Fig. 1–2.

Let us also look at a 20-percent decrease in the value of the residence. The owner-investor's position decreases to zero value, whereas liability on the loan continues. This, of course, is negative leverage. A further decrease in value might well lead to foreclosure on the loan. On the other hand, the value of the investor's position could recover with an increase in the property value back to $100,000. See Fig. 1–3.

Our second example shows how leverage works on a rate of return basis. The example is kept simple to make the principle of leverage stand out. Assume a commercial lot worth $100,000 is under a long-term net lease for $12,000 per year. The tenant pays taxes, insurance, and all other costs of operation. Without mortgage or debt financing, the rate of return to the owner is 12 percent. Suppose, however, that the owner pledges the lot as security for a long-term loan of $80,000 at 10 percent, with no amortization required. That is, only interest payments of $8,000 must be paid each year ($80,000 times 10 percent equals $8,000). The difference in income of $4,000 ($12,000 less $8,000 equals $4,000) goes entirely to the owner-investor. And the owner now has only $20,000 invested in the property ($100,000 less the $80,000 loan equals $20,000). The

FIGURE 1–3 Negative Leverage Through Value Decrease

Property Interest	Initial Financing	Financing after Property Value Decreases
Market value	$100,000	$80,000
Less debt (fixed)	− 80,000	− 80,000
Owner's equity	$ 20,000	- 0 -

FIGURE 1–4 Leveraging or Increasing Rate of Return through Borrowing

	Before Borrowing	After Borrowing
Annual net income	$ 12,000	$12,000
Less interest on debt ($80,000 × 10% = $8,000)	- 0 -	8,000
Equals net cash flow to investor	$ 12,000	$ 4,000
Divided by value of investor's equity	100,000	20,000
Equals rate of return to equity	12%	20%

owner's rate of return has now been leveraged up to 20 percent. See Fig. 1–4.

The benefits of leveraging are not obtained without a cost. An investor-borrower incurs increased risk of loss of income or of the property. If conditions become bad, the investor's position may be wiped out through negative leverage, as previously shown. If conditions become even worse, the investor may actually have to come up with additional money. A prudent investor takes this risk into account in his or her strategy and decision making.

SUMMARY

Investors and practitioners can greatly benefit from the study of real estate finance, which will better enable them to acquire a desired property or to earn higher fees and commissions. Lender-borrower conflict and cooperation is a thread that runs throughout the history of real estate finance. Since the mid 1960s, a sound knowledge of real estate finance is becoming increasingly important because of continuing inflation and periodic credit crunches.

Finance is also important in the real estate ownership cycle because money is the life blood of real estate sales and construction activity. The decision-making process surrounding real estate purchase involves five steps: (1) recognize problem situation, (2) collect data, (3) identify problem, (4) pose alternatives, and (5) make decision. Decisions are then implemented through the administrative process.

The organizational rationale of the book centers around four major sections: (1) law and instruments, (2) primary institutions and sources of funds, (3) arranging and negotiating financing, and (4) secondary institutions and sources of funds. An investor or a practitioner needs knowledge in all four of these areas to achieve the greatest success in the long run. Basic financing instruments are the (1) mortgage, (2) trust deed, (3) land contract, and (4) lease. The key considerations in negotiating a loan are: (1) loan-to-value ratio, (2) principal amount, (3) interest rate, (4) duration or term, (5) amortization provisions, and (6) debt service. Leverage, borrowing at a lower rate than a property is expected to earn, is the basic technique for maximizing return or wealth in real estate investing.

KEY TERMS

Amortization	Interest	Mortgagee
Credit Financing	Landlord	Mortgagor
Debt Financing	Lessee	Negative Leverage
Debt Service	Lessor	Power of Sale
Duration	Leverage	Principal
Equity	Loan-to-Value Ratio (LVR)	Tenant
Equity Financing	Mortgage	Term

QUESTIONS FOR REVIEW AND DISCUSSION

1. State or list at least three reasons why it is necessary to understand the financing of real estate.

2. What is the real estate ownership or decision-making cycle? How does real estate finance relate to the cycle?

3. State or list the five steps in the decision-making process, in their proper order or sequence.

4. State or list the steps in the administrative process in their proper order.

5. What are the four major divisions or sections into which the subject matter of this book is divided?

6. Explain the meaning and implications of leverage. Use an example if necessary.

7. Match the following key terms and definitions:

    a. Amortization   _____
    b. Debt Service   _____
    c. Leverage   _____
    d. Equity   _____
    e. Loan-to-Value
        Ratio   _____

    1. The market value of a property less any debt against it.
    2. An impediment to clear title of realty.
    3. The unpaid balance of a loan.

f. Mortgagee   _____

g. Principal   _____

4. Making periodic payments for interest and repayment of principal.
5. The lender.
6. The borrower.
7. Principal of a loan divided by market value.
8. The periodic payments on a loan.
9. Use of borrowed funds to increase rate of return.

two

Mortgage Basics

The mortgage is the traditional instrument for legally pledging real estate to secure a debt in our country. But mortgaging a property has varying legal implications depending on the state in which the property is located and the specific instrument used. We look at mortgage types and clauses in the next two chapters. In this chapter we concentrate on concepts that are generally important in the mortgage transaction. These concepts have proven central in the continuing struggle between borrowers and lenders as they continually seek advantage in mortgage loan negotiations.

Perhaps the most basic consideration in this struggle is whether a mortgage is regarded as a lien or a transfer of title. Use of alternative financing instruments and clauses to gain advantage is a second aspect of this competition. And the rights and duties of the parties during the life of a mortgage is a third aspect. We take up these topics early to set the stage for more specific discussion of mortgage finance in later chapters. Major topic headings are as follows:

1. History of Mortgage Law
2. Current Theories of Mortgage Law
3. Basic Mortgage Arrangements
4. Basic Mortgage Instruments

5. Transfer of Mortgaged Property
6. Assignment of Mortgage and Note
7. Termination of Mortgage

HISTORY OF MORTGAGE LAW

Our mortgage law traces from fourteenth-century England to modern-day America. In the fourteenth century, an owner who desired to borrow funds and use real property as security for the debt gave the deed to the property to the lender. The lender then had two options: (1) to allow the borrower to retain possession of the property, or (2) to take personal possession of the property. If the lender took possession, the lender was required to apply collected rents toward the reduction of the debt.

The deed contained a *defeasance clause* that provided for cancellation of the deed and the return of title to the borrower on payment of the debt. The borrower was required to pay the debt in full by the specified due date. If the debt was not paid by the due date, default occurred and the borrower's interest in the property was terminated. In these circumstances the lender took possession of and clear title to the property.

Termination of the borrower's rights was particularly harsh in some cases. For example, the mortgage debt might amount to only a small fraction of the value of the property. Or the borrower might be robbed on the way to pay the debt. Under these conditions, some borrowers petitioned the king to regain ownership of the property by being allowed to pay the debt and accrued interest after the due date. Initially this privilege to regain ownership after the due date was granted only in cases of hardship. But by the early seventeenth century it became a common law right called the *equitable right of redemption* or the *equity of redemption*.

The development of the borrower's equitable right of redemption in turn put the lenders at a disadvantage. While the lender received title to and possession of the property on default, the borrower retained the right to regain title and possession. Lenders therefore countered this borrower's equitable right of redemption with a foreclosure suit. On default, the lender asked the courts to enter an order for foreclosure. The *foreclosure decree* or *order* specified the time period in which the borrower might exercise the equitable right of redemption. If not exercised within the specified time period, the borrower's equitable right of redemption was foreclosed or terminated. This concept continues today.

A lender receiving possession and clear title to the property on termination of the borrower's equitable right of redemption is termed *strict foreclosure*. Losing a property worth $50,000 for failure to pay a debt of $10,000 seems somewhat harsh. Thus, foreclosure and public sale gradually replaced strict foreclosure in the United States. Under *foreclosure and public sale* the property is sold under court order after the foreclosure of the borrower's equitable right of redemption. If any proceeds remain after paying the court costs and the lender's claim, they are given to the borrower.

Borrowers gained an additional advantage with the passing of statutory redemption laws. *Statutory redemption* allows a borrower to redeem a property after foreclosure and public sale or after strict foreclosure. Statutory redemption requires the borrower to pay the lender's claim and associated costs to regain title. The time period for the exercise of statutory redemption varies according to state statute. This statutory right of redemption is, by definition, not based on common law.

CURRENT THEORIES OF MORTGAGE LAW

Mortgage law in the United States varies from state to state, as mentioned. States are often classified as following either the title theory, lien theory, or intermediate theory, depending on the principles underlying their laws. One method of distinguishing whether a state follows the principles of the title theory or lien theory is whether or not the mortgage passes title to the lender. If title passes, the state may be classified as following the *title theory*. A second method of classification is based on the passage of possession after default. If possession passes to the lender immediately after default, the state follows the title theory. Few states conform exactly and fully to either lien theory or title theory principles. A combination or mixture of these principles results in classification of the state as following the *intermediate theory*.

Under either classification system about 60 percent of the states are clearly in the lien theory category. All of the states west of the Mississippi River, with the exception of Missouri and Arkansas, follow the lien theory. In turn, trust deeds are used more widely in the west. A classification system that emphasizes passage of title puts approximately 25 percent of the states in the title theory category. About 15 percent would be classified as intermediate theory states. A classification system emphasizing passage of possession on default marks about 15 percent of the states as title theory states. In turn, approximately 25 percent would be classified as intermediate theory states.

TITLE THEORY

In a title theory state, a mortgage conveys title to the lender. In its strongest form the lender has the right to take possession and collect the rents immediately after the borrower signs the mortgage. A few title theory states follow this form. In other title theory states the borrower has the right to possession until default occurs. On default the lender receives the right to possession. Upon repayment of the debt, title is returned to the borrower by a provision in the mortgage termed the *defeasance clause.*

LIEN THEORY

A mortgage does not convey title to the lender in a lien theory state. The mortgage is merely a lien against the property offered as security for the debt. In its strongest form the lender receives the rights to possession and to rents only after the foreclosure sale and the expiration of any statutory redemption period. In some lien theory states, lenders use an *assignment of rents,* which gives the lender the right to possession and to collect the rents immediately on default by the borrower. In other lien theory states, the lender has the right to request the appointment of a receiver to manage the property and to collect rents on default by the borrower.

INTERMEDIATE THEORY

States that follow a theory somewhere between the title theory and the lien theory are called intermediate theory states. In a typical intermediate theory state, the mortgage is written as a lien but on default, title transfers to the lender. On default or on the initiation of foreclosure action, the lender has the right to request possession or the appointment of a receiver.

BASIC MORTGAGE ARRANGEMENTS

A real estate mortgage pledges real property as security for a debt or obligation. The mortgage may take any of several forms as a legal document or arrangement. These forms include the regular mortgage, the equitable mortgage, the trust deed, and the security deed.

REGULAR MORTGAGE

The regular mortgage is the customary mortgage form in 38 states. A *regular mortgage* is one that meets all of the statutory requirements for a mortgage in a given state. A regular mortgage might also be called a standard mortgage for the state in question. It is usually a form document on which the specific details of the mortgage agreement may be entered on blank lines at appropriate places in the instrument.

TRUST DEED

The *trust deed* or *deed of trust* is the dominant form of securing realty in 11 states. It differs from the other forms of mortgages in that it involves three parties rather than two. A trust deed in the nature of a mortgage transfers title to the property to a third party trustee. The borrower is the trustor, and the lender is the beneficiary of the trust. If the borrower repays the debt, the trustee reconveys the title to the borrower. If the borrower defaults, the trustee takes action to sell the pledged property, with the proceeds going first to satisfy the lender's claim. Trust deeds are discussed in detail in Chap. 6.

SECURITY DEED

The security deed is the customary form of mortgage instrument in Georgia. In that state, a security deed conveys title to the lender, whereas a regular mortgage merely creates a lien. Specifically, a *security deed* includes a statement that it is a deed to secure a debt and is not a regular mortgage. The amount of the debt is also stated along with a granting to the lender of the power to sell the property on default. A security deed involves two parties only, a borrower and a lender.

EQUITABLE MORTGAGE

An equitable mortgage may be created when the document intended to offer a property as security does not conform to state statutory requirements for a regular mortgage, a security deed, or a trust deed. An *equitable mortgage* is therefore a financing arrangement that functions like a mortgage, even though it is not legally termed a mortgage. For example, sale of a property under a sale and leaseback with a repurchase option may be treated as an equitable mortgage. Or a mortgage document may contain a material defect and the court declares it to be an equitable mortgage. Equitable, as used here, refers to legal fairness or fair dealing. If an equitable mortgage is recognized and title has been conveyed to the lender, courts allow borrowers to recover title upon repayment of the monies in question. Several examples may be appropriate to clarify the discussion here.

Assume a borrower gives a deed to owned property as security for a debt. The deed may not mention the debt. Thus, the situation makes it appear to be a sale of the property. If the court finds that, in fact, the deed was given to secure a debt, the arrangement will be treated as an equitable mortgage and the borrower is enabled to regain title by repaying the debt.

For another example, assume that a buyer purchases property on an installment basis, as by land contract, and makes a substantial down payment. The buyer legally has the right to obtain title after making the last installment payment. If the buyer defaults, the court may consider the arrangement to be an equitable mortgage on reviewing the situation. The seller would then have to foreclose the property to clear the title to the property.

BASIC MORTGAGE INSTRUMENTS

Mortgaging real estate usually requires that the borrower sign two documents. One is either a promissory note or a bond. The note or bond serves as evidence of the debt. The signing of a note or bond makes the borrower personally liable for payment of the debt. The second is the pledge of the property as security for the debt, or the mortgage itself.

MORTGAGE NOTE

A *mortgage note* is a promissory note that is secured by a mortgage. A mortgage note is a written instrument in which the *obligor* (the borrower) makes a promise to pay the *obligee* (the lender). A bond is similar to a mortgage note except that it is more formal and may require a seal to make it valid. The essential elements of a valid mortgage note or bond are as follows:

1. A written instrument
2. An obligor and an obligee with contractual capacity
3. The obligor's promise to pay a specific sum
4. The terms of payment
5. A default clause including mortgage covenants by reference
6. Proper execution
7. Voluntary delivery and acceptance

By signing the mortgage note or bond, the borrower recognizes the existence of the debt, promises to meet the terms of payment, and agrees to the provisions for default. *Proper execution* means that the borrower must sign the document. While not generally required by law, it is good practice to have it witnessed, acknowledged, and in some states sealed. An *acknowledgment* is a formal declaration made before a public officer such as a notary public that the document is being signed voluntarily. *Voluntary delivery* means that the borrower signs it of his or her own free will and offers the instrument to the lender. *Acceptance* means that the lender willingly agrees to be bound by the provisions of the instrument.

The main significance of signing a note or bond is that the borrower becomes personally liable for the payment of the debt. A lender holding both a note and a mortgage may seek payment of the claim under the note, the mortgage, or both. Usually a lender seeks repayment by forcing a sale of the property under the terms of mortgage or trust deed. However, if the sale proceeds are not adequate, a lender may also collect repayment from the borrower personally. For example, assume the sale only produces $50,000, whereas the lender's claim totals $60,000. Thus there is a deficiency of $10,000. The lender may seek a deficiency judgment for $10,000 in a personal suit against the borrower, under the terms of the note or bond. If the lender wins the suit, a court grants a deficiency judgment. A *deficiency judgment* is a personal judgment against the borrower-mortgagor for the amount that sale proceeds fell short of the lender-mortgagee's claim. Thus, the borrower in our example would be forced to sell other assets to raise the $10,000 difference.

MORTGAGE CONTRACT

The purpose of a mortgage or trust deed is to pledge or promise real property as security for a debt. In the event of default, the mortgage allows the lender, if necessary, to force a sale of the property to provide the funds for the payment of the debt. The trust deed, discussed in Chap. 6, serves the same purpose but is enforced in a different manner.

The essentials of a valid mortgage are typically as follows:

1. A written instrument
2. A mortgagor and mortgagee with contractual capacity
3. An interest in property that may be offered as security
4. An offer of the interest in the property as security for the payment of a debt or obligation
5. An adequate description of the property
6. The mortgagor's covenants
7. Proper execution
8. Voluntary delivery and acceptance

In some states the mortgage must also contain a statement of the debt or obligation secured by the mortgage. Mortgagor's covenants and clauses are discussed in Chap. 4. A mortgagor-borrower must sign the mortgage in order for it to be binding. The mortgage must be acknowledged and in some states, witnessed. In a few states it also must be sealed.

A mortgage is valid between a mortgagor and a mortgagee without making public record of it, because both have actual notice of the arrangement. A third party who hears of the arrangement is deemed to have actual knowledge or notice of it. *Actual notice* means to have explicit knowledge of facts or information. A third party with actual notice is bound by it. However, if the mortgage is not recorded, third parties lacking actual notice are not bound. For example, assume Smith owns a property and has mortgaged it. The lender has not recorded the mortgage, and we are not aware of the existence of the mortgage. We purchase the property. The lender will not be able to foreclose on the mortgage and force the sale of the property to recover the debt. In this instance, the lender has lost the specific lien against the property. The situation could have been avoided by recording the mortgage. The lender-mortgagee does retain a personal claim against Smith.

Recording the mortgage provides constructive notice to all third parties. *Constructive notice* means everyone is presumed to have certain knowledge because it appears in the public records. The date of recording normally establishes the priority of a mortgage lien against other claims on the property. The mortgage must be recorded in the recorder's office at the township or county in which the property is located. In most states the mortgage must be acknowledged to be eligible for recording. And in some states it must be both witnessed and acknowledged.

TRANSFER OF MORTGAGED PROPERTY

The owner of a mortgaged property is free to sell his or her interest in the property unless the mortgage contract specifically contains a clause barring sale. The sale may be made free and clear of the mortgage, subject to the mortgage or with the purchaser assuming the mortgage.

FREE AND CLEAR

The owner of the mortgaged property contracting to sell it free and clear must arrange to have the mortgage released prior to or at the time of closing. The purchaser often obtains a new mortgage loan to pay a substantial portion of the purchase or sale price. In turn, a portion of the proceeds from the sale are used to pay the debt at the closing. Sometimes the mortgage lender makes a new mortgage loan to the purchaser while releasing the seller from the existing mortgage.

SUBJECT TO THE MORTGAGE

Buying a property *subject to the mortgage* means the purchaser recognizes the existence of the debt but does not become personally liable for the debt. The seller-mortgagor continues to have personal liability for the debt. The buyer makes payments to the lender to avoid foreclosure and loss of the equity investment in the property. But assume the buyer defaults on the payment of the mortgage note for some reason and there is a foreclosure and sale. In turn, the sale does not produce sufficient funds to pay the lender's claim. The purchaser's loss is limited to any equity investment in the property. The seller may be liable for payment of a deficiency judgment.

ASSUMPTION OF MORTGAGE

In an assumption the purchaser recognizes the existence of the mortgage and agrees to pay the debt. This may be accomplished by signing the mortgage or by signing an appropriate statement in the deed. Either provides evidence that the purchaser assumes personal responsibility for payment of the debt. An assumption does not automatically release the seller from the personal liability for payment of the debt. If a lender cannot recover his or her claim by a sale of the property upon default, a deficiency judgment may be obtained against either the buyer or the seller. Thus, an *assumption of a mortgage* is an agreement by a grantee (usually a buyer) to accept responsibility and become personally liable for payment of an existing mortgage loan against the property.

A seller may request and get a complete release from liability to the lender when the mortgage is assumed by the purchaser, which is termed *novation*. This may be accomplished by a separate written agreement between the grantor (seller), the grantee (buyer), and the lender, which is recorded after signing.

In recent years lenders have increasingly inserted due-on-sale clauses in mortgages because of rising interest rates. A *due-on-sale clause* requires a lender's approval to sell the property subject to the mortgage or for the buyer to assume the mortgage. This clause is valid in some states and invalid in other states. If valid, and the lender will not agree to a transfer of the property subject to the mortgage or to an assumption, the property must be refinanced. In effect, this means the property is sold free and clear of the mortgage. A lender may agree to the sale if the interest rate on the loan is adjusted at the same time. A due-on-sale clause is also known as an alienation clause, a nonalienation clause, a call clause, or a transfer of ownership acceleration clause.

ASSIGNMENT OF MORTGAGE AND NOTE

A lender is usually free to transfer his or her interest in the note and mortgage. The note is evidence of ownership of the debt, and the mortgage shows an interest in the property offered as security for the debt. The mortgage is transferable only if it is accompanied by the note evidencing the debt. The lender's interest may be transferred by merely delivering the note and mortgage. Normally the sale of the lender's interest is facilitated by a mortgage assignment.

A *mortgage assignment* is a transfer of the lender's rights in a mortgage contract. The *assignor* is the party transferring the interest in the note and mortgage. The *assignee* is the party receiving the note and mortgage.

An assignment of mortgage instrument includes a statement of consideration, identification of the mortgage, the mortgage balance as of a given date, the interest rate, and the date to which the interest has been paid. The assignment of mortgage should be signed by the assignor, witnessed, and/or acknowledged, and recorded. Usually the assignee requests a written statement, termed an *estoppel certificate,* from the borrower agreeing to the current outstanding balance on the mortgage. This written statement prevents the borrower from later arguing that a smaller amount is due to the assignee. Estop means to stop, prevent, or bar.

TERMINATION OF MORTGAGE

The most common method of terminating a mortgage is payment of the debt. In most states the lender gives the borrower a satisfaction piece when the debt is paid. A *satisfaction piece* is written evidence that the debt has been paid; it is, in effect, a receipt. A satisfaction piece is called a *release of mortgage* in a number of states. The satisfaction piece must be recorded to clear the title. In some states the satisfaction piece or other evidence of payment of the debt is presented to the county recorder, who then enters notice of cancellation on the face of the mortgage instrument. This entry has the effect of clearing title of the mortgage lien.

A lender may release the mortgage claim at his or her discretion. For example, parents sometimes lend their offspring money to purchase a home and take a mortgage in return. They can forgive the debt and release the mortgage at any time. The release must be recorded to clear the title, however.

A mortgage may be terminated in other ways. A mortgage can be terminated by foreclosure proceedings, as discussed. A mortgage can be terminated by the merger of the mortgagor's and mortgagee's interests. For example, a mortgagor may convey his or her interest in the property by deed to the mortgagee in return for a release from the mortgage obligation. This conveyance, if done to avoid foreclosure, is termed *giving a deed in lieu of foreclosure.* A mortgage can be terminated by the passage of a time period specified by the state statute of limitations. Assume that a state statute of limitations says that a mortgagee's rights must be exercised within ten years after the due date of the debt. Failure of the mortgagee to take action to enforce the mortgage within the specified time period means the mortgagee is not allowed to bring legal action after that date.

SUMMARY

Mortgaging property originated in fourteenth-century England. Gradually borrowers gained the equitable right of redemption in property under default, which allowed recovery of title after the due date of the loan. Then lenders gained the right of foreclosure which specifies the time period in which the equitable rights of redemption must be exercised. Strict foreclosure was gradually replaced by foreclosure and sale, which allowed the borrower to receive any excess proceeds from the sale left over after paying the court costs and the lender's claim. A number of states have since passed statutory redemption laws, which allow borrowers to regain title even after the foreclosure sale.

A majority of states follows the lien theory, whereas others follow either the title theory or the intermediate theory. Under the title theory the mortgage conveys title to the lender. Under the lien theory the mortgage is merely a lien and does not transfer title to the lender. A lender can acquire possession more quickly after default in states following the title theory and intermediate theory than in states under the lien theory.

Real property may be offered as security for a debt under a regular mortgage, a trust deed in the nature of a mortgage, and a security deed. The typical real estate mortgage transaction involves two instruments—a note and a mortgage. A note provides evidence of the debt and makes the borrower personally liable for the payment of the debt. A mortgage pledges the property as security for the debt. A mortgage note and a mortgage are both contracts, and they must conform to legal requirements to be valid. Both the mortgage note and the mortgage must conform to the statutory requirements for proper execution.

The mortgagor is sometimes able to sell the mortgaged property subject to the mortgage or with the purchaser assuming the existing mortgage. If the property is sold subject to the mortgage, the purchaser is not personally liable for the payment of the debt to the lender. If the property is sold with the purchaser assuming the mortgage, the purchaser is personally liable to the lender for the payment of the debt. The purchaser's assumption of the mortgage does not automatically release the original mortgagor from personal liability to the lender.

The lender may sell his or her interest under the mortgage and the note to another investor. The mortgage note must be transferred along with the mortgage. Usually an instrument called an assignment of mortgage is used along with the delivery of the note and mortgage.

The mortgage may be terminated in a number of ways including payment of the debt, foreclosure and sale, deed in lieu of foreclosure, and the statute of limitations. On payment of the debt, the mortgagee provides the mortgagor with a receipt called a satisfaction piece or a release of mortgage. The satisfaction piece or release must be recorded to clear the mortgagor's title of the mortgage lien.

KEY TERMS

Acknowledgment

Actual Notice

Assignee

Assignment (of Mortgage or Rents)

Assignor

Assumption of Mortgage

Constructive Notice

Deed in Lieu of Foreclosure

Defeasance Clause

Deficiency Judgment

Due-on-Sale Clause

Equitable Mortgage

Equitable Right of Redemption

Estoppel Certificate

Foreclosure

Foreclosure Decree or Order

Foreclosure and Public Sale

Intermediate Theory

Lien Theory

Mortgage Note

Novation

Obligee

Obligor

Regular Mortgage

Release of Mortgage

Satisfaction Piece

Security Deed

Statutory Redemption

Strict Foreclosure

Subject to the Mortgage

Title Theory

Trust Deed

QUESTIONS FOR REVIEW AND DISCUSSION

1. Briefly, how has mortgage financing changed from fourteenth-century England to modern-day America? Have these changes been desirable? Discuss.

2. Distinguish between the lien, title, and intermediate theories of mortgages in reference to the rights of mortgagees and mortgagors. Which theory do you favor? Why?

3. What is an equitable mortgage? How does it differ from a regular mortgage? Is it possible to recognize an equitable mortgage based on the document itself? Why or why not?

4. List and discuss briefly each of the seven essential elements of a valid mortgage note or bond.

5. What is the purpose of a note or bond?

6. Identify and discuss the eight essential elements of a mortgage.

7. What is the purpose of the mortgage?

8. What are the implications of a mortgage for the transferability of ownership of the pledged property?

9. In what ways may a mortgage be terminated?

10. Match the following key terms and definitions:
    a. Actual Notice _____   1. Presumed possession of
    b. Strict Foreclosure_____   knowledge contained in public records.

c. Deficiency
   Judgment   _____

d. Novation   _____

e. Assignor   _____

f. Defeasance
   Clause   _____

2. Provision for debt cancellation and return of title to borrower.

3. Possession and clear title given lender.

4. Personal judgment against borrower for short fall in sale proceeds.

5. Possessing explicit knowledge of facts or information

6. Release of seller–borrower obligations when mortgage assumed.

7. Party transferring interest in a contract, such as a mortgage, and a note.

8. Release of an interest upon receiving satisfaction.

three

Mortgage Types

Real estate serves as security for numerous types of loans. Three commonly known types of loans are conventional, FHA insured, and VA guaranteed loans. A loan type is really independent of the method used to pledge the property; that is, a property may be pledged by means of a mortgage, a trust deed, or a security deed. Thus, there is a trust deed equivalent and a security deed equivalent for each of the various types of mortgage loans discussed in this chapter. We limit our discussion here to the mortgage type of loan arrangement for convenience only.

Anyone connected with real estate finance can greatly benefit from having a thorough knowledge of mortgage types. Investor-borrowers gain increased flexibility and therefore greater advantage in obtaining a loan. For example, lenders sometimes offer limited types of mortgage loans through design or lack of knowledge of alternatives. Thus, a lender expecting higher interest rates may encourage borrowers to consider only variable-rate or rollover loans. In actuality, the borrower might find a long-term fixed-rate loan more desirable and make it a point to shop around until the appropriate type of loan is obtained. Brokerage personnel are better able to generate additional transactions by assisting clients to obtain the most appropriate loans for their needs. In similar fashion, developers, counselors, and educators can serve themselves or their clientele in a more competent manner when they have complete knowledge of mortgage types. In short, knowledge of mortgage types is a "must" in today's real estate market.

The various types of loans fall into six categories in this discussion: (1) traditional, (2) by stage of development, (3) by priority of lien, (4) by payment pattern, (5) by type of security, and (6) other. A given mortgage loan may fall into one or more categories. For example, the loan could be an FHA insured, graduated payment, package, first mortgage loan. On the other hand, some loan types are mutually exclusive. Thus, a given mortgage loan cannot be both a conventional loan and an FHA insured loan. These distinctions become apparent after each type of loan is fully understood. In other words, the emphasis is on understanding terminology.

TRADITIONAL CLASSIFICATION

Mortgage loans are often classified on the basis of whether there is government involvement associated with the loan. Government involvement includes insurance and guarantees of mortgage loans and direct loans made by government or governmental agencies. A loan without government involvement is called a *conventional loan*. The major government insured and guaranteed loans are discussed below in relation to nongovernment loans. These major governmental loans as well as other government-related loans are taken up again in Chap. 12 in greater detail.

CONVENTIONAL MORTGAGE

A mortgage loan that is not insured, guaranteed, or granted by government or a government agency is called a *conventional mortgage loan*. The term goes back to when governmental loans were first introduced; the choice open to a borrower was governmental backing or conventional financing.

Conventional loans are the dominant method of financing. They typically account for over 75 percent of the dollar volume of loans made in a given year. Many factors contribute to the dominance of the conventional loan. Borrowers often do not meet the eligibility requirements for government guaranteed or direct loans. For example, the maximum loan limits on FHA insured loans make them impractical for financing higher priced homes. And some lenders sometimes prefer not to make FHA insured and VA guaranteed loans.

Noninsured. Noninsured conventional mortgages normally have lower loan-to-value ratios, shorter maturities, and higher interest rates than do government insured or guaranteed loans. The interest rate is determined by market conditions. The typical upper range of loan-to-value ratios on noninsured conventional loans is from 75 to 80 percent. There is no third party to absorb the loss in case of default and foreclosure. The lender must depend on the borrower's income and/or the income from the property and the value of the property for repayment of the debt. The terms of the loan are negotiated between the borrower and lender in the context of the policies of the lender and governmental regulations governing the activities of the lender. Institutional regulations and policies are discussed in Chaps. 10, 11, and 12.

Insured. The typical upper range of loan-to-value ratios on conventional mortgage loans insured by private mortgage insurance companies is from 90 to 95 percent. The use of private mortgage insurance allows the borrower to reduce the required down payment from the range of 20 to 25 percent to the range of 5 to 10 percent. The reduction in the required down payment is necessary for many borrowers. Use of private mortgage insurance reduces the lender's risk or exposure to loss to a level roughly comparable to that on a noninsured loan with a loan-to-value ratio of 75 percent. Lender acceptance and borrower demand account for the widespread use of private mortgage insurance.

Private mortgage insurance typically insures the top 20 or 25 percent of the loan. The borrower pays the premium for the insurance and benefits by obtaining a higher percentage loan. A typical premium plan requires the borrower to pay one-half of one percent for the first year and one-quarter of one percent annually on the remaining mortgage balance. The lender usually terminates the insurance policy when the loan-to-original-value ratio declines to 70 or 75 percent. The borrower pays the premium, which raises the issue whether the interest rate on the loan should be decreased by the amount of the premium.

PURCHASE MONEY MORTGAGE

A *purchase money mortgage* is a conventional mortgage given by the purchaser to the seller as part of the purchaser's consideration for the purchase price of the property. That is, the seller finances part of the transaction. Assume that the purchase price is $80,000 and the buyer pays the seller $10,000 in cash. The buyer gives the seller a mortgage securing the payment of the remaining $70,000 of the purchase price. A purchase money mortgage often takes second priority on the sold property. Assume a purchase price of $100,000. The buyer has $10,000 in cash and obtains a $70,000 first mortgage loan from an institutional lender. The buyer gives the seller a second purchase money mortgage securing the remaining $20,000 of the purchase price. The terms of payment and the interest rate are established by mutual agreement between the buyer and seller. A purchase money mortgage is often used because the owner wants to sell the property and potential buyers cannot obtain sufficient financing from other lenders. The abbreviation PMM is often used to identify a purchase money mortgage.

The deed and the purchase money mortgage are delivered as part of the same transaction. The mortgage normally includes a clause describing it as a purchase money mortgage, which gives it a special priority status. In most states, a PMM automatically has priority over existing judgment liens against the purchaser, homestead exemptions, and dower or curtesy rights of the purchaser's spouse.

A broader definition of a purchase money mortgage is sometimes used, which includes those granted by third party lenders to aid buyers in financing purchased properties. In this sense, any mortgage given to secure a loan whose entire proceeds are used as part of the purchase price of the mortgaged property is a purchase money mortgage. In some states a third party purchase money mortgage is given the same priority status as one given by a seller.

FHA Insured Mortgage

The Federal Housing Administration (FHA) operates under the U.S. Department of Housing and Urban Development (HUD). The Federal Housing Administration insures mortgage loans, which are called *FHA insured loans* or FHA loans. FHA itself does not make mortgage loans, rather the mortgage loans are made by FHA approved lenders. FHA mortgage insurance is granted only if both the property and the borrower meet FHA standards. The maximum loan-to-value ratio, the amount of the loan, and the term of the loan are specified by FHA. The HUD Secretary also establishes the allowable interest rate. The interest rate is typically set below the market rate on conventional mortgage loans.

There are numerous FHA mortgage insurance programs. The most popular program by far is the one involving Section 203b—home mortgage insurance. We therefore confine our discussion to Section 203b. The insurance protects the lender for the entire amount of the loan. The borrower pays an annual insurance premium of one-half of one percent on the average loan balance during each year. The insurance must be kept in force for the life of the loan. There is no maximum limit on the borrower's income.

The current standard maximum loan limit on a mortgage loan secured by a single-family home is $67,500. The maximum allowable loan is larger in high-cost areas like Hawaii and Alaska or if the property is equipped with solar energy devices. The basic program currently limits the loan to 97 percent of the first $25,000 plus 95 percent of "value" in excess of $25,000. A veteran can obtain a higher percentage loan. The allowable loan-to-value ratio is lower if the property was not approved prior to construction and is less than one year old or if the property will not be occupied by the owner.

To show the calculation of an insurable amount, assume that we wish to purchase a single-family home for $70,000 and finance it with an FHA loan. The allowable loan would be calculated as follows:

$$\$25,000 \times .97 = \$24,250$$
$$\$45,000 \times .95 = \$42,750$$
$$\text{Amount of loan} = \$67,000$$

We would have to make a down payment of $3,000. The entire $67,000 mortgage loan would be insured.

The maximum amount of an FHA insured loan is $67,500, as mentioned. Thus, if we desired to purchase an $80,000 home we would need a down payment of $12,500. In this case we could get a higher percentage loan by using a privately insured conventional loan.

The principal advantage of using an FHA insured mortgage loan is the relatively low required down payment on moderately priced homes. Other advantages include a somewhat lower interest rate, no prepayment penalty, and a clause that makes the loan assumable. The principal disadvantage is that the safeguards built into the program make the period between application for and approval of the loan relatively lengthy.

VA MORTGAGE LOANS

The Veterans Administration guarantees, insures, and makes direct loans. Veterans are eligible if they were on active duty for at least 90 days or 181 days, depending on the specific dates of service. Veterans who have less service are eligible if they were discharged due to a service-connected disability. The unremarried widows of veterans who died in service or from service-related disabilities are also eligible. Veterans with dishonorable discharges are denied veterans benefits.

VA loans can be used to purchase detached residences, condominium units, and mobile homes. They can also be used for home improvements and refinancing. We limit our discussion to VA loans for the purchase of detached residences and condominium units. VA loans are of interest to nonveterans because they can be assumed or taken over by nonveterans.

VA Guaranteed. A *VA or GI guaranteed mortgage loan* is one which is guaranteed by the Veterans Administration. This is the main VA mortgage loan program. VA guarantees loans only if both the property and the borrower meet VA standards. Lenders meeting these standards are termed "VA approved lenders." A down payment is not required and there is no upper limit on the amount of the loan. The VA does specify the maximum term of the loan and the interest rate. The allowable interest rate is usually the same as that for FHA insured loans.

The current maximum loan guarantee is $27,500, but the guarantee can never exceed 60 percent of the outstanding loan balance. Thus, if the loan were for $110,000, the loan guarantee would be only for $27,500. This would give the lender about the same risk exposure as a noninsured conventional loan with a 75 percent loan-to-value ratio or an insured conventional loan with about a 95 percent loan-to-value ratio with insurance coverage of the top 22 percent.

The principal attraction of the VA guaranteed mortgage is no down payment or a relative small down payment. The borrower may obtain a larger loan than is possible with FHA insurance. The effective cost to the borrower is less than for an FHA insured mortgage because there is no charge for the guarantee. There is no prepayment penalty and the loan is assumable. The loan processing for a VA guaranteed loan is normally faster than for an FHA loan, but it is usually slower than for conventional loans.

VA Insured. The VA also insures loans if a borrower and a lender agree that the loan is to be insured rather than guaranteed. The amount of a VA insured mortgage loan is limited to $6\frac{2}{3}$ times the borrower's maximum entitlement. Thus, if a borrower's entitlement is $27,500, the maximum amount of the insured loan is $183,333. The VA insurance program is basically for home loans, and only a small portion of VA home loans are insured.

VA Direct. A VA direct loan is one which is granted by the Veterans Administration from its own funds. The VA direct loan program is small relative to the VA mortgage guarantee program. A VA direct loan is currently limited to $33,000 for home loans. These loans are made only in areas designated as being short on housing credit. And the VA attempts to place the loan with a local lender before advancing its own funds. The interest rate is the same as that allowed for VA guaranteed mortgage loans.

FmHA Mortgage Loans

The Farmers Home Administration operates under the U.S. Department of Agriculture and is designated FmHA to distinguish it from the Federal Housing Administration. The Farmers Home Administration has numerous loan programs, which can be categorized as farming, community development, and rural housing programs. We limit our discussion here to individual rural home ownership loans. Rural home ownership loans are either guaranteed or insured by the Farmers Home Administration. The property must be located in a rural area. This includes unincorporated areas and communities of up to 10,000 in population that are rural in character. Loans can also be made in towns of up to 20,000 in population if they are located outside of a Standard Metropolitan Statistical Area and are designated as credit shortage areas. To qualify for the programs, the borrower must not receive an income above a specified amount.

FmHA Insured. The Farmers Home Administration uses its own funds to make insured loans. The FmHA sells notes backed by the mortgages and the FmHA insurance to investors. The FmHA insures the noteholders for 90 percent of the loan, which means that the investor bears only 10 percent of any loss.

The FmHA approves both the property and the borrower. The size of the home is limited to 1,300 square feet of living area. The borrower must be able to meet the terms of payment, but his or her income cannot exceed a specified level. The level varies from state to state, and in most states the borrower's adjusted family income cannot exceed $15,600. The adjusted family income is calculated by taking 95 percent of gross family income and deducting $300 for each minor child. If the adjusted family income is less than $11,200, the borrower may receive an interest subsidy.

The amount of the loan can be up to 100 percent of the value of the property. There is no maximum specified for the amount of the loan, but the borrower must be able to repay the loan. This effectively limits the size of the loan to less than $35,000. The maximum term of the loan is 33 years. The interest rate is set by the Secretary of Agriculture and is based on the prevailing cost of funds to the Department. About two-thirds of the loans are subsidized, and the subsidized loans carry an interest rate below the Department's cost of funds.

FmHA insured loans are granted only to borrowers who plan to occupy the home and cannot find credit elsewhere. The loans are periodically reviewed to see if they can be refinanced with private lenders.

FmHA Guaranteed. The Farmers Home Administration does not make guaranteed loans. FmHA approved lenders make the mortgage loans, and the FmHA guarantees the loans for 90 percent of their amount. The FmHA must approve the property and the borrower. In most states the borrower's adjusted family income must be between $15,600 and $20,000. The allowable loan-to-value ratio for loans secured by new or existing homes is 97 percent of the value on the first $25,000 and 95 percent of the value in excess of $25,000. The loan-to-value ratio is limited to 90 percent if the construction was not approved by FmHA and if the home is less than one year old. There is no maximum on the amount of the loan, but the size of the loan is effectively limited to approximately $40,000. The interest rate is negotiated between the borrower and the lender. The interest rate should not be above that on comparable conventional mortgage loans in the area. There is no interest subsidy and a one percent loan guarantee fee must be paid at the loan closing.

CLASSIFIED BY STAGE OF DEVELOPMENT

A number of different types of loans may be involved between the inception of the idea for a real estate development and its completion and occupancy. The loans range from a land acquisition loan to the end loan that is often used to repay interim loans. *Interim loans* are relatively short term in nature, whereas the *permanent loan* or *end loan* is a long-term loan.

LAND ACQUISITION LOAN

A land acquisition loan is used to acquire the land necessary for a development. Purchase money mortgages from the seller or installment land contracts are often used to acquire undeveloped land. Loans are also available from third party lenders.

LAND DEVELOPMENT LOAN

A *land development loan* is used to finance the installation of utilities, streets, and other site improvements, and it is often combined with a construction loan. A land development loan may be the only type of loan secured when the project is for the development of home sites for resale. The funds are usually advanced on a monthly draw system or on the basis of the stage of completion. The mortgage covers the entire property. When a developed lot is sold, the borrower pays the lender for the release of that lot in return for a previously agreed payment. This allows the borrower-developer to deliver title to the lot to a buyer free of the mortgage lien.

CONSTRUCTION LOAN

A *construction loan* is used to finance the costs of erecting a building or a building and other site improvements. The construction loan is usually either repaid from the proceeds of the sale of the property or from the proceeds of a long-term loan. If the building is constructed under a contract or on speculation, the builder or developer arranges only for a construction loan. The developer must arrange for a long-term loan if he or she intends to retain ownership of the improved property. The first step in obtaining a construction loan is usually to arrange for a commitment for a long-term loan. Large-scale home builders sometimes obtain a commitment for permanent financing for prospective home buyers. Speculative builders operating on short-term loans only must refinance at the end of a given time if a buyer with permanent financing is not found.

Commitment for Permanent Loan. Commitments are frequently used in conjunction with construction loans. There are basically two types of commitments for loans for the purpose of paying off the construction lender. A long-term lender may make a *permanent takeout commitment* and intend to advance the funds under a long-term mortgage loan on completion of the project. The lender benefits from a commitment fee and by placing funds for a long term. Some lenders also grant stand-by commitments. A *standby commitment* is an offer to loan funds if the prospective borrower elects to exercise that option. The terms of the standby loan are usually relatively unattractive, and the prospective borrower exercises the commitment only if he or she cannot obtain a more favorable loan elsewhere. Neither the lender nor the prospective borrower expect the loan to be made. The lender must keep funds available to meet the commitment and therefore demands a substantial commitment fee for the commitment.

A developer obtains a standby commitment for a number of reasons. It may be impossible to obtain a permanent takeout commitment; thus, the construction lender may accept a standby commitment in its place. The developer may believe that a more favorable loan could be obtained after the completion of the project because interest rates seem likely to decline. On completion and occupancy of the property, the appraised market value is likely to increase and justify a larger loan than offered under current commitments. Of course, the developer could be wrong, and he or she would like the assurance of some loan on completion of the project. The terms of the loan offered under a standby commitment are usually relatively unfavorable for the borrower-developer, who is likely to arrange other financing within a few years, even if the standby loan is made.

Terms of the Construction Loan. A construction loan normally terminates when the construction is completed or within a short time thereafter. The construction period seldom exceeds nine months for a single-family residence and three years for a large income property. The lender often charges loan origination fees. The loan-to-value ratio is usually lower than on permanent financing. In addition, commitment fees are charged for loans for large projects. The interest rate is above the prime rate, and on longer term construction loans the interest rate may float with the prime interest rate. For example, the rate may be the prime interest rate plus 4 percent. The accrued interest may be added to the loan balance, or for longer term construction loans there may be periodic interest payments.

The lender commits a specified sum, but the funds are advanced to the borrower only as the construction progresses. The *stage of completion method* is often used for single-family residences. Thus, the first disbursement of funds could be made when the foundation and basement walls are in place. A *monthly draw method* may be used for large-scale projects. The developer requests a draw based on the work completed in the previous month. The lender normally requests the contractors, subcontractors, and material suppliers to sign lien waivers evidencing that they have been paid for work completed and materials supplied to date. This prevents them from later filing mechanic's liens for the work completed or materials supplied up to the time of the advance and thereby having a claim against the property that is prior to, and predates, the mortgage.

PERMANENT LOAN

A *permanent loan* is a long-term loan that typically ranges from 15 to 30 years in duration. The permanent loan is the end loan in the development process. The proceeds of the *end loan* are used to pay off the interim loans created during the development process. There are two basic types of end loans—the fixed amount loan and the floor-to-ceiling loan.

Fixed Amount Loan. A *fixed amount end loan* is one for a specified sum and is not conditioned on achieving a certain occupancy ratio. For example, the borrower receives a $100,000 end loan on completion of the construction of the house.

Floor-to-Ceiling Loan. A floor-to-ceiling end loan specifies two or more amounts for the loan. The minimum or floor amount of the loan may be distributed when the project is completed. The remaining portion of the loan is distributed when a specified rental goal is reached. For example, the loan commitment may specify a distribution of $5 million on completion, an additional $2 million when the occupancy ratio reaches 60 percent, and an additional $1 million when the occupancy rate exceeds 75 percent. The floor of the loan is $5 million, and the ceiling of the loan is $8 million. If the occupancy rate is only 50 percent on completion of the project, the borrower only receives $5 million of the potential $8 million. There is a gap of $3 million. The developer must be able to finance this gap because the additional $3 million may be needed to pay off the interim loans and meet other obligations.

GAP LOAN

Gap financing may be necessary when the permanent take-out commitment provides for a floor-to-ceiling loan. The developer may have to furnish the construction lender both a permanent take-out commitment and a standby commitment for the potential gap. A *gap loan* is a short-term second mortgage loan used to make up the difference between amount received from the permanent loan and the total amount required. A substantial commitment fee is charged for a standby commitment for a gap loan. The interest rate on the gap loan is typically based on a floating rate and would be higher than the interest rate on the permanent loan. The gap loan may be paid off by the additional advances from the permanent loan as the occupancy level goes up.

CLASSIFIED BY PRIORITY OF LIEN

The priority of mortgage liens is normally determined by the date of recording the mortgage. The first recorded has the first lien and is the first mortgage. The second recorded has the second lien and is the second mortgage. The two exceptions to this rule are actual knowledge of a prior mortgage and subordination agreements. If the mortgage is recorded with actual knowledge of the existence of a prior unrecorded mortgage, the unrecorded mortgage retains its priority position in most states. A subordination agreement can be used to give a new mortgage priority over a previously recorded mortgage.

FIRST MORTGAGE

A *first mortgage* is a mortgage that has priority over all other mortgage liens on the property. The first mortgage holder is paid from the proceeds of a foreclosure sale before any funds are distributed to other mortgage holders. The first mortgage is also called the *senior mortgage*.

JUNIOR MORTGAGES

A *second mortgage* is a mortgage that is inferior in priority to the first mortgage but has superiority over any other mortgage liens. The second mortgage is paid from the proceeds of a foreclosure sale after the first mortgage holder has been satisfied. The second mortgage is also called a *junior mortgage*. Second mortgages, third mortgages, fourth mortgages, and any other mortgage except the first mortgage are all classified as junior mortgages.

Assume that there is a first, second, and third mortgage on the property. The first mortgage is the senior mortgage. The second mortgage is a junior mortgage to the first but senior to the third mortgage. The third mortgage is a junior mortgage, having lower priority of claim to both the first and the second mortgage.

Junior mortgages may be used to assist in financing the purchase of the property or to raise additional funds at a later date. The interest rate on a junior mortgage is typically higher than that on the first mortgage. Junior mortgage loans usually have a shorter duration or term than first mortgage loans.

A wraparound mortgage loan is a special form of second or junior mortgage. Assume that we have an existing first mortgage loan with an outstanding balance of $100,000 and an interest rate of 8 percent. We desire to obtain an additional $20,000. We could get a new mortgage loan for $120,000 and pay off the $100,000 balance on the old loan. But the interest rate on first mortgage loans has risen to 12 percent, so we would like to retain the existing loan. We could get a second mortgage loan for $20,000 with a 21 percent interest rate. Another alternative is a wraparound mortgage loan for $120,000 with a 10 percent interest rate. The wraparound loan of $120,000 includes the $100,000 balance on the existing first mortgage loan. The wraparound lender therefore gives the borrower only $20,000 in cash. Assume that the loans are term loans and require annual interest payments and no principal payments. The borrower would pay the wraparound lender $12,000 per year. The wraparound lender would pay the first mortgage holder $8,000 per year. The wraparound lender would retain the $4,000 difference as interest on the $20,000 advanced. The $4,000 return on the $20,000 cash investment makes the rate of return 20 percent per year. The borrower pays the equivalent of a 20 percent interest rate on the $20,000 cash advanced by the lender. In this example the wraparound mortgage loan is the least expensive alternative for the borrower.

A *wraparound mortgage* is usually a second mortgage that includes the balance of the existing first mortgage plus the amount of the additional funds advanced by the wraparound lender. The borrower makes the mortgage payment to the wraparound lender. The wraparound lender takes over the mortgage payments to the holder of the first mortgage and retains the difference. The wraparound lender does not assume a personal liability for the payment of the debt to the holder of the first mortgage, however. Since the wraparound mortgage holder receives the entire payment, the borrower would default on the wraparound mortgage before there was a default on the existing first mortgage.

A wraparound mortgage is used when the existing first mortgage cannot be prepaid or when it is desirable to preserve the first mortgage. If the first mortgage contains a clause that either prohibits the use of junior financing or requires the lender's approval, it may be impossible to use a wraparound mortgage.

CLASSIFIED BY PAYMENT PATTERN

There is a wide range of payment patterns available for the payment of a mortgage loan. For example, a nonamortizing mortgage loan requires only interest payments through the term of the loan, with the loan balance paid at the end of the term. Partially amortizing loans require payments of interest and principal throughout the term and a relatively large principal payment at the end of the term. A fully amortizing loan requires payments of interest and principal throughout the term, and the amount of the final payment for principal reduction is roughly equivalent to the periodic debt service payment.

DEMAND MORTGAGE LOAN

A *demand loan* is normally a short-term loan that either has no specified maturity date or that is callable before the specified maturity date. That is, the debt is payable on the maturity date or on demand. The interest payments may be added to the balance due, or periodic interest payments may be required throughout its life.

TERM MORTGAGE LOAN

A *straight-term mortgage loan* is one in which the entire loan balance is due in a single payment at the end of the term. The interest is normally paid by periodic payments during the life of the loan. A term mortgage for three or five years was the typical type of loan used to finance a home prior to the Great Depression of the 1930s. They were usually renewable at the end of each term by mutual consent of the borrower and lender. The lender sometimes refused to renew the loan if it came due during a period of tight money. This accounts for the early movies portraying the lender as a villain. Beginning in the 1930s, the term loan was largely replaced by the fully amortized mortgage loan as the principal means of financing the purchase of a home. The use of the term loan as described above, which is actually a rollover mortgage loan, has been revived in recent years because of the lenders' need for greater flexibility in their mortgage loan portfolio.

RENEGOTIABLE-RATE MORTGAGE

A *renegotiable-rate mortgage* (RRM) is one in which the lender and borrower renegotiate the interest rate on the loan at stated intervals, such as every three or five years. There may be a stated limitation on the size of any increase in the interest rate at any given renegotiation date and over the life of the loan.

The renegotiable-rate mortgage combines features of the pre-1930s term loan and a fully amortizing mortgage loan. The interest rate on the loan can be changed only on the renegotiation date. If the borrower accepts the new interest rate, the loan remains in effect. The borrower is free to reject the new interest rate and pay off the loan balance by refinancing the loan with another lender. The renegotiable-rate mortgage loan is a fully amortizing loan that normally requires monthly payments of interest and principal. Of course, either the monthly payment or the term of the loan may be changed if the interest rate is changed.

PARTIALLY AMORTIZING LOAN

A *partially amortizing loan* is one that requires periodic payments of interest and principal during its term and a large principal payment at the end of the term. The large payment at the end of the term is called a *balloon payment,* and a partially amortizing loan is sometimes called a *balloon loan.*

Assume that the loan is for $100,000 and the interest rate is 12 percent per annum. The lender could calculate the monthly payment on a 30-year basis and specify a 10-year term for the loan. The borrower would pay about $1,029 per month for 10 years, and the balloon payment at the end of 10 years would be approximately $82,300.

Purchase money mortgages, land contracts, and second mortgages often require balloon payments. The borrower must be prepared to meet the balloon payment, and in many cases this requires refinancing. Real estate investors who intend to sell the property in five to ten years often prefer partially amortizing loans because the lower monthly payments minimize their holding costs while maintaining maximum leverage.

FULLY AMORTIZING LOANS

A *fully amortizing loan* is one in which the periodic payments of interest and principal throughout the term pay the entire debt. No balloon payment is scheduled. Amortizing loans apply the debt service payment first to interest and second to the reduction of principal. The interest due is calculated on the unpaid balance. The two traditional types of fully amortizing mortgage loans follow either the level mortgage payment plan or the equal principal reduction plan. In recent years a number of alternative payment plans have gained in popularity. They are discussed later in this chapter.

Level Payment Loan. A *level payment loan* provides for equal periodic debt service payments throughout the life of the mortgage. The most common form of home mortgage loan requires equal monthly debt service payments. The loan balance declines each month, the interest payment declines each month, and the amount applied to the reduction of principal increases each month.

Assume that we borrow $100,000 for 20 years at an interest rate of 12 percent per annum. The monthly debt service payment would be

$1,101, and the monthly interest rate is 1 percent. The interest charge for the first month is $1,000. The remaining $101 would be applied to reduction of principal. The loan balance declines to $99,899. The next month the interest charge would be $998.99 and $102.01 applies to reduction of the principal. This process continues throughout the life of the loan. When the loan balance has declined to $10,000, the interest charge would be $100 and $1,001 would be applied to the reduction of principal. A loan of this type is also commonly termed a *fixed-rate mortgage* (FRM).

Equal Principal Reduction Loan. An *equal principal reduction loan* provides for equal principal payments plus interest on the declining balance. The payments are usually made monthly, and the debt service payment declines each month. Since the early debt service payments are higher than those under a level payment mortgage, the equal principal reduction mortgage is not frequently used. It appeals to borrowers who desire high payments in early years and low payments in later years.

Assume that we borrow $100,000 for 20 years at an interest rate of 12 percent per annum. The equal monthly principal payment is $416.67 and it is calculated by dividing 240 months into $100,000. The monthly interest rate is 1 percent. The first monthly debt service payment includes $1,000 for interest and $416.67 for principal reduction and totals $1,416.67. The loan balance declines to $99,583.33. The debt service payment for the second month includes $995.83 for interest and $416.67 for principal reduction and totals $1,412.50. This process continues throughout the life of the loan. When the loan balance has declined to $10,000, the interest charge would be $100 and $416.67 is applied to principal reduction. The debt service payment for that month totals $516.67.

INCREASING PAYMENT FULLY AMORTIZING LOANS

A mortgage loan that allows the borrower to make low monthly cash payments in the early years and higher payments in later years appeals to borrowers who expect rising incomes throughout the early portion of the term of the loan. There are at least three types of fully amortizing loans that allow lower cash monthly payments in the early years. They are the flexible payment mortgage, the graduated payment mortgage, and the FLIP or supplemental payment pledged savings account mortgage. Each of these allows the borrower to make lower cash monthly payments in the first few years than those required under a level payment mortgage loan. Of course, in later years the payments are higher.

Flexible Payment Mortgage. There are numerous possible payment schedules under a flexible payment mortgage. An example of a *flexible payment mortgage* (FPM) loan is one that provides for payments only on the interest for the first few years followed by level debt service payments sufficient to fully amortize the loan. Assume that we borrow $50,000 for 30 years at a 12 percent interest rate. For the first three years the monthly payments cover only the interest of $500 per month. The monthly debt service payment is $520.72 for the remaining 27 years. Sometimes a dual rate FPM is used. The lender charges one interest rate for the interest-only period and another interest rate for the remaining period. For example, the interest rate could be 9 percent for the interest-only period and 12 percent for the remaining years. This allows the payments in the early months to be reduced. The lender can earn a 12 percent rate of return on the entire loan by raising the rate in the amortizing period to slightly above 12 percent.

Graduated Payment Mortgage.   There are numerous payment schedules possible under a graduated payment mortgage. A *graduated payment mortgage* (GPM) loan is one that starts with low monthly payments during the first year; the payments are increased at a certain rate each year until they reach a predetermined level. The monthly payments remain at that level for the remainder of the term. The monthly payment usually begins at an amount less than the interest charge for that month. This is called negative amortization. The unpaid interest is added to the loan balance, and the loan balance increases in the early years.

Assume that we borrow $50,000 for a 30-year term with a 10 percent interest rate. Assume that the initial monthly payment is based on annual increases of 7.5 percent for 5 years. The monthly payments for the first year are $333.52. (Note that one month's interest on $50,000 at 10 percent is $416.67.) The payments increase each year and reach $478.82 in the sixth year and remain at this level throughout the remaining years. The outstanding balance on the mortgage reaches a peak of $52,763 in the fourth year.

FLIP or Supplemental Payment PAL Mortgage.   A *Flexible Loan Insurance Program* (FLIP) mortgage and a supplemental payment PAL (pledged savings account loan) mortgage both employ the use of a pledged savings account. The FLIP and the supplemental payment PAL mortgages provide for level debt service payments to the lender, but the amount of the monthly out-of-pocket payments made by the borrower gradually increases. The difference in the amounts of the debt service payments received by the lender and the out-of-pocket payments made by the borrower is withdrawn from the pledged savings account.

Assume that the loan can be fully amortized by making debt service payments of $480 per month for 30 years. The borrower may make monthly out-of-pocket payments of $334 during the first year. The difference of $146 ($480 − $334) would be withdrawn from the pledged savings account each month during the first year. Thereafter the borrower's out-of-pocket payment increases, and the amount withdrawn from the pledged savings decreases. At some point, such as at the beginning of the sixth year, the balance of the pledged savings account reaches zero. Then the borrower makes the entire $480 monthly debt service payment out of his or her pocket.

A FLIP or supplemental payment PAL mortgage is a level payment mortgage from the viewpoint of the lender. But it is a graduated payment mortgage from the viewpoint of the borrower's out of pocket payments.

VARIABLE-RATE MORTGAGE

A *variable-rate mortgage* (VRM) loan is one in which the interest rate on the loan can be changed in accordance with the movements in some index. For example, the interest rate on most mortgage loans made by Federal Land Bank associations is variable, and it is based on the cost of funds to the Federal Land Banks. The interest rate on long-term government bonds and the cost of funds to Federal Home Loan Banks are other examples of indexes that can be used. The adjustments may be made as frequently as once a month. There may be a limitation on the magnitude of the change in the interest rate on any given date and/or over the duration of the loan.

When the interest rate is changed, the lender must make some adjustment in either the monthly payment, the outstanding loan balance, or the remaining term of the loan. If the interest rate increases, the lender usually either increases the required monthly payment or extends the term of the loan. When the interest rate is adjusted downward, the lender may either decrease the monthly payment or shorten the term of the loan.

ADJUSTABLE MORTGAGE

An *adjustable mortgage loan* (AML) and an *adjustable-rate mortgage* (ARM) are more recent versions of variable-rate mortgages. The Federal Home Loan Bank Board allows federally chartered savings and loan associations and federally chartered mutual savings banks to make AMLs. The Comptroller of the Currency also allows national banks to make ARMs. There is no limitation on the total increase in the interest rate over the duration of either an AML or ARM. The interest rate on an AML can be changed as often as every 30 days, and there is no limit on the periodic change in the interest rate. The interest rate on an ARM cannot be changed more often than every six months, and the periodic increase cannot exceed one percent. The interest rate on both AMLs and ARMs must be governed by an index. Adjustments to the interest rate on an AML can be based on any index agreeable to both the borrower and lender, as long as the index is readily verifiable by the borrower and is beyond the control of the lender. Adjustments to the interest rate on an ARM must be based on either six-month U.S. Treasury rates, three-year

U.S. Treasury rates, or the FHLBB (Federal Home Loan Bank Board) series of long-term contract mortgage interest rates on previously occupied homes. Both the AML and ARM continue to evolve as of this writing.

BUDGET MORTGAGE LOAN

A *budget mortgage loan* requires the borrower to make monthly payments covering interest, principal, and one-twelfth of the annual hazard insurance premium and/or one-twelfth of the annual real estate taxes. The lender places the monthly payments for hazard insurance and real estate taxes into an escrow account and pays the taxes and insurance when due. The escrow or impound account may or may not be interest bearing.

FHA insured loans also require monthly escrow payments for the FHA insurance fee. If it is a privately insured mortgage loan, the lender may require monthly payments into an escrow account for the private mortgage insurance premium.

CLASSIFIED BY TYPE OF SECURITY

Mortgages can be classified by the type of security offered by the borrower. The borrower may offer real property and/or personal property as security for the payment of the debt. Two or more properties may be offered as security for the debt.

REAL ESTATE MORTGAGE

A *real estate mortgage* is one that offers real property as security for the payment of the debt. When we refer to a mortgage, we normally mean a mortgage secured by real property or primarily by real property.

CHATTEL MORTGAGE

A *chattel mortgage* is one that offers personal property as security for the payment of the debt. These loans are governed by the Uniform Commercial Code. The loan agreement is called a security agreement under the Code. And a shortened version called a financing statement is filed to establish the lender's interest in the property.

PACKAGE MORTGAGE

A *package mortgage* includes both real property and personal property items as security. If we purchase a home that contains appliances, we may offer both the home and the appliances as security. The mortgage will describe the real property and may list the items of personal property. Often the mortgage is recorded, and a financing statement covering the items of personal property is filed. The primary advantage of a package mortgage for the home buyer-borrower is that the monthly payments would initially be lower than on a smaller mortgage loan plus installment payments on a separate loan for the appliances.

PLEDGED SAVINGS ACCOUNT MORTGAGE

The borrower may obtain a mortgage with a higher loan-to-value ratio by pledging his or her savings account as additional security. The lender may release the pledged savings account as the monthly payments reduce the loan balance.

Sometimes the seller pledges a savings account to assist the borrower to obtain a mortgage loan to purchase the property. The buyer may not have sufficient funds for the required down payment. The seller either opens a savings account with the lender and pledges it or pledges an existing savings account with the lender. The seller typically pledges only an amount sufficient to cover the additional amount necessary for the borrower to meet the required down payment. The seller collects interest on the pledged account, and the account is released when the loan-to-value ratio declines to a specified level. The lender can apply the seller's pledged savings account to the payment of any deficiency resulting from the borrower's default and a foreclosure sale of the property.

BLANKET MORTGAGE

A *blanket mortgage* is one that pledges two or more parcels of real property as security for the debt. For example, a $1 million loan may be secured by a mortgage on 100 lots. The blanket mortgage usually includes a partial release clause. The partial release clause allows the borrower to obtain a release of an individual property or lot from the mortgage lien. The release price is often slightly more than the proportionate value of the property. In the example above 100 lots divided into the $1,000,000 loan equals $10,000 per lot. The release price of one lot might be $12,000. A blanket mortgage can also be used for other purposes. For example, we may want to buy a vacation home. We could offer both our permanent residence and the vacation home as security for the loan to purchase the vacation home.

LEASEHOLD MORTGAGE

A *leasehold mortgage* is one in which the tenant pledges his or her interest under the lease as security for the debt. Mortgages on long-term leases such as for 21 years or more are often treated as real estate mortgages rather than as chattel mortgages.

HOME IMPROVEMENT LOAN

A *home improvement loan* is one used to finance home improvements such as additional insulation, new aluminum siding, new kitchen cabinets, and remodeling the bathroom. Often they are unsecured installment loans with terms of three to seven years. Large home improvement loans may be second mortgage loans with terms of ten years or more. They can be VA guaranteed, FHA insured, FmHA insured, or conventional loans. The interest rate is usually higher than that on first mortgage loans.

MOBILE HOME LOANS

Mobile home loans are normally not considered to be real estate mortgage loans. Conventional mobile home loans usually have terms of up to 10 years. FHA insured and VA guaranteed mobile home loans are also available. The maximum term on a VA guaranteed mobile home loan is slightly over 15 years. The interest rate is substantially higher than that on first mortgage loans secured by single family houses.

In most cases a security agreement is used and a financing statement is filed. Sometimes a mortgage is used to offer the mobile home as security for the debt. When the borrower purchases the mobile home site or leases it on a long-term basis and offers both the lot or leasehold and the mobile home as security, a mortgage covering both the lot and the mobile home may be offered as security for the loan.

OTHER CLASSIFICATIONS OR TYPES OF LOANS

There are numerous types of mortgage loans and mortgage loan designations that were not included in the cateories discussed above. We discuss the main ones below.

PARTICIPATION MORTGAGE

A *participation mortgage* is one in which two or more persons own a share of the debt. Two or more lenders may join together to make the loan, or one lender may originate the loan and later sell a portion of the loan to an investor. Each party owns a separate share of the loan. Each party may have equal rights for a pro rata share, or one party may be given a priority status and the other party a subordinate position. The share having priority over another is called the senior participation.

The share having the subordinate position is called a junior participation. A document called a *participation agreement* or *ownership agreement* is used to specify the relationship between the parties owning a share of the debt and mortgage.

EQUITY PARTICIPATION MORTGAGE

An *equity participation mortgage* loan is one in which the lender receives an "equity kicker" in addition to normal debt service payments. Often the promoter-borrower has a very small investment in the property, and the lender provides almost all the funds. If the project fails, the lender has the large loss. In such cases the lender may demand extra benefits, termed *equity kickers,* if the project becomes very successful. There are numerous possible forms of equity kickers. The lender may be given a percentage of the ownership of the property or additional interest payments when the rentals or net income from the project reach a specified level. Other possible kickers include participation in rentals, gross or net income, profits from the sale of the property, or proceeds from refinancing the loan. If the kicker gives the lender a portion of the income but no ownership interest, some authorities classify it as an *income participation loan.*

CONVERTIBLE MORTGAGE

A *convertible mortgage* is a special form of equity participation mortgage. The lender usually makes an equity investment in the property in addition to making a loan on the property. A convertible mortgage loan requires the borrower to make interest payments on the unpaid loan balance, but there are no cash payments for reduction of the loan balance. The lender receives an increasing percentage equity ownership instead of cash payments for principal reduction. The mortgage loan converts into an equity interest or an increased equity interest in the property as the loan balance is reduced.

SHARED APPRECIATION MORTGAGE

A form of equity participation mortgage loan can be used in conjunction with the purchase of a home. A *shared appreciation mortgage* (SAM) loan is one in which the lender charges a reduced interest rate in return for a percentage of any appreciation in the value of the property over some specified period. For example, the borrower might be offered a 9 percent interest rate rather than the going rate of 12 percent in return for one-third of the appreciation in the value of the home. The borrower might be required to pay an amount equal to one-third of the appreciation at the end of ten years or as of the date of sale if the sale took place before the end of ten years.

The lender benefits if the amount received from the appreciation increases the effective rate of return to more than that returned on other mortgage loan arrangements. In this situation the borrower would still benefit if the lower required monthly payments enabled the borrower to purchase a home that he or she could not have otherwise afforded. If there is no appreciation, the lender loses and the borrower benefits by using the shared appreciation mortgage loan.

REVERSE ANNUITY MORTGAGE

The principal asset of many retired people is their home. The reverse annuity mortgage is intended to allow borrowers to use their homes as security for a loan to support a portion of their living expenses during retirement. A *reverse annuity mortgage* (RAM) allows the borrower to receive a monthly check from the lender for a specified number of years. The loan balances increase with each monthly receipt and as the unpaid interest accumulates. The monthly receipts end when the loan balance reaches a specified sum.

A variant of this allows the borrower to receive the entire proceeds when the loan agreement is signed. The funds are used to purchase a single premium annuity policy from a life insurance company. The life insurance company makes monthly payments to the borrower, and on the borrower's death the property may be sold to repay the loan. The borrower would make monthly interest payments to the lender, and this would absorb a substantial portion of the monthly annuity payments received from the insurance company.

OPEN-END MORTGAGE

An *open-end mortgage* is one that allows additional funds to be advanced and to be secured by the same mortgage. The total sum that may be advanced under the mortgage may be specified in the note and/or the mortgage. The total may be limited to the original amount of the loan or the original amount of the loan plus a specified sum. If the original amount of the loan was $50,000, the total could be limited to $50,000 or to $50,000 plus $10,000, which is $60,000. The most common open-end mortgage home loan limits the total loan to the amount of the original loan. In this case the amount of future advances is limited to the difference between the original loan balance and the then current loan balance.

The use of an open-end mortgage reduces the refinancing costs on future loans secured by the same mortgage. The interest rate on the additional advances may be different from that on the original loan. Even if the interest rate on the additional advances is higher than on the original loan, the interest rate is still below that on home improvement loans.

The open-end loan is also known as a *mortgage for future advances*. A construction loan in which the funds are distributed on the basis of the stage of completion or the monthly draw is another example of a mortgage for future advances. Mortgages for future advances and the potential problem of intervening liens are discussed in Chap. 5.

BRIDGE LOAN

A bridge loan is usually associated with a homeowner selling one home and buying another home. The homeowner normally expects to finance part of the purchase price of the new home from the proceeds of the sale of the old home. If the homeowner signs the contract to purchase the new home before he or she has sold the old home, the homeowner has a temporary financial problem. A *bridge loan* covers the period between the purchase of the new home and the sale of the old home. Assume that the homeowner expected to realize $15,000 from the sale of the old home that could be applied to the purchase price of the new home. The bridge loan would be for $15,000 or less. Bridge loans of this type are short-term loans with terms of from 30 to 90 days. They are usually renewable. The effective interest rate is considerably higher than those on first mortgage loans.

BASKET LOANS

Institutions such as life insurance companies and mutual savings banks are allowed to invest a small portion of their assets without regard to other regulations. Mortgage loans that would not be otherwise allowed are made under this provision and are called *basket loans*. Many of the creative equity participation mortgage loans are basket loans.

BUY-DOWN LOAN

A *buy-down loan* is one in which someone other than the borrower contributes cash to the borrower's mortgage payments during the early years of the loan. This reduces the effective interest rate to the borrower. Builders or others desiring to sell a property are sometimes willing to pay a portion of the buyer-borrower's interest for a specified period in order to bring about the sale.

The various types of mortgage loans were placed in the six following categories: (1) traditional classification, (2) stage of development, (3) priority of lien, (4) payment pattern, (5) type of security, and (6) other.

The traditional classification includes conventional mortgages and nonconventional mortgages, such as FHA insured and VA guaranteed mortgages. The loans included the stage of development category involved interim loans and the permanent end loan. When loans are classified on a basis of priority, they are either senior mortgages or junior mortgages. The payment patterns range from interest-only loans to fully amortizing loans, from declining to increasing monthly payments, and from fixed to variable interest rates. The security offered for a loan may be real property, personal property, or both. The mortgage may be secured by one or more properties. The other category includes a number of mortgages such as participation, reverse annuity, and open-end mortgages.

KEY TERMS

Adjustable Mortgage Loan (AML)

Adjustable-Rate Mortgage (ARM)

Balloon Loan

Balloon Payment

Basket Loan

Blanket Mortgage Loan

Bridge Loan

Budget Mortgage Loan

Buy-Down Loan

Chattel Mortgage

Construction Loan

Conventional Loan

Convertible Mortgage

Demand Loan

End Loan

Equal Principal Reduction Loan

Equity Kicker

Equity Participation Mortgage

FHA Insured Loan

First Mortgage

Flexible Payment Mortgage (FPM) Loan

FLIP Mortgage Loan

Floor-to-Ceiling Loan

FmHA Mortgage Loan

Fully Amortizing Loan

Gap Loan

Graduated Payment Mortgage (GPM) Loan

Home Improvement Loan

Interim Loan

Junior Mortgage

Land Development Loan

Leasehold Mortgage

Level Payment Loan

Monthly Draw Method

Mortgage for Future Advances

Open-End Mortgage

Package Mortgage

Partially Amortizing Loan

Participation Mortgage

Permanent Loan

Permanent Take-Out Commitment

Pledged Savings Account Mortgage Loan

Purchase Money Mortgage

Real Estate Mortgage

Renegotiable Rate Mortgage (RRM) Loan

Reverse Annuity Mortgage (RAM) Loan

Senior Mortgage

Shared Appreciation Mortgage (SAM)

Stage of Completion Method

Standby Commitment

Term Mortgage Loan

VA Mortgage Loan

Variable-Rate Mortgage (VRM) Loan

Wraparound Mortgage

1. What is a conventional mortgage? Why is it called a conventional mortgage?

2. What are the main differences between a conventional, an FHA, and a VA mortgage?

3. Explain the interrelationships, if any, between a construction, a permanent, and a gap loan.

4. Is a wraparound mortgage a junior mortgage? Discuss.

5. Distinguish between the following mortgage types based on loan payment patterns. Under what circumstances might each be used?
   a. Demand Mortgage
   b. Renegotiable-Rate Mortgage (RRM)
   c. Variable-Rate Mortgage (VRM)
   d. Term Mortgage

6. Identify and distinguish among the following types of mortgages, classified by type of security. Under what circumstance might each be used?
   a. Blanket
   b. Chattel
   c. Package
   d. Leasehold

7. What is a purchase money mortgage? Does a PMM have any special characteristics? If so, what are they?

8. What are the advantages and disadvantages of a VRM or an RRM from the viewpoint of (a) a borrower, (b) a lender, and (c) the general public?

9. What age group is most likely to use and benefit from (a) a graduated payment mortgage, (b) a reverse annuity mortgage, and (c) a budget mortgage?

10. Match the following key terms and definitions:
    a. Buy-Down Loan _____
    b. Equity Kicker _____
    c. Adjustable-Rate Mortgage (ARM) _____
    d. Gap Loan _____

    1. Loan used to finance costs of construction.

    2. Short-term second loan until all proceeds from permanent loan obtained.

e. Renegotiable-Rate
   Mortgage (RRM)
   Loan   _____
f. Shared Appreciation
   Mortgage (SAM)
   Loan   _____

3. Interest rate modified by
   agreement at stated intervals.
4. A second loan that includes
   the amount of the first loan.
5. A bonus for a lender, as a
   share of property ownership.
6. Interest rate adjusted
   periodically in accordance
   with a stipulated index.
7. Cash contribution by someone
   other than borrower to
   decrease debt service in early
   years of a loan.
8. Has a lower interest rate but
   the lender receives a portion
   of the increase in the property
   value.

four

Mortgage Clauses

In this chapter we examine the provisions of the note and mortgage in detail. Most provisions in a trust deed and the accompanying note are very similar to those in a mortgage and mortgage note. Further, many of these same clauses may be used in land contracts, leases, and options.

The note and mortgage are usually form documents. The lender fills in the blanks with the specific details of the transaction, such as the names of the parties, the amount of the debt, and the description of the property. These forms are often tailored to specific types of properties, such as one- to four-family residential, five- or more family residential, and commercial. In addition, different forms are used in different states to reflect variations in mortgage law from state to state. Finally, FHA insured and VA guaranteed mortgage loans have their own unique forms.

The uniform instruments developed jointly by the Federal National Mortgage Association (FNMA) and the Federal Home Loan Mortgage Corporation (FHLMC) are used in our discussion. The uniform instruments include notes, mortgages, and trust deeds for most, if not all, states. The FNMA-FHLMC forms represent an effort to provide fair treatment to the borrower while, at the same time, providing adequate protection to the lender. In an era of increasing consumerism and government regulation, these forms are appealing to lenders who want to comply with the various laws that apply to real estate finance. Although no specific form is required to satisfy this goal, it is presumed that FNMA-FHLMC forms do comply with the various laws. Some variable or nonuniform clauses to allow for differences in laws among the states are included in the instruments. These forms are more widely used than any other. In effect, they set the standard for all other mortgage instruments. It is therefore very advantageous for anyone interested in real estate finance to be familiar with the clauses in these instruments and trust deeds. Use of these uniform instruments, however, is not required to make a loan eligible for purchase by FNMA or FHLMC, but it may speed the transaction along.

In this chapter, our discussion begins with the provisions of the FNMA-FHLMC uniform note and mortgage forms for a first mortgage loan on a one- to four-family residential property in Illinois. The form provides for a fixed interest rate and level monthly payments. Later in the chapter we examine clauses not found in the particular uniform instruments, but which are found in the forms for junior mortgages, variable-rate mortgages, and other special mortgages.

THE UNIFORM NOTE

Figure 4–1 is the FNMA-FHLMC uniform mortgage note. It is followed paragraph by paragraph to point out and interpret its relevant provisions.

DATE

The most significant feature of the heading is that it specifies the date that the note was signed—September 15, 1982. While this date is important, the date of recording the mortgage is more significant.

INDEBTEDNESS, PROMISE TO PAY, AND TERMS OF PAYMENT

The first paragraph of the note supplies the following information:

The name of the lender, Anytown Bank, is identified. The persons who are liable for meeting the terms of the note, Merritt Miller and Morgan Miller, are identified by reference to their signatures at the bottom of the note.

The borrowers promise to pay $50,000 to Anytown Bank or order. When the Millers agree to the "or order" provision, they agree to pay to any party holding the note. The recognition of the debt and the promise to pay are the basic provisions of the note.

The Millers agree to the annual interest rate, 12 percent, to be paid on the unpaid balance. They agree to make level monthly payments of interest and principal of $526.60 beginning on October 1, 1982. The term

FIGURE 4–1

NOTE

US $ .50,000 . . . . Anytown . . . ., Illinois

City

. . . . September .15 . . . ., 19 82 .

FOR VALUE RECEIVED, the undersigned ("Borrower") promise(s) to pay . . Anytown .Bank . . . .
. . . . .Anytown., .Illinois . . . ., or order, the principal sum of
. . . . .Fifty .Thousand .and .no/100 .- - - - - - - - - - - - . ($50,000) . . . . . . Dollars, with
interest on the unpaid principal balance from the date of this Note, until paid, at the rate of . . .Twelve .(12) . . . .
. . . . .percent per annum. Principal and interest shall be payable at . . 200 .Smith .Street
. . . . .Anytown., .Illinois. 60111 . . . ., or such other place as the Note holder may
designate, in consecutive monthly installments of . . .Five .Hundred .Twenty-Six .and .60/100 . . . . . .
. . . . .Dollars (US $ 526..60 . . . .), on the . . . . .5th . . . .
. . . . .day of each month beginning . . Qctober .1 . . . ., 19 82 .. Such monthly installments
shall continue until the entire indebtedness evidenced by this Note is fully paid, except that any remaining indebtedness, if not sooner paid, shall be due and payable on . . . September .1, .2007 . . . .

If any monthly installment under this Note is not paid when due and remains unpaid after a date specified by a
notice to Borrower, the entire principal amount outstanding and accrued interest thereon shall at once become due
and payable at the option of the Note holder. The date specified shall not be less than thirty days from the date such
notice is mailed. The Note holder may exercise this option to accelerate during any default by Borrower regardless of
any prior forbearance. If suit is brought to collect this Note, the Note holder shall be entitled to collect all reasonable
costs and expenses of suit, including, but not limited to, reasonable attorney's fees.

Borrower shall pay to the Note holder a late charge of . . . . .Two .(2) . . . . .percent of any monthly
installment not received by the Note holder within . . . . .Fifteen .(15) . . . . . .days after the installment is due.

Borrower may prepay the principal amount outstanding in whole or in part. The Note holder may require that
any partial prepayments (i) be made on the date monthly installments are due and (ii) be in the amount of that
part of one or more monthly installments which would be applicable to principal. Any partial prepayment shall be
applied against the principal amount outstanding and shall not postpone the due date of any subsequent monthly
installments or change the amount of such installments, unless the Note holder shall otherwise agree in writing.

Presentment, notice of dishonor, and protest are hereby waived by all makers, sureties, guarantors and endorsers
hereof. This Note shall be the joint and several obligation of all makers, sureties, guarantors and endorsers, and shall
be binding upon them and their successors and assigns.

Any notice to Borrower provided for in this Note shall be given by mailing such notice by certified mail addressed
to Borrower at the Property Address stated below, or to such other address as Borrower may designate by notice to
the Note holder. Any notice to the Note holder shall be given by mailing such notice by certified mail, return receipt
requested, to the Note holder at the address stated in the first paragraph of this Note, or at such other address as may
have been designated by notice to Borrower.

The indebtedness evidenced by this Note is secured by a Mortgage, dated . . . . . September .15, .1982 .
. . . ., and reference is made to the Mortgage for rights as to acceleration of the indebtedness
evidenced by this Note.

/s/ .Merritt .Miller . . . .

. . . .1262 .Fairlawn .Court . . . .   /s/ .Morgan .Miller . . . .

. . . .Anytown, .Illinois .60111 . . . .
Property Address   *(Execute Original Only)*

ILLINOIS—1 to 4 Family—6/75—FNMA/FHLMC UNIFORM INSTRUMENT of the loan is 25 years, and the final installment is due on September 1, 2007. Payments are to be made at the office of Anytown Bank unless the lender directs otherwise.

DEFAULT, ACCELERATION, AND EXPENSES

The second paragraph concerns the failure to make the monthly payment when due and its consequences. When the borrowers fail to make their payment on time, they are in default. Under the provisions of this note, the noteholder must send written notice of default at least 30 days before taking action under the acceleration provision. If the borrowers pay the past due amount within the time period specified, which can be no less than 30 days, the noteholder cannot take further action against the borrowers. If they do not pay within the period specified, the noteholder may exercise the acceleration clause.

An *acceleration clause* allows a noteholder to declare the entire outstanding loan balance and accrued interest due and payable immediately. This note also provides that if the noteholder does not exercise the acceleration in a given default, the noteholder reserves the right to exercise it if the borrowers default again at a later date. This clause is included because some courts have held that forebearance in the case of one default prevents the exercise of the acceleration provision in future similar defaults.

If the noteholder does bring foreclosure action under the acceleration provision, this note provides that the noteholder has the right to demand reimbursement for all reasonable costs and expenses. The reasonable costs and expenses include reasonable attorney's fees.

The acceleration clause is very important to the noteholder. If there is no acceleration clause, the noteholder can only take legal action to collect the past due payments plus the costs. Without the acceleration clause, the noteholder could be forced to bring legal action numerous times to finally collect the total debt.

LATE PAYMENT PENALTY

The third paragraph is the late payment penalty clause. The noteholder is allowed to charge a late payment penalty if the past due payment is received after a specified time period. In this particular note, the Millers can be charged a penalty if the payment is not received within 15 days after its due date. The late payment penalty is two percent of the past due payment or about $10.

PREPAYMENT CLAUSE

The fourth paragraph is the prepayment or redemption clause. The note gives the borrowers the right to pay part or the entire balance of the debt before it is due. This is called the *prepayment privilege.* In the absence of this provision the borrower does not have the right to prepay the loan. The prepayment privilege is very important to the borrower if the borrower wants to refinance the loan to take advantage of lower interest rates, or if the owner-borrower wants to sell the property free of the mortgage.

In many states, including Illinois, state laws grant the borrower under a note secured by a single-family residence the right to prepay the loan. FHA and VA mortgage loans also grant the prepayment privilege.

If a prepayment privilege is given, often a *prepayment penalty* is charged. The typical prepayment penalty runs from two to six months interest on the amount prepaid. Prepayment penalties are not allowed in FHA insured and VA guaranteed mortgage loans. In some states a prepayment penalty on mortgage loans on single-family residences is illegal.

In the note signed by the Millers, a prepayment penalty is not provided for, but there are some restrictions on the prepayment privilege. The noteholder reserves the right to require any prepayments to be made on the due date of a monthly installment. The noteholder also reserves the right to set a minimum on the size of the prepayment. This prevents problems with someone who might want to prepay one dollar per day or per week throughout the year. The bookkeeping expense associated with frequent and small prepayments could sharply reduce the return earned by the noteholder.

The noteholder promises to apply the prepayment to the reduction of the loan balance. This has two implications. One, it benefits the borrower because this prevents the noteholder from applying the payments to prepaid interest. Two, it benefits the noteholder by preventing the borrower from calling the payments advance monthly payments. In some cases borrowers have prepaid substantial sums and experienced financial difficulties at a later date. Assume that a borrower prepaid enough to cover the required monthly payments for two years and then began to default on the monthly payments. The lender could not exercise the acceleration provision until two years after the defaults began.

BORROWER'S WAIVERS

In paragraph five the Millers waive their rights relative to presentment, notice of dishonor, and protest. Presentment refers to a demand for the payments due. A notice of dishonor is a notice that the amounts have not been paid. Protest refers to a document certifying that the borrower has failed to pay the amounts due. Their waiver eliminates some steps and formalities that would have been necessary to prove the noteholder's case before a court.

It is also stated that the note is the joint and several obligations of all makers. This means that each signer is liable for the entire obligation. The noteholder can take legal action against one or all of the makers to collect the debt. The noteholder is not bound by any agreement between the borrowers that specifies a division of the debt between them.

METHOD OF NOTICE TO BORROWER

The sixth paragraph allows the noteholder to satisfy any requirements for notice to the borrowers by the use of certified mail with a return receipt requested. The return receipt is to be sent to the noteholder's address shown in paragraph one. If the office is moved or the note has been sold to an investor, the current noteholder can provide notice of another address. The certified mail can be sent to the address shown at the bottom of the note unless the borrowers designate another address.

REFERENCE TO THE MORTGAGE

The seventh and last paragraph refers to the mortgage securing the note. This means that the borrower is bound by the covenants and clauses in the mortgage securing the note. The violation of covenants or clauses in the mortgage allows the noteholder to declare the loan in default and take action to collect the entire debt.

NEGOTIABILITY AND SIGNATURES

The bottom of the note includes blanks for the signatures of the borrowers. Below the signatures it says execute original only. This means that the borrowers should only sign the original copy of the note. In the second line of the first paragraph it says pay to Anytown Bank or order. The use of the term *or order* means that the noteholder is free to sell his or her rights in the note to another investor. If more than one copy of the note was signed, a dishonest individual could sell each of the signed copies of the note. Therefore, the safest practice is to sign only one copy of any note.

    The signature of any co-signer who guarantees the payment of the debt should also appear on the note. For example, parents are sometimes willing to assist their offspring by co-signing a note with them.

THE UNIFORM MORTGAGE

Figure 4–2 is the FNMA-FHLMC uniform mortgage. First, the opening section of the mortgage is discussed, paragraph by paragraph. Second, the uniform covenants are discussed, by number. Third, the nonuni-

FIGURE 4–2

This instrument was prepared by:

.....I.M..Lawyer........
(Name)

200. Smith. St.. Anytown, IL
(Address)

MORTGAGE

THIS MORTGAGE is made this.....15th................day of.....September..........,
19..82, between the Mortgagor,....Merritt..and.Morgan.Miller..........................
.....................................(herein "Borrower"), and the Mortgagee, Anytown.Bank...
...Anytown,..Illinois.., a corporation organized and
existing under the laws of.......Illinois......................, whose address is................
............200.Smith.Street,.Anytown,.Illinois.........(herein "Lender").

WHEREAS, Borrower is indebted to Lender in the principal sum of...Fifty.Thousand.and.no/100
----------------------------($50,000).Dollars, which indebtedness is evidenced by Borrower's
note dated..September.15,.1982.(herein "Note"), providing for monthly installments of principal and
interest, with the balance of the indebtedness, if not sooner paid, due and payable on.September.1,.2007...
....................;

To SECURE to Lender (a) the repayment of the indebtedness evidenced by the Note, with interest thereon, the
payment of all other sums, with interest thereon, advanced in accordance herewith to protect the security of this
Mortgage, and the performance of the covenants and agreements of Borrower herein contained, and (b) the repayment
of any future advances, with interest thereon, made to Borrower by Lender pursuant to paragraph 21 hereof (herein
"Future Advances"), Borrower does hereby mortgage, grant and convey to Lender the following described property
located in the County of.........Hill........................, State of Illinois:

Lot 12, Block C, Fairlawn Subidivsion, Hill County, Illinois.

which has the address of.....1262.Fairlawn.Court.............,...........Anytown.......,
                  [Street]   **[City]**
...Illinois..60111......(herein "Property Address");
[State and Zip Code]

TOGETHER with all the improvements now or hereafter erected on the property, and all easements, rights,
appurtenances, rents, royalties, mineral, oil and gas rights and profits, water, water rights, and water stock, and all
fixtures now or hereafter attached to the property, all of which, including replacements and additions thereto, shall be
deemed to be and remain a part of the property covered by this Mortgage; and all of the foregoing, together with said
property (or the leasehold estate if this Mortgage is on a leasehold) are herein referred to as the "Property".

Borrower covenants that Borrower is lawfully seised of the estate hereby conveyed and has the right to mortgage,
grant and convey the Property, that the Property is unencumbered, and that Borrower will warrant and defend
generally the title to the Property against all claims and demands, subject to any declarations, easements or restrictions
listed in a schedule of exceptions to coverage in any title insurance policy insuring Lender's interest in the Property.

ILLINOIS—1 to 4 Family—6/77—FNMA/FHLMC UNIFORM INSTRUMENT

FIGURE 4–2 (Continued)

UNIFORM COVENANTS. Borrower and Lender covenant and agree as follows:

1. Payment of Principal and Interest. Borrower shall promptly pay when due the principal of and interest on the indebtedness evidenced by the Note, prepayment and late charges as provided in the Note, and the principal of and interest on any Future Advances secured by this Mortgage.

2. Funds for Taxes and Insurance. Subject to applicable law or to a written waiver by Lender, Borrower shall pay to Lender on the day monthly installments of principal and interest are payable under the Note, until the Note is paid in full, a sum (herein "Funds") equal to one-twelfth of the yearly taxes and assessments which may attain priority over this Mortgage, and ground rents on the Property, if any, plus one-twelfth of yearly premium installments for hazard insurance, plus one-twelfth of yearly premium installments for mortgage insurance, if any, all as reasonably estimated initially and from time to time by Lender on the basis of assessments and bills and reasonable estimates thereof.

The Funds shall be held in an institution the deposits or accounts of which are insured or guaranteed by a Federal or state agency (including Lender if Lender is such an institution). Lender shall apply the Funds to pay said taxes, assessments, insurance premiums and ground rents. Lender may not charge for so holding and applying the Funds, analyzing said account, or verifying and compiling said assessments and bills, unless Lender pays Borrower interest on the Funds and applicable law permits Lender to make such a charge. Borrower and Lender may agree in writing at the time of execution of this Mortgage that interest on the Funds shall be paid to Borrower, and unless such agreement is made or applicable law requires such interest to be paid, Lender shall not be required to pay Borrower any interest or earnings on the Funds. Lender shall give to Borrower, without charge, an annual accounting of the Funds showing credits and debits to the Funds and the purpose for which each debit to the Funds was made. The Funds are pledged as additional security for the sums secured by this Mortgage.

If the amount of the Funds held by Lender, together with the future monthly installments of Funds payable prior to the due dates of taxes, assessments, insurance premiums and ground rents, shall exceed the amount required to pay said taxes, assessments, insurance premiums and ground rents as they fall due, such excess shall be, at Borrower's option, either promptly repaid to Borrower or credited to Borrower on monthly installments of Funds. If the amount of the Funds held by Lender shall not be sufficient to pay taxes, assessments, insurance premiums and ground rents as they fall due, Borrower shall pay to Lender any amount necessary to make up the deficiency within 30 days from the date notice is mailed by Lender to Borrower requesting payment thereof.

Upon payment in full of all sums secured by this Mortgage, Lender shall promptly refund to Borrower any Funds held by Lender. If under paragraph 18 hereof the Property is sold or the Property is otherwise acquired by Lender, Lender shall apply, no later than immediately prior to the sale of the Property or its acquisition by Lender, any Funds held by Lender at the time of application as a credit against the sums secured by this Mortgage.

3. Application of Payments. Unless applicable law provides otherwise, all payments received by Lender under the Note and paragraphs 1 and 2 hereof shall be applied by Lender first in payment of amounts payable to Lender by Borrower under paragraph 2 hereof, then to interest payable on the Note, then to the principal of the Note, and then to interest and principal on any Future Advances.

4. Charges; Liens. Borrower shall pay all taxes, assessments and other charges, fines and impositions attributable to the Property which may attain a priority over this Mortgage, and leasehold payments or ground rents, if any, in the manner provided under paragraph 2 hereof or, if not paid in such manner, by Borrower making payment, when due, directly to the payee thereof. Borrower shall promptly furnish to Lender all notices of amounts due under this paragraph, and in the event Borrower shall make payment directly, Borrower shall promptly furnish to Lender receipts evidencing such payments. Borrower shall promptly discharge any lien which has priority over this Mortgage; provided, that Borrower shall not be required to discharge any such lien so long as Borrower shall agree in writing to the payment of the obligation secured by such lien in a manner acceptable to Lender, or shall in good faith contest such lien by, or defend enforcement of such lien in, legal proceedings which operate to prevent the enforcement of the lien or forfeiture of the Property or any part thereof.

5. Hazard Insurance. Borrower shall keep the improvements now existing or hereafter erected on the Property insured against loss by fire, hazards included within the term "extended coverage", and such other hazards as Lender may require and in such amounts and for such periods as Lender may require; provided, that Lender shall not require that the amount of such coverage exceed that amount of coverage required to pay the sums secured by this Mortgage.

The insurance carrier providing the insurance shall be chosen by Borrower subject to approval by Lender; provided, that such approval shall not be unreasonably withheld. All premiums on insurance policies shall be paid in the manner provided under paragraph 2 hereof or, if not paid in such manner, by Borrower making payment, when due, directly to the insurance carrier.

All insurance policies and renewals thereof shall be in form acceptable to Lender and shall include a standard mortgage clause in favor of and in form acceptable to Lender. Lender shall have the right to hold the policies and renewals thereof, and Borrower shall promptly furnish to Lender all renewal notices and all receipts of paid premiums. In the event of loss, Borrower shall give prompt notice to the insurance carrier and Lender. Lender may make proof of loss if not made promptly by Borrower.

Unless Lender and Borrower otherwise agree in writing, insurance proceeds shall be applied to restoration or repair of the Property damaged, provided such restoration or repair is economically feasible and the security of this Mortgage is not thereby impaired. If such restoration or repair is not economically feasible or if the security of this Mortgage would be impaired, the insurance proceeds shall be applied to the sums secured by this Mortgage, with the excess, if any, paid to Borrower. If the Property is abandoned by Borrower, or if Borrower fails to respond to Lender within 30 days from the date notice is mailed by Lender to Borrower that the insurance carrier offers to settle a claim for insurance benefits, Lender is authorized to collect and apply the insurance proceeds at Lender's option either to restoration or repair of the Property or to the sums secured by this Mortgage.

Unless Lender and Borrower otherwise agree in writing, any such application of proceeds to principal shall not extend or postpone the due date of the monthly installments referred to in paragraphs 1 and 2 hereof or change the amount of such installments. If under paragraph 18 hereof the Property is acquired by Lender, all right, title and interest of Borrower in and to any insurance policies and in and to the proceeds thereof resulting from damage to the Property prior to the sale or acquisition shall pass to Lender to the extent of the sums secured by this Mortgage immediately prior to such sale or acquisition.

6. Preservation and Maintenance of Property; Leaseholds; Condominiums; Planned Unit Developments. Borrower shall keep the Property in good repair and shall not commit waste or permit impairment or deterioration of the Property and shall comply with the provisions of any lease if this Mortgage is on a leasehold. If this Mortgage is on a unit in a condominium or a planned unit development, Borrower shall perform all of Borrower's obligations under the declaration or covenants creating or governing the condominium or planned unit development, the by-laws and regulations of the condominium or planned unit development, and constituent documents. If a condominium or planned unit development rider is executed by Borrower and recorded together with this Mortgage, the covenants and agreements of such rider shall be incorporated into and shall amend and supplement the covenants and agreements of this Mortgage as if the rider were a part hereof.

7. Protection of Lender's Security. If Borrower fails to perform the covenants and agreements contained in this Mortgage, or if any action or proceeding is commenced which materially affects Lender's interest in the Property, including, but not limited to, eminent domain, insolvency, code enforcement, or arrangements or proceedings involving a bankrupt or decedent, then Lender at Lender's option, upon notice to Borrower, may make such appearances, disburse such sums and take such action as is necessary to protect Lender's interest, including, but not limited to, disbursement of reasonable attorney's fees and entry upon the Property to make repairs. If Lender required mortgage insurance as a condition of making the loan secured by this Mortgage, Borrower shall pay the premiums required to maintain such insurance in effect until such time as the requirement for such insurance terminates in accordance with Borrower's and

FIGURE 4–2 (*Continued*)

Lender's written agreement or applicable law. Borrower shall pay the amount of all mortgage insurance premiums in the manner provided under paragraph 2 hereof.

Any amounts disbursed by Lender pursuant to this paragraph 7, with interest thereon, shall become additional indebtedness of Borrower secured by this Mortgage. Unless Borrower and Lender agree to other terms of payment, such amounts shall be payable upon notice from Lender to Borrower requesting payment thereof, and shall bear interest from the date of disbursement at the rate payable from time to time on outstanding principal under the Note unless payment of interest at such rate would be contrary to applicable law, in which event such amounts shall bear interest at the highest rate permissible under applicable law. Nothing contained in this paragraph 7 shall require Lender to incur any expense or take any action hereunder.

8. Inspection. Lender may make or cause to be made reasonable entries upon and inspections of the Property, provided that Lender shall give Borrower notice prior to any such inspection specifying reasonable cause therefor related to Lender's interest in the Property.

9. Condemnation. The proceeds of any award or claim for damages, direct or consequential, in connection with any condemnation or other taking of the Property, or part thereof, or for conveyance in lieu of condemnation, are hereby assigned and shall be paid to Lender.

In the event of a total taking of the Property, the proceeds shall be applied to the sums secured by this Mortgage, with the excess, if any, paid to Borrower. In the event of a partial taking of the Property, unless Borrower and Lender otherwise agree in writing, there shall be applied to the sums secured by this Mortgage such proportion of the proceeds as is equal to that proportion which the amount of the sums secured by this Mortgage immediately prior to the date of taking bears to the fair market value of the Property immediately prior to the date of taking, with the balance of the proceeds paid to Borrower.

If the Property is abandoned by Borrower, or if, after notice by Lender to Borrower that the condemnor offers to make an award or settle a claim for damages, Borrower fails to respond to Lender within 30 days after the date such notice is mailed, Lender is authorized to collect and apply the proceeds, at Lender's option, either to restoration or repair of the Property or to the sums secured by this Mortgage.

Unless Lender and Borrower otherwise agree in writing, any such application of proceeds to principal shall not extend or postpone the due date of the monthly installments referred to in paragraphs 1 and 2 hereof or change the amount of such installments.

10. Borrower Not Released. Extension of the time for payment or modification of amortization of the sums secured by this Mortgage granted by Lender to any successor in interest of Borrower shall not operate to release, in any manner, the liability of the original Borrower and Borrower's successors in interest. Lender shall not be required to commence proceedings against such successor or refuse to extend time for payment or otherwise modify amortization of the sums secured by this Mortgage by reason of any demand made by the original Borrower and Borrower's successors in interest.

11. Forbearance by Lender Not a Waiver. Any forbearance by Lender in exercising any right or remedy hereunder, or otherwise afforded by applicable law, shall not be a waiver of or preclude the exercise of any such right or remedy. The procurement of insurance or the payment of taxes or other liens or charges by Lender shall not be a waiver of Lender's right to accelerate the maturity of the indebtedness secured by this Mortgage.

12. Remedies Cumulative. All remedies provided in this Mortgage are distinct and cumulative to any other right or remedy under this Mortgage or afforded by law or equity, and may be exercised concurrently, independently or successively.

13. Successors and Assigns Bound; Joint and Several Liability; Captions. The covenants and agreements herein contained shall bind, and the rights hereunder shall inure to, the respective successors and assigns of Lender and Borrower, subject to the provisions of paragraph 17 hereof. All covenants and agreements of Borrower shall be joint and several. The captions and headings of the paragraphs of this Mortgage are for convenience only and are not to be used to interpret or define the provisions hereof.

14. Notice. Except for any notice required under applicable law to be given in another manner, (a) any notice to Borrower provided for in this Mortgage shall be given by mailing such notice by certified mail addressed to Borrower at the Property Address or at such other address as Borrower may designate by notice to Lender as provided herein, and (b) any notice to Lender shall be given by certified mail, return receipt requested, to Lender's address stated herein or to such other address as Lender may designate by notice to Borrower as provided herein. Any notice provided for in this Mortgage shall be deemed to have been given to Borrower or Lender when given in the manner designated herein.

15. Uniform Mortgage; Governing Law; Severability. This form of mortgage combines uniform covenants for national use and non-uniform covenants with limited variations by jurisdiction to constitute a uniform security instrument covering real property. This Mortgage shall be governed by the law of the jurisdiction in which the Property is located. In the event that any provision or clause of this Mortgage or the Note conflicts with applicable law, such conflict shall not affect other provisions of this Mortgage or the Note which can be given effect without the conflicting provision, and to this end the provisions of the Mortgage and the Note are declared to be severable.

16. Borrower's Copy. Borrower shall be furnished a conformed copy of the Note and of this Mortgage at the time of execution or after recordation hereof.

17. Transfer of the Property; Assumption. If all or any part of the Property or an interest therein is sold or transferred by Borrower without Lender's prior written consent, excluding (a) the creation of a lien or encumbrance subordinate to this Mortgage, (b) the creation of a purchase money security interest for household appliances, (c) a transfer by devise, descent or by operation of law upon the death of a joint tenant or (d) the grant of any leasehold interest of three years or less not containing an option to purchase, Lender may, at Lender's option, declare all the sums secured by this Mortgage to be immediately due and payable. Lender shall have waived such option to accelerate if, prior to the sale or transfer, Lender and the person to whom the Property is to be sold or transferred reach agreement in writing that the credit of such person is satisfactory to Lender and that the interest payable on the sums secured by this Mortgage shall be at such rate as Lender shall request. If Lender has waived the option to accelerate provided in this paragraph 17, and if Borrower's successor in interest has executed a written assumption agreement accepted in writing by Lender, Lender shall release Borrower from all obligations under this Mortgage and the Note.

If Lender exercises such option to accelerate, Lender shall mail Borrower notice of acceleration in accordance with paragraph 14 hereof. Such notice shall provide a period of not less than 30 days from the date the notice is mailed within which Borrower may pay the sums declared due. If Borrower fails to pay such sums prior to the expiration of such period, Lender may, without further notice or demand on Borrower, invoke any remedies permitted by paragraph 18 hereof.

NON-UNIFORM COVENANTS. Borrower and Lender further covenant and agree as follows:

18. Acceleration; Remedies. Except as provided in paragraph 17 hereof, upon Borrower's breach of any covenant or agreement of Borrower in this Mortgage, including the covenants to pay when due any sums secured by this Mortgage, Lender prior to acceleration shall mail notice to Borrower as provided in paragraph 14 hereof specifying: (1) the breach; (2) the action required to cure such breach; (3) a date, not less than 30 days from the date the notice is mailed to Borrower, by which such breach must be cured; and (4) that failure to cure such breach on or before the date specified in the notice may result in acceleration of the sums secured by this Mortgage, foreclosure by judicial proceeding and sale of the Property. The notice shall further inform Borrower of the right to reinstate after acceleration and the right to assert in the foreclosure proceeding the non-existence of a default or any other defense of Borrower to acceleration and foreclosure. If the breach is not cured on or before the date specified in the notice, Lender at Lender's option may declare all of the sums secured by this Mortgage to be immediately due and payable without further demand and may foreclose this Mortgage by judicial proceeding. Lender shall be entitled to collect in such proceeding all expenses of foreclosure, including, but not limited to, reasonable attorney's fees, and costs of documentary evidence, abstracts and title reports.

19. Borrower's Right to Reinstate. Notwithstanding Lender's acceleration of the sums secured by this Mortgage, Borrower shall have the right to have any proceedings begun by Lender to enforce this Mortgage discontinued at any time

FIGURE 4–2 (*Continued*)

prior to entry of a judgment enforcing this Mortgage if: (a) Borrower pays Lender all sums which would be then due under this Mortgage, the Note and notes securing Future Advances, if any, had no acceleration occurred; (b) Borrower cures all breaches of any other covenants or agreements of Borrower contained in this Mortgage; (c) Borrower pays all reasonable expenses incurred by Lender in enforcing the covenants and agreements of Borrower contained in this Mortgage and in enforcing Lender's remedies as provided in paragraph 18 hereof, including, but not limited to, reasonable attorney's fees; and (d) Borrower takes such action as Lender may reasonably require to assure that the lien of this Mortgage, Lender's interest in the Property and Borrower's obligation to pay the sums secured by this Mortgage shall continue unimpaired. Upon such payment and cure by Borrower, this Mortgage and the obligations secured hereby shall remain in full force and effect as if no acceleration had occurred.

20. Assignment of Rents; Appointment of Receiver; Lender in Possession. As additional security hereunder, Borrower hereby assigns to Lender the rents of the Property, provided that Borrower shall, prior to acceleration under paragraph 18 hereof or abandonment of the Property, have the right to collect and retain such rents as they become due and payable.

Upon acceleration under paragraph 18 hereof or abandonment of the Property, and at any time prior to the expiration of any period of redemption following judicial sale, Lender, in person, by agent or by judicially appointed receiver, shall be entitled to enter upon, take possession of and manage the Property and to collect the rents of the Property including those past due. All rents collected by Lender or the receiver shall be applied first to payment of the costs of management of the Property and collection of rents, including, but not limited to receiver's fees, premiums on receiver's bonds and reasonable attorney's fees, and then to the sums secured by this Mortgage. Lender and the receiver shall be liable to account only for those rents actually received.

21. Future Advances. Upon request of Borrower, Lender, at Lender's option prior to release of this Mortgage, may make Future Advances to Borrower. Such Future Advances, with interest thereon, shall be secured by this Mortgage when evidenced by promissory notes stating that said notes are secured hereby. At no time shall the principal amount of the indebtedness secured by this Mortgage, not including sums advanced in accordance herewith to protect the security of this Mortgage, exceed the original amount of the Note plus US $.Ten.Thousand.and.no/100 ($10,000)

22. Release. Upon payment of all sums secured by this Mortgage, Lender shall release this Mortgage without charge to Borrower. Borrower shall pay all costs of recordation, if any.

23. Waiver of Homestead. Borrower hereby waives all right of homestead exemption in the Property.

IN WITNESS WHEREOF, Borrower has executed this Mortgage.

..../s/..Merritt.Miller......................
—Borrower

..../s/..Morgan.Miller......................
—Borrower

STATE OF ILLINOIS,.........Hill........................County ss:

I,........Robert.E..Trustworthy........., a Notary Public in and for said county and state,

do hereby certify that.....Merritt.Miller.and.Morgan.Miller.........................

........................, personally known to me to be the same person(s) whose name(s)...are....

subscribed to the foregoing instrument, appeared before me this day in person, and acknowledged that...they...

signed and delivered the said instrument as...their....free and voluntary act, for the uses and purposes therein

set forth.

Given under my hand and official seal, this....15th...day of.September......., 19.82...

My Commission expires: June 5th, 1983

..../s/..Robert.E..Trustworthy..............
Notary Public

——————————— (Space Below This Line Reserved For Lender and Recorder) ———————————

form covenants are discussed by number. Fourth, reference is made to the signatures and the acknowledgment.

The opening section includes the basic elements of the mortgage. The mortgagor and mortgagee are identified. The property is described and offered as security for the debt.

Identification of Parties and the Debt. The first paragraph of the opening section identifies the mortgagors (the Millers) and the mortgagee (Anytown Bank). It also shows the date of the mortgage and the address of the lender.

The second paragraph states the amount of the debt, $50,000. It also refers to the note that provides the evidence of the existence of the debt and identifies the final due date of the debt.

Pledge of the Property as Security. In the third paragraph the Millers mortgage, grant, and convey the identified property to the mortgagee as security. The property is offered as security for the payment of the debt evidenced by the note for any interest due and for any future advances under the mortgage. It is also security for the performance of the borrower's covenants and agreements. This is the basic provision of the mortgage. It allows the mortgagee to force the sale of the property to collect his or her claim if the borrower defaults on the payments or the mortgage covenants.

Identification of the Property. The third paragraph also includes the legal description and an informal description of the property offered as security. The identification of the property is one of the necessary elements of a mortgage.

The fourth paragraph provides further explanation of the property offered as security. The property includes all of the current improvements and any improvements erected on the land in the future. The property also includes all appurtenances, fixtures, rents, water rights, and so forth. All of the specified interests must remain part of the property covered by the mortgage. The removal or sale of any part or interest would violate the mortgage loan agreement unless the lender gives specific written approval.

Covenant of Seizin. In the fifth and last paragraph of the opening section, the borrowers covenant that they possess the estate that they are conveying and that they have the right to mortgage it. This is called the *covenant of seizin.* The borrowers promise that the property is free from encumbrances. In this sense encumbrances include any liens or claims against the property that may reduce its value. The borrowers are required to defend the title against all claims. This protection often is provided by the borrower's purchase of a mortgagee's title insurance policy that protects the lenders' interest in the property.

UNIFORM COVENANTS

Clauses one through seventeen in the Uniform Mortgage shown in Figure 4–2 are called the uniform covenants because they are included without variation in the mortgage and trust deed forms for each state. The clauses are discussed in the same order as they appear in the uniform mortgage.

Payment of Principal and Interest. Clause one requires the borrower to pay the debt when due, including any future advances and interest. The borrower also agrees to pay any required late charges and prepayment penalties if any exist.

Deposits for Taxes and Insurance. Clause two states that if it is allowed by state law, the lender may require monthly payments for real estate taxes, hazard insurance, and, if they exist, for special assessments, mortgage insurance, and ground rents. The lender holds these funds in trust or escrow for the borrower and pays the bills when due. The lender desires to make sure that the real estate taxes, special assessments, and ground rents are paid when due. Liens for property taxes and usually liens for ground rents have priority over the mortgage lien. The lender also wants to keep the hazard insurance and mortgage insurance in force to further protect his or her position. The use of escrow accounts is one means of making certain that the funds are available to pay these bills when due.

These escrow accounts may or may not earn interest. If they don't earn interest, the borrower may find it more favorable to employ a pledged savings account to insure payment of the bills.

In this note the lender gives the borrower an option in the event that escrow account contains excess funds. The borrower can request either the return of the excess funds or the application of the funds to reduce the required monthly payments into the escrow accounts. If the deposits are less than the charges, the borrower is required to make up the deficiency within 30 days after receiving such notice. The lender agrees to refund any deposits held at the time the debt is paid in full. Finally, the lender reserves the right to apply the escrow funds to payment of the debt in the event of foreclosure.

Application of Payments. Clause three specifies the use of the funds from the monthly mortgage payment and the monthly payment into the escrow account, if any. The lender is required to first apply the funds to the payment of property taxes, hazard insurance, mortgage insurance, and ground rents. They apply second to interest on the note and third to the reduction of the principal on the note. They apply next to interest and principal on any future advances.

Charges and Liens. In clause four the borrower agrees to pay any charges and liens against the property that may have priority over the mortgage. These charges and liens must be paid when due unless the lender agrees otherwise. This is an important clause particularly when there is no escrow account or pledged savings to guarantee the payment of the liens. If prior liens such as real estate taxes are not paid, the property might be sold at a tax sale or foreclosure sale. Such a sale would extinguish the lender's claim on the property unless the lender redeems the property.

Hazard Insurance. Clause five requires the borrower to maintain an extended coverage hazard insurance policy that protects against such things as fire, windstorms, hail, and smoke. The lender also has the right to require insurance against other hazards such as floods and earthquakes. The clause does not allow the lender to require insurance coverage in excess of the lender's claim. Of course, it is normally in the best interest of the borrower to carry a larger amount of insurance coverage. The lender has the right to approve or reject the insurer chosen by the borrower as long as the lender uses reasonable standards in the decision. The policy must contain a *mortgage clause* that makes the lender an insured party. The lender holds physical possession of the insurance policy. If there is a loss, the borrower must promptly notify the insurer and lender. In the event of loss, the lender may use the insurance proceeds to restore the property, if it is economically feasible. If it is not economically feasible or if the security of the lender would be impaired, the lender can apply the proceeds to the payment of the mortgage claim. The lender is also given this option if the property is abandoned and the borrower does not answer the lender's notice. In any event, if the proceeds are used to pay the lender's claim, any excess funds must be given to the borrower.

Preservation and Maintenance of Property. In clause six the borrower promises to maintain the property in good repair and not to permit its waste or deterioration. This prohibits the removal or demolition of any of the improvements on the land without the lender's approval. The borrower also promises to conform to the terms of any lease, condominium, or planned-unit development agreement. The clause also provides for a rider for condominium or planned-unit developments.

Protection of Lender's Security. In clause seven the lender reserves the right to protect the secured property if the borrower fails to do so. The lender is allowed to pay such expenses as the hazard insurance premiums, real estate taxes, and rental. The lender has the right to enter the property to make repairs. If legal action is brought against the property involving such things as code enforcement, eminent domain, or bankruptcy, the lender has the right to appear at the proceedings to defend the property. The lender has all of the rights of the borrower at such legal proceedings, which means he can act in the place of the borrower. This is sometimes called the *subrogation of rights provision.* This applies only if the borrower fails to act. The lender has the option to perform or not to perform these acts. If the lender does incur expenses on behalf of the borrower, the lender has the right to request reimbursement. If the borrower does not reimburse the lender, the lender can add the expenditures to the debt. The lender can then collect interest on these expenditures at interest rate of the loan or the highest interest rate allowed by law, whichever is lower.

Inspection. Clause eight grants the lender the right to inspect the property if reasonable cause is shown and notice is given to the borrower. This provides the lender an opportunity to verify whether or not the property is in an adequate state of repair.

Condemnation. Clause nine describes the lender's rights in the event that a portion of or the entire property is taken through condemnation proceedings under the government's right of eminent domain. If the entire property is taken, the proceeds from the condemnation are first applied to payment of the lender's claim. If any funds are left, they must be given to the borrower. If there is a partial taking of the property, the lender is allowed to apply a proportionate share of the proceeds to reduction of the mortgage claim. The remaining funds go to the borrower. Any partial payment of the lender's claim does not postpone or reduce the monthly payments due to the lender.

If the property is abandoned or the borrower does not reply to the lender's notice within 30 days, the lender may settle with the condemnor. The lender has the option to apply the funds either to restoration of the property or to settlement of the lender's claim.

Borrower Not Released. Clause ten states that the lender's extension of the time for payment or modification of the loan amortization schedule does not release the original borrower or the borrower's successors. This clause relates to the assumption of a mortgage without a release of the original borrower from his or her obligations. In the absence of this clause the original borrower must approve any adjustments made in the terms of the loan or the original borrower is released from the obligation to the lender. This clause allows adjustments in the terms of the loan without the approval of the original mortgagor, who continues to be bound by the obligation to the lender. The original borrower is therefore advised to obtain a release when the loan is assumed by another party, if possible.

Forbearance by Lender. Clause eleven states that any forbearance by the lender is not a waiver of the lender's right to take action in the future. For example, if the lender has accepted late payments from the borrower and not taken action to enforce the acceleration of the debt, this is forbearance. Some courts have held that since the lender has not taken action in this situation in the past, the lender cannot take action under the acceleration clause in future similar situations. The purpose of the *forbearance by lender* clause is to allow the lender to forbear in a given situation without losing the right to take action at a later time.

Remedies Cumulative. Clause twelve states that the lender's remedies under the mortgage or afforded by law or equity are distinct and cumulative. The remedies may be exercised concurrently, independently, or successively. In some states the lender can foreclose under the mortgage and ask for a deficiency judgment under the note at the same time. The lender can enter the property to restore it, add the expenses to the debt, and not take action to accelerate the debt.

Extent of Borrower's Obligations. Any party who takes the lender's place under the mortgage such as an investor obtains the lender's rights. Any party who takes the borrower's place under the mortage, such as someone assuming the mortgage or an heir, is bound by the borrower's covenants in the mortgage. The covenants and agreements are joint and several. If there are two or more borrowers, any one borrower can be named in the action for the collection of the debt. In the absence of this clause in the mortgage or note, the borrowers are assumed to have a joint obligation. In that case the lender would have to serve notice on and name each of the borrowers in any legal action.

Notice. Clause fourteen states that certified mail is sufficient for notice to the borrower or lender unless state law specifies otherwise. The notice to the lender is sent to the lender's address as shown on the face of the mortgage or to any other address specified by the lender. The notice to the borrower is sent to the borrower's address shown on the face of the mortgage or to any other address specified by the borrower. This clause is important in serving notice when it is impossible to deliver notice in person.

Uniform Mortgage and Governing Law. Clause fifteen states that the mortgage and note shall be governed by the law of the state or other jurisdiction in which the secured property is located. If the state law overrules a provision or provisions of the mortgage or note, the remaining provisions of the documents are not affected.

Borrower's Copy. Clause sixteen requires the lender to deliver a copy of the mortgage note and the mortgage to the borrower at execution or after recording.

Property Transfer and Loan Assumption. Clause seventeen is the due-on-sale or alienation clause. The *due-on-sale clause* allows the lender to exercise the acceleration clause and declare the entire debt and accrued interest due when the property is sold or transferred in some other manner. This note exempts certain transfers from the due-on-sale clause. For example, it does not apply to transfers as a result of one of the joint tenant's death or to the granting of a leasehold interest for three years or less if there is no option to purchase clause in the lease.

If part or all of the property is sold or transferred without the lender's prior written approval excluding certain stipulated transfers, the lender has the option to declare the entire debt and accrued interest due. If the lender exercises the option to accelerate, the borrower must be notified by certified mail. The lender must give the borrower at least 30 days from the date of notice before taking legal action to collect the debt. If the borrower pays the debt within the time period specified, legal action becomes unnecessary.

The lender can allow the assumption of the mortgage loan agreement by reaching a written agreement with the party receiving title to the property. The written agreement must specify that the lender approves the credit of the prospective owner and that the interest rate on the loan is acceptable. The lender is allowed to raise the interest rate as a condition of approval of the assumption.

The due-on-sale clause has been an area of controversy in recent years. When the parties who assumed the loans were faced with paying a higher interest rate than those on the original loans, a number of law suits were filed. In most states the due-on-sale clause is valid. In a few states the due-on-sale clause has been declared invalid when the security position of the lender is not weakened by the assumption. And at least five states have passed laws that prohibit the inclusion of a due-on-sale clause. This clause is also prohibited in FHA insured and VA guaranteed mortgages.

Some mortgages include a due-on-encumbrance clause, which allows the lender to accelerate the payments if the borrower creates another lien on the property, such as a second mortgage. Clause seventeen specifically excludes an acceleration because of the creation of a lien or encumbrance subordinate to this mortgage or the creation of a purchase money mortgage interest for household appliances.

NONUNIFORM COVENANTS

Clauses eighteen through twenty-two in the mortgage shown in Figure 4–2 are called the nonuniform covenants, because they vary among the states. The clauses are discussed in the same order as they appear in the uniform mortgage.

Acceleration and Remedies. Clause eighteen describes the procedure that must be followed to accelerate the debt and foreclose for any breach other than an unauthorized transfer of the property. The lender must send written notice to the borrower, which must specify the following:

1. The breach.
2. The action required to cure the breach.
3. A date, at least 30 days after notice, by which the breach must be cured.
4. That failure to cure may result in acceleration of the sums due on foreclosure by judicial proceeding and sale of the property.
5. That the borrower has a right to reinstate after the acceleration.
6. That the borrower has a right to present a defense at the foreclosure proceeding.

If the borrower does not cure the breach on or before the date specified, the lender can accelerate all sums due and begin foreclosure proceedings. The note also specifies that the lender is entitled to collect all expenses of foreclosure, which include reasonable attorney's fees and costs of documentary evidence, abstracts, and title reports.

Borrower's Right to Reinstate. Clause nineteen—the *borrower's right to reinstate clause*—gives the borrower the right to stop the foreclosure proceedings at any time prior to the entry of the decree for the sale of the property. Essentially this is the borrower's equitable right of redemption. The borrower must meet the following requirements to stop the foreclosure proceedings:

1. Pay all sums which would have been due if the lender had not exercised acceleration.
2. Cure all breaches of any other covenants or agreements.
3. Pay all the lender's expenditures incurred to enforce the covenants and the remedies.
4. Assure the lender's interest in the property and the note shall continue unimpaired.

If the borrower meets these conditions, the mortgage is reinstated as if no acceleration had occurred.

Assignment of Rents. Clause twenty is an assignment of rents provision that provides additional security for the lender. The *assignment of rents* transfers the rights to collect the rents of the property to the lender. The mortgage allows the lender to take possession and collect the rents on acceleration or abandonment through to the expiration of the statutory redemption period. The borrowers are allowed to continue to occupy the property by paying reasonable rent. The lender or a judicially appointed receiver is allowed to take possession, manage the property, and collect the rents. Under this provision the lender or receiver is accountable for only those rents actually collected. The funds from the rents are applied first to the costs of operating and managing the property. The remaining funds are used to satisfy the debt, accrued interest, and other claims of the lender.

The assignment of rents gives the lender greater rights to possession and rents and lesser liability for management than the mortgage would otherwise provide.

Future Advances. Clause twenty-one allows the borrower to obtain *future advances* or additional funds by signing new notes that are secured by this mortgage. The amount of the future advances are not allowed to increase the debt in excess of $60,000. Of course, the lender has the right to refuse to make future advances. And the lender can charge a different interest rate on the future advances.

Release. Clause twenty-two requires the lender to provide the borrower with a written release of the mortgage when the borrower pays the debt in full. The borrower should record the release to clear the mortgage lien from the title to the property. The lender is required to provide the release without charge, but the borrower is responsible for any fees to record the release.

Waiver of Homestead. Clause twenty-three requires the borrower to release any right to a homestead exemption; it is therefore referred to as a *waiver of homestead exemption.* In Illinois the borrower has a homestead exemption of $10,000 unless the proceeds of the loan are used to purchase the homestead. If the homestead exemption applies against the loan, the first $10,000 of the net proceeds of the sale are given to the borrower. The waiver of the homestead exemption means that the net proceeds of the sale will apply first to the payment of the lender's claim and then the borrower receives the remaining funds, if any.

EXECUTION AND ACKNOWLEDGMENT

At the bottom of the mortgage form there are blanks for signatures and an acknowledgment. The borrowers must sign the mortgage to make it binding. The acknowledgment is completed to attest to the fact that the borrowers signed the mortgage of their own free will.

OTHER MORTGAGE LOAN CLAUSES

There are a number of mortgage clauses that were not contained in the particular uniform mortgage and note discussed above. Different states have some different variable clauses in the uniform mortgage. Junior mortgages require some clauses that are not found in first mortgages. Construction and land development loans require some additional clauses. Large-scale residential and commercial mortgages contain some provisions that are not appropriate for a mortgage on a single-family residence. The clauses are discussed under the headings of other residential mortgage loan clauses, junior mortgage clauses, and clauses in other types of mortgage loans. But it should be noted that some of the clauses could be used in more than one category of loan.

OTHER RESIDENTIAL MORTGAGE LOAN CLAUSES

Some of the more common clauses associated with residential loans that are not discussed as uniform clauses are explained below.

Variable-Rate Provision. A variable-rate mortgage loan contains a provision in the note that the interest rate on the debt may be increased or decreased in accordance with the movement of some index. Federally chartered savings and loan associations sometimes use the cost of funds as determined by the Federal Home Loan Bank Board as the reference index for changing the interest rate. The *variable-rate provision* is favorable to the borrower if the cost of funds declines in the future. It is favorable to the lender if the cost of funds increases in the future.

Interest Escalator Clause. The note may contain a clause that allows the lender to increase the interest rate on the debt after the occurrence of some specified event. The most common *interest escalator clause* provides for an increase in the interest rate when the borrower defaults on the loan agreement. Some developers have used this type of clause to offer low interest rates to the buyer-borrower for the first few years and to raise the rate to a higher level after some specified date.

Payment Escalator Clause. The note associated with a graduated payment or flexible payment mortgage loan allows the lender to increase the required monthly payment at some specified date. This is a *payment escalator clause.*

Cognovit Provision. The note may contain a *cognovit provision,* which means that the lender's attorney may appear in court and confess judgment against the borrowers. This provision is only exercised when the borrower is in default. It allows the lender's attorney to admit that the borrower has defaulted. This shifts the burden of proof to the borrower. The cognovit provision speeds court action and is therefore not favorable to the borrower. The cognovit provision is prohibited in a number of states.

Defeasance Clause. A defeasance clause is included in mortgages in title theory states. The *defeasance clause* states that on payment of the debt the mortgagee is divested of title and title is returned to the mortgagor.

Power-of-Sale Clause. In some states a *power-of-sale clause* is inserted in the mortgage or trust deed. Where applicable, the inclusion of the power-of-sale clause allows foreclosure by sale without a judicial proceeding. This reduces the cost of foreclosure action. Power of sale is discussed in the chapter entitled "Mortgage Default and Its Implications."

Receiver Clause. A *receiver clause* allows the lender to request the appointment of a receiver to protect the lender's interests after default, pending action to foreclose. The inclusion of this clause speeds the process of the appointment of a receiver.

Mortgagee in Possession Clause. The *mortgagee in possession clause* grants the lender the right to request possession as foreclosure action is initiated. This is prohibited in some lien theory states, and it is allowed only in conjunction with an assignment of rents in some other states.

Owner Rent Clauses. The *owner rent clause* allows the lender or receiver to charge the owner reasonable rent for occupancy of the property after foreclosure action is begun. This clause is necessary in some states to charge and collect rents from a borrower-owner who remains in possession after default.

Waiver of Defense Clause. In most states a negotiable note makes the mortgage negotiable. In some states this rule is not followed, and in some states events such as a past due payment can prevent the negotiability of the mortgage. In these states a *waiver of defense* or *estoppel clause* is included in the mortgage. The clause requires the borrower, on the request of the lender, to deliver a written statement acknowledging the outstanding balance of the debt and stating whether or not the borrower has any defenses against the mortgage. The written statement is called by a number of names including waiver of defenses, certificate of no defense, or estoppel certificate.

If the *estoppel certificate* states the balance of the loan and that there are no defenses against the mortgage, the borrower is prevented from denying the statement in the future. This makes the mortgage acceptable to investors, which means that it is negotiable.

Waiver of Dower and Curtesy. In states in which one or both of the spouses have dower or curtesy rights, the mortgagee may include a clause that requires the borrowers to waive these rights. This makes the foreclosure sale free of dower and curtesy.

JUNIOR MORTGAGE CLAUSES

Junior mortgages contain clauses that are not found in first mortgages. The junior mortgage holder is concerned with any default on a prior mortgage that would lead to a foreclosure that would, in turn, extinguish the junior mortgage. The borrower is concerned with the effect of the existence of a junior mortgage on his or her ability to refinance the first mortgage loan. Five common clauses that deal with these problems are discussed below.

Covenant to Meet Terms of Prior Mortgage. The borrower promises to meet the payments on the first mortgage and to perform all its covenants. This allows the junior mortgage lender to declare a breach in the junior mortgage and accelerate the debt in the event of any default on the first mortgage.

Right to Notice. The borrower promises to provide the junior mortgage lender any notice received from the first mortgage holder. This keeps the junior mortgage lender informed of any action being taken by the holder of the first mortgage.

Default in Prior Mortgage Clause. If a borrower breaches the terms and covenants of the first mortgage, a junior mortgage holder is given the right to correct the breach by a *default in prior mortgage clause.* For example, the junior mortgage holder is given the authority to pay such things as past due mortgage payments and real estate taxes and to add the expenditures to the debt owed on the second mortgage. This allows the junior mortgage holder to prevent a default in the prior mortgage while foreclosing the junior mortgage.

Due-on-Encumbrance Clause. Junior mortgages often include a clause prohibiting any other new mortgages or liens on the property. If new mortgages or liens are created, the junior mortgage holder is allowed to accelerate the debt and foreclose.

Subordination Clause. The subordination clause usually benefits the borrower. The *subordination clause* allows the borrower to retire the existing first mortgage and replace it with a new first mortgage. Without this clause when the existing first mortgage is retired, the second mortgage becomes the first mortgage. There may be a limitation on the subordination clause regarding an increase in the dollar amount of the first mortgage loan. The second mortgage holder could require that the balance owed on the second be reduced by an amount equal to the increase in the first mortgage loan.

CLAUSES IN OTHER TYPES OF MORTGAGE LOANS

Construction loans, land development loans, multifamily residential loans, and commercial loans often contain clauses not found in single-family mortgage loan agreements. Our discussion here is limited to the most important of these clauses.

Sole Security Clause. In many large projects the developer's or investor's net worth is small relative to the amount of the loan, and the lender looks to the value of the property for security. The mortgage loan agreement may contain a sole security clause. A *sole security clause* says that the lender will not hold the borrower personally liable in the event of default. A sole security clause prevents the lender from seeking a deficiency judgment under the note. The lender's only action is to foreclose on the mortgage. This is also called the *exculpatory clause.* Exculpatory means free from blame or guilt.

An exculpatory clause is usually agreed to by a lender in financing a large income property, such as an apartment house. This is reasonable with an income property loan in that the property is more looked to than the borrower for security. Default may have the potential for loss equal to or in excess of all the borrower's assets. Without an exculpatory clause this risk might be too great for an investor. A lender in a junior mortgage is not likely to agree to such a clause because all lien rights in the property offered as security may be given up as a result.

Sale in One Parcel Clause.   If the mortgage covers two or more parcels of real property such as a number of lots, any foreclosure sale must offer each parcel for sale separately. In some situations the sale of each lot separately would produce less funds than the sale of all the lots as one parcel. The *sale in one parcel clause* allows the property to be sold either as one parcel or as separate parcels.

Partial Release Clause.   A land developer may have a blanket mortgage loan covering a number of lots, and he or she desires to sell a portion of the lots. The lender could require payment of the entire debt to release the claim on any given lot. A *partial release clause* requires the lender to release a portion of the parcels or lots upon the payment of a specified portion of the debt. Since the best lots usually sell first and the worst lots sell last, a lender often requires a larger payment for the release of the first lots sold.

Take-Over Clause.   A construction loan contains a *take-over clause* that gives the lender the right to complete the construction if the borrower defaults on the loan. This allows the lender to make the property marketable prior to the foreclosure sale.

Equity Participation Clause.   The loan agreement may contain an *equity participation clause* that allows the lender to collect both interest and receive a share of the borrower's equity. The equity participation can take many forms. The lender may receive a percentage of any net income above a specified level or a percentage of the ownership of the property.

SUMMARY

The note and mortgage or trust deed are usually form documents. One of the most commonly used sets of forms is the FNMA-FHLMC uniform note and mortgage or trust deed. These forms provide the basis of our discussion in this chapter. The basic elements of the uniform note are (1) identification of the parties to the transaction, (2) recognition of the existence of the debt, (3) the borrower's promise to pay, (4) specification of the terms of payment, (5) reference to the mortgage, (6) the lender's right to accelerate on default, and (7) the borrower's right to prepay. The basic elements of the mortgage are (1) identification of the parties and the debt, (2) a pledge of the property as security, (3) identification of the property, and (4) numerous covenants. The mortgage includes 17 uniform covenants. The more notable covenants are for (1) payment of interest and principal, (2) escrow accounts for taxes and insurance, (3) adequate hazard insurance coverage, (4) proper maintenance of the property, (5) payments by the lender to protect his or her interest, (6) denial of forbearance as a defense, and (7) the conditions necessary for loan assumption. The mortgage used in our discussion includes six non-uniform covenants. Some of these are for (1) the method of foreclosure allowed, (2) the borrower's right of redemption, (3) the assignment of rents, (4) future advances, and (5) release of the mortgage.

A number of relatively common clauses are not included in the uniform documents examined for various reasons. Clauses sometimes used in other residential mortgage loan agreements include (1) escalator clauses, (2) a defeasance clause, (3) a power-of-sale clause, (4) a receiver clause, (5) an owner rent clause, and (6) an estoppel clause. The most notable additional clauses included in a junior mortgage are the default in prior mortgage clause and the subordination clause. Multifamily residential and nonresidential loans include numerous clauses not found in the typical single-family mortgage loan agreement. Some of these provisions are the (1) sole security clause, (2) sale in one parcel clause, (3) partial release clause, (4) take-over clause, and (5) equity participation clause.

KEY TERMS

Acceleration Clause

Assignment of Rents

Borrower's Right to
  Reinstate

Cognovit Provision

Covenant of Seizin

Default in Prior Mortgage
  Clause

Due-on-Sale Clause

Equity Participation Clause

Exculpatory Clause

Forbearance by Lender

Future Advances

Interest Escalator Clause

Mortgagee in Possession
  Clause

Owner Rent Clause

Partial Release Clause

Payment Escalator Clause

Power-of-Sale Clause

Prepayment Penalty

Prepayment Privilege

Receiver Clause

Sale in One Parcel Clause

Sole Security Clause

Subordination Clause

Subrogation Clause

Take-Over Clause

Variable-Rate Provision

Waiver of Defense Clause

Waiver of Homestead
  Exemption

1. What is the reason that a note is a separate document from the mortgage?

2. Why include both an acceleration and a prepayment clause in a mortgage note?

3. How important is the covenant of seizin in a mortgage?

4. What is the purpose of each of the following uniform clauses or covenants in a mortgage?
   a. Application of payments
   b. Hazard insurance
   c. Preservation of property
   d. Forbearance
   e. Property transfer and loan assumption

5. What is the purpose of each of the following clauses in a mortgage?
   a. Power-of-sale
   b. Receiver
   c. Owner rent

6. For whose benefit are the following clauses included in a mortgage?
   a. Subordination
   b. Default in prior mortgage
   c. Exculpatory
   d. Subrogation
   e. Alienation or due-on-sale

7. What three clauses are most important to a borrower in your judgment? To a lender? To a junior lender?

8. Match the following key terms and definitions:

   a. Due-on-Sale Clause _____
   b. Exculpatory Clause _____
   c. Subordination Clause _____
   d. Subrogation Clause _____
   e. Acceleration Clause _____

   1. Provision allowing holder of loan to declare outstanding balance due and payable immediately.
   2. Leniency by a lender at one time does not mean right to take action lost at a later time.
   3. Provision for acceleration of payments if property ownership transferred for consideration.

f. Forbearance by
   Lender Clause   _____

4. Provision giving borrower the
   right to stop foreclosure
   proceedings and redeem
   property and loan.
5. Provision that borrower not
   be held personally liable for
   debt in case of default.
6. Provision giving lender all the
   rights of the borrower for
   defending the property.
7. Provision allowing a borrower
   to replace one first loan with
   another, ahead of an existing
   loan.
8. Provision allowing a property
   to be sold as one unit or as
   several parcels.

five

Mortgage Default and Its Implications

A mortgage *default* occurs when one party fails to live up to the duties and obligations agreed to in the mortgage, or trust deed, contract and note. A borrower is most likely to go into default, because a lender has few obligations once the subject monies are advanced. Failure to pay principal and interest payments when due is the most common cause of default. Failure to pay real estate taxes or mechanic's liens is sometimes the cause of default. Default also occurs through failure to keep the property adequately insured or in a reasonable state of repair. In brief, a borrower is in default when any of the covenants or clauses in the contract is violated.

A borrower defaults for a number of reasons. Loss of income due to illness, death, or general economic conditions is a major cause of default. Divorce and family problems are other causes. Of course, the mismanagement of the borrower's finances may also result in default. A borrower in default may lose the property and face a deficiency judgment. In most cases, the borrower facing default is advised to discuss the problem with the lender. Arrangements or adjustments in the agreement can usually be made to avoid foreclosure action by the lender.

On default, a lender considers alternative actions to protect his or her interests. Basically, a lender must choose between two alternatives. First, the lender may work with the borrower to correct or clear up the deficiency or violation, which is termed an *adjustment*. Second, the lender may take legal action, which is essentially foreclosure.

This chapter is written from the viewpoint of the lender, mainly because default means the borrower no longer has much freedom of decision or action. Effectively, the lender controls the situation. An understanding of the lender's position enables a borrower to make the best of his or her position in some situations, however. For example, a borrower who is about to default and who has an understanding of possible mortgage adjustments is more apt to attempt to arrange an adjustment prior to the default. Thus, a borrower out of work and drawing unemployment compensation can make arrangements to make reduced payments, perhaps interest only, until a regular job is found again. In similar fashion, an investor-owner of a newly built apartment house may request management assistance and additional time for a rent-up because of a recession. Whether lender or borrower, the content of this chapter is important; loan payments are missed and loans do get classified as delinquent.

A relatively small portion of the outstanding mortgage loans remain delinquent for 60 days or more, and an even smaller portion involve foreclosure action. The 60-day or more delinquency rate for all mortgage loans held by insured savings and loan associations seldom exceeded one percent in any year during the 1970s. And the foreclosure rate on these loans seldom exceeded two-tenths of one percent in any year during the 1970s. The foreclosure rates on VA guaranteed and FHA insured mortgage loans runs substantially higher than those on conventional mortgage loans. Thus, during the 1970s the foreclosure rate on FHA insured mortgage loans was above one percent in some years. Of course, in the case of VA guaranteed and FHA insured loans, the lender's risk of loss is reduced by the existence of the guarantee or insurance.

Major topics in this chapter are as follows:

1. Default and possible reactions
2. Priority of liens and interests
3. Foreclosure, redemption, and deficiencies
4. Mortgage insurance and guarantees
5. Soldiers and Sailors Civil Relief Act

DEFAULT AND POSSIBLE REACTIONS

There are a number of possible sources of losses if the lender decides to foreclose. The sale of the property may produce insufficient funds to pay the lender's claim for the accrued interest and the unpaid balance of the loan. If a deficiency judgment is prohibited by law or is impractical due to the financial circumstances of the borrower, the lender may lose the interest for a time on the money tied up in the defaulted loan. The foreclosure process is often lengthy, and the lender has holding costs during this period. The lender may have to pay the real estate taxes, the premiums for property insurance, and in the case of a condominium unit the monthly assessment. The borrower may not properly maintain the property when faced with foreclosure, and the lender may be forced to bear the costs of rehabilitation to make the property marketable. Costs to be covered are attorney's fees, other legal fees, and the opportunity costs of the lender's time. And there are costs for the foreclosure sale itself.

The proceeds from the foreclosure sale are sometimes not sufficient to pay the lender's entire claim. Even if it is possible to collect on a deficiency judgment, the lender is forced to bear the opportunity cost of lost time. Often it is impossible to collect on a deficiency judgment because the borrower goes into bankruptcy. The lender's possible loss is reduced but not eliminated by the use of mortgage insurance or guarantees. The lender is faced with potential losses that increase with the period of time required to foreclose. The lender is normally reluctant to foreclose if there are any other feasible alternatives that will bring about a more immediate and less costly solution. The alternatives open to a lender are shown in Fig. 5–1.

FIGURE 5–1   Alternative Decisions and Actions Open to a Lender Concerning a Mortgage in Default

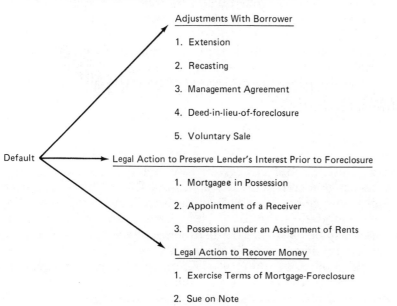

Adjustments With Borrower

1. Extension

2. Recasting

3. Management Agreement

4. Deed-in-lieu-of-foreclosure

5. Voluntary Sale

Legal Action to Preserve Lender's Interest Prior to Foreclosure

1. Mortgagee in Possession

2. Appointment of a Receiver

3. Possession under an Assignment of Rents

Legal Action to Recover Money

1. Exercise Terms of Mortgage-Foreclosure

2. Sue on Note

Mortgage adjustments are an alternative that is often less costly to both the borrower and lender. *Mortgage adjustments* refer to changes in the terms of the loan agreement. In this chapter we are largely concerned with mortgage adjustments made to avoid foreclosure. They include extensions, recasting, a management agreement, a deed in lieu of foreclosure, and a voluntary sale. Mortgage adjustments are much more frequent than foreclosure actions for a number of reasons. Adjustments may avoid losses suffered in foreclosure action. Adjustments create goodwill for the lender, whereas foreclosure results in a loss of goodwill. The federal government encourages lenders to make adjustments rather than to foreclose, particularly in times of depressed economic conditions. Holders of FHA insured and VA guaranteed mortgages are directed to make an effort to make adjustments before foreclosing.

When the borrower has temporary difficulty in meeting the mortgage payments (because of a strike or layoff due to recession), the lender may grant the borrower a moratorium on the mortgage payments. A *moratorium* waives the principal payment and/or interest payment for some reasonable time. The lender's act of not taking legal action when the borrower is in default is called *forbearance.* Forbearance creates a problem for the lender holding an assumed mortgage in which the original borrower also has personal liability for the payment of the debt. The forbearance may release the original borrower from any personal liability, which of course is not in the lender's best interest.

Extension. A lender granting a borrower a temporary moratorium may follow it with an extension. An *extension* delays or postpones the maturity date of the debt. The lender will still collect all interest and debt due, but the borrower gets additional time to make the payments. An extension agreement may therefore require the borrower to pay accrued interest but extend the time for repayment of the principal. It does not change the priority of the lender's lien, and it may sharply reduce the debt service payment. An extension agreement can be oral or written, but a written agreement is generally advised.

Recasting. A simple delay in the maturity date of the debt may not give the borrower sufficient relief to prevent future default. Therefore, the loan may be recast. *Recasting* means changing the terms of the loan agreement. Recasting normally implies more than just extending the due date of the principal of the loan. The interest rate and amount of debt service may also be changed. If the amount of the loan is changed, the adjustment is classified as *refinancing.* When the loan is recast or refinanced, a lender may encounter a problem with liens that arose between the time of recording the original mortgage and the recasting of the mortgage. This problem is best solved by obtaining approval from the intervening lien holders before recasting the mortgage.

An extension of the due date of the debt gives the borrower little relief in the typical monthly payment amortizing loan because the principal payment is usually a small portion of the total monthly payment. The lender may extend the maturity of the loan and add any unpaid interest to the amount of the debt. If the existing debt represents a small portion of the value of the property, the lender may refinance the debt. The refinancing may allow the borrower to obtain additional funds to better meet temporary difficulties. Or the refinancing could be primarily to extend the term and reduce the required monthly payments. A lender may negotiate an increase in the interest rate in the recasting. There are many ways in which the loan can be recast to make it possible for the lender to be adequately compensated while avoiding foreclosure proceedings. A knowledgable borrower may be able to obtain a favorable recasting or refinancing by suggesting it to the lender.

Management Agreement. If an income producing property is in default or approaching default, the lender may combine a recasting of the loan with a management agreement. A *management agreement* transfers responsibility for property operation from the borrower to a competent manager. The lender believes that improved management will result in a flow of funds adequate to meet the terms of the mortgage agreement. If the change of management does not prevent default, the lender still has the option to foreclose.

Deed in Lieu of Foreclosure. A *deed in lieu of foreclosure* means that the borrower voluntarily conveys title to the lender and the lender forgives the debt. Foreclosure is avoided and no deficiency judgment results. Deed in lieu of foreclosure also reduces time and costs to the lender and borrower. If the value of the property is less than the amount of the lender's claim and deficiency judgment is not allowed or is impractical, a lender may combine forbearance with a suggestion for later use of a deed in lieu of foreclosure. This combination serves to give the borrower time to make alternative arrangements while avoiding lender-borrower litigation. Typically, with the use of a deed in lieu of foreclosure, the lender offers the borrower some cash consideration plus forgiveness of the debt to avoid other possible legal difficulties. A deed in lieu of foreclosure must be the voluntary action of the borrower to be legally valid. Accepting a deed in lieu of foreclosure means that the lender takes the property subject to existing junior liens. If the total of all claims against the property exceeds its value, a deed in lieu of foreclosure is not a satisfactory alternative for the first mortgage lender.

Voluntary Sale. The lender may combine forbearance with a suggestion that the borrower sell the property and use a portion of the proceeds to pay the lender's claim. This is appropriate when the borrower's situation has permanently changed and the borrower is not able to meet any reasonable payment schedule. This is most feasible when the value of the property exceeds the amount of the lender's claim. A lender may assist in financing the sale by allowing the assumption of the mortgage or by granting a new mortgage loan.

ACTIONS TO RECOVER MONEY

Sometimes adjustments are not possible. An aggressive lender may refuse to make an adjustment in order to foreclose on a mortgage that has a low interest rate. Also, if the borrower is uncooperative, the lender is likely to refuse to make an adjustment. And sometimes, even after adjustments are made, the borrower with the financial capacity to do so does not meet the payments and refuses to sell the property or to give a deed in lieu of foreclosure. At this point the lender's best alternative is to take action to collect the debt. The lender can either sue on the note or take action under the mortgage.

Exercise Terms of the Mortgage. The most common method of action for the lender to recover money owed is to sue in a court of equity for a decree of foreclosure and an order for the sale of the mortgaged property. If the mortgage contract includes a power of sale, it is usually exercised. In either method the funds from the sale are used to pay the lender's claim and any remaining funds are given to the borrower. If the sale does not produce sufficient funds to pay the lender's claim, in some states the lender is allowed to obtain a deficiency judgment under the note for the remainder of the claim.

Sue on Note. In some states the lender may sue on the note or debt itself, independent of the mortgage. This action, called a judgment lien, has advantages and disadvantages relative to action under the mortgage. In suing on the debt, the lender seeks to enforce a general lien rather than a specific lien. A judgment to enforce a general lien is directed against the individual borrower rather than against the specific property. The judgment attaches to all of the borrower's assets. This is advantageous when the borrower has substantial net assets and when the lender's claim plus foreclosure costs is likely to exceed the value of the property. At the same time, the lender gives up a priority position relative to the property offered as security for the debt, if other judgment liens have been entered against the borrower. And while foreclosure may terminate the liens that arose against the specific property after recording the mortgage, a judgment on the debt does not.

PRESERVATION OF THE LENDER'S INTEREST PRIOR TO FORECLOSURE

Upon making the decision to foreclose, the lender is advised to obtain possession of the property. If the borrower abandons the property, the lender should make arrangements to have it properly maintained. A borrower remaining in possession may not maintain the property in good condition due to a lack of funds or other reasons. A borrower with a bitter attitude may even intentionally damage the property. Furthermore, in the case of an income producing property, the borrower may collect the rents and divert the funds to personal use during the foreclosure period. In extreme cases the borrower may even attempt to collect advance rentals to obtain more funds for personal use.

Possession of the property and the right to collect the rents should be obtained as quickly as possible. The right of possession and receipt of rents may be transferred to the lender or a receiver to prevent waste of the property and diversion of the rental income. The fastest means is a voluntary transfer of these rights. An owner-occupant transferring the rights to possession and rents while retaining occupancy must usually pay rent. A voluntary transfer of the rights to possession and rents is allowed in all states.

If the borrower is not willing to voluntarily transfer the rights to possession and rents, in some states the lender may take legal action to force their transfer. In title theory and intermediate theory states, the lender automatically has the right to take possession and collect rents on default or to request the appointment of a receiver. In lien theory states the lender does not have the right to possession unless there is a special clause to this effect in the mortgage. Therefore, in most lien theory states, a clause in the mortgage or a separate document called an assignment of rents are used to enable the lender to take possession and collect rents on default. An assignment of rents is also used in title and intermediate theory states because it has the advantage of not terminating existing leases. In some lien theory states the lender cannot obtain possession under either the mortgage or an assignment of rents. In these states it is usually possible, however, to obtain the appointment of a receiver to protect the property from destruction.

Mortgagee in Possession.   A lender occupying the property through the voluntary act of the mortgagor or through court action is called *mortgagee in possession.* A mortgagee in possession is responsible for proper management and collection of rents, and he or she must account to the court for all revenues and expenditures. The rentals collected are applied first to the operating costs of the property and second to the payment of the interest and the debt. Failure to properly manage the property makes the mortgagee liable to the mortgagor and junior lien holders. Therefore, many mortgagees prefer to request the appointment of a receiver rather than become a mortgagee in possession. Also court action to place the mortgagee in possession may be a lengthy process, whereas a receiver can often be appointed in a matter of days.

Appointment of a Receiver.   Normally a receiver is a disinterested third party appointed by a court to preserve and manage the property in the best interests of both the borrower and lender. Sometimes the court allows the mortgage lender to serve as the receiver. The receiver is given the right to possession and rents. The receiver does not have to dispossess the owner-occupant. The receiver may determine a reasonable rental rate and allow the borrower to continue to occupy the property by paying the agreed rental. The receiver pays the operating costs and holds the remaining funds for the payment of the interest and mortgage debt. In some lien theory states the mortgagee is not allowed to take possession; rather the court will appoint a receiver. In states in which both options are available, the appointment of a neutral receiver has the advantage of relative speed and the avoidance of liability.

Possession Under an Assignment of Rents.   An *assignment of rents* transfers the borrower's interest in the existing leases and future leases to the lender. The assignment of rents may be contained in the mortgage or it may be a separate document. The existing tenants must usually be notified of the assignment; and if the assignment is a separate document, it is recorded. In title, intermediate, and some lien theory states the assignment of rents is activated on default by giving the tenants notice to pay the rents to the lender or a receiver. In most other lien theory states that recognize an assignment of rents, it is activated by filing a foreclosure suit and requesting the appointment of a receiver. In some lien theory states an assignment of rents is not allowed.

Use of an assignment of rents has a number of advantages. In some states an assignment of rents is the only way that the rents may be collected. In other states the assignment of rents shortens the process of placing the mortgagee in possession or of obtaining the appointment of a receiver. An action under an assignment of rents does not terminate the leases signed after the mortgage was recorded, whereas placing the mortgagee in possession under the mortgage may terminate the leases. Under the assignment of rents the lender may be responsible for only the rents actually collected; otherwise the lender may be accountable for all the rents that should have been collected.

PRIORITY OF LIENS AND INTERESTS

The priority of liens becomes a major concern when a mortgagee considers foreclosure action. A lien senior to a mortgage is not extinguished or terminated by foreclosure. A lien with a lesser priority, however, may be extinguished by foreclosure. A similar situation exists relative to the interests of the tenant under a lease or the purchaser under a land contract. If the lease or contract is prior to the mortgage, foreclosure action does not terminate it. If the mortgage has priority over the lease or land contract, either can be terminated by the foreclosure action.

The basic rule of priority is "first in time is first in line." This means that the first notice that can be proven or documented, actually or constructively, has first priority.

PRIORITY OF LIENS

The general rule of priority of liens is that the time of recording or filing establishes the priority of the lien. For example, the liens recorded first, second, and third have first, second, and third priority, respectively. Subordination agreements allow a reordering of priority. This general rule does not apply to liens for real estate taxes and special assessments. Mechanics' liens are also an exception in that in most states their priority is determined by the time the work was begun rather than the time of filing. Special rules also apply to purchase money mortgages and mortgages for future advances.

Real Estate Tax Liens.   Liens for real estate taxes and special assessments have priority over all other liens.

Federal Tax Liens.   The priority of federal tax liens follows the general rule and is therefore dependent on the time of filing, with one exception: A mortgage recorded after the filing of a lien for unpaid federal income taxes may be given priority over the tax lien. If the mortgagee does not have actual notice of the federal tax lien and disburses the loan within 45 days after the filing of the tax lien, the mortgage is given priority.

Judgment Liens.   A judgment lien is usually a general lien on both the personal and real property of the debtor. The priority of the judgment lien relative to the real property is usually determined by the date of recording the lien in the jurisdiction in which the real property is located.

Mortgage Liens.   The priority of the mortgage lien is usually determined by the time of recording except for a purchase money mortgage, which has a special status. A purchase money mortgage taken back by a seller to secure part of the purchase price is given priority over prior or subsequent liens attaching to the property through the purchaser-mortgagor. A mortgage given to a third party with the entire net proceeds paid to the seller as part of the purchase price is treated as a purchase money mortgage in most states. In both cases the purchase money mortgage must be recorded to gain priority against subsequent liens.

A mortgage for future advances such as a construction loan or an open-end mortgage loan allows funds to be advanced under the existing mortgage after it has been recorded. There is a question about the priority of the funds advanced *after* recording in relation to liens that arise after recording but prior to the advance. The general rule is that the future advances have priority over the intervening liens if the advances are obligatory. In a few states this rule does not apply against mechanics' liens. If the future advances are optional or nonobligatory, the relative priority is uncertain. The optional future advances are given priority over intervening mortgages up to a specific dollar amount in a majority of the states. In some states the optional advances are not given priority.

Mechanics' Liens.   In nearly all the states a mechanics' lien must be filed within a specified time after the completion of the work to be legally valid and enforceable. But in most states the priority of the mechanics' lien is determined by the time the job was started. In other states the priority is determined by the time the contract was signed, and in a few states priority is established by the time of filing the lien.

Subordination and Waiver of Liens.   The priority of liens may be reordered by subordination agreements. For example, a mortgage recorded on June 15 could be given priority over one recorded on March 30 by a subordination agreement. Lien holders are allowed to waive their priority in favor of a mortgage, and this is valid if consideration is given for the waiver. Lenders often employ waivers and releases to protect against mechanics' liens.

INTERESTS OF THE OCCUPANTS

The mortgaged property may be occupied by the owner-borrower, a tenant under a lease, the purchaser under a land contract, or a trespasser at the time of default. Legal action will dispossess a trespasser. Foreclosure action will dispossess the owner-borrower. Whether or not the tenant under a lease or the purchaser under a land contract can be dispossessed depends on the circumstances.

Leases.   If the lease existed prior to recording of the mortgage being foreclosed, the tenants have the right to remain in possession by paying rent to the mortgagee. Notice of foreclosure action must be given tenants to bring this about. A lease may contain a provision that subordinates it to any future mortgage. This provision gives the mortgagee the option to terminate the lease by foreclosure or to extend and continue the lease. If the lease was made after the mortgage was recorded, the mortgagee automatically has the option to terminate or extend the lease. If the lender offers to extend the lease, the tenant is free to accept or reject the offer.

Land Contracts.   An occupant under a land contract that was recorded before a mortgage has the right to remain in possession by making payments to the mortgagee. In most states, this would be also true if the buyer moved into possession before the mortgage was recorded; the lender would be presumed to have actual knowledge of the occupant's rights. Sometimes the land contract contains a clause that makes it subordinate to any future mortgage, which makes the rights of the mortgagee automatically superior to those of the purchaser under the contract. If a land contract was not recorded and the purchaser was not occupying the property, the lender would not have actual notice and the mortgage recorded after the signing of the land contract would have priority. A mortgage recorded before a land contract clearly has priority. In this situation the mortgagee has the option to dispossess the purchaser occupying through the land contract or to extend the contract.

FORECLOSURE, REDEMPTION, AND DEFICIENCIES

Most lenders attempt to make adjustments or to obtain a voluntary transfer to avoid the necessity for foreclosure. Even so, foreclosures total well in excess of 100,000 per year nationally. After a lender decides to foreclose, a borrower can still redeem the property prior to foreclosure by exercising the equitable right of redemption. The lender may foreclose in a number of ways, including judicial sale, power of sale, strict foreclosure, and foreclosure by entry. If the value of the property received or the proceeds of the sale are insufficient to compensate the lender, the lender may seek a deficiency judgment for the remainder of the claim. In a number of states the borrower retains an opportunity to redeem ownership following foreclosure under the statutory right of redemption.

EQUITY REDEMPTIONS

The borrower's *equitable right of redemption* is a common-law right that allows the borrower to redeem the property prior to foreclosure. The equitable right of redemption, also known as the equity of redemption, may be exercised by the mortgagor or any party whose interest would be terminated by the foreclosure. These parties include junior lienholders, the lessee, the purchaser under a land contract, or an individual who has purchased the equitable right of redemption from the mortgagor. The equitable right of redemption is exercised by paying the outstanding principal, accrued interest and any expenses of the mortgagee. The equitable right of redemption is terminated by the passage of the time specified in the decree of judicial foreclosure or by the sale in a power-of-sale foreclosure.

FORECLOSURE

An action for foreclosure is a request to terminate the mortgagor's equitable right of redemption. Although a sale normally follows foreclosure, it is not necessary. In a *strict foreclosure* there is no sale.

The original mortgagee or the subsequent holder of the mortgage has the right to sue for foreclosure on default by the mortgagor. The party taking the foreclosure action names the mortgagor or any individual purchasing the property subject to the mortgage as the chief defendant. In addition, anyone having a junior interest in the property, which arose after the recording of the mortgage, is best named as a defendant. This includes junior mortgage holders, judgment creditors, tenants, and a spouse who has dower or homestead rights. Foreclosure action terminates the rights of all parties having an interest in the property that is junior to the lender's rights. The rights of a party not named in the suit are not extinguished by the suit.

Parties having interests superior to those of the mortgagee bringing action are not affected by the foreclosure. A junior mortgage holder therefore need not name a senior mortgage holder in a foreclosure action. The senior mortgage continues as a claim against the property, and the title is taken subject to the senior mortgage. The senior mortgage may be named in the foreclosure action to establish the amount of the claim, however.

There are four basic types of foreclosure: (1) judicial sale, (2) power of sale, (3) strict foreclosure, and (4) foreclosure by entry. Judicial sale is allowed in all states, and it is the customary method of foreclosure under a mortgage in a majority of states.

Foreclosure and Judicial Sale. Under foreclosure and public sale the mortgagee requests the court to foreclose the mortgagor's equitable right of redemption and to sell the property if the claim is not paid. The lender has the title searched to identify all parties having an interest in the property and to name any parties having junior claims as defendants in the suit. Upon deciding to foreclose, a lender often files a *lis pendens,* which is a notice of pending legal action, to discourage any further transactions involving the subject property. Upon filing for foreclosure, legal notice of the action is served to all interested parties and a court date is set. The defendants are given an opportunity to present their case in court. Usually there is no valid defense and the court enters a judgment for foreclosure. The court specifies the time period in which the equitable right of redemption must be exercised. If it is not exercised within the specified time period, a date is set for the sale of the property. The court normally appoints the sheriff or referee to conduct the sale.

The mortgagee has a right to bid at a foreclosure sale. Bid amounts must be paid in cash immediately at the sale, except that the debt is considered the equivalent of cash by the court. The highest bidder is the winning bidder. The lender typically makes an offer equal to the amount of the debt, which usually turns out to be the winning bid. Competitive bidders are the few who can produce cash on the spot. Court acceptance of certified checks would probably increase competition, raise bid prices, and be more equitable to the borrower-mortgagor being fore-closed.

The sale ends upon confirmation of the transaction by the court. The court confirms the sale if the bid is considered to be reasonable. In a few states a minimum acceptable price such as two-thirds of ap-praised value is necessary for confirmation of the sale. After the sale is confirmed, a sheriff's deed or a referee's deed in foreclosure is issued to the successful bidder.

If there is a statutory redemption period, the successful bidder may receive an interim certificate of sale followed by a deed after the expira-tion of the statutory redemption period. The title received by the pur-chaser at the foreclosure sale is that which the borrower held, but it is free from the interest of the junior claimants named in the foreclosure suit. Defects in the title that existed before the mortgage was recorded are not extinguished by a foreclosure sale.

The proceeds of the sale may fail to cover the lender's entire claim. The expenses of the sale are paid first. The lender's claim for expenses, interest, and debt principal is paid next. Remaining funds are then paid to satisfy claims of junior lienholders. Any residual funds are paid the borrower. If funds are insufficient and it is not prohibited by the statute, the lender may seek a deficiency judgment for the remaining portion of the mortgage claim. In some states a decree for a deficiency judgment is entered at the same time the decree for foreclosure is entered and the sale is confirmed. In other states the deficiency judgment is sought in a separate action after the foreclosure sale.

Foreclosure by Power of Sale. A mortgage or security deed may include a power-of-sale provision. This allows the mortgagee to employ foreclo-sure by power of sale, which is called sale by advertisement in some states. Foreclosure through a power of sale in a mortgage is allowed in over 20 states, and it is the customary method of foreclosure under a mortgage in ten or more states.

Under the *power of sale* there is no need for a judicial decree for foreclosure and sale. This usually shortens the time required for fore-closure and reduces the costs of the foreclosure process.

The mortgagee must meet the statutory requirements of the state to exercise the power of sale. These requirements vary from state to state. The first is usually to file notice of default in the public recorder's of-fice. There is normally a waiting period between the time of the default and the time of the sale. The borrower has the right to redeem the prop-erty during this waiting period. The second requirement is to provide public notice of the time and place of the public sale. The public notice is usually given by publication in a local newspaper and by posting no-tice on the subject property. Usually the mortgagee must give personal notice or notice by certified mail to the borrower, and sometimes notice must be given to the junior lienholders.

The sale must be public. The mortgagee may usually bid if the sale is held by a public officer or if the mortgage grants the right. The highest bid is normally made by the lender. The proceeds of the sale are distributed in the same manner as in a foreclosure and sale. If the statutory requirements are met, the title received through the nonjudicial sale has the same quality as that received through a judicial sale. The sale terminates the borrower's equitable right of redemption. The deed is granted by the mortgagee. If there is a statutory redemption period, a certificate of sale may be issued and the deed delivered later if the property is not redeemed within the statutory time.

The sale is subject to judicial review. Separate court action is required to obtain a deficiency judgment. In some states no deficiency judgment is allowed or, if it is, it is more limited than under foreclosure and sale.

Strict Foreclosure. *Strict foreclosure* is a judicial process to terminate the borrower's equitable right of redemption and eliminate the mortgagor's rights and the rights of those claiming through the mortgagor such as junior lienholders. Under strict foreclosure there is no sale. The foreclosure results in the mortgagee perfecting title to the property. The process is the same as that for a foreclosure and sale except there is no court order for a sale. There may or may not be a statutory redemption period. If the mortgagee seeks a deficiency judgment, the court would probably order a sale to establish the value of the property. Strict foreclosure is common only in Connecticut and Vermont. It is used in special circumstances in other states when a deficiency judgment is not sought, and it is prohibited in a number of states.

Foreclosure by Entry. Foreclosure by entry is allowed in Maine, Massachusetts, New Hampshire, and Rhode Island, and its use is common only in Maine. There are two types of foreclosure by entry. Foreclosure by peaceable entry does not require court action. A writ of entry requires court action, and it is not allowed in Rhode Island. Entry by peaceable possession is possible if the mortgagor gives written permission in the presence of witnesses. If the entry is opposed, the mortgagee requests the court for a writ of entry. The court establishes the amount due to the mortgagee and enters a judgment granting the mortgagee possession if the amount due is not paid within a specified time. Under foreclosure by entry, the time period for terminating the mortgagor's right of redemption varies from one to three years. On termination of the period for redemption, the mortgagee has clear title to the property.

DEFICIENCY JUDGMENTS

A deficiency results when the value of the property received or the proceeds of the sale are insufficient to cover the lender's claim. For example, if the lender's claim (foreclosure expenses, interest, principal) is for

$100,000 and the lender only realizes $90,000 from the sale, the deficiency is $10,000. The lender could then seek a *deficiency judgment* for the $10,000. Most states allow deficiency judgments, but a number of states place some restrictions on them. Arizona, California, Montana, North Carolina, Oregon, and South Dakota prohibit deficiency judgments on purchase money mortgages. At least eight states limit the amount of the deficiency judgment to the difference between the lender's claim and the fair market value as established by an appraisal.

The trend is toward restricting deficiency judgments under the note. The FHA prohibits deficiency judgments on residential mortgage loans. The VA strongly discourages them unless the borrower actually has the ability to pay the deficiency judgment. Even when deficiency judgments are decreed, they are seldom enforced on home loans. This probably is because it would be an additional hardship on the borrower. A deficiency judgment is probably not worth seeking unless the borrower has hidden assets or strikes it rich by receiving a large inheritance, for example.

STATUTORY REDEMPTION

While foreclosure and/or sale extinguishes the borrower's equitable right of redemption, several states have passed laws that allow redemption after foreclosure. *Statutory redemption* is redemption after the foreclosure sale under the provisions of a state statute. Where statutory redemption is allowed, the typical period for the exercise of the right is either six months or one year after the date of the foreclosure sale. Under the state law, the borrower and often any party whose rights have been foreclosed can redeem the property. The borrower is usually free to sell this redemption right to a third party who then can redeem the property. The redemption amount equals the price paid at the foreclosure sale, accrued interest as established by the statute, and expenses.

In some states the mortgagee may select a method of foreclosure to avoid statutory redemption. Statutory redemption exists under some method of foreclosure in over 30 states. It can be avoided in six of these states by foreclosing under power of sale. In one or more additional states statutory redemption can be avoided by an agreement not to request a deficiency judgment, by a borrower's waiver of the right to redemption, and by a foreclosure sale to a third party.

In some states FHA insured, VA guaranteed, and Small Business Administration loans have been held to be exempt from statutory redemption laws. Also, the federal government has the right to redeem from a foreclosure sale under federal law, even if there is not a state statutory redemption law.[1]

---

[1] Robert Kratovil, *Modern Mortgage Law and Practice* (Englewood Cliffs, N.J.: Prentice-Hall, Inc., 1972), p. 335.

A mortgagor has the right to continue in possession through the statutory redemption period in most states. But the lender or receiver can usually obtain possession if cause is shown.

If statutory redemption exists, the purchaser at the sale obtains either a deed that can be canceled by redemption or a certificate of sale. If the purchaser receives a certificate of sale, it can be used to obtain the deed after the expiration of the statutory redemption period.

MORTGAGE INSURANCE AND GUARANTEES

Lenders can limit their foreclosure losses by the use of insured or guaranteed loans. The two principal types of insured mortgage loans are FHA insured loans and privately insured loans. The Veterans Administration is the principal guarantor of mortgage loans. On foreclosure the lender presents a claim. The insurer or guarantor then either purchases the property from the lender or pays a portion of the loss suffered by the lender.

PRIVATE MORTGAGE INSURANCE

Private mortgage insurance companies offer insurance coverage ranging from 12 to 30 percent on residential mortgage loans. The premiums on the private mortgage insurance policy are paid by the borrower. There are numerous premium plans. The premium for a loan with a loan-to-value ratio of 95 percent and with 25 percent insurance coverage would be 1 percent for the first year and about one-quarter of 1 percent for years two through ten under the constant payment plan. Assume that the value of the property is $110,000 and the amount of the mortgage loan is $100,000. With 25 percent coverage on the $100,000 loan, the private mortgage insurance company is committed to absorb up to $25,000 of any loss. If the lender suffered a $20,000 loss on the foreclosure, the insurance company would pay the lender $20,000. If the lender suffered a $30,000 loss, the insurance company would only pay the lender $25,000.

Under a typical mortgage insurance policy, the lender is required to notify the insurer within ten days after the borrower has been in default for four months. Monthly reports on the status of the loan are required thereafter. The insurer has the right to request the lender to start action to foreclose after the mortgage loan has been in default for nine months. The lender must notify the insurer of the amount owed by the borrower at least 15 days before the foreclosure sale. The lender is required to bid at least that amount at the foreclosure sale.

The lender is required to file a claim for the loss within 60 days after completion of the foreclosure proceedings. If title is obtained through foreclosure, the lender is also required to send an offer of conveyance of title to the insurance company. The claim form includes

1. The outstanding principal balance
2. Accrued interest from the date of default to the date of the claim
3. Real estate taxes and hazard insurance premiums necessarily advanced
4. Any expenses necessary to preserve the property
5. Necessary expenses of the foreclosure proceedings, such as court costs and filing fees
6. Reasonable attorney's fees, but not in excess of three percent of the principal and interest claimed

The insurer has two alternatives if the lender acquires title through foreclosure—(1) the insurer may pay the lender 25 percent of the claim up to the dollar maximum of the coverage, and (2) the insurer may pay the lender the entire claim and take title to the property.

FHA INSURANCE

The Federal Housing Administration has two basic types of insurance for residential mortgage loans. One type is a coinsurance policy similar to a private mortgage insurance policy that covers only the top portion of the loan. The second and common form of FHA insurance insures the entire amount of the loan. The borrower pays the annual premium for the FHA insurance. The annual premium on a policy covering the entire loan is one-half of one percent on the average outstanding loan balance for that year.

The lender must follow the required procedure to collect on the insurance policy. The lender must file a notice of default with the local FHA office within 60 days of the default. An effort must usually be made to make adjustments. If adjustments fail, the FHA may accept an assignment of the mortgage from the lender prior to foreclosure and may pay the lender's claim. If the FHA does not desire an assignment, the lender must acquire title in some way within 12 months after the default or begin foreclosure action. If there is a foreclosure sale, the lender is expected to bid the debt and is usually the winning bidder. The lender is required to submit the claim and deliver title to the FHA within 30 days of the acquisition of title. FHA takes title and pays the lender part of the claim. The claim can be paid in debentures, but it is normally paid in cash.

The lender's claim is divided into two classes. The first class includes the unpaid balance on the mortgage, real estate taxes, special assessments, property insurance, costs necessary for the preservation and operation of the property, and part of foreclosure costs including attorney's fees up to $350. The second class includes accrued interest to the date of foreclosure, expenditures for repairs to restore the property, and the remaining foreclosure costs. The FHA pays the claim for the first class on presentation of the claim. The lender has a contingent claim for the second class. They are paid out of the net receipts realized by FHA's sale of the property. The FHA rehabilitates the property and deducts these costs from the sale price to determine the net receipts from the sale. The amount received on the contingent claim can vary from nothing to the entire contingent claim. The total amount collected on both claims will not exceed the dollar amount of the insurance policy.

VA GUARANTEE

The Veterans Administration offers mortgage loan guarantees as veterans' benefits, and there is no charge for the guarantee. The guarantee is currently limited to 60 percent of the amount of the loan or $27,500, whichever is lower. The VA guarantee never exceeds 60 percent of the outstanding balance on the loan. For example, if the original loan is $80,000, the guarantee is $27,500. When the outstanding loan balance has declined to $30,000, the guarantee declines to $18,000. Thus, VA guarantee is similar to private mortgage insurance in that it only covers the top portion of the loan.

The lender must notify the local VA office of any default. The VA encourages mortgage adjustments and may assist in the process. If the adjustments fail, the lender presents a claim for payment to the VA. The VA has the option to pay the lender's claim and request an assignment of the mortgage, or it can suggest that the lender foreclose. If there is a foreclosure sale, the lender is usually the winning bidder. The VA has the option to pay the lender's claim and take title. If the VA does not desire to take title, the lender keeps title. If this option is selected, the VA pays the difference between the predetermined value of the property at the time of the foreclosure and the amount of the lender's claim up to the amount of the guarantee.

The lender's claim includes all those allowed under FHA insurance, but there is a different limit for attorney's fees. Attorney's fees are limited to 10 percent of the maximum unpaid loan balance or $250, whichever is less, unless specific approval is granted for higher amounts.

SOLDIERS AND SAILORS CIVIL RELIEF ACT

The *Soldiers and Sailors Civil Relief Act* only applies to individuals drafted into the armed services who do not make military service a career. If involuntary service materially affects the individual's ability to make mortgage payments, the court can delay any foreclosure action until 90 days after separation from military service. The interest rate on the mortgage loan is limited to six percent while the individual is in the service. And if the individual's mortgage has been foreclosed and a right to statutory redemption is involved, the right is extended until the person's service time ends.

SUMMARY

Upon mortgage default, both the borrower and the lender usually attempt to negotiate an adjustment to avoid foreclosure action. Adjustments include extensions, recasting the loan, management agreements, a deed in lieu of foreclosure, and voluntary sales.

If an adjustment is not possible or proves unsatisfactory, the lender can sue on the note or enforce the terms of the mortgage. The lender usually chooses to foreclose and is concerned with the preservation of the property. A receiver may be appointed or the mortgagee may be put in possession to prevent wasteful use of the property. An assignment of rents assists the lender to obtain possession.

The lender should determine what interests are prior to the mortgage, because prior interests are not terminated by the foreclosure action. Foreclosure action extinguishes the junior interests if the parties are named in the suit or are properly notified.

There are four basic types of foreclosure action. These are foreclosure and sale, power of sale, strict foreclosure, and foreclosure by entry. Foreclosure and sale is the most common method of foreclosing on a mortgage. Strict foreclosure is in common usage in only two states. Foreclosure by entry is in common usage in only one state. In foreclosure and sale the court sets the time period for the exercise of the equitable right of redemption. If the property is not redeemed within the time period, the property is sold at a court supervised sale. Under foreclosure by power of sale the lender or trustee holds the sale without court supervision. The sale terminates the borrower's equitable right of redemption.

If the foreclosure does not fully compensate the lender for his or her claim, the lender is allowed to sue for a deficiency judgment under the provisions of the note. Deficiency judgments are prohibited in some states and on some types of mortgage loans. In a number of states the borrower is given a statutory right to redeem the property after the equitable right of redemption has been terminated and the property sold.

Mortgage insurance and guarantees can be used to reduce the lender's loss on foreclosure. Conventional mortgages can be insured by private mortgage insurance that provides coverage on the top portion of the loan. The most common FHA insurance program covers the entire amount of the loan. The VA guarantee covers the top portion of the loan. Under each of these programs the lender presents a claim. The insurer or guarantor has the option to take title or pay a portion of, or the entire, claim.

KEY TERMS

Assignment of Rents

Deed in Lieu of Foreclosure

Equitable Right of
   Redemption

Extension

Foreclosure by Entry

Judgment Lien

Management Agreement

Mechanics' Lien

Moratorium

Private Mortgage Insurance

Recasting

Receiver

Soldiers and Sailors Civil
   Relief Act

Statutory Redemption

Strict Foreclosure

Sue on the Note

QUESTIONS FOR REVIEW AND DISCUSSION

1. Five adjustments to default by a borrower are possible. What are they? Explain each briefly.

2. What alternatives does a lender have to recover money upon default? Explain each.

3. Three alternatives are open to preserve or protect a lender's interest pending foreclosure. Explain each.

4. What is the basic rule of priority of liens and interests in real estate? Explain fully.

5. What is strict foreclosure? What alternatives to strict foreclosure are there?

6. How valuable is the right to a deficiency judgment to a lender-mortgagee?

7. Distinguish between the equitable right of redemption and the statutory right of redemption?

8. From the viewpoint of a lender, explain the relative benefits of using private mortgage insurance, FHA insurance, or a VA guarantee.

9. How are the proceeds of the sale of a foreclosed property distributed? That is, what gets first priority on the proceeds, second, and so forth?

10. Match the following key terms and definitions:

    a. Extension   _____

    b. Deed in Lieu of
       Foreclosure   _____

    c. Recast   _____

    d. Moratorium   _____

    1. Temporary waiver of principal and interest payments.

    2. Right of borrower to redeem property prior to foreclosure decree or sale.

e. Statutory Right of
   Redemption _____

f. Equitable Right of
   Redemption _____

3. A postponement of the
   maturity date of a loan.

4. Changing the terms of a loan
   agreement, such as the
   interest rate or amount of
   debt service.

5. Voluntary conveyance of title
   to lender by borrower and
   forgiveness of debt by lender.

6. Right of borrower to redeem
   property within limited time
   after foreclosure decree or
   sale.

7. Right of lender to occupy and
   manage property.

six

Trust Deed Financing

The basic purpose of a *trust deed,* which is also called a deed of trust, a trust deed in the nature of a mortgage, or a trust deed mortgage, is the same as that of a mortgage. Both are used to hypothecate real property. *Hypothecate* means to pledge specific property as security for a debt of obligation without surrendering possession of the property. If the debt is not paid, the property is usually sold and the proceeds used to pay the debt.

The trust deed may be used for the hypothecation of real property in almost every state. The trust deed is the most common method of hypothecating real property in 11 states and the District of Columbia.[1] The trust deed is frequently used in at least eight additional states. In the remaining states it is used in special circumstances such as in mortgage bond issues where numerous notes are secured by the trust deed. Power of sale is being recognized as a means of foreclosure in more and more states. The use of the power of sale in a trust deed tends to weaken the borrower's position in the loan arrangement. The trust deed will therefore probably continue to increase in importance.

---

[1]The 11 states are Alaska, California, Colorado, Idaho, Mississippi, Missouri, North Carolina, Tennessee, Texas, Virginia, and West Virginia.

In this chapter we discuss the following topics:

1. Nature of a trust deed
2. Reasons for use of a trust deed
3. Similarity to a mortgage
4. Reconveyance of title
5. Foreclosure

NATURE OF A TRUST DEED

If a mortgage is used, the borrower delivers the note and mortgage to the lender. The lender records the mortgage and holds the note and mortgage until the debt is paid. If the debt is paid, the lender releases the mortgage. If the borrower defaults, the lender forecloses.

If a trust deed is used, three parties are involved: a borrower, a lender, and a trustee. Figure 6–1 shows the structure of a loan agreement employing a trust deed. The owner-borrower grants title to the trustee through a trust deed and is called the *trustor* or grantor. The *trustee* holds title and safeguards the interests of both the borrower and the lender. The lender is the *beneficiary* of the trust deed. In practice, the borrower usually delivers the note and the trust deed to the lender. The lender records the trust deed. In some cases the trust deed and/or the note are delivered to the trustee after the trust deed is recorded. And in such cases the trustee holds the trust deed in a long-term escrow. Regardless of who physically holds the trust deed, the trustee holds title to the property until the debt is paid. If the debt is paid, the trustee reconveys title to the borrower. If the borrower defaults, the lender requests the trustee to foreclose.

TRUSTEE

The trustee is intended to be a neutral third party. In a few states the trustee must be a *public trustee,* such as a county clerk. In most states a

FIGURE 6–1   The Trust Deed Financing Arrangement

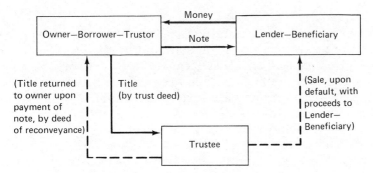

private trustee is allowed. In a number of states the private trustee must be an attorney, a financial institution, a trust company, or a title insurance company. In the remaining states a private trustee can be anyone who has contractual capacity. In some states an employee of the lender is appointed as trustee, which avoids the cost of employing an outside trustee. If the lender's employee is the trustee and foreclosure is necessary, a neutral third party is then usually substituted as the trustee. In a number of states only residents can serve as trustees. No matter who the trustee is, the trustee is expected to act with strict impartiality.

The trustee holds legal title to the property pledged as security, but the title is limited to what is necessary to perform the terms of the trust agreement.

BENEFICIARY

The lender-beneficiary does not hold title to the property. The lender usually has the only right to request the trustee to act, that is, to sell the property. In foreclosure the proceeds of the sale are used to pay the lender-beneficiary.

A beneficiary usually has the right to sell the note and lender position or interest in the trust deed to other investors. The new noteholder has the same rights to enforce the contract and to collect the proceeds from any sale of the property in foreclosure as were held by the original lender-noteholder.

TRUSTOR

The owner-borrower-trustor holds equitable title to the property and retains possession. The borrower has essentially the same rights under a trust deed as under a mortgage. Barring default, the borrower can sell or lease the property or do anything that an owner might otherwise do, subject however to the covenants of the loan agreement.

REASONS FOR USE

The use of the trust deed is usually associated with the power of sale. Exercise of the power of sale is the common method of foreclosing in each of the 11 states and the District of Columbia in which the trust deed is the dominant method of hypothecating real property. Power of sale is less expensive and usually faster than judicial foreclosure and sale. Eight additional states make frequent use of the trust deed, but in two of these states, including Illinois, the use of power of sale is prohibited. Power of sale is the typical method of foreclosure in ten states in which the mortgage is dominant and in Georgia where the security deed is dominant. The availability of power of sale in a given state does not mean that the trust deed is the dominant method of hypothecation. And a prohibition against the exercise of the power of sale in a given state does not preclude the use of a trust deed in that state. The use or lack of use of the trust deed in a given state is the result of a combination of advantages and disadvantages of various methods of hypothecation of real property in that state.

ADVANTAGES

Foreclosure through power of sale is less expensive and usually faster than other means of foreclosure. The exercise of the power of sale is allowed under a trust deed in about ten states in which its exercise is otherwise prohibited under a mortgage. This accounts for the use of the trust deed in about one-half of the states in which it is dominant. In about 20 states the exercise of power of sale is allowed under both the mortgage and the trust deed. In using the trust deed, a lender avoids a conflict of interest situation by using a neutral third party, such as a trustee, to conduct the public sale. This use of a third party helps the lender retain goodwill and encourages the use of the trust deed in these states.

In at least nine states the use of a trust deed is also favored because the exercise of the power of sale eliminates the statutory redemption period. The same is accomplished under the exercise of the power of sale in a mortgage in some of these states. In other words, in most of the states that the trust deed is dominant, there is no statutory redemption after a sale under the power of sale. And in the other states in which the trust deed is dominant, the statutory redemption period is relatively short or can be shortened by the use of the trust deed.

In a few states the lender or trustee may find it easier to obtain possession and rents under the trust deed than under the mortgage. In some states the enforcement of the trust deed is not governed by the statute of limitations, whereas the enforcement of a mortgage is governed by the statute of limitations. Thus, use of the trust deed gives a lender greater flexibility.

The trust deed may also be used to hide the identity of the lender. This can be accomplished with the use of a bearer note and by providing in the trust deed that sale proceeds upon foreclosure are payable to the trustee. A *bearer note* means it is payable to the party having possession of the note rather than to a specified party, usually the lender. The use of a bearer note and a trust deed payable to the trustee can be used to make the note and the trust deed assignable without the necessity of recording the assignment. This has risks, should the note and trust deed fall into the hands of an unscrupulous trustee. Trustee bonding may therefore be desirable in this situation.

The advantages cited above are advantages to the lender. But they can also work to the advantage of the borrower, to the extent that they lower the lender's costs and make it easier to obtain a loan. In some states, if the lender exercises the power-of-sale clause in a trust deed, the lender is prohibited from obtaining a deficiency judgment against the borrower. This is also an advantage for the borrower.

DISADVANTAGES

One disadvantage of the use of the trust deed is the cost of the services of the third party trustee. This expense may be reduced by use of a lender's employee as the trustee.

In some states the use of the power of sale in a trust deed eliminates the lender's right to a deficiency judgment, which acts as a disadvantage to the lender. It may not be too great a disadvantage in most cases because deficiency judgments are seldom enforced, at least on home loans.

There are some disadvantages related to administrative problems. If the trustee cannot be located, delays in obtaining action under the trust deed may be encountered. If the note has been misplaced, it may be time consuming to obtain the deed of reconveyance. Administrative problems also occur with the use of a mortgage, but they tend to be more difficult to solve under a trust deed because the trustee will insist on proper documentation to meet the terms of the trust agreement.

There are a number of possible disadvantages to the borrower in some states. Foreclosure through the power of sale in a trust deed is faster than judicial foreclosure under a mortgage. This is a definite disadvantage in states in which the power of sale is allowed in a trust deed but prohibited in a mortgage. In some states the use of the trust deed with a power of sale eliminates or shortens the statutory redemption period. In a few states the borrower may lose possession more quickly after default if a trust deed is used. And in some states the statute of limitations does not apply against actions to collect a debt secured by a trust deed. It is clear that in some states it is to the advantage of the borrower to negotiate the use of a mortgage rather than a trust deed. Of course, if the borrower does not default on the terms of the loan, it does not matter whether a mortgage or a trust deed is used.

MULTIPLE NOTES AND THE TRUST DEED

One major advantage of a trust deed is that it can be used to facilitate borrowing large sums of money against a major property. For example, a trust deed can be used in every state to offer corporate property as the security for a large number of notes. Assume that a corporation desires to raise a large sum of money and use its real property as security for the debt. The corporation may transfer title to a trustee by a trust deed, with a large number of notes or bonds secured by the trust deed. The notes or bonds are then sold to a number of investors. Even though the notes or bonds are secured by a trust deed, they are typically called mortgage bonds.

The trustee represents the interests of the bondholders, and if there is a default the trustee can take action to foreclose. The trustee can exercise power of sale if applicable or seek a judicial foreclosure and sale. In most states the trustee is allowed to bid in the name of the bondholders at the foreclosure sale. In some states the trustee is allowed to bid in the name of the bondholders only if such a clause is contained in the trust deed.

A trust deed may also be used in most states to transfer title to noncorporate property to a trustee in order to secure multiple notes against a given property. The trustee then acts to protect the interests of the various noteholders, as explained above.

SIMILARITY TO A MORTGAGE

There are FHA insured trust deeds, purchase money trust deeds, blanket trust deeds, junior trust deeds, wraparound trust deeds, and so forth. In short, there is a trust deed arrangement equivalent for every type of mortgage arrangement. FNMA-FHLMC has developed a uniform trust deed note and trust deed for every state in which the arrangement is legal. Most of the convenants are the same as those in the uniform mortgage instruments. Thus, except for the differences noted above, the arrangements are much alike.

NOTE

The uniform mortgage note is identical to the uniform note accompanying a trust deed with one exception. The mortgage note says that the note is secured by a mortgage, and the trust deed note says that the note is secured by a trust deed.

TRUST DEED

Figure 6–2 is the uniform FNMA-FHLMC trust deed for the state of Texas. The opening portion of the uniform trust deed differs from the opening of the uniform mortgage discussed in Chap. 4. It identifies the document as a deed of trust. It identifies the grantor-borrower, the trustee, and the beneficiary-lender. The major difference is that it contains a provision in which the borrower grants title to the trustee. And if it is allowed by law, the clause grants the trustee power of sale. The remain-

FIGURE 6–2 A Uniform FNMA-FHLMC Trust Deed

DEED OF TRUST

THIS DEED OF TRUST is made this . . . . day of . . . . ,
19 . . . ., among the Grantor, ...
. . . . (herein "Borrower"), ...
. . . . (herein "Trustee"), and the Beneficiary,
. . . ., a corporation organized and
existing under the laws of . . . . , whose address is . . . .
. . . . (herein "Lender").

BORROWER, in consideration of the indebtedness herein recited and the trust herein created, irrevocably grants
and conveys to Trustee, in trust, with power of sale, the following described property located in the County of
. . . . , State of Texas:

Which has the address of . . . . , ... ,
[Street]   [City]
. . . . (herein "Property Address");
[State and Zip Code]

TOGETHER with all the improvements now or hereafter erected on the property, and all easements, rights,
appurtenances, rents (subject however to the rights and authorities given herein to Lender to collect and apply such
rents), royalties, mineral, oil and gas rights and profits, water, water rights, and water stock, and all fixtures now or
hereafter attached to the property, all of which, including replacements and additions thereto, shall be deemed to be
and remain a part of the property covered by this Deed of Trust; and all of the foregoing, together with said property
(or the leasehold estate if this Deed of Trust is on a leasehold) are herein referred to as the "Property";

TO SECURE to Lender (a) the repayment of the indebtedness evidenced by Borrower's note dated . . . .
. . . . (herein "Note"), in the principal sum of . . . .
. . . . Dollars, with interest thereon, providing for monthly installments
of principal and interest, with the balance of the indebtedness, if not sooner paid, due and payable on . . . .
. . . . ; the payment of all other sums, with interest thereon, advanced
in accordance herewith to protect the security of this Deed of Trust; and the performance of the covenants and
agreements of Borrower herein contained; and (b) the repayment of any future advances, with interest thereon, made
to Borrower by Lender pursuant to paragraph 21 hereof (herein "Future Advances").

Borrower covenants that Borrower is lawfully seised of the estate hereby conveyed and has the right to grant
and convey the Property, that the Property is unencumbered, and that Borrower will warrant and defend generally
the title to the Property against all claims and demands, subject to any declarations, easements or restrictions listed
in a schedule of exceptions to coverage in any title insurance policy insuring Lender's interest in the Property.

TEXAS—1 to 4 Family—1/76—**FNMA/FHLMC UNIFORM INSTRUMENT**

FIGURE 6–2 (*Continued*)

UNIFORM COVENANTS. Borrower and Lender covenant and agree as follows:

1. Payment of Principal and Interest. Borrower shall promptly pay when due the principal of and interest on the indebtedness evidenced by the Note, prepayment and late charges as provided in the Note, and the principal of and interest on any Future Advances secured by this Deed of Trust.

2. Funds for Taxes and Insurance. Subject to applicable law or to a written waiver by Lender, Borrower shall pay to Lender on the day monthly installments of principal and interest are payable under the Note, until the Note is paid in full, a sum (herein "Funds") equal to one-twelfth of the yearly taxes and assessments which may attain priority over this Deed of Trust, and ground rents on the Property, if any, plus one-twelfth of yearly premium installments for hazard insurance, plus one-twelfth of yearly premium installments for mortgage insurance, if any, all as reasonably estimated initially and from time to time by Lender on the basis of assessments and bills and reasonable estimates thereof.

The Funds shall be held in an institution the deposits or accounts of which are insured or guaranteed by a Federal or state agency (including Lender if Lender is such an institution). Lender shall apply the Funds to pay said taxes, assessments, insurance premiums and ground rents. Lender may not charge for so holding and applying the Funds, analyzing said account or verifying and compiling said assessments and bills, unless Lender pays Borrower interest on the Funds and applicable law permits Lender to make such a charge. Borrower and Lender may agree in writing at the time of execution of this Deed of Trust that interest on the Funds shall be paid to Borrower, and unless such agreement is made or applicable law requires such interest to be paid, Lender shall not be required to pay Borrower any interest or earnings on the Funds. Lender shall give to Borrower, without charge, an annual accounting of the Funds showing credits and debits to the Funds and the purpose for which each debit to the Funds was made. The Funds are pledged as additional security for the sums secured by this Deed of Trust.

If the amount of the Funds held by Lender, together with the future monthly installments of Funds payable prior to the due dates of taxes, assessments, insurance premiums and ground rents, shall exceed the amount required to pay said taxes, assessments, insurance premiums and ground rents as they fall due, such excess shall be, at Borrower's option, either promptly repaid to Borrower or credited to Borrower on monthly installments of Funds. If the amount of the Funds held by Lender shall not be sufficient to pay taxes, assessments, insurance premiums and ground rents as they fall due, Borrower shall pay to Lender any amount necessary to make up the deficiency within 30 days from the date notice is mailed by Lender to Borrower requesting payment thereof.

Upon payment in full of all sums secured by this Deed of Trust, Lender shall promptly refund to Borrower any Funds held by Lender. If under paragraph 18 hereof the Property is sold or the Property is otherwise acquired by Lender, Lender shall apply, no later than immediately prior to the sale of the Property or its acquisition by Lender, any Funds held by Lender at the time of application as a credit against the sums secured by this Deed of Trust.

3. Application of Payments. Unless applicable law provides otherwise, all payments received by Lender under the Note and paragraphs 1 and 2 hereof shall be applied by Lender first in payment of amounts payable to Lender by Borrower under paragraph 2 hereof, then to interest payable on the Note, then to the principal of the Note, and then to interest and principal on any Future Advances.

4. Charges; Liens. Borrower shall pay all taxes, assessments and other charges, fines and impositions attributable to the Property which may attain a priority over this Deed of Trust, and leasehold payments or ground rents, if any, in the manner provided under paragraph 2 hereof or, if not paid in such manner, by Borrower making payment, when due, directly to the payee thereof. Borrower shall promptly furnish to Lender all notices of amounts due under this paragraph, and in the event Borrower shall make payment directly, Borrower shall promptly furnish to Lender receipts evidencing such payments. Borrower shall promptly discharge any lien which has priority over this Deed of Trust; provided, that Borrower shall not be required to discharge any such lien so long as Borrower shall agree in writing to the payment of the obligation secured by such lien in a manner acceptable to Lender, or shall in good faith contest such lien by, or defend enforcement of such lien in, legal proceedings which operate to prevent the enforcement of the lien or forfeiture of the Property or any part thereof.

5. Hazard Insurance. Borrower shall keep the improvements now existing or hereafter erected on the Property insured against loss by fire, hazards included within the term "extended coverage", and such other hazards as Lender may require and in such amounts and for such periods as Lender may require; provided, that Lender shall not require that the amount of such coverage exceed that amount of coverage required to pay the sums secured by this Deed of Trust.

The insurance carrier providing the insurance shall be chosen by Borrower subject to approval by Lender; provided, that such approval shall not be unreasonably withheld. All premiums on insurance policies shall be paid in the manner provided under paragraph 2 hereof or, if not paid in such manner, by Borrower making payment, when due, directly to the insurance carrier.

All insurance policies and renewals thereof shall be in form acceptable to Lender and shall include a standard mortgage clause in favor of and in form acceptable to Lender. Lender shall have the right to hold the policies and renewals thereof, and Borrower shall promptly furnish to Lender all renewal notices and all receipts of paid premiums. In the event of loss, Borrower shall give prompt notice to the insurance carrier and Lender. Lender may make proof of loss if not made promptly by Borrower.

Unless Lender and Borrower otherwise agree in writing, insurance proceeds shall be applied to restoration or repair of the Property damaged, provided such restoration or repair is economically feasible and the security of this Deed of Trust is not thereby impaired. If such restoration or repair is not economically feasible or if the security of this Deed of Trust would be impaired, the insurance proceeds shall be applied to the sums secured by this Deed of Trust, with the excess, if any, paid to Borrower. If the Property is abandoned by Borrower, or if Borrower fails to respond to Lender within 30 days from the date notice is mailed by Lender to Borrower that the insurance carrier offers to settle a claim for insurance benefits, Lender is authorized to collect and apply the insurance proceeds at Lender's option either to restoration or repair of the Property or to the sums secured by this Deed of Trust.

Unless Lender and Borrower otherwise agree in writing, any such application of proceeds to principal shall not extend or postpone the due date of the monthly installments referred to in paragraphs 1 and 2 hereof or change the amount of such installments. If under paragraph 18 hereof the Property is acquired by Lender, all right, title and interest of Borrower in and to any insurance policies and in and to the proceeds thereof resulting from damage to the Property prior to the sale or acquisition shall pass to Lender to the extent of the sums secured by this Deed of Trust immediately prior to such sale or acquisition.

6. Preservation and Maintenance of Property; Leaseholds; Condominiums; Planned Unit Developments. Borrower shall keep the Property in good repair and shall not commit waste or permit impairment or deterioration of the Property and shall comply with the provisions of any lease if this Deed of Trust is on a leasehold. If this Deed of Trust is on a unit in a condominium or a planned unit development, Borrower shall perform all of Borrower's obligations under the declaration or covenants creating or governing the condominium or planned unit development, the by-laws and regulations of the condominium or planned unit development, and constituent documents. If a condominium or planned unit development rider is executed by Borrower and recorded together with this Deed of Trust, the covenants and agreements of such rider shall be incorporated into and shall amend and supplement the covenants and agreements of this Deed of Trust as if the rider were a part hereof.

7. Protection of Lender's Security. If Borrower fails to perform the covenants and agreements contained in this Deed of Trust, or if any action or proceeding is commenced which materially affects Lender's interest in the Property, including, but not limited to, eminent domain, insolvency, code enforcement, or arrangements or proceedings involving a bankrupt or decedent, then Lender at Lender's option, upon notice to Borrower, may make such appearances, disburse such sums and take such action as is necessary to protect Lender's interest, including, but not limited to, disbursement of reasonable attorney's fees and entry upon the Property to make repairs. If Lender required mortgage insurance as a condition of making the loan secured by this Deed of Trust, Borrower shall pay the premiums required to maintain such insurance in effect until such time as the requirement for such insurance terminates in accordance with Borrower's and Lender's written agreement or applicable law. Borrower shall pay the amount of all mortgage insurance premiums in the manner provided under paragraph 2 hereof.

Any amounts disbursed by Lender pursuant to this paragraph 7, with interest thereon, shall become additional indebtedness of Borrower secured by this Deed of Trust. Unless Borrower and Lender agree to other terms of payment, such amounts shall be payable upon notice from Lender to Borrower requesting payment thereof, and shall bear interest from the date of disbursement at the rate payable from time to time on outstanding principal under the Note unless payment of interest at such rate would be contrary to applicable law, in which event such amounts shall bear interest at the highest rate permissible under applicable law. Nothing contained in this paragraph 7 shall require Lender to incur any expense or take any action hereunder.

8. Inspection. Lender may make or cause to be made reasonable entries upon and inspections of the Property, provided that Lender shall give Borrower notice prior to any such inspection specifying reasonable cause therefor related to Lender's interest in the Property.

FIGURE 6–2 *(Continued)*

9. Condemnation. The proceeds of any award or claim for damages, direct or consequential, in connection with any condemnation or other taking of the Property, or part thereof, or for conveyance in lieu of condemnation, are hereby assigned and shall be paid to Lender.

In the event of a total taking of the Property, the proceeds shall be applied to the sums secured by this Deed of Trust, with the excess, if any, paid to Borrower. In the event of a partial taking of the Property, unless Borrower and Lender otherwise agree in writing, there shall be applied to the sums secured by this Deed of Trust such proportion of the proceeds as is equal to that proportion which the amount of the sums secured by this Deed of Trust immediately prior to the date of taking bears to the fair market value of the Property immediately prior to the date of taking, with the balance of the proceeds paid to Borrower.

If the Property is abandoned by Borrower, or if, after notice by Lender to Borrower that the condemnor offers to make an award or settle a claim for damages, Borrower fails to respond to Lender within 30 days after the date such notice is mailed, Lender is authorized to collect and apply the proceeds, at Lender's option, either to restoration or repair of the Property or to the sums secured by this Deed of Trust.

Unless Lender and Borrower otherwise agree in writing, any such application of proceeds to principal shall not extend or postpone the due date of the monthly installments referred to in paragraphs 1 and 2 hereof or change the amount of such installments.

10. Borrower Not Released. Extension of the time for payment or modification of amortization of the sums secured by this Deed of Trust granted by Lender to any successor in interest of Borrower shall not operate to release, in any manner, the liability of the original Borrower and Borrower's successors in interest. Lender shall not be required to commence proceedings against such successor or refuse to extend time for payment or otherwise modify amortization of the sums secured by this Deed of Trust by reason of any demand made by the original Borrower and Borrower's successors in interest.

11. Forbearance by Lender Not a Waiver. Any forbearance by Lender in exercising any right or remedy hereunder, or otherwise afforded by applicable law, shall not be a waiver of or preclude the exercise of any such right or remedy. The procurement of insurance or the payment of taxes or other liens or charges by Lender shall not be a waiver of Lender's right to accelerate the maturity of the indebtedness secured by this Deed of Trust.

12. Remedies Cumulative. All remedies provided in this Deed of Trust are distinct and cumulative to any other right or remedy under this Deed of Trust or afforded by law or equity, and may be exercised concurrently, independently or successively.

13. Successors and Assigns Bound; Joint and Several Liability; Captions. The covenants and agreements herein contained shall bind, and the rights hereunder shall inure to, the respective successors and assigns of Lender and Borrower, subject to the provisions of paragraph 17 hereof. All covenants and agreements of Borrower shall be joint and several. The captions and headings of the paragraphs of this Deed of Trust are for convenience only and are not to be used to interpret or define the provisions hereof.

14. Notice. Except for any notice required under applicable law to be given in another manner, (a) any notice to Borrower provided for in this Deed of Trust shall be given by mailing such notice by certified mail addressed to Borrower at the Property Address or at such other address as Borrower may designate by notice to Lender as provided herein, and (b) any notice to Lender shall be given by certified mail, return receipt requested, to Lender's address stated herein or to such other address as Lender may designate by notice to Borrower as provided herein. Any notice provided for in this Deed of Trust shall be deemed to have been given to Borrower or Lender when given in the manner designated herein.

15. Uniform Deed of Trust; Governing Law; Severability. This form of Deed of Trust combines uniform covenants for national use and non-uniform covenants with limited variations by jurisdiction to constitute a uniform security instrument covering real property. This Deed of Trust shall be governed by the law of the jurisdiction in which the Property is located. In the event that any provision or clause of this Deed of Trust or the Note conflicts with applicable law, such conflict shall not affect other provisions of this Deed of Trust or the Note which can be given effect without the conflicting provision, and to this end the provisions of the Deed of Trust and the Note are declared to be severable.

16. Borrower's Copy. Borrower shall be furnished a conformed copy of the Note and of this Deed of Trust at the time of execution or after recordation hereof.

17. Transfer of the Property; Assumption. If all or any part of the Property or an interest therein is sold or transferred by Borrower without Lender's prior written consent, excluding (a) the creation of a lien or encumbrance subordinate to this Deed of Trust, (b) the creation of a purchase money security interest for household appliances, (c) a transfer by devise, descent or by operation of law upon the death of a joint tenant or (d) the grant of any leasehold interest of three years or less not containing an option to purchase, Lender may, at Lender's option, declare all the sums secured by this Deed of Trust to be immediately due and payable. Lender shall have waived such option to accelerate if, prior to the sale or transfer, Lender and the person to whom the Property is to be sold or transferred reach agreement in writing that the credit of such person is satisfactory to Lender and that the interest payable on the sums secured by this Deed of Trust shall be at such rate as Lender shall request. If Lender has waived the option to accelerate provided in this paragraph 17, and if Borrower's successor in interest has executed a written assumption agreement accepted in writing by Lender, Lender shall release Borrower from all obligations under this Deed of Trust and the Note.

If Lender exercises such option to accelerate, Lender shall mail Borrower notice of acceleration in accordance with paragraph 14 hereof. Such notice shall provide a period of not less than 30 days from the date the notice is mailed within which Borrower may pay the sums declared due. If Borrower fails to pay such sums prior to the expiration of such period, Lender may, without further notice or demand on Borrower, invoke any remedies permitted by paragraph 18 hereof.

NON-UNIFORM COVENANTS. Borrower and Lender further covenant and agree as follows:

18. Acceleration; Remedies. Except as provided in paragraph 17 hereof, upon Borrower's breach of any covenant or agreement of Borrower in this Deed of Trust, including the covenants to pay when due any sums secured by this Deed of Trust, Lender prior to acceleration shall mail notice to Borrower as provided in paragraph 14 hereof specifying: (1) the breach; (2) the action required to cure such breach; (3) a date, not less than 30 days from the date the notice is mailed to Borrower, by which such breach must be cured; and (4) that failure to cure such breach on or before the date specified in the notice may result in acceleration of the sums secured by this Deed of Trust and sale of the Property. The notice shall further inform Borrower of the right to reinstate after acceleration and the right to bring a court action to assert the non-existence of a default or any other defense of Borrower to acceleration and sale. If the breach is not cured on or before the date specified in the notice, Lender at Lender's option may declare all of the sums secured by this Deed of Trust to be immediately due and payable without further demand and may invoke the power of sale and any other remedies permitted by applicable law. Lender shall be entitled to collect all reasonable costs and expenses incurred in pursuing the remedies provided in this paragraph 18, including, but not limited to, reasonable attorney's fees.

If Lender invokes the power of sale, Lender or Trustee shall give notice of the time, place and terms of sale by posting written notice at least 21 days prior to the day of sale at the courthouse door in each of the counties in which the Property is situated. Lender shall mail a copy of the notice of sale to Borrower in the manner prescribed by applicable law. Such sale shall be made at public vendue between the hours of 10 o'clock a.m. and 4 o'clock p.m. on the first Tuesday in any month. Borrower authorizes Trustee to sell the Property to the highest bidder for cash in one or more parcels and in such order as Trustee may determine. Lender or Lender's designee may purchase the Property at any sale.

Trustee shall deliver to the purchaser Trustee's deed conveying the Property so sold in fee simple with covenants of general warranty. Borrower covenants and agrees to defend generally the purchaser's title to the Property against all claims and demands. The recitals in Trustee's deed shall be prima facie evidence of the truth of the statements contained therein. Trustee shall apply the proceeds of the sale in the following order: (a) to all reasonable costs and expenses of the sale, including, but not limited to, reasonable Trustee's fees and attorney's fees and costs of title evidence; (b) to all sums secured by this Deed of Trust; and (c) the excess, if any, to the person or persons legally entitled thereto.

If the Property is sold pursuant to this paragraph 18, Borrower or any person holding possession of the Property through Borrower shall immediately surrender possession of the Property to the purchaser at such sale. If possession is not surrendered, Borrower or such person shall be a tenant at sufferance and may be removed by writ of possession.

19. Borrower's Right to Reinstate. Notwithstanding Lender's acceleration of the sums secured by this Deed of Trust, Borrower shall have the right to have any proceedings begun by Lender to enforce this Deed of Trust discontinued at any time prior to the earlier to occur of (i) the fifth day before sale of the Property pursuant to the power of sale contained in this Deed of Trust or (ii) entry of a judgment enforcing this Deed of Trust if: (a) Borrower pays Lender all sums which would be then due under this Deed of Trust, the Note and notes securing Future Advances, if any, had no acceleration occurred; (b) Borrower cures all breaches of any other covenants or agreements of Borrower contained in this Deed of Trust; (c) Borrower pays all reasonable expenses incurred by Lender and Trustee in enforcing the covenants and agreements of Borrower contained in this Deed of Trust and in enforcing Lender's and Trustee's remedies as provided in paragraph 18 hereof,

FIGURE 6–2 (*Continued*)

including, but not limited to, reasonable attorney's fees; and (d) Borrower takes such action as Lender may reasonably require to assure that the lien of this Deed of Trust, Lender's interest in the Property and Borrower's obligation to pay the sums secured by this Deed of Trust shall continue unimpaired. Upon such payment and cure by Borrower, this Deed of Trust and the obligations secured hereby shall remain in full force and effect as if no acceleration had occurred.

20. Assignment of Rents; Appointment of Receiver; Lender in Possession. As additional security hereunder, Borrower hereby assigns to Lender the rents of the Property, provided that Borrower shall, prior to acceleration under paragraph 18 hereof or abandonment of the Property, have the right to collect and retain such rents as they become due and payable.

Upon acceleration under paragraph 18 hereof or abandonment of the Property, Lender, in person, by agent or by judicially appointed receiver, shall be entitled to enter upon, take possession of and manage the Property and to collect the rents of the Property including those past due. All rents collected by Lender or the receiver shall be applied first to payment of the costs of management of the Property and collection of rents, including, but not limited to, receiver's fees, premiums on receiver's bonds and reasonable attorney's fees, and then to the sums secured by this Deed of Trust. Lender and the receiver shall be liable to account only for those rents actually received.

21. Future Advances. Upon request of Borrower, Lender, at Lender's option prior to release of this Deed of Trust, may make Future Advances to Borrower if the Property is not the homestead of Borrower. Such Future Advances, with interest thereon, shall be secured by this Deed of Trust when evidenced by promissory notes stating that said notes are secured hereby.

22. Release. Upon payment of all sums secured by this Deed of Trust, Lender shall release this Deed of Trust without charge to Borrower. Borrower shall pay all costs of recordation, if any.

23. Substitute Trustee. Lender at Lender's option, with or without cause, may from time to time remove Trustee and appoint a successor trustee to any Trustee appointed hereunder by an instrument recorded in the county in which this Deed of Trust is recorded. Without conveyance of the Property, the successor trustee shall succeed to all the title, power and duties conferred upon the Trustee herein and by applicable law.

24. Subrogation. Any of the proceeds of the Note utilized to take up outstanding liens against all or any part of the Property have been advanced by Lender at Borrower's request and upon Borrower's representation that such amounts are due and are secured by valid liens against the Property. Lender shall be subrogated to any and all rights, superior titles, liens and equities owned or claimed by any owner or holder of any outstanding liens and debts, however remote, regardless of whether said liens or debts are acquired by Lender by assignment or are released by the holder thereof upon payment.

25. Partial Invalidity. In the event any portion of the sums intended to be secured by this Deed of Trust cannot be lawfully secured hereby, payments in reduction of such sums shall be applied first to those portions not secured hereby. In the event that any applicable law limiting the amount of interest or other charges permitted to be collected is interpreted so that any charge provided for in this Deed of Trust or in the Note, whether considered separately or together with other charges that are considered a part of this Deed of Trust and Note transaction, violates such law by reason of the acceleration of the indebtedness secured hereby, or for any other reason, such charge is hereby reduced to the extent necessary to eliminate such violation. The amounts of such interest or other charges previously paid to Lender in excess of the amounts permitted by applicable law shall be applied by Lender to reduce the principal of the indebtedness evidenced by the Note, or, at Lender's option, be refunded.

26. Vendor's Lien; Renewal and Extension. The Note secured hereby is [primarily secured by the Vendor's Lien retained in the Deed of even date herewith conveying the Property to Borrower, which Vendor's Lien has been assigned to Lender, this Deed of Trust being additional security therefor.]* [in renewal and extension, but not in extinguishment, of that certain indebtedness described as follows:]*

*Delete bracketed clauses as appropriate.

IN WITNESS WHEREOF, Borrower has executed this Deed of Trust.

....
—Borrower

....
—Borrower

STATE OF TEXAS,.................................County ss:

BEFORE ME, the undersigned, a Notary Public in and for said County and State, on this day personally appeared
...., known to me
to be the person(s) whose name(s).............subscribed to the foregoing instrument, and acknowledged to me
that ..he.. executed the same for the purposes and consideration therein expressed.

GIVEN UNDER MY HAND AND SEAL OF OFFICE, this.................day of..................., 19.....

....
Notary Public

———————————— (Space Below This Line Reserved For Lender and Recorder) ————————————

ing portion of the uniform trust deed is identical to that of the uniform mortgage except the words *deed of trust* are substituted for the word *mortgage.* Thus, there is no need to discuss further the 17 uniform covenants of the trust deed shown in Fig. 6–2.

Nonuniform covenants vary from state to state, however. For example, the uniform trust deed for Texas contains some nonuniform covenants that differ from those in the uniform mortgage for Illinois, which we examined in Chap. 4. Most of these differences result from differences in state law and/or practice.

The two basic differences between the nonuniform covenants found in mortgages and trust deeds are found in clauses 23 and 18.

If a private trustee is used in the state, the trust deed contains a *substitute trustee clause* that allows the lender to appoint a substitute trustee. This clause is necessary if the original trustee was a private trustee who has died or who has gone out of business, such as in the case of a corporate trustee. This clause is also advisable if an employee of the lender is the original trustee and foreclosure is necessary.

In clause 18 the power of sale is specified as a remedy. The procedure of public notice before the sale is recited in detail. But these are not unique to a trust deed. Power of sale may be exercised under a mortgage in some states, and the clause in the mortgage specifies the procedure for public notice prior to sale. The unique portion of clause 18 is the involvement of the trustee. In Texas either the lender or the trustee can mail a copy of notice of sale to the borrower. In some states the lender must give the trustee written notice of the default and of the lender's desire to foreclose. The trustee then files a notice of default. Under either system the trustee gives public notice of the sale and then the trustee conducts the sale.

RECONVEYANCE OF TITLE

When the note is paid in full, the borrower-trustor is entitled to regain full title. The exact procedure depends on the state law. Essentially, the process is as follows. The noteholder-beneficiary marks the note paid, dates it, and signs it. "Cancelled" is also written on the trust deed, along with a date and signature. The borrower presents the note and trust deed to the trustee. The trustee issues a *deed of release* or a *deed of reconveyance,* which returns title to the borrower-owner. In some states a different method is used. The lender sends a request for reconveyance to the trustee, which is accompanied by the note and trust deed if they are not already in the trustee's possession. The *request for reconveyance* directs the trustee to issue a deed of release or reconveyance to the borrower. The trustee cancels the note if it has not been canceled by the lender and issues the release deed to the borrower. In Virginia and perhaps in a few other states the noteholder rather than the trustee grants the release.

The deed of reconveyance or deed of release is signed by the trustee, and it is usually acknowledged. The borrower records the release deed. This provides constructive notice and clears the title of the pledged property. The release is also often noted in the margin of the recorded trust deed.

FORECLOSURE

The exercise of power of sale is the typical method of foreclosing under a trust deed in all the states in which the trust deed is the dominant method of hypothecating real property. Beyond this, foreclosure under a trust deed may differ from that under a mortgage due to the applicable state laws. In some states a judicial proceeding for foreclosure and sale is the only method of foreclosing under both the mortgage and trust deed. In some states power of sale is allowed under both the mortgage and trust deed. In about ten states it is possible to exercise power of sale under a trust deed, whereas it is prohibited under a mortgage.

The difference in the procedure for exercising the power of sale under a mortgage and a trust deed is due to the existence of a trustee. When the borrower defaults, the lender accelerates the debt. The lender gives written notice to the trustee of the default and of the lender's desire to foreclose through the exercise of the power of sale. In some states the trustee must file a notice of default. It provides constructive notice of the trustee's intention to sell the property unless the borrower corrects the default. In some other states certified mail must be used to notify the parties. There is a waiting period prior to the sale, which varies widely among states and ranges from approximately 20 days to 4 months. The trustee is required to give notice of the sale date a number of times during the waiting period. If the default is not corrected during the waiting period, the trustee sells the property at a public sale.

The trustee grants a *trustee's deed* to the purchaser at the sale. This is equivalent to the lender's deed given after the exercise of the power of sale under a mortgage. If statutory redemption is allowed, the trustee may grant a trustee's certificate of sale at the time of the sale and the trustee's deed at the expiration of the statutory redemption period. The trustee's deed conveys all the rights that the borrower possessed. If proper notice has been given, the sale terminates all of the junior liens against the property.

The proceeds of the sale are used to pay the claims of the lender-beneficiary. Surplus funds are used to pay junior liens and claims first, with any remainder given to the borrower. The lender is usually the winning bidder at the sale. If the proceeds of the sale or the value of the property received by the lender are insufficient to pay the lender's claim, the lender-beneficiary can seek a deficiency judgment if allowed by state law.

SUMMARY

The trust deed involves three parties. The owner-borrower is the trustor and conveys title to the trustee. The trustee accepts title and safeguards the interests of both the borrower and the lender. The lender is the beneficiary of the trust.

There is a trust deed equivalent for every type of mortgage. The borrower may sell the property subject to the trust deed with the lender's approval. At the same time the lender is free to sell the note that is secured by the trust deed.

The clauses in a trust deed are nearly identical to those in a mortgage, with two exceptions. The trust deed usually provides for replacement of the original trustee with a substitute trustee. And, the remedies clause requires notification of the trustee and action by the trustee when foreclosure is necessary.

If the property is sold under the power of sale, the trustee issues the purchaser a trustee's deed. If the debt is paid, the trustee issues the borrower either a deed of release or reconveyance. The borrower records the reconveyance to clear title of the pledged property from the trust deed.

Power of sale is the common means of foreclosing a trust deed in the states in which it is the dominant method of hypothecating real property. The statutory redemption period is relatively short or nonexistent in most of these states. The trust deed can be used to hide the identity of the lender. The use of a bearer note and a trust deed payable to the trustee allows the assignment of the trust deed without the necessity of recording the assignment.

The trust deed may be used in situations in which a large number of bonds or notes are secured by a given property. The trustee acts to protect the interests of the noteholders or bondholders.

One disadvantage of using a trust deed is the cost of employing the trustee. Another disadvantage to the lender is that in some states it eliminates the lender's right to seek a deficiency judgment.

KEY TERMS

Bearer Note	Hypothecate	Trustee
Beneficiary	Public Trustee	Trustee's Deed
Deed of Reconveyance	Request for Conveyance	Trustor
Deed of Release	Substitute Trustee Clause	

1. In using a trust deed to finance property, who is the trustee? The beneficiary? The trustor?

2. Explain the advantages and disadvantages of a trust deed as a financing instrument.

3. Compare a trust deed to a mortgage for securing a loan.

4. Are there any situations when it is more appropriate to use a trust deed rather than a mortgage to secure a loan?

5. How is a trust deed foreclosed?

6. Match the following key terms and definitions:

   a. Beneficiary _____
   b. Deed of Release _____
   c. Hypothecate _____
   d. Trustee _____
   e. Trustor _____

   1. Pledge property to secure a debt while retaining possession.
   2. Owner-borrower under a trust deed arrangement.
   3. A lender in a trust deed arrangement.
   4. Holds title in a trust deed arrangement.
   5. Instrument conveying title to the trustee.
   6. Instrument used to return title to borrower.

seven

Land Contract and Option Financing

A *land contract* is a written agreement between the buyer and seller for the purchase of real property that requires the buyer to make payments over a number of years while the seller holds title until the payments are completed. The seller, *vendor,* retains legal title, but the right of possession is normally given to the buyer when the contract is signed. The buyer-*vendee* makes installment payments over a number of years and usually receives the deed only after the purchase price is paid in full. A land contract is also known as a land sale contract, an installment land contract, an installment sales contract, and a contract for deed. In many ways, contract for deed is the most appropriate term.

The land contract is a form of seller financing and is very versatile as a means of financing. It can be used for intermediate-term or long-term financing, for senior or junior financing, and in a variety of situations. It makes transactions possible when mortgage and trust deed financing is not available. Potential buyers and sellers and real estate brokerage personnel are therefore at an advantage if they are familiar with land contract financing.

The major topics included in this chapter are

1. Uses of land contracts
2. The nature of a land contract

3. Land contract compared to a purchase money mortgage
4. Options

USES OF LAND CONTRACTS

The land contract received its name because at one time it was the principal method of financing the sale of vacant land. At that time most institutional lenders would not lend money for the sale of vacant land. Land contracts are still frequently used in the sale of recreational and retirement home sites when the buyer does not plan to build on the lot immediately. Land contracts are also used in the sale of improved properties such as homes, apartment buildings, farms, and other income properties.

Both the vendee and vendor may benefit from the use of land contracts. For example, poorly located or substandard property may not qualify for mortgage financing from an institutional lender. In this situation, the owner may offer land contract financing to attract a buyer. An owner may also employ a land contract to reduce taxes on the capital gain from the sale. In other situations a prospective buyer may benefit from land contract financing. If the buyer cannot meet traditional lending standards such as the minimum down payment or a good credit rating, the seller's assistance to purchase the property may be arranged through the use of a land contract.

A land contract may have a long term requiring monthly payments that fully amortize the debt over a 15- to 20-year period. Or a land contract may be an intermediate-term agreement requiring monthly payments over a 3- to 5-year period followed by a large balloon payment. In the interim, the buyer's equity is built up and the buyer's financial condition is improved. Thus, the buyer expects to qualify for a mortgage loan from a third party lender to pay the balloon payment.

Land contracts as an alternate form of financing are widely used. When interest rates rise rapidly and the availability of mortgage loans is sharply restricted, a potential borrower who expects interest rates to decline to lower levels within one or two years is reluctant to commit to a long-term mortgage with a high interest rate. Such a person might prefer an intermediate-term land contract with the expectation of obtaining a mortgage loan to prepay the contract or to make the balloon payment when interest rates decline.

In periods of tight money, many potential borrowers who meet traditional mortgage lending standards are unable to obtain mortgage loans. If an owner desires to sell the property, seller financing becomes necessary. The owner can sell on an intermediate-term land contract basis. The buyer is expected to arrange for a mortgage loan when mortgage funds become available.

A land contract serves as both a sales and a financing instrument. As a sales device it contains the elements of a valid contract, such as the mutual agreement between competent parties, consideration, a legal property description, and the signatures of the seller and the seller's spouse, if appropriate. As a financing instrument it may contain many of the clauses found in a mortgage. It should also be signed by the buyer and buyer's spouse, if appropriate.

RIGHTS AND DUTIES OF THE VENDOR AND VENDEE

A land contract may be a relatively informal document drafted by the buyer and/or the seller. In an informal document many of the rights and duties may not be spelled out in the contract. In this case, the local customs would govern. In other instances, the seller or, on occasion, the buyer employs a lawyer, and the rights and duties of the parties are fully spelled out in the land contract. The provisions in the formal land contract prevail over local custom, unless state statutes prohibit such provisions. For example, state statutes may forbid a provision preventing recording of the land contract.

Vendor. The vendor retains legal title to the property. The vendor has the right to receive the payments promised under the land contract. The vendor has the right to prevent waste of the property. And if the vendee defaults on the land contract, the vendor has the right to take legal action to regain possession of the property. The vendor also has the right to mortgage the property to obtain a loan, but the vendee should attempt to limit the amount of the loan to a sum no greater than that due under the land contract, that is, the seller's equity. The vendor has the right to assign his or her interest in the land contract or to sell the property subject to the rights of the vendee.

The vendor's primary duty is to deliver marketable title to the vendee when the vendee fulfills his or her obligations under the land contract. The vendor is not required to have marketable title when the land contract is signed, but the vendor must be in a position to deliver it when full payment of the debt is made.

Vendee. The vendee has equitable title when the land contract is signed. *Equitable title* gives the vendee the right to obtain legal title when the debt is paid in full. Equitable title transfers the rights and duties of ownership to the vendee. The vendee has the right to possession only if it is given in the contract or if it is delivered by the vendor. The vendee has the right to use the property for any lawful purpose. The vendee is allowed to make improvements on the property. The vendee has the right to sell or assign his or her rights under the land contract, but the vendee is not relieved of the obligations under the land contract unless the vendor specifically grants a release. The vendee is allowed to pledge his or her interest under the land contract as security for a loan.

The vendee has the duty to make the payments required by the contract. When the vendee is given the right to possession, the vendee is typically responsible for keeping the property insured and paying the real estate taxes.

TYPICAL PROVISIONS OF A LAND CONTRACT

Figure 7–1 shows a typical land contract, in which can be included most of the clauses found in a mortgage. The typical land contract is written to protect the seller. The buyer often makes a small down payment and is in a relatively weak bargaining position. The contract dictates the type of deed to be delivered and the time of delivery. Although an *escrow for deed* is not a standard clause in a seller drafted land contract, the buyer should seek to have the deed placed in escrow. The escrow agent would maintain possession of the deed and deliver it to the buyer when the buyer fulfills the terms of the contract. Delivery of the deed into escrow would make the completion of the transaction possible in spite of death, disability, or stubbornness on the part of the seller.

The typical land contract grants the buyer the right to possession of the property. The contract makes the buyer responsible for maintenance of the property and gives the seller the right to inspect the property. The buyer is usually given the responsibility for the payment of real estate taxes and special assessments and for keeping the property properly insured. A well-drawn contract specifies the amount, time, and place of payments. And it specifies that the payments are applied first to interest, then to unpaid real estate taxes and insurance premiums, and finally to reduction of the debt. It would also include an acceleration clause in event of default by the buyer.

The contract specifies the allowable use of the property. It requires the seller's approval to remove or to add any improvements to the property. The contract might require the seller's approval of any assignment of the buyer's rights or of any lease made by the buyer.

The contract usually grants the buyer a prepayment privilege, which may be limited in some way when there is a mortgage on the property or when the seller is attempting to derive income tax benefits from an installment sale. The land contract may be prepayable only two to to four years after the contract is signed.

The contract usually contains a *mortgage clause,* which allows the property to be mortgaged after the land contract is signed. This allows the land contract to be subordinated to a future mortgage. The buyer

FIGURE 7-1 Contract for Deed (Land Contract)

FORM No. 854—CONTRACT—REAL ESTATE—Partial Payments—Deed in Escrow. STEVENS-NESS LAW PUBLISHING CO., PORTLAND, OR. 97204

CONTRACT—REAL ESTATE

THIS CONTRACT, Made this 29th *day of* February *, 19* 82 *, between* William E. & Ellen Cellars (H&W)
, hereinafter called the seller,

and Raymond & Amy Beyers (H&W)
, hereinafter called the buyer,

WITNESSETH: That in consideration of the mutual covenants and agreements herein contained, the seller agrees to sell unto the buyer and the buyer agrees to purchase from the seller all of the following described lands and premises situated in Rustic *County, State of* Anystate *, to-wit:*

Lot 91, University South Subdivision
Rustic County, Anystate

for the sum of One Hundred Ten Thousand and no/100 *Dollars* ($110,000.00) *(hereinafter called the purchase price) on account of which* Ten Thousand *Dollars* ($10,000.00) *is paid on the execution hereof (the receipt of which is hereby acknowledged by the seller), and the remainder to be paid at the times and in amounts as follows, to-wit:*

Two thousand dollars ($2,000) on the first day of April, 1982 and two thousand dollars ($2,000) on the first day of each and every month thereafter until all principal and interest has been paid. Payments go first to interest second to reduce principal.

All of said purchase price may be paid at any time; all deferred balances shall bear interest at the rate of one *per cent per* month from March 1st, 1982 *until paid, interest to be paid* monthly *and • {being included in the minimum regular payments above required. Taxes on said premises for the current tax year shall be prorated between the parties hereto as of this date.*

*The buyer warrants to and covenants with the seller that the real property described in this contract is
(A) primarily for buyer's personal, family, household or agricultural purposes.

The buyer shall be entitled to possession of said lands on ___, 19 ___ , and may retain such possession so long as he is not in default under the terms of this contract. The buyer agrees that at all times he will keep the premises and the buildings, now or hereafter erected thereon, in good condition and repair and will not suffer or permit any waste or strip thereof; that he will keep said premises free from construction and all other liens and save the seller harmless therefrom and reimburse seller for all costs and attorney's fees incurred by him in defending against any such liens; that he will pay all taxes hereafter levied against said property, as well as all water rents, public charges and municipal liens which hereafter lawfully may be imposed upon said premises, all promptly before the same or any part thereof become past due; that at buyer's expense, he will insure and keep insured all buildings now or hereafter erected on said premises against loss or damage by fire (with extended coverage) in an amount not less than $ ___ in a company or companies satisfactory to the seller, with loss payable first to the seller and then to the buyer as their respective interests may appear and all policies of insurance to be delivered as soon as insured to the seller. Now if the buyer shall fail to pay any such liens, costs, water rents, taxes, or charges or to procure and pay for such insurance, the seller may do so and any payment so made shall be added to and become a part of the debt secured by this contract and shall bear interest at the rate aforesaid, without waiver, however, of any right arising to the seller for buyer's breach of contract.
The seller has exhibited unto the buyer a title insurance policy insuring marketable title in and to said premises in the seller; seller's title has been examined by the buyer and is accepted and approved by him.
Contemporaneously herewith, the seller has executed a good and sufficient deed (the form of which hereby is approved by the buyer) conveying the above described real estate in fee simple unto the buyer, his heirs and assigns, free and clear of incumbrances as of the date hereof, excepting the easements, building and other restrictions now of record, if any, and ___ and has placed said deed, together with an executed copy of this contract and the title insurance policy mentioned above, in escrow with Hi Fidelity Escrow Services, Urbandale, Anystate *, escrow agent, with instructions to deliver said deed, together with the fire and title insurance policies, to the order of the buyer, his heirs and assigns, upon the payment of the purchase price and full compliance by the buyer with the terms of this agreement. The buyer agrees to pay the balance of said purchase price and the respective installments thereof, promptly at the times provided therefor, to the said escrow agent for the use and benefit of the seller. The escrow fee of the escrow agent shall be paid by the seller and buyer in equal shares; the collection charges of said escrow agent shall be paid by the* buyer

(Continued on Reverse)

IMPORTANT NOTICE: Delete, by lining out, whichever phrase and whichever warranty (A) or (B) is not applicable. If warranty (A) is applicable and if seller is a creditor, as such word is defined in the Truth-in-Lending Act and Regulation Z, the seller MUST comply with the Act and Regulation by making required disclosures; for this purpose, use Stevens-Ness Form No. 1308 or similar. If the contract becomes a first lien to finance the purchase of a dwelling use Stevens-Ness Form No. 1307 or similar.

And it is understood and agreed between said parties that time is of the essence of this contract, and in case the buyer shall fail to make the payments above required, or any of them, punctually within 20 days of the time limited therefor, or fail to keep any agreement herein contained, then the seller at his option shall have the following rights: (1) to declare this contract null and void, (2) to declare the whole unpaid principal balance of said purchase price with the interest thereon at once due and payable, (3) to withdraw said deed and other documents from escrow and/or (4) to foreclose this contract by suit in equity, and in any of such cases, all rights and interest created or then existing in favor of the buyer as against the seller hereunder shall utterly cease and determine and the right to the possession of the premises above described and all other rights acquired by the buyer hereunder shall revert to and revest in said seller without any act of re-entry, or any other act of said seller to be performed and without any right of the buyer of return, reclamation or compensation for moneys paid on account of the purchase of said property as absolutely, fully and perfectly as if this contract and such payments had never been made; and in case of such default all payments theretofore made on this contract are to be retained by and belong to said seller as the agreed and reasonable rent of said premises up to the time of such default. And the said seller, in case of such default, shall have the right immediately, or at any time thereafter, to enter upon the land aforesaid, without any process of law, and take immediate possession thereof, together with all the improvements and appurtenances thereon or thereto belonging.
The buyer further agrees that failure by the seller at any time to require performance by the buyer of any provision hereof shall in no way affect his right hereunder to enforce the same, nor shall any waiver by said seller of any breach of any provision hereof be held to be a waiver of any succeeding breach of any such provision, or as a waiver of the provision itself.

The true and actual consideration paid for this transfer, stated in terms of dollars, is $ 110,000 *However, the actual consideration consists of or includes other property or value given or promised which is the whole consideration (indicate which).*

In case suit or action is instituted to foreclose this contract or to enforce any provision hereof, the losing party in said suit or action agrees to pay such sum as the trial court may adjudge reasonable as attorney's fees to be allowed the prevailing party in said suit or action and if an appeal is taken from any judgment or decree of such trial court, the losing party further promises to pay such sum as the appellate court shall adjudge reasonable as the prevailing party's attorney's fees on such appeal.
In construing this contract, it is understood that the seller or the buyer may be more than one person or a corporation; that if the context so requires, the singular pronoun shall be taken to mean and include the plural, the masculine, the feminine and the neuter, and that generally all grammatical changes shall be made, assumed and implied to make the provisions hereof apply equally to corporations and to individuals.
This agreement shall bind and inure to the benefit of, as the circumstances may require, not only the immediate parties hereto but their respective heirs, executors, administrators, personal representatives, successors in interest and assigns as well.
IN WITNESS WHEREOF, said parties have executed this instrument in triplicate; if either of the undersigned is a corporation, it has caused its corporate name to be signed and its corporate seal affixed hereto by its officers duly authorized thereunto by order of its board of directors.

/S/ Raymond Beyers   /S/ William E. Cellars

/S/ Amy Beyers   /S/ Ellen Cellars

SOURCE: Reproduced with permission of the Steven–Ness Law Publishing company, Portland, Oregon.

should seek to limit the amount of the mortgage to an amount no greater than the seller's equity in the contract.

The contract usually contains a *forfeiture clause* or a *liquidated damages clause.* This clause allows the seller to have the land contract forfeited upon default by the buyer. It allows the seller to keep the buyer's payments as liquidated damages. Whether or not this provision can actually be enforced depends on state law and the particular circumstances involved. The remedies the seller can take for a breach of contract are discussed in more detail later in this chapter.

ADDITIONAL BUYER CONSIDERATIONS

The buyer should inspect the property and request a title search. The inspection of the property reveals any existing tenants and the possibility of mechanic's liens not yet filed, and a title search would reveal any existing judgment liens on the property. The buyer receives the property subject to the rights of existing tenants, any existing liens, and to any possible mechanic's liens not yet filed. A buyer should therefore request the right to pay any liens against the property and to deduct them from the amount due under the land contract.

A buyer can protect against judgments that arise after the land contract is signed by occupying the property and/or recording the land contract. If the buyer occupies the property, it gives third parties actual notice of the buyer's claim of ownership. Recording the land contract provides constructive notice to third parties. Recording is particularly necessary to protect the buyer's rights, especially if the buyer does not occupy the property. The seller may negotiate to prohibit the recording of the land contract. This allows the seller to avoid the difficulty and expense involved with clearing the title of the land contract in the event of default by the buyer. In some states the seller is allowed to prohibit recording the land contract.

If there is an existing mortgage on the property, the buyer receives the property subject to the mortgage. Since it is a sale, it may activate the due-on-sale clause in the mortgage, and the sale would thus require the lender's approval. If the seller makes the mortgage payments, it is advisable for the buyer to reserve the right to correct any default in payments. The buyer can request the right to make the mortgage payments directly to the lender. Another alternative is for the buyer to make the payments to an escrow agent, who, in turn, makes the mortgage payment to the lender and forwards the balance to the seller.

REMEDIES FOR BREACH OF CONTRACT

In some states some remedies for the breach of a land contract are governed by statute. The land contract may include clauses that specify the remedies for the breach of contract. Historically the courts have enforced the terms of the contract if they do not violate statutes. In recent years many courts have looked beyond the terms of the contract and have sought to bring about an equitable settlement between the parties.

Remedies of the Vendor.   The vendor has numerous possible remedies if the purchaser defaults on the terms of the land contract. The remedies can be either informal or legal (enforced in court). The vendor may informally attempt to collect any past due payments and keep the land contract in force. If the buyer abandons the property, the vendor may get the buyer to voluntarily waive any further claim against the property. If voluntary action fails, the vendor may serve notice of default after some period, such as one to three months, and then take legal action.

The vendor can sue for specific performance, damages, rescission, forfeiture, or foreclosure. The vendor can sue for specific performance of the terms of the land contract or for the balance of the purchase price. This approach is only successful when the buyer is financially able to meet the terms of the contract. The vendor can sue for return of the property and damages for actual losses suffered. The measure of the damages is the difference between the price stated in the land contract and the price at which the vendor could presently sell the property. The vendor would have to sell the property to prove the damages, and the vendor has to give the buyer credit for that portion of the purchase price already paid and the value of any improvements made by the buyer.

The vendor can seek *rescission* of the contract. In this case, the vendor receives possession of the property, but the vendor is required to refund the payments already received less the fair rental of the property. If the payments exceed the fair rental, the court might allow the buyer to continue in possession until his or her equity is extinguished.

The typical land contract contains a forfeiture clause that allows the vendor to retain all the payments made by the buyer as liquidated damages. *Liquidated damages* are those specified in a clause in the land contract. Forfeiture and the retention of the payments as liquidated damages are the common legal remedies in a majority of the states. In most states, the courts enforce the provision for liquidated damages unless the court finds it to be a penalty rather than compensation for damages. If the buyer has established a substantial equity either through payments or by making improvements, the vendor may be prevented from using forfeiture as a remedy. In a few states forfeiture is prohibited if the buyer has occupied the property for more than five years or if the buyer has an equity in excess of 20 percent. In such cases, the land contract must be foreclosed.

In a few states a land contract must be foreclosed like a mortgage even if it has been in existence for only a short period of time and the buyer has a small equity in the property. Even if forfeiture is allowed, in a number of states the buyer is entitled to a refund of payments made to the vendor less reasonable compensation to the vendor.[1]

In a few states the vendor must bring a foreclosure suit to recover the property from the buyer. In some states the vendor can employ strict foreclosure, and in others the court may order a foreclosure sale. The buyer has an equitable right of redemption in all states and in some states there is a statutory redemption period.

Remedies of the Vendee.   If the seller has the ability to deliver the deed but refuses to deliver the deed, the vendee can sue for *specific performance* of the terms of the land contract. If the seller is unable to deliver the deed, the vendee can sue for rescission of the land contract, enforcement of a vendee's lien, or damages. If the contract is rescinded, the vendee recovers all payments made less the fair rental of the property and the value of improvements made by the vendee that increase the value of the property. The purchaser has a *vendee's lien* for the repayment of the funds applied to the purchase price. If the purchaser exercises the vendee's lien, it ties up the property and makes it difficult for the vendor to sell the property to a third party. If the vendee sues for damages, the damages are limited to the amount of the loss that the vendee can prove.

It is often difficult to prove the amount of damages, and sometimes a money judgment is difficult to collect. If the vendee contemplates seeking money damages, he or she is advised to insert a penalty clause in the land contract, which specifies the amount of money due to the vendee on default by the seller. It is the vendee's equivalent to the vendor's forfeiture and liquidated damages clause.

LAND CONTRACT COMPARED TO A PURCHASE MONEY MORTGAGE

The land contract and a purchase money mortgage granted by the seller are both types of seller financing. If a purchase money mortgage is used, the purchaser receives the title immediately and gives the seller a mortgage to secure the debt. When the land contract is used, the seller retains legal title until the buyer makes the agreed payments. Both require the buyer to make installment payments to the seller. If the buyer-borrower defaults on the purchase money mortgage, the seller-lender must foreclose to recover the property. If the buyer defaults on a land contract, the seller can usually either rescind the contract or request a forfeiture of the contract.

The use of a purchase money mortgage rather than a land contract

---

[1]Robert Kratovil and Raymond J. Werner, *Real Estate Law,* 7th ed. (Englewood Cliffs, N.J.: Prentice-Hall, Inc., 1979), p. 130.

has some advantages and disadvantages for the buyer and seller. The borrower-buyer receives title simultaneously with signing the mortgage and mortgage note. The seller must be able to deliver the deed at that time while delivery of the deed is delayed when using a land contract. If the buyer-borrower defaults, the seller-lender must foreclose on the mortgage, and it may be a relatively lengthy process to clear title. The buyer-borrower has an equitable right of redemption and in some states a statutory right of redemption. In some states, the buyer-borrower may be liable for a deficiency judgment when a purchase money mortgage is accompanied by a mortgage note. The potential deficiency judgment is the principal disadvantage to the buyer-borrower. It is an advantage to the seller-lender, but it is of limited significance to the seller in most cases because the buyer can declare bankruptcy.

The principal advantage of a land contract to the buyer is that the buyer is not liable for a deficiency judgment. The disadvantages to the buyer are that the buyer does not receive title immediately and his or her rights can be terminated more quickly. One advantage to the seller is that the seller does not have to possess title at the time of the sale. The seller also can regain possession more rapidly. And if the seller is allowed to forbid recording the contract, there is no expense associated with clearing title. The seller cannot get a deficiency judgment against the buyer, but in most cases this is not a significant disadvantage to the seller.

In states where the seller-lender cannot obtain a deficiency judgment under a purchase money mortgage, the purchase money mortgage is preferable to a land contract from the buyer's viewpoint. If the buyer makes a relatively small down payment and there is a high probability of default or if the seller does not currently hold title, the land contract is preferable to a purchase money mortgage from the seller's viewpoint.

Both the purchase money mortgage and the land contract can be used for either intermediate-term or long-term financing. Sometimes both a land contract and a purchase money mortgage are used in the same transaction. The land contract is sometimes replaced by a purchase money mortgage when the buyer builds up sufficient equity to justify the seller's delivery of title to the buyer.

Both the purchase money mortgage and the land contract can be used as either first or second liens. The purchaser can buy the property subject to an existing mortgage or obtain a new first mortgage loan and use a second purchase money mortgage as partial payment. If there is an existing mortgage on the property, the buyer receives the property subject to the mortgage and the land contract represents a type of secondary financing similar to a second purchase money mortgage.

A purchase money mortgage and a land contract transaction both qualify as an installment sale for federal income tax purposes. If the seller receives less than the entire selling price in the year of sale and payments are received over two or more years, the seller can recognize any capital gain on an installment basis. For example, assume that the seller's adjusted tax basis is $40,000, and the selling price of the property is $100,000. The seller's capital gain is therefore $60,000, which is 60 percent of the selling price. A contract might call for the seller to receive $25,000 of the selling price in the first year as well as in years two, three, and four. The seller, in turn, recognizes a capital gain of $15,000, which is 60 percent of $25,000 received, in each of the four years. An installment sale therefore allows the lender to spread the recognition of the capital gain over a number of years, and to pay taxes at a lower rate. If the full $100,000 is received in year one, the seller would have to recognize the entire $60,000 gain immediately. The use of the installment sale provision therefore allows the seller to defer the payment of taxes and also to pay taxes at a lower rate. Thus, the total amount of the income tax paid on the gain is reduced.

Since the payments on land contracts and purchase money mortgages include both interest payments and principal payments, a reduction in the portion of the payment attributable to interest increases the portion for principal reduction. If the payments remain fixed and the interest rate is lowered, the selling price of the property is increased. This will increase the seller's capital gain. It should be noted that the buyer may object to having a smaller portion of the payment allocated to interest because the interest is a tax-deductible expense for the buyer.

OPTIONS

An option may serve as a temporary means of financing. An *option* is an agreement in which one party holds open an offer. The option is usually for a specified period of time. An *option to purchase* is an agreement in which an owner commits to sell a property at a stated price to a potential buyer usually within a specified period of time. The potential buyer has the right to either exercise or to decline to exercise the option. An *option to sell* is an agreement in which the potential buyer agrees to buy the property at a stipulated price usually within a specified period of time. The owner has the right to either exercise or to decline to exercise the option. The option to purchase is the typical type of option used in real estate transactions. And it is an extremely powerful device for the control of property with a minimum initial investment.

An option to purchase is the common means used by developers to acquire control of the land prior to making engineering and feasibility studies and arranging for permanent and construction financing. Options are sometimes combined with leases. For example, a residence might be rented under a lease that also contains an option to purchase. This gives the tenant time to decide whether or not to purchase the property and, if so, to arrange for long-term financing. Often a portion of the rental payments is applied as partial payment for the property if the option is exercised. The seller can use an option to defer recognition of income from the sale. The money received for the option is not taxable until either the option period expires or the buyer exercises the option.

A binding option must meet the requirements for a valid contract and be signed by the optionor. The party making the offer is called the *optionor* and the party to whom the offer is made is called the *optionee. The optionee must give consideration for the option to make a binding contract.* The price of the option can vary from one dollar to a substantial sum. The price paid for the option normally increases as the length of the option period increases and as the price for the property offered approaches its current market value. Normally, the amount paid for the option is applied toward the purchase price of the property if the option is exercised. If the option is not exercised, the optionor usually keeps the option money.

An option should specify the time period in which it can be exercised and the price that must be paid for the property if the option is exercised. The price is usually a fixed amount, but sometimes the price of the property increases over the term of the option agreement. Ideally the other terms of the sale should be specified in the option. An option for development purposes includes a clause granting the developer the right to enter for the purpose of surveying and making engineering studies.

The holder of an option to purchase is free to assign the option to a third party unless it is expressly forbidden. The owner of the property can sell the property to a third party during the option period, but the property would still be subject to the option if the third party had knowledge of the existence of the option.

SUMMARY

A land contract is a written agreement between the buyer and seller for the purchase of real property that requires the buyer to make payments over a number of years while the seller holds title until the payments are completed. The land contract is usually used when the buyer and/or the property does not meet traditional lending standards. The buyer usually makes a small down payment, and the probability of default is reasonably high.

A land contract serves as both a sales and a financing instrument. And as such it must meet the requirements for a valid real estate sales contract. Thus, it normally includes many of the clauses found in a mortgage. The vendee receives equitable title and the rights and responsibilities of ownership. The vendee is free to assign the land contract and lease the property unless it is prohibited in the contract. The vendor is free to assign his or her interest under the land contract and to mortgage the property unless it is prohibited in the contract. The two common remedies of the vendor in event of default by the vendee are rescission and forfeiture.

The land contract and the purchase money mortgage are alternative methods of seller financing. The purchase money mortgage is usually preferable from the buyer's viewpoint because the buyer receives title immediately and the seller must foreclose to terminate the buyer's rights. The land contract is preferable from the seller's viewpoint particularly when there is a high probability of default. The buyer's rights can usually be terminated by rescission or forfeiture. The use of either a land contract or a purchase money mortgage can be designed to allow the seller to recognize the capital gain on an installment basis.

Options to purchase are used to control property prior to actual purchase of the property. They are often used by developers, and sometimes the option is combined with a lease. A binding option must meet the requirements for a valid contract. The holder of the option may realize his or her profit by selling the option to a third party.

KEY TERMS

Equitable Title	Mortgage Clause	Option to Sell
Escrow for Deed	Option	Rescission
Forfeiture Clause	Optionee	Specific Performance
Land Contract	Optionor	Vendee
Liquidated Damages Clause	Option to Purchase	Vendor

QUESTIONS FOR REVIEW AND DISCUSSION

1. What is a land contract?

2. Explain conditions under which land contracts are commonly used.

3. Give other names by which a land contract is commonly known.

4. What are the rights and duties of the vendor in a land contract? The vendee?

5. Identify and explain at least three critical considerations of a buyer under a land contract.

6. An owner sells a mortgaged property by land contract. What precautions should the buyer take concerning future borrowing by the seller where the subject property might be used as security?

7. How does a land contract differ from a purchase money mortgage as a technique of seller financing?

8. What is an option? How is an option used?

9. Match the following key terms and definitions:

   a. Option to
      Purchase   _____
   b. Escrow for Deed   _____
   c. Mortgage Clause   _____
   d. Rescission   _____
   e. Specific
      Performance   _____
   f. Land Contract   _____

   1. Provision that land contract would be subordinated to new mortgage after land contract is signed.

   2. Legal requirement that contract be fulfilled or completed exactly as stated.

   3. In land contract arrangement, deed delivered to escrow agent for delivery to buyer when contract fulfilled.

   4. Charges or payments required exactly as stated in contract.

   5. Cancellation of a contract, with adjustments for payments made or consideration provided.

   6. Commitment by owner to sell at a stated price within an agreed period of time upon the decision or choice of a specific person.

   7. Written agreement to sell realty with payments made over extended time and legal title remaining with seller.

eight

Lease Financing

A *lease* is an agreement between a landlord and tenant that transfers the right to possession and use of the property to the tenant in return for a specified rental payment. The lease is both a conveyance of possession and a contract to pay rent and meet other obligations, such as preventing waste to the property. The landlord is called the *lessor,* and the tenant is called the *lessee.* The lessee's interest in the property is called the *leasehold estate,* which consists of the right to possess and use the property. The lessor's interest in the property is called the *leased fee estate,* which consists of the right to the rent and to the return of the right of possession on termination of the lease.

A lease must meet the requirements for a valid contract to be binding on both parties. It must be a mutual agreement between competent parties for a legal purpose. Leases with a term of more than one year usually must be in writing to be enforceable in court. Usually, the lease must grant actual possession, describe the property, specify the term of the lease, and state the lessee's consideration, which normally is the rental payment. The lease must be signed by the lessor and usually the lessor's spouse. The lessee technically does not have to sign because taking possession and paying rent is sufficient to show acceptance of the terms of the lease. But good business practice normally demands the lessee's signature for leases with durations of more than one year. In a number of states leases with durations in excess of a specified period, such as one or three years, must be recorded to provide constructive notice of their existence. Good business practice also dictates recording such leases.

Leases are of interest to us because they represent an alternative means of financing and controlling real estate. Major topics in this chapter are as follows:

1. Types of leases
2. Interrelationship between lease and mortgage financing
3. Long-term leases
4. Leasehold mortgage financing
5. Sale and leaseback
6. Hybrid sale arrangements

TYPES OF LEASES

Leases may be classified in a number of ways. They can be classified as residential leases or as nonresidential leases such as commercial or industrial leases. They can be classified as leases of improved property or as land leases. A *ground lease* is a lease of land that usually gives the lessee the right to erect an improvement on the land. Leases can also be classified as gross leases or net leases. A *gross lease* is one in which the lessee pays a stated rental and the lessor bears the usual costs of ownership, such as real estate taxes and insurance. A *net lease* is one in which the lessee pays a stated rental and some or all of the usual costs of ownership. A *triple net lease* is one in which the lessee bears all of the costs of ownership including real estate taxes, insurance, and all operating expenses such as utilities and maintenance. On occasion it even requires the lessee to make the payments on the lessor's mortgage loan. Residential leases are usually gross leases. Ground leases are usually net leases, and many commercial and industrial leases are also net leases.

Leases can be classified by their duration as well. Leases may be of indefinite duration *such as from month to month* that are terminated only after proper notice, or they may be for a definite duration such as one year.

Leases are sometimes classified as long term or short term. This classification is arbitrary and varies according to the types of leases being discussed. Residential or agricultural leases for two or three years are usually considered to be long term. But when we consider nonresidential leases and ground leases, two or three years is a short term. Generally, nonresidential leases would have to have a term of at least five years to be considered long term. Some institutional lenders can make leasehold mortgage loans only if the term of the loan is at least 21 years. In this context a long-term lease must have a term of at least 21 years, and it will often have a life of 99 years or longer.

Leases are often classified by the type of the specified rental payment. Most leases are either flat leases, graduated leases, percentage leases, or escalator leases. A *flat lease* or a straight lease provides for a fixed sum to be paid periodically throughout its life, as for example, $1,000 per month. A *graduated lease* is one that calls for periodic increases or decreases in the rental over the term of the lease. A *percentage lease* usually bases the rental payment on a percentage of the gross sales of the tenant or on a flat amount plus a percentage of gross sales. An *escalator lease* or index lease provides for rental adjustments in direct proportion to increases in such things as real estate taxes, insurance, and operating costs or to changes in an index such as the cost of living index.

INTERRELATIONSHIP BETWEEN LEASE AND MORTGAGE FINANCING

Lease financing can be used as an alternative for mortgage financing. Both the lessor and the lessee have the right to offer their interests in the lease as security for a debt. The relative priority of mortgages and leases is therefore of considerable significance to lenders, landlords, and tenants.

LEASING AS A FINANCING TECHNIQUE

Space may be leased as well as purchased. A potential homebuyer may lease with an option to buy, and a later decision to buy may be exercised on a land contract basis or with mortgage or trust deed financing. The homebuyer may purchase the building and lease the land under a long-term ground lease, which reduces the immediate dollar expenditure necessary to purchase a home. Residential ground leases have a long history of use in Baltimore and in Pennsylvania. They are also sometimes used in some other states such as California and Hawaii.

Businesses also use leases as a means of financing. Financial analysts, accountants, and the Internal Revenue Service recognize certain long-term leases as financing agreements. The financial analyst defines a financial lease as one which is noncancelable and in which the lessee provides the maintenance while the lease payments fully amortize the lessor's investment. Generally accepted accounting principles require the lessee who enters into a financial lease *to restate the balance sheet in order to report the leased asset* as a fixed asset and the present value of the future lease payments as a debt. The Internal Revenue Service finds that some leases are in fact installment loans.[1] Whether or not a long-term lease meets any or all of the definitions used by financial analysts, accountants, and the Internal Revenue Service, it does represent an alternate means of financing.

Businesses lease improved properties and sometimes they lease only the land and erect the improvements themselves. A *build-to-suit lease* is a case in which it is clear that a lease is an alternate means of financing. Assume that a firm needs space to operate its business and that no suitable facilities are available in the area. The firm could obtain a loan to purchase land and to erect a building to meet its needs. An alternative is to request an investor to purchase the land, to erect the building, and to lease it to the firm. The investor will agree to the arrangement if the promised rental is sufficient to yield a satisfactory rate of return and if the firm has an acceptable credit rating.

An investor or firm that currently owns property may employ a sale and leaseback as an alternative to mortgage financing. Assume that a firm purchased and improved a site at a certain location for its business, but it now needs additional funds to finance a major advertising campaign and to increase its working capital. The firm might offer the property as security for a loan. An alternative means of raising the funds would be to sell the property to an investor and at the same time lease it back under a long-term lease.

RELATIVE PRIORITY OF LEASES AND MORTGAGES

A lease has priority over the mortgage on the underlying or leased fee estate if the lease became effective before the mortgage was recorded. The mortgage is prior to the lease if the mortgage was recorded before the lease was made. The relative priority of the lease and the mortgage can be changed by a subordination agreement. A lender can agree to subordinate a mortgage to a leasehold estate. Or a lessee can agree to subordinate an existing leasehold estate to a new mortgage on the leased fee.

An owner-lessor is free to mortgage the leased fee estate unless prohibited by the lease. If leases are subordinate to the mortgage, the lender realizes greater security. Thus, later, if the lender forecloses and obtains ownership of the leased fee, he or she is entitled to collect rents from the leases or to evict the tenant-lessee.

A lease may provide the basic security necessary for an owner to obtain a mortgage loan. Thus, if a property were up for lease to the federal government or to a private firm with a sound credit rating for a duration equal to or in excess of that of the mortgage, the lender would

---

[1]Eugene F. Brigham, *Fundamentals of Financial Management,* 2nd ed. (Hinsdale, Ill.: The Dryden Press, 1980), pp. 571–73.

probably make the loan and consider the lease to be the primary security for the mortgage loan. This is called a *credit loan*. That is, the lender looks primarily to the credit of the tenant when deciding whether or not to grant the loan and when determining the terms of the loan. A credit loan normally has a lower interest rate and/or a higher loan-to-value ratio than a loan on a leased fee in which the real property is the primary source of security to the lender. Many of the build-to-suit leases are made to tenants with high credit ratings.

A lessee is free to mortgage the leasehold unless prohibited by the lease agreement. If the lessee-borrower defaults on a leasehold mortgage, foreclosure may result in the leasehold-lender becoming the owner of the leasehold. The lender would then be responsible for rental payments on the lease. The lender might immediately attempt to lease the property for a greater rental to a third party or to sell the leasehold to a third party. If a lessee-borrower defaults on a mortgaged leasehold estate under a long-term ground lease where a building has been erected, the foreclosure often results in the lender becoming the owner of the leasehold estate and therefore of the building. As the new owner, the lender now has to make the rental payments on the ground lease.

A lender on the leasehold would usually prefer to avoid any obligation to make rental payments due on a lease. This can be accomplished by getting the landlord to subordinate the leased fee estate to the leasehold mortgage. If the fee is subordinated and the lender is forced to foreclose on the leasehold mortgage, the leasehold lender may become the owner of both the leased fee estate and the leasehold estate. Of course, the owner of the leased fee would probably demand and get the right to make the mortgage debt service payments to protect his or her ownership position. Lenders on leasehold estates give more favorable terms to the lessee-borrower when the leased fee estate is subordinated to the leasehold mortgage.

LONG-TERM LEASES

Long-term leases can be leases of improved property or leases of land only. In a long-term ground lease the lessee usually expects to immediately erect a building on the site. Long-term leases have a number of possible advantages for both the lessor and lessee and some disadvantages as well.

ADVANTAGES OF LONG-TERM LEASES

An owner of real property realizes benefits from the property by using, selling, or leasing it. If the owner sells the property, possible future appreciation in the value of the property is lost. And a capital gain tax on the sale will probably have to be paid. By leasing the property, an owner avoids the probable tax and at the same time retains ownership of the property, which may appreciate in value. Even if the owner desires to sell, a favorable lease on the property may increase the value of the property and its marketability. Alternatively, or at a later date, if the owner needs immediate cash, the property may be used as security for a loan. An owner can often shift some of the burdens and risks of ownership to the tenant through a net lease. A net lease allows the lessor to collect the rental free of the problems of increasing taxes, insurance, and maintenance. If it is a net ground lease, the owner-lessor may have greater security because a building is constructed on the land. And finally, some leases, such as percentage leases, allow an owner-lessor to participate in the success of the lessee during the term of the lease.

Advantages accrue to the lessee-tenant as well. For example, a particular site or location may be needed by a prospective user or business. The prospective user of the property can either buy or lease the property in question. In some cases an owner might refuse to sell the property but agree to lease it. Thus, control is gained. Leasing the property reduces the lessee's investment in the property. In time, the lessee has a potential capital gain if the value of the leasehold interest increases and a sale is arranged. And the leasehold position might be sold outright or sold on an immediate leaseback arrangement.

Another advantage to a tenant is that the rental payments are tax deductible. An owner of property can deduct depreciation on the improvements and interest payments in a tax return. But an owner is not allowed to depreciate land for federal income tax purposes. When the land represents a large portion of the property value, rental payments will yield a larger tax deduction than would depreciation and interest expense.

IMPORTANT LEASE CLAUSES

A long-term lease agreement is a relatively complex document. It often contains many of the clauses found in a mortgage or trust deed plus clauses unique to lease contracts. Some of the more important clauses most likely to be used are as follows.

Rental. The time, the place, and the amount of the rental payment should be specified. Rental payments are the equivalent of debt service on a mortgage loan. In a percentage or escalator lease, the manner of calculating the rent is also specified. In a net lease, the real estate taxes, insurance premiums, and maintenance are classified as additional rent. This classification makes the failure to pay these charges a default of the payment of rent rather than a breach of contract. In turn, this speeds possible eviction of the lessee and reduces risk of loss to the landlord.

Security Deposit. The lessee is usually required to make a security deposit; however a deposit is not likely to be required with a ground lease. Ground leases do often require the lessee to construct a building on the land, with a surety bond or a pledge of assets to guarantee construction of the building.

Lessee's Right to Make Payments. A lessee's interest may be terminated if the lessor's rights in the property are extinguished. A lessee will therefore often demand a clause that allows the lessee to make payments on the lessor's mortgage to prevent default and foreclosure. The lessee may also reserve the right to make any other payments necessary to protect the lease. The lessor is of course free to sell the leased fee subject to the lease, unless it is otherwise prohibited in the lease.

Maintenance and Improvements. The lease specifies which party is responsible for maintenance. In long-term leases the lessee is typically responsible for maintenance. The lessor may make alterations and improvements requested by the lessee and may charge additional rent. Or the lessee may be allowed to make alterations and improvements with the approval of the lessor. If the life of improvements is expected to extend beyond the term of the lease, the lease will specify the compensation to be paid to the lessee on expiration of the lease. The lack of such a provision will result in the improvements reverting to the lessor, without any compensation paid the lessee.

Destruction of the Premises and Insurance. The lessee is normally responsible for keeping the property adequately insured. An alert lessee will insist on a clause in the lease that requires the proceeds of the insurance policy be used to repair or rebuild the premises unless the lessee is allowed to terminate the lease. The lessor will desire to require the lessee to continue to make the rental payments while the premises are being restored. The lessee may negotiate a clause that allows a reduction in the rental during the restoration period or termination of the lease if the restoration period extends beyond the expiration date of the lease. In some states the law provides that complete destruction of the premises terminates the lease.

Assignment of Leasehold. A long-term lease usually contains a clause that allows the lessee to assign the lease to a third party or to sublet only with the lessor's approval. The lessor will generally approve if the new tenant has a credit rating equal to or superior to that of the existing tenant. Some leases forbid any assignment or subletting. An *assignment of lease* transfers the lessee's entire interest under the lease, whereas a *sublease* transfers something less than the lessee's entire interest.

Mortgages and Subordination. The lease may be negotiated to contain a provision subordinating the lease to any future mortgage on the leased fee. Or a clause may be negotiated subordinating the leased fee to any future mortgages on the leasehold estate. Of course there may be no subordination clause in the lease.

Option to Renew. The lease may include an *option to renew clause*. The option to renew may require the lessee to notify the lessor of a desire to renew within a specified period prior to the expiration of the lease. Or the lease may require notice to prevent renewal. The rental may be increased or decreased on renewal, depending on the negotiations.

Option to Purchase. The lease may give the lessee an option to purchase the leased fee at a specified price. The lessee usually gives consideration to the lessor to make the option binding. The lease specifies the manner for determining the price of the property. The option price may be specified so that it increases or decreases with time. Sometimes the price of the property is to be established by an appraisal at the time of the exercise of the option. The lease will specify whether or not any portion of the rental payments apply to the purchase price of the property.

A lessor may desire not to sell the property, and so will not agree to an option to purchase. But the same lessor may agree to a right of first refusal. A *right of first refusal* gives the lessee the right to buy the property on the terms demanded by the lessor in event that the lessor decides to sell the property at a later date. The right may be worded to give the lessee the right to buy at the terms of sale agreed to between the lessor and a neutral third party.

Default and Termination. A lease usually specifies the lessor's remedies in the event that the lessee defaults on the terms of the lease. To begin with the lessor seeks the right to regain possession upon default. The lessor may negotiate a provision that in event of default and reentry by the lessor the lease is not terminated and the lessee remains liable for all damages resulting from the default. This makes the lessee responsible for rental payments if the lessor is unable to lease the property to another tenant. On the other hand, the lessee may negotiate a provision requiring that the lessor give notice of probable default in prior instruments, therefore giving the lessee reasonable time to avoid or cure the default.

Other Clauses. The lessor is likely to include a clause that requires the lessor's approval for any change in the use of the property. It is also desirable that a lease specify what happens if the property is condemned under the right of eminent domain. The lease may specify that the lessee is responsible for the payment of rental until the condemner is entitled to take possession. The application of the proceeds of the taking should be specified. Thus, the lease may provide for compensation for any improvements constructed by the lessee and possibly for a complete buy-out of the leasehold interest.

A leasehold estate may have a market value and, as such, can provide security for a loan, thus giving rise to a leasehold mortgage. Assume that a certain lessee holds a leasehold estate and must pay rental of $10,000 per year for the next 20 years. Assume that because of increases in rental levels, our lessee could sublease at an annual rental of $15,000 for the next 20 years. Since the holder of the leasehold estate could sublease and realize a net return of $5,000 per year for the next 20 years, an investor would be willing to purchase the leasehold estate from the lessee. Leasehold mortgage loans are often arranged with the financial worth of the leasehold estate serving as security. Alternatively, a loan may be arranged on a site controlled by a ground lease in order to create a leasehold estate. The loan proceeds would be used to erect improvements (a building) on the site. In this case, the worth of the leasehold estate would depend on the demand for the services of the improved property. Thus, this situation would involve much greater risk for the lender.

RESIDENTIAL LEASEHOLD MORTGAGE LOANS

Mortgage loans have basically the same provisions and must meet the same lending standards, whether made to an owner of a complete fee simple estate or of a leasehold estate. The worth of the property pledged as security is a major concern, of course. And for owner-occupants of one-family residential units, income, assets, and credit rating are critical factors.

FHA insured, VA guaranteed, and conventional mortgage or trust deed residential leasehold loans are available if the term of the ground lease is sufficiently long. FHA insurance can be given if the lease has a remaining term of at least 50 years at the time of the loan or if the lease had an original term of at least 99 years and is renewable. A VA guarantee can be made if the lease extends at least 14 years beyond the term of the loan. Conventional loans are generally available if the lease extends at least ten years beyond the due date of the loan.

NONRESIDENTIAL LEASEHOLD MORTGAGE LOANS

Lenders can make mortgage loans secured by leaseholds on improved properties or on ground leases and the improvements constructed by the lessee. The unexpired term of the lease must meet various minimums relative to the length of the mortgage. The minimum unexpired term varies among institutional lenders, and when the lenders are governed primarily by state law the minimum varies from state to state. Leasehold mortgage lenders prefer leases that contain options to renew, options to purchase, a clause requiring notice to the lender of default on the lease, and a clause allowing the lender to correct any default on the lease.

A leasehold lender would like to have the leased fee and any mortgage on the leased fee subordinated to the leasehold mortgage. If the *leased fee mortgage* is subordinated to the leasehold mortgage, foreclosure by the holder of the leased fee mortgage does not terminate the lease. A *subordinated fee leasehold mortgage* gives the leasehold lender a first lien position. In foreclosure the leasehold lender is likely to be the winning bidder at the foreclosure sale and to become the owner of the leased fee, the leasehold estate, and any improvements erected by the lessee. If the mortgage on the leased fee is not subordinated, the leasehold lender makes the loan subject to the mortgage on the leased fee and to rights of the owner of the leased fee.

Subordination of the leased fee allows the lessee-borrower to obtain better terms on the leasehold mortgage loan. In a few states life insurance companies cannot make a leasehold mortgage loan unless the leased fee is subordinated, except under the basket clause. The subordinated fee leasehold mortgage loan is most common when the lessee has a ground lease and intends to construct a building on the land. The lessee may convince the lessor to join in the financing by offering to pay higher rental and in some cases by offering participation in the profits of the project.

An owner of a leased fee may refuse to subordinate the fee. But, to make a mutually satisfactory arrangement, the owner of the fee may be willing to waive or reduce the rental in event of default on the leasehold mortgage loan. This may satisfy the leasehold mortgage lender. If there is no subordination or waiver, the leasehold mortgage lender may require the lessee-borrower to pledge other assets such as marketable securities to assure payment of ground rentals. A borrower with a strong credit rating, for example, a triple A rating, may be able to obtain favorable terms in a leasehold mortgage loan without subordination of the fee.

SALE AND LEASEBACK

A sale and leaseback or a *sale-leaseback* is a financing technique in which the owner sells a property to an investor and simultaneously leases it back from the investor. A classical example of a sale-leaseback is one in which the seller has owned the property for a number of years. The improvements have been largely written off or depreciated for income tax purposes, whereas the market value of the property has increased. The owner-seller wishes to raise additional funds to expand business operations while retaining control of a particular property or location. In this situation, more funds may be raised through a sale-leaseback than through a mortgage loan. The rental payments on the lease would probably be slightly higher than the mortgage payments on a loan in an amount equal to the funds raised by the sale. But, of course, more money has been obtained. Also the higher rental is partially offset because the rental payments are tax deductible. Although interest on a loan and depreciation on the improvements are tax deductible expenses for an owner, in this example depreciation deductions would be relatively small because the improvements have already been depreciated for tax purposes.

A sale-leaseback arrangement can involve improved properties which have been owned for a number of years or buy-build-sell lease-backs. In a *buy-build-sell leaseback* the firm buys land, constructs a building and other improvements to meet its needs, and on completion sells and immediately leases the property back. The buy-build-sell leaseback may now be the most common type of sale-leaseback. Some sale-leaseback transactions involve land only. A developer therefore obtains control of a site in return for rental payments while not committing his or her equity funds to holding the site. The rental payments are tax deductible, but land is not allowed to be depreciated for tax purposes. Improvements added to the land by a lessee are, of course, fully depreciable for tax purposes.

TERMS OF THE SALE-LEASEBACK

An investor usually purchases the property at a price equal to 80 to 100 percent of the market value of the property. If the sale is based primarily on the financial stability of the lessee rather than on the property, the purchase price will be 100 percent of market value. If the sale is based primarily on the property and only incidentally on the credit standing of the lessee, the purchase price could be as low as 80 percent of the market value of the property.

The lease is usually a net lease in which the seller-lessee is responsible for the payment of real estate taxes, insurance, and all operating costs. The rental payments are calculated to allow the buyer-investor to recover the purchase price plus a rate of return equal to that on high-grade bonds over the term of the lease. The duration of the lease typically runs from 20 to 40 years, with an option to renew.

If the lease contains an option to purchase, it must be worded with care to prevent the Internal Revenue Service from determining that the intent of the transaction is in fact to make a loan. If the intent is found to be a loan, the IRS will disallow the deductibility of a portion of the rental. The option price should not be below the projected market value of the property at the time that the option is exercised.

A willing owner-seller-lessee and a willing buyer-investor-lessor are all that are required to create a sale-leaseback arrangement. Retailers such as supermarket and restaurant chains are the leading seller-lessees, and industrial corporations are second. A sale-leaseback can be used with office buildings, warehouses, shopping centers, land, or any property.

Life insurance companies are a major source of sale-leaseback financing. Pension funds, real estate investment trusts, subsidiaries of industrial corporations, and tax-exempt institutions such as universities, charitable organizations, and religious institutions also purchase real estate and lease it back. State or local government agencies provide sale and leaseback financing to attract industry to the state or community. Sometimes wealthy individuals and real estate syndicates purchase property and lease it back.

A sale-leaseback arrangement has a number of possible attractions to investors. The rental payments over the term of the lease may be negotiated to amortize the purchase price of the property and to yield a satisfactory rate of return that is equal to or greater than that on high-grade bonds. At the end of the lease, the investor still owns the property, which increases the rate of return even more. At that time the owner may sell it for a gain or retain ownership and lease it to another party.

The investor may also increase the return by borrowing the money to finance the purchase. This is called a *leveraged sale-leaseback,* and it reduces the owner's equity investment in the property. If tax-exempt institutions such as universities, charitable organizations, and religious institutions use a leveraged lease, the income from the lease is called unrelated business income and, as such, the income is taxable. State and local government agencies make leveraged leases and their profits are not taxed. They also have the advantage of issuing securities on which the interest paid is not subject to federal income taxes. This gives them a lower cost of funds and they pass the benefits of the lower cost funds to the lessee to attract industry to a state or an area.

ADVANTAGES AND DISADVANTAGES OF SALE-LEASEBACK

There are many possible advantages and disadvantages in a sale-leaseback arrangement for the seller-lessee and the buyer-lessor. Whether or not a particular factor is an advantage or a disadvantage depends on the type of sale-leaseback, the circumstances of the lessee and lessor, and future events.

Advantages to the Lessee. The following are some of the possible benefits that may accrue to the seller-lessee:

> *1.* A sale-leaseback may provide financing up to 100 percent of the value of the property, whereas a mortgage loan would probably be limited to 75

percent of the value of the property. The differential is reduced if a portion of proceeds must be used to pay taxes on a capital gain from the sale. The differential is increased if there is a capital loss and the seller's income taxes are reduced by the sale.

2. The funds freed by the sale are expected to earn at a higher rate of return by use elsewhere in the seller's business than the cost of funds paid for rentals under the lease.

3. The rental payments are a tax-deductible expense. Therefore the tax deduction realized may be greater than the interest paid on a mortgage plus the depreciation on the improvements if the property were retained. If the lease is for land only, the lessee can deduct the ground rental payments, depreciation on any improvements erected, and interest paid on a leasehold mortgage.

4. The cost of funds may be lower under the sale-leaseback than under a mortgage. This may occur when the state or local government agency makes the leaseback.

5. The lessee is free to relocate when the lease expires or if it is cancelable. The lessee does not own the property, and therefore is not forced to bear the possible loss on the sale of the property.

Disadvantages to the Lessee.   The following are some of the possible disadvantages to the lessee:

1. Since the lessee is not the owner of the property, he or she does not receive the benefit of appreciation in the value of the property. This can be partially offset by including an option to purchase in the lease. Or the lessee may realize a portion of the benefits from the increase in value by subleasing or by assigning the lease.

2. The lessee may be forced to relocate at the expiration of the lease. This problem can be deferred by including an option to renew in the lease. An option to purchase may allow the lessee to avoid this problem entirely.

3. Under a net lease the lessee bears the burden of increasing taxes, insurance, and operating costs. Of course these same increases would be incurred if the lessee owned the property.

4. The lease requires the lessee to make rental payments for an extended period of time. Of course a mortgage loan would also commit the owner to mortgage payments for a number of years.

Advantages to the Lessor.   The following are some of the possible benefits to the buyer-lessor:

1. The yield on the lease may be higher than that under a mortgage. This is due in part to the fact that the lessor can deduct the depreciation on the improvements for tax purposes.

2. The value of the property may appreciate and the lessor is free to sell it for a gain. If the lessor desires to retain ownership after the expiration of the lease, the lessor is free to lease it and continue to collect rent.

3. It may be possible to invest a large sum for an extended period of time. And if there is no option to purchase, the lessor does not have the problem of prepayment.

4. State and local governments may use a sale-leaseback to attract industry to the area. Hopefully this would bring greater prosperity to the area.

5. If the lessee defaults, the lessor can regain possession faster under the lease than under foreclosure on a mortgage.

Disadvantages to the Lessor. The following are some of the possible disadvantages to the lessor:

1. The property may decline in value. If the lessor did not foresee the decline in value, the lease payments may yield a less than satisfactory rate of rcturn.

2. Since the sale-leaseback involves higher percentage financing, there may be a greater chance for default, all other things being equal. The lessor normally limits the transaction to lessees with strong credit standings or to general use properties that could hopefully be leased again without too much delay.

3. If the lessee is declared bankrupt, the lessor's claim may be limited to a claim for one to three years rental. Of course the lessee would be free to lease the property to another party after the lessee regained possession of the property.

HYBRID SALE ARRANGEMENTS

The owner may use a sale-contract-back, which may also be called a sale-buyback. A *sale-contract-back* is a financing technique in which the owner sells the property to an investor and simultaneously repurchases the property under a long-term land contract. Since the original owner now has equitable title to the property, he or she retains the right to depreciate the property for tax purposes. The buyer-investor may receive a share of the net income from the property in addition to interest on the contract as an inducement to participate in the transaction.

An owner may also engage in a sale-condo-back transaction. A *sale-condo-back* arrangement is one in which the owner sells the property to an investor and the investor deeds part of the property back as a condominium unit. If the property is already improved, the seller will receive cash plus a condominium unit in the building. If the sale consists of land only, the seller may or may not receive cash in addition to the condominium unit in the building erected by the purchaser. A sale-condo-back transaction would appeal to an owner who wanted to raise funds plus retain an ownership of space located on that particular site.

SUMMARY

A lease gives the lessee the right to possess and use the property in return for rental payments to the lessor. Long-term leases can be used as an alternative to mortgage or trust deed financing and to land contract financing. The priority of a lease relative to a mortgage can be changed by a subordination agreement. A long-term lease has a number of advantages for both the lessee and lessor. A long-term lease is a relatively complex document that contains many of the clauses found in a mortgage plus several clauses unique to leases.

A leasehold estate alone or a leasehold estate including a building to be owned by the lessee can be used as the security for a leasehold mortgage loan. Leasehold lenders prefer the additional security offered by subordination of the leased fee to the leasehold mortgage loan. If the fee is subordinated and the leasehold mortgage lender is forced to foreclose, the lender may become the owner of both the leased fee and the leasehold.

A sale and leaseback is a financing technique in which an owner sells a property to an investor and simultaneously leases it back. A sale-leaseback effectively gives a lessee higher percentage financing than is possible with mortgage financing. Over the term of the lease, the buyer-lessor normally recovers the purchase price plus a rate of return equal to or higher than that on high-grade bonds. And in addition the buyer-lessor may realize a capital gain by sale of the property on expiration of the lease.

A sale-contract-back is a financing technique in which an owner sells property to an investor and simultaneously purchases the property back under a land contract. In a sale-condo-back the owner sells the property and receives a condominium unit in the property as partial payment.

KEY TERMS

Assignment of Lease	Leased Fee Estate	Right of First Refusal
Build-to-Suit Lease	Leased Fee Mortgage	Sale-Condo-Back
Buy-Build-Sell Leaseback	Leasehold Estate	Sale-Contract-Back
Credit Loan	Leasehold Mortgage	Sale-Leaseback
Escalator Lease	Lessee	Sublease
Flat Lease	Lessor	Subordinated Fee
Graduated Lease	Leveraged Sale-Leaseback	Leasehold Mortgage
Gross Lease	Net Lease	Triple Net Lease
Ground Lease	Percentage Lease	

QUESTIONS FOR REVIEW AND DISCUSSION

1. Define and distinguish between the following types of leases:
   a. Ground
   b. Gross
   c. Net
   d. Flat
   e. Percentage
   f. Index

2. Explain the use of a lease as a financing technique.

3. Distinguish between short-term and long-term leases.

4. Explain the significance of the following lease clauses:
   a. Assignment of Leasehold
   b. Security Deposit
   c. Option to Renew
   d. Subordination

5. Explain how a leasehold may be mortgaged. What serves as the basis for the value of the leasehold?

6. Explain the sale and leaseback arrangement.

7. What are the advantages and disadvantages of sale and leaseback financing to a lessee?

8. What are the advantages and disadvantages of sale-leaseback financing to a lessor?

9. Match the following key terms and definitions:

   a. Leasehold Mortgage _____
   b. Graduated Lease _____
   c. Ground Lease _____
   d. Right to First Refusal _____
   e. Sublease _____
   f. Subordinated Fee Leasehold Mortgage _____
   g. Net Lease _____
   h. Percentage Lease _____

   1. Lease of land with right to add improvements given to the tenant.
   2. Arrangement in which lessee pays stated rental and some or all of the usual costs of ownership as taxes, insurance, and maintenance.
   3. Arrangement in which rental payment is a proportion of gross sales.
   4. Periodic increases or decreases in rental payments.
   5. A transfer of something less than the entire interests of a lessee.
   6. Right of a lessee to buy a property at same terms as given a neutral third party.
   7. Leasehold lender has first lien on the entire property.
   8. Debt financing of the leasehold estate.

nine

Mortgage Market Overview

Mortgage financing is one of the most substantial uses of credit in our country. This fact is often overlooked in our usual concern over the massive debt piled up by our corporations, governments, and consumers. In this chapter, we begin with a look at mortgage debt relative to these other forms of debt. We also look at who provides this money and the types of properties financed. We then move on to a discussion of residential finance. We conclude with an overview of the regulations of the financial institutions that make up the mortgage market. Our overall purpose is to provide an introduction and a setting for further discussion of the primary lenders in our mortgage markets. Our immediate intent is to understand the institutions in our mortgage markets with whom borrowers are most likely to come into contact.

Specific topics taken up in this chapter are as follows:

1. Mortgage market in perspective
2. Mortgage market participants
3. Mortgage debt by property type
4. Residential financing
5. Federal regulations affecting depository institutions

The *mortgage market* is the coming together and interaction of those seeking to borrow against real estate and others seeking to make loans secured by real estate. Loans are negotiated and interest rates and fees are determined in this interaction. The loans may have a duration of 1 day to 40 years or more. Thousands of people and institutions, operating without any central organization or clearing house, make up this market. Yet each transaction has an impact upon all the others.

The mortgage market is a distinct component of our financial markets. Our *financial markets* are where all types of loans are made and where such loans are bought and sold. A financial market is made up of money markets and capital markets. The term *money market* pertains to loans and instruments of short duration, typically less than one year. *Capital market,* on the other hand, involves longer term debt instruments, generally more than one year, and stocks. While this dividing line between the two is certainly arbitrary, it is also very useful.

The mortgage market is the largest single component of our capital markets. Corporate debt exceeds mortgage debt in total, but nearly half of corporate debt is short term, and short-term debt is a component of money markets rather than of capital markets.

The mortgage market involves debt secured by real property, through either a mortgage or a trust deed. The debt is held by primary and secondary lenders. A *primary lender* originates and often services mortgage loans. Savings and loan associations, mutual savings banks, commercial banks, life insurance companies, and mortgage companies make up the bulk of primary lenders. A *secondary lender* buys loans from or originates loans through primary lenders. Governmental agencies make up the bulk of secondary lenders. The buying and selling of existing loans takes place in what is called the *secondary mortgage market.*

Let us begin with a brief look at mortgage debt relative to net public and private debt. Figure 9–1 shows the percentage distribution of our debt in 1940 and 1976. The data in Fig. 9–1 are based on those in Fig. 9–2, which shows debt distribution for selected years from 1940 to 1976; 1976 is the last year for which complete data is available.

Figure 9–1 shows that consumer debt accounted for just over 10 percent of our debt in both 1940 and 1976. Public debt dropped from one-third of the debt to one-fourth. Corporate debt, short- and long-term, increased slightly to just under 40 percent of the total. And mortgage debt increased substantially from 18.2 to 25.1 percent of the total.

As shown in Fig. 9–2, net public and private debt amounted to slightly more than $3.54 trillion at the end of 1976. In this same year, the value of all goods and services produced in our nation (our gross national product) totaled $1.7 trillion. Thus, net debt was 2.1 times the GNP. In

FIGURE 9–1 Percentage Distribution of Net Public and Private Debt, 1940 and 1976

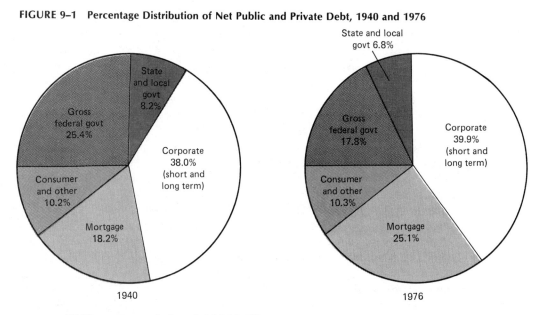

1940   1976

1940, our net debt of $200 billion was exactly 2 times our GNP of $100 billion. So, our ratio of debt to output appears not to have changed appreciably in the interim. Note also that in 1976 mortgage debt was slightly larger than our total public debt.

Mortgage debt increased by over 24 times from 1940 to 1976, much faster than any other type of debt. By way of comparison, our gross fed-

FIGURE 9–2 Net Public and Private Debt, 1940–1980 for Selected Years

(Billions of Dollars)

End of Year	Total Public and Private	PUBLIC			PRIVATE			
		Gross Federal[1]	State and Local[2]	Total	Corporate Long- and Short-Term	Mortgage[3]	Consumer and Other[4]	Total
1940	$ 200.0	$ 50.7	$ 16.4	$ 67.1	$ 76	$ 36.5	$ 20.4	$ 132.9
1950	539.2	256.9	24	280.9	142	72.8	43.5	258.3
1960	970.6	290.9	70	360.9	303	207.5	99.2	609.7
1970	2,024.8	382.6	143.6	526.2	797	474.2	227.4	1,498.6
1975	3,183.1	544.1	219.9	764.0	1,287	801.5	330.6	2,419.1
1976	3,543.7	631.9	241.0	872.9	1,415	889.2	366.6	2,670.8
1977	—	718.9	259.7	978.6	NA	1,023.5	NA	—
1978	—	789.2	280.4	—	NA	1,172.8	NA	—
1979	—	845.1	NA	—	NA	1,333.6	NA	—
1980	—	930.2	NA	—	NA	1,450.0	NA	—

[1]*Federal Reserve Bulletin,* September 1981, Table 1.41.
[2]*1980 U.S. Statistical Abstract,* Table 499.
[3]*Economic Report of the President,* 1981, Table B–69, and *Federal Reserve Bulletin,* December 1980, Table 1.55.
[4]*The Bond Buyers Municipal Finance Statistics,* June 1978, p. 56.
SOURCES: *1978 Statistical Abstract of the U.S.,* Table 881, with supplements as indicated.

eral debt increased only 12.5 times. Corporate and consumer debt both increased about 18 times. Overall, debt increased 17.7 times during this 36-year period. Inflation, apart from other considerations, accounts for the fourfold increase in debt during this period.

We are talking of huge amounts of money, of course. The amount $3.54 trillion is the same as $3,540 billion. Based on our population of 215 million people, we had nearly $16,500 of debt per capita in 1976.

The numbers presented here may seem large and somewhat out of context for many people. Even so, it is important to remember that our mortgage debt is over one-third larger than our federal debt. Further, though not shown in Figs. 9–1 and 9–2, mortgage debt is several percentage points larger than long-term corporate debt. Finally, by way of comparison, mortgage debt is 2.5 times the amount of consumer debt.

The term, mortgage debt, as used here includes debt secured by either mortgages or trust deeds, as mentioned. Both instruments are actively used by lenders making up the mortgage market. In turn, mortgage debt serves as an excellent measure of the size and significance of our mortgage markets.

Two other terms need definition before proceeding further with our discussion of the mortgage market. The terms are intermediation and disintermediation. Financial institutions are commonly referred to as *financial intermediaries,* meaning they channel money from people with excess funds to people with a need for funds. Thus, people with excess funds deposit them in banks or savings and loan associations. The banks and associations, in turn, lend the funds to businesses, consumers, or home buyers. The process is called *intermediation.* Sometime people withdraw the monies from their savings or time accounts and lend them directly to borrowers to earn higher rates of return. This process is called *disintermediation.* Disintermediation, when it occurs, greatly decreases the amount of funds available for mortgages from lenders and therefore reduces the activity in the mortgage market.

MORTGAGE MARKET PARTICIPANTS

As mentioned, mortgage debt makes up one-fourth of the net public and private debt created in our financial markets. It seems appropriate, therefore, that we now look at who borrows, or demands, this money and, more importantly, who lends, or supplies, this money. An overview of the mortgage market and its participants is provided in Fig. 9–3. The relative roles of borrowers, primary lenders, secondary lenders, and other institutions of mortgage finance are all indicated in the figure.

DEMANDERS OF MORTGAGE FUNDS

Demand for mortgage funds is from households, builders and developers, investors, and businesses. Households demand mortgage credit to

FIGURE 9–3 The Mortgage Market

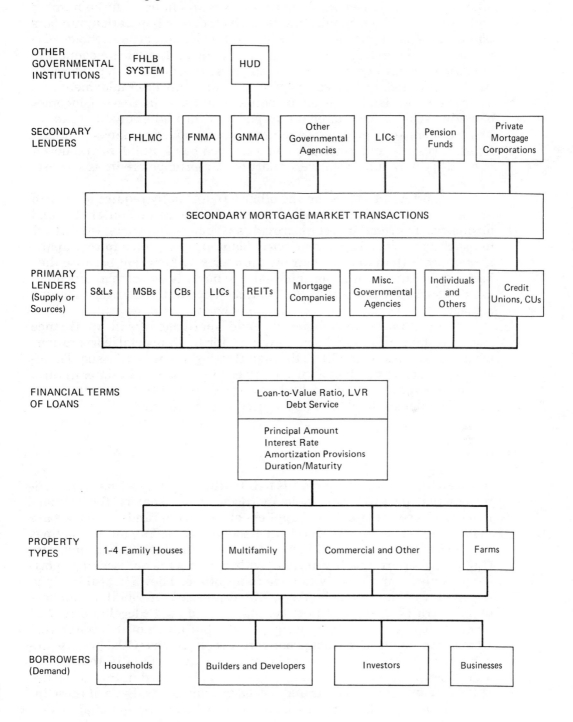

buy or remodel homes as well as to borrow money on owned homes for other purposes. Household demand shifts with changes in the number and structure of households, that is, with changing population numbers and lifestyle characteristics. Change in the location of households also influences demand. As people move from one section of the country to another or from central cities to suburbs, the demand for mortgage funds is affected. Increases or decreases in income or employment also affect demand. Higher levels of employment and increasing incomes cause households to demand more space and/or higher quality space.

Builders and developers operate to satisfy space demands of households, investors, and businesses on a derived basis. Builders and developers usually require relatively short-term mortgage credit as a consequence.

Real estate investors, on the other hand, usually require long-term credit as they strive to satisfy demands for space of households and businesses. In effect, investors provide space for nonowners, whether or not such nonownership is by choice. Some people prefer to rent apartments rather than to own their own property. Others rent because they have neither the income nor the wealth to buy. Likewise, investors often provide space for businesses, as in large office buildings and shopping centers.

Finally, many businesses demand mortgage credit to finance stores, restaurants, warehouses, and so forth. Industrial corporations usually finance new facilities through floating a new bond issue. Therefore much corporate debt actually serves to finance real estate. In turn, this means that mortgage debt does not reflect the full amount of real estate credit actually demanded or used in our economy.

SUPPLIERS OF MORTGAGE FUNDS

At this point, our main concern is to introduce the major financial institutions that originate and hold mortgage loans, that is, the primary lenders. These are the main suppliers of mortgage funds. Thus, we are mainly talking of savings and loan associations (S&Ls), mutual savings banks (MSBs), commercial banks (CBs), and life insurance companies (LICs). These are the institutions with which someone seeking mortgage monies is most likely to have to negotiate. They are also likely to negotiate with mortgage bankers, who originate considerable numbers of loans which they pass on to secondary lenders. Federal and related agencies hold considerable mortgage debt, but much of it is purchased from others, such as mortgage bankers. Credit unions (CUs) are also becoming increasingly active in the mortgage market. Finally, individuals and others originate and hold mortgage debt. Included in this group are real estate investment trusts and mortgage companies. Each of these institutions or agencies is discussed more fully in subsequent chapters.

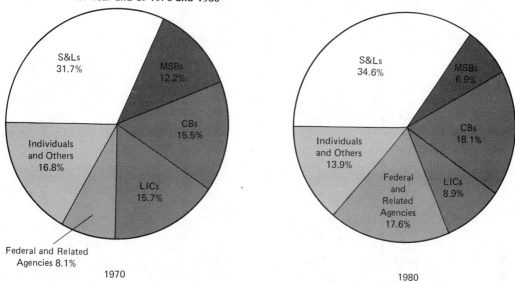

FIGURE 9–4 Percentage Distribution of Mortgage Debt Outstanding by Holder for Year-End of 1970 and 1980

1970

1980

The percentage distribution of mortgage debt held in 1970 and 1980 is shown in Fig. 9–4. The total amount of mortgage debt for selected years is shown in Fig. 9–5, along with the institution or individual who owns or holds the debt, as depicted in Fig. 9–3. Originations of long-term loans on residential properties are listed in Fig. 9–6. This information serves as the framework for our summary discussion of the various suppliers of mortgage funds. Let us now briefly consider each of these institutions.

Savings and Loan Associations. Savings and loan associations (S&Ls) are easily the most dominant institution of real estate finance. At the end of 1980, they held 34.6 percent of all mortgage debt (see Figs. 9–4 and 9–5). Savings and loans specialize in financing residential properties, primarily one- to four-family houses. Their expertise in this area includes both construction and permanent financing. Savings and loan associations obtain most of their funds through time deposits; consequently they have a relatively stable source of funds. Savings and loans are the second largest group of financial institutions in the United States, behind commercial banks. In 1979, S&Ls originated 43.3 percent of all long-term residential financing (see Fig. 9–6). S&Ls were first in originations of both one- to four-family home loans and multifamily building loans.

Mutual Savings Banks. Mutual savings banks (MSBs) are much like savings and loan associations in their emphasis on financing residential properties. They are declining in importance in mortgage lending and accounted for only 6.9 percent of mortgage debt in late 1980 (see Figs.

FIGURE 9–5 Mortgage Debt Outstanding by Holder for End of Selected Years, 1940–1980

(Billions of Dollars)

End of Year	Total	MAJOR FINANCIAL INSTITUTIONS					Federal and Related Agencies	Individuals and Others
		Total	S&Ls	MSBs	CBs	LICs		
1940	$ 36.5	$ 19.5	$ 4.1	$ 4.9	$ 4.6	$ 6.0	$ 4.9	$ 12.0
1950	72.8	51.7	13.7	8.3	13.7	16.1	2.8	18.4
1960	207.5	157.6	60.1	26.9	28.8	41.8	11.5	38.4
1970	474.2	355.9	150.3	57.9	73.3	74.4	38.3	79.9
1975	801.5	581.2	278.6	77.2	136.2	89.2	101.0	119.3
1978	1,172.8	848.1	432.9	95.2	214.0	106.2	170.5	154.2
1979	1,333.6	939.5	475.8	98.9	246.0	118.8	216.6	177.5
1980 est.[1]	1,450.0	992.0	501.0	99.5	263. 0	128.5	256.0	202.0
Percent of 1980 Totals[2]	100.0%	68.4%	34.6%	6.9%	18.1%	8.9%	17.6%	13.9%
Percent Increase 1975–1980	80.9	70.7	79.8	28.9	93.1	44.1	153.5	69.3

[1]Estimate is extrapolation of trend for year from end of third quarter.
[2]Percentages may not total to 100.0 because of rounding.

SOURCES: Economic Report of the President, 1981, Table B–69, and *Federal Reserve Bulletin,* Table 1.55.

9–4 and 9–5). MSBs are concentrated in the eastern states of New York, Massachusetts, Connecticut, Pennsylvania, and New Jersey. In effect, MSBs tend to be in abundance whenever there are few S&Ls. Thus their importance is undoubtedly substantial in the northeast. MSBs are also similar to S&Ls in that their main source of funds is time deposits; MSBs are therefore reasonably stable institutions. MSBs only originated 4.9 percent of all new long-term residential financing in 1979 (see Fig. 9–6).

Commercial Banks. CBs specialize in short-term lending to businesses and consumers. Even so, they are the second largest real estate lender, with emphasis on one-family homes and commercial properties. They also are very active in short-term lending for construction, mortgage companies, and real estate investment trusts (REITs). In fact they lead in loans for new construction and for commercial properties. They obtain funds through both demand and time deposits, which means less stability in their source of funds by comparison with other financial institutions. As of December 31, 1980, CBs held 18.1 percent of all mortgage debt. This percentage is up from 15.5 percent in 1970; see Fig. 9–4. As shown in Fig. 9–6, CBs were third in originating residential financing in 1979, with 21.4 percent of the total.

Life Insurance Companies. LICs specialize in long-term financing of commercial investment properties, like shopping centers, office build-

FIGURE 9–6 Total Originations of Long-Term Mortgage Loans on Residential Properties by Selected Lender Groups, 1970, 1978, and 1979

(Billions of Dollars)[1]

	1970		1978		1979	
	$	%	$	%	$	%
SAVINGS & LOAN ASSNS.	16.7	37.6	96.2	47.8	87.7	43.3
1 to 4 family	14.8		90.0		82.8	
Multifamily	1.9		6.2		4.9	
MUTUAL SAVINGS BANKS	3.5	7.9	10.6	5.3	9.9	4.9
1 to 4 family	2.1		9.4		9.0	
Multifamily	1.4		1.2		.9	
COMMERCIAL BANKS	8.1	18.3	46.0	22.8	43.4	21.4
1- to 4-family	7.8		43.9		41.4	
Multifamily	.3		2.1		2.0	
LIFE INSURANCE COMPANIES	2.5	5.6	2.6	1.3	3.6	1.8
1- to 4-family	.3		.8		2.0	
Multifamily	2.2		1.8		1.6	
MORTGAGE COMPANIES	10.3	23.2	36.2	18.0	47.3	23.4
1- to 4-family	8.9		34.4		45.3	
Multifamily	1.4		1.8		2.0	
OTHERS	3.3	7.4	9.8	4.8	10.5	5.2
1- to 4-family	1.7		6.5		6.6	
Multifamily	1.6		3.3		3.9	
TOTAL ORIGINATIONS	44.4	100.0	201.4	100.0	202.4	100.0
1- to 4-family	35.6		185.0		187.1	
Multifamily	8.8		16.4		15.3	

[1]Based on Mortgage Loan Gross Flows, HUD.
SOURCE: Seller Servicer, May–June 1980, p. 25.

ings, hotels and motels, and large apartment buildings. They avoid financing small properties, such as one-family homes. The reason for this is almost certainly because they operate from a single national office or possibly several regional offices. Returns tend to be higher and administrative problems fewer with larger properties. However, LIC's are acquiring more one-family loans in recent years from mortgage bankers. The LIC's source of funds—policy premiums—is quite stable, hence the preference for long-term financing. They often depend on mortgage companies and commercial banks to originate their loans. In late 1980, LICs held only 8.9 percent of all mortgage debt, down sharply from their 15.7 percent share in 1970 (see Fig. 9–4). As shown in Fig. 9–6, LICs originated only 1.8 percent of all new residential financing in 1979.

Federal and Related Agencies.   More than doubling their share during the 1970s, federal and related agencies accounted for 17.6 percent of mortgage debt held at the end of 1980. Most of this debt was acquired from primary lenders and mortgage bankers or mortgage companies. The main federal agencies are the Federal Home Loan Mortgage Corporation (FHLMC), the Federal National Mortgage Association (FNMA), and the Government National Mortgage Association (GNMA). The Federal Home Loan Bank System backs up the FHLMC, whereas the Department of Housing and Urban Development serves as a secondary support institution for GNMA. A series of problems in financial markets has caused these agencies to steadily increase their share of mortgage debt held, which came about through a substantial increase in mortgage pools.

Individuals and Others. Mortgage companies, real estate investment trusts, pension funds, credit unions, and individuals held 13.9 percent of all mortgage debt in late 1980. Mortgage companies include both mortgage bankers and mortgage brokers. *Mortgage bankers* originate and service loans even though the loans may have been sold to a life insurance company, a federal agency, or some other secondary lender. *Mortgage brokers* bring borrowers and lenders together for a fee, much like a real estate broker brings buyers and sellers together. However, mortgage brokers do not service loans on a continuing basis like mortgage bankers. Figure 9–6 shows that mortgage companies originated 23.4 percent of all new residential financing in 1979, whereas others, individuals and other miscellaneous lenders, originated 5.2 percent.

MORTGAGE DEBT BY PROPERTY TYPE

Mortgage debt outstanding is reported by type of property securing the loan as well as by holders of the loan. The classifications are one- to

FIGURE 9–7 Percentage Distribution of Mortgage Debt Outstanding for End of Years 1970 and 1980 by Type of Property

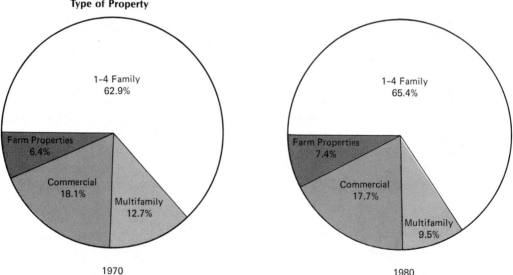

| 1970 | 1980 |

SOURCE: *Economic Report of the President,* 1981, Table 68. See Fig. 9–8 in this text for supporting data.

FIGURE 9–8 Mortgage Debt Outstanding by Type of Property for Selected Years, 1940–1980

(Billions of Dollars)

End of Year	All Properties	Farm Properties	NONFARM PROPERTIES			
			Total	Family	Multi-Family	Commercial
1940	$ 36.5	$ 6.5	$ 30.0	$ 17.4	$ 5.7	$ 6.9
1950	72.8	6.1	66.7	45.2	10.1	11.5
1960	207.5	12.8	194.7	141.9	20.3	32.4
1970	474.2	30.3	443.8	298.1	60.1	85.6
1975	801.5	50.9	750.7	490.8	100.6	159.3
1978	1,172.8	76.2	1,096.6	761.8	122.0	212.7
1979	1,333.6	92.4	1,241.2	872.1	130.7	238.4
1980 est.[1]	1,450.0	108.0	1,342.0	948.0	138.0	256.0
Percent of Total 1980	100.0%	7.4%	92.6%	65.4%	9.5%	17.7%
Percent Increase 1975–1980	80.9	112.2	78.8	93.2	37.2	60.7
Times Increase 1940–1980	39.7	16.6	44.7	54.5	24.2	37.1

[1]Estimate is extrapolation of trend for year from end of third quarters.

SOURCE: Economic Report of the President, 1981, Table B68, and *Federal Reserve Bulletin,* Chart 1.55.

four-family, multifamily, farm, and commercial loans. Commercial, one- to four-family, and multifamily loans are frequently combined into an additional classification—nonfarm property loans. Let us look at the distribution of mortgage debt by property type. We then examine the distribution of one- to four-family debt by type of holder.

At year end 1980, one- to four-family loans accounted for nearly two-thirds (65.4 percent) of the total mortgage debt outstanding—$1.33 trillion (see Figs. 9–7 and 9–8). Multifamily loans accounted for nearly 10 percent of the total, meaning that residential loans made up about three-fourths of all mortgage debt outstanding. Commercial loans accounted for 17.9 percent of all loans, and farm loans trailed way behind with 7.4 percent of the total. Obviously residential financing dominates the mortgage market.

Over the years 1940–1980, debt on one- to four-family homes increased over 50 times, much faster than any other category. Since 1975, loans on farms and on one- to four-family homes have increased fastest, each with over a 90 percent increase.

Note that life insurance companies dropped out of one- to four-family lending for all practical purposes. MSBs' share declined, although traditionally these institutions are steady lenders on residential properties. We saw earlier that MSBs are declining in importance in the overall mortgage market as well. This is just further evidence of the shifting dominance and patterns of institutions in our mortgage markets.

RESIDENTIAL FINANCING

Our intent is to develop the best possible understanding of the mortgage market. We have seen that residential properties account for three-fourths of all mortgage debt outstanding. So, let us extend our mortgage market overview with some further discussion of residential financing. A brief look at residential construction and homeownership is therefore included in our discussion to complete the picture of mortgage markets as they have developed to date.

GOVERNMENT VERSUS CONVENTIONAL FINANCING

FHA and VA loans dominated residential real estate finance for decades following World War II. Such loans are said to be government underwritten, meaning the federal government is liable to lenders for any losses they suffer in making such loans. With the advent of private mortgage insurance and rapidly fluctuating interest rates beginning about 1960, conventional lending has steadily expanded its share of the

FIGURE 9–9   Percentage Distribution of Nonfarm Mortgage Debt by Type of Financing for End of Years 1970 and 1980

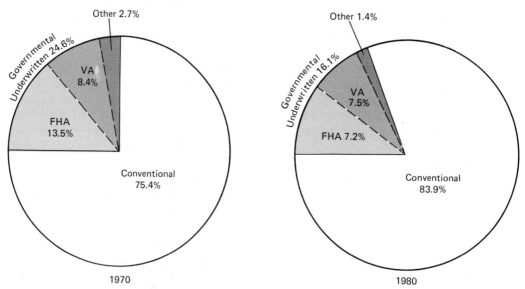

SOURCE: *Economic Report of the President,* 1981, Table B–69. See Fig. 9–10 in this text for supporting data.

FIGURE 9–10 Nonfarm Mortgage Debt by Type of Financing for End of Selected Years, 1940–1980

(Billions of Dollars)

End of Year	Total All Nonfarm Properties	GOVERNMENT UNDERWRITTEN				CONVENTIONAL	
		Total	1- to 4-Family Houses			Total	1- to 4-Family Houses
			Total	FHA Insured	VA Guaranteed		
1940	$ 30.0	$ 2.3	$ 2.3	$ 2.3	—	$ 27.7	$ 15.1
1950	66.7	22.1	18.9	8.6	$ 10.3	44.6	26.3
1960	194.7	62.3	56.4	26.7	29.7	132.3	85.5
1970	443.8	109.2	97.3	59.9	37.3	334.6	200.8
1975	750.7	147.0	127.7	66.1	61.6	603.7	363.0
1978	1,096.6	176.4	153.4	71.4	82.0	920.2	608.5
1979	1,241.2	199.0	172.9	81.0	92.0	1,042.2	699.1
1980 est.[1]	1,342.0	216.0	196.0	96.0	100.0	1,126.0	751.0
Percent of 1980 Total	100.0%	16.1	14.6%	7.2%	7.5%	83.9%	56.0%
Percent Increase 1975–1980	78.8	46.9	53.5	45.2	62.3	86.5	106.9

[1]Estimate is extrapolation of trend for year from end of second and third quarters.

SOURCE: Economic Report of the President, 1981, Table B–68.

mortgage market, as evidenced by Figs. 9–9 and 9–10. At year end 1980, five-sixths (83.9 percent) of all financing was of the conventional type.

Actually FHA and VA loans never accounted for more than one-third of all outstanding mortgage debt. But because of the governmental underwriting and standardized terms, these loans were much more liquid than conventional loans. This greater liquidity caused them to be the basis for the development of the secondary mortgage market. In more recent years, the standardized terms of FNMA-FHLMC uniform instruments and the loss protection of private mortgage insurance has greatly lessened this difference. As a result, conventional loans are now freely traded in the secondary mortgage market as well. In numerical terms, governmentally underwritten loans declined from one-fourth of all nonfarm mortgage debt in 1970 to less than one-sixth in 1980. Again see Figs. 9–9 and 9–10. In other words, conventional loans increased their share from three-fourths of the total in 1970 to slightly over five-sixths in 1980.

Even with one- to four-family debt, four dollars are out in conventional loans for every one dollar in FHA or VA loans. FHA and VA are roughly equal in their share of all mortgage debt outstanding, each with about ten percent. Thus, FHA and VA loans no longer dominate the mortgage markets.

Figure 9–11 summarizes the changing nature of mortgage debt by providing an overview of debt by type of property, type of holder, and

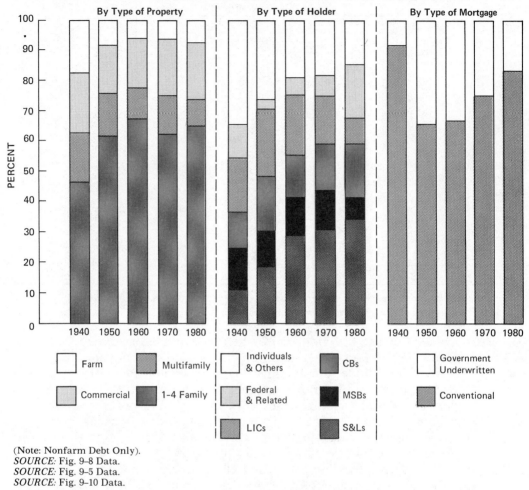

FIGURE 9–11 The Changing Anatomy of Mortgage Debt, 1940–1980

End of Decade Distribution of Mortgage Debt by Type of Property, Holder, and Mortgage (by Percent)

(Note: Nonfarm Debt Only).
SOURCE: Fig. 9–8 Data.
SOURCE: Fig. 9–5 Data.
SOURCE: Fig. 9–10 Data.

type of mortgage (conventional versus government underwritten) for selected years from 1940 to 1980.

NUMBER OF HOUSING UNITS

Let us now look at the growth in the number of housing units in the United States since 1940 to improve our perspective of residential finance. As shown in Fig. 9–12, the number more than doubled from 34.9 million units in 1940 to an estimated 80.1 million units in 1980. The increase amounts to about1.0 million units per year from 1940 to 1970 and to about 1.7 million units per year during the 1970s. The inverse rela-

FIGURE 9–12   Occupied Housing Units—Tenure and Population per Occupied Unit from 1940 to 1980

(In thousands, except percents. Prior to 1960, excludes Alaska and Hawaii)

| Year | Total Population | OCCUPIED UNITS | | | | | Population per Occupied Unit |
| | | Total | Owner Occupied | | Renter Occupied | | |
			Number	Percent	Number	Percent	
1940	132,164,569	34,855	15,196	43.6	19,659	56.4	3.8
1950	151,325,798	42,855	23,560	55.0	19,266	45.0	3.4
1960	179,323,175	53,024	32,797	61.9	20,227	38.1	3.3
1970	203,211,926	63,450	39,885	62.9	23,565	37.1	3.1
1980[1]	222,807,000	80,135	52,088	65.0	28,047	35.0	2.8

[1]1980 estimates by authors based on latest data available.

SOURCE: U.S. Bureau of the Census, *U.S. Census of Population of Housing, 1960 and 1970.*

tionship between private housing starts and interest rates on conventional new home loans is depicted in Fig. 9–13.

Home ownership in the United States increased most sharply on a percentage basis between 1940 and 1960, largely because of the stable interest rates. During this period, owner-occupancy averaged a 1 percent increase per year, going from 43.6 to 61.9 percent. From 1960 to 1980, the proportion of owner occupied units increased only slightly to an estimated 65.0 percent.

FEDERAL REGULATIONS AFFECTING DEPOSITORY INSTITUTIONS

Our overview of the mortgage market would not be complete without a brief look at the Depository Institutions Deregulation and Monetary Control Act of 1980 (DIDMICA). The Act is one of the most comprehensive and far-reaching pieces of legislation affecting our financial institutions ever to be passed. The Act, for the first time, authorizes interest-bearing checking accounts for savings and loan associations. These accounts are technically termed negotiated order of withdrawal, or NOW, accounts. The Act also phases out interest rate ceilings on deposits, which discourage savings and therefore slow down the economy while stimulating inflation. The Act also expands and gives greater flexibility to S&Ls in their investing activity.

The Act consists of nine separate titles, the first six of which contain important provisions for our purposes. The specific provisions of the Act and their implications as they affect individual institutions are integrated into subsequent chapters.

Title I: Monetary Control Act. Reserve requirements are extended to all transaction accounts at all depository institutions and are made uniform for all commercial banks. Likewise, fees for services rendered by the Federal Reserve System are to be uniform for both member and

FIGURE 9–13 **Inverse Relationship between Mortgage Loan Interest Rates and Private Housing Starts, 1965–1981**

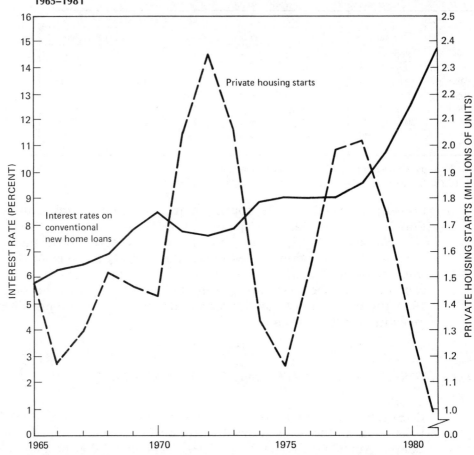

SOURCE: *Savings and Loan Sourcebook,* 1980 and 1981 and *Federal Reserve Bulletins.*

nonmember banks. Finally, both member and nonmember banks are to have equal discount and borrowing privileges from the Federal Reserve.

   Title II: Depository Institutions Deregulation Act. Limitations on interest rates payable on deposits are to be phased out in an orderly manner by 1986. The Depository Institutions Deregulation Committee (DIDC) is to oversee the phase-out.

   Title III: Consumer Checking Account Equity Act. Interest-bearing checking accounts are authorized for all depository institutions. Thus, banks may provide automatic transfer of funds from savings to checking accounts, S&Ls may offer NOW accounts, and credit unions may offer share draft accounts. Deposits are also insured up to $100,000 per account under this title.

   Title IV: Powers of Thrift Institutions and Miscellaneous Provisions. Portfolio restrictions on thrift institutions (S&Ls, MSBs, and CUs) are removed, and services they can offer are expanded. For example, credit unions are authorized to make real estate loans, whereas savings and loans may issue credit cards. The intent is greater flexibility for the institutions.

Title V: State Usury Laws. Changing economic conditions often caused interest rates to go above state usury ceilings prior to 1980. Title V of the Act removes state usury ceilings on loans secured by residential real property or manufactured homes (mobile homes). A floating usury ceiling based on the discount rate of the Federal Reserve is substituted for the state usury ceilings. States may reimpose their own usury ceilings by explicit action prior to April 1, 1983. State interest rate ceilings on deposits are also suspended by this title. These provisions are intended to maintain the flow of funds in our financial markets during times of variable interest rates.

Title VI: Truth in Lending Simplification and Reform Act. This title requires the Federal Reserve Board to issue model forms and clauses for consumer loans. The intent is to increase consumer understanding of credit terms while facilitating lender-creditor compliance with the Truth in Lending (TIL) Act.

The full impact of the Depository Institutions Deregulation and Monetary Control Act are unknown as of this writing. The Act expands the powers and flexibility of all depository institutions and promises to increase competition among them.[1] In so doing, it is intended to improve the functioning of our financial markets. The Act is almost certain to have a significant impact on our mortgage markets.

The Act also gives the Federal Reserve Board the right to establish reserve requirements for all depository institutions rather than only for member banks. The effect will be to increase the Federal Reserve's ability to implement monetary policy.

SUMMARY

Real estate purchasers are one of the chief users of credit in our economy along with businesses, governments, and consumers. The mortgage market is where real estate loans are negotiated and where interest rates and fees are determined. Primary lenders originate and often service these loans. S&Ls, MSBs, CBs, LICs, and mortgage companies make up the bulk of the primary lenders. Secondary lenders, primarily governmental agencies, buy loans from the primary lenders. The buying and selling of existing loans is termed the secondary mortgage market.

The main demanders of mortgage funds are householders, builders

---

[1]"Banks and S&Ls Gird for Price War When NOW Accounts Go National," *Wall Street Journal,* October 3, 1980, p. 29.

and developers, investors, and businesses. Nonfarm properties account for about 93 percent of total mortgage debt outstanding. Urban residential properties, with 75 percent of the total debt outstanding, are easily the main type of property financed. Governmental backed loans are decreasing in importance, and as of 1980 they accounted for only one-seventh of all mortgage debt outstanding. It is estimated that, in 1980, we have about 80 million dwelling units in the United States, with approximately 1.5 million units added each year. Figure 9–12 visually summarizes much of this information.

The Depository Institutions Deregulation and Monetary Control Act of 1980 is to be implemented during the 1980s. The Act promises to reshape the roles of our various financial institutions and to increase competition in our financial markets.

KEY TERMS

Capital Market	Money Market	Primary Lender
Disintermediation	Mortgage Banker	Secondary Lender
Financial Intermediary	Mortgage Broker	Secondary Mortgage Market
Financial Market	Mortgage Market	
Intermediation		

QUESTIONS FOR REVIEW AND DISCUSSION

1. What is a primary lender? A secondary lender?

2. Distinguish between financial markets, money markets, and capital markets. In which of these does the mortgage market best fit?

3. What do financial intermediation and disintermediation mean? What is the significance of each?

4. Who are the main borrowers in our mortgage market?

5. Who are the main lenders in our mortgage market and what is their relative importance? Who are the main originators of long-term mortgage loans?

6. Briefly explain the nature and significance of the Depository Institutions Deregulation and Monetary Control Act of 1980. Does the Act impact real estate finance?

7. Match the following key terms and definitions:
   a. Disintermediation _____
   b. Capital Market _____
   c. Mortgage Market _____

   1. Where loans and instruments of short duration, less than one year, are arranged or bought and sold.

d. Financial Market _____
e. Money Market _____
f. Mortgage Banker _____
g. Mortgage Broker _____

2. Where loans are arranged or bought and sold.
3. Where stocks and debt instruments of more than one year are created or are bought and sold.
4. Where loans secured by real estate are arranged or are bought and sold
5. Originates and services mortgage loans for a fee.
6. Withdrawal of funds from financial institutions for direct investment or lending.
7. Brings borrowers and lenders together for a fee but does not service loans arranged.
8. Where existing mortgage loans are bought and sold.

ten

Private Depository Lenders

Savings and loan associations, mutual saving banks, commercial banks, and credit unions act as financial intermediaries by accepting deposits from savers and making loans to borrowers. Recent years have seen numerous changes in the regulation of these private depository institutions, as evidenced by the Depository Institutions Deregulation and Monetary Control Act of 1980. All depository institutions have been given the authority to offer some type of interest-bearing checking account under the Act. At the same time, the mortgage-lending powers of depository institutions have been liberalized, and S&Ls have been given broadened consumer lending powers. However, rising interest rates have made it less profitable to borrow funds on a short-term basis and to lend on a long-term basis at fixed interest rates. Indeed, some lenders say that fixed-rate mortgage loans are a thing of the past.

These depository institutions were the leading source of mortgage financing during the 1970s and will probably remain so during the 1980s. S&Ls and MSBs traditionally invest over one-half of their assets in mortgage loans. CBs invest less than one-quarter of their assets in mortgage loans, but they are second only to S&Ls in dollar volume of mortgage loan holdings. CUs emphasize consumer installment credit, but they are increasingly using their authority to make residential mortgage loans as well.

In this chapter we discuss: (1) organization and regulation, (2) sources of funds, (3) investment policies, (4) mortgage lending authority, and (5) mortgage-lending activities of depository institutions. We discuss these institutions in the following order:

1. Savings and Loan Associations
2. Mutual Savings Banks
3. Commercial Banks
4. Credit Unions

Selected characteristics concerning the mortgage-lending activities of these institutions are presented as a summary of our discussion in Fig. 10–4 at the end of the chapter.

SAVINGS AND LOAN ASSOCIATIONS

Savings and loan associations are the largest source of loans to finance the ownership of homes. Savings and loan associations are also sometimes called building and loan associations, cooperative banks, homestead associations, building associations, and savings associations. Early building and loan associations were organized primarily to assist members in acquiring homes. Present-day associations have a dual goal of financing home ownership and, at the same time, providing an adequate rate of return to saver–depositors. At the end of 1980, approximately 4,600 savings and loan associations held assets of about $630 billion.

Organization and Regulation

A savings and loan association may be either a mutual or a stock organization. A mutual savings and loan is owned by its depositors, who expect interest earnings on their deposits. A stock savings and loan is owned by stockholders who expect a profit on their investment. All federally chartered savings and loans were established as mutual organizations, but they may convert to stock organizations. State chartered associations can be either mutual or stock organizations. Stock associations represented nearly 19 percent of all savings and loans (at the end of 1980), and they held about 28 percent of all savings and loan assets. Thus, stock companies are slightly larger than the typical S&L.

Nearly 2,000—over 40 percent of all associations—are federally chartered. These federally chartered associations held over 55 percent of all savings and loan assets at the end of 1980. Federally chartered savings and loan associations are automatically members of the Federal Home Loan Bank System (FHLBS) and are subject to regulation by the Federal Home Loan Bank Board (FHLBB). Over 76 percent of the state chartered associations were members of the FHLBS at the end of 1980. However, the lending authority of member state chartered savings and loans is primarily regulated at the state level. FHLBS member savings and loans hold over 98 percent of all assets of the savings and loan business.

All federally chartered savings and loans and about 75 percent of the state chartered savings and loans are insured by the Federal Savings and Loan Insurance Corporation (FSLIC). The FSLIC insures each account for up to $100,000. Massachusetts, Ohio, Maryland, and North Carolina have state organizations that insure accounts of approximately 400 savings and loan associations located in their state.

SOURCES OF FUNDS

Deposits accounted for nearly 79 percent of the funds held by S&Ls at the end of 1980. Passbook savings accounts represented about 21 percent of these deposits. Money market certificates represented another 36 percent of the deposits, while other market rate certificates and certificates of deposits represented approximately 43 percent. A *money market certificate* (MMC) is a short-term (182-day) savings instrument that carries an interest rate based on the average yield of U.S. Government six-month treasury bills in the most recent auction. Thus, while MMCs are fixed-rate instruments, the interest rate may fluctuate from week to week with the interest rate established at the weekly auction for treasury bills. A *certificate of deposit* (CD) is an intermediate-term instrument (two- to ten-year maturity) that earns at a higher interest rate than a passbook account. Cashing in a CD early results in the loss of the premium interest rate. Savings and loan associations and other depository institutions gained the authority to offer NOW (negotiable order of withdrawal) accounts as of January 1, 1981. NOW accounts are the equivalent of interest-bearing checking accounts. They may become a significant source of funds for savings and loans.

Advances from Federal Home Loan Banks were the second most important source of funds and accounted for ten percent of funds at the end of 1980. Other sources include loans from commercial banks, escrow accounts, net-worth and mortgage-backed bonds.

The principal sources of funds available for investment in a given year are increases in deposits, interest on loans, and loan repayments. Additional funds may be obtained by borrowing from Federal Home Loan Banks, selling securities, or selling mortgage loans.

INVESTMENT POLICIES

One of the principal goals of savings and loan associations is to finance homeownership; thus they emphasize mortgage lending. In fact, mortgage loans accounted for about 80 percent of S&L assets in 1980. Cash and short-term securities represented another 8 percent of assets. Other assets such as GNMA mortgage-backed securities, FHLMC participation certificates, stock in Federal Home Loan Banks, and consumer loans represented the remaining 12 percent of S&L assets at this same time.

The Depository Institutions Deregulation and Monetary Control Act of 1980 greatly expanded the investment powers of federally chartered savings and loans associations. The Act allows them to invest up to 20 percent of their assets in consumer loans, commercial paper, and corporate debt securities. This change may cause federally chartered associations to significantly increase investments in these alternative areas, particularly if the tax law is changed to encourage it. If these expanded investment powers give federal associations a competitive advantage, similar powers are likely to be granted to state chartered associations.

Income tax law may act to set an upper limit on consumer loans, investments in corporate bonds, and commercial mortgage loans. Thrift institutions are allowed a deduction of 40 percent of their net income as an addition to bad debt reserves if 82 percent or more of their assets are invested in residential mortgage loans and other qualifying assets. The deduction sharply reduces their income tax liability. As the percentage of assets invested in residential mortgage loans and other qualifying assets declines, the allowable deduction declines. Consumer loans, corporate bonds, and commercial mortgage loans are nonqualifying assets unless they are government insured or guaranteed. Thus, the incentives of the S&L are presently toward residential mortgage lending.

MORTGAGE-LENDING AUTHORITY

The Federal Home Loan Bank Board regulates the lending authority of federally chartered associations, as previously mentioned. The Board therefore controls 43 percent (by number) and 55 percent (by value of assets) of savings and loans. The DIDMC Act of 1980 liberalized the mortgage-lending authority for federally chartered S&Ls. State laws and regulations define the lending authority for state chartered S&Ls. Some states have parity clauses that allow a state chartered association to make any mortgage loan that a federally chartered association may make. Therefore, if federally chartered associations obtain a competitive advantage from the DIDMC Act, state regulations are likely to be changed to grant equal powers to state chartered associations. The discussion here, therefore, concentrates on regulations that apply only to federally chartered associations.

Percent of Assets. S&Ls have no limit on the percentage of assets that may be invested in mortgage loans. At the same time, no more than 20 percent of assets may be invested in mortgage loans secured by commercial property.

Lending Area. While the FHLBB imposes no territorial lending regulations, the Federal Savings and Loan Insurance Corporation restricts loans to the United States and to its territories and possessions. The FSLIC limits placed on a loan secured outside the savings and loan associations' normal lending territory were set at $200,000 in 1981 and at $200,000 with allowances for changes in the Consumer Price Index thereafter. An association's normal lending territory is defined as the state in which its principal office is located plus any portion of a circle within a radius of 100 miles from its principal office that falls outside the home state.

Government-Backed Loans. Federal associations are allowed to make government-backed mortage loans on the terms specified by any of the various federal agencies. This applies to loans secured by either residential or nonresidential property. Thus, federal S&Ls may make loans insured or guaranteed by the FHA, VA, FmHA, Economic Development Administration, or Small Business Administration.

Improved Residential and Nonresidential. Federal associations may make conventional uninsured mortgage loans on properties improved with buildings for up to 90 percent of their value. The maximum allowable maturity is 40 years for one- to four-family residences and 30 years for multifamily and commercial properties. The loans can be nonamortizing, partially amortizing, or fully amortizing.

The loan-to-value ratio on home loans may be raised to 95 percent if the property is owner occupied, if the balance exceeding 90 percent of value is insured by private mortgage insurance, if it is either partially or fully amortizing, and if the monthly payments include real estate taxes. The loan-to-value ratio may also exceed 90 percent if a savings account is pledged to cover the excess.

Unimproved Property. Federal associations may make loans on unimproved properties for up to two-thirds of their value for a three-year term. They may make loans on single-family building lots for up to 75 percent of value. The term may be for up to fifteen years if the lot is intended as the borrower's principal residence.

Construction Loans. Federal S&Ls may make secured construction loans for up to 75 percent of value. The maximum term for loans to finance the construction of single-family dwellings is 18 months, but the loan may later be extended for six months. Construction loans on other types of improved property are limited to a three-year term. Land development loans may have a term of up to five years, and they may be extended for up to three years.

Nonconforming Loans. Federal S&Ls are allowed to invest up to five percent of their assets in residential construction loans that are not secured by real property. Effectively, this means they may make personal loans for property modernization and rehabilitation. They are also allowed to invest up to five percent of their assets in nonconforming loans secured by either residential real estate or real estate used for commercial farming.

Other Loans. Federal associations may make leasehold mortgage loans if the initial lease, or an option to renew, extends the life of the lease for at least five years beyond the maturity date of the loan. S&Ls may also make junior mortgage loans. They may participate in mortgage loans with other lenders, and they are allowed to make alternate types of mortgage loans, such as flexible payments, graduated payment, variable-rate, and renegotiable-rate mortgage loans. They may also make bridge loans, home improvement loans, and loans on mobile homes.

Regulation versus Lending Policies. S&Ls have more liberal lending policies for conventional mortgage loans on single-family residences than other institutional lenders. Even so, S&Ls do not, as a policy, lend up to the limits of their authority. The average loan on an existing single-family home granted by associations in 1980 had a loan-to-value ratio of approximately 74 percent and a maturity of slightly over 28 years. Since the terms are more liberal, the loans have more risk and the interest rate is higher. The new regulations make it possible for associations to grant loans with even higher percentage loan-to-value ratios and longer maturities.

MORTGAGE-LENDING ACTIVITY

Figure 10–1 shows the mortgage holdings of savings and loan associations at the end of 1980. A total of $502.8 billion in mortgage debt was held. About 83 percent of this amount was secured by one- to four-family residences. Somewhat less than 8 percent was secured by multifamily residences, and an additional 9 percent was secured by commercial properties.

FIGURE 10–1 Total Assets and Mortgage Holdings of Savings and Loan Associations at the End of 1980

Type of Property	Dollars (in Billions)	Percent of Mortgage Loans
One- to Four-Family	$419.4	83.4%
Multifamily	38.1	7.6
Commercial	45.3	9.0
Farm	—	—
Total Mortgage Loans	$502.8	100.0
Total Assets	$629.8	

SOURCE: *Federal Reserve Bulletin,* June 1981, pp. A27, A39. Percentages by authors.

Associations held 34.6 percent of all mortgage debt outstanding in 1980. They held 43.7 percent of all one- to four-family residential mortgage debt and 27.9 percent of mortgage debt secured by multifamily residences. S&Ls also held 17.5 percent of the debt secured by mortgages on commercial property.

Savings and Loans traditionally emphasize mortgage lending, and they are the dominant lender on residential properties. They are primarily local lenders. S&Ls also buy and sell mortgage loans and partial interests in mortgage loans, in the secondary mortgage market.

Compared with the other three main private institutional lenders (CBs, MSBs, and LICs), S&Ls are the leading mortgage lender, especially in loans to purchase both one- to four-family residences and multifamily residences. They are usually the leading source of loans to construct one- to four-family residences as well. They rank above the other three large institutional lenders in the dollar volume of holdings of FHA insured and VA guaranteed mortgage loans. They rank third in holdings of mortgage loans on commercial property, and they rank second as a source of home improvement loans and loans secured by mobile homes. In short, S&Ls are probably the most important institution in our primary mortgage market.

SERVICE CORPORATIONS

Savings and loan associations are allowed to invest up to three percent of their assets in service corporations. At least one-half of any investment in service corporations above one percent of assets must be invested for community, inner-city, and community development purposes. A service corporation may be a statewide organization owned by several savings and loans within a state; or a service corporation may be wholly owned by a single savings and loan association.

One of the principal attractions of service corporations is that they may engage in activities otherwise forbidden to a savings and loan association. Thus, service corporations may develop land, renovate improved properties, own rental properties, and enter into joint ventures. They may operate as an insurance, property management, or appraisal firm. Also, they may originate, purchase, and sell mortgages, as well as provide clerical and other services to several savings and loan associations.

MUTUAL SAVINGS BANKS

The first mutual savings bank (MSB) in the United States was established in 1816. Mutual savings banks thrived because at that time commercial banks did not accept deposits from individuals. Therefore, mutual savings banks provided a safe place for individual savers to store their money and to earn a return on their funds. In the latter half of the nineteenth century, the midwestern, southern, and western sections of the country were developing quite rapidly. Commercial banks soon learned to accept both savings and demand deposits from individuals in order to obtain funds to help finance the growth of the nation. As a result, MSBs did not spread but remained concentrated in the New England and Middle Atlantic states.

In 1980, 463 mutual savings banks were located in 17 states plus Puerto Rico. They had assets of about $172 billion at the end of 1980. About 90 percent of these assets are held by MSBs in New York, Massachusetts, Connecticut, Pennsylvania, and New Jersey. On the national level MSBs have steadily declined in importance relative to CBs, S&Ls, and LICs, because of their concentration in the Northeast. The South and West have simply experienced a more rapid rate of growth in economic activity than the Northeast, which is reflected in the relative size and importance of the financial institutions serving these regions.

ORGANIZATION AND REGULATION

Mutual savings banks are *mutual organizations,* as their name implies. That is, they are owned by their depositors. However, management authority is exercised by a self-perpetuating board of trustees. Current board members select the new board members.

Most mutual savings banks are state chartered and are governed by state law. In 1979 existing MSBs were given the right to convert to a federal charter, if the conversion would not violate state law. The first conversion took place in September 1980. The Federal Home Loan Bank Board grants the federal charter and governs operations of federally chartered mutual savings banks. A grandfather clause allows a federal mutual savings bank to carry on any activities it was engaged in on December 31, 1977, subject to a limitation on its equity, corporate bond, and consumer loan investments. The board of trustees of a federal MSB must be elected by its depositors. The primary advantage of a federal charter is more liberal rights to operate branch offices. About 30 percent of all state chartered mutual savings banks were members of the FHLBS in 1980. As such they are allowed to borrow funds from Federal Home Loan Banks.

About two-thirds of the deposits in mutual savings banks in Massachusetts are insured by the Mutual Savings Central Fund, Inc. of Massachusetts. The deposits in the remaining savings banks in Massachusetts and the state chartered mutual savings banks in all other states were insured by the Federal Deposit Insurance Corporation in 1980.

SOURCES OF FUNDS

Deposits are the source of over 88 percent of the funds held by mutuals. The largest source is time deposits, which includes certificates of deposit (CDs) and money market certificates (MMCs). Ordinary savings accounts are the second most important source. NOW accounts and checking accounts are currently a relatively small source, but they may assume greater importance in the future. Other sources of funds are general reserves and other liabilities, such as advances from Federal Home Loan Banks or loans from CBs. The principal sources of funds available for investment in any given year are increases in deposits and loan repayments. Additional funds may be generated by borrowing or by selling securities and mortgages in the secondary market.

INVESTMENT POLICIES

The goal of state chartered MSBs is to provide savers with a safe place to invest their funds and to pay the depositors an adequate return. Federally chartered MSBs have the additional goal of providing for the financing of homes. In actuality, state chartered mutuals strongly favor home mortgage lending as well.

Mortgage loans represented 58 percent of MSB assets in 1980. GNMA mortgage-backed securities represented an additional 8 percent. Corporate bonds are their second biggest investment. Corporate, state and local government, and federal agency notes and bonds accounted for 14 percent of assets. U.S. government obligations made up 5 percent of assets, and common and preferred stock accounted for another 3 percent. Other loans such as consumer loans and loans of federal funds accounted for over 7 percent of assets. In 1980, the remaining assets were comprised of cash, bank premises, and miscellaneous assets.

MSBs follow conservative lending and investment policies. State law and regulations govern the eligibility and standards of the quality of loans and investments. About 77 percent of assets are in mortgage loans, GNMA mortgage-backed securities, and bonds. When the returns on bonds rise relative to the yields on mortgage loans, mutual savings banks increase the percentage of assets invested in bonds. If mortgage yields are higher than those on bonds, they increase the percentage of assets invested in mortgage loans.

MORTGAGE-LENDING AUTHORITY

There are relatively few federally chartered mutual savings banks; and the powers of state chartered mutual savings banks vary among the states. The following regulations provide generalizations about lending powers of state chartered mutuals.

Percent of Assets.   Mortgage loans are generally limited to 60 to 75 percent of deposits or assets. In some states such as New York, FHA and VA loans are not limited by this percent of deposits or assets rule. In Massachusetts, savings banks are allowed to invest up to 75 percent of deposits in conventional mortgage loans plus an additional 15 percent of deposits in FHA insured and VA guaranteed mortgage loans.

Lending Area.   There are no lending area restrictions for FHA insured and VA guaranteed mortgage loans. About one-third of the states, including Delaware, Maryland, and Washington, have no territorial limitations on conventional mortgage loans. In the remaining states, conventional mortgage loans are usually limited to those made in the home state and adjoining states.

Some states limit out-of-state mortgage loans to a specified percentage of deposits or assets. In Massachusetts conventional out-of-state mortgages are limited to 25 percent of deposits. In a number of states the allowable loan-to-value ratios are lower for out-of-state mortgages, unless they are insured.

Government-Backed Loans.   Mutual savings banks are allowed to make FHA insured and VA guaranteed loans on the terms specified by the Federal Housing Administration and the Veterans Administration. MSBs are generally also allowed to lend on mortgages insured or guaranteed by the state in which the savings bank is chartered.

One- to Four-Family Residences.   In New York and Massachusetts, MSBs are allowed to make conventional mortgage loans on one- to four-family residences for up to 95 percent of appraised value. These loans are available only to owner occupants, and a portion of the loan must be insured by a private mortgage insurance corporation. In New York the monthly payments on a 95 percent loan must include real estate taxes and insurance premiums, and the term is limited to the either three-fourths of the remaining useful life of the building or 40 years, whichever is the shorter period. In Massachusetts the monthly payments on 95 percent loans must include real estate taxes, and the term is limited to 35 years. Dollar limitations may be specified according to the loan-to-value ratios. Loans with loan-to-value ratios of 80 percent or less have higher dollar limits, and private mortgage insurance is not required.

Regulations vary among the states. Uninsured conventional mortgage loans on one- to four-family residences are usually limited to 75 to 80 percent of value. However, Massachusetts allows a 90 percent loan-to-value ratio. The maximum maturities range from 25 to 40 years.

Multifamily and Nonresidential.   Mutual savings banks may make mortgage loans on multifamily and nonresidential properties for up to 75 to 80 percent of appraised value for terms of up to 30 years and in New York of up to 40 years. In some states the maximum maturity is limited to 25 years.

Other Mortgage Loans. MSBs may also make leasehold mortgage loans and participate in loans with other lenders. They are allowed to make construction loans, particularly for home construction. In 13 states MSBs may make loans on unimproved property. In some states mutual savings banks are allowed to make alternate types of mortgage loans, such as graduated-payment, variable-rate, and renegotiable-rate mortgage loans. They may also make home improvement loans.

Regulations versus Lending Policies. Regulations specify the permissible loan limitations, but the lending policies of the individual savings banks determine the actual loans and terms granted. The average mortgage loan on an existing single-family home granted by mutual savings banks in 1980 had a loan-to-value ratio of about 68 percent and a maturity of over 26 years.

MORTGAGE-LENDING ACTIVITY

Figure 10–2 shows the mortgage holdings of mutual savings banks at the end of 1980, which totaled $100 billion in mortgage debt. About 65 percent of the dollar holdings was secured by one- to four-family residences, over 17 percent was secured by multifamily residences, and an additional 17 percent was secured by commercial properties.

Mutual savings banks held 6.9 percent of all mortgage debt outstanding in 1980. They held 6.8 percent of one- to four-family residential mortgage debt and 12.7 percent of multifamily residential mortgage debt. MSBs also held 6.6 percent of the debt secured by mortgages on commercial property.

Mutual savings banks emphasize residential lending. The smaller savings banks, which are typically located in small cities and rural areas, emphasize lending in the local area. The large savings banks, which are usually located in larger metropolitan areas, also lend locally, but historically, when they have had excess funds, they have made substantial purchases of mortgages in the secondary mortgage market.

FIGURE 10–2   Total Assets and Mortgage Holdings of Mutual Savings Banks at the End of 1980

Type of Property	Dollars (in Billions)	Percent of Mortgage Loans
One- to Four-Family	$ 65.3	65.4
Multifamily	17.3	17.4
Commercial	17.1	17.1
Farm	0.1	0.1
Total Mortgage Loans	$ 99.8	100.0
Total Assets	$171.6	

SOURCE: Federal Reserve Bulletin, June 1981, pp. A27, A39. Percentages by authors.

These purchases of out-of-state mortgages serve to transfer funds from one section of the country to another, for example, from the Northeast to mainly the West and South. About one-quarter of the mortgage holdings of MSBs represent loans in nonsavings bank states. In the 1960s nearly all of the out-of-state mortgages were either FHA insured or VA guaranteed. In the 1970s savings banks continued to purchase FHA insured and VA guaranteed mortgages from mortgage bankers and other lenders. However, they increasingly purchased conventional mortgage loans from lenders in high-growth states as California, Texas, and Florida.

Mutual savings banks are the largest holders of mortgage loans in New York, Massachusetts, New Hampshire, and Maine. They are significant purchasers in the secondary mortgage market and are also one of the largest holders of GNMA mortgage-backed securities.

Mutual savings banks, compared with the other three main institutional lenders, rank fourth in both total mortgage loans held and commercial mortgage loans held. They rank third in the holdings of one- to four-family mortgages, multifamily mortgages, and construction loans. They rank second in the holdings of FHA insured and VA guaranteed loans. Their holdings of farm mortgage loans are negligible.

COMMERCIAL BANKS

Commercial banks were originally organized to finance business and agriculture. They made mortgage loans, but only as a secondary activity. National banks were prohibited from making mortgage loans from the Civil War through 1916. Currently commercial banks make business and agricultural loans, mortgage loans, consumer installment loans, and other loans.

Commercial banks are the main type of financial institution in the United States, with approximately 15,000 commercial banks located throughout our nation. Commercial banking institutions had total assets of $1,704 billion at the end of 1980. As the dominant financial institution, they provide financing for the other mortgage lenders in addition to making mortgage loans.

ORGANIZATION AND REGULATION

Commercial banks are owned by stockholders. Their goal is to make a profit for the stockholders while serving the local community. (Stockholder owned profit oriented organizations are called *stock organizations*). Commercial banks may be either state or federally chartered. The activities of state chartered banks are regulated by state commissions. Federally chartered commercial banks are called national banks, and their activities are regulated by the Comptroller of the Currency.

About one-third of all commercial banks are federally chartered, and this one-third holds slightly less than 60 percent of the assets of all commercial banks. It follows that federally chartered banks are much larger than state chartered banks, on the average. National banks are required to be members of the Federal Reserve System. State chartered banks are free to become members of the Federal Reserve System if they so desire. In 1979 about one thousand state chartered banks were members of the Federal Reserve System, and they held over 10 percent of all assets held by commercial banks. Thus, about 40 percent of all CBs were members of the Federal Reserve System in 1980 and they accounted for over 70 percent of the assets.

Membership of banks in the Federal Reserve System declined in importance from the viewpoint of monetary policy as a result of the DIDMC Act of 1980. The Act extended the authority of the Federal Reserve to control reserve requirements for all depository institutions. The intent and effect is to increase the Federal Reserve's power to regulate the money supply. Of course, this means that nonmember commercial banks are now also subject to regulation by the Fed.

Over 98 percent of CBs are members of the Federal Deposit Insurance Corporation. FDIC insures their deposit accounts for up to $100,000, and the member banks are governed by FDIC regulations.

SOURCES OF FUNDS

Deposits are the source of over 72 percent of the funds held by commercial banks. In 1980 demand deposits provided about 27 percent of funds. Time deposits provided another 34 percent, and savings deposits represented 12 percent of funds. Other sources of funds are borrowings, other liabilities, and stockholders' equity.

The principal sources of funds available for new investments in any given year are increases in deposits and loan repayments. Additional funds may be obtained by borrowing, selling securities, or selling mortgage loans.

INVESTMENT POLICIES

CBs place greater emphasis on short- and intermediate-term loans and securities than do S&Ls and MSBs. This is due, at least in part, to commercial banks obtaining nearly 30 percent of their funds from demand deposits. That is, if they borrow on a short term, they want to lend on a short term. This manner of operation also serves to achieve their primary goal of providing short-term and intermediate-term financing for business and agriculture.

Loans accounted for about 55 percent of the assets of commercial banks at the end of 1980. The three major categories are commercial and industrial, mortgage, and consumer installment credit loans. In 1980 commercial and industrial loans represented over 19 percent of assets, mortgage loans over 15 percent, and consumer installment credit loans over 8 percent. Loans to other financial institutions, agricultural loans, and term loans to individuals accounted for the balance of CB assets in loans—about 13 percent.

Securities represented about 19 percent of the assets of CBs at this same time. The major securities held were U.S. Treasury, state and local government, and U.S. Government agency obligations. Holdings of corporate bonds and stock were less than one-half of 1 percent of assets in 1980. A substantial portion of all securities held had a remaining maturity of less than five years, which conforms to the desire of CBs to emphasize short- and intermediate-term investments.

Cash, reserves with the Federal Reserve, balances with depository institutions, and cash items in the process of collection represented about 13 percent of CB assets in 1980. The remaining assets were accounted for by bank premises, direct lease obligations, real estate, bankers' acceptances, and other assets.

CBs emphasize safety in their lending and investment activities. They emphasize local lending over investment in securities. They place a priority on serving the credit demands of regular depositors and the local community. They have historically preferred short- and intermediate-term, self-liquidating business and agricultural loans. Commercial banks are active in consumer installment credit loans. These loans are either short-term or intermediate-term, and they serve the needs of the depositors, local business, and the community. CBs make mortgage loans in their communities to serve the needs of their depositors, even though this activity conflicts with their desire to lend on a short-term basis. Commercial banks are usually agreeable to other lenders dominating residential mortgage lending. Commercial banks sometimes increase their residential lending activity temporarily, depending on alternative lending opportunities.

MORTGAGE-LENDING AUTHORITY

The approximately one-third of the CBs that are federally chartered hold about 60 percent of the assets held by all commercial banks. The *Comptroller of the Currency* regulates the lending activities of these national banks. Comptroller regulations, as given below, apply to these national banks.

State banking laws and regulations specify the mortgage-lending authority of state chartered commercial banks. A few states have parity clauses that allow a state charted CB to make any mortgage loans that a federally chartered CB can make. If the national banks have more favorable lending authority, which gives them a significant competitive advantage, state laws are usually changed within a few years to make the remaining state chartered banks competitive.

Percent of Assets.   The real estate loans of national banks are limited to either the unimpaired capital plus the unimpaired surplus of the bank or 100 percent of the time and savings deposits of the bank, whichever is greater. The law defines real estate loans as any loan secured by real estate, if the bank relies on the real estate as the primary security for the loans. FHA insured and FmHA insured or guaranteed mortgage loans are not considered real estate loans under this definition. VA insured or guaranteed mortgage loans are also exempt if the insurance or guarantee covers at least 20 percent of the loan. There are numerous other conditions under which a loan is not classified as a real estate loan as defined above. When all of these exceptions are taken into account, the typical commercial bank could legally hold well over 50 percent of its assets in loans secured by real estate.

Lending Area.   There are no restrictions on the lending area for national banks.

Government-Backed Loans.   National banks are allowed to make FHA insured and VA guaranteed loans on any terms specified by FHA and VA. They are allowed to make mortgage loans insured, guaranteed, or backed by the full faith and credit of the federal government or a state government on the terms specified by the insurer or guarantor.

Improved Residential and Nonresidential.   National banks are allowed to make conventional mortgage loans on properties improved with buildings for up to 90 percent of value and for up to 30 years. This applies to residential, commercial, industrial, and farm properties. The loan-to-value ratio may exceed 90 percent if the excess over 90 percent is fully guaranteed or is secured by a pledged savings account or other security.

Loans on one- to four-family residences or loans having loan-to-value ratios above 75 percent must be amortized. The payments may be calculated on amortization over a 30-year period, even though the loan is for a shorter term; this means there would be a balloon payment.

Unimproved Property.   National banks may make loans for up to two-thirds of value on properties that have no onsite or offsite improvements, that is, on raw land. If offsite improvements are present, such as streets and utilities, the maximum loan-to-value ratio is 75 percent.

Construction Loans.   National banks may make construction loans for up to 75 percent of value and for up to 60 months.

Nonconforming Loans.   National banks are allowed to make real estate loans not governed by specific regulations. These nonconforming mortgage loans are limited to up to ten percent of the amount that the bank is allowed to invest in real estate mortgage loans. National banks may therefore make loans for maturities in excess of 30 years and for higher than the specified loan-to-value ratios.

Other Mortgage Loans.   National banks are authorized to make leasehold mortgage loans if the term of the lease, including an option to renew, extends the term of lease for at least ten years beyond the maturity date of the loan. They may also make junior mortgage loans, and they may participate in large loans with other lenders. National banks may make alternate types of mortgage loans, such as graduated payment, variable-rate, and renegotiable-rate mortgage loans. Finally, they are allowed to make home improvement loans.

Regulation versus Lending Policies.   While national banks have liberal mortgage-lending powers, they usually follow more conservative policies than either S&Ls or MSBs. The average mortgage loan on an existing single-family home granted by commercial banks in 1980 had a loan-to-value ratio of approximately 67 percent and a maturity of less than 24 years.

Mortgage-Lending Activity

Figure 10–3 shows the mortgage holdings of commercial banks. At end of year 1980, $265 billion in mortgage debt was held. Over 60 percent of the dollar holdings was secured by one- to four-family residential properties, whereas about 5 percent was secured by multifamily properties. Over 31 percent was secured by commercial property, and over 3 percent by farm properties.

Commercial banks held 18.2 percent of all mortgage debt outstanding in 1980; they held 16.7 percent of the debt secured by one- to four-family residences and 9.0 percent of the debt secured by multifamily residences. In addition, CBs held 32.0 percent of the debt secured by commercial property and 9.2 percent of the debt secured by farms.

Commercial banks traditionally devote less than 20 percent of their total assets to mortgage lending. They emphasize construction loans and

FIGURE 10–3   Total Assets and Mortgage Holdings of Commercial Banks at the End of 1980

Type of Property	Dollars (in Billions)	Percent of Mortgage Loans
One- to Four-Family	$ 160.7	60.7
Multifamily	12.3	4.6
Commercial	82.7	31.3
Farm	8.9	3.4
Total Mortgage Loans	$ 264.6	100.0
Total Assets	$1,703.7	

SOURCE: Federal Reserve Bulletin, June 1981, pp. A17, A39. Percentages by authors.

mortgage loans on commercial properties and for one- to four-family residences. They appear to avoid lending on large residential properties. Small commercial banks devote a substantially higher percentage of their assets to mortgage loans than do large commercial banks. This is probably due to a greater relative demand for mortgage funds in areas outside major cities and to the commercial banks' desire to serve local needs. Commercial banks often originate loans to serve the needs of their community and, in turn, sell the loans in the secondary mortgage market.

Commercial banks, when compared with the other three main institutional lenders, rank second to savings and loan associations in mortgage debt held. They are the leading source of construction loans, particularly construction loans on multifamily and commercial properties. They are usually second to savings and loan associations as a source of construction loans for one- to four-family residences. They rank first as a holder of loans on commercial properties. They rank second as a holder of mortgage loans on one- to four-family residences and on farm properties. They rank fourth in terms of the dollar holdings of both FHA insured and VA guaranteed loans and loans on multifamily residences. Commercial banks are the leading source of home improvement loans and loans secured by mobile homes.

Commercial banks frequently provide short-term funds to other real estate lenders. They lend to mortgage companies, real estate investment trusts, savings and loan associations, and mutual savings banks. These short-term loans are used to assist the other lenders to temporarily finance a portion of their mortgage holdings. The other lenders repay these loans through sale of the mortgages in the secondary market or from internally generated funds.

CREDIT UNIONS

Credit unions are mutual organizations that accept deposits from and make loans to their members. The common bond for about three-fourths of credit unions is that all the members work for a single employer.

At the end of 1980, the approximately 23,000 credit unions in the United States held assets of nearly $72 billion. About 13,000 credit unions are federally chartered, and the remainder are state chartered. Federally chartered credit unions are regulated by the National Credit Union Administration. State chartered credit unions are regulated by the chartering state. The National Credit Union Share Insurance Fund insures the accounts in all federal credit unions plus approximately 4,000 state chartered credit unions.

Share deposits were the source of nearly 90 percent of the funds held by credit unions during 1980. Regular reserves, undivided earnings, and borrowings are the sources of the remaining funds. The major use of funds is loans to members, and, in 1980, loans to members represented approximately two-thirds of the assets for most credit unions. Other major asset holdings include cash, deposits, and government securities.

Credit unions emphasize consumer installment credit loans, and they make a wide range of short- and intermediate-term consumer installment credit loans. Automobile loans represented nearly 50 percent of their loan holdings during 1980. They are also significant sources of home improvement loans and mobile home loans. Federally chartered credit unions can make mobile home loans and home improvement loans for terms of up to 15 years.

Federally chartered credit unions have the authority to make FHA insured and VA guaranteed mortgage loans on the terms specified by the FHA and VA. Federal credit unions that have assets of $2 million or more also have the authority to make conventional home mortgage loans for a term of up to 30 years. The sales price or value of the real estate cannot exceed 150 percent of the median price of residential real estate in the local area. Uninsured conventional mortgage loans may have loan-to-value ratios of up to 90 percent. The loan-to-value ratio may be increased up to 95 percent if the excess over 90 percent is covered by private mortgage insurance. No more than 25 percent of a federal credit union's assets may be invested in mortgage loans secured by one- to four-unit dwellings.

While federal credit unions and some state chartered credit unions have the authority to make long-term residential mortgage loans, few credit unions make such loans. Credit unions held more than $4 billion in mortgage loans at the end of 1980.

SUMMARY

Savings and loan associations, mutual savings banks, commercial banks, and credit unions raise their funds from deposits. This places them in the position of raising their funds on a short-term basis, whereas mortgage loans are made on a long-term basis. They are faced with the problems of disintermediation and fluctuations in the cost of their funds. Even so, they hold from about 60 to 70 percent of all categories of conventional long-term mortgage loans except farm loans. They all are allowed to make FHA insured and VA guaranteed loans. Commercial banks and savings and loan associations are the dominant construction lenders. They all are significant sources of home improvement loans and mobile home financing.

Figure 10–4 summarizes selected characteristics of the depository institutions in the mortgage market. With the exception of credit unions, each of the deposit institutions is a large holder of mortgage

	Savings and Loan Associations	Mutual Savings Banks	Commercial Banks	Credit Unions
Total Assets, 1980	$630 billion	$172 billion	$1,704 billion	$72 billion
Total Mortgages, 1980	503 billion	100 billion	264 billion	4 billion
Percent of Assets Invested in Mortgages	80%	58% +	15% +	5% +
Type of Properties Financed (Loan Portfolio)				
One- to Four-Family	83%	65%	61%	99%
Multifamily	8%	17%	5%	—
Commercial	9%	17%	31%	—
Farm	—	—	3%	—
Construction Lending	Largest lender one- to four-family building	Relatively little construction lending	Largest construction lender—first for multifamily and commercial property	Little
Mortgage-Lending Authority, Conventional Uninsured				
One- to Four-Family	90%, 40 years	75–90%, 25–40 years	90%, 30 years	90%, 30 years
Multifamily	90%, 30 years	75–80%, 25–30 years	90%, 30 years	—
Commercial	90%, 30 years	75–80%, 25–30 years	90%, 30 years	—
Typical Lending Terms on Single-Family Homes				
Loan-to-Value Ratio	74%	68%	67%	—
Maturity	28 years	26 years	24 years	—

loans. Both savings and loans associations and mutual savings banks devote a high percentage of their funds to mortgages. Commercial banks and credit unions devote a relatively small percentage of their funds to mortgages; nevertheless commercial banks are the second largest holder of mortgages. They all emphasize one- to four-family mortgages within their mortgage portfolio. In addition, commercial banks emphasize mortgage loans on commercial properties.

KEY TERMS

Certificate of Deposit
Commercial Bank
Comptroller of the Currency
Credit Union

Federally Chartered
Money Market Certificate
Mutual Organization
Mutual Savings Bank
National Bank

Savings and Loan Association
Service Corporation
State Chartered
Stock Organization

QUESTIONS FOR REVIEW AND DISCUSSION

1. Distinguish between a certificate of deposit and a money market certificate.

2. Compare the mortgage-lending authority of S&Ls with their actual activity in relation to property types financed, loan-to-value ratios, and loan durations.

3. Explain why there are not more mutual savings banks in the South and West. Are MSBs more liberal than S&Ls in their mortgage-lending activities?

4. What are the top four types of asset investment of commercial banks, ranked by dollar amount? What percent of CB assets is typically invested in real estate loans? Does this percentage mean CBs are not important in real estate finance? Explain.

5. Discuss briefly the *modus operandi* of credit unions. Is this method of operation likely to change as a result of DIDMCA? Discuss.

6. Match the following key terms and definitions:

   a. Certificate of Deposit _____
   b. Money Market Certificate _____
   c. Service Corporation _____
   d. Stock Organization _____
   e. Mutual Organization _____

   1. Short-term savings instrument.
   2. Business organization wholly owned by one or more S&L.
   3. Owned by depositors who expect interest earnings on their deposits.
   4. Intermediate-term savings instrument.
   5. Owned and managed by professional executives.
   6. Owned by shareholders who expect a return or profit on their investment.
   7. Long-term savings instrument.

eleven

Private Nondepository Lenders

Private, nondepository lenders—life insurance companies, mortgage companies, pension funds, real estate investment trusts (REITs), finance companies, and individuals—taken together, account for about 30 percent of all mortgage loan originations, and they account for nearly 23 percent of all loan holdings, in dollar terms. Further, LICs rank third to S&Ls and CBs in total loan holdings, and mortgage companies rank third in loan originations. Mortgage companies, of course, sell many of these loans to other investors in the secondary mortgage market.

These nondepository lenders are taken up in the same sequence as listed above. The topics of discussion are: (1) organization and regulation, (2) sources of funds, (3) investment policies, (4) mortgage-lending authority, and (5) mortgage-lending activity. LICs and mortgage companies are discussed at some length. Pension funds, REITs, finance companies, individuals, and other private mortgage lenders are discussed only briefly. The objective, as in the previous two chapters, is to provide useful insights into the *modus operandi* of these lenders and the nature of our financial markets for actual or potential investor–borrowers.

By way of an overview of these lenders, mortgage companies are the third largest originators of mortgage loans. These loans, most of which are sold to other investors in the secondary mortgage market, serve to transfer funds from capital surplus areas to areas with relative shortages of mortgage funds. Pension funds hold large sums of money, and they promise to become a more important investor in the mortgage market. Real estate investment trusts were significant mortgage lenders at one time, but high short-term interest rates and loan defaults have sharply reduced their lending activity in recent years. Finance companies actively solicit second mortgage loans and have large mortgage loan holdings. Individuals are significant mortgage lenders, and their importance increases when mortgage funds are not readily available from institutional lenders. The essential characteristics concerning the activities of each of these mortgage lenders are summarized in Fig. 11–4 at the end of the chapter.

LIFE INSURANCE COMPANIES

Life insurance companies (LICs) were founded to offer financial protection for the beneficiaries of the insurance policies. The premiums for whole life insurance and endowment policies include a savings element or a reserve. Life insurance companies invest these funds. LICs are interested in the expected return and the safety of the investment, as eventually each policy must be paid off. Real estate mortgage lending is one of a number of ways in which life insurance companies invest their funds.

Over 1,800 life insurance companies operate in the United States. They held assets totaling $476 billion at the end of 1980. The large asset holdings of LICs make them an extremely important factor in our financial markets.

ORGANIZATION AND REGULATION

LICs are either stock or mutual companies. Over 90 percent of all life insurance companies are owned by stockholders; these are called stock companies. Mutual companies, however, account for approximately 60 percent of LIC assets, even though they account for less than 10 percent of all LICs.

Life insurance companies are state chartered. Even though the federal government regulates life insurance companies in matters of national concern, the states exercise the principal regulatory control over them. Each must follow the regulations of the state in which it is chartered. And if it does business in another state, the investment of policy reserves generated in the other state are also governed by the regulations of that state. For example, some states require that a specified percentage of the policy reserves generated in a state must be invested within that state.

SOURCES OF FUNDS

Policy reserves, including those of pension funds administered by life insurance companies, represent over 80 percent of the funds held by LICs. *Policy reserves* are monies set aside and invested to meet future or contingent liabilities, such as funds to pay off on policies. Other sources of funds include accumulated policy dividends, reserves for future dividends, mandatory reserves, and surplus funds. The principal sources of funds available for investment in a given year are net-premium income, pension fund contributions, loan repayments, maturing securities, and investment income. Additional funds may be generated by selling existing investment holdings.

INVESTMENT POLICIES

The contractual obligations of LICs are primarily long term in nature; thus long-term investments are emphasized. LICs greatly differ from depository institutions in this respect. As the relative rates of return on the various investment alternatives vary, life insurance companies vary the composition of their investment portfolios. For example, life insurance companies decreased their holdings of one to four-family mortgage loans during the late 1960s and the 1970s, whereas they increased their holdings of commercial mortgage loans and corporate bonds. This policy is related to the economics of lending or investing; overhead per dollar of investment is less on large investments.

Mortgage loans were the second most important investment area for LICs, and they accounted for over 27 percent of LIC assets at the end of 1980. Corporate bonds represented the most important investment area, with over 40 percent of assets at the end of 1980. Corporate stock accounted for nearly an additional 10 percent of assets. Government securities represented less than 5 percent of assets, and policy loans represented over 8 percent of assets. Life insurance companies invested approximately 3 percent of assets in real estate. The remaining 7 percent of assets represented cash, due and deferred premiums, due and accrued income, real estate joint ventures, and other assets.

Policy loans are loans to policyholders under the terms of the insurance policy. The level of policy loans is determined by the wishes of the policyholders rather than by any decisions of LIC executives. Fluctuations in the demand for policy loans creates uncertainty and increases the liquidity needs of life insurance companies.

MORTGAGE-LENDING AUTHORITY

The mortgage-lending authority of life insurance companies is specified by state law and regulations of both the states in which they are chartered and the states in which they are doing business. For example, if a company is chartered in New York and is doing business in Pennsylvania, New York law would apply to the LIC's overall operation, whereas Pennsylvania law would govern the investment of reserves generated from the sales of policies in Pennsylvania. The mortgage-lending authority of life insurance companies varies from state to state; thus these comments on regulations are necessarily generalized.

Percent of Assets. California, Pennsylvania, Texas, and Ohio have no upper limit on the percentage of assets that LICs can invest in conventional mortgage loans. More conservative states, such as New York and Illinois, do have an upper limit on the percent of assets that can be invested in mortgage loans, namely 50 percent in New York and 60 percent in Illinois. These limits often exclude government guaranteed or insured mortgage loans. For example, in New York there is no limit on VA guaranteed mortgage loans that may be held. In addition, 10 percent of assets can be invested in FHA insured loans. In summary, then, LICs may invest from 50 to 100 percent of their assets in real estate loans.

Lending Area. LICs are generally allowed to lend anywhere in the United States, and in some cases they are also allowed to lend in Canada.

Government-Backed Loans. As mentioned, LICs are allowed to make government guaranteed or insured loans (for example, FHA insured, VA guaranteed, and state insured or guaranteed) on the terms specified by the federal or state government agency sponsoring the insurance or guarantee.

One- to Four-Family Residences. Life insurance companies are generally allowed to make conventional mortgage loans on one- to four-family residences for up to 75 to 80 percent of value and for up to 30 years. In New York, life insurance companies may lend up to 90 percent of the value for up to 40 years. However, no more than 10 percent of these assets may be invested in mortgage loans involving loan-to-value ratios in excess of 75 percent, unless the loans are guaranteed.

Improved Multifamily and Nonresidential. Life insurance companies are typically limited to 75 to 80 percent loan-to-value ratios and maturities of up to 30 years on mortgage loans on multifamily and nonresidential properties.

Basket or Leeway Clause. The regulations in a number of states contain a *basket* or *leeway clause* that allows life insurance companies to invest a small portion of their funds, such as 3 or 4 percent, without regard to regulations. A portion of these "unrestricted" funds are often used to make income or equity participation loans with high loan-to-value ratios or to engage in real estate joint ventures.

Other Mortgage Loans. Life insurance companies are allowed to make leasehold mortgage loans. They are also allowed to participate in loans with other lenders. And in some states they are allowed to make construction loans.

Regulations versus Lending Policies. Regulations specify the permissible limits of loans and terms. At the same time, the lending policies of the individual life insurance companies may be more restrictive and may actually be used to determine the actual loans and terms granted. LICs are not required to make mortgage loans up to the limits of the regulations governing them.

MORTGAGE-LENDING ACTIVITY

Life insurance companies prefer to make large multifamily and commercial mortgage loans. These loans generally have higher interest rates and lower loan servicing costs, which make them more profitable than mortgage loans on one- to four-family residences. These loans also sometimes involve equity or income participations, which promise an additional return. Life insurance companies substantially decreased their holdings of one- to four-family mortgages from 1965 through 1978.

Figure 11–1 shows the mortgage holdings of life insurance companies at the end of 1980. Over 61 percent of their dollar mortgage holdings was secured by commercial properties. Over 13 percent was secured by one- to four-family residences, and 15 percent was secured by multifamily residences. An additional 10 percent was secured by farm properties.

Life insurance companies held 9 percent of all mortgage debt outstanding in 1980. They held 31.3 percent of commercial mortgage debt but only 1.9 percent of one- to four-family residential mortgage debt. And they held 14.3 percent of the mortgage debt secured by multifamily residences and 13.3 percent of that secured by farms.

Life insurance companies employ a number of methods to acquire mortgage loans. They originate loans through their home office and/or branch offices. Another method is through loan correspondents. A *loan correspondent* is a party that negotiates mortgage loans for lenders or investors. Mortgage bankers and mortgage brokers are loan correspond-

FIGURE 11–1   Total Assets and Mortgage Holdings of Life Insurance Companies at the End of 1980

Type of Property	Dollars (in Billions)	Percent of Mortgage Loans
One- to Four-Family	$ 17.9	13.7
Multifamily	19.6	15.0
Commercial	80.8	61.6
Farm	12.8	9.7
Total Mortgage Loans	$131.1	100.1[1]
Total Assets	$476.2	

[1]Due to rounding error.

SOURCE: Federal Reserve Bulletin, June 1981, pp. A27, A39. Percentages by authors.

ents; they actively seek a correspondent relationship with life insurance companies and other lenders, because of the great importance of the contact or relationship.

Compared with the three other major institutional lenders (S&Ls, CBs, and MSBs), life insurance companies rank third in total mortgage holdings. Life insurance companies rank first in holdings of farm mortgages. They rank second in the holdings of both multifamily mortgages and commercial mortgages. And they rank a distant fourth in holdings of one- to four-family mortgage loans.

MORTGAGE COMPANIES

Mortgage companies emphasize mortgage banking activities and are often called mortgage bankers. *Mortgage bankers* originate mortgage loans and sell them to other parties, usually retaining the servicing of the loans. *Loan origination* refers to loan underwriting and advancing the funds to the borrower. Mortgage brokers differ in that they only bring the borrower and lender together for a fee but do not originate loans in their own name. Also, brokers do not service existing loans.

Some mortgage companies engage in both mortgage brokerage and banking, along with sideline activities such as real estate brokerage, property management, insurance sales, and real estate joint ventures. The primary source of revenue from the mortgage banking portion of the business is servicing fees.

Mortgage companies are important sources of mortgage loans. They are the dominant originators of FHA insured and VA guaranteed loans. Mortgage companies make the mortgage market more efficient by assisting in transferring funds from areas that have capital surpluses to those having capital shortages.

There are in excess of 2,000 mortgage companies in the United States, but many of them are small, closely-held firms. A number of mortgage companies have merged with or have been purchased by financial institutions, such as commercial banks and S&L service companies, which operate them as subsidiaries. Mortgage companies had assets of approximately $16 billion at the end of 1979.[1] The largest 5 percent of the mortgage companies do about 50 percent of the mortgage banking business.

ORGANIZATION AND REGULATION

Mortgage companies are state chartered corporations. They are regulated by the states, but they have much less restrictive regulations than the

---

[1]Schuyler E. Schell, "Capital Adequacy and the Mortgage Banker," *Mortgage Banker,* 41, no. 1 (October 1980), 41.

large institutional lenders. This is because they do not have a fiduciary relationship to depositors, policyholders, or pensioners.

Since they originate FHA insured and VA guaranteed mortgage loans and sell loans to quasi-government agencies such as FNMA and FHLMC, mortgage companies must conform to the regulations of these organizations. For example, the FHA requires originators to have a net worth of at least $100,000. Also the loans they make must conform to the loan restrictions of the purchasers if they are to be sold in the secondary market. This is the principal restriction on the lending activities of mortgage companies.

SOURCES OF FUNDS

The owner's equity investment is the source of over ten percent of the funds employed by mortgage companies. Most of the remainder of the funds is borrowed. Mortgage warehouse loans from commercial banks are a major source of borrowed funds. A *mortgage warehouse loan* is secured by a specified pool of mortgage loans from the mortgage company's inventory. Unsecured loans from commercial banks are another major source of funds. The largest mortgage companies also issue commercial paper and collateral trust notes. The commercial paper is unsecured, and the collateral trust notes are secured by pools of mortgage loans. Collateral trust notes are sold to the general investing public and provide an alternative to borrowing from commercial banks.

INVESTMENT POLICIES

If we ignore sideline activities, almost all of the assets of mortgage companies are invested in mortgage loans. Over 75 percent of their loan holdings represents an inventory of long-term mortgage loans that they intend to sell to other investors. Their remaining loan holdings represent construction loans and land loans. Mortgage companies invest in relatively short-term loans for at least three reasons. One, the interest rates are high and they are profitable loans in their own right. Second, these loans allow mortgage companies to originate the long-term loans that replace the construction loans and land loans when the projects are completed. Loan origination fees are often realized in both cases. Third, mortgage companies, in limiting themselves to short-term loans, turn over their portfolios more often and thereby maintain a higher level of activity; thus they don't tie up their capital.

MORTGAGE LOAN ACTIVITY

There are no significant limitations on the lending authority of mortgage companies. Mortgage companies originate long-term loans with

FIGURE 11–2 Mortgage Holdings of Mortgage Companies at the End of 1980

Long-Term Loans	Dollars (in Billions)	Percent of Mortgage Loans
One- to Four-Family	$4.4	47.8
Multifamily	1.4	15.2
Commercial and Farm	1.0	10.9
Construction Loans	2.4	26.1
		100.0
Total Loans	$9.2	

SOURCE: *Mortgage Banking,* October 1981, p. 135.

the intention of selling them to other investors. They must make loans that have a high potential for resale. So they originate loans that meet the investment desires or needs of investors in the secondary mortgage market.

Figure 11–2 shows the mortgage holdings of the approximately 700 members of the Mortgage Bankers Association of America at the end of 1980. Most of the $6.8 billion of long-term mortgages are held for resale, whereas some of the $2.4 billion of construction and some land loans are held until maturity.

The mortgage holdings of mortgage companies substantially understate their importance in the mortgage market. The volume of mortgage loan originations provides a better indication of their significance. Mortgage companies usually rank third after savings and loan associations and commercial banks as originators of both total mortgage loans and those on one- to four-family residences. (Refer back to Fig. 9–6 for details.) Occasionally, such as in 1979 and 1980, they rank second in the origination of mortgage loans on one- to four-family residences. They are the dominant originators of FHA insured and VA guaranteed loans, with about 75 percent of the loan activity. Mortgage companies also originate over $10 billion in conventional mortgage loans annually. Finally, mortgage companies are the third most important source of construction loans.

At one time mortgage companies sold most of their loans to life insurance companies, mutual savings banks, and other institutional investors. In recent years mortgage companies have sold about 75 percent of their originations of FHA insured and VA guaranteed in the form of GNMA mortgage-backed securities. The mortgage companies assemble a pool of mortgages and issue securities backed by the pool of mortgages, and the securities are guaranteed by GNMA. Mortgage companies also continue to sell substantial amounts of mortgage loans to private financial institutions, the Federal National Mortgage Association, and the Federal Home Loan Mortgage Corporation. Mortgage companies are often the local loan correspondent for one or more life insurance companies and sometimes for mutual savings banks.

The principal source of income for mortgage companies in addition to origination fees is servicing fees. *Servicing* involves collection of loan payments, bookkeeping, preparation of tax and insurance records, follow-up on delinquent loans, and a number of other duties. The servicing fee generally ranges from one-quarter to one-half of one percent of the unpaid balance of the mortage loan. Mortgage companies were servicing over $260 billion of mortgage loans at the end of 1979. This included about one-quarter of the dollar volume of all one- to four-family residence mortgage loans. Mortgage companies also realize profits and sometimes losses from the sale of mortgages.

PENSION FUNDS

The purpose of pension funds is to act as a trustee for funds accumulated during the employment years of individuals, in order to provide those individuals with retirement income. There are four types of pension funds: (1) insured, (2) noninsured, (3) state and local government, and (4) federal government. Insured pension reserves are managed by life insurance companies, which is why they are called insured. Noninsured pension funds are called trusteed pension funds, and the trustee is often a commercial bank. Insured and noninsured funds are also termed private pension funds.

The two sources of funds for pension funds are retirement contributions from individuals and employers and investment income. The assets of pension funds exceeded $700 billion at the end of 1980. Figure 11–3 shows the total assets of the various types of pension funds, excluding OASI (Social Security) at that time. The assets of insured pension funds are included in the assets of life insurance companies. And except for separate accounts, their funds are invested the same as those of life insurance companies. The assets of U.S. government retirement funds are invested in federal securities. So our main interest is in private non-

FIGURE 11–3   Assets of Private and Public Pension Funds, Book Value at the End of 1980

	Dollars (in Billions)	Percent of Total
Insured Pension Funds	$164.6	22.6
Private Noninsured Pension Funds	286.1	39.2
State and Local Government Retirement Funds	202.7	27.8
U.S. Government Retirement Funds	76.4	10.5
Total	$729.8	100.1[1]

[1]Total does not equal 100 percent due to rounding error.

SOURCE: SEC Monthly Statistical Review, September 1981, p. 14. Percentages by authors.

insured pension funds and in state and local government retirement funds.

Noninsured pension funds are state chartered and are managed by trustees. Commercial banks are the trustees for most pension funds; the remainder are managed by investment counselors or are self-administered. Pension fund investments are governed by state and federal law and the prudent man rule. State and local government retirement plans are typically regulated by state law and the prudent man rule. The *prudent man rule* is that any investment administrator or trustee must handle funds entrusted to him or her in the same rational, careful manner that a prudent man would exercise in investing his own monies.

Both noninsured private pension funds and state and local government retirement funds invest over 75 percent of their assets in stocks and corporate bonds. Both also invest in mortgage loans. At the end of 1980 noninsured private pension funds held approximately $4 billion of mortgage loans, which represented somewhat over 1 percent of their assets. About one-half of the total represents commercial mortgages. Over one-third of the total represented one- to four-family mortgages, and less than one-fifth were multifamily mortgages. At the end of 1980, state and local government retirement funds held approximately $11 billion in mortgage loans, which represented about 5 percent of their assets. One- to four-family home mortgages, commercial mortgages, and multifamily mortgages each represented roughly one-third of the total.

Pension funds generally invest in FHA insured, VA guaranteed, and large mortgage loans. State and local government retirement funds generally limit their mortgage lending to their particular state. In some states they invest in state guaranteed mortgage loans. And some states have made an effort to require some retirement funds to be invested in conventional home mortgage loans. Some noninsured private pension funds, particularly those related to the building trades, have attempted to make funds available for conventional home mortgage loans in order to stimulate home construction.

Pension funds also engage in sale and leaseback financing and some direct ownership of real estate. They have the asset potential to substantially increase their mortgage holdings. However, this same potential was often mentioned throughout the 1970s, but no dramatic increase in the percentage of assets invested in mortgage loans came about. Pension funds have been important purchasers of GNMA mortgage-backed securities, however. Mortgage-backed securities may be the most promising way to attract more pension fund money into the mortgage market.

REAL ESTATE INVESTMENT TRUSTS

In 1960 real estate investment trusts were given a tax status similar to that of mutual funds investing in corporate securities. A qualifying

REIT is not taxed on the earnings that it distributes to its shareholders or certificate holders. The basic requirements for the special tax status are as follows:

1. It must be organized under a state charter as a corporation, trust, or association and be managed by one or more trustees or directors. And the shares or certificates of beneficial interest must be transferable.

2. Five or fewer investors cannot own in excess of 50 percent of the trust, and the trust must have at least 100 investors.

3. The trust cannot hold property for sale to customers in the ordinary course of business. Income from the sale of securities held for less than one year and from the sale of real property or mortgages held for less than four years must represent less than 30 percent of the trust's income.

4. At least 95 percent of its income must be derived from dividends, interest, rentals on real property, and the gain on the sale of stock, securities, mortgages, or real property. And at least 75 percent of its income must be generated from rents, interest, dividends from other REITs, and gains on the sale of real property including mortgages.

5. The trust must distribute at least 90 percent of its earnings.

There are no restrictions on the types of mortgage loans that they are allowed to make.

REITs were founded to allow small investors to participate in large real estate investments. There are three types of REITs: equity, mortgage, and mixed or hybrid. Equity REITs invest in the ownership of real estate. Mortgage REITs invest in mortgage loans. Mixed REITs invest in both real estate equity interest and mortgage loans. REITs grew from about $1 billion in assets in 1968 to over $20 billion in assets in 1973. In 1973 they held about $16 billion in mortgage loans. They were major sources of construction loans and multifamily residential loans.

Mortgage REITs raise their funds through the sale of shares or certificates and by borrowing. They borrow from commercial banks and sell commercial paper. In the past, they borrowed primarily on a short-term basis and lent on an intermediate- or long-term basis. In 1973 and 1974, short-term interest rates rose sharply and made it less profitable or even unprofitable to borrow short term and lend long term. Then in 1974 and 1975, many borrowers defaulted on loans made by REITs. As a result, a number of REITs were forced into voluntary reorganization. As a group, REITs halted mortgage-lending activities. Those REITs that continued to lend emphasized construction loans. If short-term interest rates fall below long-term interest rates, REITs may regain their importance in the mortgage market.

REITs held somewhat over $4 billion in mortgage loans at the end of 1980. Commercial mortgages represented over one-half of the total. Multifamily mortgages accounted for about one-third, and one- to four-family home mortgages accounted for the remainder.

FINANCE COMPANIES

The term *finance companies* includes sales finance companies, consumer finance companies, and commercial finance companies. Finance companies had over $150 billion in assets at the end of 1980. About 15 percent of their funds is raised from equity. They raise about one-half of the remainder from short-term debt, primarily commercial paper. The remainder of their funds are provided by long-term debt and lease financing. They invest about 90 percent of their funds in consumer and business loans.

At the end of 1980 finance companies held nearly $13 billion in mortgage loans. Mortgage loans on one- to four-family residences represented over 68 percent of the total. Multifamily mortgages accounted for over 12 percent, and commercial mortgages represented the remainder. Finance companies are also important sources of mobile home financing.

Consumer finance companies actively solicit applications for second mortgage loans. They accept a second mortgage on a home as security for loans used for a variety of purposes. They usually charge higher interest rates than commercial banks and other institutional lenders, but they often grant loans that do not meet the standards of other lenders. Sales finance companies are major sources of mobile home financing. And commercial finance companies occasionally grant mortgage loans.

INDIVIDUALS

Individuals are a significant source of real estate financing, holding mortgage loans totaling about $125 billion at the end of 1980. They are important sources of all types of mortgage loans, particularly second mortgages. One- to four-family residence mortgages represent over one-half of the total. They are the second largest grantor of farm mortgage loans, and farm mortgage loans represent about one-quarter of individuals' total mortgage holdings. Individuals also hold a large dollar volume of multifamily mortgages and commercial mortgages.

Individuals, as lenders, fall into three major categories. They are sellers, relatives and associates, and wealthy individuals. Except in the case of wealthy individuals, the primary motivation for mortgage lending by individuals is either to bring about the sale of their property or to assist a relative or an associate to purchase a property.

A buyer should inquire whether or not the seller of the property will assist in the financing. Often the seller is willing to take back a second mortgage to bring about the sale. When mortgage funds are not available from institutional lenders, the seller may be forced to sell on a land contract basis or to take back a first purchase money mortgage in order to bring about the sale. On occasion the seller may prefer to sell on an installment basis because of tax advantages. Seller financing to bring about the sale of the property accounts for the largest portion of mortgage lending by individuals.

Relatives, friends, and employers may be willing to assist in the financing of the purchase of real estate, particularly homes. Wealthy individuals sometimes engage in mortgage lending because it offers a better rate of return than other investment alternatives of equal risk.

With the exception of usury laws, there are no restrictions on the lending authority of individuals. Individual lenders may offer either lower or higher interest rates than institutional lenders. Individuals often prefer shorter maturities than institutional lenders.

OTHER PRIVATE MORTGAGE LENDERS

Numerous other private organizations engage in the extension of credit to finance real estate either occasionally or on a regular basis. Corporations and other organizations that own real property sometimes take back purchase money mortgages to assist in the sale of the property. Other organizations such as property and casualty insurance companies, foundations, endowment funds, and personal trusts hold a large amount of assets, a small percentage of which is invested in mortgages.

Title insurance companies or their subsidiaries sometimes engage in mortgage lending. Private mortgage insurance companies or their subsidiaries sometimes grant mortgage loans and assist other lenders to form pools of mortgages and issue mortgage-backed securities. Real estate syndicates are significant sources of sale and leaseback financing and often take back purchase money mortgages to assist in the sale of their property.

SUMMARY

Figure 11–4 shows selected characteristics of private nondeposit institutions in the mortgage market. Life insurance companies and pension funds raise their funds through contractual arrangements, and they can forecast their cost of funds and liquidity requirements with a relatively high degree of accuracy. Long-term investments such as mortgage loans are well suited to their investment needs. REITs, finance companies, and mortgage companies obtain a large portion of their funds from

FIGURE 11–4 Selected Characteristics of Private Nondepository Institutions in the Mortgage Market

(in billions)

	Life Insurance Companies	Mortgage Companies	Pension Funds	REITs	Finance Companies
Main Source of Funds	Policy Reserves and Pension Funds	Debt	Deductions and Contributions	Equity and Debt	Debt
Total Mortgages, 1980	$131	$9	$15	$4	$13
Percent of Assets Invested in Mortgages	25% +	80% +	3%	30% +	9%
Type of Property (Loan Portfolio)					
One- to Four-Family	14%	80%	35%	14%	77%
Multifamily	16%	8%	25%	33%	10%
Commercial	60%	11%	40%	53%	13%
Farm	10%	1%	—	—	—
Construction Lending	Some	Substantial	Little	Significant	Little
Mortgage-Lending Authority Conventional Uninsured					
One- to Four-Family	75–90%, 30–40 yrs.	No	Prudent Man	No	No
Multifamily	75–80%, 30 yrs.	Restrictions		Restrictions	Restrictions
Commercial	75–80%, 30 yrs.				

debt, particularly short-term debt. Fluctuations in the cost of short-term credit cause them substantial problems.

While the deposit institutions emphasize lending on one- to four-family residences, life insurance companies, pension funds, and REITs do not. The latter emphasize commercial lending, which in the case of REITs includes construction lending. Mortgage companies emphasize the origination of mortgages on one- to four-family residences, but their holdings of such loans represent an inventory and not long-term investments. Finance companies emphasize second mortgage loans on one- to four-family residences, but usually the proceeds are not used to assist in the purchase of the home. None of these institutions emphasize long-term investments in first mortgages on homes.

Life insurance companies and pension funds emphasize commercial mortgages. Mortgage companies and REITs emphasize construction lending. Mortgage companies employ over 80 percent of their funds in mortgage lending. REITs invested almost as high a percentage before the large loan defaults in 1974 and 1975. At that time they became property owners through foreclosure actions.

Life insurance companies and pension funds have limitations on their mortgage-lending authority, but the other institutions and individuals are unrestricted. Individuals and other property owners may be willing to take back a purchase money mortgage to assist in the sale of their property.

KEY TERMS

Basket or Leeway Clause

Finance Company

Life Insurance Company

Loan Correspondent

Loan Origination

Mortgage Banker

Mortgage Broker

Mortgage Company

Mortgage Warehouse Loan

Noninsured Pension Fund

Policy Loan

Policy Reserves

Prudent Man Rule

Real Estate Investment
   Trust (REIT)

Servicing

State and Local
   Government Retirement
   Funds

QUESTIONS FOR REVIEW AND DISCUSSION

1. How are life insurance companies regulated? Does the regulation affect the manner in which LICs invest their assets?

2. What is the principal source of funds of life insurance companies? Does this source influence the investment policies of LICs? Explain.

3. What is a basket clause? What is its significance?

4. LICs tend to invest more heavily in large projects or to make large loans. Is there any rationale for this type of activity? Explain.

5. What is a loan correspondent? Explain the function of a correspondent.

6. What is a mortgage company? Explain the function and operation of a mortgage company.

7. Mortgage companies are less subject to regulation than most other lenders. Why? Are there any restrictions on the lending activities of mortgage companies? Explain.

8. Are pension funds significant investors in mortgage loans? Might they be? Discuss.

9. What are the three basic types of REITs? Are REITs relatively significant as mortgage lenders? Might they be? Discuss.

10. What are the categories of individuals who invest in mortgage loans? Are they similar in their motivations and manner of operation? Explain.

11. Match the following key terms and definitions:

    a. Loan
       Correspondent   _____

    b. Mortgage Warehouse
       Loan   _____

    1. A provision setting restrictions aside and allowing leeway in investing funds.

c. Basket Clause   _____

d. Prudent Man
   Rule   _____

e. Servicing   _____

f. Policy Reserves   _____

2. Monies set aside and invested to meet contingent liabilities.

3. A typical or *modus operandi* loan.

4. Someone that negotiates mortgage loans for lender-investors.

5. Collecting payments, maintaining records, follow-up on delinquent payments, and generally looking after a loan.

6. Handle and invest funds in a careful and rational manner.

7. A loan secured by a specific group of mortgages.

twelve

Government and Related Agencies

Government, government agencies, and government sponsored agencies play an important role in the mortgage market. The Federal Reserve System acts to control the money supply and the availability of credit. The Federal Deposit Insurance Corporation, FSLIC, and others insure the accounts of depositors at financial institutions. The Federal Home Loan Banks provide liquidity for savings and loans associations, which allows them to keep a high percentage of their assets invested in mortgage loans on a continuing basis. The U.S. Department of Housing and Urban Development and others subsidize low-income renters and homeowners. The Federal National Mortgage Association (FNMA), the Government National Mortgage Association (GNMA), the Federal Home Loan Mortgage Corporation (FHLMC), and others purchase existing mortgages in the secondary mortgage market. Federal Land Bank associations, the Farmers Home Administration, state housing finance agencies, and other organizations originate and sometimes provide monies for mortgage loans. The Veterans Administration, the Federal Housing Administration, and other agencies insure or guarantee mortgage loans to enable borrowers to finance the purchase of homes with low down-payment mortgage loans.

Our intent here is to look at and discuss these agencies and their roles and/or activities in the primary mortgage market. Our discussion proceeds in the following order:

1. Federal Reserve System
2. Deposit Insurance
3. Federal Home Loan Bank System
4. Department of Housing and Urban Development
5. Farmers Home Administration and Federal Land Banks (FmHA and FLBs)
6. Federally Related Secondary Market Institutions (FNMA, GNMA, and FHLMC)
7. Veterans Administration
8. Federal Housing Administration
9. State and Local Governments and HFAs

The discussion may seem disjointed at times because of the variety of agencies and programs. Even so, our coverage of real estate finance would be less than complete without mention of each of these agencies and programs.

FEDERAL RESERVE SYSTEM

The federal government promotes conditions favorable to high employment, price stability, and economic growth through both fiscal and monetary policy. *Fiscal policy* involves the use and control of taxation and government expenditures to achieve economic goals. *Monetary policy* involves the use and control of the currency or the money supply and interest rates to reach these goals. The Federal Reserve System is the main federal agency that implements monetary policy. Our discussion is limited to the Federal Reserve System and the monetary policy because of the close and direct effects they have on real estate financing.

ORGANIZATION

The Board of Governors of the Federal Reserve System is responsible for the coordination of the system. The United States is divided into 12 districts, each of which is served by a Federal Reserve Bank. All national banks and many state chartered banks are members of the Federal Reserve System. The Board of Governors regulates the money supply through control of required reserve ratios for member banks. Member banks operate up to the limit of their reserves and often borrow funds from a Federal Reserve Bank to maintain required reserve ratios.

The DIDMC Act of 1980 provides for the phasing-in of reserve requirements on all transaction accounts and nonpersonal time and savings accounts at all depository institutions. DIDMC also grants all these institutions the authority to obtain loans from a Federal Reserve Bank in order to meet these reserve requirements. *Transaction accounts* are any checking account-like arrangement, such as NOW accounts, automatic transfer accounts, and share draft accounts.

The Federal Reserve Banks derive about two-thirds of their funds from the issuance of Federal Reserve notes; most of the remainder comes from deposits made by financial institutions. Federal Reserve notes are the currency that individuals use in their everyday cash transactions, that is, dollar bills, and so forth. U.S. government and federal agency securities represent about 80 percent of the asset holdings of Federal Reserve Banks.

GENERAL CONTROLS

The Federal Reserve directly controls the required reserve ratios in our financial system. The Federal can also influence the level of reserves by indirect methods or activities. When financial institutions have excess reserves, they are in a position to increase the availability of credit, which tends to decrease interest rates and to increase the availability of money for mortgage loans. If the financial institutions have a shortage of reserves, they restrict their lending activity, interest rates tend to rise, and mortgage loans become more difficult to obtain.

When actual reserves exceed required reserves, they are called *excess reserves*. A shortage of reserves occurs when required reserves exceed the level of reserves held. Financial institutions may borrow reserves from Federal Reserve Banks to maintain required reserve levels, and they may usually pay back these advances or loans within a relatively short period of time. Therefore, many experts watch the level of free reserves and excess reserves to determine whether or not the Federal Reserve is trying to increase or decrease the availability of credit.

The Federal Reserve employs three basic tools to control reserves and, in turn, the availability of credit in the economy. These tools are open market operations, changes in the discount rate, and changes in required reserve ratios.

Open Market Operations. The Federal Reserve may purchase or sell government securities in the financial markets, which is termed *open market operations.* Purchases act to create excess reserves in financial institutions, which, in turn, increase the availability of credit. The sales of government securities by the Federal Reserve System absorb assets of financial institutions and lead to a shortage or deficiency of reserves, which, in turn, decreases the availability of credit in the economy.

The Discount Rate. A commercial bank or other depository institution having a deficiency in reserves may borrow reserves from its district Federal Reserve Bank. The *discount rate* is the rate charged by a Federal Reserve Bank for such borrowings. If the discount rate is increased relative to market interest rates, institutions tend to borrow less. The discount rate therefore represents a potential cost of funds to financial institutions, and it serves as a reference point to them in determining interest rates borrowers are charged. An increase in the discount rate tends to cause an increase in the interest rates charged on all types of loans, including mortgage loans. If the discount rate equals or exceeds rates obtainable from borrowers, financial institutions cut back on borrowing from Federal Reserve Banks. In turn, credit availability is limited.

Reserve Requirements. The Federal Reserve Board may change the required reserve ratios to create either an excess or deficiency of reserves. Increasing required reserve ratios leads to a deficiency in reserves of financial institutions, meaning availability of credit is restricted. Lowering reserve ratios leads to excess reserves for financial institutions and increased credit availability.

SELECTIVE CREDIT CONTROLS

The Board of Governors of the Federal Reserve System has the authority, subject to congressional approval, to impose credit controls on various types of loans. This power enables the Federal to direct the use of available credit. For example, the Federal has consistently limited the loan-to-value ratio for loans used to purchase stocks and convertible bonds. The Board only imposed credit controls on mortgage loans during the Korean War era; it seems unlikely that such controls will be imposed on mortgage loans in the near future.

DEPOSIT INSURANCE

Deposit insurance protects savers against loss on monies placed with financial institutions up to a specified dollar amount. Deposit insurance therefore encourages individuals to deposit their savings in commercial banks, mutual savings banks, savings and loan associations, and credit unions. To the extent that deposit insurance leads to larger deposits in such institutions, the availability of mortgage loans is increased.

Both federal and state agencies or sponsored agencies insure accounts in depository institutions. The federally related organizations are the Federal Deposit Insurance Corporation (FDIC), the Federal Savings and Loan Insurance Corporation (FSLIC), and the National Credit

Union Share Insurance Fund (NCUSIF). These organizations insure the vast majority of accounts for up to $100,000. The FDIC insures the accounts of all national banks, most state chartered commercial banks, and a majority of mutual savings banks. The FSLIC insures the accounts of all federally chartered savings and loan associations, most state chartered savings and loans, and a number of mutual savings banks. The NCUSIF insures the share accounts in all federally chartered credit unions and about 4,000 state chartered credit unions.

FEDERAL HOME LOAN BANK SYSTEM

The Federal Home Loan Bank System was founded in 1932 to provide credit to thrift institutions, to establish a program of deposit insurance, and to regulate member institutions.

ORGANIZATION

The Federal Home Loan Banks Board (FHLBB) is responsible for the coordination of the Federal Home Loan Bank System (FHLBS). The FHLBS is comprised of Federal Home Loan Banks, the Federal Savings and Loan Insurance Corporation (FSLIC), the Federal Home Loan Mortgage Corporation (FHLMC), and member institutions. The United States is divided into 12 districts, each of which contains a Federal Home Loan Bank. FSLIC provides insurance for deposit accounts and imposes reserve requirements on member institutions. FHLMC provides a secondary market for mortgage loans, which is discussed later in this chapter. All federally chartered savings and loan associations are required to be members of the FHLBS. In addition, over 80 percent of state chartered savings and loans, about 100 mutual savings banks, and a few insurance companies belong to the FHLBS.

ACTIVITIES OF FEDERAL HOME LOAN BANKS

A member of the FHLBS may borrow an amount up to 50 percent of its savings deposits from a Federal Home Loan Bank. While loans from a Federal Reserve Bank are considered loans of last resort, it is common for an S&L to obtain advances from a Federal Home Loan Bank for an extended period of time. Member institutions' borrowings from Federal Home Loan Banks totaled over $47 billion at the end of 1980.

The principal activity of the Federal Home Loan Banks is to provide liquidity to member institutions, which are primarily savings and loan associations. When savings and loans experience a shortage of funds, they increase their borrowings from the Federal Home Loan Banks. This allows them to continue to originate mortgage loans. When

S&Ls experience an inflow of funds, they repay a portion of the advances from the Federal Home Loan Banks.

The Federal Home Loan Banks raise funds from reserve deposits, capital stock, retained earnings, short-term loans, and consolidated debt offerings. The majority of the funds are raised by issuing consolidated debt securities, primarily bonds, in the capital market. The Federal Home Loan Banks raise the interest rates on advances to member institutions as their costs rise, which, in turn, forces savings and loan associations to raise the interest rates charged on mortgage loans. Demand for loans drops as interest rates go higher. Alternatively, decreasing costs lead to lower interest rates and greater demand for loans.

DEPARTMENT OF HOUSING AND URBAN DEVELOPMENT

The department of Housing and Urban Development (HUD) has a multi-billion dollar annual budget, which it uses to provide adequate housing for low- and moderate-income households and to improve the surrounding environment. About one-half of its budget is used to make housing payments and to subsidize public housing. About one-third of its budget is devoted to community development grants, which are used for street improvements, water and sewer facilities, rehabilitation of private property, historic preservation, and other activities. The remainder of the budget provides for the routine services provided by HUD.

These community development grants allow localities to make low interest rate loans for the rehabilitation of private homes and the preservation of historic buildings, including homes. In addition, HUD administers a separate Section 312 loan program for the rehabilitation of residential properties in selected areas. As of February, 1981, these low interest rate loans were available for up to a 20-year term and for an amount up to $33,500 for a single-family residence. If a home buyer is considering rehabilitating a property or preserving a historic home, contact with local government officials or HUD may be worthwhile to determine if subsidized loans are available.

HUD also supervises the activities of FHA, GNMA, and FNMA. Each of these organizations is discussed later in this chapter.

FARMERS HOME ADMINISTRATION AND FEDERAL LAND BANKS

The Farmers Home Administration and the Federal Land Banks engage in rural lending activities including rural housing loans and farm ownership loans. The Farmers Home Administration (FmHA) is an agency in the U.S. Department of Agriculture. Its activities are supported by Federal funds. The Federal Land Banks (FLBs) are part of the Cooperative Farm Credit System, which is administered by the Farm Credit Administration. The various components of the System including the Federal Land Banks were initially capitalized by the federal government, but now the System is completely owned by its users. The System is financed primarily through the issuance of Federal Farm Credit Banks Consolidated Systemwide Bonds. Additional funds are obtained from common stock and the issuance of consolidated discount notes. The System therefore is no longer supported by federal monies.

FARMERS HOME ADMINISTRATION

The FmHA has the largest direct loan program of any federal agency, and it operates a wide range of programs for rural development. These programs fall into three broad categories, which are farmer programs, rural housing programs, and community programs. The community programs include water and waste disposal loans and grants, community facility loans, and business and industrial loan guarantees. The farmer programs include farm operating loans, emergency loans, and farm ownership loans. The principal rural housing programs are low- and moderate-income housing loans and rural rental housing loans. The FmHA also administers a disaster aid program that includes low interest rate loans to assist victims to repair, rebuild or replace their homes.

Applications for loans may be made at FmHA county and district offices. The FmHA makes rural housing and farm ownership loans only if funds are not available from private lenders on reasonable terms.

Figure 12–1 shows the mortgage holdings of the FmHA and FmHA pools securing mortgage-backed securities at the end of 1980. The FmHA held less than $3.5 billion in mortgage loans, but this understates the significance of the FmHA as a lender. In 1980 the FmHA originated $2.7 billion in rural single-family mortgage loans, nearly $800 million in rural rental housing mortgage loans, and over $800 million in farm mortgage loans. The FmHA's mortgage holdings are small compared with its loan originations because the FmHA places the mortgages into pools and issues mortgage-backed securities called *certificates of bene-*

FIGURE 12–1   Total Mortgage Holdings of the FmHA and FmHA Pools at the End of 1980
(in millions)

Type of Property	FmHA	FmHA Pools
One- to Four-Family	$ 916	16,683
Multifamily	610	2,612
Commercial	411	5,271
Farm	1,355	6,964
Total Mortgage Loans	$3,492	31,530

ficial ownership. In recent years these mortgage-backed securities have been purchased by the Federal Financing Bank, which is a federal agency.

The Farmers Home Administration both insures or guarantees loans. The guarantees protect private lenders originating FmHA loans. The insurance protects the purchasers of insured loans originated by FmHA or the holders of FmHA mortgage-backed securities.

Rural Homeownership Loans. Rural homeownership loans are available in nonurban communities of less than 10,000 in population and in certain designated communities between 10,000 and 20,000 in population. These mortgage loans are available for terms of up to 33 years. The FmHA's Section 502 homeownership loan program is described in Chap. 3. The FmHA originates the Section 502 insured loans. The interest rate on the insured loan is determined by the cost of funds to the Department of Agriculture, which is generally below the rates charged by private mortgage lenders. When the borrower's income becomes adequate to obtain financing from a private mortgage lender, the borrower is required to refinance.

Section 502 guaranteed loans are made by private mortgage lenders with the interest rate negotiated between the borrower and lender. There is no refinancing requirement for Section 502 mortgage loans.

Rural Rental Housing Loans. The FmHA also makes direct insured mortgage loans for rental multifamily housing. The housing must be for low- or moderate-income persons, for individuals over 62 years of age, or for handicapped individuals. The loans are for up to 40-year terms if for housing low- and moderate-income individuals, and for up to 50-year terms if for senior citizens or handicapped individuals. Nonprofit organizations and government bodies may borrow up to 100 percent of appraised value or development cost, whichever is less. Individuals and others may borrow up to 95 percent if the project was inspected by the FmHA or if the property is at least one year old.

Farm Ownership Loans. The FmHA makes direct insured farm ownership loans, and it guarantees such loans made by other mortgage lenders. The loans may be used to buy land, construct, or repair farm homes and service buildings, and for other agricultural development. The loans are available only for family-sized farms and only if the borrower will operate the farm.

The FmHA can make low interest rate insured mortgage loans for up to 40 years and up to $200,000 in amount. The borrower is expected to refinance with another mortgage if possible. The FmHA can guarantee farm ownership loans made by other lenders for up to $300,000. Interest rates on guaranteed loans are negotiated between the borrower and lender.

There are 12 Federal Land Banks, each of which is located in a Farm Credit District. The stock in the Federal Land Banks is owned by the approximately 500 Federal Land Bank associations. The stock in the Federal Land Bank associations is owned by their individual member-borrowers.

The mortgage loans are originated and serviced by the Federal Land Bank associations. The Federal Land Banks advance the funds to make the loans and hold the mortgages. The Federal Land Bank associations originated over $10 billion in mortgage loans in 1980. Their originations included nearly $700 million in rural housing loans, about $9.6 billion in farm mortgages, and a small volume of farm-related business loans. The Federal Land Banks held over $38 billion in mortgage loans at the end of 1980. They are the largest source of farm mortgage loans, and they held approximately $36 billion at the end of 1980. They also held over $2 billion in rural housing loans.

Rural housing loans are only available for financing moderate-priced single-family housing in communities of 2,500 or less in population. Farm loans may be made only to bona fide farmers or ranchers. Farm and rural housing mortgage loans can be made for terms from 5 to 40 years, but loans for 30 years or more are not common. Conventional loans are limited to an 85 percent loan-to-value ratio. The loans are variable-rate mortgage loans, and the interest rate varies with the cost of funds to the Federal Land Banks. The interest rate is normally a little below that charged by private institutional lenders.

The effective interest rate is increased by the requirement that a borrower purchases stock in the Federal Land Bank association in an amount equal to 5 percent of the sum borrowed. In recent years most Federal Land Bank associations paid either no dividends or small dividends on their stock.

FEDERALLY RELATED SECONDARY MARKET INSTITUTIONS

The federal government has actively promoted the development of an active secondary mortgage market, in which existing loans may be bought and sold. FNMA, GNMA, and FHLMC are instrumental in the effort to maintain secondary mortgage markets.

FEDERAL NATIONAL MORTGAGE ASSOCIATION

The Federal National Mortgage Association is often called *Fannie Mae*. FNMA was created by Congress in 1938 to purchase FHA insured mortgages; in 1948 FNMA began purchases of VA guaranteed mortgages. In

1969, FNMA was converted from a government agency into a profit-oriented corporation whose common stock is listed on the New York Stock Exchange. In 1970 FNMA was given the authority to purchase conventional mortgage loans, which it began to exercise in 1972.

Currently, FNMA provides a secondary mortgage market for residential mortgages. It buys and sells FHA insured and VA guaranteed mortgage loans secured by either one- to four-family dwellings or multi-family properties. Purchases and sales of conventional mortgages are limited to those securing one- to four-family residences. FNMA purchases mortgages when loanable funds are in short supply and sells them when funds are plentiful. It does not originate mortgage loans.

FNMA purchased over $8 billion of mortgage loans and sold no loans during 1980. Loans are purchased on both an immediate delivery and an advance commitment basis. These mortgage purchases are financed primarily through the sale of notes and bonds.

GOVERNMENT NATIONAL MORTGAGE ASSOCIATION

The Government National Mortgage Association is often called *Ginnie Mae.* GNMA is an agency within HUD. GNMA was formed in 1968 to assume the special assistance function and the management and liquidation functions that FNMA performed prior to its conversion to a profit-oriented corporation. GNMA was also given the authority to guarantee mortgage-backed securities.

Special Assistance Function. FNMA purchases FHA insured and VA guaranteed mortgage loans from private lenders under its special assistance function. GNMA's special assistance function involves helping to finance housing in underdeveloped areas and purchasing mortgage loans to stabilize housing construction. The loans purchased carry below-market interest rates, which were made to subsidize housing, primarily multifamily, for individuals otherwise unable to obtain adequate housing. GNMA purchases the loans at or near their face value—par— and then sells them to other investors on a discounted basis to raise the yield to the market interest rate. Mortgages are purchased on both an immediate delivery basis and an advance commitment basis. Occasionally GNMA originates loans.

In 1975 GNMA was granted emergency stand-by authority to purchase federally insured and conventional mortgage loans at below-market interest rates to stimulate housing production. This program operates only upon the declaration of an emergency.

Mortgage-Backed Security Program. GNMA may guarantee mortgage-backed securities. The use of this authority goes about as follows. Private organizations, such as mortgage companies and commercial banks, put together pools of FHA insured and VA guaranteed mortgages and issue mortgage-backed securities against them. GNMA guarantees the purchasers of these securities that they will receive the interest and principal due them. The guarantee increases the marketability of the mortgage-backed securities and serves to attract more money from our financial markets for financing real estate.

Management and Liquidation Function. GNMA is also responsible for the management and liquidation of mortgages transferred to it in 1968 when it was founded. Of course, GNMA is also responsible for the management and liquidation of mortgages that it acquired after 1968 and that it still holds.

FEDERAL HOME LOAN MORTGAGE CORPORATION

The Federal Home Loan Mortgage Corporation is known by a number of names, including *Freddie Mac* and the Mortgage Corporation. The Federal Home Loan Banks own all the stock in the FHLMC. The FHLMC was founded in 1970 to develop a secondary mortgage market in residential mortgages primarily to benefit savings and loan associations. It was given the authority to purchase FHA insured, VA guaranteed, and conventional mortgage loans. At that time neither FNMA or GNMA provided a market for conventional mortgage loans.

While the FHLMC may purchase FHA and VA loans, it primarily purchases conventional mortgage loans on either a whole or participation (partial) basis. Loans are purchased on both an immediate delivery and advance commitment basis. Freddie Mac does not originate mortgage loans; it raises funds for purchases by placing mortgages in pools and issuing mortgage-backed securities against the pools.

VETERANS ADMINISTRATION

The Veterans Administration (VA) was established in 1944 to provide benefits for veterans. Mortgage loan guarantees and insurance and direct mortgage loans are among the benefits offered. Home, farms, business buildings, and mobile homes may all be used as security for VA mortgage loans. Our discussion here is limited to GI home loans.

VA home loans may be obtained to finance the purchase or construction of a one- to four-family residence or the purchase of a condominium unit. They may also be used for home improvement and refinancing existing mortgage loans. In all cases the applicant must occupy or intend to occupy the residence.

To qualify for a VA loan, veterans must have served at least 90 days since September 16, 1940 in "war time" periods, or at least 181 days in "nonwar time" periods. In addition, an unmarried spouse of an individual who died as a result of service or the unmarried spouse of service personnel classified as prisoners of war or as missing in action, qualify for VA mortgage loans. VA mortgage loans may be assumed by non-veterans if certain credit standards are met.

DIRECT MORTGAGE LOANS

The VA may make direct mortgage loans to veterans living in rural areas experiencing a shortage of capital. To qualify, a veteran must show that he or she cannot obtain a loan from a private lender or through another government program. Loans are available for the construction of a residence, the purchase of a farm or residence, or home improvement.

VA direct mortgage loans are usually limited to $33,000, and the terms on direct loans are the same as those for VA guaranteed loans. As a result of these restrictions, the VA direct loan program is relatively small; the total volume of VA direct mortgage loans made during 1979 was $37 million.

GUARANTEED MORTGAGE LOANS

A VA loan guarantee is for up to 60 percent of the mortgage balance, with a maximum guarantee of $27,500. The amount of this maximum guarantee is changed periodically in response to economic conditions. There is no legal upper limit on the amount of the mortgage loan, but there are practical limits. A lender normally wants a guarantee to cover at least the top 25 percent of a mortgage loan. The VA does not require that the borrower make a down payment, but it does require the borrower pay at least the closing costs. If we assume that a lender demands a 25 percent guarantee and the borrower makes no down payment, $110,000 becomes the practical limit to the size of the VA guaranteed mortgage loan.

The VA guaranteed about $14.5 billion in home mortgage loans during 1979. Approximately $92 billion in VA guaranteed mortgage loans were outstanding at the end of 1979.

Terms of the Loan. The maximum interest rate on VA mortgage loans is set by the Administrator of Veterans Affairs in consultation with the Secretary of HUD. This interest rate is usually the same as that on FHA insured loans. The rate is usually below the market rate of interest. This means that the loan must be discounted to make it yield the market rate. The discount points on a VA loan may not be paid by the borrower, except when the borrower is refinancing or building a home. That is, the seller must absorb any loan discount.

The maximum maturity of a VA home mortgage loan is 30 years and 32 days. A VA loan may be prepaid at any time without a prepayment penalty. The VA does not require monthly payments of debt service to cover real estate taxes and hazard insurance as most lenders do.

Loan Procedure.   The first step in obtaining a VA loan is securing a certificate of eligibility, which documents that the borrower is entitled to a VA guarantee. Application is then made to a private lender, such as a mortgage company, commercial bank, or savings and loan association. The lender studies the application to determine whether or not the applicant has the financial ability to meet the monthly payments. If the determination is positive, the lender requests the VA to determine the reasonable value of the property. The VA requests an approved appraiser to make an appraisal of the property, which serves as the basis of a *certificate of reasonable value* (CRV) to be issued by the VA. If the purchase price exceeds the CRV, the applicant must sign a statement acknowledging the fact and must pay the excess in cash to obtain the loan.

Lenders of VA guaranteed loans are divided into three categories. Supervised lenders are those that are subject to examination and supervision by a state or federal agency. They can make VA guaranteed loans on an automatic basis. If they qualify the borrower, obtain a VA appraisal, and determine that the property meets VA minimum property standards, they can make the loan without VA approval. After the loan is made, the VA is required to issue the guarantee.

The second category—the nonsupervised lender who qualifies for automatic loan processing—can also make the loan without prior approval. The third category—the nonsupervised lender—must forward the application for a VA guarantee and accompanying documents such as a credit report and verification of employment to the VA. If the application is approved by the VA, it issues a Certificate of Commitment. The lender can then make the loan and receive a VA guarantee. In many cases even supervised lenders do not lend before receiving a certificate of commitment.

At closing, a VA lender usually charges a one percent origination fee. The borrower must pay this fee plus other closing costs. The VA does not charge for the loan guarantee because it is a veteran benefit.

INSURED MORTGAGE LOANS

A small portion of VA loans are insured rather than guaranteed. The terms of insured loans and the procedure for obtaining them is essentially the same as that for guaranteed loans. However, the lender must request insurance rather than a guarantee.

FEDERAL HOUSING ADMINISTRATION

The Federal Housing Administration (FHA) was established in 1934 and became a part of HUD in 1968. FHA has made a number of major contributions to the field of mortgage financing through its loan insurance programs. FHA pioneered the long-term, high loan-to-value ratio, fully amortizing mortgage loan. It formalized appraisal standards and borrower qualification procedures to determine whether or not a property and a borrower qualified for a loan. FHA also instituted minimum property standards to keep borrowers from buying substandard homes with FHA insured loans.

FHA insures but normally does not make direct loans. Even so, FHA makes some purchase money mortgage loans to finance the sale of some of the properties it acquires through foreclosures. FHA made less than $100 million in purchase money mortgage loans during 1979, which is a negligible amount in comparison with its loan insurance activity. FHA insured $22 billion in loans originated during 1980, which included about $16.5 billion in one- to four-family mortgage loans and about $4 billion in multifamily mortgage loans. About $81 billion in one- to four-family FHA insured mortgage loans were outstanding at the end of 1979.

PROGRAMS

FHA has a number of different loan insurance programs. Nearly all of the loan insurance activity involves Title I and Title II of the National Housing Act of 1934, as amended. Title I programs provide loan insurance for relatively short-term home improvement loans and for mobile home loans. The average Title I insured loan was for about $5,300 during 1979. Under Title I the FHA insures the lender for 90 percent of the loan balance. Title II programs include loan insurance for loans to construct or purchase one- to four-family residences, multifamily rental properties, condominium housing, and cooperative housing. Title II programs also include loan insurance for loans to repair or rehabilitate residences. The standard Title II arrangement insures the lender against loss for 100 percent of the loan balance.

In 1976 the FHA instituted a coinsurance program for housing loans meeting the standards of Section 203(b) of Title II. Under this program the lender is insured for only 90 percent of the loan balance for the first five years and for 100 percent thereafter. The primary advantage of the coinsurance program is that the lender can make the loan prior to receiving a conditional commitment from the FHA. This is intended to make FHA insurance more comparable to private mortgage insurance, particularly in terms of the time lag between the borrower's submission of an application and the granting of the mortgage loan. While the coinsurance program has a time advantage, the standard 100 percent loan insurance still accounts for almost all the insurance issued under Title II.

There are over 30 different FHA mortgage insurance programs under Title II. Yet four programs accounted for over 95 percent of the FHA home mortgage insurance granted in 1979. Many of the programs available apply to specific parties and have a very low level of activity. The four programs involve Sections 203(b), 245/203, 221(d)(2), and 235 revised. Both Sections 203(b) and 245/203 are applicable to the general population. Section 203(b) provides mortgage insurance on loans for the construction or purchase of one- to four-family residences, and it accounted for over 60 percent of FHA home mortgage loan insurance granted in 1979. Section 245/203 differs from 203(b) in that it insures graduated payment mortgages rather than level payment mortgages. Section 245/203 accounted for over 25 percent of FHA home mortgage insurance granted in 1979. Section 221(d)(2) is applicable to low- and moderate-income families and individuals over 62 years of age that have been displaced by government action such as urban renewal. Section 235 is applicable primarily to low-income families receiving government subsidies to purchase a home.

In 1979 two sections, 221(d)(3) and (4) and 223(f), accounted for over 90 percent of the FHA mortgage insurance for multifamily loans. Section 221 multifamily mortgage insurance is for the construction or rehabilitation of low- and moderate-income housing. Section 223(f) insures loans for the improvement, sale, or refinancing of existing multifamily projects without long-term financing.

FHA INSURANCE AND LOAN TERMS

The FHA limits the dollar amount of insurance available for a given loan. It also regulates the term of the mortgage, the contract interest rate, and other factors. The restrictions vary among programs; our discussion emphasizes the limits and regulations for Section 203(b) mortgage insurance.

Term. The term of the loan may be limited to three-fourths of the remaining life of the property or to a specified maximum, whichever is shortest. The standard limit on the term of a Section 203(b) loan is 30 years. It may be raised to 35 years if the borrower cannot meet the income standards for a 30-year loan and if the property was constructed under FHA inspection. Other programs, such as 221(d)(2) and some multifamily insured loans, are allowed to have a term up to 40 years.

Mortgage Loan Limits. The limits on the maximum dollar amount of a mortgage loan eligible for FHA insurance vary among the programs, and they are periodically adjusted for rising home prices. The standard limits under Sections 245 and 234 (condominium units) are identical to those under Section 203(b). The following are the standard limits on the dollar amount of a mortgage loan insured under Section 203(b) as of the beginning of 1981:

Single-family homes	$ 67,500
Two-family homes	$ 76,000
Three-family homes	$ 92,000
Four-family homes	$107,000

These limits may be increased by up to one-third if the property is located in an area that is designated as a high-cost area. A loan on a single-family house in a high-cost area is further limited to no more than 95 percent of the median price of single-family homes in the area.

Maximum Insurance Commitment.   The mortgage insurance is also limited to a percentage of the acquisition price plus closing costs or the appraised value plus closing costs, whichever is the lesser amount. The percentages vary among programs, and some even allow loan insurance up to 100 percent of appraised value plus closing costs less a nominal cash sum. The following percentage limits apply to Section 203(b) mortgage insurance, though variations occur within this section. The first two regulations apply in cases in which the applicant intends to become an owner-occupant.

1.   If construction was started under FHA approval or was completed one year or more prior to the submission of the application, the following percentages are applied to appraised value plus closing costs:
        97 percent on the first $25,000
        95 percent on the excess over $25,000

2.   If the property was started prior to or without FHA approval and was completed less than one year prior to the application, the mortgage insurance is limited to 90 percent of appraised value plus closing costs.

3.   If the property will not be owner occupied, the insurance is limited to no more than 85 percent of that provided for owner-occupants.

    Veterans who have served for 90 or more days and who intend to become owner-occupants qualify for higher percentage loans.
    Lenders typically desire FHA insurance for the full amount of the loan. Thus, the amount of the mortgage insurance is identical to the amount of the mortgage loan. Of course, the mortgage loans are limited to maximum amounts stated above, such as $67,500 for a single-family home.

Down Payment.   The costs associated with the purchase of a home with an FHA insured loan are the purchase price, closing costs, prepaid items, and the loan discount. Under FHA regulations, closing costs include the lender's loan origination fee, the cost of title insurance, attorney's fees, recording fees, and similar charges. The FHA allows either the seller or purchaser to pay the closing costs. The prepaid items include the first year's hazard insurance premium plus two month's additional premium, payments into an escrow account for real estate taxes, one month's FHA insurance premium, and often interest to the date of the first monthly mortgage payment. FHA requires the purchaser to prepay these items. The loan discount acts to raise the effective interest rate on the loan. With an existing house, a buyer-borrower is not allowed to pay a loan discount, so the seller must pay the discount in order for a sale to take place.

The down-payment requirement is best explained by the following example. A prospective purchaser wants to buy a five-year-old house in a normal cost area using a Section 203(b) insured mortgage loan. The purchase price and the FHA appraised value are identical and equal $50,000. The closing costs are $1,000 and the prospective purchaser agrees to pay them. Both the acquisition cost and the appraised value plus closing costs equal $51,000. The purchaser has to prepay on items totaling $700.

Since the appraised value plus closing costs equal $51,000, the mortgage insurance can be calculated by multiplying 97 percent times $25,000 and adding 95 percent of $26,000. The total equals $48,950, and the purchaser receives a $48,950 mortgage loan. The purchaser must pay the $50,000 purchase price, $1,000 in closing costs, and $700 for prepaid items. This totals $51,700, and, as noted above, the loan totals $48,950. The $2,750 difference is the required down payment.

If the purchase price was $55,000—$5,000 above the appraised value—the prospective purchaser could still obtain a $48,950 loan. In this event the purchaser would have to pay the difference of $5,000, which would raise the required down payment to $7,750.

Interest Rate. The maximum contract interest rates on FHA insured mortgage loans is set by the Secretary of HUD. The interest rates vary among the programs, and they are frequently changed in response to conditions in the mortgage market. In early 1981, the contract interest rate on Section 203(b) loans was 13.5 percent and 14 percent on Section 245/203 graduated payment mortgage loans.

The contract interest rate on FHA insured loans is normally set below the market interest rate. Lenders discount the loans to raise the effective rate to the market rate of interest. A one percent discount is usually referred to as a *point*. The borrower is not allowed to pay the discount on the loan except when refinancing or constructing the property. A seller is therefore forced to absorb the points to bring about the sale. In turn, sellers usually consider this in establishing the asking price.

The Housing and Community Development Act of 1980 authorizes HUD to institute a demonstration plan that permits the interest rate on some FHA Section 203 mortgages to be set by negotiation between the borrower and lender, that is, at the market interest rate. The program is authorized for the greater of ten percent of FHA Section 203 loans or 50,000 mortgages.

Monthly Payments. The monthly payments include interest and principal. The graduated payment mortgage loans are an exception. In the early repayment years, the monthly payments may not even fully cover the interest requirement. In later years, the monthly payments are raised sufficiently to pay the interest and to fully amortize the loan. The FHA also requires the monthly payments to include escrow payments for real estate taxes, hazard insurance, and FHA mortgage insurance.

Other Features. Lenders are allowed to charge a 1.0 percent origination fee for loans on existing homes and a 2.5 percent origination fee for construction loans.

The FHA mortgage insurance premium is 0.5 percent of the average outstanding loan balance for the year. And the insurance must be maintained for the life of the loan.

FHA insured mortgage loans grant the borrower a prepayment privilege without penalty. The FHA also allows insured mortgage loans to be assumed.

FHA APPROVED LENDERS

Members of the Federal Reserve System, the FDIC, the FSLIC, and some other agencies are automatically approved to make FHA insured loans. This category includes commercial banks, savings and loan associations, and mutual savings banks. Lenders who are not automatically approved can apply for the authority to make FHA insured loans. This includes mortgage companies. Interestingly, mortgage companies originate about three-quarters of all FHA insured mortgage loans.

OBTAINING AN FHA INSURED LOAN

The first step in obtaining an FHA insured mortgage loan is locating a lender that makes FHA insured loans. The prospective borrower applies to the lender for the loan. The lender does a preliminary analysis of the applicant to determine whether or not he or she will probably qualify for an FHA insured mortgage loan. Next the lender submits a request for an appraisal of the property. An FHA approved appraiser estimates the value of the property and reports on the condition of the property. The property must meet FHA minimum property standards. Upon receiving the appraisal, the FHA issues a *conditional commitment* for mortgage insurance. The commitment is conditional on the approval of the borrower and in some cases on bringing the property up to FHA standards. For example, the FHA may require that the heating system be repaired.

During this time the lender verifies the potential borrower's employment history, checking and savings account balances, and obtains a credit report. This information on the potential borrower's financial situation is forwarded to the FHA. If the FHA approves the potential borrower, the FHA issues a *firm commitment* for mortgage insurance. After any final conditions are fulfilled, the lender makes the loan. The lender submits copies of the settlement statement, note, and mortgage to the FHA. The FHA then issues a mortgage insurance certificate to the lender, and the loan is insured.

The FHA has some underwriting standards regarding the relationship of the borrower's income and expenses that are worthy of mention. The FHA usually defines the borrower's effective income as that average income likely to prevail during the next five years. Net effective monthly income is effective income less federal income tax. Monthly housing costs include the debt service on the mortgage, the FHA mortgage insurance premium, hazard insurance premiums, real estate taxes, maintenance expenses, heating costs, and utilities. Generally monthly housing costs are limited to 35 percent of net effective income. For example, if the borrower's net effective monthly income is $2,000, monthly housing costs are limited to $700.

A second general rule is that total monthly fixed obligations are limited to 50 percent of net effective monthly income. Total monthly fixed obligations include housing costs, state and local income taxes, Social Security and retirement payments, and installment obligations that extend for more than 11 months. In our example, total monthly fixed obligations are limited to $1,000. These general rules may be relaxed if the borrower makes a larger down payment or has other substantial assets.

STATE AND LOCAL GOVERNMENTS AND HFAs

State and local governments have issued securities that are exempt from federal income taxation and have used the proceeds to make financing available below the market interest rate. State governments participate in the mortgage market primarily through state housing finance agencies (HFAs). Their programs are primarily aimed at low- and moderate-income families. In 1978 Chicago issued tax-exempt securities to provide mortgage financing for middle-income buyers in Chicago. Thereafter numerous other cities and counties issued tax-exempt securities to subsidize home buyers within their respective cities or counties.[1] State and local governments or their agencies also engage in some commercial and industrial financing to attract industry.

State and local governments and primarily state housing finance agencies held over $20 billion in mortgage loans at the end of 1979 and over $30 billion by the end of 1980. They originated about $3 billion in mortgage loans during 1979. Single-family residential mortgage loans represented over 40 percent of their holdings and mortgages on multi-family properties accounted for an additional 45 percent at the end of 1979. Commercial and farm mortgages accounted for somewhat over 10 percent of their holdings in the same year.

Their funds are raised primarily through the issuance of tax-exempt bonds. This allows state and local governments or agencies to offer mortgage loans at interest rates below those charged by private mortgage lenders.

The federal government became concerned with the revenue losses from tax-exempt securities particularly after cities started to subsidize middle-income families. In 1980 Congress passed the Mortgage Subsidy Bond and Interest Exclusion Tax Act. The Act places restrictions on the issuance of tax-exempt residential mortgage revenue bonds beginning January 1, 1981, and it denies the tax-exempt status of such bonds issued after December 31, 1983. The Act will diminish the provision of mortgage financing by state and local governments and associated agencies, but will not eliminate it.

State and local governments and/or their agencies engage in a wide range of activities related to mortgage financing. State HFAs play the largest role in housing loan financing. In addition, state, cities, and counties also act independently of HFAs. There are also a number of states, counties, and cities, or their agencies, and local nonprofit organizations that provide lease financing, mortgage loans, and/or loan guarantees to encourage commercial and industrial development.

About one-half of state HFAs make direct construction loans to public, nonprofit, or limited profit organizations to provide multifamily housing to low- and moderate-income families and in a few cases to finance the developers of single-family subdivisions. Over one-half of HFAs make direct permanent loans to developers of multifamily projects, whereas less than one-quarter make direct permanent loans to low- and moderate-income buyers. About three-quarters of HFAs purchase single-family mortgage loans, and about one-quarter purchase multifamily mortgages. Over one-quarter of HFAs make loans to lenders to finance mortgage loans for low- and moderate-income home buy-

---

[1]James A. Verbrugge, *Tax-Exempt Bonds for Single-Family Housing: An Evaluation of State Housing Finance Agency and Local Government Programs* (Chicago: U.S. League of Savings Association, 1979), pp. 5, 16.

ers, and a few HFAs have similar programs for multifamily projects. In many cases even the direct loans by HFAs are actually originated and serviced by private lenders. Some of the mortgage purchase plans used by HFAs employ advance commitments to lenders, which make them somewhat similar to direct loans.

The municipal and county plans are primarily direct loans or loans to lenders to assist middle-income families to purchase single-family homes. Some states such as California, Oregon, and Wisconsin operate programs that are independent of state HFAs and that provide home mortgage loans to veterans. Some states also have plans to provide low-interest-rate mortgage loans to farmers. Some states and HFAs also insure or guarantee residential mortgage loans.

SUMMARY

The Federal Reserve influences credit availability and interest rates. FDIC, FSLIC, and NCUSIF insure accounts in depository institutions. The Federal Home Loan Bank System regulates savings and loans, and Federal Home Loan Banks lend to savings and loans. HUD performs a number of functions to assist low- and moderate-income families to obtain adequate housing.

The Farmers Home Administration and Federal Land Banks both originate a large number of mortgage loans in rural areas. Fannie Mae (FNMA), Freddie Mac (FHLMC), and Ginnie Mae (GNMA) are active participants in the secondary mortgage markets.

The Veterans Administration guarantees a large number of mortgage loans, and the Federal Housing Administration insures a large number of loans.

State and local governments and related agencies such as housing finance agencies participate in the mortgage market. They make direct loans, purchase loans, provide funds to lenders, and insure or guarantee mortgage loans.

KEY TERMS

Certificate of Reasonable Value (CRV)
Discount Rate
Excess Reserves
Fannie Mae (FNMA)
FHA Conditional Commitment

FHA Firm Commitment
Freddie Mac (FHLMC)
FSLIC
Ginnie Mae (GNMA)
Open Market Operations

Point
Reserve Requirements
Section 203(b)
Section 245/203
Transaction Account

1. Distinguish between fiscal and monetary policy, including the implications of each for real estate finance.

2. Explain the use of open market operations by the Federal Reserve Bank to change the money supply and to influence the level of interest rates.

3. What federal agencies insure deposits of savers? In light of DIDMC, is it likely that these agencies will be merged?

4. What down payment would be required on a one-family residence purchased for and having a market value of $72,000, assuming an FHA 203(b) loan was obtained?

5. Distinguish between an FHA conditional commitment and a firm commitment.

6. What income and expense criteria must a potential borrower meet to qualify for an FHA loan?

7. Match the following key terms and definitions:

    a. Discount Rate   _____

    b. Point   _____

    c. Reserve Requirements   _____

    d. Excess Reserves   _____

    e. Open Market Operations   _____

    f. Fiscal Policy   _____

    1. NOW, automatic transfer, and share draft accounts.

    2. Buying and selling of securities by the Federal Reserve in our financial markets.

    3. Interest rate charged borrowers by the Federal Reserve Banks.

    4. A discount of one percent.

    5. Controlled government taxation and spending to achieve economic goals.

    6. Actual reserves exceeding required reserves.

    7. Reserve standards for financial institutions set by the Federal Reserve System.

thirteen

Equity Planning and Funding

An investor needs a working knowledge of financing techniques, sources of funds, and the real estate financing process to arrange and/or negotiate the best possible financing for a specific property. Thus far we have discussed techniques and sources of funds in some depth. We now therefore turn our attention to the real estate financing process.

Equity financing must first be provided for. If the equity financing cannot be arranged, it is almost certain that debt financing cannot be obtained.

Equity is, of course, the interest or value of an owner or owners in an investment. Owning the equity position carries many benefits as well as many obligations and risks. Cash flows and increases in value accrue to the equity position, along with tax benefits, even though debt financing is used. On the other hand, owners must manage and maintain the property, pay taxes, insurance, and other operating expenses, and meet debt service. Failure to meet these obligations may mean loss of the property. Further, declines in value act to wipe out the equity position before any losses are suffered by creditors.

A prudent investor takes time to study the investment and to balance the chance for gain or profit against the risk of loss before undertaking any venture. And, if a particular property promises high profits and low risks but is too large to be handled on an individual basis, our investor may share the equity position.

An equity investor is generally the initiator, the decision maker, the risk taker, and the driving force in any venture undertaken. Being the initiator and the organizer gives our investor many opportunities to maximize self-interest if he or she is prepared. Thus, in addition to the real estate financing process and equity or investment planning, our discussion includes alternative ways of arranging equity financing. These condiderations apply whether a personal residence or an apartment house is to be financed.

THE FINANCING PROCESS

Acquisition, ownership, and disposition are the three major phases of the real estate investment cycle. Financing is usually a major concern in acquiring ownership unless a buyer can pay the entire price from personal resources. Most frequently, however, much of the purchase price must be borrowed. Let us consider the major steps or elements involved in arranging financing for a typical real estate acquisition. The debt–equity financing process is outlined in Fig. 13–1.

Initially an earnest money deposit is required in making an offer to purchase a house or other property. Acceptance of the offer by the owner creates a buy-sell contract. The earnest money deposit becomes a down payment. Typically the offer is conditional upon the buyer being able to obtain acceptable debt financing.

Title must be cleared and financing arranged to complete the acquisition. The purchaser must now apply for a loan to one or more of several potential lenders. It is helpful for the purchaser to understand the many concerns and methods of operation of prospective lenders. Application may then be made to lenders most suitable to the purchaser's needs.

In deciding whether or not to make the loan, the lender carefully

FIGURE 13–1 The Debt-Equity Financing Process

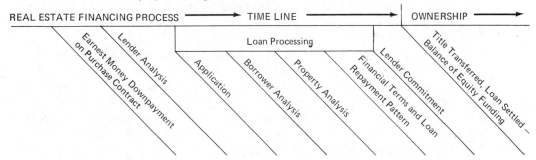

studies the prospective borrower and the property. If both meet certain criteria, the financial terms of the loan may be negotiated. For home loans, most lenders set forth financial terms at the time application is made. Finally, having processed the loan application and finding it acceptable, the lender sends a letter of commitment to the borrower.

Assuming the seller can provide a marketable title, the transaction is completed, the title is transferred, and the loan is closed. The purchaser comes up with additional equity funds or down payment as necessary. At this point, the acquisition phase of the real estate investment cycle ends and the ownership phase begins.

One chapter or more is included here on each of the major steps or elements of the financing process, as shown in Fig. 13–1. The remainder of this chapter is devoted to a discussion of equity planning and funding. Note that equity funds are usually put in at the beginning and at the end of an acquisition. Coming up with the second payment is often a major problem and challenge for the buyer–borrower because of the uncertainty in the amount and in time. Careful planning helps alleviate much of this problem.

The next chapter, which is on loan underwriting and settlement procedures, covers regulations such as the Real Estate Settlement Procedures Act (RESPA), Truth in Lending Act, and the Equal Credit Opportunity Act. The FNMA–FHLMC application form is also explained in a subsequent chapter.

Not all properties can be financed in the traditional ways. Sometimes atypical or unusual methods must be used. This section of the book therefore also includes a chapter on creative financing. Effectively, creative financing involves combining instruments or techniques with motivations of involved parties to create a transaction where none would be possible if traditional methods alone were used.

EQUITY PLANNING

In making an equity investment it is important to have the money available when needed. For an individual investor, this is mainly a matter of personal financial planning and budgeting. As the investment becomes larger and more parties become involved, planning and coordination become more difficult.

Let us look at some of the major considerations in making a group investment on one large property. The considerations break down into three phases: (1) organization, which parallels the acquisition phase in the ownership cycle, (2) ownership or investment administration, and (3) dissolution, which is generally the equivalent of property disposition. These same considerations must be taken up by the individual investor, but they are much less complex.

The main considerations in the organization of a group for real estate investment are objectives of the parties, the contributions by the parties, and the distribution of benefits to the parties. Agreement is necessary on these for a successful venture. Agreement must also be reached on investment management and dissolution, but discussion of these considerations is delayed for now.

The nature of the venture should first be made clear. It may be to acquire an existing property, to buy land and develop it, or to buy land for resale. Each of these choices has different implications insofar as the objectives of the parties are concerned. Obviously the investors should be in agreement concerning objectives, property type, and risks to be incurred.

The contributions, hard cash, know-how, or commissions expected of each party must also be agreed upon. Typically, organizers and developers put up know-how, termed *soft money,* and the less active investors put up dollars, termed *hard money.* At the same time, the proportional share attributed to each party must be agreed upon. Usually parties putting up hard cash get a preferred position against losses. All parties are usually expected to put up an equity contribution of substance so that each has a strong interest in the success of the venture.

Planning a successful venture also requires providing for the distribution of benefits, mainly cash flow, equity reversion, tax depreciation, and management fees. These benefits may be split up any way that is agreeable to all the parties. Profits, of course, are only realized after all operating expenses and interest requirements have been satisfied. Cash flow might then be divided according to proportional shares of ownership, whereas tax depreciation and equity reversion may be allocated to those able to use it to best advantage.

INVESTMENT ADMINISTRATION

Over and above contributions and shares, responsibility for management is an important consideration when several investors are involved in a venture. Administration includes keeping operating costs associated with an existing investment under control. It also includes keeping improvement and interest costs within limits in a new development. At the same time, leverage must be established and maintained to maximize return to equity. Finally, management means keeping rental income up and maintaining the property.

Who is responsible for administrative management? Typically limited partners and institutional investors are passive relative to day-to-day operation of a property. Hence, the organizer of the venture or the developer of the property becomes responsible for administration of the investment, almost by default. In a well-structured venture, management responsibility becomes a part of the contribution of the organizer or developer. Even so, compensation may be provided only after the break-even or default point has been reached in order to increase the incentive for sound management.

DISSOLUTION OR DISPOSITION

Typically, upon sale of an investment property, all parties get their initial equity investment returned before any profits or other benefits are distributed. Often, in a partnership, a buy–sell agreement between the partners may be included so that partners desiring to continue the arrangement may do so. Likewise, by agreement, all partners may be insured for the amount of their equity contribution by the partnership. Then, in the event of death of a partner, the insurance is paid the estate of the deceased and the surviving partners continue as a partnership without interruption.

EQUITY FUNDING ALTERNATIVES

Investors must come up with equity to acquire and control a property, since 100 percent debt financing is seldom possible. The most obvious source of equity funding is one's own capital, which also gives the greatest freedom and flexibility. Many ventures are too large for an individual investor, however, and require a sharing of the equity position. Let us look more deeply at the various ways of arranging equity funding.

PERSONAL RESOURCES

There are numerous possible sources of equity funds from personal resources. A number of the potential sources are shown in Fig. 13–2.

Personal savings accounts are the most convenient source of equity funds. Money is simply withdrawn from the account when needed. Sale of a car, boat, or other property also releases cash for investment. Borrowing on a personal note, often with personal property such as a car or boat put up as collateral, also releases funds for investment. However, it should be recognized that a debt obligation is created at the same time.

Aggressive investors use an extension of the idea of borrowing against property already owned, which is called pyramiding. For example, John and Marcia own a duplex worth $110,000 on which they owe $60,000. By refinancing to $90,000, John and Marcia can obtain $30,000

FIGURE 13–2 Borrower Sources of Funds

SOURCE	EXPLANATION OF HOW FUNDS OBTAINED
1. Personal savings account	Simple withdrawal
2. Personal property (car, boat, jewelry, etc.), stocks and bonds, equipment	Sale and/or using as collateral for loan
3. Other real property	Sale and/or refinancing; amounts to pyramiding
4. Sweat equity	Value of labor contributed toward construction/rehabilitation
5. Advance on future income/bonuses	Employer gives advance to keep employee satisfied; generally limited to highly valued employees
6. Life insurance	Request cash value from company
7. Income tax refund	Provide income tax return made out by accountant to verify that refund is to be received
8. Friends and/or relatives	Gift letters, stating loan not repayable and interest rate to be low or zero
9. Business loan	Obtain loan from family business
10. Co-signers	Obtain more funds from lender, and higher LVR, because of high credit standing of co-signer

to acquire an additional property, perhaps another duplex. *Pyramiding,* then, is using real property that is already owned to serve as collateral in acquiring additional property. Leverage is kept near a maximum under a pyramiding strategy.

Pyramiding is a high-risk strategy best suited to a rising market or to inflationary times. As long as values increase and cash to meet debt service requirements flows, the base of the pyramid may be expanded. A downward turn or even a slowdown in the economy carries the risk of a complete collapse of the pyramid, much like a house of cards. Inability to meet debt service on one property may eventually mean that all properties will go into default and be foreclosed.

People without much in the way of personal savings may generate an initial down payment on a home through a contribution of personal services, called *sweat equity.* Thousands of GIs used this technique, in conjunction with VA loans, to acquire first homes when they had little or no cash. Typically, a builder would allow a GI and his or her friends to do some of the construction work, such as painting, electrical work, plumbing, roofing, or clean-up, depending on their skills. This technique may again become popular because of the rapidly rising prices of houses and the increasingly higher down payments.

Finally, loans from close friends or relatives are a means of generating equity funds from personal resources. Loans of this type are likely to be interest-free and repayable only after the borrower has cleared other financial hurdles. Loans of this type are risk-free and are essentially gifts.

PARTNERSHIP

A partnership is a convenient way of arranging equity funding when a venture is too large to be handled individually. A partnership is an organizational arrangement whereby two or more people join together as co-owners to conduct a business or to make investments. Profits and losses are shared by the partners according to contributions of capital and expertise. Partnerships of consequence usually have written articles of agreement. Even so, a partnership is easily dissolved, which lends uncertainty to its usefulness as an investment vehicle.

Partnerships are legally recognized as being either general or limited. In a *general partnership,* all partners share in the operation of the enterprise and have unlimited liability in the event of losses. A *limited partnership* must have at least one general partner to manage the affairs of the entity. Limited partners are exempt by law from liability in excess of their individual contributions and cannot participate in management. For example, a broker may organize a limited partnership to acquire an apartment building. The broker would personally act as the general or managing partner, with the others being silent or limited partners. The success of a limited partnership depends directly on the competence of the general partner.

CORPORATION

A *corporation* is a legal entity with business rights that are essentially the same as those of an individual. The entity is owned by stockholders, who may be many in number. The liability of a stock owner is limited to the amount of his or her individual investment. Substantial amounts of money for equity may be raised through the corporate vehicle. A corporation ceases to exist only if dissolved according to proper legal process. Thus, changes in ownership of stock do not affect its existence.

Corporate organization has several major disadvantages for purposes of real estate investment. For one thing, costs of organizing and maintaining the entity are relatively high. For another, profits are subject to double taxation—once at the corporate level and once at the shareholder level. Finally, corporations are subject to more governmental regulation than most other forms of business organization.

A *Subchapter S corporation,* which is a hybrid of the partnership and corporate forms of organization, is frequently used in holding real estate. A Subchapter S is limited to 25 shareholders, who enjoy the limited liability of the corporate form. At the same time, corporate profits are exempt from corporate income taxes if distributed to shareholders immediately at the end of each accounting period. Operating losses may also be passed through to shareholders for deduction on their tax returns. A Subchapter S corporation is also called a *tax-option corpora-tion;* the shareholders may elect to have profits retained by the corporation to be taxed at corporate rates rather than distribute the profits and be taxed like a partnership.

REAL ESTATE INVESTMENT TRUSTS

A *trust* is a fiduciary arrangement whereby property is turned over to an individual or an institution, termed a *trustee,* to be held and administered for the profit and/or advantage of some person or organization, termed the *beneficiary.* The person setting up a trust is termed a *trustor* or *creator. Fiduciary* means based on faith and confidence, primarily in the trustee. The trustee acts for the trust, which may hold property in its own name, just as a general partner or a corporation does. The trustee is obligated to act solely for the benefit of the beneficiary or beneficiaries. The most usual trust arrangement is the real estate investment trust (REIT).

A Real Estate Investment Trust works much like a corporation. People buy shares (of beneficial interest) and thereby join together for the ownership of real estate with limited liability. At the same time, double taxation of profits may be avoided by meeting the requirements of the trust laws.

REITs are subject to considerable regulation and the initial costs are very high. Sizable investments with substantial revenues must therefore be contemplated to justify the organizational effort.

SYNDICATES AND JOINT VENTURES

Syndicates and joint ventures are the coming together of individuals or of individuals and organizations to conduct business and to make investments. Personal and financial abilities are pooled because the syndicate members believe that, by acting together, they can accomplish things that each could not undertake and complete by acting separately. A syndicate may also be formed when members want to limit individual investment in a project. A *syndicate* is not an organizational form per se, in the sense of a corporation or trust. A syndicate, in fact, may have the legal form of a partnership, corporation, or trust. The term syndicate continues to be used because it connotes an organization that has limited goals, usually of an investment nature. A *joint venture,* as its name implies, is a joint effort; however, the organizational structure is usually less formal than that of a syndicate, and one shot arrangement is implied. An equity participation arrangement between a developer and a lender is an example of a joint venture.

Institutional lenders sometimes join investors or developers as equity investors in return for providing debt financing, in what is termed an *equity participation.* The most usual form of equity participation is one in which the lender receives a percentage of gross or net income from a property above an agreed-upon base figure. In return, the lender may commit to a loan with a higher than usual loan-to-value ratio. For example, a 90 percent loan may be made on a $5 million property with monthly debt service of $50,000. In turn, it may be agreed that 15 percent of all net operating income in excess of $60,000 goes to the lender as a "kicker." This arrangement reduces the amount of equity funding required for a venture and therefore certainly deserves mention in any discussion of equity funding.

CONDOMINIUM OR COOPERATIVES

An individual desiring ownership of a dwelling unit in a large multi-family structure could conceivably get others to join in an effort to convert the property into a condominium or cooperative units. The individual might take the role of a developer–promoter and realize profits in addition to the desired unit. Such profit would be well deserved because the effort required is considerable.

LONG-TERM LEASE

A long-term lease may serve as a device to share equity financing also. A ground lease and a leasehold mortgage provide an example. Effectively the owner of the leased fee shares equity financing with the owner of the leasehold interest. The owner may mortgage the leased fee to reduce his or her equity investment. And the tenant–investor borrows against the leasehold interest to finance improvements.

In a simple example, a tenant–investor may lease a vacant lot for $20,000 per year. The productivity of the property, if improved, promises a net operating income to the tenant–investor of $100,000. Improvements are added and financed by a leasehold mortgage that requires $70,000 per year in debt service. The tenant–investor nets $10,000 per year.

The lease must be long enough, of course, for the lessee–investor to recapture the cost of improvements from the property's income. It is conceivable that another investor may be induced to buy the land for purposes of creating a suitable investment opportunity for both parties. A partnership, corporate, or trust arrangement is not needed with the use of a long-term lease.

SUMMARY

The real estate financing process involves arranging for both equity funding and debt financing. Loan processing, in order to arrange for debt financing, involves application, borrower analysis, property analysis, negotiation of financial terms, and lender commitment.

The group forms of raising equity funds are usually necessary for larger properties that are beyond the capability of individuals. The main concerns in these group forms are investor objectives, contributions and shares, distribution of benefits, investment management, and group dissolution. Careful organization and planning are necessary to successfully arrange equity funding for larger properties.

There are many ways of arranging for equity funding, for instance: (1) personal resources, (2) partnership, (3) corporation, (4) trust, (5) condominium and cooperative, and (6) long-term lease. A syndicate arrangement is also used, although it actually takes the form of a partnership, corporation, or trust.

KEY TERMS

Corporation	Joint Venture	Subchapter S Corporation
Equity	Kicker	Sweat Equity
Fiduciary	Limited Partnership	Syndicate
General Partnership	Pyramiding	Tax-Option Corporation
Hard Money	Soft Money	Trust

QUESTIONS FOR REVIEW AND DISCUSSION

1. Identify and discuss briefly at least three important reasons a real estate investor gives thought to equity planning and funding.

2. Outline the steps of the real estate financing process in the sequence most likely to be taken by an investor.

3. The equity planning function breaks down into three phases. What are they? Indicate at least two functions or activities likely to be required of an investor in each phase.

4. List at least four alternative arrangements for funding an equity position. Indicate briefly the conditions under which each might be most appropriate for use.

5. Match the following key terms and definitions:
   a. Soft Money   _____
   b. Kicker   _____
   c. Sweat Equity   _____
   d. Pyramiding   _____

   1. Using owned property as collateral to acquire additional property.
   2. Two or more people joining together as co-owners to

e. Syndicate   _____

f. Fiduciary   _____

conduct business and make investments.

3. Based on trust and confidence, as in financial matters.

4. Know-how and contacts put up by investment organizers and property developers.

5. Using personal effort or services to make down payment on a home.

6. Loans from relatives or close friends.

7. A portion of increases in income or value reserved to a lender in return for favorable financing terms.

fourteen

Loan Underwriting and Settlement Procedures

A prospective borrower needs a knowledge of the underwriting and settlement process to negotiate the best possible loan. The prospective borrower requests a loan and is interviewed by the lender to initiate the process. If prospects for arranging a loan are reasonable, the borrower files a loan application and the lender requests an appraisal of the property. The lender then begins the underwriting process, which involves analyzing the risks involved with the loan and deciding whether or not to grant the loan.

Underwriting means to finance as well as to insure or guarantee. Thus, underwriting, as used in real estate finance, has a dual meaning. A lender financing a property for an investor is underwriting a loan. Likewise, the FHA or VA, in insuring or guaranteeing the lender against loss on the loan, is also underwriting the loan.

The person analyzing the risks and making the decision in either case is called an *underwriter.* An underwriter analyzes the requested loan terms, the characteristics of the applicant, and the characteristics of the property in making the decision. If the loan is granted, the lender issues a loan commitment, subject to the borrower, showing valid title and adequate hazard insurance. Upon acceptance of the loan commitment by the borrower, the loan is arranged. At settlement the lender collects or deducts various charges and disburses the balance of the loan. The final step is recording the mortgage and/or trust deed.

A number of consumer protection laws must be observed by the lender in the underwriting and settlement process. They include the Equal Credit Opportunity Act, the Real Estate Settlement Procedures Act (RESPA), and the Truth in Lending Act. These and other laws are discussed in the appendix to this chapter. Treating these laws separately concentrates our discussion on the loan underwriting process and settlement procedures in the main body of this chapter.

Our discussion involves five basic topics: (1) the loan interview, (2) the loan application, (3) the underwriting decision, including analysis of the loan terms, the borrower, and the property, (4) the loan commitment and the events through recording the mortgage, and (5) the settlement statement. An institutional lender is assumed. The process is not likely to be this formal in getting a loan from an individual, although the same steps are desirable. Also, the prospective borrower is assumed to be seeking a loan to finance the purchase of a residence.

LOAN INTERVIEW

The loan officer typically begins the loan interview by explaining the general underwriting guidelines or policies of the institution. The interviewer is also likely to explain the importance of not defaulting on the mortgage loan agreement and the consequences of default. The applicant is also advised that, if default becomes imminent, he or she should immediately contact the lender about possible adjustments to alleviate the situation.

At this point, the applicant may question the loan officer about application and likely loan terms. The applicant may also ask about the probability of the loan being approved at the requested terms. If approval is uncertain, the applicant and loan officer may discuss possible changes to improve the probability of the loan terms being mutually agreeable. For example, the down payment might be increased to reduce the required monthly payments. A relative might give the applicant money for the increased down payment. Alternatively, the debt service might be reduced by using a longer amortization time with a balloon payment. If the loan is not likely to be granted, the applicant either should not apply or should withdraw the application. Denial of the request might raise an issue about the borrower's credit worthiness in the future. If the loan request is denied, the lender will inform the applicant of the reason for rejection.

The officer gathers information during the interview to supplement the loan application. The applicant should be cooperative and provide accurate information. A request by the interviewer to visit the applicant's home often means that the application is borderline. In effect, the interviewer is attempting to obtain information and to make judgments about the applicant's lifestyle and probability of properly caring for any property purchased.

If the applicant already owns the property and is seeking to refinance, the interview and underwriting procedure may be somewhat more relaxed. The same is true if the lender and applicant have previously engaged in mutually satisfying loan arrangements.

LOAN APPLICATION

The loan application and the appraisal report are the primary sources of information used for making the underwriting decision. The FHLMC-FNMA residential loan application, shown in Fig. 14–1, is the most commonly used application form for home mortgages. A lender who intends to sell the loan in the secondary mortgage market should use the FHLMC-FNMA form.

The beginning of the application shows the amount of the loan and the terms requested. The second section identifies the property, the purpose of the loan, and the source of the down payment. The third section contains information about the borrower and the co-borrower, if any. The co-borrower is normally the borrower's spouse. It requests their addresses, marital status, and places of employment. The fourth section contains information about the borrower's and co-borrower's gross monthly incomes, present and proposed monthly housing expense, and the financial details of the purchase. The fifth section requests details on any other income, such as that from self-employment. The sixth section requests information on former employment. The seventh section requests the disclosure of factors, generally regarded as negative, such as prior foreclosures, current law suits, and money borrowed to finance the down payment. The eighth section requires the applicant to provide a statement of assets and liabilities. The ninth section requires the applicant to provide credit references. The remaining sections request information toward compliance with the Equal Credit Opportunity Act and the fair housing laws.

Truthful statements are advised because most of the requested information can be verified with other parties. Substantial misrepresentations are almost certain to cause the loan request to be rejected. The applicant should be prepared to explain any recent sizable increases in cash or other asset balances and any past credit difficulties.

Upon accepting the loan application, the lender usually requests an appraisal of the property and begins the verification of the information presented in the loan application. The lender is required to give the applicant a booklet explaining settlement costs at this time. A good faith estimate of settlement costs is usually provided the applicant a few days after submission of the application.

FIGURE 14–1 Residential Loan Application

ANYTOWN BANK
200 Smith Street
Anytown, Illinois 60111

RESIDENTIAL LOAN APPLICATION

| MORTGAGE APPLIED FOR | [X] Conventional [ ] FHA [ ] VA | Amount $50,000 | Interest Rate 12% | No. of Months 300 | Monthly Payment Principal & Interest $526.60 | Escrow/Impounds (to be collected monthly) [X] Taxes [ ] Hazard Ins. [ ] Mtg. Ins. [ ] |

Prepayment Option
Prepayable without penalty in amounts of $100 or more

SUBJECT PROPERTY

Property Street Address	City	County	State	Zip	No. Units
1262 Fairlawn Court	Anytown	Hill	Illinois	60111	1

Legal Description (Attach description if necessary)
Lot 12, Block C, Fairlawn Subdivision, Hill County, Illinois Year Built 1976

Purpose of Loan: [X] Purchase [ ] Construction-Permanent [ ] Construction [ ] Refinance [ ] Other (Explain)

Complete this line if Construction-Permanent or Construction Loan
| Lot Value Data Year Acquired | Original Cost $ | Present Value (a) $ | Cost of Imps. (b) $ | Total (a + b) $ | ENTER TOTAL AS PURCHASE PRICE IN DETAILS OF PURCHASE. |

Complete this line if a Refinance Loan
| Year Acquired | Original Cost $ | Amt. Existing Liens $ | Purpose of Refinance | Describe Improvements [ ] made [ ] to be made Cost: $ |

Title Will Be Held In What Name(s)	Manner In Which Title Will Be Held
Merritt and Morgan Miller	Joint Tenancy

Source of Down Payment and Settlement Charges
Savings

This application is designed to be completed by the borrower(s) with the lender's assistance. The Co-Borrower Section and all other Co-Borrower questions must be completed and the appropriate box(es) checked if [X] another person will be jointly obligated with the Borrower on the loan, or [ ] the Borrower is relying on income from alimony, child support or separate maintenance or on the income or assets of another person as a basis for repayment of the loan, or [ ] the Borrower is married and resides, or the property is located, in a community property state.

BORROWER			CO-BORROWER		
Name Merritt Miller	Age 39	School Yrs 14	Name Morgan Miller	Age 37	School Yrs 14
Present Address No. Years 4 [ ] Own [x] Rent			Present Address No. Years 4 [ ] Own [X] Rent		
Street Apt. 3B 300 West Hill Street			Street Apt. 3B 300 West Hill Street		
City/State/Zip Anytown, Illinois 60111			City/State/Zip Anytown, Illinois 60111		
Former address if less than 2 years at present address			Former address if less than 2 years at present address		
Street			Street		
City/State/Zip			City/State/Zip		
Years at former address [ ] Own [ ] Rent			Years at former address [ ] Own [ ] Rent		

Marital Status [X] Married [ ] Separated [ ] Unmarried (incl. single, divorced, widowed)	DEPENDENTS OTHER THAN LISTED BY CO-BORROWER NO. 2 AGES 16, 12	Marital Status [X] Married [ ] Separated [ ] Unmarried (incl. single, divorced, widowed)	DEPENDENTS OTHER THAN LISTED BY BORROWER NO. -- AGES --

Name and Address of Employer	Years employed in this line of work or profession?	Name and Address of Employer	Years employed in this line of work or profession?
AXT Distributors 420 South Fourth Street Anytown, Illinois 60111	11 years Years on this job 4 [ ] Self Employed*	Anytown Elementary School 111 East Hill Street Anytown, Illinois 60111	13 years Years on this job 3 [ ] Self Employed*
Position/Title Office Manager	Type of Business Wholesalers	Position/Title Secretary	Type of Business School
Social Security Number*** 954-21-4352	Home Phone 752-1267 Business Phone 752-2525	Social Security Number*** 926-34-5695	Home Phone 752-1267 Business Phone 752-2000

GROSS MONTHLY INCOME				MONTHLY HOUSING EXPENSE**			DETAILS OF PURCHASE	
Item	Borrower	Co-Borrower	Total		Present	Proposed	Do Not Complete If Refinance	
Base Empl. Income	$1,700	$960	$2,660	Rent	$400		a. Purchase Price	$60,000
Overtime	50		50	First Mortgage (P&I)		$527	b. Total Closing Costs (Est.)	2,050
Bonuses				Other Financing (P&I)			c. Prepaid Escrows (Est.)	360
Commissions				Hazard Insurance	25	30	d. Total (a + b + c)	$62,410
Dividends/Interest				Real Estate Taxes		92	e. Amount This Mortgage	(50,000)
Net Rental Income				Mortgage Insurance		10	f. Other Financing	(--)
Other† (Before completing, see notice under Describe Other Income below.)				Homeowner Assn. Dues			g. Other Equity	(--)
				Other:			h. Amount of Cash Deposit	(2,000)
				Total Monthly Pmt.	$425	$659	i. Closing Costs Paid by Seller	tax 750
				Utilities	100	160	j. Cash Reqd. For Closing (Est.)	$9,660
Total	$1,750	$960	$2,710	Total	$525	$819		

DESCRIBE OTHER INCOME

[ ] B–Borrower C–Co-Borrower   NOTICE: † Alimony, child support, or separate maintenance income need not be revealed if the Borrower or Co-Borrower does not choose to have it considered as a basis for repaying this loan. Monthly Amount $

IF EMPLOYED IN CURRENT POSITION FOR LESS THAN TWO YEARS COMPLETE THE FOLLOWING

B/C	Previous Employer/School	City/State	Type of Business	Position/Title	Dates From/To	Monthly Income $

THESE QUESTIONS APPLY TO BOTH BORROWER AND CO-BORROWER

If a "yes" answer is given to a question in this column, explain on an attached sheet.	Borrower Yes or No	Co-Borrower Yes or No	If applicable, explain Other Financing or Other Equity (provide addendum if more space is needed).
Have you any outstanding judgments? In the last 7 years, have you been declared bankrupt?	No	No	
Have you had property foreclosed upon or given title or deed in lieu thereof?	No	No	
Are you a co-maker or endorser on a note?	No	No	
Are you a party in a law suit?	No	No	
Are you obligated to pay alimony, child support, or separate maintenance?	No	No	
Is any part of the down payment borrowed?	No	No	

*FHLMC/FNMA require business credit report, signed Federal Income Tax returns for last two years, and, if available, audited Profit and Loss Statements plus balance sheet for same period.

**All Present Monthly Housing Expenses of Borrower and Co-Borrower should be listed on a combined basis.

***Neither FHLMC nor FNMA requires this information.

FHLMC 65 Rev. 8/78   FNMA 1003 Rev. 8/78

236

FIGURE 14–1 *(Continued)*

This Statement and any applicable supporting schedules may be completed jointly by both married and unmarried co-borrowers if their assets and liabilities are sufficiently joined so that the Statement can be meaningfully and fairly presented on a combined basis; otherwise separate Statements and Schedules are required (FHLMC 65A/FNMA 1003A). If the co-borrower section was completed about a spouse, this statement and supporting schedules must be completed about that spouse also.   ☒ Completed Jointly   ☐ Not Completed Jointly

ASSETS			LIABILITIES AND PLEDGED ASSETS			
Indicate by (*) those liabilities or pledged assets which will be satisfied upon sale of real estate owned or upon refinancing of subject property						
Description	Cash or Market Value		Creditors' Name, Address and Account Number	Acct. Name If Not Borrower's	Mo. Pmt. and Mos. left to pay	Unpaid Balance
Cash Deposit Toward Purchase Held By	$ 2,000		Installment Debts (include "revolving" charge accts)		$ Pmt./Mos. /	$
Anytown Realty					/	
Checking and Savings Accounts (Show Names of Institutions/Acct. Nos.)					/	
Anytown Bank Checking- 29-30-125	800				/	
Savings - 42072	14,500				/	
Stocks and Bonds (No./Description)					/	
					/	
					/	
Life Insurance Net Cash Value Face Amount ($ 40,000)	2,500		Other Debts Including Stock Pledges		/	
SUBTOTAL LIQUID ASSETS	$ 19,800					
Real Estate Owned (Enter Market Value from Schedule of Real Estate Owned)			Real Estate Loans		✕	
Vested Interest in Retirement Fund Merritt Morgan	4,800 7,000				✕	
Net Worth of Business Owned (ATTACH FINANCIAL STATEMENT)						
Automobiles (Make and Year) 1981 Escort 1977 Pinto	3,500 1,000		Automobile Loans Anytown Bank Anytown, Illinois-12-523		119 / 24	2,500
Furniture and Personal Property	6,000		Alimony, Child Support and Separate Maintenance Payments Owed To		✕	
Other Assets (Itemize)						
					✕	
			TOTAL MONTHLY PAYMENTS		$ 119	
TOTAL ASSETS	A $ 42,100		NET WORTH (A minus B) $		TOTAL LIABILITIES	B $ 2,500

SCHEDULE OF REAL ESTATE OWNED (If Additional Properties Owned Attach Separate Schedule)

Address of Property (Indicate S if Sold, PS if Pending Sale or R if Rental being held for income) ⬦	Type of Property	Present Market Value	Amount of Mortgages & Liens	Gross Rental Income	Mortgage Payments	Taxes, Ins. Maintenance and Misc.	Net Rental Income
		$	$	$	$	$	$
TOTALS ➡		$	$	$	$	$	$

LIST PREVIOUS CREDIT REFERENCES

⬦ B–Borrower C–Co-Borrower	Creditor's Name and Address	Account Number	Purpose	Highest Balance	Date Paid
B	Anytown Bank Anytown, Illinois	12-478	Car Loan	$ 4,000	2/80
B	Hill County Bank Hillside, Illinois	225-357	Car Loan	3,000	10/77

List any additional names under which credit has previously been received _____

AGREEMENT: The undersigned applies for the loan indicated in this application to be secured by a first mortgage or deed of trust on the property described herein, and represents that the property will not be used for any illegal or restricted purpose, and that all statements made in this application are true and are made for the purpose of obtaining the loan. Verification may be obtained from any source named in this application. The original or a copy of this application will be retained by the lender, even if the loan is not granted.   The undersigned ☐ intend or ☐ do not intend to occupy the property as their primary residence.

I/we fully understand that it is a federal crime punishable by fine or imprisonment, or both, to knowingly make any false statements concerning any of the above facts as applicable under the provisions of Title 18, United States Code, Section 1014.

/s/ Merritt Miller _____ Date 8/30/82   /s/ Morgan Miller _____ Date 8/30/82
Borrower's Signature   Co-Borrower's Signature

INFORMATION FOR GOVERNMENT MONITORING PURPOSES

Instructions: Lenders must insert in this space, or on an attached addendum, a provision for furnishing the monitoring information required or requested under present Federal and/or present state law or regulation. For most lenders, the inserts provided in FHLMC Form 65-B/FNMA Form 1003-B can be used.

FOR LENDER'S USE ONLY

(FNMA REQUIREMENT ONLY) This application was taken by ☒ face to face interview ☐ by mail ☐ by telephone

/s/ I.M. Lender _____   Anytown Bank
(Interviewer)   Name of Employer of Interviewer

FHLMC 65 Rev. 8/78   REVERSE   FNMA 1003 Rev. 8/78

237

Successful underwriting involves careful analysis of the risks in an undertaking and making a decision whether or not to accept the undertaking based on the analysis. Most obviously unacceptable loan undertakings are turned down in the interview stage. However, a prospective borrower may submit an application even if the interviewer says that the request clearly violates the lender's guidelines. For example, the applicant may request a below-market interest rate, a 60-year term, and a loan in excess of the value of the property. The lender is almost certain to reject such requests. In other cases, it may be obvious that the loan requested is easily within the lender's guidelines and is almost certain to be granted. And sometimes, a specific guideline might be violated, but strengths in other areas may make the loan acceptable.

The lender, of course, desires to only make loans for which the rate of return exceeds the associated risk. The primary risks associated with a given loan are that the borrower may not repay the loan and that the security offered may be insufficient to allow the lender to recover its investment in foreclosure.

Underwriting guidelines differ among VA guaranteed loans, FHA insured loans, and conventional loans. Some of the underwriting standards for VA and FHA loans are discussed in Chap. 12. In this chapter our attention is devoted to underwriting policies for conventional home mortgage loans. Loan terms are discussed first, followed by consideration of borrower and property characteristics.

Loan Terms Analysis

Loan terms include the principal amount, the loan-to-value ratio, interest rate, the term, the monthly debt service, the associated monthly escrow or impound payments, and a possible prepayment option. In addition lenders increasingly emphasize variable-rate and renegotiable-rate mortgage loans.

Loan terms vary among lenders and change over time. The terms offered by a given lender are determined by regulations, current availability of funds, competition, and by the lender's expectations concerning business conditions, price levels, interest rates, and future availability of funds.

A loan officer normally informs an applicant about the available terms at the loan interview. The important consideration is that the loan terms may be negotiable. The prospective borrower can inquire about the negotiability of the loan terms at the interview. The borrower may obtain a lower interest rate if he or she increases the down payment or decreases the length of the loan. The borrower may avoid monthly payments into escrow accounts by pledging a savings account. And possibly a prepayment option without a prepayment penalty may be obtained merely by a request.

The loan officer analyzes the requested loan terms and makes a determination of whether or not the proposed interest rate and other lender charges combine to provide an adequate rate of return on the lender's funds. The officer may reject the terms requested but suggest changes that will make them acceptable.

BORROWER ANALYSIS

Borrower analysis has three primary goals. One is to determine whether or not the borrower has the necessary funds or assets for the down payment and associated settlement costs. The second is to determine the probability that the borrower will have adequate income necessary to meet the required debt service and other monthly expenses. The third is to determine the borrower's willingness to meet his or her monthly obligations.

Assets. The applicant lists the source of the funds for the down payment and the settlement charges in the loan application. The application also contains a statement of assets and liabilities, including checking and savings account balances and any cash deposit made in connection with the real estate purchase contract. The applicant is required to have signed a request for verification of deposit form, which the underwriter uses to verify the account balances and the cash deposit. If the deposits are sufficient to cover the down payment and settlement charges, the applicant has passed test one.

Next, the underwriter further examines the accounts to see if there have been recent sizable increases in the deposit balances. If there has been a sizable increase, an explanation is necessary. If the increase resulted from a gift from relatives, the underwriter requests a *gift letter* that states that the amount truly is a gift and not a loan. If the increase resulted from delaying the payment of other obligations or from an unsecured loan, it is a negative factor.

The statement of assets and liabilities also provides other information. The applicant's net worth can be related to the applicant's income and provides a measure of the applicant's financial management ability. If the borrower's assets are more than sufficient to close the transaction, a portion may be used to pay the costs of moving, immediate repairs, appliances, and furniture, if needed. This sufficiency allows the applicant to devote a larger portion of current income to monthly debt service and other housing expenses and may make possible a slightly larger loan.

Expense-to-Income Ratios. The Federal Home Loan Mortgage Corporation has two general expense-to-income ratio requirements for the conventional home mortgage loans that it purchases. One is that monthly housing expense generally should not exceed from 25 to 28 percent of the borrower's stable gross monthly income. FHLMC defines the borrower's monthly housing expenses as the monthly debt service on the loan, hazard insurance premium, real estate taxes, and, if applicable, mortgage insurance premiums, homeowners' association dues other than unit utility charges, and ground rental payments. The other is that the total monthly debt payments generally should not exceed from 33 to 36 percent of the borrower's stable gross monthly income. FHLMC defines the borrower's total monthly debt payments as the sum of (1) the monthly housing expenses defined above, (2) the monthly payment on any installment debt which has more than ten remaining payments, (3) alimony, and (4) child support or maintenance payments.[1]

FHLMC does not include utility charges in monthly housing expenses or in total monthly payments because the charges vary due to differences in utility rates, family size, and living styles. However, utility costs are considered in analyzing the borrower's ability to meet housing expenses and other obligations.

The FHLMC requirements for the expense-to-income ratio are flexible. Higher ratios can be justified by a number of other factors, such as a large down payment, a substantial net worth, or the demonstrated ability of the borrower to devote a larger portion of income to housing expenses.

Stable Income.   FHLMC defines *stable monthly gross income* as the borrower's gross monthly income from primary base earnings plus recognizable secondary income. Bonuses, commissions, overtime, and part-time jobs are examples of secondary income. FHLMC includes secondary income in stable monthly income if it meets a number of conditions. It must be typical for the occupation, it must be earned for at least the preceding two years, and it must be probable that it will continue in the future.

The Equal Credit Opportunity Act requires the lender to give equal status to the income of both the husband and wife for meeting housing expenses. Each spouse's income must be sustainable or likely to continue over the early portion of the mortgage term.

The underwriter submits the request for verification of employment forms that were signed by the applicants. If the applicant is self-employed, the lender requests income statements and balance sheets and/or federal income tax returns for the preceding two years. This data serves as a check on the accuracy of the information provided in the loan application.

The most difficult problem is the prediction of future income. The

---

[1]*Underwriting Guidelines: Home Mortgages* (Washington, D.C.: Federal Home Loan Mortgage Corporation, 1979), pp. 13, 14.

length of employment and the type of work are two factors of importance. In manufacturing industries, seniority often determines which employees are most subject to layoffs. Salaried employees and professional workers are usually less subject to layoffs. The underwriter must assess the applicant's relative education and skills and the future demand for those skills. The length of time in a particular business and future prospects for the business are important considerations when the applicant operates a small business.

Willingness to Pay. An applicant's credit history and attitude, or willingness to pay, is the concern of the third major decision to be made by a loan underwriter.

The underwriter requests a credit report on the applicant. The *credit report* serves to verify information concerning the debts owed by the applicant. Occasionally it reveals debts not reported by the applicant. The credit report describes the usual manner of payment of the applicant's obligations. A pattern of delinquent payments increases the risk associated with the loan. The credit report may also reveal a foreclosure, bankruptcy, or pending law suit. The analysis of the credit report allows the lender to judge the applicant's willingness to pay and ability to manage financial affairs.

Past credit difficulties do not automatically cause rejection of a loan request. However, there must be strong evidence that the applicant will meet future obligations to offset a negative credit report. The applicant must provide reasonable explanations for past credit difficulties and evidence that these difficulties will not reappear in the foreseeable future.

The motivation for the loan is a significant factor. A loan for the purchase of a home is viewed more favorably than a refinancing loan to consolidate debts. A large down payment is viewed more favorably than a small down payment. With a small down payment, a small decline in the value of the property could eliminate the borrower's equity. In this event, the borrower might have little reason to continue to make loan payments, unless significant other assets would be lost due to a deficiency judgment.

PROPERTY ANALYSIS

An underwriter also requests and studies a market value appraisal of the property. The FNMA-FHLMC residential appraisal report form is shown in Fig. 15–3 in the following chapter. The use of the appraisal is discussed briefly here. A more detailed discussion of the appraisal and the property to be financed is provided in the following chapter.

The appraisal is prepared either by a staff appraiser of the lender or by an independent fee appraiser. It is important to realize that an appraisal is an estimate or opinion of value at a specific point in time. The underwriter reviews the appraisal to see that the estimate of value is supported by the evidence included in the appraisal report. Assuming that the underwriter accepts the indicated value, he or she can calculate the loan-to-value ratio rather than the loan-to-price ratio. The underwriter is equally concerned with judging the probable trend in the value of the property over the early years of the loan, during which time the risk of default is usually highest. Property may decrease in value, which is a major risk to a lender. To avoid or minimize this risk, an underwriter carefully studies the marketability of the property and its probable market value during the early years of the loan. Design, functional and physical adequacies and inadequacies, needed repairs, and the value of the property relative to others in the neighborhood all impact the marketability of the subject property. A purchase price exceeding the appraised value raises concerns of marketability. The underwriter is also interested in the future of the real estate market in the area and the stability of the neighborhood, as each affects the future value and marketability of the property.

LOAN RATING GRID

A loan rating grid is a convenient method of summarizing an underwriter's analysis of the factors concerning the loan request. A *loan rating grid* lists the factors of concern on the vertical axis and either comments or numerical ratings for the factors on the horizontal axis. The grid may cover only one set of factors, such as the borrower analysis, or it may cover the loan terms, borrower, and the property. Some rating grids give weights to the factors of concern and numerical ratings for the loan under consideration. For example, assume that the adequacy of income is given a weight of ten and the borrower scores an eight. These ratings can be totaled to arrive at a score for the loan request. If the score is adequate, the loan request is granted. If the score is too low, the loan request is denied. Figure 14–2 shows a hypothetical mortgage loan rating grid. An underwriter makes the decision to accept or reject the loan request after analyzing the various factors. If the loan request is rejected, the lender may still make a loan with less generous terms. If the loan request is approved, the lender issues a loan commitment.

LOAN COMMITMENT THROUGH RECORDING THE MORTGAGE

If the underwriter approves the loan application, the lender usually issues a loan commitment and the borrower normally accepts. The lender usually discloses the annual percentage rate on the loan and agrees to make advance disclosure of the settlement statement at this time. The loan commitment may contain a number of conditions.

At settlement the borrower must show valid title to the property

FIGURE 14–2 Mortgage Loan Rating Grid

FACTORS	COMMENTS	SCORE
Loan Terms		
Interest rate		_____
Term		_____
Amortization		_____
Escrow Provisions		_____
Loan-to-Value Ratio		_____
Junior Financing		_____
Borrower Characteristics		
Adequacy of Assets		_____
Adequacy of Income		_____
Stability of Income		_____
Credit Characteristics		_____
Motivation for the Loan		_____
Importance of the Equity		_____
Property Characteristics		
Appraised Value versus Price		_____
Marketability		_____
Stability of Future Value		_____

and adequate hazard insurance, and, if applicable, flood insurance and private mortgage insurance. The borrower or borrowers also sign the mortgage and mortgage note at settlement. If the loan is to purchase a property, the seller delivers the deed at settlement. The borrower makes the required down payment, pays the lender's charges, and if applicable makes deposits into escrow accounts for real estate taxes and hazard insurance. The lender disburses the loan funds and arranges for prompt recording of the deed and mortgage.

LOAN COMMITMENT

A *loan application* is technically an offer to exchange a mortgage lien and promissory note at specified terms for a loan. And legally, a *loan commitment* constitutes acceptance of the offer, making a loan agreement or a binding contract.[2]

In practical terms, the typical commitment is an offer by a lender

---

[2]Robert Kratovil and Raymond J. Werner, *Real Estate Law,* 7th ed. (Englewood Cliffs, N.J.: Prentice-Hall, Inc., 1979), p. 233.

to make a mortgage loan at terms specified in the commitment. The lender usually sets a time, such as ten days, in which the applicant must accept the offer. In accepting a loan commitment, a borrower also accepts its conditions.

The typical loan commitment requires the borrower to provide evidence of valid title and adequate property insurance. The commitment often requires the borrower to provide a mortgagee's title insurance policy. The commitment may require flood insurance and private mortgage insurance. And the commitment may require either a pledged savings account or escrow deposits for real estate taxes and hazard insurance.

EVIDENCE OF TITLE

The borrower may show evidence of valid title by any one of three methods: (1) an abstract and opinion of title, (2) a Torrens certificate, or (3) a title insurance policy. The evidence of title depends on a search of the public records and ideally includes a survey of the property. A survey is used to disclose unrecorded easements or encroachments affecting the property.

Abstract and Opinion of Title. An *abstract of title* is a condensed history of the property's ownership. A lawyer's opinion of title is his or her opinion of the significance of any defects revealed by a search of the public records. Ideally the lawyer's opinion is also based on a search of the public records for outstanding liens against personal property received along with the purchase of the real estate. The principal advantage of an abstract and a lawyer's opinion or certificate of title is that it is available throughout the country. The principal disadvantage of an abstract and opinion of title is that neither the party preparing the abstract nor the lawyer issuing the opinion guarantees against latent or hidden defects.

Torrens System. Title evidence by the Torrens system is available in only a few counties in the United States. The most prominent areas using the Torrens system are New York City, Chicago, Boston, Minneapolis–St. Paul, Duluth, and Honolulu. The Torrens system guarantees a purchaser against loss of a property due to claims not filed with the Registrar of Titles. The Torrens system has a serious defect, however. The Registrar of Titles is not required to provide a legal defense of the title. A purchaser must defend against any litigation at his or her own expense. Due to the possibility of legal expenses, in Chicago, some purchasers buy title insurance policies even though the property is registered under the Torrens system.

Title Insurance. Lenders generally prefer title insurance. *Title insurance* guarantees compensation to a policyholder for any losses suffered due to a defect in title not excepted in the policy. The title insurance company also agrees to defend, at its own expense, against any lawsuit involving a defect in title covered by the policy. Title insurance also increases negotiability of the loan in the secondary mortgage market. In case of a faulty title, the buyer of the loan gets paid off by the insurance company rather than having to fight a lawsuit in a distant city.

Title insurance companies offer both owner's policies and mortgagee's policies. A lender typically requests a borrower to provide a mortgagee's title insurance policy. The mortgagee's policy offers protection to the lender, which is not terminated by foreclosure. A purchaser usually obtains both an owner's and a mortgagee's policy.

A seller usually requests the commitment for the title insurance policies as part of his or her obligation to provide evidence of a marketable title. The title insurance company makes a report of title, with any exceptions listed. Most exceptions relate to the rights of parties in possession claiming under an unrecorded document, and/or to unrecorded interests that would be shown by a survey. A survey or a survey rider in the policy removes exceptions due to questions of boundaries. The borrower and lender should note the exceptions included in the title insurance policy. Ideally, the borrower should have legal council to determine the significance of any exceptions.

An extended mortgagee's title insurance policy provides protection against unrecorded mechanics' liens, and it is desirable when the improvements on a property were recently built or modified.

SETTLEMENT STATEMENT

A *settlement statement* is a detailed accounting of a mortgage loan transaction and/or a real estate sales transaction. A settlement statement is also known as a *closing statement.* Preparation of a settlement statement for the purchase of a home involves a number of calculations including the proration of expenses and classifying these and other items as credits or charges to the buyer or seller. The final result shows the cash payment required from the buyer and the cash due to the seller at settlement or closing.

A transaction involving a loan secured by a one- to four-family residence is usually governed by the Real Estate Settlement Procedures Act (RESPA). According to RESPA the lender is responsible for preparation of the settlement statement. The lender may delegate the actual preparation of the settlement statement to a third party, but the lender retains responsibility for its accuracy and conformance to various provisions of RESPA.

FINANCING COSTS

The lender may make a number of charges to the borrower at settlement. A loan origination fee is a charge for the services provided and materials used in initiating the mortgage loan. A *loan discount* is a charge used to increase the rate of return to the lender. An appraisal fee is a charge to cover the costs of the appraisal ordered by the underwriter. A credit report fee is the charge to cover the cost of the credit report. A lender's inspection fee covers an inspection of the improvements either conducted or ordered by the underwriter. A mortgage insurance application fee is usually charged when FHA insurance is involved. An assumption fee is the charge to a borrower assuming an existing loan. A document preparation fee may be levied for preparation of the mortgage and mortgage note. The lender also usually requires the borrower to make an interest payment for the remaining portion of the month following the day of the closing. The interest payment covers the period from the day of closing to the beginning of the month when the first regular monthly payment of debt service is scheduled.

RESERVES DEPOSITED WITH THE LENDER

A lender may require the borrower to establish escrow or impound accounts for hazard insurance, mortgage insurance, real estate taxes, and annual assessments. An *escrow* or *impound account* is an account established to accumulate funds for future needs, such as real estate taxes or the hazard insurance premium. For example, a hazard insurance premium of $300 might be due on January 1 of the following year. If the borrower deposited $25 per month into the escrow account, at the end of 12 months there would be $300 available to pay the hazard insurance premium. Assume, however, that the settlement is made on September 15 and that the borrower makes monthly escrow payments on November 1, December 1, and January 1. These three payments of $25 only total $75, whereas a $300 hazard insurance premium is due on January 1. The lender avoids a deficit problem by requiring a $225 deposit into the escrow account at closing.

PRORATIONS

A *proration* is a division or distribution of proportionate shares of expenses, income, or other items between two or more parties. At a title closing, expenses and income may be prorated between the buyer and seller. Prepaid expenses and accrued income items result in a credit to the seller and a charge to the buyer, whereas accrued expenses and prepaid income items result in a credit to the buyer and a charge to the seller. The income and expenses are usually prorated as of the date of possession or closing, whichever comes first. The date of settlement or possession is usually regarded as a day of expense and income for the seller.

Assume that the settlement date is June 15 and the annual real estate taxes are $1,200. The seller is responsible for the real estate taxes from January 1 through June 15. The real estate taxes for $5\frac{1}{2}$ months total $550. If the seller has prepaid the real estate taxes of $1,200, $650 would be credited to the seller and charged to the buyer. If the real estate taxes are paid in the following year, $550 would be credited to the buyer and charged to the seller.

COMPLETED SETTLEMENT STATEMENT

Figure 14–3 shows a completed HUD settlement statement as required by RESPA. The form is relatively self-explanatory. Our comments are limited to explaining items requiring calculations. The items are identified by citing the line number in the HUD settlement statement.

The settlement date is September 15, 1982. The month of September contains 30 days. Monthly charges and credits are calculated by dividing the annual amount by 12 months. Daily charges and credits are calculated by dividing the monthly amount by 30 days.

Proration of Real Estate Taxes—Lines 210, 211, 510, and 511.   The real estate taxes are payable in 1983 and are estimated to be $1,080. The monthly rate is $90. Eight and one-half months times $90 totals $765. The $765 is a credit to the buyer and a charge to the seller.

Accrued Interest on Existing Mortgage—Line 506.   The outstanding balance on the existing mortgage is $26,896.50. The interest rate is 9 percent per annum. The interest for one month is $201.72, and it is due with the October 1 payment. The daily rate is $6.724. Fifteen days interest at $6.724 totals $100.86. This is a charge to the seller.

Loan Discount—Line 802.   The lender charges a two point or 2 percent loan discount. Two percent times $50,000 totals $1,000. The borrower is charged $1,000.

Interest on New Loan—Line 901.   The interest rate on the $50,000 loan is 12 percent. One month's interest totals $500. The daily rate is $16.667. The borrower pays 16 days interest at settlement to bring the loan current as to interest as of the end of September. Sixteen times $16.667 totals $266.67. This is a charge to the borrower at settlement. The first regular monthly payment, to be made on November 1, would include interest accrued to the end of October.

Reserve for Real Estate Taxes—Lines 1003 and 1004.   The real estate taxes payable in 1983 are estimated at $1,080. They are due in two equal installments, payable on June 1 and September 1. The lender requires the borrower to establish an escrow account for real estate taxes. The lender requires the monthly payments to accumulate to $1,080 as of the 1 June 1983 payment. Conceptually the escrow payments should have begun on 1 July 1982. The borrower must make the deposits for July, August, Sep-

FIGURE 14–3 Settlement Statement

Form Approved OMB NO. 63-R-1501

A. U.S. DEPARTMENT OF HOUSING AND URBAN DEVELOPMENT
SETTLEMENT STATEMENT

B. TYPE OF LOAN

1. ☐ FHA   2. ☐ FMHA   3. ☐ CONV. UNINS.

4. ☐ VA   5. ☒ CONV. INS.

Anytown Bank
200 Smith Street
Anytown, Illinois 60111

6. FILE NUMBER:
4224MV

7. LOAN NUMBER:
23-429-0

8. MORT. INS. CASE NO.:
81-312-462

C. **NOTE:** This form is furnished to give you a statement of actual settlement costs. Amounts paid to and by the settlement agent are shown. Items marked "(p.o.c.)" were paid outside the closing; they are shown here for informational purposes and are not included in the totals.

D. NAME OF BORROWER:
Merritt Miller
Morgan Miller

E. NAME OF SELLER:
Robert Harrison
Betty Harrison

F. NAME OF LENDER:
Anytown Bank

G. PROPERTY LOCATION:
1262 Fairlawn Court
Anytown, Illinois

H. SETTLEMENT AGENT:
Anytown Bank
PLACE OF SETTLEMENT:
Anytown Bank

I. SETTLEMENT DATE:
9/15/82

J. SUMMARY OF BORROWER'S TRANSACTION:		**K. SUMMARY OF SELLER'S TRANSACTION:**	
100. GROSS AMOUNT DUE FROM BORROWER		**400. GROSS AMOUNT DUE TO SELLER**	
101. Contract sales price	59,600.00	401. Contract sales price	59,600.00
102. Personal property	400.00	402. Personal property	400.00
103. Settlement charges to borrower (line 1400)	2,412.67	403.	
104.		404.	
105.		405.	
Adjustments for items paid by seller in advance		*Adjustments for items paid by seller in advance*	
106. City/town taxes to		406. City/town taxes to	
107. County taxes to		407. County taxes to	
108. Assessments to		408. Assessments to	
109.		409.	
110.		410.	
111.		411.	
112.		412.	
120. GROSS AMOUNT DUE FROM BORROWER	62,412.67	**420. GROSS AMOUNT DUE TO SELLER**	60,000.00
200. AMOUNTS PAID BY OR IN BEHALF OF BORROWER		**500. REDUCTIONS IN AMOUNT DUE TO SELLER**	
201. Deposit or earnest money	2,000.00	501. Excess deposit (see Instructions)	
202. Principal amount of new loan(s)	50,000.00	502. Settlement charges to seller (line 1400)	3,913.00
203. Existing loan(s) taken subject to		503. Existing loan(s) taken subject to	
204.		504. Payoff of first mortgage loan	26,896.50
205.		505. Payoff of second mortgage loan	
206.		506. Accrued Interest on	
207.		507. Existing Loan	100.86
208.		508.	
209.		509.	
Adjustments for items unpaid by seller		*Adjustments for items unpaid by seller*	
210. City/town taxes ⟩1/1/82 to 9/15/82	765.00	510. City/town taxes ⟩1/1/82 to 9/15/82	765.00
211. County taxes to		511. County taxes to	
212. Assessments to		512. Assessments to	
213.		513.	
214.		514.	
215.		515.	
216.		516.	
217.		517.	
218.		518.	
219.		519.	
220. TOTAL PAID BY/FOR BORROWER	52,765.00	**520. TOTAL REDUCTION AMOUNT DUE SELLER**	31,675.36
300. CASH AT SETTLEMENT FROM OR TO BORROWER		**600. CASH AT SETTLEMENT TO OR FROM SELLER**	
301. Gross amount due from borrower (line 120)	62,412.67	601. Gross amount due to seller (line 420)	60,000.00
302. Less amounts paid by/for borrower (line 220)	52,765.00	602. Less reduction amount due seller (line 520)	31,675.36
303. **CASH** (☒ FROM) (☐ TO) **BORROWER**	9,647.67	603. **CASH** (☒ TO) (☐ FROM) **SELLER**	28,324.64

(44502-3) 5/76*
HUD-1A SETTLEMENT STATEMENT

SAF Systems & Forms
(American Savings & Accounting Supply, Inc.)

WORKSHEET — DETACH AND COMPLETE BEFORE TYPING

FIGURE 14–3 (*Continued*)

```
        Anytown Bank
        200 Smith Street              U.S. DEPARTMENT OF HOUSING AND URBAN DEVELOPMENT
        Anytown, Illinois  60111                     SETTLEMENT STATEMENT
                                                           PAGE 2
```

L. SETTLEMENT CHARGES

		PAID FROM BORROWER'S FUNDS AT SETTLEMENT	PAID FROM SELLER'S FUNDS AT SETTLEMENT
700.	**TOTAL SALES/BROKER'S COMMISSION based on price** $ 60,000 @ 6 % = 3,600		
	Division of commission (line 700) as follows:		
701.	$ 2,160 to Anytown Realth		
702.	$ 1,240 to Hillside Realty		
703.	Commission paid at Settlement		3,600.00
704.			
800.	**ITEMS PAYABLE IN CONNECTION WITH LOAN**		
801.	Loan Origination Fee %		
802.	Loan Discount 2 %	1,000.00	
803.	Appraisal Fee to I.M. Appraiser	50.00	
804.	Credit Report to Anytown Bank	40.00	
805.	Lender's Inspection Fee		
806.	Mortgage Insurance Application Fee to		
807.	Assumption Fee		
808.			
809.			
810.			
811.			
900.	**ITEMS REQUIRED BY LENDER TO BE PAID IN ADVANCE**		
901.	Interest from 9/15/82 to 10/1/82 @ $ 16.667 /day (16 days)	266.67	
902.	Mortgage Insurance Premium for 12 mos. to Brokers Mortgage Ins. Co.	375.00	
903.	Hazard Insurance Premium for 1 yrs. to Fireside Insurance Co.	240.00	
904.	yrs. to		
905.			
1000.	**RESERVES DEPOSITED WITH LENDER FOR**		
1001.	Hazard insurance mos. @ $ /mo.		
1002.	Mortgage insurance mos. @ $ /mo.		
1003.	City property taxes 4 mos. @ $ 90 /mo.	360.00	
1004.	County property taxes mos. @ $ /mo.		
1005.	Annual assessments mos. @ $ /mo.		
1006.	mos. @ $ /mo.		
1007.	mos. @ $ /mo.		
1008.	mos. @ $ /mo.		
1100.	**TITLE CHARGES**		
1101.	Settlement or closing fee to		
1102.	Abstract or title search to		
1103.	Title examination to		
1104.	Title insurance binder to		
1105.	Document preparation to Anytown Bank	25.00	
1106.	Notary fees to		
1107.	Attorney's fees to		
	(includes above items No.:)		
1108.	Title insurance to Brokers Title Insurance Company	50.00	250.00
	(includes above items No.: 1109 and 1110)		
1109.	Lender's coverage $ 50,000		
1110.	Owner's coverage $ 60,000		
1111.			
1112.			
1113..			
1200.	**GOVERNMENT RECORDING AND TRANSFER CHARGES**		
1201.	Recording fees: Deed $ 3 ; Mortgage $ 3 ; Release $ 3	6.00	3.00
1202.	City/county tax/stamps: Deed $ -- ; Mortgage $ --		
1203.	State tax/stamps: Deed $ 60 ; Mortgage $ --		60.00
1204.			
1205.			
1300.	**ADDITIONAL SETTLEMENT CHARGES**		
1301.	Survey to		
1302.	Pest inspection to		
1303.			
1304.			
1305.			
1400.	**TOTAL SETTLEMENT CHARGES** (enter on line 103, Section J and line 502, Section K)	2,412.67	3,913.00

The Undersigned Acknowledges Receipt of This Settlement Statement and Agrees to the Correctness Thereof.

/s/ Robert Harrison
/s/ Merritt Miller & Morgan Miller   /s/ Betty Harrison
              Buyer   **Seller**

(44503-1) 5/76*
HUD-1B SETTLEMENT STATEMENT

SAF Systems & Forms
American Savings & Accounting Supply, Inc.)

WORKSHEET — DETACH AND COMPLETE BEFORE TYPING

tember, and October at settlement. Four monthly escrow payments of $90 per month total $360, which is a charge to the borrower.

SUMMARY

In seeking a loan, a prospective borrower files an application and is interviewed by the lender, which begins the underwriting process. The underwriter analyzes the terms of the requested loan, the borrower characteristics, and the property characteristics in determining whether the loan should be made. If the loan request is approved, the lender issues a loan commitment, conditional on the borrower providing proper evidence of title and adequate hazard insurance. If the borrower accepts the loan commitment, a contract has been made. A settlement statement is prepared. If the transaction involves the purchase of a property, the settlement statement shows cash due from the buyer and the cash due to the seller. The seller delivers the deed to the buyer at closing. The buyer–borrower signs the mortgage and mortgage note, and the deed and the mortgage are recorded. The lender disburses the funds and the loan is made.

KEY TERMS

Abstract
Abstract and Opinion of Title
Borrower Analysis
Closing Statement
Credit Report
Escrow Account
Expense-to-Income Ratio
Gift Letter
Impound Account
Loan Application

Loan Commitment
Loan Discount
Loan Interview
Loan Rating Grid
Loan Terms Analysis
Loan Underwriting
Mortgagee's Title Insurance Policy
Owner's Title Insurance Policy

Property Analysis
Proration
Settlement Statement
Stable Monthly Gross Income
Title Insurance
Torrens System
Underwriter
Underwriting
Willingness to Pay

QUESTIONS FOR REVIEW AND DISCUSSION

1. What is the essential purpose of the loan interview?

2. Is it to the advantage of a lender to use the FHLMC-FNMA residential loan application form? Why?

3. What is an underwriter? What does an underwriter look at in his or her work relative to evaluating a mortgage loan?

4. What requirements or guidelines does the FHLMC have regarding expense-to-income ratios of potential borrowers? What is the purpose of these guidelines?

5. What is "willingness to pay"? How is it judged? Why is it important?

6. What evidence may be used to show valid title in obtaining a loan? Which is a lender likely to prefer?

7. What does RESPA mean? What is the purpose of RESPA procedures?

8. Match the following key terms and definitions:

a. Underwriting _____
b. Proration _____
c. Stable Monthly Gross Income _____
d. Loan Discount _____
e. Escrow Account _____
f. Loan Commitment _____

1. Accumulating funds for future needs with a lender, such as for real estate taxes or insurance premiums.

2. Base earnings plus recognizable secondary income, such as bonuses, commissions, overtime, and part-time jobs.

3. Making a loan to an investor; insuring a lender against loss on a loan.

4. Dividing expenses, income, or other income between parties on a proportionate basis.

5. Motivation of applicant in seeking a loan.

6. An offer to exchange a mortgage lien and promissory note for a loan at specified terms.

7. An offer by a lender to make a mortgage loan at specified terms.

8. Charge on borrower to increase rate of return to lender.

Appendix
to
Chapter Fourteen

Consumer protection laws apply to the extension of credit to finance residential real estate. The essentials of these laws are discussed here. The laws are taken up in the following order.

1. Fair Credit Reporting Act
2. Equal Credit Opportunity Act
3. Home Mortgage Disclosure Act
4. Community Reinvestment Act
5. Truth in Lending Act
6. Real Estate Settlement Procedures Act
7. National Flood Insurance
8. Usury Laws

FAIR CREDIT REPORTING ACT

The Fair Credit Reporting Act protects individuals by requiring that information in credit reports be accurate and relevant. The Act also requires the recipient of the credit report to treat it with confidentiality and to use it only for the purpose specified. If a prospective lender or seller denies credit due to information in the credit report, the applicant must be informed about it. The individual has the right to request examination of his or her file at the credit agency. The individual may correct any errors and file explanatory statements to counteract negative information in the credit agency's files.

Certain information is considered either unreliable or irrelevant. The Fair Credit Reporting Act prohibits investigative reports derived from interviews of an individual's neighbors regarding his or her mode of living, general reputation, and character. If less than $50,000 is involved, certain historical credit information is prohibited. In general, most adverse information that predates the credit report by more than seven years is prohibited. However, with bankruptcies, the period is 14 years.

EQUAL CREDIT OPPORTUNITY ACT

The Equal Credit Opportunity Act (ECOA) forbids discrimination in the granting of credit because of race, color, religion, national origin, age, sex, marital status, or the fact that all or part of the applicant's income is derived from a public assistance program. ECOA is implemented through Regulation B of the Board of Governors of the Federal Reserve and is sometimes referred to as Regulation B.

A lender may not ask questions about the spouse except under one of the following conditions: The applicant lives in a community property state; the spouse is to be contractually liable for the debt; the spouse's income is to be used to qualify for the loan; or the applicant will use child support, alimony, or maintenance to qualify for the loan.

A lender may not automatically reject part-time income when calculating an applicant's income. The lender must assess the probability of the part-time income continuing in the future. A lender cannot assume that a pregnancy will prevent a woman's employment. ECOA has forced lenders to give equal weight to a woman's income.

Applicants must be furnished with notice of their rights, under ECOA, prior to submitting a request for credit. The applicant must be informed of the rejection or acceptance of the request for credit within 30 days after the receipt of the completed application for credit. If a request for credit is denied and if the applicant requests, the applicant must be informed of the reason for rejection.

HOME MORTGAGE DISCLOSURE ACT

The Home Mortgage Disclosure ACT (HMDA) requires covered lenders to disclose the geographic distribution of their one- to four-family residential mortgage-lending activities by zip codes or census tract numbers. HMDA applies to depository institutions that have assets of more than $10,000,000, that have at least one office within a Standard Metropolitan Statistical Area, and that make federally related mortgage loans. Any mortgage made by an institution whose accounts are insured by an agency of the federal government or which is regulated by an agency of the federal government is classified as a federally related mortgage loan. Also, a mortgage loan sold to FNMA, FHLMC, or GNMA is classified as a federally related mortgage loan.

The purpose of the disclosure is to assist in the prohibition of redlining on the basis of race under the Civil Rights Act of 1968, Federal Home Loan Bank Board regulations, and various state laws. *Redlining* is the practice of imposing unjustifiably higher standards for mortgage-lending activity in certain areas within a community. An extreme form of redlining is a case in which a lender refuses to make any mortgage loans in redlined sections of the community regardless of the merits of the loan request.

COMMUNITY REINVESTMENT ACT

The Community Reinvestment Act (CRA) requires regulated financial institutions to serve the convenience and needs of the communities in which they operate. Each institution covered by CRA must prepare a map showing the communities that it serves. A community is defined as the contiguous areas surrounding each office or group of offices, including any low- or moderate-income neighborhoods in those areas. The institution must prepare a CRA statement for each community in which it has an office, and the statement must list the specific types of credit that it offers in each community.

The institution's service to its community is reviewed by the appropriate regulatory agencies, which are the Comptroller of the Currency, the Board of Governors of the Federal Reserve System, the FDIC, and the Federal Home Loan Bank. The intent is to prohibit lenders from redlining.

TRUTH IN LENDING ACT

Title I of the Consumer Credit Protection Act is called the Truth in Lending Act. The Truth in Lending Act authorizes the Board of Governors of the Federal Reserve System to interpret, implement, and amplify the law. The Board of Governors publishes the regulations as Federal Reserve Regulation Z; consequently the Truth in Lending Act is sometimes called *Regulation Z*. The Truth in Lending Act requires the disclosure of the costs of credit from alternative sources, so a consumer may choose the least cost source, other things being equal. The lender provides advance disclosure of the loan terms, such as the interest rate, finance charges, the due date of repayments, prepayment penalties, and late payment charges. The Act does not regulate the cost of credit or set maximum allowable interest rates.

Loans and Creditors Covered

Regulation Z applies to consumer credit and real estate loans to individuals for nonbusiness purposes, unless the business purpose is agriculture. Personal property and agriculture credit arrangements involving in excess of $25,000 are exempt. Loans secured by multifamily properties containing more than four units are exempt. Loans secured by properties containing two or more dwelling units are exempt if one or more of the units will be rented or sold as a condominium unit. Loans to corporations, trusts, partnerships, estates, cooperatives, associations, or units of government are exempt. Loan assumptions are not covered.

Regulation Z applies only to loans requiring five or more repayment installments. It applies to new loan transactions including refinancing, consolidation, or an increase in an existing obligation.

Only creditors who regularly extend or arrange for the extension of credit are required to comply with the provisions of Regulation Z.

Disclosure

The creditor's disclosure statement must disclose a number of specifics, the most important of which are the finance charges and the annual percentage rate. The finance charge is the total of all costs that the creditor requires the consumer or borrower to pay, directly or indirectly, to obtain the credit or loan. The *annual percentage rate* (APR) is the effective interest rate on the credit. The APR disclosed by the lender must be accurate within one-eighth of one percent.

The creditor's disclosure must also include the following: the total dollar amount of the finance charge and an itemization of the finance charge; the date on which the finance charge begins to apply; the number, amounts, and due dates of payments; the total of payments; the amount charged for any default, delinquency, or late payment; a description of the property and the security interest retained; any penalty charge for prepayment; the identification of the method used to compute any refund resulting from prepayment of the principal; the total amount of credit made available to the borrower; and the amounts deducted as prepaid finance charges.

It should be noted that if the loan is a first mortgage loan for the purpose of purchasing or constructing the pledged property, the lender does not have to disclose the total dollar amount of the finance charge and the total of the payments.

The creditor must make the disclosure before the credit is granted.

In the case of mortgage loans, the lender usually makes the disclosure at the time that the loan commitment is issued.

FINANCE CHARGES

Real estate purchase costs that are incurred in the absence of the extension of credit are not included in the finance charge. However, they must be itemized and disclosed to the customer. Examples of such costs are title insurance, recording fees, survey fees, appraisal fees, inspection fees, credit report fees, legal fees, and transfer taxes. Hazard insurance premiums are excluded if the lender provides a cost statement of the insurance and notifies the borrower of the right to obtain equivalent insurance elsewhere.

Finance charges include interest, loan origination fees, loan discounts, finder's fees, and service or carrying charges. Mortgage insurance premiums are included if they are required by the lender. Any credit life insurance premiums are included unless the borrower desired to purchase the insurance.

RESCISSION

Regulation Z gives the customer or the borrower the right to rescind the credit transaction. The customer or borrower must exercise this right in writing by midnight of the third business day following the date of the transaction or delivery of all material disclosures, whichever is later. This right of rescission does not apply to a loan whose proceeds are used to purchase a personal residence by the borrower and which is secured by a lien on that property.

REAL ESTATE SETTLEMENT PROCEDURES ACT (RESPA)

The Real Estate Settlement Procedures Act (RESPA) is implemented by the Board of Governors of the Federal Reserve System through Regulation X. RESPA applies to loans for the purchase of one- to four-family residences. It also applies to transactions such as when the purchaser assumes the loan or takes the property subject to an existing mortgage, when the loan terms are changed, or when the lender charges an assumption fee of more than $50. It does not cover refinancings, home improvement loans, construction loans, and loans secured by properties containing over 25 acres.

RESPA covers federally related first mortgage loans and loans made by lenders with more than $1 million per year invested in residential loans.

DISCLOSURE REQUIREMENTS

RESPA requires the lender to give the loan applicant a copy of the HUD publication *Settlement Costs and You* or an approved equivalent publication within three days after the submission of the loan application. The lender must give the borrower a written, good faith estimate of settlement costs other than those required in escrow deposits within three business days after the submission of the loan application. The party conducting the settlement is required to allow the borrower to inspect the settlement statement one day prior to settlement. The HUD uniform settlement form must be used as the financial settlement statement, and a copy must be given to both the buyer and the seller.

OTHER PROVISIONS

RESPA prohibits the payment of kickbacks or unearned fees. Real estate brokers are explicitly allowed the split fees with cooperating brokers, but they are prohibited from receiving any kickbacks or unearned fees. An example of a prohibited kickback is a payment to the lender for referring the borrower to a particular insurance agency or to a particular title insurance company.

Sellers cannot make the use of a particular title insurance company a condition of sale. Lenders are required to disclose their relationship to the title insurance company used.

RESPA limits the amount that the lender can require the borrower to place in escrow accounts for items such as real estate taxes and hazard insurance. RESPA limits required payments into escrow accounts at settlement to the amount necessary to bring the account up to the date of the first mortgage payment plus two additional months. Thereafter, monthly escrow payments are limited to one-twelfth of the projected cost for items such as real estate taxes and hazard insurance premiums.

The lender is responsible for preparation of the settlement statement, for which a fee may not be charged. The lender may delegate the preparation of the settlement statement to another party who is allowed to charge a preparation fee, but the lender has the ultimate responsibility for the preparation of the statement and for its conformance to the provisions of RESPA.

NATIONAL FLOOD INSURANCE

The National Flood Insurance Act established a program to provide insurance for losses due to floods. Flood insurance is offered by private insurance companies and is subsidized by the federal government. If the community or a portion of the community is located in a HUD designated special flood hazard area, the community is directed to develop a land use plan and to provide zoning of flood plains. Any new structures must be elevated above the one-hundred-year flood level or be properly floodproofed.

Communities are encouraged to participate in the national flood insurance program. If the community does not participate, federal agencies and federally insured or regulated institutions are prohibited from making mortgage loans on properties located in the HUD designated special flood hazard areas. There are exemptions to this rule including one for mortgage loans on residential dwellings occupied as a residence prior to 1 March 1976 or one year following the designation of the area as a special flood hazard area, whichever is later.

If the property is located in a designated special flood hazard area, the lender is responsible for informing the borrower. If flood insurance is available through the national flood insurance program, the lender must require flood insurance as a condition for granting the loan. The borrower is required to initiate, maintain, and renew the flood insurance. If flood insurance is not available and the property is not exempt, the lender is prohibited from making a mortgage loan on the property.

USURY LAWS

A *usury law* establishes a maximum allowable interest rate that may be charged by a lender. The allowable interest rate can be a specified rate or it can be a rate that floats with some index. If the lender charges and collects at a higher rate than that allowed by law, the lender is committing *usury.* Loans made to corporations are usually not covered by usury laws.

In 1979 Congress permanently exempted FHA and VA mortgage loans from state usury laws. In 1980 Congress passed an exemption of conventional residential mortgage loans from state usury laws. Residential mortgage loans made after 31 March 1980 are exempt from state usury laws. A state is allowed to reinstate the usury provision applicable to conventional residential mortgage loans if the state passes a law reinstating coverage of conventional mortgage loans prior to 1 April 1983. A number of states are expected to pass laws to limit the allowable loan discount, and some are expected to pass laws limiting the loan discount and reestablishing a maximum allowable interest rate.

SUMMARY

The Fair Credit Reporting Act is intended to protect the individual from inaccurate reporting by a credit agency. The Equal Credit Opportunity

Act forbids discrimination in the granting of credit on the basis of race, color, religion, national origin, age, sex, marital status, or the fact that all or part of the individual's income is derived from a public assistance program. The Home Mortgage Disclosure Act and the Community Reinvestment Act require disclosures of information that could be used to reveal any redlining activity. The Truth in Lending Act requires the lender to provide disclosure of the cost of credit including the APR. Lenders must make flood insurance a condition for obtaining a loan secured by a property located in the flood plain unless it qualifies as an exemption. Usury laws establish the maximum allowable interest rate that a lender can lawfully charge. Congress preempted state usury laws on residential mortgage loans in 1979 and 1980, but the states may reinstate their usury regulations by explicit acts.

KEY TERMS

Annual Percentage Rate (APR)

Community Reinvestment Act

Equal Credit Opportunity Act

Fair Credit Reporting Act

Flood Insurance

Home Mortgage Disclosure Act

Redlining

Regulation B

Regulation X

Regulation Z

RESPA

Truth in Lending Act

Usury

Usury Law

fifteen

Property Analysis

The value of the property being financed provides security, both initially and during the life of the loan. The value is therefore of primary interest to a lender, as it is to the seller and buyer in a real estate buy-sell agreement as well. However, our attention and concern are primarily with the relationship between the loan amount and the property value.

Most primary and secondary lenders are limited by regulations or policy to a maximum loan-to-value ratio (LVR) for the loans they originate or acquire. The LVR is based on market value or purchase price, whichever is lower. Loan underwriters also look to the value outlook for the subject property to ascertain whether the LVR is likely to increase during the life of the loan. An increasing LVR would mean that the risk of loss to the lender is also increasing. That is, a mortgage holder wants the property value to exceed the loan amount by some percentage at all times during the life of the loan. A holder is likely to be particularly concerned with the risk of a decline in the property's value in the early years of the loan. The possibility of an increasing loan-to-value ratio goes up with loan repayment patterns in which the principal amount may actually get larger in the early years, such as with a graduated payment plan. See Fig. 15–1.

As previously mentioned, loan underwriters look to the buy-sell price of a property being financed as well as to its market value estimate in making risk judgments. Secondary lenders prefer that the estimate be made by an independent appraiser. An FNMA-FHLMC standardized residential report form is increasingly being used by appraisers in reporting their value estimates for several reasons. Data about the property may be collected more quickly. The form acts as a checklist, thereby helping to insure against omissions. The standard format facilitates understanding and review of the appraisal by underwriters, review appraisers, and secondary lenders, and it is therefore widely accepted. The document is often referred to as *Form 70,* based on the number assigned it by the FHLMC.

MARKET VALUE

Two basic definitions of *value* are: (1) the dollar amount of the goods or services that the property commands in exchange and (2) the present value of the future benefits associated with the ownership of the property. Value to a specific owner-seller or buyer, is often termed *subjective value.* Subjective value varies from individual to individual. Value to the typical buyer and seller is called *market value* or value in exchange. Market value, as an objective value, should be verifiable or documented in the market. Market value, being objective and verifiable, carries much greater assurance that the property can be converted to its cash equivalent. Market value is also considered the "most probable selling price."

There are other definitions of market value. The California Supreme Court defined market value in the case of Sacramento R. R., et al. vs. Heilborn, 156 Calif. 408. In that case, market value was defined as "the highest price in terms of money which a property will bring if exposed for sale on the open market, with a reasonable time to find a purchaser, buying with full knowledge of all uses to which it is adapted and for which it is capable of being used." Another definition of market value is "the price at which a property will sell, assuming a knowledgeable buyer and seller both operating with reasonable knowledge and without undue pressure."[1] The market value definition currently used by FNMA-FHLMC is shown in Fig. 15–2.

The various definitions of market value explicitly state or imply a number of assumptions. These are

1. Payment, on sale, is on a cash or cash equivalent basis. The buyer utilizes financing on the terms generally available in the area.
2. Buyers and sellers have reasonable, but not perfect, knowledge.

---

[1]Alfred A. Ring and Jerome Dasso, *Real Estate Principles and Practices,* 9th ed. (Englewood Cliffs, N. J.: Prentice-Hall, Inc., 1981), p. 722.

FIGURE 15–1 Possible Interrelationships between the Value of the Subject Property and Mortgage Debt under Alternative Repayment Plans

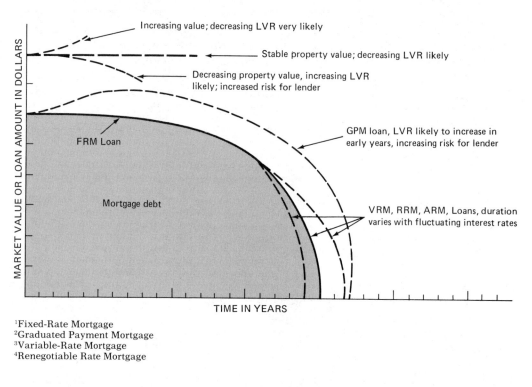

Increasing value; decreasing LVR very likely

Stable property value; decreasing LVR likely

Decreasing property value, increasing LVR likely; increased risk for lender

GPM loan, LVR likely to increase in early years, increasing risk for lender

FRM Loan

Mortgage debt

VRM, RRM, ARM, Loans, duration varies with fluctuating interest rates

MARKET VALUE OR LOAN AMOUNT IN DOLLARS

TIME IN YEARS

[1]Fixed-Rate Mortgage
[2]Graduated Payment Mortgage
[3]Variable-Rate Mortgage
[4]Renegotiable Rate Mortgage

FIGURE 15–2 Definition of Market Value Used by FNMA-FHLMC

DEFINITION OF MARKET VALUE: The highest price in terms of money which a property will bring in a competitive and open market under all conditions requisite to a fair sale, the buyer and seller, each acting prudently, knowledgeably and assuming the price is affected by undue stimulus. Implicit in this definition is the consummation of a sale of a specified date and the passing of title from seller to buyer under conditions whereby: (1) buyer and seller are typically motivated; (2) both parties are well informed or well advised, and each acting in what he considers his own best interest; (3) a reasonable time is allowed for exposure in the open market; (4) payment is made in cash or its equivalent; (5) financing, if any, is on terms generally available in the community at the specified date and typical for the property type in its locale; (6) the price represents a normal consideration for the property sold unaffected by special financing amounts and/or terms, services, fees, costs, or credits incurred in the transaction.

SOURCE: FHLMC Form 439; FNMA Form 1004B, Revised 1978; and Byrl N. Boyce, *Real Estate Appraisal Terminology,* rev. ed. (Cambridge, Mass.: Ballinger, 1981), p. 160. *Real Estate Appraisal Terminology* is jointly sponsored and endorsed by the American Institute of Real Estate Appraisers and the Society of Real Estate Appraisers.

3. Buyers and sellers are not under undue pressure to buy or sell, and they have a reasonable time period in which to conduct their business.
4. The buyer and seller are typically motivated and act indepently in their own best interests.

Market price, as distinct from market value, is the amount negotiated between a particular buyer and seller in an actual transaction. The market price may be equal to, less than, or more than the market value of the property. The market price may exceed market value if the buyer must act quickly or if the buyer receives financing terms more favorable than typically available. Market price is a fact; market value is an abstraction.

Underwriters and lenders frequently use market value in determining the amount they will lend on a property. Typically, this is accomplished through a loan-to-value ratio set by policy. However, a lower LVR may be used, as when the buy-sell price is less than market value. Also, when speculation is rampant in an area, prices are driven above a level considered reasonable by the lender. The appraiser might view speculators as typical buyers, whereas the lender might view them as special types of buyers. In this situation, the lender would exert more caution and apply a lower LVR in deciding the amount to lend.

THE APPRAISAL PROCESS

Lenders use appraisers to perform the analysis leading to an estimate of market value. An appraiser forms an estimate or opinion of market value based on specific data, hopefully in an impartial manner. Even so, estimates of market value for a given property may vary among appraisers, depending on assumptions made. An appraiser's estimate must be documented or rationalized and, in most cases, it must be in a written appraisal report. The FHLMC-FNMA standard form constitutes an abbreviated report, which is adequate for most one-family properties.

The appraiser follows a series of steps in reaching the estimate of value given in the appraisal report. The series of steps is called the *appraisal process.* The process is related to the FHLMC-FNMA residential report shown in Fig. 15–3 later in this chapter. The steps, with comments, are as follows:

1. *Definition of the Problem.* The problem is to estimate the market value for loan purposes of the fee simple interest in the property located at Lot 12, Block C. Fairlawn Subdivision, Hill County, Illinois (1262 Fairlawn Court, Anytown, Illinois), on the sale date of 28 August, 1982.

2. *Preliminary Survey and Appraisal Plan.* The appraiser determines the data needed, the sources of the data, and the number of work hours necessary to complete the appraisal. This allows the appraiser to estimate the date by which the appraisal report can be delivered and to determine the fee.

3. *Data Collection and Analysis.* The appraiser gathers general data and specific data. There are four general forces that influence the value of property—social, economic, governmental, and physical factors. In some appraisals these factors are examined on the national, regional, community, neighborhood, and specific site level. The FHLMC-FNMA residential report only requires the disclosure of data for the neighborhood and specific site levels. In addition, the improvements on the site are analyzed in some detail. Other specific data include comparable sales prices, rental levels, and local building costs.

4. *Application of the Three Approaches to Value.* The national, regional, city, and neighborhood data provide a general background for the application of the specific data under the market, cost, and income approaches. A value indication is reached by each of these three approaches.

5. *Reconciliation.* After reaching the value indications, the appraiser examines and compares them. When there is an active market for comparable properties, the direct sales comparison approach, or the *market approach to value,* is the most reliable approach, it is then given the greatest consideration in making a final value estimate. With single-family houses, the market approach is by far most often used. In such cases, the indications of *cost* and *income approachs* to value are then used as checks on the value indication derived via the market approach. The appraiser uses his or her judgment and experience to arrive at the final value estimate.

6. *Appraisal Report.* When the appraisal is completed, the appraiser makes an appraisal report, which shows the appraised value and the supporting data and analysis. The appraisal report can be a narrative report containing numerous pages or a form report such as the FHLMC-FNMA residential appraisal report.

FHLMC-FNMA RESIDENTIAL APPRAISAL REPORT

Figure 15–3 shows a completed FHLMC-FNMA residential appraisal report form. The form has several distinct sections, as indicated along its left-hand margin. These sections are as follows:

1. To be completed by lender
2. Neighborhood
3. Site
4. Improvements
5. Interior finish and equipment
6. Property rating (indicated at low center)
7. Cost approach
8. Market data analysis

FIGURE 15–3   Residential Appraisal Report

RESIDENTIAL APPRAISAL REPORT   File No. ____

Borrower	Merritt and Morgan Miller Census Tract ____ Map Reference ____
Property Address	1262 Fairlawn Court
City	Anytown County Hill State Illinois Zip Code 60111
Legal Description	Lot 12, Block C, Fairlawn Subdivision, Hill Country, Illinois

Sale Price $ 60,000 Date of Sale 8/28/82 Loan Term 25 yrs Property Rights Appraised [X]Fee [ ]Leasehold [ ]DeMinimis PUD
Actual Real Estate Taxes $ 1,080 (yr) Loan charges to be paid by seller $ None Other sales concessions None
Lender/Client Anytown Bank   Address 200 Smith Street, Anytown, Illinois 60111
Occupant Vacant   Appraiser I. M. Appraiser Instructions to Appraiser Call broker for keys

NEIGHBORHOOD

Location [ ]Urban [X]Suburban [ ]Rural
Built Up [X]Over 75% [ ]25% to 75% [ ]Under 25%
Growth Rate [X]Fully Dev. [ ]Rapid [ ]Steady [ ]Slow
Property Values [ ]Increasing [X]Stable [ ]Declining
Demand/Supply [ ]Shortage [X]In Balance [ ]Over Supply
Marketing Time [X]Under 3 Mos. [ ]4–6 Mos. [ ]Over 6 Mos.
Present Land Use 100 % 1 Family ___% 2–4 Family ___% Apts. ___% Condo ___% Commercial ___% Industrial ___% Vacant ___%
Change in Present Land Use [X]Not Likely [ ]Likely (*) [ ]Taking Place (*)
(*) From _____ To _____
Predominant Occupancy [X]Owner [ ]Tenant ___% Vacant
Single Family Price Range $ 55,000 to $ 75,000 Predominant Value $ 65,000
Single Family Age 2 yrs to 8 yrs Predominant Age 5 yrs

	Good	Avg.	Fair	Poor
Employment Stability		[XX]		
Convenience to Employment	[X]			
Convenience to Shopping	[X]			
Convenience to Schools	[X]			
Adequacy of Public Transportation				[X]
Recreational Facilities		[X]		
Adequacy of Utilities		[X]		
Property Compatibility	[X]			
Protection from Detrimental Conditions	[X]			
Police and Fire Protection		[X]		
General Appearance of Properties	[X]			
Appeal to Market	[X]			

Note: FHLMC/FNMA do not consider race or the racial composition of the neighborhood to be reliable appraisal factors.
Comments including those factors, favorable or unfavorable, affecting marketability (e.g. public parks, schools, view, noise).
View of small river, 3 blocks to elementary school, 6 blocks to public park. Neighborhood of moderate priced single family residences – There is no public transportation in Anytown thus this neighborhood is not at a relative disadvantage – Income range $18,000 - $28,000.

SITE

Dimensions 100' on Fairlawn Court + x 120' deep = 12,000 Sq. Ft. or Acres [ ]Corner Lot
Zoning classification Single family residential Present improvements [ ]do [ ]do not conform to zoning regulations
Highest and best use: [X]Present use [ ]Other (specify) _____

	Public	Other (Describe)
Elec.	[X]	
Gas	[X]	
Water	[X]	
San.Sewer	[X]	

OFF SITE IMPROVEMENTS
Street Access: [X]Public [ ]Private
Surface Concrete
Maintenance: [X]Public [ ]Private
[X]Storm Sewer [X]Curb/Gutter
[ ]Underground Elect. & Tel [X]Sidewalk [X]Street Lights

Topo Gently rolling
Size Average
Shape Regular
View Overlooks small river
Drainage Average
Is the property located in a HUD Identified Special Flood Hazard Area? [ ]No [ ]Yes

Comments (favorable or unfavorable including any apparent adverse easements, encroachments or other adverse conditions) _____
The subject site is slightly above average as compared to others in the neighborhood.

IMPROVEMENTS

[X]Existing [ ]Proposed [ ]Under Constr. No. Units 1 Type (det, duplex, semi/det., etc.) Detached Design (rambler, split level, etc.) Ranch Exterior Walls Wood siding
Yrs. Age: Actual 6 Effective 4 to 8 No. Stories 1
Roof Material Composition Gutters & Downspouts Aluminum [ ]None Window (Type): Sliding – Aluminum Insulation [ ]None [ ]Floor
[ ]Storm Sash [X]Screens [ ]Combination [X]Ceiling [X]Roof [X]Walls
[ ]Manufactured Housing
Foundation Walls Poured concrete
[ ]Slab on Grade [ ]Crawl Space

BSMT: 90 % Basement [ ]Outside Entrance [X]Sump Pump [X]Concrete Floor 0 % Finished Evidence of: [ ]Dampness [ ]Termites [ ]Settlement
[ ]Floor Drain Finished Ceiling _____ Finished Walls _____ Finished Floor _____

Comments The basement is dry and could be finished to provide additional living space.

ROOM LIST

Room List	Foyer	Living	Dining	Kitchen	Den	Family Rm.	Rec. Rm.	Bedrooms	No. Baths	Laundry	Other
Basement										Yes	
1st Level	No	Yes	Yes	Yes	No	Yes	No	3	2	–	None
2nd Level											

Finished area above grade contains a total of 7 rooms 3 bedrooms 2 baths. Gross Living Area 1,658 sq. ft. Bsmt Area 1,540 sq.ft.

INTERIOR FINISH & EQUIPMENT

Kitchen Equipment [X]Refrigerator [X]Range/Oven [ ]Disposal [ ]Dishwasher [X]Fan/Hood [ ]Compactor [ ]Washer [ ]Dryer
HEAT: Type Forced air Fuel Gas Cond. Good AIR COND: [ ]Central [X]Other 3 window units [X]Adequate [ ]Inadequate

Floors	[ ]Hardwood [X]Carpet Over sub floor
Walls	[X]Drywall [ ]Plaster
Trim/Finish	[ ]Good [X]Average [ ]Fair [ ]Poor
Bath Floor	[ ]Ceramic [X]carpet
Bath Wainscot	[ ]Ceramic [X]drywall

Special Features (including energy efficient items) Smoke detector

PROPERTY RATING

	Good	Avg.	Fair	Poor
Quality of Construction (Materials & Finish)		[X]		
Condition of Improvements	[X]			
Room sizes and layout		[X]		
Closets and Storage		[X]		
Insulation—adequacy		[X]		
Plumbing—adequacy and condition		[X]		
Electrical—adequacy and condition		[X]		
Kitchen Cabinets—adequacy and condition		[X]		
Compatibility to Neighborhood	[X]			
Overall Livability		[X]		
Appeal and Marketability		[X]		

ATTIC: [X]Yes [ ]No [ ]Stairway [X]Drop-stair [ ]Scuttle [ ]Floored [ ]Heated
Finished (Describe) No
CAR STORAGE: [ ]Garage [ ]Built-in [X]Attached [ ]Detached [ ]Car Port
No. Cars 2 [X]Adequate [ ]Inadequate Condition _____
Yrs Est Remaining Economic Life 35 to 45 .Explain if less than Loan Term

FIREPLACES, PATIOS, POOL, FENCES, etc. (describe) None

COMMENTS (including functional or physical inadequacies, repairs needed, modernization, etc.) None - but will need washer and dryer.

FIGURE 15–3 (*Continued*)

VALUATION SECTION

Purpose of Appraisal is to estimate Market Value as defined in Certification & Statement of Limiting Conditions (FHLMC Form 439/FNMA Form 1004B). If submitted for FNMA, the appraiser must attach (1) sketch or map showing location of subject, street names, distance from nearest intersection, and any detrimental conditions and (2) exterior building sketch of improvements showing dimensions.

COST APPROACH

Measurements		No. Stories	Sq. Ft.
43' x 36'	x	1	1,548
10' x 11'	x	1	110
x	x		
x	x		
x	x		
x	x		

Total Gross Living Area (List in Market Data Analysis below) __1,658__

Comment on functional and economic obsolescence: __None__

ESTIMATED REPRODUCTION COST – NEW – OF IMPROVEMENTS:

Dwelling __1,658__ Sq. Ft. @ $ __28__	=	$46,240
Basement 1,540 Sq. Ft. @ $ __5__	=	7,700
Extras Refrigerator and range	=	1,000
Special Energy Efficient Items _____	=	
Porches, Patios, etc.	=	
Garage/Car Port __400__ Sq. Ft. @ $ __10__	=	4,000
Site Improvements (driveway, landscaping, etc.)	=	1,000
Total Estimated Cost New	=	$59,940

Less Depreciation $ __9,290__ | Physical | Functional $ – | Economic $ – | = $(9,290)

Depreciated value of improvements . . . . = $50,650

ESTIMATED LAND VALUE . . . . = $9,000
(If leasehold, show only leasehold value)

INDICATED VALUE BY COST APPROACH . . . $59,650

The undersigned has recited three recent sales of properties most similar and proximate to subject and has considered these in the market analysis. The description includes a dollar adjustment, reflecting market reaction to those items of significant variation between the subject and comparable properties. If a significant item in the comparable property is superior to, or more favorable than, the subject property, a minus (-) adjustment is made, thus reducing the indicated value of subject; if a significant item in the comparable is inferior to, or less favorable than, the subject property, a plus (+) adjustment is made, thus increasing the indicated value of the subject.

MARKET DATA ANALYSIS

ITEM	Subject Property	COMPARABLE NO. 1		COMPARABLE NO. 2		COMPARABLE NO. 3	
Address	1262 Fairlawn Ct.	1264 Fairlawn Ct.		1322 Fairlawn Ct.		823 Fairlawn Ct.	
Proximity to Subj.		next door		1 block		4 blocks	
Sales Price	$ 60,000		$62,800		$62,00		$6,000
Price/Living area	$ 36.19	$36.73		$36.26		$3.78	
Data Source	Contract/Appraisal	Contract/Appraisal		Contract/Appraisal		Contract/Appraisal	
		DESCRIPTION	Adjustment	DESCRIPTION	Adjustment	DESCRIPTION	Adjustment
Date of Sale and Time Adjustment	Aug. 27, 1982	Aug. 1, 1982	–	March 12, 1982	+1,900	March 5, 1982	+1,700
Location	Average	Average	–	Average	–	Average	
Site/View	Good	Good	–	Good	–	Average	+1,000
Design and Appeal	Average/Average	Average/Average	–	Average/Average	–	Average/Average	–
Quality of Const.	Average	Average		Average		Average	
Age	6	6	–	5	–1,000	7	+1,000
Condition	Good	Good		Good		Good	
Living Area Room Count and Total	Total 7 B-rms 3 Baths 2	Total 7 B-rms 3 Baths 2		Total 7 B-rms 3 Baths 2		Total 7 B-rms 3 Baths 2	
Gross Living Area	1658 Sq.Ft.	1710 Sq.Ft.	–1,450	1,710 Sq.Ft.	–1,450	1,658 Sq.Ft.	–
Basement & Bsmt. Finished Rooms	90%/none	Full/none	–450	Full/none	–450	Full/none	
Functional Utility	Average	Average	–	Average		Average	
Air Conditioning	3 window units	3 window units		3 window units	–	3 window units	
Garage/Car Port	Att. 2 car	Att. 2 car	–	Att. 2 car	–	Att. 2 car	
Porches, Patio, Pools, etc.	None	Patio	–600	Patio	–600	None	–
Special Energy Efficient Items	None	None		None		None	
Other (e.g. fireplaces, kitchen equip., remodeling)	Refrigerator & Range	Refrigerator, range, washer, dryer & disposal	–500	Refrigerator, range, washer, dryer & disposal	–500	Refrigerator & Range	–
Sales or Financing Concessions	Conventional/None	Conventional/None	–	Conventional/None	–	Conventional/None	–
Net Adj. (Total)		☐ Plus; ☒ Minus $ 3,000		☐ Plus; ☒ Minus $ 2,100		☒ Plus; ☐ Minus $ 3,700	
Indicated Value of Subject		$ 59,800		$ 59,900		$ 59,700	

Comments on Market Data __All comparables are in the same subdivision. Comparable No. 3 the same model - comparables Nos. 1 & 2 very similar models.__

INDICATED VALUE BY MARKET DATA APPROACH . . . . . . $ 59,800

INDICATED VALUE BY INCOME APPROACH (If applicable) Economic Market Rent $ __500__ /Mo. x Gross Rent Multiplier __120__ = $ 60,000

This appraisal is made ☒ "as is" ☐ subject to the repairs, alterations, or conditions listed below ☐ completion per plans and specifications.

Comments and Conditions of Appraisal: _____

Final Reconciliation: __The market data approach was given the greatest consideration because of the comparability of the properties and the recent sales dates. The cost and income approaches were used primarily as checks.__

Construction Warranty ☐ Yes ☒ No Name of Warranty Program _____ Warranty Coverage Expires _____

This appraisal is based upon the above requirements, the certification, contingent and limiting conditions, and Market Value definition that are stated in ☒ FHLMC Form 439 (Rev. 10/78)/FNMA Form 1004B (Rev. 10/78) filed with client __March 15__ 19 __79__ ☐ attached.

I ESTIMATE THE MARKET VALUE, AS DEFINED, OF SUBJECT PROPERTY AS OF __August 28__ 1982 to be $59,800

Appraiser(s) /s/ I. M. Appraiser   Review Appraiser (If applicable) /s/ I. M. Lender

☒ Did ☐ Did Not Physically Inspect Property

FHLMC Form 70 Rev. 7/79   REVERSE   FNMA Form 1004 Rev. 7/79

The completed form provides the essential data relating to the neighborhood, the site, and the improvements and the indicated value under each of the three approaches to value. The information should support the appraiser's final value estimate. A user of the appraisal may make judgments about the neighborhood, the site, the improvements, and the appraiser's analysis based on the data. The influence of a particular factor, positive or negative, is usually obvious. If it is not obvious, comment will be made on it. A lender is particularly interested in any factors that may adversely affect the current and future marketability of the property. If the negative factor is fully reflected in the value estimate and if it does not make the property difficult to market, the lender will not reject the loan because of that factor.

With this introduction, the FHLMC-FNMA standardized residential appraisal report form is taken up section by section.

TO BE COMPLETED BY LENDER

The lender completes the first portion of the appraisal report. The borrower, the location of the property, and the property rights to be appraised are identified. The purpose of the appraisal is to estimate the market value for financing purposes. The date of sale, which is the date for valuation purposes, is also stated. The lender lists the loan terms, the annual real estate taxes, the sale price, any loan changes to be paid by the seller, and any other sales concessions. The existence of sales concessions would mean that the $60,000 sales price overstates the true transaction price of the property.

NEIGHBORHOOD

The FHLMC directs the appraiser and lender to consider economic, governmental, social, and physical factors in the analysis of the neighborhood. It should be noted that FHLMC and FNMA prohibit the consideration of race or the racial composition of the neighborhood as a factor in the valuation of the property.

The appraiser is required to furnish considerable information on the neighborhood in which the subject property is located. The possible negative features include under 25 percent built-up, a slow growth rate, declining property values, an over supply, a long marketing time, a probable change in land use, tenant occupancy with substantial vacancies, and a price outside of the normal price range. Rapid decline in neighborhood quality is one of the most likely reasons for a rapid decline in property value, an increasing LVR, and, hence, an increased risk of loss to a lender due to default of the borrower. In our case example, however, the neighborhood and property passes all of these tests.

The right-hand side of the neighborhood section shows a rating grid for neighborhood, involving factors ranging from employment stability to appeal to the market of the subject. The only negative factor for the neighborhood is that it has no public transportation. However, this is not a relative disadvantage because there is no public transportation in the entire community.

Any below average rating for any factor in the rating grid must be explained in the blanks provided for comments. Any other significant factors about the neighborhood not covered elsewhere should be explained by comments.

The analysis of the neighborhood factors suggests that there is no reason to expect a decline in property values in the neighborhood.

SITE

The FHLMC-FNMA form requires the appraiser to provide information about the site. The site is zoned single-family residential and is approximately one-quarter acre in size. It is at its highest and best use. It is served by all the standard utilities, and it has all the typical offsite improvements. The factors from topography through to drainage are all average or better. No flood hazard exists. The subject site is slightly above average for the neighborhood.

IMPROVEMENTS

The appraiser describes the improvements including the basement and provides a room list. The structure is a detached ranch-type single-family residence that is six years old. The exterior walls, the roof, gutters and downspouts, windows, and insulation are adequate and indicate average construction. The house contains approximately 1,650 square feet of gross living space and seven rooms including three bedrooms plus two bathrooms. The house has an unfinished basement of approximately 1,500 square feet in size, and it contains a laundry room. The improvements are average in quality and size and conform to the standards of the neighborhood.

INTERIOR FINISH AND EQUIPMENT/PROPERTY RATING

The structure has an unfinished attic and an adequate two-car attached garage. The materials used in the floors, walls, and the trim indicate average quality construction. The heating system is a gas fueled forced-air system, which is in good condition. Adequate air conditioning is provided by three window units. Kitchen equipment includes a refrigerator, stove with oven, and a fan with hood, but the purchasers will have to furnish their own washer and dryer.

The appraiser rates the property on a number of factors ranging from the quality of construction through appeal and marketability. The improvements are average in most categories, but they are in good condition and comparable to other houses in the area. The subject improvements have a good appeal to individuals who desire to move to this neighborhood, so the property appears to have good marketability. The estimated remaining economic life of the improvements is 35 to 45 years, so a 25-year loan term seems acceptable.

VALUATION SECTION

The valuation section (second page) concerns the application of the three basic approaches to estimate the market value of the subject property. Each approach requires the use of data obtained from the market. If there is an active market for the type of property being appraised, the market approach, also called the direct sales comparison approach, is the preferred method. The other two approaches are the cost approach and the income approach.

COST APPROACH

The first portion in the valuation section is the analysis leading to the market value estimate by the cost approach. The appraiser first determines that the property is at its highest and best use. The appraiser employs the cost-per-square-foot method. The number of square feet in the dwelling, the basement, and the garage are determined and multiplied by the cost per square foot for each. The cost for extras—special energy efficient items, porches, patios, and site improvements—is added. The total estimated cost if the house were new would be $59,940.

The next step is the calculation and deduction of depreciation. *Depreciation* is the loss in value from reproduction cost new due to any cause. There are three classes of depreciation. *Physical depreciation* or physical deterioration results from the wear and tear of use, the actions of the elements, or any other physical cause. *Functional depreciation* or functional obsolescence results from design deficiencies and obsolete or inadequate equipment, wiring, plumbing, and other such features. *Economic depreciation* or economic obsolescence results from external factors such as declining employment opportunities in the area, which reduce the demand for the property.

The appraiser also classifies the depreciation as either curable or incurable in an economic sense. *Incurable depreciation* occurs when the cost to cure is greater than the value added by the cure. *Curable depreciation* occurs when the value added is greater than the cost to cure. In the case of incurable depreciation, the appraiser includes the loss in market value in the total depreciation. If the depreciation is curable, the appraiser includes the cost to cure in the total description. The total depreciation of $9,290 is deducted from the $59,940 reproduction cost of the improvements. The depreciated cost of the improvements is $50,650.

The next step is to calculate the land value and to add it to the depreciated cost of the improvements. The appraiser has estimated the land value at $9,000. The resulting indicated value by the cost approach is $59,650.

MARKET DATA APPROACH

The direct sales comparison approach involves the adjustment of the sales prices of comparable properties to estimate the market value of the subject property. The FHLMC-FNMA form requires the appraiser to cite three recent sales of the properties that are most similar and located closest to the subject property. The appraiser makes a time adjustment for the change in the value of the comparable properties between the dates that they sold and the date of appraisal for the subject property. Adjustments are made for any difference between the subject property and the comparable properties. If the comparable properties have superior features, a deduction must be made to make them equivalent to the subject property. If the comparable properties have inferior features, an addition must be made to make the comparable properties equivalent to the subject property. Adjustments are always made from the comparable to the subject property in the analysis.

Let us consider comparable property number two. It was sold on 12 March 1982, and the appraiser estimates that it has increased in value by $1,900 by 28 August 1982. The appraiser adds the $1,900 to arrive at the comparable property market value as of 28 August, 1982. The comparable property is one year newer than the subject property, and the appraiser deducts $1,000 for the difference. The comparable property contains about 50 square feet of gross living space more than the subject property, and the appraiser deducts $1,450. The comparable property has a larger basement, and the appraiser deducts $450. The comparable property has a patio, whereas the subject property does not, and the appraiser deducts $600. When comparable property two was sold, it had a washer, dryer, and garbage disposal. The subject property does not have these, so the appraiser deducts $500. The total deductions are $4,000, and are partially offset by the $1,900 addition for the time adjustment. The net minus deduction is $2,100, which indicates that the value of the subject property is $59,900.

The appraiser adjusts each of the three comparable properties to arrive at a value for the subject property. The appraiser uses his or her judgment and experience to arrive at a $59,800 value indication for the subject property by the direct sales comparison, or market, approach.

INCOME APPROACH

Since the property is a single-family dwelling, the appraiser uses the gross rent multiplier version of the income approach. The appraiser estimates the economic market rent at $500 per month and the gross monthly rent multiplier at 120. This results in a $60,000 estimate by the gross rent multiplier version of the income approach.

RECONCILIATION

The appraiser arrived at a $59,650 value by the cost approach, a $59,800 value by the market approach, and a $60,000 value by the income approach. *Reconciliation* is the process of considering the differences in the value indications and arriving at a single value estimate for the subject property. Since there is an active market for this type of property, the appraiser relies heavily on the $59,800 value estimate arrived at by the market approach. The cost and income approaches are used as checks of the reasonableness of the value indication arrived at under the market approach. Note the final statement, *"I estimate the market value, as defined, of subject property as of* August 28, 1982 to be $59,800," followed by the appraiser's signature. This statement and value estimate provides the basis of a lend decision by the bank, and a possible buy decision of a loan at a later date by a secondary lender.

SUMMARY

Market value of a property provides the basis for using the property to secure a mortgage loan. The loan-to-value ratio is a typical indication upon which this decision is based. The appraisal process is used to estimate market value. The appraisal process consists of a series of steps ranging from the definition of the problem to the completion of the appraisal report.

The FHLMC-FNMA standardized residential appraisal report form serves as an abbreviated appraisal report that is widely accepted by secondary lenders. The form contains information about the neighborhood, site, and improvements. Analysis and value indications under the cost, market, and income approaches and the final value estimate are also shown on the form. An underwriter, lender, and any purchaser in the secondary mortgage market review the form report in detail prior to making a decision to make or to buy a loan secured by the subject property.

KEY TERMS

Appraisal Process	Functional Depreciation	Market Value
Cost Approach to Value	Income Approach to Value	Physical Depreciation
Curable Depreciation	Incurable Depreciation	Reconciliation
Depreciation	Market Approach to Value	Subjective Value
Economic Depreciation	Market Price	

QUESTIONS FOR REVIEW AND DISCUSSION

1. Give two reasons a property must be appraised or valued in the real estate financing process.

2. Give at least two reasons for a primary lender to use an FHLMC-FNMA standard appraisal form to document the market value of a property being considered as security for a loan.

3. Give two alternative definitions of market value.

4. What are the main data required of a lender in a Form 70?

5. Identify the main sections of a Form 70 pertaining to data about the subject property.

6. Which of the three approaches to value is usually the most important in finding the market value of one-family residences?

7. Match the following words or phrases to their correct definitions:

   a. Curable Depreciation   1. Area values increasing.

   b. Market Price _____   2. Most probable selling price.

   c. Market Value _____   3. When cost to correct deficiency exceeds value increase after correction.

   d. Reconciliation _____

   e. Subjective Value _____   4. Value to an individual.

      5. Price in fact.

      6. When cost to correct deficiency is less than value increase after correction

      7. Price in theory.

      8. Method of reaching final market value.

sixteen

Lender Considerations and Analysis

Mortgage lenders are concerned with the safety, liquidity, and relative profitability of the loans. Risks are attached to loans on an individual and a portfolio basis. The long duration of the loan necessitates that lenders forecast conditions for a number of years into the future to broadly assess and to manage these risks. This long duration of the loans also means the portfolio is relatively illiquid.

Lenders engage in profit planning because of the long life and the many risks associated with their mortgage loan investments. They must take into account the cost of funds as well as the costs of loan servicing in this planning. They also must continuously and carefully manage their portfolio to obtain an adequate rate of return and to maintain solvency.

The purpose of this chapter is to give an overview of a lender's concerns in originating mortgage loans and managing a mortgage loan portfolio. Toward this end, the following major topics are discussed:

1. Lenders' Broad Considerations
2. Lending Risks
3. Decision Costs
4. Profit Planning

5. Loan Portfolio Management
6. Loan Servicing

The expectation is that the overview will give the reader a much better perspective of the real estate financing process.

LENDERS' BROAD CONSIDERATIONS

Economic conditions directly affect the safety and profitability of mortgage lending. Thus, expectations about future economic conditions have a major impact on the willingness of individuals and institutions to lend (and borrow) and on the terms offered by lenders. Lenders, therefore, forecast a number of factors including the expected levels of economic activity, of real estate activity, of interest rates, and of the rate of inflation. Also, since government policies have a major impact on these factors, lenders must consider government actions and policies when making their forecasts.

LEVEL OF ECONOMIC ACTIVITY

The lender must forecast the level of economic activity at both the national and local levels because both impact local property values. The lender must take into account both the secular, or long-term, trends and cyclical, or short-term, movements in the level of economic activity.

The level of economic activity has a direct impact on the value of properties. As the level of economic activity declines, income declines and unemployment increases. This leads to an increase in defaults on mortgage loans and to declines in property values. If lenders expect a major recession, they are likely to adopt very conservative lending standards. Expected levels of economic activity at or near full employment lead to opposite conclusions. With high levels of economic activity, property values would remain stable or increase and mortgage defaults would be at a low level.

REAL ESTATE ACTIVITY

The general level of real estate activity has an impact on both property values and the demand for real estate financing. The lender should be aware of trends at both the national and local levels. When there is a high level of real estate activity, the demand for real estate financing is high and property values tend to be either stable or increasing. When the level of real estate activity falls, the demand for mortgage funds tends to decline and property values tend to decline. In turn, a rational lender would follow more conservative policies.

Interest rates have a twofold impact for lenders. First, the level of interest rates has an impact on the availability and cost of funds to financial institutions. Second, the level of interest rates determines the value of existing mortgage loans.

Savings and loan associations and other financial institutions need a 1.25 to 2 percent spread or differential between their cost of funds and the interest rate that they charge on mortgage loans. Traditionally, most mortgage loans had long terms and fixed interest rates. The cost of funds for a large portion of the funds held by savings and loan associations and other depository institutions is tied to market interest rates, so the cost of funds fluctuates periodically. The Depository Institutions Deregulation and Monetary Control Act of 1980 provides for the phase-out of interest rate ceilings on all deposits at financial institutions. This phase-out may result in the cost of funds of depository institutions fluctuating even more widely.

The combination of long-term fixed interest rate loans and rising interest rates, which increase the lender's cost of funds, has caused substantial problems for most thrift institutions. This combination caused many savings and loan associations and mutual savings banks to realize losses in the early 1980s. Some institutions became insolvent and were absorbed or acquired by other institutions.

Lenders forecast interest rates in order to forecast their cost of funds. If interest rates are expected to fluctuate widely, lenders must either abandon long-term loans or use variable-rate loans to shift the problem or part of the problem to the borrowers.

Forecasting interest rates is also necessary to forecast expected returns from the lender's holdings. Falling interest rates encourage the prepayment of loans; the lender-investor must then accept lower interest rates when reinvesting these prepaid funds. Of course, rising interest rates allow lenders to make new loans at higher interest rates.

Rising interest rates cause another problem for depository institutions. When interest rates rise, some depositors withdraw their deposits and invest them directly or in money market funds. This withdrawal reduces the funds at depository institutions. The savings and loan associations and other depository institutions may then be forced to cut back on mortgage-lending activity. Alternatively, they might sell existing loans from their portfolio in the secondary mortgage market to gain new funds.

As the current market interest rate on new loans rises above the contract interest rate on existing loans, an existing mortgage loan falls in value and sells at a discount in the secondary mortgage market. If current market rates decline, the value of an existing loan increases. Lenders must forecast the level of interest rates to calculate the value of their mortgage portfolio.

The availability of funds and the level of interest rates are also important determinants of the level of economic activity, the level of real estate activity, and property values.

VALUE OF THE DOLLAR

Lenders also project changes in the general price level or the purchasing power of the dollar. With a substantial rise in the general price level, the lender is repaid in dollars with less purchasing power. This is a major concern for lenders that make loans from their own equity funds. With a projection of inflation, a lender either raises the interest rate charged or requires an equity participation.

Depository institutions obtain most of their funds from deposits. They then lend or invest the funds. They are, in a sense, both borrowers and lenders, so the spread between the cost of funds and the returns is much more important to them then changes in the purchasing power of the dollar. Of course, when there is inflation, depositors demand a higher rate of return to protect the purchasing power of their funds. This higher rate of return raises the cost of funds to depository institutions.

GOVERNMENT POLICY

Lenders forecast government policy because it has an impact on the entire economy. Government fiscal policy involves taxation and government expenditures. In turn, fiscal policy directly influences the levels of economic activity, of real estate activity, of inflation, and of interest rates. Monetary policy as exercised by the Federal Reserve Board also has an influence on these factors. Monetary policy can also be used to directly influence the level of interest rates.

Government agencies, including the Federal Reserve Board, regulate the activities of financial insitutions. Quasi-government corporations are active purchasers in the secondary mortgage market. GNMA guarantees mortgage-backed securities, and limits on its activity can reduce the liquidity of FHA and VA mortgages. Government agencies such as FHA, VA, and FmHA insure and/or guarantee mortgage loans, and their activities have an impact on the mortgage market and real estate market.

The Depository Institutions Deregulation and Monetary Control Act (DIDMCA) of 1980 is an example of a change in government policy that will have a major impact on the mortgage market. It allows federal savings and loan associations to engage in increased consumer installment credit lending, which may reduce the percentage of their assets that they invest in mortgage loans. The planned phase-out of interest rate ceilings on deposits seems likely to raise the cost of funds to financial institutions generally. In recent years, regulators have also allowed financial institutions to make new types of mortgage loans, such as graduated payment and variable-rate mortgage loans. Changes in regulations allow significant changes in operations within the mortgage market, so mortgage lenders must be aware of the impact of current regulations and must anticipate future changes in laws and regulations.

LENDING RISKS

Lenders assume a number of risks when they engage in mortgage lending. These risks are usually classified as either individual loan risks, which include borrower risk and property risk, and portfolio risks. Both classes of risks are discussed below.

INIDIVIDUAL LOAN RISK

Individual loan risk refers to the probability of a default on the given mortgage loan and the probable magnitude of the loss on the given loan in the event of default. The probability of a loss on an individual mortgage loan can be kept at a minimum by proper underwriting policy and implementation of that policy. In the underwriting process, the lender makes an assessment of the borrower risk and the property risk.

Borrower risk is the chance that a borrower either will not have the funds necessary to repay the loan or will be unwilling to repay the loan. The lender analyzes the borrower's (a) credit rating, (b) assets, (c) income, and (d) motivation to determine the nature of the borrower risk. The guidelines or procedures for assessing the borrower risk are discussed in Chap. 14, "Loan Underwriting and Settlement Procedures" and in Chap. 20, "Residential Income Property Financing."

Property risk is the risk that the value of the property pledged as security will be insufficient to pay the lender's claim when the lender forecloses. In the case of income property loans in which the repayment of the loan is dependent on the income generated from the property, property risk also refers to the possibility that the property will generate insufficient income.

The value of the property is estimated by the appraisal, which was discussed in Chap. 15. The value is dependent upon the property's onsite characteristics, location, and marketability. The lender also must forecast future trends in the real estate market and property values. The analysis of income from a property is discussed in Chap. 20.

The assessment of the borrower and property risks allows the lender to determine the appropriate terms for the loan. The lender may make only first mortgage loans, reduce the loan-to-value ratio, and/or require mortgage insurance to limit the individual loan risk. Individual loan risks cannot be entirely eliminated because random events such as divorce, death, illness, or unemployment will cause losses on some loans. The losses associated with these events are a normal cost of mortgage lending.

PORTFOLIO RISKS

A mortgage loan portfolio is the sum or total of all mortgage loans held by a lender-investor. Chances of loss that apply to the portfolio are called *portfolio risks*. These risks can be categorized as (a) administrative, (b) business, (c) financial, (d) interest rate, (e) liquidity, and (f) purchasing power risk.

In corporate finance, the traditional definition of business risk is that it is the risk inherent in the operation of the business, while financial risk is the added risk associated with the use of borrowed funds and preferred stock. These definitions of risk are appropriate for nondepository lenders, but depository institutions are major lenders. By their nature depository institutions accept deposits which represent debt, so they inherently use this type of financing in the operation of their business. Depository institutions obtain only a small portion of their funds from debt financing other than deposits and certificates. Thus we shall define business and financial risk somewhat differently than it is defined in corporate finance when we discuss depository institutions and their mortgage portfolios.

There are a number of administrative actions involved with the closing and servicing of mortgage loans. The possibility of errors in the contract terms at closing, errors in record keeping, and the failure to note significant deterioration in the pledged property are examples of *administrative risks*. They increase the costs of administering a mortgage loan. Lenders can control administrative risks and keep them at a minimum by devising and implementing standard operating procedures.

The mortgage lender expects a small percentage of the loans to result in losses. *Business risk* as related to the portfolio is the risk that a higher than expected percentage of the loans will result in losses. This reduces the rate of return to the lender, and in a major recession or depression it could result in the lender's insolvency or bankruptcy. Diversification and mortgage insurance can reduce the business risk associated with the portfolio.

Depository institutions and others are subject to financial risk on the loan portfolio. They need a positive spread between the return on the mortgage loan portfolio and the cost of their funds. The *financial risk* on the portfolio is the chance that the spread will be too thin. The spread is reduced by falling returns from the portfolio, an increasing cost of funds, or a combination of the two. When the spread becomes too small or negative, it can result in the insolvency and possible bankruptcy of the lender. The use of adjustable-rate loans can reduce the financial risk associated with the portfolio.

The classic *interest rate risk* is that the market interest rate will rise and cause a decrease in the value of the loan portfolio. Another aspect of an interest rate risk relates to the spread which was discussed above. Rising market interest rates are often accompanied by disintermediation, and depository institutions are forced to raise the interest rates paid on deposits, which increases their cost of funds.

Liquidity risk refers to the ability to convert the mortgages into cash. Since increases in the market rate of interest cause declines in the value of existing mortgages, there is the risk that a mortgage cannot be converted into cash at its face value. In times of disintermediation, many lenders attempt to sell mortgages. There is no assurance that the lender can sell loans even at or near the current market price because FNMA, FHLMC, and others purchase only a portion of the loans offered for sale.

The *purchasing power risk* is the risk that the general price level will rise and that the lender will be repaid in dollars with reduced purchasing power. The purchasing power risk associated with the portfolio is a major concern to lenders that employ a substantial amount of their own equity funds in their lending activities. The purchasing power risk is of secondary concern to depository lenders except to the degree that changes in the price level affect the spread, and this relates more closely to financial risk.

Loan portfolio management is discussed in more detail later in this chapter.

DECISION COSTS

Lending decision costs include the loan origination costs, servicing costs, and costs associated with defaults, foreclosures, and other unfavorable events. Loan origination costs include the salaries of loan officers and the expenses associated with support services. Loan servicing costs include personnel costs, computer services, and other support services. Decisions costs are also sometimes termed administrative costs.

Decision costs tend to be highly dependent on future events; thus they may vary widely from year to year. Decision costs include (1) the costs for collecting delinquent payments through to adjustments or foreclosure, (2) the losses involved with liquidating the pledged properties, (3) the losses from increases in the market interest rates above the contract interest rate on the mortgages, and (4) the costs associated with selling a portion of the mortgage portfolio if additional funds are needed to maintain the institution's liquidity.

Collecting payments on delinquent loans increases servicing costs. In some cases the lender makes adjustments to avoid foreclosure, and this sometimes involves the forgiveness of a portion of the interest. In any event, delinquent loans require increased personnel time, which increases costs.

Foreclosure also requires additional personnel time. Often the sale of the pledged property does not produce sufficient funds to pay the lender's claim. Court costs, maintenance costs, and selling costs have priority over the lender's claim at foreclosure. Often there is only enough left to pay a portion of the balance of the loan. The lender will probably not collect the expected interest and will lose a portion of the principal. Although the lender may seek a deficiency judgment, in most cases, the enforcement of a deficiency judgment produces only a small amount of additional funds.

When market interest rates rise, the value of the mortgage portfolio falls. If the market interest rate rises above the contract interest rate on the loan, the market value of the loan declines below the outstanding balance on the loan. If the loan is sold, the lender realizes a loss. Even if market interest rates have remained stable, there are selling costs involved in the sale of mortgages in the secondary market. The lender must consider these costs associated with the necessary sale of mortgages to meet liquidity needs.

Fluctuating interest rates may also impose an opportunity cost. Assume that the lender has made a 20-year loan at a 10 percent interest rate and that the market interest rate has risen to 15 percent. By making the long-term loan at 10 percent, the lender has foregone the opportunity to invest the funds at 15 percent today. Today, lenders are very concerned with fluctuating interest rates and the cost of funds, so they are promoting the use of adjustable-rate mortgage loans.

Lenders must also estimate the magnitude of the lending decision costs and reflect them in the charges for mortgage loans.

PROFIT PLANNING

Mortgage lenders must engage in profit planning, that is, in managing to ensure that income exceeds costs. Lenders must estimate and attempt to control both their income and costs on a continuing basis. With long-term, fixed interest rate mortgage loans it is relatively easy to estimate the probable income from the existing loan portfolio. However, it is relatively difficult to estimate costs, particularly the cost of funds relating to the loan portfolio. Rising costs can convert a profitable loan portfolio into an unprofitable one. When lenders make variable-rate loans, the income and the costs become relatively difficult to estimate. However, the spread between the income and costs can be estimated more accurately. With adjustable-rate loans, the chances of the loan portfolio becoming unprofitable are reduced.

Costs

The major cost for depository institutions is the cost of funds. The cost of funds equals approximately 80 percent of the total costs for savings and loan associations and mutual savings banks. Operating expenses account for approximately 20 percent of their costs. Employee compensation represents about one-half of these operating expenses. Office occupancy, advertising, and deposit insurance fees are other significant operating expenses. Reserves for bad debts is another significant operating expense, even if it is not fully recognizable for income tax purposes.

The cost of funds is obviously the major cost, and it deserves the most attention. The cost of funds is a fluctuating cost, since the cost for a large portion of the funds held by depository institutions is linked to market interest rates, and the interest rate on six-month money market certificates is tied to the interest rates on U.S. Treasury bills. Limitations on the interest rates paid for various types of deposits are to be phased out by the mid 1980s. This may increase both the cost of funds for depository institutions and the variability of the cost of funds. Institutional competition for funds takes place on both a price and a nonprice basis. Interest rates paid on deposits represent the price basis. Advertising, convenient office locations, and other services are the nonprice methods used to attract deposits. Escrow or impound accounts for taxes and insurance, in addition, provide some relatively low-cost funds for depository institutions. Many depository mortgage lenders also encourage the borrowers to maintain savings accounts with them as an additional source of funds.

Income

Income of mortgage lenders is derived primarily from interest and fees. Lenders often charge loan application fees, inspection fees, and mortgage origination fees to offset the costs of making loans. Service fees for mortgage banking activities are another source of income. Overall, interest from loans is the most important source of lender income.

Lenders tend to relate the fees and the interest rate charged on the loan to the costs and risks inherent in the loan. When the costs and/or risks are higher, lenders charge a higher interest rate and/or fees. Construction loans have substantially higher servicing costs and often more business risk than loans on existing properties. Loans on income properties usually have more business risk than home mortgage loans. Loans with high loan-to-value ratios typically have more business risk than loans with lower loan-to-value ratios, when the same type of property is involved. A junior mortgage loan has more business risk than the first mortgage loan on the same property. Graduated payment mortgage loans tend to have more business risk. Fixed-rate mortgage loans usually have greater financial risk than variable-rate mortgages, thus the initial interest is lower for variable-rate mortgage loans. Shared appreciation loans and equity participation provide greater protection against inflation, and they have lower contract interest rates than the nonparticipating loans when inflation is expected.

Lenders must keep their funds invested to earn an adequate rate of return. Since lenders must compete to keep their funds invested, competition places a limit on the interest rate and fees that can be charged. The demand for loans as well as the availability and cost of funds are major determinants of the interest rates that can be charged on mortgage loans. Lenders are forced to lower interest rates when they have excess funds and when there is a lack of other good investment alternatives.

LOAN PORTFOLIO MANAGEMENT

Portfolio management is aimed at relating the rate of return with associated risk. The portfolio manager's problem is to select the combination of assets that produces either the lowest level of risk for a specified rate of return or the highest rate of return for a given level of risk.

The institution or investor must specify the goals for the portfolio and the procedures to achieve the goals. Policy decisions include determining the percentage distribution of the portfolio among different types of assets and the acceptable level of risk for the various types of investments. The allowable investments of some institutions such as savings and loan associations are specified by regulations, and this must be reflected in the portfolio planning.

The institution must decide what percentage of assets should be invested in mortgage loans and what standards should be required for those mortgage loans. We limit our discussion here to the management of the mortgage loan portfolio, which is only one aspect of the total portfolio management problem.

DIVERSIFICATION AND BUSINESS RISK

Diversification serves to reduce the risk associated with a mortgage loan portfolio. Given normal business conditions, a small percentage of the loans in the portfolio produce losses due to random events such as divorce, illness, death, and unemployment. Increasing the number of loans in the portfolio makes the likelihood of such losses more predictable. This is true if there is not a common element or relationship among the loans that would result in losses on most loans in a portfolio from a single event. An example seems appropriate here.

Assume that general business conditions are normal and a lender's loans are concentrated in a local area largely dependent on the income and employment of a naval base. Closing the naval base would cause a sharp decline in income, employment, and property values for the entire area. The lender would probably suffer losses on a large portion of its loans. The dependence of the entire area on the naval base is the common element of risk in the lender's portfolio.

The purpose of diversification is to reduce the portfolio risk by reducing the chance that one element would affect all loans. Diversification may be achieved through decisions or policy concerning the area of lending, type of property accepted for security, type of borrowers accepted, and time of lending.

Area of Lending. A lender reduces the common area risk by making loans over a wide geographic area and thereby avoiding excessive concentration of loans in one small area. Institutions such as savings and loan associations can accomplish this even while serving local needs. First, the lender sells whole loans or participations in loans originated from the local area. Second, the lender buys whole loans or participations in loans secured by properties in other areas of the country.

Types of Property. The lender can diversify by avoiding overconcentration in construction loans, loans on commercial properties, apartment building loans, loans on condominium units, and loans on detached single-family residences. Since construction loans and loans on income properties promise higher rates of return, this diversification problem is typically solved by avoiding overconcentration in these types of loans.

Types of Borrowers. The lender should avoid lending a large portion of the funds to a single borrower. The lender should also avoid concentrating loans to borrowers employed by one company or even to borrowers employed in one industry.

Time of Lending. There is a tendency for people to become overly optimistic or overly pessimistic. When property values are rapidly increasing, there is a tendency to believe that it will continue and the lender tends to reduce lending standards. Then the trend changes and some marginal borrowers speculating on increasing property values default on their loans. The lender can guard against this tendency by limiting the amount of funds devoted to mortgage lending in any given time period. Also, newly originated loans tend to have more risk than seasoned loans. Thus, placing limits on the percentage of new loans reduces risk from unseasoned loans.

Other Aspects. A lender may justifiably assume more risk if its magnitude can be estimated and the compensation is adequate. The lender should estimate the costs of the risks and establish reserves and include them as a normal cost.

Even after a lender has diversified as much as possible, there may still be common elements among the loans. For example, in a depression, a large number of borrowers would default. Losses due to a depression may be reduced or offset by using mortgage loan insurance or governmental mortgage loan guarantees.

PROTECTION AGAINST INTEREST RATE RISK

The lender may suffer losses from interest rate changes in either an upward or downward direction. When interest rates increase, the market value of fixed-rate loans decreases. When interest rates decrease, the market value of fixed-rate loans increases, but many borrowers prepay their loans. When a borrower prepays a loan because of falling interest rates, the lender loses by having to reinvest these funds at lower interest rates.

When allowed by law, the lender may charge a prepayment penalty to discourage prepayment. Thus, the prepayment penalty offers some compensation for the loss due to reinvestment at lower rates.

The lender can offset the risk or a portion of the risk associated with rising interest rates by using variable-rate mortgages. Since the cost of funds is related to interest rates, the use of variable-rate loans has the advantage of helping to maintain the lender's spread between the interest rate earned and the cost of funds.

The lender can diversify by making both fixed-rate mortgage loans and variable-rate mortgage loans. In areas in which certain types of loans are prepayable without penalty, variable-rate mortgages may be more appropriate. If the lender can prevent prepayment on other classes of loans when prepayment is due to refinancing, fixed-rate loans may be appropriate. The lender should diversify by making both varible-rate and fixed-rate mortgages. The proportions would depend on the risk associated with each type of loan and expectations, and the overall level of risk that the lender is willing to accept.

PROTECTION AGAINST PURCHASING POWER RISK

Lenders investing equity in mortgage loans want and need protection against a decline in the purchasing power of the money invested. Several approaches are used to obtain this protection.

One approach is to estimate the future inflation rate and, in turn, adjust the interest rate charged on loans to offset the inflation rate. Another approach is to use shared appreciation mortgage (SAM) loans and/or equity participation loans. The underlying assumption of this approach is that income, property values, and the general price level will move in the same direction at about the same rate. A third approach is to use adjustable-rate loans—variable-rate mortgage (VRM) and renegotiable-rate mortgage (RRM)—with the expectation that interest rates and the general price level will move up and down together.

Depository institutions are vitally concerned with the impact of inflation on the cost of funds. Depositors typically demand higher interest rates on their savings to offset inflation or the decline in the purchasing power of the dollar. VRM and RMM loans give the depository institution a degree of protection against both rises in the cost of funds and declines in the purchasing power of the dollar.

PROTECTION AGAINST LIQUIDITY RISK

An institution's primary defenses against liquidity risk are forecasting liquidity needs, investing a portion of its funds in liquid assets, such as U.S. Treasury bills, and borrowing additional funds. Our discussion is limited to the liquidity risk of the mortgages in the portfolio.

Mortgage loans can provide the security for obtaining loans. Mortgage loans or loan participations can be sold in the secondary market. Lenders can increase the liquidity of their mortgage loan portfolio by including FHA insured, VA guaranteed, and FHLMC-FNMA conforming conventional loans in the portfolio, because of the relatively strong secondary market for these loans. Lenders increasingly use the standardized FHLMC-FNMA forms and conform to FHLMC-FNMA guidelines such as loan-to-value ratios and dollar amounts. This conformity increases the liquidity of those loans with very little cost.

LOAN SERVICING

The purpose of mortgage loan servicing is to see that the borrower meets his or her obligations under the mortgage. If the borrower does not meet the obligations, servicing extends to maintaining or preserving the investment as much as possible through adjustments or foreclosure. An institution servicing loans for others must also remit funds and make periodic status reports to the mortgage holder.

Servicing mortgage loans involves several functions. The *cashier function* consists of receiving and depositing the payments from the borrowers and conveying the information to the accounting department. The *accounting function* consists of recording the payments received and entering the information in the appropriate accounts, such as interest, principal, and escrow accounts. If the servicing is done for another investor, the accounting or report function includes preparation of reports for the investor and the remittance of funds to the investor. The *collection function* involves the collection of past due payments, and the *insurance function* is to see that each property has adequate hazard insurance, that losses are properly adjusted, and, in general, that the lender's position is protected. The *tax function* is to make sure that all real estate taxes and special assessments on the mortgaged properties are paid on schedule.

The collection function is the most complicated area of loan servicing, in that past due payments must be obtained or foreclosure initiated. Preventive collection procedures are often used by lenders, in which they stress the importance of making payments when due to borrowers.

The collection department reminds each borrower when a payment is past due and attempts to find out the reason for the tardiness with the purpose of helping correct it if possible. For a borrower that is delinquent or in default, the collection office seeks to determine the cause and the appropriate action. If the borrower's financial position has declined temporarily due to a strike or illness and if the borrower has a good attitude, the collection officer will attempt to make an adjustment. If the borrower's financial position appears to have deteriorated permanently, the collection officer may suggest that the borrower sell the property and find less expensive housing. For a borrower with a negative attitude and/or a situation that seems hopeless, the collection officer may suggest a deed in lieu of foreclosure or foreclosure action.

When the borrower's delinquencies become a significant problem, the collection officer is likely to arrange for more frequent property inspection to guard against unreasonable depreciation. If the loan is insured or guaranteed, the collection officer must file the reports of default in conformance with regulations in order to be able to collect on the insurance or guarantee.

SUMMARY

Lenders forecast economic variables including the level of economic activity and interest rates in order to make a broad assessment of the risks of mortgage lending. The lender is concerned with both individual loan risks and portfolio risks. The principal costs of lending, other than normal servicing costs, are the cost of collecting delinquent payments and the losses associated with liquidating pledged properties. Lenders engage in profit planning to better manage their activities and thereby avoid insolvency and bankruptcy. Major concerns for depository lenders are the wide fluctuations in their cost of funds and the maintaining of an adequate spread between the yield on the portfolio and the cost of funds. The major concern in portfolio management is the controlling of risk through diversification.

The purpose of mortgage loan servicing is to see that each borrower meets his or her obligations. The most complex area of loan servicing is the collection of delinquent or defaulted payments.

KEY TERMS

Accounting Function
Borrower Risk
Business Risk
Cashier Function
Collection Function
Diversification

Financial Risk
Individual Loan Risk
Insurance Function
Interest Rate Risk
Liquidity Risk

Mortgage Loan Servicing
Portfolio Risk
Property Risk
Purchasing Power Risk
Tax Function

QUESTIONS FOR REVIEW AND DISCUSSION

1. Lenders have broad concerns with each of the following: (a) level of economic activity, (b) level of real estate activity, (c) interest rates, (d) value of the dollar, and (e) government policy. Describe and discuss the nature of the concern in each of these areas.

2. Lenders have individual loan risks and portfolio risks. Distinguish between these two types of risks and explain each fully.

3. What are lender decision costs?

4. In how many ways may a lender diversify to avoid business risk? Are there any residual business risks that lenders generally cannot avoid? Explain.

5. Can lenders protect themselves from purchasing power and liquidity risks? If so, how?

6. What is the most difficult function or activity in loan servicing? Why? Explain.

7. Match the following key terms and definitions:
   a. Collection
      Function _____
   b. Interest Rate Risk _____
   c. Portfolio Risk _____
   d. Diversification _____
   e. Business Risk _____
   f. Financial Risk _____
   g. Purchasing Power
      Risk _____

   1. The chance that the spread between cost of borrowing and return on an investment will become too thin.
   2. Reducing the chance of loss by spreading risks.
   3. Chance of inflation and getting repaid with money of reduced value.
   4. Chance the rate of return will be less than expected.

5. Chance that the value of a loan will fall because of an increase in the interest rate.
6. Obtaining overdue payments on a loan.
7. Chance of loss on all loans or investments held.
8. Chance that loan or investment will not be readily saleable at or near market value.

seventeen

Borrower Considerations and Analysis

The property, the lender, and the borrower are the basic ingredients of any debt financing arrangement. The site, improvements, neighborhood or location, and ultimately the market value are the chief concerns relative to the property, as discussed in Chap. 15. A lender balances many considerations in making a loan, as discussed in Chap. 16. These considerations include economic and financial outlook, decision costs, portfolio management, and portfolio servicing. Operating on a large number or portfolio basis allows a lender to offset bad decisions with good ones, and thereby avoid or offset risks; this is termed a *pooling effect.* Lenders may also require borrowers to obtain mortgage insurance to protect against risks. Thus, one bad loan does not mean disaster for a lender.

Individual borrowers, particularly homeowners, have little or no possibility of pooling to spread their risks. If they are unable to meet the requirements or terms of a loan, disaster soon follows by way of default and foreclosure. The most usual causes of default and foreclosure are separation, divorce, illness, death, and loss of employment or income. Borrowers therefore face risks of breakdown of marriage or health, in addition to many of the economic risks faced by lenders.

Covered in this chapter are the concerns of both the lender and the borrower as they pertain to the evaluation of a borrower being able to repay a loan. Major topics covered are as follows:

FHLMC QUALIFICATION GUIDELINES

Ability and motivation to repay are basic determinants of a successful loan. These considerations are particularly important with the high LVR of home loans because the proceeds of a foreclosure sale are unlikely to cover principal repayment, accrued interest, plus all foreclosure costs in the early years.

No "cut and dried" formula exists to determine a borrower's ability and motivation to repay a loan. But, certain pertinent information is invariably collected by lenders to evaluate this ability and motivation. FHLMC Form 65, shown in Chap. 14 as Fig. 14–1, is an excellent illustration of the nature of this information. In addition to a description of the subject property and the requested loan, Form 65 includes information concerning borrowers, such as: (1) identification, (2) monthly income and housing expenses, (3) assets and liabilities or net worth, (4) credit references, and (5) certification of the accuracy of the information provided.

Given the basic format and an understanding of the applicable standards, a borrower may personally assess the risks associated with taking out a loan prior to entering the real estate market.

Making this determination before making an offer on a house is likely to help the potential buyer-borrower to better search out a property within his or her means. Making the determination should also enable the potential buyer-borrower to do a more effective job of obtaining a loan.

With this brief introduction, let us move on to a more specific discussion of annual stabilized income, assets and liabilities, credit worthiness, and motivation as required by Form 65.

NET WORTH

Net worth equals assets minus liabilities. The assets may be liquid or nonliquid. Liabilities take the form of unpaid balances on loans or debt. In most cases debt carries an obligation to make periodic, usually monthly, payments. Alimony, child support, and maintenance payments also constitute monthly or periodic obligations, even though no debt exists. The reverse side of FHLMC Form 65, shown in Fig. 14–1, provides a format to summarize a potential borrower's assets, liabilities, and obligations. In Fig. 14–1, net worth equals $39,600 ($42,100 minus $2,500).

FHLMC Form 65 and applicable supporting schedules may be completed jointly by both married and unmarried co-borrowers. Then assets and liabilities must be sufficiently joined so that the statement can be meaningfully and fairly presented on a combined basis. Otherwise separate statements and schedules are required (FHLMC Form 65A).

Assets. *Liquid assets* include (1) cash deposits toward purchase of a subject property, (2) checking and savings account balances, (3) stocks and bonds at market value, and (4) the net cash value of life insurance policies. *Nonliquid assets* include the cash or market value of (1) owned real estate, (2) vested interests in retirement funds, (3) net worth of an owned business, (4) furniture and other personal property, and (5) any other assets, such as notes of others or an interest in a trust. The combined value of liquid and nonliquid assets equals total assets owned by a borrower or by co-borrowers.

The purchase of a home is a major investment for most people. Younger couples frequently have only limited assets. But ownership of even some stocks, bonds, savings accounts, and other assets indicates a desire and ability to save for security and to establish a life style. Cars, boats, furniture, and personal property are often over valued by potential borrowers. Even so, ownership of such items means the borrower is likely to have fewer pressures to acquire these assets after obtaining a loan. In turn, the borrower will remain more able to meet the debt service requirements on any loan obtained.

Liabilities and Obligations. Most liabilities take the form of debt. The most common kinds of debt are (1) installment, (2) auto, (3) real estate, and (4) stock pledges. These liabilities typically include an obligation to make monthly payments to amortize the debt. Payments for (1) alimony, (2) child support, and (3) separate maintenance are another source of monthly or periodic obligations of borrowers though they technically involve no debt.

Liabilities are deducted from assets to determine the net worth of a potential borrower. Obligations are deducted from stabilized income to determine a borrower's expense-to-income ratio. The expense-to-income ratio and the net worth of a potential borrower are both important in determining ability to meet loan obligations.

ANNUAL STABILIZED INCOME

The annual stabilized income of borrowers is often difficult to determine. Two or more borrowers may be involved. Each may hold one or more jobs. They may have supplemental income, some of which is highly uncertain. Income must be evaluated by source, amount, and certainty before qualifying as stabilized gross monthly income on Form 65. Basic employment income is of greatest concern in qualifying a residential borrower.

The salary of a borrower or co-borrower may easily be ascertained with an employer. Likewise, income from retirement funds and trusts is easily ascertained. Both tend to be stable and certain. Earnings from hourly wages and piece work in a primary job tend to fluctuate more than salaries but still qualify as basic employment income. Likewise, income from second or part-time jobs qualifies if the job has been held for several years. Finally, income of self-employed and professional people must have a regular pattern to count as basic income.

Time on the job and the nature of the work both affect the weight given base income in qualifying an applicant for a loan. Generally two or three years in a given line of work is minimum to qualify for full recognition of the income. Income tax records are typically required to verify income as to amount, certainty, and duration. Lenders avoid commitments to potential borrowers of short tenure and experience.

Type of work also affects the weighting given income. Seasonal jobs (agriculture, construction) have lighter weights than salaried jobs, for example. The least weight is given income of an applicant with short tenure in a job with uncertain income, such as an aspiring sales representative working on a commission basis.

Income from overtime, bonuses, commissions, dividends, interest, and net rents may also qualify as gross income. Mainly, the income must have been received on a continuing basis for several years. The possible sale of the bonds, stocks, or realty is usually noted by the lender.

Income from alimony, child support, and welfare payments may count in qualifying for a loan. With alimony and child support, the size and certainty depend on the court decree as well as the ability of the person making the payments. The pattern and outlook for the payments must be stable in order for them to count. Alimony and child support income need not be reported by an applicant if the payments are not to be the basis for qualifying for a loan. Finally, welfare payments must be counted at face value in qualifying a potential borrower.

Some income may not be given weight in qualifying a borrower. Income that is from illegal activities, such as pushing drugs, or that is not reported for tax purposes does not count. Likewise, earnings from children of borrowers does not qualify as income for qualifying a borrower, unless the children become co-borrowers. The rationale is that the children have no continuing obligation on the loan otherwise.

HOUSING EXPENSES

For a residential loan, FHLMC underwriting guidelines indicate that housing expenses should not exceed from 25 to 28 percent of gross income. This ratio may be calculated on a monthly or annual basis. Housing expense generally includes (1) rent, (2) loan payments for principal and interest, (3) hazard insurance, (4) property taxes, and (5) mortgage insurance. Other housing expenses might include (1) homeowner association dues and (2) ground rental payments. While the FHLMC 25 to 28 percent of gross income guideline excludes utility expenses, the prospective borrower should consider them and FHLMC considers utility expenses in deciding what percentage of gross income can be devoted to the housing expenses listed above.

In Fig. 14–1, the Millers' current monthly housing expenses excluding utility expenses, while renting, are $425. They need or want their own home. After the proposed purchase, their monthly housing expenses excluding utility costs are expected to increase to $659. The $659 monthly housing expenses represents less than 25 percent of the Millers' gross monthly income, and they meet the FHLMC guideline.

WILLINGNESS TO PAY

Willingness to pay involves credit worthiness and motivation. Both are important in the lend-borrow decision, though extremely difficult to analyze and judge.

Credit worthy means a person has consistently met financial commitments or obligations in a satisfactory manner. Credit worthiness is determined largely from the credit experience of the potential borrower, as evidenced by a credit report. Testimony by credit references also serves as evidence. Figure 17–1 shows a typical credit report. Credit references are listed on the reverse side of Form 65 (see Fig. 14–1). Lenders also frequently check out a borrower-buyer with the sales agent or the seller in the transaction. And some lenders make a personal visit to the potential borrower's residence to observe his or her life style, from which judgments about credit worthiness are sometimes made.

Three basic types of information may be gleaned from a credit report such as that shown in Fig. 17–1: (1) employment history, (2) credit history, and (3) attitude toward credit. Employment stability and type as well as earnings are usually shown. Current employment and earnings data are also usually given for the spouse. The amount and type of credit used by subject of the credit report are given as well. Thus, experience on auto loans, real estate loans, and credit card purchases are all available. This information may be used by lenders to cross check information provided by a loan applicant concerning net worth and monthly payment obligations. Finally, the performance on these loans provides evidence of attitude toward credit. Meeting payments on schedule and successfully retiring loans represent a positive attitude. Bankruptcies, foreclosures, and judgments would indicate a poor attitude and performance, unless they could be fully explained as being beyond the applicant's control.

FIGURE 17–1 Sample Credit Report

NAME AND ADDRESS OF CREDIT BUREAU MAKING REPORT		☐ SINGLE REFERENCE	☐ IN FILE REPORT	☐ TRADE REPORT

NAME AND ADDRESS OF CREDIT BUREAU MAKING REPORT
CREDIT REPORTING SERVICES
P. O. BOX 78910
URBANDALE, ANYSTATE, USA

☐ SINGLE REFERENCE   ☐ IN FILE REPORT   ☐ TRADE REPORT
☐ FULL REPORT   ☐ EMPLOY & TRADE REPORT   ☐ PREVIOUS RESIDENCE REPORT

☒ OTHER Mortgage Loan Report

	Date Received 11/6/82	CONFIDENTIAL

FOR Urbandale Savings and Loan Association
P. O. Box 99999
Urbandale, Anystate 00000

Date Received 11/6/82
Date Mailed 11/8/82
In File Since 10/76

CONFIDENTIAL

STANDARD FACTUAL DATA REPORT

PREVIOUS INQUIRIES
9/82 coast to coast credit corp.
10/82

REPORT ON: LAST NAME	FIRST NAME	INITIAL	SOCIAL SECURITY NUMBER	SPOUSE'S NAME
Beyers	Richard	U.	555-55-5555	Amy

ADDRESS:	CITY	STATE:	ZIP CODE	SINCE:	SPOUSE'S SOCIAL SECURITY NO.
10055 Wayside Drive, Urbandale, Anystate			00001	5 years	444-44-4444

COMPLETE TO HERE FOR TRADE REPORT AND SKIP TO CREDIT HISTORY

PRESENT EMPLOYER:	POSITION HELD:	SINCE:	DATE EMPLOY VERIFIED	EST. MONTHLY INCOME
Head, Count, and Tally, Inc.	Accountant, CPA	4 years	10/7/99	$ 3,333

COMPLETE TO HERE FOR EMPLOYMENT AND TRADE REPORT AND SKIP TO CREDIT HISTORY

DATE OF BIRTH	NUMBER OF DEPENDENTS INCLUDING SELF: 5				
Age 37		LENGTH OF TIME MARRIED 10 years	☐ OWNS OR BUYING HOME	☒ RENTS HOME	

FORMER ADDRESS:	CITY:	STATE:	FROM:	TO:
3456 River Road, Urbandale, Anystate			10/93	8/95 (2 years)

FORMER ADDRESS:	CITY:	STATE:	FROM:	TO:
2222 Apple Way, #33, Emerald City, Somestate			7/89	10/93

FORMER EMPLOYER:	POSITION HELD:	FROM:	TO:	EST. MONTHLY INCOME
Accidental Accountants	Accountant, CPA	7/89	8/95	$ 2,222

SPOUSE'S EMPLOYER:	POSITION HELD:	SINCE:	DATE EMPLOY VERIFIED	EST. MONTHLY INCOME
X-cello Manufacturing	Clerk-Typist	10/98	10/7/99	$ 600 (half-time)

CREDIT HISTORY *(Complete this section for all reports)*

WHOSE	KIND OF BUSINESS AND ID CODE	DATE REPORTED AND METHOD OF REPORTING	DATE OPENED	DATE OF LAST PAYMENT	HIGHEST CREDIT OR LAST CONTRACT	PRESENT STATUS BALANCE OWING	PAST DUE AMOUNT	NO. OF PAYMENTS	NO. MONTHS HISTORY REVIEWED	TIMES PAST DUE 30-59 DAYS ONLY	60-89 DAYS ONLY	90 DAYS AND OVER	TYPE & TERMS (MANNER OF PAYMENT)	REMARKS
J	Visa	10-99M	7/90	10/99	888	138	-0-			Acct. # 98765432]00]2345				
J	Sears	9-99M	6/92	10/99	357	-0-				Acct. # 444 090 11511 Revolving Acct.				
J	MC	10-99	7/92	10/98	432	-0-				Acct. # 6666 0000 7777 0000				
J	Emerald City First National Bank													
	Mortgage Loan				$48,000	-0-	closed						Prepaid 10/95 $448/monthly	
	No public record of lawsuits, judgments, bankruptcy, etc.													
	No previous trade checking													

REMARKS: 1. Amplify his employment history. (this report shall contain information as to the subject's previous employment status, location and salary, if there has been a change in employment status within the past two years.)

2. The reporting bureau certifies that: (a) ☒ public records have been checked for suits, judgements, foreclosures, garnishments, bankruptcies, and other legal actions involving the subject with the results indicated below: or, (b) ☒ equivalent information has been obtained through the use of a qualified public records reporting service with the results indicated below. (Give details). (The records of real estate transfers which do not involve foreclosure may be excluded).

3. The reporting bureau certifies that the subject's credit record in the payment of bills and other obligations has been checked: (a) ☒ through the credit accounts extended by a combined minimum of 75% of the larger department stores and larger consumer and unsecured credit granters of the community in which the subject resides, with the results indicated below: or, (b) ☒ through accumulated credit records of such credit granters of the community in which the subject resides, with the results indicated below.

The information in this report is provided under the contract between the Department of Housing and Urban Development Federal Housing Administration and Credit Reporting Services. The information is not to be divulged to anyone other than the named Department of Housing and Urban Development organizational element, Veterans Administration and USDA-Farmers Home Administration, except as required by Public Law 91-508, and the contract.

SOURCE: Copy provided by Credit Reporting Services.

FIGURE 17–1 (*Continued*)

					CREDIT HISTORY		(*Complete this section for all reports*)							

Table headers:

WHOSE	KIND OF BUSINESS AND ID CODE	DATE REPORTED AND METHOD OF REPORTING	DATE OPENED	DATE OF LAST PAYMENT	HIGHEST CREDIT OR LAST CONTRACT	PRESENT STATUS			HISTORICAL STATUS				TYPE & TERMS (MANNER OF PAYMENT)	REMARKS
						BALANCE OWING	PAST DUE AMOUNT	NO. OF PAYMENTS	NO. MONTHS HISTORY REVIEWED	TIMES PAST DUE 30-59 DAYS ONLY	60-89 DAYS ONLY	90 DAYS AND OVER		

A. Column 1, "Whose Account", provides a means of showing how a credit grantor maintains the account for ECOA purposes. Examples: 0 – Undesignated, 1 – Individual account for individual use, 2 – Joint account contractual liability, 3 – Authorized user spouse, 4 – Joint, 5 – Co-maker, 6 – On behalf of account.

B Column 3, "Method of Reporting", indicates how a trade item was placed in file: A – Computer tape or TVS, M – Manual

C. When inserting dates, use month and year only (Example: 12-76)

D. Manner of Payment using present common language coding (1-175-1) will be printed in column 15 for in-file trade items which do not contain information for columns 9 through 14.

E. Remarks codes (Examples)

ACC – Account closed by consumer.	RLD – Repossession. Paid by dealer.
AJP – Adjustment pending.	RLP – Repossession. Proceeds applied to debt.
BKL – Account included in Bankruptcy	RPO – Repossession
CCA – Consumer counseling account. Consumer has retained the services of an organization which is directing payment of his accounts.	RRE – Repossession, redeemed.
	RVD – Returned voluntarily. Paid by dealer.
	RVN – Returned voluntarily.
	RVP – Returned voluntarily, proceeds applied to debt.
CLA – Placed for collection.	
DIS – Dispute following resolution.	RVR – Returned voluntarily, redeemed.
DRP – Dispute resolution pending.	STL – Plate stolen or lost.
JUD – Judgment obtained for balance shown.	WEP – Wage Earner Plan Account (Chapter XIII of the Bankruptcy Act).
MOV – Moved. Left no forwarding address.	
PRL – Profit and loss write-off.	

F. Account Numbers, if shown, should appear on second line just below each trade item.

G. Disputes and comments associated with specific trade lines should be printed on second or third line in cases where account numbers are printed.

Motivation is the desire, incentive, or impulse that drives a person to some act or goal. Needless to say, lenders prefer borrowers with high motivation for homeownership. Motivation may be judged from many things. A family unit with children is traditionally regarded as having a strong motivation. Desire for privacy, independence, and freedom to practice one's own life style are also recognized as strong incentives. Finally, the drive to create an estate, to save and invest, and to avoid continuing to pay rent are also strong incentives for some people.

Lenders use everything from rating grids to individual or personal "systems" in judging motivation. But regardless of the method used, lenders must respect the Equal Credit Opportunity and Fair Credit Reporting Acts (see Appendix to Chap. 14). Marital status or sex, for example, are no longer justifiable grounds for rejecting credit under these acts.

BORROWER CAPABILITY: A CASE EXAMPLE

The FHLMC underwriting guidelines may be used by a buyer to determine the size and type of house that can be afforded. The guidelines can also help the lender decide whether or not to accept a loan applicant. Let us look at a case example for an illustration of the process. The approach is to present a typical problem situation of a family desiring a larger home. The FHLMC guidelines are then applied to the family to calculate how much they can reasonably afford to pay for housing. The reader is encouraged to note well the facts of the situation because the case is carried over to Chap. 21, "Creative Financing."

A Typical Problem Situation

Richard and Amy Beyers wish to buy a house. Their annual stabilized income is $50,000. They have two children: Ann (aged 8) and Kevin (aged 5). Richard and Amy have enough cash assets to make a $20,000 down payment and to cover reasonable closing costs. The Beyers also have continuing installment obligations of $250 per month, including $110 per month for support of Richard's daughter, Kathy, by a prior marriage. Richard has steady employment as an accountant; his income has been increasing steadily, and his occupational outlook is promising. Amy works part-time as a secretary–typist. She expects to return to full-time work in two years when the children are older and more established in school. How much can they reasonably pay per month for housing expenses?

Capability Analysis

The FHLMC guidelines for the expense-to-income ratio are based on long experience in evaluating borrowers for successful loan transactions. The guidelines, which are used by most financial institutions in making conventional loans, indicate that, except in unusual circumstances, a residential borrower should not pay more than 25 percent of gross stabilized income for housing expenses. The guidelines further state that no more than 33 percent of gross stabilized income should be allocated to installment payments. With a higher percentage, chances of default sharply increase. What are the implications of these guidelines for the Beyers?

With an annual stabilized gross income of $50,000, the Beyers should not pay more than $12,500 (25 percent) for housing expenses. This breaks down to $1,042 per month. The guideline limits for selected income levels are set forth in Fig. 17–2. Housing expenses, remember, include payments for principal, interest, hazard insurance, property taxes (PIIT), and, if applicable, mortgage insurance, homeowner association dues, and ground rental payments. None of these charges outside of PIIT are expected to apply to the Beyer's situation.

Total installment payments, at 33 percent of gross stabilized income, should not exceed $16,500 per year for the Beyers, according to Fig. 17–2. Installment payments include housing expenses plus utilities and periodic payments for installment debt, alimony, and child support. The upper limit on all installment payments for the Beyers, on a monthly basis, would therefore be $1,375.

The problem statement says that the Beyers have continuing installment obligations of $250 per month, including $110 per month for child support. Thus, the Beyers would have continuing obligations be-

FIGURE 17–2 Annual and Monthly Borrower Qualifying Payment Limits for Selected Income Levels Based on FHLMC Expense-to-Income Ratio Guidelines

(Add 10 percent for Absolute Maximum Payment Amounts justified by large down payment, substantial net worth, or demonstrated ability and willingness to devote larger portion of income for housing expenses)

ANNUAL STABILIZED INCOME	25% HOUSING EXPENSES		33% TOTAL INSTALLMENT PAYMENTS	
Primary earnings plus "experience" earnings from bonuses, commissions, overtime, and other secondary sources for previous two years which are likely to continue	Principal repayment, interest, hazard insurance, and property taxes (PITI) and, if applicable, mortgage insurance, homeowner association dues, and ground rental payments. Excludes utility charges.		Housing expense, plus required periodic payments for utilities, installment debt, alimony, and child support	
	Annual	Monthly	Annual	Monthly
$20,000	$5,000	416.67	$6,600	$ 550
30,000	7,500	625	9,900	825
40,000	10,000	833.33	13,200	1,100
50,000	12,500	1,041.67	16,500	1,375
60,000	15,000	1,250.00	19,800	1,650
70,000	17,500	1,458.33	23,100	1,925
80,000	20,000	1,666.67	26,400	2,200

FIGURE 17–3 Calculation of the Net Amount Available to Richard and Amy Beyers for Payments on Any Debt Financing Obtained according to the FHLMC Expense-to-Income Ratio Guidelines

	Yearly	Monthly
Stabilized Income	$50,000	$4,167
Times 33%		
Equals Limit for Total Installment Payments	16,500	1,375
Less Continuing Installment Obligations	3,000	250
Equals Amount Available for Housing Expenses	$13,500	$1,125
Less Projected Hazard Insurance		
and Property Tax Expense	3,600	300
Equals Net Amount Available for Debt Financing	$ 9,900	$ 825

yond housing expenses of $3,000 per year. Deducting this $3,000 from the $16,500 means that the Beyers really have only $13,500 per year, or $1,125 per month, for housing expense. This $13,500 is slightly more than the $12,500 or 25 percent of annual stabilized income suggested by the guidelines. However, the Beyers consider they have a strong credit rating and decide this $1,000 additional would be acceptable to most lenders.

Upon inquiry to their friends occupying houses similar to what they want, Richard and Amy determine that hazard insurance, taxes, and utilities for the type of housing they want typically amount to $300, $2,100, and $1,200 per year, respectively. The total is therefore $3,60C per year, or $300 per month. Deducting the $3,600 per year from the $13,500 available for housing expense leaves $9,900 per year for principal and interest payments on any debt financing obtained. On a monthly basis, $9,900 per year amounts to $825. The calculations leading to this $825 per month are summarized in Fig. 17–3.

Amy and Richard Beyers now know they have the capability to obtain financing if payments run less than $825 per month. They also know they have the capability to meet total housing expense of $1,125 per month. They are now much better prepared to shop for housing.

The Beyers, like most people, stretch the limit in their search for housing. They select a house that may be beyond their capability. And interest rates are high. This case problem is continued in Chap. 21, "Creative Financing," in which we discuss some other financing possibilities that are open to them.

BORROWERS' PERSONAL CONSIDERATIONS

A lender is barred from asking a borrower for certain personal information, according to the Equal Credit Opportunity Act (ECOA). For example, questions concerning birth control practices or expectation of children in the future are prohibited. The topics of personal and marital health are also essentially off limits for lender's questions. However, a lender may make judgments about an applicant's earnings outlook based on his or her occupation or business.

As mentioned earlier, default results mainly because of illness, death, separation, divorce, or a loss of income through loss of job or business failure. Thus, it is important for the borrower to realize that such information is pertinent to his or her chances of successfully meeting the requirements of any loan obtained, and he or she is advised to take these considerations into account upon entering into a loan contract. Foreclosure is an expensive process in which both the lender and the borrower lose. Default and foreclosure carry particularly high financial and emotional costs for the residential borrower. Let us look, therefore, at each of these areas from a borrower's perspective.

PERSONAL HEALTH

Undertaking heavy debt service obligations when in poor physical or emotional health could be disastrous for a borrower. Default and foreclosure might well lead to the loss of any cash equity invested in the residence plus a deficiency judgment. If a member of the family requires considerable medical attention, the high costs could also lead to the same result. On the other hand, a well-insured person with terminal cancer might buy a residence to assure housing for his or her family, the expectation being that the insurance would pay off the loan. In any event, potential borrowers are advised to take the risk of illness or death into account in deciding when and if to borrow.

Risk of disability or death due to an unexpected event, such as an auto accident, is a continuing concern for the borrower. Insurance provides some protection against this risk. However, an accident cannot be anticipated with any degree of certainty by borrower or lender.

MARITAL HEALTH

Buying a dream house is likely to make a good marriage better. At the same time, it may be the final straw for a faltering marriage.

Breakdown of a marriage, followed by separation and divorce, involves high emotional and financial costs. Separation usually means that two places of residence must be maintained. The associated stress also often leads to reduced earning ability. And typically, housing expenses when buying are greater than when renting. Therefore a couple experiencing serious marital difficulty is advised not to take on the additional burden and stress of buying a house.

EARNINGS OUTLOOK

A borrower-applicant may have a strong credit rating and therefore may look very able and willing to an underwriter. At the same time, the prospective borrower may know that his or her earning ability is in serious jeopardy. Severe friction may exist between the applicant and his or her boss. The borrower's job may be about to be done away with in a company reorganization. The business may be in serious financial straits and about to go into bankruptcy. In circumstances of this type, a prospective borrower is advised to defer action until the outlook improves.

THE INCOME PROPERTY BORROWER

Income properties tend to have high value relative to a borrower's assets. In turn, income property borrowers prefer not to pledge their personal assets in obtaining financing. To avoid pledging personal assets, a sole security or exculpatory clause is negotiated, meaning that the property is the only security provided for the loan and that the borrower is free from personal liability on the loan. At the same time, an assignment of rents on default is usually included in the loan agreement. An exculpatory clause acts to disallow a deficiency judgment under the note as well. In case of default, the lender's only real course of action, therefore, is to foreclose on the mortgage. The use of an exculpatory clause means, in short, that the lender must place much greater emphasis on analyzing the property and its value prior to making the loan.

A sole security clause may or may not be negotiated into a loan agreement. The relative bargaining strengths of the parties is likely to govern. In any event, the relative financial ability of the borrower is important for both personal decision making and underwriter reassurance.

The financial strength of potential borrowers, as individuals, must usually be judged from credit reports and personal financial statements. Successful business experience and net worth are the key items in evaluating individual borrowers. However, wealthy borrower-investors generally avoid committing their personal net worth to secure real estate loans. Thus, they either negotiate a sole security clause or operate and borrow as a business firm.

The financial statements of business firms, especially corporations, are the primary source of information in judging their financial ability. An operating, or profit and loss, statement and a balance sheet are the basic statements used. An underwriter would prefer the statements to have been prepared or audited by a certified public accountant (CPA) to assure their completeness and accuracy. Credit reports from firms like Dun and Bradstreet are also useful in judging financial ability.

The main items of concern in financial statements of business firms are an acceptable current ratio, profitable use of assets, and net worth. The *current ratio* is current assets divided by current liabilities. The current ratio indicates ability to meet short-term obligations and thereby remain liquid or solvent. Profitable use of assets is judged from net return on sales or assets. Profit is the ultimate financial objective of a business firm. Hence, poor performance here indicates a basic failure that, if not corrected, would probably mean the firm's going out of business. The return-on-total-assets ratio is probably the best overall basis for judging profitability. *The return-on-total-assets ratio* equals net income plus interest expense divided by total assets. Note that interest expense is included in calculating the ratio, because interest expense is the return to borrowed capital. The industry norm is the standard in applying and interpreting these ratios.

A projected pro forma operating statement and balance sheet, based on the assumption that the loan has been arranged, are usually prepared for the prospective borrowers. The object is to judge the effect of the loan on the borrower's financial picture. If the postloan outlook is satisfactory for both the lender and the borrower, the loan is arranged.

SUMMARY

Lenders look to both the borrower and the property as security for a loan. Lenders are also able to spread or pool their risk because they operate on a portfolio basis. In taking out a loan, individual borrowers face many of the same risks as lenders do plus some additional ones, that cannot be pooled. Individual borrowers are therefore advised to evaluate their own risks in taking out a loan and not to rely totally on the lender's judgment.

The FHLMC guidelines are extremely useful in evaluating these risks. The guidelines take into account net worth, ability to pay, and willingness to pay. Not more than 25 percent of a borrower's gross income should go for housing expense, according to the guidelines. And total installment obligations should not exceed 33 percent of gross income. Willingness to pay is largely determined by a credit report. A case example illustrates application of the guidelines.

Personal considerations of a prospective borrower that are not covered by the guidelines include personal health, marital health, and earnings outlook. A negative judgment on any of these may mean a loan should not be obtained.

Income property investor-borrowers prefer to include a sole security clause in any loan arrangement. In turn, the lender must rely more heavily on the property as security for the loan. The current ratio and the return-on-total-assets ratio are critical data to a lender in evaluating corporate borrowers.

KEY TERMS

Credit Worthy

Current Ratio

Liquid Assets

Motivation

Nonliquid Assets

Pooling Effect

Return-on-Total-Assets
Ratio

QUESTIONS FOR REVIEW AND DISCUSSION

1. List and explain briefly the items that make up annual stabilized income according to the FHLMC guidelines.

2. What items make up housing expenses?

3. What is "willingness to pay"? How is willingness to pay determined?

4. Identify and briefly explain the personal risks of a borrower and their implications.

5. What criteria might a lender look to in evaluating a corporate applicant for a loan?

6. Match the following key terms with their most appropriate definitions:

   a. Return-on-Total-Assets Ratio _____

   b. Current Ratio _____

   c. Motivation _____

   d. Credit Worthy _____

   e. Pooling Effect _____

   1. $\dfrac{\text{Net Income}}{\text{Total Assets}}$

   2. Making many similar decisions with the expectation that good ones will offset bad ones.

   3. Experience showing a person has consistently met financial commitments and obligations in a satisfactory or successful manner.

   4. Desire to meet commitments necessary to achieve home ownership.

   5. $\dfrac{\text{Current Assets - Inventory}}{\text{Current Liabilities}}$

   6. $\dfrac{\text{Current Assets}}{\text{Current Liabilities}}$

   7. $\dfrac{\text{Net Income \& Interest Expense}}{\text{Total Assets}}$

eighteen

Loan Repayment Patterns

The loan repayment pattern is probably the most basic and the most often overlooked aspect of negotiation in real estate debt financing. It is, however, increasingly becoming a tool for negotiation for several reasons. Tight money with its high interest rates and the rapid inflation in property values make it difficult for many households to afford adequate housing with traditional repayment patterns. Investors encounter this same difficulty. At the same time, lenders need flexibility in adjusting loan interest rates to fluctuating conditions in financial markets. Alternative loan repayment patterns allow borrowers and lenders to solve these problems. Of course, some compromise by each in the negotiations may be necessary for a loan to actually be made. Each is seeking the greatest possible personal advantage, of course.

Alternative repayment patterns basically reflect manipulation of the interest rate, the term, and the frequency of payments (debt service). Alternative repayment plans, in other words, require an understanding of the mechanics of time value of money (TVM) as well as a means of making fast and accurate calculations. TVM calculations pertinent to loan negotiations are taken up in the next chapter, and calculators and computers, of course, provide the means for fast, accurate calculations. Our discussion in this chapter is limited to the most common repayment patterns and their implications. An understanding of TVM mechanics should enable anyone to quickly understand the nature and implications of patterns not taken up here.

We begin this chapter with a brief look at borrower and lender goals in loan negotiation. We then take up nonamortizing, fully amortizing, and partially amortizing loans, and their advantages and disadvantages as loan repayment patterns. We follow with an examination of several popular new patterns.

The principles discussed here apply whether a loan is secured by a mortgage, trust deed, or land contract arrangement, and even, with slight modification, to lease and option arrangements.

An $8,000 loan at ten percent per year with a scheduled repayment period of four years is initially used to explain and illustrate the individual plans. Annual payments are used for simplicity and clarity; in practice, monthly payments are much more common. Subsequent discussion may involve a 20- to 25-year term loan to explain and illustrate the long-run implications of the plans.

OBJECTIVES OF PARTIES

A loan is negotiated between a lender and a borrower because both expect to be better off after the contract is made. What are the objectives of each of the parties that make this mutually advantageous contract feasible? Let us take a brief look at the goals of the borrower and the lender to see how this balance of goals is achieved.

BORROWER GOALS

The two basic reasons debt financing is used are need and leverage. These reasons often reinforce each other. An owner takes on additional risk, termed *financial risk,* in borrowing to finance a property. The need to borrow or the advantage of leverage must be weighed against the financial risk.

Home buyers acquire real estate primarily for consumption. Most do not have the resources to finance the home from personal wealth, consequently, leverage is secondary to need in obtaining a loan. Many would probably prefer avoiding debt financing altogether. But the basic need and concern is to get the money so that the desired dwelling unit may be obtained. The amount that a particular buyer-owner can borrow depends on personal wealth, income, and credit worthiness. These items, in turn, limit the maximum value of housing that may be arranged.

An investor-borrower, on the other hand, acquires real estate to maximize return. Leverage assists in realizing this goal. Typically, the property itself is the main security for the loan. That is, the personal as-

FIGURE 18-1   Return to the Equity Investor in Real Estate

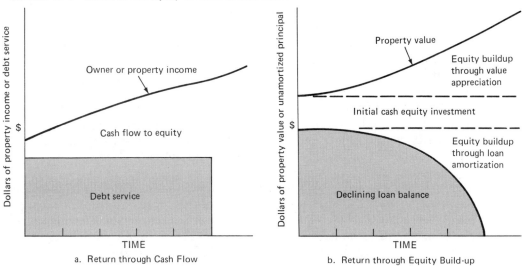

a. Return through Cash Flow

b. Return through Equity Build-up

sets of the borrower are often omitted as security for the loan under an exculpatory clause. The borrower's main concern is to balance potential returns against chances of loss of the property through default and foreclosure.

Returns may be realized through periodic cash flow or through equity reversion. *Equity reversion* is the after-tax proceeds realized on sale at the end of the holding period. Cash flow to equity occurs as long as property net operating income (NOI) exceeds debt services. NOI equals gross income less operating expenses. Equity reversion is available as long as disposition value of the property exceeds loan balance and disposition costs. Equity build-up occurs, meaning equity reversion increases, either through loan amortization or value appreciation (see Fig. 18-1).

The crucial ratios in debt financing are the loan-to-value ratio and the default ratio. We defined the LVR in Chap. 1. The *default ratio* is debt service divided by property income. The higher the default ratio the greater the probability of default. Obviously, it is desirable that income be greater than debt service. A property that must be "fed" cash because debt service exceeds income is termed an *alligator:* It eats cash. These ratios are also crucial from a lender's viewpoint. We will be looking at them from time to time throughout the chapter.

LENDER GOALS

Financial institutions, as intermediaries, have traditionally put themselves in the position of *borrowing short term* and *lending long term* when making loans on real estate. Passbook deposits are subject to withdrawal on demand. Certificates of Deposits (CDs) and Money Market Certificates (MMCs) have relatively short terms compared with mortgage loans and must be repaid at maturity. Borrowing short results in a lender having to continually pay the going market rate to attract and hold funds. At the same time, lending long has traditionally meant that the rate earned on the loan portfolio is fixed or subject to change only very slowly.

In times of increasing interest rates, this situation squeezes the institutions spread between the rate paid to borrower from depositors and the rate earned on loans made. Too tight a squeeze results in losses, and may eventually lead to insolvency and bankruptcy.

Lenders strive to avoid this squeeze by negotiating more flexible loan terms. One way is to shorten the life of loans, which means more frequent renewal. At each renewal, the interest rate can then be adjusted. A second way is to make the contract interest rate responsive to changing conditions in the financial markets. Either way acts to shift more of the risk of increasing interest rates to the borrower.

Lenders must also keep the loan-to-value ratio in mind when negotiating a repayment plan. A market value appraisal when the loan is made is necessary to set the initial LVR. The pattern of value for the property must be predicted during the life of the loan to maintain an acceptable ratio. If the property value declines more rapidly than the loan is amortized, the lender's risk in default and foreclosure is increased. On the other hand, maintaining or reducing the LVR reduces this lender risk.

NONAMORTIZING LOANS

A nonamortizing loan is also called a *term loan,* a *straight loan,* or a *straight-term loan.* A straight-term loan agreement calls for repayment of the principal sum, in full, at the end of the life of the loan. Interest is usually payable on a monthly, quarterly, semi-annual, or annual basis in the interim.

Up to the 1930s, most mortgage loans were nonamortizing, or straight, with a three- to five-year life. At the end of the agreed life, the loan was generally renewed for a subsequent three- to five-year term, or it was refinanced with another lender if payment was demanded. With increasing interest rates prevalent in the late 1970s, nonamortizing loans were reintroduced into real estate finance.

A brief example shows why a nonamortizing loan is also called a straight loan. The payments on a four-year, ten percent, $8,000-loan with interest payable annually would be as follows:

End of year 1	$800
End of year 2	800

End of year 3   800
End of year 4 $8,800 ($8,000 + $800)

The payments and principal outstanding, in graphic terms, would be as shown in Fig. 18–2.

A straight-term loan with a long-term (20-year) appears as shown in Fig. 18–3. With increasing or stable income and value (lines *a* and *b* in Fig. 18–3), risk to both the borrower and the lender is minimal. With decreasing income or value (line C), the default and LVR ratios increase, meaning the risks increase steadily. It follows that a short-term straight loan with decreasing income or value may be rational in a situation of decline. A long-term loan, on the other hand, would be extremely risky.

A term mortgage is advantageous to an investor-borrower for two reasons. First, debt service requirements are smaller than those on amortizing mortgages of equal amount. This means higher cash flow to the investor's equity position on a continuing basis. Second, leverage is maintained in the investment because no equity build-up occurs through loan amortization. That is, the loan balance remains constant or unchanged. The main deficiency of a straight-term loan is its traditional short life. The borrower must periodically pay refinancing fees and risk interest rate increases. Of course, interest rate decreases would benefit an owner-borrower. If a long-term straight loan is obtained and income and value increase, an investor-borrower would eventually find it advantageous to refinance with a larger loan to maintain leverage.

FIGURE 18–2 Straight-Term Loan Payments and Balances

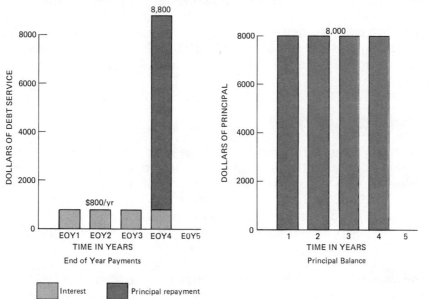

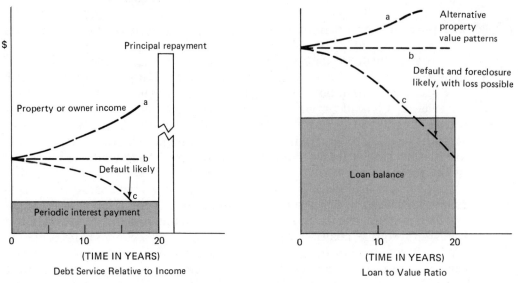

FULLY AMORTIZING LOANS

A *fully amortizing loan* is one in which periodic debt service pays accrued interest on the principal and at the same time repays a portion of the principal. The entire principal is repaid over the life of the loan agreement. The interest rates, the term, and the frequency of payments may be fixed or allowed to vary within this definition. Considerations beyond interest rate and amortization period, such as income or equity participation arrangements, are explained in a later section of this chapter.

FIXED-RATE MORTGAGE (FRM) LOAN

The traditional fully amortizing loan is now termed a fixed-rate mortgage (FRM) loan. Level or equal periodic payments of debt service are made over the life of the loan while the interest rate is held constant.

The $8,000, ten percent, four-year loan introduced earlier is helpful in explaining the inner workings of the FRM loan.

Debt service on the $8,000 loan works out to be $2,523.77 per year. Steps in the amortization of the principal over the four years are shown in Fig. 18–4. The interest accrued and payable is calculated by taking the principal balance at the beginning of each year (BOY) times the ten percent interest rate. This interest is deducted from the level debt service of $2,523.77 to find the amount by which the principal is reduced at the end of each year, EOY, upon payment of the debt service.

Note in the fourth or last year that debt service is decreased by $0.03 so that the principal is amortized exactly. This situation comes up because debt service must be rounded off to the nearest penny. Sometimes a slight adjustment is needed to make the numbers work out. Some amortization schedules call for the adjustments to be made in the debt service for the first period rather than for the last period.

The reader should not feel a need to reproduce the arithmetic. The important thing is to know that the arithmetic works out; let the tables or the calculator do the rest. It is also helpful to note that the proportion of the payment going to interest declines with each passing period, and the proportion going to principal reduction increases (see Figs. 18–4 and 18–5).

A fixed-rate mortgage loan is suitable for any financing situation with three exceptions. When owner or property income is expected to decline, the default ratio increases, and default becomes more likely. When property value declines at a faster rate than the loan is amortized, the LVR increases, and the chance of loss in default is increased. The third exception concerns changes in interest rates. When the market rate goes below the contract rate, the borrower suffers, though at some point it may be advantageous to absorb prepayment penalties and other refinancing costs to get a lower interest rate. When the market interest rate increases above the contract rate, an FRM loan is undesirable from the lender's point of view. The lender typically is locked in, however,

FIGURE 18–4 Annual Amortization of a Ten Percent, Four-Year, $8,000 Loan by a Level or Constant Payment Plan

PRINCIPAL BALANCE, BOY1		$8,000.00
Year 1 debt service	$2,523.77	
Interest (10% × $8,000)	800.00	
Principal reduction	1,723.77	1,723.77
PRINCIPAL BALANCE, EOY1, BOY2		$6,276.23
Year 2 debt service	$2,523.77	
Interest (1% × $6,276.23)	627.62	
Principal reduction	1,896.15	1,896.15
PRINCIPAL BALANCE, EOY2, BOY3		$4,380.08
Year 3 debt service	$2,523.77	
Interest (10% × $4,380.08)	438.01	
Principal reduction	2,085.76	2,085.76
PRINCIPAL BALANCE, EOY3, BOY4		$2,294.32
Year 4 debt service	2,523.74	
Interest (10% × $2,294.32)	229.43	
PRINCIPAL REDUCTION	$2,294.31	2,294.31
PRINCIPAL BALANCE, EOY4		$ 000.00

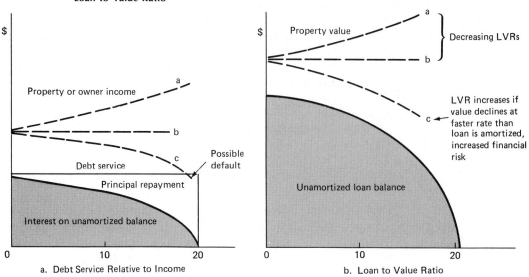

a. Debt Service Relative to Income

b. Loan to Value Ratio

and must await action by the borrower to gain relief. Lenders have, therefore, increasingly gone to more flexible financing arrangements.

Desirable features of a fixed-rate amortizing mortgage loan to an owner-occupant of a house (or other property) include the following:

1. Combined payments covering principal, interest, insurance, and taxes (PIIT) may be arranged and paid once a month like rent.
2. Interest is charged and payable on the remaining balance only.
3. Owner equity is built up automatically over a period, usually from 10 to 30 years, once the arrangement has been made. The borrower moves steadily toward 100 percent, a mortgage-free ownership. Fear of not being able to repay or replace a large debt sometime in the future is therefore removed.

An amortizing mortgage loan has the following two favorable features for the lender as well.

1. The loan usually continues to be well secured because the loan-to-value ratio remains level or decreases. Loan principal repayments usually equal or exceed losses in property value due to wear, tear, and obsolescence. Amortizing loans are therefore less risky than straight-term loans, other things being equal.
2. Loan maturities are spread out over a long time. And loan-to-value ratios may vary from a high of 97 percent down to almost zero, with an average of perhaps 60 percent. Not only do these considerations make for a portfolio of well-seasoned loans, they also make for stability in the portfolio. In turn, this stability makes it possible for a lender to make additional high loan-to-value ratio loans.

Variable-rate mortgage (VRM) and renegotiable-rate mortgage (RRM) loans surfaced in the late 1970s as two distinct ways to keep loan contract rates in adjustment with market rates. The intent is to have instruments that are simultaneously responsive to the needs of borrowers and lenders. The need is also to develop and maintain instruments that are acceptable in the secondary mortgage market. In April 1981, the Federal Home Loan Bank Board (FHLBB) issued regulations concerning origination, purchase, participation in, and other involvement in alternative mortgage loan (AML) instruments by federal S&Ls and MSBs. The regulations preempt all state laws that would otherwise prevent federally chartered thrift institutions from dealing in AML instruments. Roughly comparable regulations were issued by the office of the controller of the currency (OCC) in March 1981 for national banks. Subsequently, FNMA issued guidelines concerning the types of ARM loans it would purchase, which were slightly more restrictive than the FHLBB regulations.

In essence, the FHLBB regulations are as follows:

1. Changes in market interest rates may be reflected by adjustments in the amount of debt service, the outstanding loan balance, or the life of the loan, provided the term or life does not exceed 40 years. Thus, a higher market interest rate may result in higher debt service, in allowing the principal amount to increase, or in extending the time debt service must be paid.

2. Adjustments in the interest rate on the loan must be based upon the movement of an index that is beyond the control of the lender and readily verifiable. The index selected must be agreed to by the borrower and the lender. Lenders therefore are prohibited from using their own cost of funds or loan rates as the index for AMLs. Acceptable indexes include the FHLBB's national average mortgage rate index, the FHLBB average cost of funds to FSLIC institutions, the three- or six-month U.S. Treasury bill rates, or the average monthly yield on one-, two-, three-, or five-year Treasury securities.

3. Adjustments are not limited for any one period or in the aggregate, even as they may apply to the amount of debt service. The FHLBB expects competition among lenders in negotiating the instruments or contracts to limit the types of adjustments that might be made. The intent is to give the thrifts maximum flexibility in designing the AML instruments. An outside constraint is that debt service must be adjusted at least once every five years to assure that the loan will be amortized over its remaining term.

4. Notice of payment adjustments must be given at least 30 days, but no more than 45 days, prior to the adjustment.

5. Borrowers are entitled to prepay their loans in full or in part at any time during the loan term without penalty.

In some cases, the FNMA guidelines provide for a maximum interest rate adjustment per year (*interest rate cap*) and a maximum periodic payment adjustment per year (*payment* or *debt service cap*). Further, FNMA stated very clearly that a due-on-sale clause is mandatory in all ARM loans it purchases.

All the agencies appear to agree on the following two points: Interest rate increases are at the option of the lender. Decreases are mandatory. Charging fees for interest rate adjustments are prohibited.

ARM Risks. An ARM loan is similar to an FRM loan insofar as TVM calculations are concerned. However, negative amortization or principal build-up due to increasing interest rates might well raise the LVR and in turn lender risk of loss in foreclosure. Higher interest rates might also extend the life of the loan. This longer life also increases lender risk of loss in default if the LVR is increased because the property ages and decreases in value at a faster rate than the loan is amortized. A level property income might cause problems if the initial default ratio is too high and if rising interest rates require a higher debt service. However, a level property value would not increase lender risk of loss in default followed by a foreclosure sale, assuming some amortization of the loan occurs. Increasing income and value would sharply reduce risks to both borrowers and lenders.

RRM Risks. An RRM loan is a special version of the ARM loan. The main difference is that debt service adjustments are made every 3 or 5 years rather than every 6 or 12 months. A borrower would experience increased chance of default and foreclosure with RRM debt financing under two sets of circumstances. First, if income decreased, risk of default is increased. And, second, if debt service increases more rapidly than income, risk of default increases. This would be true whether the income were personal or property. A borrower's equity would also suffer if value declined more rapidly than the loan was amortized.

The lender's risks essentially run parallel to those of the borrower. A decreasing LVR would substantially increase chances of a capital loss to the lender in default and foreclosure.

PARTIALLY AMORTIZING LOANS

A *partially amortizing loan* is one in which a portion, but not all, of the principal is repaid by the borrower during the life of the loan. A partially amortizing loan obviously has features similar to a nonamortizing and a fully amortizing loan. It has several advantages. For an investor, cash flow to equity is relatively high because debt service is low relative to a fully amortizing loan. Also, leverage in an investment is maintained because the loan is not amortized rapidly since the debt service is kept low. The advantage of a partially amortizing loan to a lender is that the security is maintained because the loan-to-value ratio is kept stable. The loan is paid off at about the same rate as the property depreciates.

FIGURE 18–6 A Partially Amortizing Loan

Year	Debt Service on $8,000 Non-amortizing Loan (from Fig. 18–2)	Debt Service on $8,000 Fully Amortizing Loan (from Fig. 18–4)	Total Debt Service on $16,000 Partially Amortizing Loan
1	$ 800	$2,523.77	$ 3,323.77
2	800	2,523.77	3,323.77
3	800	2,523.77	3,323.77
4	8,800	2,523.77	11,323.77

Also, the calculations are easy and there is great flexibility in setting up the loan.

One common way of setting up a partially amortizing loan is to treat one portion of the principal as fully amortizing and one portion as nonamortizing. For example, a four-year, $16,000 loan with a ten percent interest rate may be split into two loans of $8,000 each. The first might be a fully amortizing loan and the second a nonamortizing, or straight-term loan. Total debt service is then determined by combining the debt service on the smaller portions (See Figs. 18–2, 18–4, and 18–6). The calculations for each of these smaller loans are shown in earlier examples.

Fig. 18–7 shows the total debt service payments and their allocation and the outstanding loan balance for the four year loan term.

An alternative and increasingly popular way of setting up partially amortizing loans is to use a long amortization period to calculate debt service, but to require an early or balloon prepayment. This arrangement is particularly appropriate where property value is expected to decline sharply. For example, our $16,000 loan could be set up on a 20-year amortization schedule for debt service purposes, with a balloon payment at the end of year four. (See Fig. 18–8).

In this case, annual end-of-year debt service would equal $1,879.35. The balloon payment, due at the end of year four, would be fourteen thousand seven hundred three dollars and fifty-two cents. That is, one thousand two hundred ninety-six dollars and forty-eight cents of the initial principal is paid off in the first four years.

Now that we've completed our discussion of nonamortizing, fully amortizing, and partially amortizing loans, we are ready to move on to alternative loan patterns. For the most part, they are variations of patterns already discussed.

ALTERNATIVE REPAYMENT PATTERNS

According to a Louis Harris poll, 93 percent of people aged 25 to 34, who make up the prime first time home buying group, want to own their

FIGURE 18–7 Partially Amortizing Loan Payments and Balances

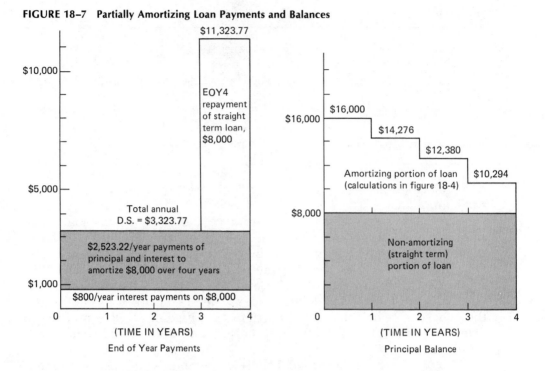

End of Year Payments

Principal Balance

own homes. To achieve this end, many sacrifices are made. Couples have children later to enable both partners to work and save the required down payment. Couples also buy lower cost existing homes in the inner city rather than new homes in the suburbs, because the former are cheaper. Even so, rising home prices and interest rate increases make ownership increasingly difficult. The traditional standard that

FIGURE 18–8 Partial Amortization of a 20-Year, Ten Percent Loan, with Balloon Repayment at End of Year Four

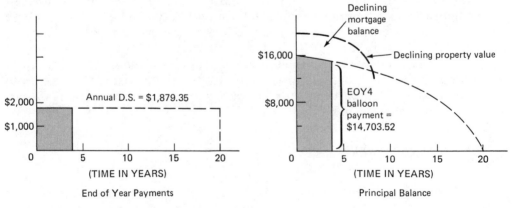

End of Year Payments

Principal Balance

housing payments should not exceed 25 percent of a borrower's income is being revised upward to 33 percent. Graduated payment adjustable mortgage (GPAM) and shared appreciation mortgage (SAM) loans are alternatives that improve chances of ownership by first time buyers.

Any number of alternative repayment plans might be negotiated to help first time homeowners. Let us look at some of the more popular representative types, beginning with the graduated payment adjustable mortgage (GPAM) and then with equity and income participation loans.

GRADUATED PAYMENT ADJUSTABLE MORTGAGE (GPAM)

The graduated payment adjustable mortgage (GPAM) loan has low initial payments that increase as the loan ages. At the same time, the amount of the principal increases in the early years and is later amortized by the larger payments. Additionally, every three to five years, rates are adjusted up or down in response to market conditions. This type of loan is sometimes called a budget or young people's loan. The reason is that it enables a young couple to qualify for the loan earlier than they otherwise would, with the expectation of paying larger payments when their income increases. Let us take an example.

Assume a $100,000 loan, with a 30-year term and an initial interest rate of 12 percent. Initially monthly payments might be set at $800 for the first five years, which is only enough for the interest on $80,000. This means that the $20,000 balance will grow 12 percent compounded monthly during these five years. The $20,000 therefore increases to $36,333 during the five years, giving a total loan at EOY5 of $116,333 ($80,000 + 36,333). The loan now has only a 25-year remaining term. If the market interest rate has not changed, debt service would increase to $1,225.25 for the sixty-first month. An increase or decrease in the inter-

FIGURE 18–9 Patterns of Debt Service and Principal Amounts on a Graduated Payment Adjustable Rate Mortgage

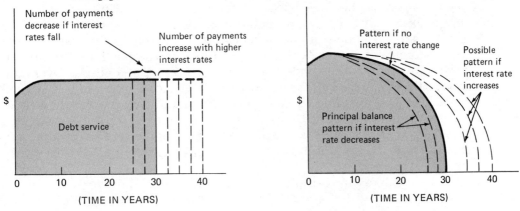

est rate would be directly reflected in higher or lower debt service. By this time, the borrowers have presumably increased their earning capacity to handle the increased debt service.

Note that GPAM loan is not appropriate for a property expected to decline rapidly in value, since the LVR and risk of default would increase.

SHARED APPRECIATION MORTGAGE (SAM) LOANS

A *SAM* or *shared appreciation mortgage loan* typically involves equity participation by the lender and lower interest rates to the borrower. The lender advances monies on a home at below-market interest rates in return for a partial claim on any appreciation in value after ten years or sooner if the home is sold before the end of year ten. A SAM loan is particularly advantageous for the first time home buyer. A typical SAM loan might reduce the interest rate by 30 percent in return for 30 percent of value appreciation during the upcoming ten years. Note that the lender is only providing financing for 75 percent of the home's value, whereas he or she will realize a share of the appreciation on 100 percent of the value.

For a home not sold within ten years, the borrower would pay the lender a lump sum, termed *contingent interest,* equal to the agreed share of appreciation. The home would be valued by an appraiser to determine the amount of appreciation. Costs of improvements and the appraisal would be deductions from the ten-year value. The lender is required to refinance the home if the borrower wishes, with the new loan covering at least the remaining loan balance plus the contingent interest.

SAM mortgages contain risks and benefits for both lenders and borrowers. Slight appreciation would mean the lender earns less than the prevailing rate of interest. Alternatively, a sharp increase in value would mean the borrower paid more than the prevailing rate. Also, relinquishing some of the appreciation gives homeowners less equity to apply to a subsequent home purchase. The winner in the trade-off depends upon the extent of the interest rate cut, the portion of appreciation conveyed to the lender, and the rate of appreciation. Over and above these considerations, however, a SAM loan may well be a good deal. Many prospective homeowners cannot qualify for a mortgage loan to buy a home without this below-market interest rate. So, even if a lender gets 30 percent of the appreciation, 70 percent of realized appreciation is much better for a borrower than 100 percent of zero appreciation.

Let us take an example of how a SAM loan might work. A home is purchased for $100,000 with the aid of a 30-year SAM loan for $75,000. The current market interest rate is 12 percent. The arrangement includes an interest rate one-quarter below the market rate (9 percent) in return for 40 percent of the appreciation during the first ten years of ownership or sooner if sold before end of year ten. The current market rate applies on any refinancing. The property doubles in value during the seven years before it is sold. Monthly debt service at 9 percent amounts to $603.47. Without the SAM loan, it would have been $771.46. At the end of the seventh year, the property is worth $200,000. Of this amount $40,000 belongs to the lender. The remaining balance of the loan is $70,230. Given these facts, the borrower paid slightly more than 13.5 percent, compounded monthly, for the loan. In turn, however, the borrower now has an equity of nearly $90,000 ($200,000 less $70,230 and −$40,000 equals $89,770). Without the SAM loan, the borrower might not have been able to purchase any home.

INCOME PARTICIPATION LOAN

Income properties were traditionally financed with fixed-rate mortgage loans. However, with the high inflation and fluctuating interest rates of recent years, lenders pointed out they are not adequately compensated for the considerable risk they incurred. Investors borrowed when interest rates were low and realized high profits due to inflation. At times, lenders actually paid more for deposits than they realized from loans made. At the very least, the lenders' profits were limited. Thus, lenders increasingly turned to more flexible financing arrangements, such as income participation loans, to realize higher rates of return from successful projects.

A typical arrangement is financing of projects at a fixed rate plus a percentage of net operating income over the breakeven point. The breakeven point is determined or defined as NOI exceeding operating expenses, debt service, and some minimal rate of return to the equity position. Above this level, some portion, perhaps one-fourth, of the NOI goes to enhance the lender's rate of return on successful projects. If an investor-borrower does not agree to the participation, the financing may not be obtained. The arrangement is often quite complex and may take the form of a joint venture.

Let us take an example. A property is projected to earn $2,300,000 effective gross income in the year a loan is negotiated. Total project cost is agreed to be $12,000,000, of which $10,000,000 is accounted for by debt financing. Operating expenses are judged to account for 40 percent of EGI. The current market interest rate is 12 percent. A ten-year straight-term loan is negotiated at 10 percent, with the lender to get 25 percent of all NOI after the investor-borrower also realizes 10 percent on initial cash equity invested. NOI is projected to go up 8 percent per year.

Effective gross income (EGI)	$2,333,333
less 40% for operating expenses	933,333
Net operating income (NOI)	1,400,000
less debt service at 10% of	
$10,000,000 loan	−1,000,000
Cash throw-off to borrower	
and income participation	400,000
Less 10% to investor's equity	
(10% × 2,000,000)	200,000
Cash available for income	
participation	200,000
Portion to lender (25%)	.25
Additional participation	$ 50,000
payments to lender	

In year one, the lender therefore nets $1,050,000 on the $10,000,000 advanced, for a 10.50 percent rate of return. In year two, the net increases to $1,078,000 for a 10.78 percent rate of return. And in year three, an 11.08 percent rate of return is realized. Soon the lender's rate of return increases to well over 12 percent.

The net effect is that the project is made feasible for both the investor-borrower and the lender. The investor gets the project and a higher rate of return on the early years. At the same time, the lender gets an overall rate of return well above the market rate. The lender shares in both the risks and the higher rate of return usually reserved for the investor. Both the lender and the borrower benefit by modifying the traditional repayment pattern.

SUMMARY

With interest rates varying between 10 and 16 percent, loan repayment patterns must often be negotiated to enable many prospective home buyers to realize their desires. Lenders, for their part, aim to keep rates of return on loans above their cost of money by varying repayment patterns.

A nonamortizing loan better enables a borrower-investor to keep debt service low while keeping leverage high. Fully amortizing loans may have fixed or variable rates and are typically for long periods of time, often 20 to 30 years. Meeting debt service for the contracted time enables a borrower to gradually realize 100 percent equity ownership.

Three repayment patterns introduced in recent years are the GPAM, the SAM, and income participation loans. Each is designed to make the initial cost of borrowing affordable. A graduated payment adjustable mortgage has initial payments that are less than the interest cost, which results in an increase in principal in the early years. A Shared Appreciation Mortgage loan provides for a lower interest rate in exchange for a portion of any increase in a property's value. An income participation mortgage gives the lender a portion of cash throw-off in exchange for a lower interest rate and basic debt service.

KEY TERMS

Alligator	Equity Participation Loan	Income Participation Loan
Borrowing Short–Lending Long	Equity Reversion	Partially Amortizing Loan
	Financial Risk	SAM Loan
Default Ratio	GPAM Loan	
Equity Build-up		

QUESTIONS FOR REVIEW AND DISCUSSION

1. Identify the two basic motivations for borrowing against real estate. Explain each briefly, including the associated risks involved.

2. Identify the basic motivations for lending on real estate. Explain the main risks involved.

3. Explain the benefits and the risks of a nonamortizing or straight-term loan from a borrower's viewpoint. From a lender's viewpoint.

4. Explain the benefits and the risks of a fully amortizing, fixed-rate loan from a borrower's viewpoint. From a lender's viewpoint.

5. Are risks increased or decreased by using adjustable interest rates with fully amortizing loans? Explain.

6. Compare the risks of a VRM loan with the risks of a RRM loan from a borrower's viewpoint. A lender's viewpoint.

7. Compare GPAM, RRM and SAM loans in terms of the repayment patterns involved, the risks involved, and other characteristics or benefits.

8. How do income and/or equity participation loans work? Who benefits? Who faces the greatest risk or losses?

9. Match the following key terms and definitions:
   a. Default Ratio _____ 1. Value appreciation plus loan
   b. Alligator _____ amortization.

c. Equity Reversion _____

d. Income Participation _____

e. Equity Build-up _____

2. Disposition price less transaction costs, taxes, and liens.

3. Reduced interest rate obtained in return for a share of value appreciation.

4. Property income divided into debt service.

5. Debt service exceeds property net operating income.

6. Reduced interest rate obtained in return for a portion of the operating income.

nineteen

Loan Negotiation Calculations

The time value of money (TVM) is the central financial issue in borrowing, lending, or investing funds. Simply stated, time value of money means a dollar in hand is worth more than a dollar to be received in the future. "A bird in hand is worth two in the bush," has about the same meaning.

Money to be received in the future has reduced value for at least four reasons. First, most of us prefer current consumption over future consumption. We therefore expect interest as compensation for giving up current consumption when we lend money to others. Second, investors have alternative investment opportunities and allocate money to the various opportunities on the basis of comparative rates of return to be earned. The highest rate of return is usually preferred, other things being equal. Third, inflation causes people to demand a return or premium on money loaned out just to maintain purchasing power. Fourth, in lending out or investing money, the risk that the money will not be recovered must be recognized. Risk acts to decrease the value of dollars to be received in the future. In short, these reasons create a reality in which money cannot be borrowed without paying interest. Or, looking at the transaction from a lender's viewpoint, money will not be loaned out without the expectation of interest earnings.

Understanding TVM is crucial to brokers, sales personnel, appraisers, and counselors, as well as to borrowers, lenders, and investors. The earnings of a property or prospective buyer relative to the debt service of a loan may determine whether a transaction holds together or not. Likewise, an appraiser or counselor must use realistic TVM relationships in valuing a property or in advising a client. To do less may mean the opinions rendered are faulty, and in turn a lawsuit for incompetent professional services may be incurred.

In this chapter emphasis is on the mechanics of the time value of money as it pertains to borrowing or lending money, such as in arranging a mortgage loan. Understanding this material is basic to understanding later chapters on income property financing, creative financing, and the buying and selling of existing first mortgages in the secondary mortgage market. Major topics covered in this chapter are as follows:

1. Terms of Financing Reviewed
2. Basic Time Value of Money Calculations
3. Calculation of a Loan Amortization Schedule
4. Calculation of Interest Paid
5. Analysis of Mortgage Loan Alternatives

As mentioned, this material is fundamental and the calculations are not difficult. Once the basic concepts are understood, the main requirements are to keep the time differentials firmly in mind and to concentrate on one calculation at a time. The problems discussed here are too involved to work easily by hand. Therefore, use of a calculator is advised. Tables of TVM factors are provided in the appendices to this text. Many calculators have the TVM factors built in, which greatly speeds up the computational process. Hewlett-Packard and Texas Instruments are the leading producers of calculators with built-in TVM factors.

TERMS OF FINANCING REVIEWED

As discussed briefly in Chaps. 1 and 9, there are six key terms or considerations that must be negotiated in arranging a loan. These items are

1. Loan-to-value ratio
2. Principal or loan amount
3. Interest rate
4. Duration or life of the loan
5. Loan amortization provisions
6. Debt service

A *loan-to-value ratio (LVR)* is the proportion of a property's appraised market value or sale price, whichever is less, that is financed by borrowed money. The ratio is usually expressed as a percentage.

$$\frac{\text{loan or principal amount}}{\text{sale price or market value}} = \frac{\$80{,}000}{\$100{,}000} = 80 \text{ percent}$$

The *principal* or loan amount is the number of dollars actually borrowed. The *interest rate* is the price paid to borrow money and is usually stated as a percent per year of the number of dollars borrowed. The *duration or life* of a loan is the number of years or months until the loan is repaid. The pattern of repayment constitutes the *loan amortization* or *repayment provisions.* The pattern of repayment also determines the number of dollars of debt service required, usually on a monthly or annual basis. *Debt service* is the periodic payment of interest or of interest and principal to satisfy the mortgage loan. With high interest rates, the pattern of repayment may be critical, as pointed out in the previous chapter.

BASIC TIME VALUE OF MONEY CALCULATIONS

The traditional residential mortgage loan is one made on a level or constant payment plan with a fixed interest rate. The important calculations in initiating these loans are the determination of the required debt service and of the amortization schedule. TVM (time value of money) tables are helpful in understanding these calculations. Calculators with built-in TVM factors may be used also, but they do not facilitate understanding. TVM calculations are also frequently called *compound interest* or *present value* calculations, but both these terms are narrower in meaning than time value of money.

Time value of money factors or calculations relate payments and/or values at two different points in time. A factor is also a multiplier. The key to selecting a specific factor is the interest or discount rate and the time or number of compounding periods. TVM tables are intended primarily for instructional purposes, thus only monthly and annual factors are included. Sample application or use of these factors is shown herein. The diagrams illustrate what each factor does and how it is to be used. Do not be unduly concerned about the mathematics behind the factors. If the tables and factors are properly used, the mathematics will work out. The convention with mortgage loans is to assume monthly payments unless otherwise stated.

TVM calculations for mortgage loan purposes require an understanding of three basic concepts: (1) present value of one (*PVI factor*),

(2) present value of one per period (*PVI/P factor*), and (3) principal recovery (*PR factor*). Our discussion is aimed at developing this understanding and at enabling the reader to put the concepts into practice.

FUTURE VALUE

TVM tables were originally called compound interest tables because of the process involved. Compound means to mix and combine. The idea of compound interest meant to calculate interest on principal and to mix or combine the interest with the principal in the next period. In turn, interest was then earned, or paid, on interest as well as on the original principal. Interest earned on money deposited in a savings account illustrates the process of compounding.

Consider $100 paid into a savings account to earn interest at 5 percent, compounded annually. What amount or future value will the account contain at the end of one year? A simple calculation solves the problem. EOY means end of year, and EOM means end of month, FV means future value, and i means the interest rate.

$$FV\ (EOY1) = \text{amount of deposit times } (1 + i)$$

$$FV\ (EOY1) = \text{deposit } (1 + i)$$

$$= \$100\ (1 + 0.05)$$

$$= \$105$$

The amount in the account accumulates to $110.25 at EOY2. The additional $0.25 represents interest earned on interest.

$$FV\ (EOY2) = FV\ (EOY1)\ (1.05)$$

$$= \$1.05\ (1.05) \text{ or } \$100\ (1.05) + \$5\ (1.05)$$

$$= \$110.25 \text{ or } \$105.00 + \$5.25$$

At EOY3 the account contains $115.76, calculated as follows:

$$FV\ (EOY3) = \$110.25\ (1.05)$$

$$= \$115.76$$

Note that the interest earned in year one is added to the principal for calculating interest earned in year two. And interest earned in year two is added to the principal for calculating interest earned in year three. The same result may be obtained by multiplying one plus the interest rate times itself for the number of periods involved.

$$\text{FV (EOY1)} = \$100 \ (1.05)^1 = \$105.00$$

$$\text{FV (EOY2)} = \$100 \ (1.05)^2 = \$110.25$$

$$\text{FV (EOY3)} = \$100 \ (1.05)^3 = \$115.76$$

Generalizing, the future amount in an account at the end of any year may be calculated by this formula:

$$\text{FV (EOY}_n = \text{deposit} \ (1 + i)^n$$

where

$$n = \text{number of years}$$
$$i = \text{interest rate}$$

The accumulation of interest for ten years on a \$1,000 deposit earning 10 percent is shown in Fig. 19–1. Interest being earned on interest shows up clearly in the interest earned column. Note that at 10 percent, a deposit grows much faster than at 5 percent.

PRESENT VALUE

Having discussed future value or compounding, let us now take up the calculation of present values. To illustrate present value calculations, let us take the case of an investor with the right to receive \$1,000 at the end of each of the next two years who wishes to sell the right. Other investors earn 10 percent per year on comparable investments. So what is the value of our investor's position? What might other investors pay for the right to receive \$1,000 at the end of each of the next two years? By

FIGURE 19–1   Compound Interest on a \$1,000 Deposit at 10 Percent for Ten Years

Year	BOY[1] Value	Interest Earned During Year at 10 Percent	Future or EOY Value
1	\$1,000.00	\$100.00	\$1,100.00
2	1,100.00	110.00	1,210.00
3	1,210.00	121.00	1,331.00
4	1,331.00	133.10	1,464.10
5	1,464.10	146.41	1,610.51
6	1,610.51	161.05	1,771.56
7	1,771.56	177.16	1,948.72
8	1,948.72	194.87	2,143.59
9	2,143.59	214.36	2,357.95
10	2,357.95	235.79	2,593.74

[1]Beginning of year.

comparing this to our earlier compounding example, we can ask, What amounts invested today at 10 percent would grow to $1,000 at the end of each of the next two years? Calculating the future value of an immediate deposit involves multiplying the initial deposit by $(1 + i)$, where i equals the interest rate. Here, the future values and the interest rate are known. Our need is to solve for the initial or present value. The process calls for dividing the future value by $1 + i$. For our example, a payment of $1,000 to be received at the end of year one would have a present value of $909.09.

$$PV \text{ (BOY1)} = \frac{\text{future payment (EOY1)}}{(1 + i)^1}$$

$$PV \text{ (BOY1)} = \frac{\$1,000}{1.10} = \$909.09$$

In like fashion, the present value of the $1,000 to be received at the end of year 2 is $826.45.

$$PV \text{ (BOY1)} = \frac{\text{future payment (EOY2)}}{(1 + i)^2}$$

$$PV \text{ (BOY1)} = \frac{\$1,000}{(1.10)^2} = \frac{\$1,000}{(1.21)} = \$826.45$$

Thus, the investor's position is worth $1,735.54 ($909.09 + 826.45).

The general formula for finding the present value of a future payment to be received at the end of year n, discounted at rate i, is

$$PV \text{ (BOY1)} = \frac{\text{future payment (EOY}n)}{(1 + i)^n}$$

The process of finding the present value of a future payment is called *discounting*. And the interest rate in present value calculations is often called the *discount rate*. The discounting of a future value always gives a present value that is less than the future value, assuming a positive interest or discount rate.

The process of discounting involves making an adjustment for differences in the time of receipt of future payments and the discount rate. The concept may be related to the everyday usage of the term *discount*. For example, we are sometimes advised to discount a statement or rumor made by a commonly known gossip or liar; that is, we are advised to take the statement at less than face value. Merchants also have sales at discounted prices, meaning reductions from regular or list prices. In discounting, the present value is always less than the amount to be received if the discount rate is greater than zero percent, as mentioned. In turn, discounting results in the present value getting smaller and smaller as the time of expected receipt extends further and further into the future.

In summary, compounding or future worth is the opposite of discounting. That is, a deposit today in a savings account earns compound interest and becomes worth more in the future. It stands to reason therefore that an expectation of future dollars are worth less when discounted to the present (see Fig. 19–2).

PRESENT VALUE OF ONE FACTOR (PV1)

Tables of precalculated factors or multipliers are available to solve common problems. In calculating the data for such tables, $(1 + i)$ is defined as the *base* of each table. Thus for a five percent table, $(1 + .05)$ is the base. For a ten percent table, $(1 + .10)$ is the base.

To illustrate the construction of PV1 tables, let us calculate present value factors for payments to be received at the end of one, two, and three years. The general equation is

$$PV1^{x\%}_{n\ periods} = \frac{1}{(1 + i)n}$$

$$PV1^{10\%}_{1\ year} = \frac{1}{(1.10)^1} = 0.090909$$

$$PV1^{10\%}_{2\ years} = \frac{1}{(1.10)^2} = \frac{1}{1.21} = 0.826446$$

$$PV1^{10\%}_{3\ years} = \frac{1}{(1.10)^3} = \frac{1}{1.331} = 0.751315$$

FIGURE 19–2 **The Relationship of Present or Discounted Value to Future or Compounded Value**

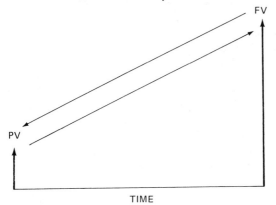

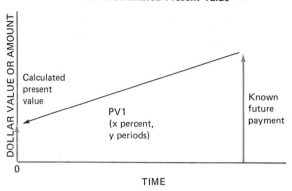

FIGURE 19-3 The Function of a PV1 Factor Is to Convert a Known Future Payment into a Calculated Present Value

The PV1 factors we have just calculated are shown in the PV1 column of the ten percent *annual* TVM table in an appendix to this book, along with factors for other years. The PV1 factor converts a single payment to be received in the future into a present, lump-sum value. Figure 19-3 shows the function of the PV1 factor.

Several PV1 factors may be used in solving a single problem. Suppose we expected to receive $10 one year from now, $20 two years from now, and $30 three years from now. What is the present value of this series of payments using a discount rate of 10 percent? The answer is $48.16, rounded off.

Time	Payment Expected		PV1 Factor		Present Value
EOY1	$10	×	0.909091	=	$9.09091
EOY2	20	×	0.826446	=	16.52892
EOY3	30	×	0.751315	=	22.53945
			Total present value		$48.15928

PRESENT VALUE OF ONE PER PERIOD (PV1/P) FACTOR

Given a PV1 table, we can calculate the present value of any series of future cash flows in a similar manner. However, if the future cash flows are equal in size, the procedure may be simplified for faster calculation. Suppose that a series of $10 payments are to be received at the end of each of the next three years. What is the present value of the series at a 10 percent discount rate? Using the procedure outlined above, the value of the series is $24.87, rounded off.

Time	Payment Expected		PV1 Factor		Present Value
EOY1	$10	×	0.909091	=	$9.09091
EOY2	10	×	0.826446	=	8.26446
EOY3	10	×	0.751315	=	7.51315
	Total of factors and values		2.486852		$24.86852

Note, however, that the total of the PV1 factors equals 2.486852. And multiplying the equal payment, $10, times this 2.486852 also gives us $24.87. Thus, totaling PV1 factors gives us a new short-cut factor, which is termed the present value of one-per-period factor (PV1/P). The PV1/P factor is used as a multiplier to convert a series of equal or level payments, which are to be received in the future, into a calculated present value. The PV1/P factor is also called the present value of an ordinary annuity, one-per-period, factor. See Fig. 19–4.

As stated, the PV1/P factor equals the total of all PV1 factors for the time involved. This means that when monthly payments are involved, PV1 factors for all previous months must be totaled. TVM tables usually only include PV1 factors per year end; that is, a PV1 factor for 39 months is not provided because 39 months does not round off to a full year. In turn, PV1 factors in a table involving monthly compounding do not total to the PV1/P factor in the table. This is because 11 out of 12 of the PV1 factors are not included in the table. A comparable situation exists when quarterly or semi-annual compounding is involved.

Another example now seems in order. Suppose we wish to know the present value of a series of $20 payments to be received at the end of

FIGURE 19–4 The Function of a PV1/P Factor Is to Convert a Series of Equal or Level Payments into a Calculated Present Value

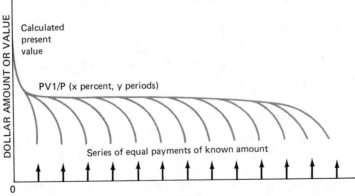

each of the next four years. The discount rate is 12 percent. Calculation of the present value of the series is as follows:

$$\text{Periodic, Level Payment} \times \text{PV1/P} \quad {}^{12\%}_{\text{4 years}} = \text{Calculated PV}$$

$$\$20 \times 3.037349 = \$60.74698$$

The factor is obtained from the PV1/P column of the 12 percent, annual table in the appendix. The present value thus equals $60.75 when rounded off.

Present value factors may also be used in combination. One common use is to value a mortgage loan that involves a balloon payment. Suppose a loan calls for annual debt service of $12,000 to a lender at the end of each of the next five years plus a lump-sum payment of $100,000 at EOY5. The discount rate is 12 percent. The cash flows look as follows:

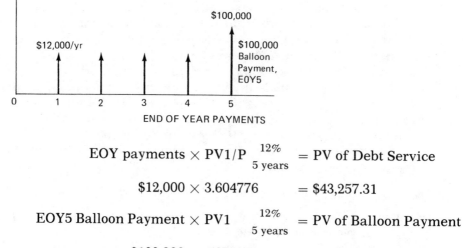

$$\text{EOY payments} \times \text{PV1/P} \quad {}^{12\%}_{\text{5 years}} = \text{PV of Debt Service}$$

$$\$12,000 \times 3.604776 = \$43,257.31$$

$$\text{EOY5 Balloon Payment} \times \text{PV1} \quad {}^{12\%}_{\text{5 years}} = \text{PV of Balloon Payment}$$

$$\$100,000 \times .567427 = \$56,742.70$$

The value of the loan equals $100,000 ($43,257.31 + $56,742.70, rounded off to one cent). The loan is straight term or nonamortizing. The EOY payment of $12,000 represents accrued interest for the year or interest in arrears.

PRINCIPAL RECOVERY (PR) FACTOR

A principal recovery (PR) factor is a multiplier used to convert a present, lump-sum value, such as a mortgage loan, into a series of equal or level payments to be received in the future. The payments include interest on the borrowed money as well as repayment of the borrowed money. This is sometimes referred to as *return on* and *return of* the bor-

FIGURE 19–5 The Function of a Principal Recovery Factor Is to Convert a Known Present Value into a Series of Equal Future Payments That Include Principal and Interest

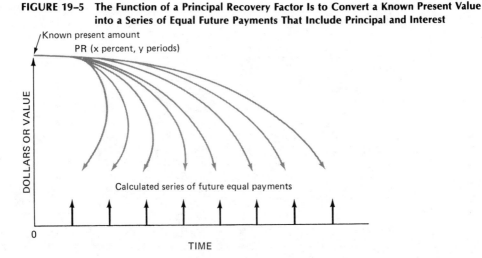

rowed money. The principal recovery factor is also more technically called the *amount to amortize one factor*. Figure 19–5 illustrates the payment and value relationships involved when a PR factor is used.

Let us take an example to illustrate the application of the PR factor. Assume the Urbandale Savings and Loan Association agrees to make a $100,000 loan to Raymond and Amy Beyers. The proposed interest rate is 12 percent, compounded monthly, and the life of the loan is 25 years or 300 months. Monthly payments amount to $1,053.20. Using a factor from the 12 percent monthly TVM table in the appendix, the calculation is as follows:

$$\text{Loan amount} \times \text{PR} \ {}^{\text{12 mo.}}_{\text{25 years}} = \begin{array}{l}\text{Required monthly}\\\text{debt service}\end{array}$$

$$\$100,000 \times \begin{array}{l}\text{PR factor}\\\text{(from table)}\end{array} = \begin{array}{l}\text{Required monthly}\\\text{debt service}\end{array}$$

$$\$100,000 \times .010532 \qquad = \$1,053.20$$

Thus, the Beyers must agree to make payments of $1,053.20 per month for 300 months in return for the immediate advance of $100,000 by the Urbandale Savings and Loan Association. Using a calculator, the debt service amounts to $1053.22. This is because the TVM tables often involve some rounding off.

Since this calculation calls for monthly payments, a monthly principal recovery factor is used. Figure 19–6 illustrates the calculation graphically.

Let us return to Raymond and Amy Beyers to see the interrelationship of the principal recovery and the present value of one-per-period factor. In extending our example, let us consider that Raymond and Amy Beyers have an annual income of $48,000, which qualifies them

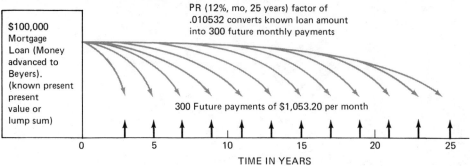

PR (12%, mo, 25 years) factor of .010532 converts known loan amount into 300 future monthly payments

$100,000 Mortgage Loan (Money advanced to Beyers). (known present present value or lump sum)

300 Future payments of $1,053.20 per month

TIME IN YEARS

with the Urbandale Savings and Loan Association to support a debt service of $1,050 per month toward purchase of a home. Using the traditional standard of 25 percent of income for debt service, the Beyers could allocate only $1,000 per month for debt service.

$$\frac{\$48,000}{12 \text{ months}} = \$4,000 \text{ per mo.}$$

$$\$4,000 \times 25\% = \$1,000$$

The FHA standard allows the Beyers to devote 35 percent of net effective monthly income to monthly housing costs. If the FHA estimates the Beyers' net effective monthly income at $3,600, the Beyers can devote $1,260 per month to monthly housing costs. If monthly housing costs total $200 for other than debt service, the Beyers can allocate $1,060 per month to debt service.

The FHLMC standard allows the Beyers to devote 28 percent of gross monthly income to real estate taxes, hazard insurance, and debt service. This totals $1,120 per month ($4,000 × 28 percent). If real estate taxes and hazard insurance total $80 per month, the Beyers can allocate $1,040 per month to debt service.

Both the loan officer and the Beyers agree that the monthly debt service of about $1,050 would be satisfactory. Terms required by the bank are 12 percent compounded monthly and a loan life of 25 years. How large a loan can they obtain?

$$\frac{\text{Monthly}}{\text{payment}} \times \text{PV1/P} \begin{smallmatrix} 12\% \text{ mo} \\ 25 \text{ years} \end{smallmatrix} = \frac{\text{Obtainable}}{\text{loan}}$$

$$\$1,050 \times \frac{\text{PV1/P factor}}{\text{(from table)}} = \frac{\text{Obtainable}}{\text{loan}}$$

$$\$1,050 \times 94.9465.38 = \$99,693.86$$

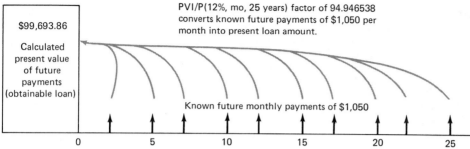

With a little additional negotiation, the loan officer and the Beyers agree that a loan of $100,000 is mutually acceptable. Debt service on the loan would be $1,053.20 as calculated earlier with the PR factor. The use of a PV1/P factor is illustrated in Fig. 19-7. A comparison of Figs. 19-6 and 19-7 illustrates the opposite manner in which the PR and PV1/P factors are used.

CONTRACT MUTUALLY ADVANTAGEOUS

The traditional level payment (fixed-rate mortgage) loan may be considered from two different viewpoints—the lender's and the borrower's. To the borrower, the loan represents the receipt of a lump-sum amount that is used to finance the purchase of real estate. To obtain the amount, the borrower agrees to make equal periodic payments over a specified period. Making the payments is the price paid to receive the lump-sum amount. To the lender, the loan represents an investment, the right to receive a series of equal periodic payments at equal time intervals in the future for the return of principal and interest. In other words, the lender is purchasing an annuity whose present worth is the amount advanced to create the loan. The price of the annuity is the principal amount advanced. The parties enter into the loan contract to gain mutual advantage. Both parties are better off after the loan has been arranged, because each obtains what was desired. The borrower finances a residence. The lender obtains a secured annuity.

CALCULATION OF A LOAN AMORTIZATION SCHEDULE

We have now gone through the basic calculations of real estate debt financing. All financing terms, no matter how sophisticated, actually involve some combination of these three basic calculations. Working examples, along with thought and explanation by an instructor, should enable anyone to master the use of TVM calculations. Gaining this mastery is very worthwhile.

Let us now consider the development of a loan amortization schedule. Loan amortization is the repayment or reduction of the principal balance. The amount amortized is the original amount less the remaining unpaid balance. Thus, the amount amortized at any given time may be determined by calculating the unpaid balance at any given time and subtracting it from the initial balance. For example, how much has been amortized on the Beyers' loan at the end of years 5, 10, 15, 20, and 25? Once we learn how to determine the remaining balances at these times, we will be able to calculate the balances at any point in the life of the loan.

At the end of five years, the Beyers still have to make monthly payments of $1,053.20 for 20 years. The loan balance at EOY5 is $95,651, which is the discounted value of the remaining payments.

$$\frac{\text{Monthly}}{\text{debt service}} \times \text{PV1/P} \begin{array}{l} \text{12\% mo} \\ \text{20 years} \end{array} = \frac{\text{Loan balance,}}{\text{EOY5}}$$

$$\$1,053.20 \times \begin{array}{l} \text{PV1/P factor} \\ \text{(from table)} \end{array} = \frac{\text{Loan balance,}}{\text{EOY5}}$$

$$\$1,053.20 \times 90.819405 = \$95,651.00$$

Thus, the amount amortized is $4,349 ($100,000 − $95,651).

Comparable calculations give the loan balance at the end of year ten.

$$\$1,053.20 \times \text{PV1/P} \begin{array}{l} \text{12\% mo} \\ \text{15 years} \end{array} = \frac{\text{Loan balance,}}{\text{EOY10}}$$

$$\$1,053.20 \times 83.321655 = \$87,754.37$$

The amount amortized, based on the full schedule of loan balances, is as follows:

Time	Loan Balance	Amortized Amount
Initial	$100,000.00	$ −0−
EOY5	95,651.00	4,349.00
EOY10	87,754.37	12,245.63
EOY15	73,408.58	26,591.42
EOY20	47,346.64	52,653.36
EOY25	$ 00,000.00	$100,000.00

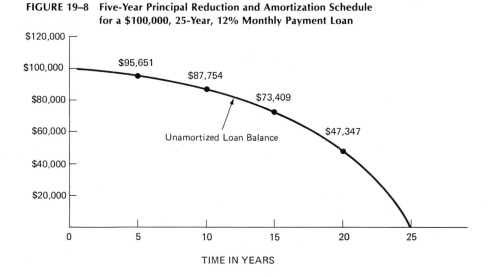

FIGURE 19–8 Five-Year Principal Reduction and Amortization Schedule for a $100,000, 25-Year, 12% Monthly Payment Loan

TIME IN YEARS

These balances and the amount amortized are graphically illustrated in Fig. 19–8.

CALCULATION OF INTEREST PAID

A borrower often wishes to know the amount of interest paid during a given time. For example, interest payments in any given year are deductible expenses for income tax purposes. Let us consider how the amount of interest paid in a given year might be calculated with TVM tables. Interest is usually due and charged at the end of each month or payment period. Mortgage debt service payments are customarily made at the beginning of each month. The payment therefore includes interest accrued for the previous month plus the principal reduction amount for the current period. Interest payable at the end of each month is termed *interest in arrears.* Interest is sometimes payable at the beginning of a payment period, which is termed *interest due* or *interest due in advance.*

Several ways of making calculations for interest in arrears can be used, depending on the situation. For single periods, when the loan balance is known, the interest may be calculated in two ways. (See Fig. 19–9 for the calculations of these two methods. Assume a $100,000, 12 percent, 25-year loan calling for monthly payments.) The single period method has a limitation, in that the exact balance at the beginning of the period must be known, which is not a usual situation. In the example in Fig. 19–9, the debt service is $1,053.20, which leaves $53.20 for amortization after interest for month one. The principal balance at EOM1 is therefore $99,947 when rounded off.

	Method A		Method B

PERIOD 1

$100,000	loan balance, BOM1	interest rate	12%
× .12	times annual interest rate	divided by number	
12,000	equals interest per year	of months in year	÷12
		equals monthly	
$1,000	equals interest	interest rate	1%
12)12,000	for month 1	times loan balance	× $100,000
		equals interest	
		for month 1	$1,000

PERIOD 2

$99,947	loan balance BOM2	loan balance BOM2	$99,947
× .12	times annual interest rate	times monthly	
11,993.62	equals interest per year	interest rate	×1%
		equals interest	
$999.47	equals interest for	for month 2	$999.47
12) 11,993.62	month 2		

Interest payments made during a year are usually considered more important because they are tax deductible. Let us therefore calculate an annual principal reduction and interest paid schedule for the first three years of the $100,000 loan. Annual debt service on the loan is $12,638.40 (12 × $1,053.20). Interest paid in any year equals annual debt service less amortization or principal reduction during the year. That is, debt service not going to principal reductions goes to interest and vice versa. Therefore, interest paid on the $100,000 loan in years one, two, and three amounts to $11,964, $11,878, and $11,782, respectively. (See Fig. 19–10.) The numbers are rounded off since interest need only be listed to the nearest dollar on an income tax return.

ANALYSIS OF MORTGAGE LOAN ALTERNATIVES

Our discussion of calculations for loan negotiation would not be complete without a brief comparison of five common mortgage loan alter-

FIGURE 19–10 Schedule of Annual Principal Reduction and Interest Paid for the First Three Years on a 25-Year, $100,000, 12% Monthly Payment Loan

(Annual Debt Service Equals $12,639 Rounded Off)

Time	Loan Balance	Principal Reduction during Year	Interest Paid during Year
BOY1	$100,000	—	—
EOY1	99,325	$675	$11,964
EOY2	98,564	761	11,878
EOY3	97,707	857	11,782

natives. The alternatives have financial implications for both the buyer and the seller of a property that greatly influence the type of loan that might best be obtained. Our comparison also examines the financial requirements of a potential buyer for a given property.

Let us take a one-family residence that sells for $70,526. This figure is used because it gives the maximum LVR under FHA section 203(b). The alternatives compared are three conventional loans (at 80 percent, 90 percent, and 95 percent of value, respectively), an FHA loan, and a federal VA loan. Figure 19–11 summarizes the comparison.

Note first that as we go from an 80 percent conventional loan to a federal VA loan, the total move-in costs (that is, the cost to actually move into the home) steadily decline. The decrease is basically because of a higher loan-to-value ratio. Thus, as a buyer has less ready cash for a

FIGURE 19–11   Financial Implications of Common Mortgage Loan Alternatives for Seller and Probable Buyer-Borrower of $70,526 One-Family Residence

ITEM OF COMPARISON	LOAN TYPE				
	80% Conventional	90% Conventional PMI	95% Conventional PMI	FHA 203b Maximum	Federal VA Maximum
Loan Amount	$56,421	$63,473	$67,000	$67,500	$70,526
Loan-to-Value Ratio (LVR)	80%	90%	95%	95.7%	100%
Required Down Payment	$14,105	$7,053	$3,526	$3,026	-0-
Estimated Additional Closing Costs	1,918	3,491	3,685	2,902	1,763
Total Move-in Costs	$16,023	$10,544	$7,211	$5,928	$1,763
Relative Interest Rates Required	12%	12¼%	12½%	11½%	11¼%
Mortgage Term or Duration	25 years	25 years	25 years	30 years	30 years
Required Monthly Debt Service (PI[1] only)	$594.24	$680.27	$730.54	$668.45	$684.99
Required monthly payment for insurance and taxes (PITI)[2]	$120	$120	$120	$120	$120
Total Required Monthly Payment	$714.24	$800.27	$850.54	$788.45	$804.99
Required Monthly Income to Qualify[3]	$2,857	$3,201	$3,402	$3,154	$3,220
Required Annual Income to Qualify[4]	$34,284	$38,412	$40,824	$37,848	$38,640
Likely Discount Required of Seller: Points (% of Loan)	-0-	-0-	-0-	6%	7%
Dollars	-0-	-0-	-0-	$4,050	$4,937

[1]PI means principal and interest.
[2]PITI means payments of principal, interest, taxes, and insurance.
[3]Four times PITI, meaning housing expenses should only be 25 percent of income.
[4]Twelve times required monthly income.

down payment and closing costs, the greater the need to move toward a high loan-to-value ratio, that is, to obtain an FHA or VA loan. The required monthly income to qualify for the various loans is also shown in Fig. 19–11. Basically, the higher the down payment, the lower the required monthly PITI debt service payment, which includes payments on the principal, interest, taxes, and insurance.

PITI payments are frequently required by a lender. The taxes and insurance are placed in an escrow or impound account by the lender, and used to pay taxes and insurance as appropriate. PITI is sometimes referred to as *total debt service.* Many lenders consider that maximum total monthly debt service should not exceed one-fourth of a borrower's income. This ratio is considered to better relate the cost of carrying the property to the borrower's income.

The higher down payment on a conventional loan is partially offset by longer and lower interest rates on the FHA and VA loans. In turn, the FHA and VA alternatives are not freely available because of the subsequential discounts required of a seller.

This type of analysis is particularly useful for a seller or a broker. It clearly indicates income requirements of a potential buyer for an owned or listed property. The numbers would change as the value of the property changes. FHA insured financing would rapidly lose out as the property value increased, because of the $67,500 loan limit.

A potential buyer might work from known annual income, in a comparable type of analysis, to determine the most suitable financing for his or her situation. This type of analysis can also be used to ascertain the upper limit that might be paid for a residence by a buyer.

SUMMARY

The time value of money is the central issue in financial negotiations between a borrower and a lender and in investment analysis. The three basic TVM calculations involve the PV1, PV1/P, and PR factors. The PR factor converts a present lump sum into a series of equal payments to be received in the future. The PV1 factor converts a single future payment into a lump-sum present value amount, whereas the PV1/P factor discounts a series of uniform future payments into a single, lump-sum present value amount. Therefore, the PV1/P factor and the PR factor act in exactly the opposite manner.

TVM applications include calculating required debt service on a loan and the size of a loan justified by a given income. TVM mechanics may be used to determine wealth and income requirements of a potential buyer for a property of known value. Alternatively, an interested buyer might use TVM calculations to determine the affordability of residential units available in the market place.

KEY TERMS

BOY	EOY	Present Value
Compound Interest	Future Value	PR Factor
Discount	Interest Due in Advance	PV1 Factor
Discounting	Interest in Arrears	PV1/P Factor
Discount Rate	PITI	

QUESTIONS FOR REVIEW AND DISCUSSION

1. Give at least three reasons why money to be received in the future has less value than money in hand.

2. Ima Elderly buys a three-year certificate of deposit for $2,000, to earn nine percent, compounded annually. What amount will she receive at EOY3?

3. Ima Elderly needs money at the end of a year and decides to sell the CD. Using a nine percent discount rate, how much could she sell the certificate for? (Note that if she turns the certificate in, a substantial interest penalty applies. This caution is not part of the problem.) Is the answer related to the EOY1 value of the initial $2,000 in any way?

4. John and Linda Hunter jointly earn an annual income of $36,000. The annual real estate taxes and hazard insurance on the desired home total $840. Under FHLMC rules, how much can the Hunters devote to monthly debt service? The lender is willing to make a loan at a 10 percent interest rate for a 20-year term. What is the amount of the loan that the Hunters can obtain under FHLMC standards?

5. What considerations are likely to enter into the decision of the Hunters as to the maximum value property they might buy?

6. What size loan might the Hunters get, assuming they decide to devote one-fourth of their income to debt service (principal and interest only), that is $9,000 per year or $750 per month. Assume the current market interest rate is 12 percent, compounded monthly, and the typical loan term is 25 years. What is the maximum they could pay for a home, assuming an 80 percent LVR?

7. The market interest rate increases to 15 percent, compounded monthly. What is the effect on the size of loan obtainable? On the maximum price they could pay for a home?

8. The Parktown Savings and Loan agrees to make a $75,000 loan to the Hunters for 20 years at 12 percent, compounded monthly. How much debt service would be required on the loan?

9. Property taxes on the property to be acquired by the Hunters are estimated to be $2,100 for the coming year. Hazard insurance is expected to cost $312 for the year. How much PITI, or total debt service, for the Hunters given the monthly debt service in eight above?

10. Match the following key terms and definitions?

a. Discounting	_____	1. Paying interest on interest.
b. Total Debt Service	_____	2. Interest due and payable at the beginning of a period.
c. Interest in Arrears	_____	3. Unearned interest.
d. Compounding	_____	4. Determining the present value of a future payment.
e. Interest Due	_____	5. Interest due and payable at the end of a period.
		6. PITI.

twenty

Financing Residential Income Property

This chapter focuses on arranging *permanent debt* financing for existing residential income properties. The lender and potential borrower-buyer are presumed to be known. The buyer is also presumed to have determined that the property will make an acceptable investment if suitable debt financing can be obtained.

The essentials of the loan negotiation are covered. Understanding this process prepares the reader to undertake more complicated transactions, such as the financing of income residential properties to be developed on a vacant site or the use of a real estate investment trust (REIT) as a vehicle to finance an existing property. Possibilities of income or equity participation by the lender in the property are touched on in our discussion.

Completed FHLMC standard forms, featuring the Redwood Apartments as a case property, are used to add substance to the discussion and to illustrate the forms.

The format of our discussion roughly parallels our previous discussion of the financing process; however, all the topics are condensed into this one chapter. Major topics included are as follows:

1. Application
2. Annual Operating Statement

3. The Appraisal Report
4. Borrower Analysis
5. Underwriting Analysis
6. Loan Closing

Note that in financing income property, much greater emphasis is given to the property, compared with that given to the borrower. The reason for this, touched on briefly in the chapter on mortgage clauses, is that the property becomes the primary security for the loan rather than the borrower, since the borrower's net worth may be small relative to the size of the loan. The borrower, therefore, wishing to avoid personal liability in the event of default, requests that the loan agreement for the income property contain an exculpatory or sole security clause.

Our discussion here is equally beneficial to the borrower as it is to the lender, even though the perspective appears to be mainly that of the lender. Use of the financial ratios, for example, could enable a borrower to avoid obtaining a loan likely to result in default and foreclosure. Further, the ratios may point to alternative ways to structure a loan that will satisfy an investor's goals.

APPLICATION

The loan application opens the negotiations for an income property loan much as it does for a one-family loan. However, as mentioned previously, the emphasis is on the property rather than the borrower. The concern is also on the source of the equity funds, with the capability of management being an additional consideration. See the completed multifamily unit loan application FHLMC Form 75 in Fig. 20–1.

The subject property is the Redwood Apartments (32 units), which are being purchased for $1,000,000. A loan of $750,000 is being sought at an interest rate of 12 percent, compounded monthly, and a term of 25 years. A prepayment penalty declining by one percent per year from five percent in year one is part of the initial loan negotiation. Items usually submitted as part of the application, as noted on page two of the application, are: (1) sale agreement, (2) partnership agreement, (3) recorded survey, (4) area map, with arrow to the site, and (5) a property income and expense statement for the previous ten years. These items are not included in this chapter, however.

The lender is the Anytown First National Bank. ABC Real Estate Investors, a limited partnership, is the loan applicant. Joe Aesop is the general partner representing ABC. Al King is the person assigned to analyze and underwrite the loan for the Anytown Bank. Al immediately requests an appraisal from Mike Meter, SRPA/MAI.

FIGURE 20–1 Multifamily Loan Association

MULTIFAMILY LOAN APPLICATION

LOAN APPLIED FOR	Amount	Interest Rate	Monthly Payment Principal & Interest	Amortization Basis	Term	Escrow/Impounds (to be collected monthly)
▶	$ 750,000	12 %	$ 7,899.18	300 Mos.	300 Mos.	☑ Taxes ☒ Hazard Ins. ☐ ___

Prepayment Option

Prepay w/5% penalty in year one, declining by 1% per year; no penalty after EOY5.

PURPOSE OF LOAN

☒ **PURCHASE SUBJECT PROPERTY** — Settlement Date August 31, 1982 ___ per sales agreement (attach copy)

Sales Price	Cash Down Paymt.	Source of Equity Funds (cash down and/or other - explain)
$ 1,000,000	$ 250,000	$50,000 down; balance at closing from limited partners of ABC Real Estate Investors

Secondary Financing	Interest Rate	Monthly Payment Principal & Interest	Term	To Be Payable To:
$ None	– %	$ –	– Mos.	–

☐ **REFINANCE SUBJECT PROPERTY**

Describe Significant Improvements Made.

FUNDS TO BE USED TO PAY: ▼	Date Acquired	Purchase Price
		$

First Lien Balance	Maturity Date	Payable To:	(name & address)		Cost $ ___
$					Account No.

Second Lien Balance
$

Remaining Funds to be used to

☐ **CONSTRUCT NEW MULTIFAMILY BUILDING(S)**

Estimated time to complete construction ___ mos.

Date Property Acquired	Cost	Existing Lien(s)	Payable to: (Name & Address)
	$	$	

USE OF FUNDS: ▼		SOURCE OF FUNDS: ▼		
Pay Existing Lien(s)	$	Loan Applied For	$	Attach copies of plans; specifications; site plan; construction contract (if applicable); detailed breakdown of estimate of land development, direct & indirect construction costs; and, if applicable, details of performance and payment bonds or completion bond.
Land Dev. Costs	$	Funds invested by Owner	$	
Direct Constr. Costs	$	Other:	$	
Indirect Constr. Costs	$			
TOTAL:	$	TOTAL:	$	

General Contractor (name & address)	Explain source of funds to be invested by owner and/or other.

SUBJECT PROPERTY

Street Address	City	County	State	ZIP Code
2020 Columbus Avenue	Anytown	Rustic	IL	60606

Legal Description (attach separate sheet, if necessary)	Site/Lot Size	No. Bldgs.	No. Stories	No. Units	No. Pkg. Spaces	Yr. Built
Lots 5-8, Sampson's Sub'd, Rustic Co., IL	300'x125' 37,500 S.F.	2	4	32	40	1971

Title is in ☒ Fee Simple
☐ Leasehold (attach copy of ground lease)

Brief Description of Improvements, incl. type structural frame, exterior walls, heat & A/C system, recreation facilities.

Two 16 unit structures, wood frame with brick veneer, individual heating, and A/C, gas, central recreation room for pool, pingpong, cards; swimming pool (summer use only), sauna and Jacuzzi.

☐ Annualized estimates based on present levels of income & expenses—OR ☒ Pro-forma estimates for: 1982–83

Gross Rental Income from apartments	$	168,750
Other gross rental income from ___ None	$	–
Less vacancy (4 %)	(	6,750)
Other income (explain) ___	$	–
Less operating expenses	(	62,000)
Net effective income before debt service and depreciation	$	100,000

No. Apts. Vacant	Is project subject to rent control?	Name of current resident manager	Telephone No.
	☒ No ☐ Yes If yes, attach copy of Rent Control Law	None	

Management will be by: (individual or firm's name & address)
Everready Real Estate Mgmt., Inc.

Apts. are rented	☐ Furnished No. ___	6006 Madison Blvd., Anytown

Individual or firm manages following multifamily buildings:
☒ Unfurnished No. 32

Utilities Incl. in rent	☐ Water ☐ Gas ☐ Elec.	(Address)	(No. Units)
		Condominium Towers	60
☒ Heat ☒ A/C ☐		Southgate	48
		Douglas Manor	16
		Heaven's Gate	128

Attach signed, certified current income and expense statement and balance sheet for subject property as well as statements for the previous two calendar or fiscal years (pro-forma statements are required for new properties). Attach signed, certified current rent schedule showing occupant's name (if vacant, so indicate); apartment no. and type; monthly rent and lease expiration date; whether rented furnished or unfurnished; and type of utilities furnished by owner.
Expense statements should itemize expenditures for repairs and/or replacements.

BORROWER(S) TYPE

BORROWER(S) WILL BE ☐ Individual(s) ☒ Partnership ☐ Corporation ☐ ___

Name of Borrower(s) (name of individual[s], partnership, corp.)	Title Will Be Vested In: (name of individual[s], partnership, corp.)
ABC Real Estate Investors	ABC Real Estate Investors

PARTNERSHIP TYPE ☐ General ☒ Limited ☐ Joint Venture (Attach partnership agreement)

Principal Business of Partnership	Partnership Address	Telephone No.
Real Estate Investments	800 Madison Blvd., Anytown, IL 60602	(815)333-6006

CORPORATION	Corporation Address	Telephone No.	Date of Incorp.	State of Incorp.
		( )		

FHLMC FORM 75 9/80

343

FIGURE 20–1 (*Continued*)

List below names of: individual borrowers; general partners, if partnership; or officers, if corporation. Under "Title", indicate "Indiv.". Gen'l Ptnr", "Pres." "V. Pres.", "Treas.", etc. "Stockholder", as appropriate.

PERSONAL INFORMATION

	Name	Phone	Age	Home Address	Title	Ownership
A	John Aesop	815-686-8484	41	1960 Lakeside Anytown IL 60605	General Partner	20 %
B						%
C						%
D						%

ENTER INFORMATION BELOW ON LINES WITH LETTER CORRESPONDING TO THE PERSON NAMED ABOVE

EMPLOYMENT SUMMARY

	Primary Employer (name & address)	Type Business	Position	Years in this Business	Social Security No.
A	Self employed, 707 Viking, Anytown IL 60606	Real Estate Brokerage	Owner-Pres.	12	888-88-8888
B					
C					
D					

NAME OF GUARANTORS OF LOAN (If none, so state) ▶ None

FINANCIAL STATEMENTS. Satisfactory financial statements are required to be submitted with this application. Use of FHLMC Form 75A as a form of **personal financial statement** is optional.

ATTACHMENTS

CHECK ITEMS ATTACHED TO THIS APPLICATION

- ☒ Sales agreement (if purchase)
- ☐ Ground lease (if leasehold)
- ☒ Partnership agreement (if partnership)
- ☒ Recorded plat or survey
- ☒ Area map with arrow to site
- ☐ Copy of rent control laws or ordinances (if applicable)

- ☐ Construction contract or breakdown of est. costs; plans, specs., & site plan (if construction)
- ☒ Property income & exp. statements for previous 2 years (or pro-forma, if new or proposed)
- ☐ Description of repairs; replacements (if indicated in expense statement)

- ☐ Current income & expense statement and balance sheet regarding subject property.
- ☐ Current rent schedule, per instructions on front (unless construction)
- ☐ Financial statements
- ☐ Statement of management plan
- ☐ Statement of borrower's experience in owning, managing or building multifamily buildings
- ☐ Other _____

FOR LENDER'S USE

INFORMATION FOR GOVERNMENT MONITORING PURPOSES (complete if borrower[s] are individual[s])

Instructions: Lenders must insert in this space, or on an attached addendum, a provision for furnishing the monitoring information required or requested under present Federal and/or present state law or regulation. For most lenders, the inserts provided in FHLMC Form 65-B/FNMA Form 1003-B may be used.

AGREEMENT: The undersigned applies for the loan indicated in this application to be secured by a first mortgage or deed of trust on the property described herein, and represents that the property will not be used for any illegal or restricted purpose, and that all statements made in this application and the attachments, are true and are made for the purpose of obtaining the loan. Verification may be obtained from any source named in this application and/or in attachments.

I/we fully understand that it is a federal crime punishable by fine or imprisonment, or both, to knowingly make any false statements concerning any of the above facts as applicable under the provisions of Title 18, United States Code, Section 1014.

John Aesop
/s/ John Aesop _____ Date 6/12/82 _____ Date _____

_____ Date _____ _____ Date _____

FHLMC Form 75 9/80   REVERSE

The heart of the analysis in the valuation of the Redwood Apartments is the annual pro forma operating statement (see Fig. 20–2). A *pro forma operating statement* is an analyst's best estimate or forecast of income and expenses for a subject property in the coming year. The *subject property* is the property under study. In our case example, the Redwood Apartments is the subject property. A pro forma statement takes account of past experience along with adjustments for changes in conditions likely to be encountered in the coming year.

A pro forma annual operating statement is the beginning point for both market value and investment analyses. In the investment analysis, it provides the basis of cash flow projections. In the market value analysis, it provides the figures for capitalization by the gross income multiplier (GIM) and direct capitalization techniques.

The Redwood Apartments, as shown in the operating statement, are expected to generate a gross income of $168,960 for the coming year, if fully rented. The rents are based on market rents rather than on exist-

FIGURE 20–2   Annual Pro Forma Operating Statement, Redwood Apartments

GROSS SCHEDULED INCOME			$168,960
Less vacancy and credit losses (4%)			− 6,758
EFFECTIVE GROSS INCOME (EGI)			$162,202
Less Operating Expenses:			
FIXED			
Property taxes	32,880		
Hazard insurance	2,256		
License and permits	396		
		$35,532	
VARIABLE			
Gas, water, and electricity	3,180		
Supplies	2,100		
Advertising	600		
Payroll, including payroll taxes	3,300		
Management (5% of EGI)	8,110		
Interior maintenance	2,880		
Miscellaneous services	1,800		
		$21,970	
RESERVES FOR REPLACEMENTS			
Ranges	1,200		
Heating and A/C units	2,300		
Dishwashers and disposals	1,200		
		$4,700	
TOTAL OPERATING EXPENSES		$62,202	− 62,202
NET OPERATING EXPENSES			$100,000

ing, or contract, rents. *Market rent* is based on documented current rental rates for comparable properties. *Contract rent* is the rental rate included in a lease agreement. For the Redwood Apartments, market rent is documented on page two of the appraisal report, FHLMC Form 71B, shown as Fig. 20–3 in the next section. Adjustments made on the actual or contract rents for the past year in order to arrive at market rent are shown in the report.

Gross rent per month for all 32 apartments is calculated to be $14,080, which translates to a gross scheduled income of $168,960 on an annual basis. *Gross scheduled income* is therefore the potential income for one year for the property if all spaces are rented out and payments received. If the apartments are rented on signed leases, this adjustment could not occur until the leases come up for renewal. With month-to-month rental agreements, the rental can be adjusted rather quickly with proper notice. Some *vacancies and credit losses* (V&CL) occur as tenant turnover occurs or tenants hold over and are unable to pay for the unit occupied. In either case, V&CL is money not collected for space rental. A deduction of four percent for V&CL yields effective gross income. *Effective gross income* (EGI) is the amount of money actually collected for space rented.

Operating expenses must be incurred to maintain the property and provide services to tenants. These expenses break down into fixed and variable expenses and into reserves for replacements. Only items pertaining to operation of the property are included. That is, items like income taxes of the owner or payments for debt financing are not included. These items are independent of the property's ability to generate income. Likewise, security deposits of tenants, which are one-time deposits returnable to tenants, are not included. Deducting operating expenses from EGI gives *net operating income* (NOI). NOI is termed net annual income in the FHLMC form. NOI indicates the productivity of a property on its own. For the Redwood Apartments, NOI equals $100,000 for the coming year.

THE APPRAISAL REPORT

An appraisal report provides vital background data for financial analysis and the underwriting decision. FHLMC Form 7 is a standardized appraisal report to document and facilitate secondary mortgage market transactions involving loans of $750,000 or less for income properties. Form 71B is a modified version of Form 70, which was explained earlier as a standardized appraisal form for single-family properties. Major sections of Form 71B are as follows:

1. To be completed by lender
2. Neighborhood

3. Site
4. Description of improvements
5. Cost approach
6. Comparable rental data
7. Monthly rent schedule subject
8. Market approach
9. Income approach
10. Reconciliation and value conclusion
11. For lender's use only

Each of these sections has been completed in Fig. 20–3 for the Redwood Apartments. Since our purpose is understanding loan underwriting for income residential properties and not market value appraising, our discussion will only highlight portions of the appraisal report. The reader is referred to each of these sections and to the content therein at various times in the discussion. In most sections, the content and its implications for value should be apparent. For an in-depth treatment of income property appraising, the reader is referred to Chaps. 17 to 22 of *The Appraisal of Real Estate*[1] and to *Income Property Valuation* by William N. Kinnard, Jr.[2]

To Be Completed by Lender

In the first section of the appraisal report, the property is identified along with information about it. The lender and borrower are also identified. The person from whom an appraisal is requested is identified along with the underwriter assigned to analyze the loan. Exhibits requested of the appraiser are also indicated.

Neighborhood, Site, and Improvements

The three sections on neighborhood, site, and description of improvements contain important information and judgments about the subject property. This information aids the appraiser in selecting comparables and in making an analysis. The information also allows the underwriter to quickly review and check the factual data underlying the appraisal and to make judgments therefrom. The data allow the underwriter and others to judge whether the comparable properties are really comparable.

---

[1]American Institute of Real Estate Appraisers, Chicago: 1978.
[2]Lexington, Mass.: D.C. Heath & Co. 1971.

FIGURE 20-3 Appraisal Report—Residential Income Property

APPRAISAL REPORT—RESIDENTIAL INCOME PROPERTY
This Form may be used for appraisal of income producing properties provided the loan requested does not exceed $750,000.

Borrower/Client __ABC Real Estate Investors__ File No. _____
Property Address __2020 Columbus Ave.__ Map Reference _____
City __Anytown__ County __Rustic__ State __IL__ Zip Code __60606__ Census Tract _____
Legal Description __Lots 5-8, Sampson's Sub'd, Rustic Co., IL__

Current Sale Price (if applicable) $ __1,000,000__ Date of Sale __6/7/82__ Loan Requested $ __750,000__
Terms of Sale __25% down, remainder by debt financing, to close 8/31/82 or before.__
Property Rights Appraised [X] Fee [ ] Leasehold (attach completed Lease Analysis FHLMC Form 461)
Lender __Anytown First National Bank__ Lender's Address __One Columbus Ave., Anytown IL 60601__
Instructions to Appraiser: The purpose of this Appraisal is to estimate the current Market Value of the Subject Property. The Definition of Market Value is as set forth in Certification And Statement Of Limiting Conditions (FHLMC 439).
Note: FHLMC/FNMA do not consider the racial composition of the neighborhood to be a relevant factor and it must not be considered in the appraisal.
Other Information: _____
Appraisal requested from __Mike Meter, S.R.P.A./MAI__ Date __6/16__ 19__82__ By: __Al King, Underwriter__
Items 1, 2, 4, 5 & 6 are required. Attach additional items and check box if items are considered appropriate for this appraisal or are requested by Lender.

1. [X] Descriptive photographs of subject property
2. [X] Descriptive photographs of street scene
3. [X] Photographs of __Typical unit interior__
4. [X] Sketch or floor plan of typical units
5. [X] Owner's current certified rent roll if existing, or
   pro forma if proposed or incomplete
6. [ ] Owner's income and expense statement 19 ____ , or
   pro forma income and expense statement

7. [X] Map(s) __area, city__
8. [X] Plot plan or survey
9. [ ] Qualifications of Appraiser.
10. [ ] Lease Analysis FHLMC Form 461 (required if leasehold interest appraised)
11. [ ] Summary of reciprocal agreements with other owners for use of parking, driveways, recreational facilities, private streets, (required if applicable)
12. [ ]
13. [ ]

NEIGHBORHOOD

Location . . . . [X] Urban . . . [ ] Suburban . . [ ] Rural
Built-up . . . . [X] Over 75% . . [ ] 25% to 75% . [ ] Under 25%
Present land use: . . . ____ % Condominiums ____ % 1-Family __80__ % Apartments
____ % Commercial __20__ % Duplex & vacant
Change in present land use . . [X] Not likely . . [ ] Likely(*) . . [ ] Taking Place(*)
(*)From _____ To _____
Property values . . . . [ ] Increasing . [X] Stable . . . [ ] Declining
Housing demand/supply . . [ ] In balance . . [X] Shortage . . [ ] Oversupply
Predominant occupancy . . [ ] Owner . . [X] Tenant . . __3__ % Vacant
Condominium: Price range $ _____ to $ _____ Predominant $ _____
Age _____ yrs. to ____ yrs. Predominant _____ yrs
Single Family: Price range $ _____ to $ _____ Predominant $ _____
Age _____ yrs. to ____ yrs. Predominant _____ yrs
Typical apartment: Type __2 BR__ No. Stories __one__
No. Units __8__ Age __8__ yrs. Condition __good__
Rent Levels: [X] Increasing [ ] Stable [ ] Declining

OVERALL RATING	Good	Avg	Fair	Poor
Employment Stability	✓			
Adequacy of Utilities	✓			
Convenience of Schools		✓		
Police and Fire Protection . . .	✓			
Recreational Facilities	✓			
Property Compatibility	✓			
Protection from Detrimental Conditions	✓			
General Appearance of Properties	✓			
Appeal to Market	✓			

	Distance	Access or Convenience	
Public Transportation	1 block	✓	
Employment Centers	1-2 mi	✓	
Shopping Facilities	1/2 mi	✓	
Grammar Schools	3/4 mi	✓	
Freeway Access	1 mi		

Estimated neighborhood apartment vacancy rate __3-4__ %, [ ] Decreasing [X] Stable [ ] Increasing. Rent Controls [X] No [ ] Yes (comment on page 4 if Yes)
Describe any incompatible land uses and overall property appeal and maintenance level __No incompatible uses in immediate area.__
__Some highway/industrial use - 6 blks.__

Describe any oversupply of units in area by type and rental __None__

Describe any shortage of units in area by type and rental __Shortage of one BR, also units at lower rent levels.__

Describe potential for additional units in area considering land availability, zoning, utilities, etc. __Excellent. Rent levels increasing.__
__Some vacant sites with multi-family zoning. Streets & utilities in.__

Is population of relevant market area of insufficient size, diversity and financial ability to support subject property and its amenities? __✓__ If yes, specify.
__Area is well established as to shopping, work areas, and general character.__
__Continued growth and development likely   population in mid-to-upper income levels.__
Describe any probable changes in the economic base of neighborhood which would favorably or adversely affect apartment rentals (e.g. employment centers, zoning)
__Area has had steady growth of 15-20% per decade since 1960.__

General comments including either favorable or unfavorable elements not mentioned (e.g. public parks, view, noise, parking congestion) _____
__Some congestion developing in major thoroughfares to CBD and work areas.__

SITE

Dimensions __300' x 125' (300' on Columbus Ave.)__ Area __37,500__ Sq. Ft. or Acres
Zoning (classification, uses and densities permitted) __Residential three (allows 1 DU/1,000 SF, some small offices.__
Present improvements [X] do [ ] do not conform to zoning regulations.
Highest and best use: [X] Present use [ ] Other (specify) __Zoning allows five more units, however, layout of__
__parcel and structures preclude adding additional units while retaining amenities.__

	Public	Comm.	Individual		
Electricity	[X]	[ ]	[ ]	Street [X] Public [ ] Private	Surface __Asphalt__
Gas	[X]	[ ]	[ ]	[X] Storm Sewer	
Water	[X]	[ ]	[ ]	[X] Curb & Gutter	
Sanitary Sewer	[X]	[ ]	[ ] Sep. Tnk.	[X] Sidewalk [X] Alley	

[X] Underground Electricity & Telephone   [X] Street Lights

Ingress and Egress (Adequacy) __Both easy; good visability__
Topography __Level__
View Amenity __Typical__
Drainage and Flood Conditions __None that__
__subject property__
Is the property located in a HUD Identified Special Flood Hazard Area? __No__

COMMENTS (including any easements or encroachments or any nonconforming use(s) of present improvements)
__None__

FHLMC Form 71B—Rev. 8/77   Page 1

FIGURE 20–3 (*Continued*)

<table>
<tr><td colspan="2">

[X] Existing Approx. Year Built 19 71 [ ] Proposed [ ] Under Construction [ ] Elevator [ ] Walk-up No. of Stories_____ [ ] Row or Townhouse

No. of Bldgs. 2 No. of Units 32 No. of Rooms 128 No. of Baths 56 Parking Spaces: No 40 Type Carport - covered

Basic Structural System wood frame Exterior Walls Brick veneer Roof Covering Asphalt

Interior Walls Wallboard; sanded joints Floors Oak Bath Floor and Walls Linoleum

Insulation 4" ceiling; 3" sidewalls - Fiberglas Adequacy very good Adequacy of Soundproofing Typical

Heating: [ ] Central [X] Individual Type Forced air Fuel Gas Condition Fair

Air Conditioning: [ ] Central [ ] Individual Describe Integrated w/heating system Adequacy and Condition Fair

Elevator(s): Number 2 Automatic_____ Adequacy and Condition Good condition; good maintenance experience, slow

Security Features Heavy front door, opened by tenant "buzzer," intercom. service.

</td></tr>
</table>

DESCRIPTION OF IMPROVEMENTS

Kitchen cabinets, drawers and counter space [ ] Adequate [ ] Inadequate	OVERALL PROPERTY RATING	Good	Avg.	Fair	Poor
[X] Range/Oven [X] Fan/Hood [X] Dishwasher [X] Disposal	General appearance of property	√			
[ ] Refrigerator [ ] Washer [ ] Dryer [ ]	Quality of construction (materials and finish) .		√		
Hot Water Heater(s) Individual	Condition of improvements		√		
Plumbing Fixtures Adequate, Kohler	Rooms size and layout		√		
Electrical Service 220	Closets and storage	√			
Recreational Facilities swimming pool, recreation room	Plumbing—adequacy and condition	√			
w/pool, pingpong, sauna, & Jacuzzi	Electrical—adequacy and condition	√			
	Amenities and parking facilities			√	
Effective Age 8 Yrs. Estimated Remaining Economic Life 32 Yrs.	Appeal to Market	√			

COMMENTS: (Special features, functional or physical inadequacies, repairs needed, modernization, etc.)_____
Exterior just repainted.

COST APPROACH

LAND SALES (complete ONLY if appropriate for this appraisal) Zoning Area Sales Price Date Price per Sq. Ft. or per Unit

1.	(Cost approach not used; adequate		Ø $			$	Per
2.	data for income and direct sales		Ø $			$	Per
3.	comparison approaches)		Ø $			$	Per

Comments & Reconciliation

Estimated Land Value $_____

APARTMENT BUILDING(S)—ESTIMATED REPRODUCTION COST NEW

x _____ = _____ sq.ft. x _____ (Stories) = _____ sq. ft. x $_____ $_____

x _____ = _____ sq.ft. x _____ (Stories) = _____ sq. ft. x $_____ $_____

x _____ = _____ sq.ft. x _____ (Stories) = _____ sq. ft. x $_____ $_____

OTHER IMPROVEMENTS _____ $_____

_____ $_____

TOTAL ESTIMATED COST NEW OF IMPROVEMENTS . . . . . $_____

LESS DEPRECIATION _____

DEPRECIATED VALUE OF IMPROVEMENTS . . . . $_____

ADD—ESTIMATED LAND VALUE . . . . $_____

INDICATED VALUE BY THE COST APPROACH (IN FEE SIMPLE) . . . . $_____

IF LEASEHOLD DEDUCT VALUE OF FEE INTEREST (ATTACH CALCULATIONS) . . $_____

INDICATED VALUE BY THE COST APPROACH (LEASEHOLD) . . . . $_____

COMPARABLE RENTAL DATA

ITEM	COMPARABLE No. 1	COMPARABLE No. 2	COMPARABLE No. 3
Address	1720 Columbus Ave.	1120 W. 20th	1963 Columbus Ave.
Proximity to subj.	3 blocks south	2 blocks west	1 block south
Rental survey date			
Brief description of property improvements	No. Units 28 No. Vacant 1 Age 8 yrs One building wrapped around swimming pool	No. Units 40 No. Vacant 1 Age 8 yrs Brick veneer, excellent landscaping & appearance	No. Units 80 No. Vacant 8 Age 0 yrs Brick New

Individual unit breakdown

	Rm. Count		Size	Monthly Rent			Rm. Count		Size	Monthly Rent			Rm. Count		Size	Monthly Rent		
	Tot	BR	b	Sq.Ft.	$	#	Rm	Tot	BR	b	Sq.Ft.	$	#	Rm	Tot	BR	b	Sq.Ft.	$	#	Rm
	4	2	1 1/2	960	420	44	105	4	2	2	900	450	50	112.50	4	2	1 1/2	900	500	55.5	125
	5	3	2	1120	490	44	98								5	3	2	1060	580	55.	116

| Utilities, furniture and amenities included in rent | Heat & A/C not included Recreation center Fireplace | Heat & A/C included fireplace Recreation center | Fireplace Heat & A/C included, Recreation center, sauna, Jacuzzi, covered patio, one month's free w/ one year lease. |
| Comparison to subject including rental concessions, if any | Property slightly newer No concession; B Very comparable | Better location, appearance Rent high by comparison | New, still filling up. Better than subject. Rent/SF adjusted to subject 45¢. |

MONTHLY RENT SCHEDULE SUBJECT

Utilities included in actual rents: [ ] Water [ ] Gas [ ] Heat [ ] Electric [ ] Air Conditioning [ ]_____

Utilities included in forecasted rents: [ ] Water [ ] Gas [ ] Heat [ ] Electric [ ] Air Conditioning [ ]_____

No. of Units	Unit Rm Count			Total Rooms	Sq. Ft. Area Per Unit	No. Units Vacant	ACTUAL RENTS		Total Rents	FORECASTED RENTS		Total Rents	Per Sq. Ft. or Room	
	Tot. BR	b					Per Unit			Per Unit				
							Unfurnished	Furnished		Unfurnished	Furnished			
16	4 2	2		64	1,024	1	$ 440	$ –	$ 7,040	$460	$	$7,360	44.9 ¢	$115
16	4 2	1 1/2		64	1,008	0	410	–	6,560	420		6,720	41.7	105
TOTAL									$			$		

FHLMC Form 71B—Rev. 8/77 Page 2

FIGURE 20–3 (*Continued*)

ITEM	SUBJECT	COMPARABLE No. 1	COMPARABLE No. 2	COMPARABLE No. 3
Address	2020 Columbus Ave.	1760 Columbus Ave.		1120 W. 20th
Proximity to subject		3 blocks north		2 blocks west
Map code				
Lot size	37,500 SF	27,200 SF		
Brief description of building improvements	No. Units: 32 No. Vac.: 1 Year Built: 1971 Brick veneer, individual heat & A/C Basement	No. Units: 28 No. Vac.: 1 Year Built: 1966 Brick veneer, w/ window A/C, basement	No. Units: 40 No. Vac.: 1 Year Built: 19 72 Stucco, w/individual heat & A/C	No. Units: 40 No. Vac.: 1 Year Built: 1974 Brick veneer, excellent landscaping, and maintenance
Quality	High	Fair	High	High
Condition	Good	Good	Good	Very good
Recreational facilities	Swimming pool Rec. room	Rec. Room Pool	Rec. room, swimming pool	Rec. room, swim pool Fireplace
Parking	1.25 space/DU	One space/DU	1.2 space/DU	1.25/DU
Tenant appeal	Strong; some functional obsolescence but well maintained	Moderate; some functional obsolescence	Strong, well maintained. Recently painted.	Strong. Better location and appearance.

	Unit breakdown	No. of Units	Tot.	BR	b	No. of Units	Tot.	BR	b	No. of Units	Tot.	BR	b	No. of Units	Tot.	BR	b
		16	4	2	2	28	4	2	1 1/2	40	4	2	2	40	4	2	2
		10	4	2	1 1/2												

	SUBJECT	COMPARABLE No. 1	COMPARABLE No. 2	COMPARABLE No. 3
Util. paid by owner	No	None, exc.for Bldg		
Data source	Buyer-Borrower	Seller		
Price	$840,000 [x]Unf. []F	$840,000 [x]Unf. []F	$1,360,000 [x]Unf. []F	$1,285,200 []Unf. []F
Sale–Listing–Offer				
Date of sale	6/7/82	1/12/82	2/27/82	4/1/82
Terms (Including conditions of sale and financing terms)	Subject to fin. 75% LVR at 12% or less. for 25 yrs.or longer	Subject to fin.	Subject to fin.	Subject to fin.

Complete as many of the following items as possible using data effective at time of sale

	SUBJECT	COMPARABLE No. 1	COMPARABLE No. 2	COMPARABLE No. 3
Gross Annual Income	$ 168,960	$ 137,760	$ 225,166	$ 216,000
Gross Ann. Inc. Mult.(1)	5.92	6.1	6.04	5.95
Net Annual Income	$ 100,000	$ 82,000	$ 135,550	$ 131,328
Expense Percentage (2)	40.8 %	40.5 %	39.8 %	39.2 %
Overall Cap. Rate (3)	10 %	9.76 %	9.97 %	10.2 %
Price per unit	$ 31,250	$ 30,000	$ 34,000	$ 32,130
Price per room	$ 7,812	$ 7,500	$ 8,600	$ 8,032
Price gross bldg. area	$ 26.94 /sq. ft. bldg. area	$ 27.93 /sq. ft. bldg. area	$ 27.31 /sq. ft. bldg. area	$ 28.17 /sq. ft. bldg. area

(1) Sale Price ÷ Gross Annual Income (2) Total Annual Expenses ÷ Total Gross Annual Income (3) Net Annual Income ÷ Price

RECONCILIATION: Sale price per unit range from $30,000 to $34,000, which brackets subject property purchase price per unit of $31,250. On a per room basis, prices from $7,500 to $8,600 bracket the subjects $7,812, and prices from $27.03 to $28.17 make the $26.04 per gross square foot paid for the comparable look very reasonable. A market value of $1,000,000 for the subject is therefore indicated and reasonable.

INDICATED VALUE BY MARKET APPROACH $

INCOME

Total Monthly Apartment Forecasted Rents	$	14,080
Other Monthly Income (Itemize)		
	$	
Total Gross Monthly Forecasted Income	$	14,080
Total Gross Annual Forecasted Income	$	168,960
Less Forecasted Vacancy and Collection Loss (4 %)	$(	6,758)
Effective Gross Annual Income	$	162,202
Less Forecasted Expenses & Replacement Reserves	$(	62,202)
Net Annual Income from Total Property	$	100,000
Less Return on and Recapture of Depreciated Value of Furnishings ($ _____ @ _____ %)	$(	-)
Net Annual Income from Real Property	$	100,000

Capitalized as follows:

NOI $100,000 ÷ R .101 = $990,100

GIM 168,960 x 6.0 = $1,013,760

*Real Estate Taxes []Actual [x]Est. Tax Rate Per $100 $ 5.59 A.V.
Total Assessed Value $ 588,000   3.29 M.V.

Comments:

EXPENSES

	ACTUAL	FORECASTED
Real Estate Taxes* $		$ 32,880
Other taxes or licenses		396
Insurance		2,256
Unsubordinated ground rent		-
Fuel		
Gas		-
Electricity		-
Water and sewer		-
Trash removal		
Advertising		600
Maintenance and repairs		2,890
Interior and exterior decorating		2,100
Cleaning expenses and supplies		8,100
Management (Off-site)		-
Res. Mgr. salary & apartment		
Janitor(s) salary		3,300
Miscellaneous		1,800
Gas, water, & El-Bldg.		3,180
REPLACEMENT RESERVES		
Carpeting and drapes		1,200
Ranges and ovens		1,200
Dishwashers and disposals		2,300
Individual heating & AC units		
TOTAL EXPENSES & REPL. RES. $		$ 62,202

INDICATED VALUE BY INCOME APPROACH . . . . . . $ 1,000,000

FIGURE 20–3 (*Continued*)

General Comments (including comments on any items rated poor or fair) _____

_____

_____

_____

_____

_____

_____

_____

CONDITIONS AND REQUIREMENTS OF APPRAISAL (include required repairs, replacements, painting, termite inspections, etc.): _____

_____

_____

_____

_____

_____

RECONCILIATION AND VALUE CONCLUSION

Indicated Value by the Cost Approach . . . . $ ____–____

Indicated Value by the Market Approach . . . $ __1,000,000__

Indicated Value by the Income Approach . . . $ __1,000,000__

FINAL RECONCILIATION: Value indications by income and market approach both support a market
value of $1,000,000 for the subject property.

_____

_____

_____

_____

_____

_____

_____

I certify, that to the best of my knowledge and belief, the statements made in this report are true and I have not knowingly withheld any significant information; that I have personally inspected subject property, both inside and outside, and have made an exterior inspection of all comparable sales listed herein; that I have no interest, present or contemplated, in subject property or the participants in the sale; that neither the employment nor compensation to make said appraisal is contingent upon any value estimate; and, that all contingent and limiting conditions are stated herein. ☐ Certification and Statement of Limiting Conditions (FHLMC Form 439 Rev. 9/75) applies (☐ On file with client ☐ Attached).
As a result of my investigation and analysis, my estimate of Market Value of the subject property as of ____8/5____ 19_82_ is . . . .

$ 1,000,000

Date ___8/12/82___ Appraiser /S/ Michael Meter M.A.I., S.R.P.A.
If applicable, complete the following

Date _____ Appraiser _____

Date _____ ☐ Supervising or ☐ Review Appraiser _____
☐ Did ☐ Did Not Physically Inspect Property

FOR LENDER'S USE ONLY (completion optional)

Loan Recommended: $__750,000__ @ _12_ %. Term _25_ yrs. Principal & Interest $_7,899.18_ /mo. $_94,790.20_ /annually
Subject to: Income participation of 30% of any increase in NOI for 12 years, and Balloon
repayment of loan at EOY12.

Borrower's Cost or Purchase Price $__1,000,000__ Appraised Value $__1,000,000__ Loan to Appraised Value _75_ %
Loan: Per Unit $_23,437.50_ Per Room $_5,859.38_ Per Sq. Ft. of Building Area $_201.81_
Gross Annual Forecasted Income $_168,960_ Gross Annual Income Multiplier _5.95_ Overall Capitalization Rate _10.1_ %
Forecasted Annual Expenses and Replacement Reserves $_68,960_ (_40.8_ % of Gross Annual Forecasted Income)
Break-even Point (this loan): (Annual Exp. & RR $_68,960_ + Annual P&I pymts $_94,780_) ÷ (Gross Annual Income $_168,960_) = _96.9_ %
(All financing) : (Annual Exp & RR $_68,960_ + Annual P&I pymts. for all financing $_94,790_) ÷ (Gross Annual Inc. $_168,960_) = _96.9_ %
Borrower's Return on Appraised Equity: (Net Annual Inc. $_100,000_ (−) Annual P&I pymts $_94,790_) = $_5,210_ (1)
(Appraised Value $_1,000,000_ (−) Loan Amt. $_750,000_) = $_250,000_ (2)
$_5,210_ (1) ÷ $ _250,000_ (2) = _2.08_ %
Comments or Committee action Debt service coverage Ratio = NOI ÷ Annual D.S. = $100,000/94,790=1.055
Loan is marginally secured to present with limited room for decline in revenues. However,
demand is strong for space and rents have steadily increased in the area. Income participation at 30% of increase in NOI offsets risk of loss. Alternative is a 25 yr. loan at
14% interest, compounded monthly.

FHLMC Form 71B—Rev. 8/77

Page 4

The approaches to value are taken up one at a time. Modern appraisal theory says that when adequate market data is available, the cost approach need not be applied in that it is usually the least reliable guide to value for existing properties. Therefore, Mike Meter only applies the market and income approaches.

In the market approach, sales of comparable properties show a price per unit ranging from $30,000 to $34,000 for the comparables. And the price per gross square foot ranged from $27.03 to $28.17. Both these figures make the figures for the subject property—$31,250 per unit and $26.04 per gross square foot—appear quite reasonable. A $1,000,000 market value for the subject is therefore indicated as reasonable. In the income approach, the gross income multiplier (1) supports a value for the subject of $1,013,760. The expense percentages (2) are all near 40 percent, indicating they are realistic, thereby increasing the validity of any capitalization value of net operating income. Direct capitalization (3) (NOI/R) indicates a value of $990,100. The R represents the capitalization rate. Again, a $1,000,000 market value is supported by the income data from the market.

In the reconciliation and value conclusion section, a market value of $1,000,000 seems warranted. Note that an actual appraisal and discussion might be more detailed. Our intent, again, is only to relate the appraisal and the appraisal value to loan underwriting.

UNDERWRITER'S REVIEW

Upon receiving the report, an underwriter reviews the entire appraisal report to insure that proper documentation concerning the subject property's market value were included. A checklist as shown in Fig. 20-4 might well be used for this purpose. In our example, Al King makes this review.

BORROWER ANALYSIS

As indicated earlier, the income property is the primary security for the loan. Even so, the income and net worth of borrowers might well be obtained and checked, along with a credit report on them. The intent, of course, would be to determine the amount of additional security the borrower might provide for the loan. The analysis would parallel the analysis of a borrower seeking a single-family home loan.

_____ Personal inspection
_____ FHLMC Form 71A_____or 71B _____
_____ Descriptive photos of subject
_____ Descriptive photos of immediate environment of subject
_____ Descriptive photos of interior of typical units
_____ Sketch of floor plan of typical unit
_____ Owner's certified rent roll or pro forma rent roll
_____ Owner's income and expense statement, pro forma
_____ Maps of property neighborhood _____ and urban area _____
_____ Plot plan
_____ Structural plans and specifications (required for proposed development; optional for existing construction)
  _____ Floor plan
  _____ Wall sections
  _____ Elevations
  _____ Footing and foundation
  _____ Interior walls and finish
  _____ Floors and floor finish
  _____ Electrical wiring system
  _____ Plumbing system
_____ Zoning conformance
_____ Building code conformance
_____ Soil tests
_____ Ratio Analysis
  _____ Parking area: total   _____
  _____ No. parking spaces per dwelling unit   _____
  _____ Operating ratio   _____
  _____ Building efficiency ratio
    (net rentable area ÷ gross building area)   _____
  _____ Land-to-building ratio   _____
  _____ _____   _____
  _____ _____   _____

UNDERWRITING ANALYSIS

The purposes of an underwriting analysis are (1) to estimate the relative risks associated with the loan under study, (2) to estimate the proper amount of financing for the subject property, and (3) to determine the optimal structuring of financing to balance risk and return for the lender. Ultimately, the concern is with the ability of the borrower and the property to meet debt service and to repay the loan. Toward making this determination, an underwriter reviews certain critical financial ratios as well as data about the property and the borrower.

FINANCIAL RATIOS

Four of the most commonly used ratios in financial analysis for income property loan underwriting are the (1) loan-to-value ratio, (2) operating ratio, (3) debt service coverage ratio, and (4) breakeven occupancy ratio. Figure 20–5 gives financial data for the Redwood Apartments, which will serve as inputs to show how these ratios are calculated. After showing the calculation of each ratio, its significance is discussed.

Loan-to-Value Ratio. For the Redwood Apartments, the proposed loan-to-value ratio is 75 percent and is calculated as follows:

$$LVR = \frac{\text{Initial Loan Amount}}{\text{Market Value}}$$

$$= \frac{\$750,000}{\$1,000,000} = 75\%$$

Maximum loan-to-value ratios for lending institutions are usually set by law. In practice, most institutions lend at lower ratios by their own policy. The LVR ratio is a crude indicator of risk in real estate financing. The higher the ratio, the higher the risk associated with a loan, other things being equal. That is, a 90 percent LVR carries more risk to a lender than a 75 percent LVR, and a 100 percent LVR means that the lender would carry 100 percent of the financial risk for a property, for all practical purposes.

LVRs of 90 percent for income residential real estate have become accepted when supplemented with FHA or private mortgage insurance. However, with higher interest rates and a greater scarcity of funds, loan-to-value ratios of 70 to 75 percent have become more common. In

FIGURE 20–5   Financial Data for the Redwood Apartments

Item	Amount
Market value	$1,000,000
Gross annual income	$ 168,960
Total annual expenses	
(V&CL plus operating expenses)	$ 68,960
Net operating income (NOI), annual	$ 100,000
Loan requested	$ 750,000
Terms requested	12%, mo., 25 years
Annual debt service	$ 94,790

the case of the Redwood Apartments, a 75 percent LVR would be acceptable to an underwriter.

The underwriter, Al King, would also look at the loan repayment pattern and the probable value of the Redwood Apartments during the early years of the loan. If the apartments are in a declining area, resulting in a probable drop in value, the LVR could conceivably increase rather than decrease, meaning greater risk to the Anytown First National Bank. However, the neighborhood data and economic trends stated in the appraisal report indicate rising rent levels and increasing values for the apartments. Thus, the LVR should steadily decrease, which would mean reduced risks to the bank.

Operating Ratio. Total annual operating expenses divided by gross annual scheduled income equals the *operating ratio.* For the Redwood Apartments, the operating ratio is 40.8 percent and is computed as follows:

$$\text{Operating Ratio} = \frac{\text{Total Annual Operating Expenses}}{\text{Gross Annual Scheduled Income}}$$

$$= \frac{\$68,960}{\$168,960} = 40.8\%$$

The operating ratio is important in ascertaining if the annual net operating income necessary to cover debt service is realistic. For residential income properties, a ratio below 35 percent is unusual and would be highly suspect. The Institute of Real Estate Management of the National Association of Realtors and the Building Owners and Managers Association both publish ratio data for income properties. Operating ratios typically start at about 38 percent for a new multifamily property and increase as the structures age.

The operating ratio presented here is a combination of two or more refined ratios: (1) the vacancy and credit loss ratio and (2) the operating expense ratio. That is, total annual operating expenses are made up of vacancy and credit losses and of operating expenses, both of which tend to increase as management quality decreases.

A 40.8 percent operating ratio for the Redwood Apartments is certainly in line with industry standards. And, as shown in the appraisal report, it is slightly higher than that of comparable properties. Likewise, the forecast rents for the Redwood Apartments are well documented. Al King, the underwriter, would therefore be justified in believing that the $100,000 NOI is realistic and that the risks associated with this NOI are acceptable.

Debt Service Coverage Ratio. The third critical financial relationship in income property financing is the debt service coverage ratio. The *debt service coverage ratio* equals net operating income divided by annual debt service. For the proposed loan on the Redwood Apartments, the ratio is 1.055 and is calculated as follows:

$$\text{Debt Service Coverage Ratio} = \frac{\text{Net (Annual) Operating Income}}{\text{Annual Debt Service}}$$

$$= \frac{\$100,000}{\$94,790} = 1.055$$

The debt service coverage (DSC) ratio is widely used by income property lenders. Acceptable ratios are traditionally based on experience. That is, DSC ratios of loans going into default tend to become minimum acceptable ratios in subsequent loans. A DSC ratio of 1.25 has been a popular minimum, though loans are often made on ratios as low as 1.10. With higher interest rates and more income and equity participations by lenders, this lower standard seems likely to become more widely accepted.

The DSC ratio of 1.055 for the Redwood Apartments seems low. Al King, therefore, has a warning flag concerning the acceptability of this loan.

Breakeven Occupancy Ratio. The point at which a property's earnings exactly equals all required expenses plus debt service is the breakeven occupancy ratio. For the Redwood Apartments and the proposed loan, a ratio of 96.9% is calculated as follows:

$$\begin{array}{c}\text{Breakeven} \\ \text{Occupancy} \\ \text{Ratio}\end{array} = \frac{\begin{array}{c}\text{Total Annual Expenses} \\ + \text{ Annual DS (V\&CL + Operating)}\end{array}}{\text{Gross Annual Scheduled Income}}$$

$$= \frac{\$68,960 + \$94,790}{\$168,960} = \frac{\$163,750}{\$168,960} = 96.9\%$$

In effect, the Redwood Apartments can only have a vacancy and credit loss rate of 3.1 percent to achieve the ratio. The appraisal indicates a V&CL rate of 4 percent; consequently, in view of this ratio and the debt service coverage ratio, the requested loan appears to carry too much risk to the Anytown First National Bank. A ratio under 90 percent must generally be achieved for a loan to be reasonably acceptable for income property financing.

FINANCING ALTERNATIVES

The DSC ratio and the breakeven occupancy ratio both indicate that the $750,000 loan, as proposed, is too much for the Redwood Apartments to carry. The expenses on the operating statement are not likely to decrease. A way to lower debt service and, in turn, the ratios must therefore be found. The targets are a DSC ratio of 1.10 or higher and a breakeven occupancy ratio under 90%. These limiting ratios can be inserted in the equations and the maximum debt service "formed" to fit both requirements.

$$\frac{\text{Maximum}}{\text{Breakeven}} = \frac{\text{Total Annual Expense} + \text{Maximum Annual DS}}{\text{Gross Annual Scheduled Income}}$$

$$90\% = \frac{\$68,960 + \text{Maximum Annual DS}}{\$168,960}$$

$$\$152,064 = \$68,960 + \text{Maximum Annual DS}$$

$$\$83,105 = \text{Maximum Annual DS}$$

$$\frac{\text{Minimum DSC}}{\text{Ratio}} = \frac{\text{Net Annual Operating Income}}{\text{Maximum Annual DS}}$$

$$1.10 = \frac{\$100,000}{\text{Maximum Annual DS}}$$

$$1.10 \times \text{Maximum Annual DS} = \$100,000$$

$$\text{Maximum Annual DS} = \$90,909$$

At this point, the underwriter might investigate several alternatives. A longer term on the loan is one possibility. A lower amount is another. And the interest rate might even be reduced, assuming that Anytown First National is pressed to get its money invested in loans. However, a lower interest rate is not likely to be considered as an acceptable alternative to a lender in times of high inflation.

Al King might decide that a debt service of $90,000 per year ($7,500 per month) is the absolute maximum that would be acceptable. Effectively, this means that all the debt service would go to interest and no amortization would occur—$750,000 × 1 percent = $7,500 = maximum monthly debt service. Alternatively, a $7,500 monthly debt service would support a 40-year amortization schedule on a $743,678 loan; a balloon payment at some earlier time, say EOY12, might be a part of the loan agreement, however. Even so, the arrangement leaves no room for possible increases in interest rates. Something more is needed.

UNDERWRITER'S RECOMMENDATION

After due deliberation, Al King proposes a $750,000, 12 percent straight-term loan for 12 years with a fixed interest rate, with a "sweetener" for his bank. The net operating income of Redwood Apartments promises to increase by at least six percent per year. Therefore, the apartments promise to be sound security for the principal. Al therefore proposes that in return for making the loan at a fixed 12 percent rate, Anytown First National Bank is to get 30 percent of any increases in NOI above $100,000 per year. Of course, Anytown First National would be entitled to audit the books of ABC Real Estate Investors and to require capable management.

The loan committee accepts Al King's recommendation concerning possible restructuring of the loan. A letter of commitment containing the proposal is sent to the ABC Real Estate Investors.

LOAN CLOSING

After some additional negotiation on details, the ABC Real Estate Investors group accepts the proposal and the loan is closed. The 30 percent income participation provision promises to reward Anytown First National for taking a slightly marginal loan and for agreeing not to increase the interest rate on the loan for 12 years.

Additional documentation of the loan is still necessary, should Anytown subsequently wish to sell it in the secondary mortgage market. Included in the documentation would be the note and mortgage or trust deed. Clear title would have to be evidenced by a recorded deed, an abstract of title and an attorney's opinion of title, or by a title report and a title insurance policy. In the use of title insurance, a lender's policy would be required. A hazard insurance policy would also be required of the borrowers.

SUMMARY

Underwriting analysis for a residential income property loan focuses mainly on the property's value and income, because the property represents the main security for the loan. Many investors will not borrow against an income property if personal responsibility for the loan is required. An exculpatory or sole security clause limits the borrower's liability for the loan.

A pro forma annual operating statement serves as probably the most important item considered in determining the market value of an income property. Market rental rates and realistic expenses must be used in making up the statement and estimating annual net operating income for the property. In turn, the statement provides basic inputs for key financial ratios considered in underwriting analyses.

The two most important ratios in loan underwriting are the debt service coverage ratio and the breakeven occupancy ratio. The DSC ratio equals NOI divided by annual debt service and must be 1.10 or greater for a loan to be acceptable. The breakeven occupancy ratio equals total annual expenses plus annual debt service divided by gross annual scheduled income. A breakeven occupancy ratio must be 90 percent or less for a loan to be acceptable to most lenders. That is, the vacancy rate for the property could reach 10 percent and the investor-borrower could still meet debt service requirements. A loan request may have to be restructured to provide acceptable ratios.

KEY TERMS

Breakeven Occupancy Ratio

Contract Rent

Debt Service Coverage (DSC) Ratio

Effective Gross Income (EGI)

Gross Scheduled Income

Market Rent

Market Value

Net Operating Income (NOI)

Occupancy Ratio

Operating Ratio

Pro Forma Operating Statement

Subject Property

Vacancy and Credit Loss (V&CL)

QUESTIONS FOR REVIEW AND DISCUSSION

1. Why is greater emphasis placed on the property than on the borrower in income property underwriting?

2. Name and explain the four dominant numbers of an annual operating statement. Show their relationships by outlining a pro forma statement.

3. Identify at least five sections of the standard FNMA-FHLMC standard appraisal form for a residential income property. What is the probable source and nature of the content of each?

4. What are the purposes of loan underwriting analyses?

5. Identify and define the four key financial ratios used in income property loan underwriting.

6. Using the following data, calculate the LVR, operating, DSC, and breakeven occupancy ratios for the subject property.

Market value	$940,000
Gross annual income	$130,000
Total annual expenses	$42,000
(V&CL plus operating)	
NOI	$88,000
Loan principal	$672,000
Monthly debt service	$7,400

7. Analyze the ratios calculated above from an underwriter's perspective. Would the loan as proposed be acceptable based on generally accepted criteria? If not, how might it be restructured?

8. Match the following terms and definitions:
   a. Breakeven Occupancy   ———
   b. NOI   ———
   c. DSC Ratio   ———
   d. Subject Property   ———
   e. EGI   ———

   1. Rentals actually collected.
   2. NOI divided by annual debt service.
   3. Investment property.
   4. Point at which NOI equals annual debt service.
   5. EGI — operating expenses.
   6. Property being studied.
   7. Point at which gross scheduled income equals annual debt service.

twenty-one

Creative Financing

Potential homebuyers and investors are kept out of the real estate game because increasing property values and high interest rates seem to make real estate ever more difficult to finance. Higher values mean larger down payments. High interest rates mean high loan payments. For example, from late 1979 to early 1981, interest rates increased from 11 to 16 percent. An interest rate of 16 percent means a family needing a $50,000, 30-year loan must be able to pay $672 per month to obtain the loan. At an interest rate of 11 percent, only $476 is required. The 41 percent increase in debt service requirements during this period sharply reduced the number of homebuyers.

Creative or flexible techniques are increasingly being used to solve financing problems. A 1981 survey by the National Association of Realtors® found that over one-half of all resale transactions involved some form of creative financing. Mortgage loan assumptions and seller takeback of second loans were the most frequently used techniques. Overall, the techniques used in descending order of importance were as follows:

- Assumption of existing mortgage loans
- Owner takeback of second mortgage loans
- Land contracts
- Owner takeback of first mortgage loans

- Assistance from friends and relatives
- Wraparound mortgage loans
- REALTORS® taking back part of commission as mortgage loan or unsecured note
- Rent with option to buy

These techniques center around making more money available for a down payment, keeping debt service payments low, or a combination of the two. That is, the issue is primarily financial and not legal. The need is to make the numbers fit the buyer's or owner's resources and income. The study also indicated that alternative mortgage instruments (VRMs, GPMs, SAMs, and RRMs) were widely used when new financing was obtained. But in many situations the new instruments did not solve the immediate problem.

Obviously a full understanding of each of these techniques is important to buyers, sellers, builders, and brokerage personnel. These techniques are discussed in previous chapters, but generally without TVM calculations taken into account, and TVM calculations are covered in Chap. 19. Let us therefore include TVM effects in a standardized case example to show that the numbers can be worked out. The example also serves to demonstrate that a financing problem may be solved in several ways. The decision maker is then in a position to select or negotiate the best way.

Problem situations in financing parallel the ownership cycle. The most critical situations generally occur when ownership is acquired. Subsequently, an owner-investor may use creative financing to maintain leverage, to build an estate, and to avoid unnecessary taxes. Finally, innovation is sometimes necessary to dispose of realty under acceptable conditions; disposition, of course, is the other side of the acquisition problem.

The approach in this chapter is to take up creative financing techniques in order of their importance and frequency of use, as indicated by the NAR survey. This chapter is actually, therefore, an integration of material discussed in earlier chapters. This chapter concludes with an overview of creative financing and miscellaneous creative financing techniques. Creative financing ultimately boils down to a legal arrangement in which the numbers work out to solve the problem at hand. With calculators and computers, it is increasingly easier to make the many calculations necessary to see which way the numbers work out best. "Long shot" or any possible arrangements are tried if the more traditional techniques don't work. Numerous workshops, seminars, and books now feature the "long shot" arrangements. Experience shows these techniques are often precarious and special purpose.

All the ingredients for successful creative financing are included in this book, that is, all except one—the reader or practitioner need only add imagination. Let us now look at the more basic techniques.

For our discussion of acquisition financing, the case problem involving Richard and Amy Beyers is continued from Chap. 17, "Borrower Considerations and Analyses." Problem recognition and developing a systematic plan to work toward solution are taken up next. Alternatives involving completely new financing are then compared with alternatives that build on existing financing. The result of this approach is that commonly used creative financing techniques are applied to a single problem to facilitate understanding.

THE PROBLEM SITUATION

Richard and Amy Beyers determined that they could reasonably afford total housing expenses of $1,125 per month according to FHLMC guidelines presented in Chap. 17. Further, after taking account of expected costs for hazard insurance, property taxes, and utilities, they judged they could afford $825 per month in principal and interest payments to obtain a loan. Remember that their annual stabilized income is $50,000, and that Richard's income is likely to increase steadily. Remember also that Amy expects to return to full-time work in two years when their children, Ann and Kevin, are well established in school.

The Beyers locate a ten-year-old ranch house at 2001 Milky Way, Anytown, USA, through Helen Ardent. Helen is a sales agent for the Everready Realty Company. The asking price is $107,000. After much thought, the Beyers offer $100,000 for the property in light of the slow real estate market. The offer is subject to clear title and to financing being arranged within the FHLMC/FNMA guidelines for conventional loans. The owners of the house, William and Ellen Cellars, accept the offer. The listing contract, also with the Everready Realty Company, calls for a commission at six percent, or of $6,000.

The Cellars bought the house new, with the assistance of a 30-year, nine percent loan. The loan has a remaining balance of $50,000. Monthly debt service for principal and interest is $449.86, effectively $450. The loan still has 20 years, or 240 payments, to maturity. Property taxes for the coming year are estimated at $2,100; hazard insurance costs $300 per year. Cost of utilities (electricity, water, and sewer) is expected to be $100 per month in the coming year. Therefore, the Beyers have only $825 a month available for payments on any debt financing arranged.

Mortgage loans are reasonably difficult to arrange in Anytown. The current interest rate on loans is 15 percent, with monthly compounding. The longest term available is 30 years. Local lenders will only consider making loans involving floating rates.

RECOGNIZING THE PROBLEM

Helen Ardent, the sales agent for Everready Realty, immediately recognizes that the Beyers-Cellars contract represents a problem situation. She therefore arranges with Richard and Amy Beyers to analyze the situation in an orderly manner to determine how it might best be handled. This orderly approach, termed the decision-making process, is discussed in Chap. 1. By way of a quick review, the steps in the process are as follows:

1. Recognize problem situation
2. Collect data as necessary
3. Identify problem or problems
4. Pose alternative solutions
5. Make decision

Helen has already taken step one by recognizing the situation. Steps two and three are often inter-active or interwoven, as in this situation. The need is to identify alternative ways to arrange the necessary financing and to select the one that is most realistic and workable.

DEVELOPING A SYSTEMATIC WORK PLAN

Helen Ardent and the Beyers, working together, agree to study the facts in the following sequence:

1. Investigate new financing
   Local financial institutions are making adjustable-rate mortgage (ARM) loans, graduated payment mortgage (GPM) loans, and sometimes shared appreciation mortgage (SAM) loans. If the Beyers can qualify for any of these, they are at least sure of getting the house they want. If needed, assistance from the Cellars may be possible by way of a "buy-down" or a new purchase money first loan from the Cellars.

2. Investigate assumption of the existing loan of the Cellars plus other financing. The alternatives to be investigated are as follows:
   (*a*) Assumption plus takeback of a second mortgage from the Cellars. Assumption plus junior financing from a combination of sources, such as friends and relatives or the broker, is directly parallel to the takeback of a second mortgage by the Cellars.
   (*b*) Finance with a contract for deed from the Cellars.
   (*c*) Arrange a wraparound mortgage (WAM) loan.
   (*d*) Rent with option to buy.

3. Select the best of the alternative methods promising an adequate solution and work out the details.

4. If no solution is reached, review entire situation.

The question immediately becomes "how much debt can be financed with $825 per month by the alternative mortgage techniques available?" Remember, the Beyers need to borrow $80,000. Remember also that the going market interest rate is 15 percent, with monthly compounding. According to the case problem, the Beyers appear to be credit worthy and otherwise able to readily qualify for a loan.

Adjustable-Rate Mortgage (ARM) Loan. Helen Ardent says that local lenders will not make fixed-rate mortgage (FRM) loans, and that any adjustable-rate loans (VRM or RRM) have a maximum term of 30 years. Basic TVM calculations show that monthly debt service of $825 for 30 years in a 15 percent market only justifies a loan of $65,246. An $80,000 loan at percent with a 30-year term requires monthly debt service of $1,011.56. Too much! Other alternatives must be considered.

FNMA Refinancing. Helen Ardent notes that if FNMA holds or owns the Cellars' $50,000, nine percent loan, FNMA will refinance the property at a rate between the current market rate and the rate on the old loan. The maximum amount available in such a refinancing on a one-family home is $98,500. The borrower and the property must meet all FNMA credit and appraisal requirements for a new conventional loan. Helen believes a 13 percent, $80,000 loan with a 25-year term could be negotiated. Monthly payments would come to $902.26. The Beyers consider this debt service too high. Also, inquiry with the lender shows that the Cellars' loan is not held by FNMA. FNMA refinancing is therefore clearly not an available alternative.

Graduated Payment Mortgage (GPM) Loan. A GPM loan is one with debt service that is initially low and which gradually increases over several years. The low initial payments may result in negative amortization or an increasing principal. A GPM loan is generally limited to borrowers whose income is likely to steadily increase. The Beyers appear to qualify.

The Beyers can absorb payments of $825 per month. They need $80,000. Richard and Amy consider annual increases of $50 per month in debt service feasible and acceptable. That is, in year two, their payments would increase to $875 per month, in year three to $925 per month, and so forth. These increases would be necessary until a level of debt service was reached that would amortize the loan in the remainder of the 30-year term, assuming no change from the 15 percent interest rate. This rate of increase in payments is consistent with professional judgment. Dr. Joseph Hu, FNMA economist, states that an annual increase of 10 percent per year is realistic.[1]

---

[1]"In Search of the Ideal Mortgage," *Seller Servicer,* April–June 1981, p. 21. *Seller Servicer* is a publication of the Federal National Mortgage Association.

At the beginning of the sixth year, debt service would reach $1,125 per month; and $1,125 per month would be adequate to amortize the loan over the 24 years and 8 months or less than the 25 years remaining in the original term. Also, at the beginning of the sixth year, the loan balance would have increased to $87,715 due to the negative amortization. Any increase in interest rates would make this amount greater.

The Beyers recognize a GPM loan as a possibility, but prefer to look at less risky alternatives. Additional calculations show that should interest rates go up, it might be eight or ten years before their payments would amortize the loan. A GPM loan with adjustable rates is termed a graduated payment adjustable mortgage (GPAM) loan.

Shared Appreciation Mortgage (SAM) Loan.   Helen and the Beyers also consider a SAM loan to be an alternative. Local lenders are offering an interest rate reduction of three percent for ten years in return for one-third of the property's appreciation in value during the 10 years. Refinancing is required at the end of the 10 years. Debt service would be based on a 30-year amortization schedule.

Monthly debt service for an $80,000, 12 percent loan with a 30-year amortization schedule calculates to $822.89. After due deliberation, the Beyers decide not to pursue a SAM loan. With a GPAM loan a strong possibility, they prefer to avoid giving up one-third of any appreciation and being forced at the same time to refinance in 10 years. If necessary, they decide they can reconsider the possibility of a SAM loan.

Straight-Term Loan.   Debt service of $825 per month only justifies a loan of $66,000 for a straight-term loan at 15 percent, compounded monthly. That is, 1.25 percent of $66,000 equals $825. And $66,000 is not a large enough loan. A straight-term loan is a no-go under the circumstances.

Buy-Down by Seller.   The Beyers heard that home builders and other sellers sometimes prepay a homebuyers' interest during the early years of a loan, which is termed a *buy-down*. That is, the debt service is reduced for the borrower through a buy-down, thereby enabling the potential buyer-borrower to qualify for a loan and to purchase the house. One- to five-year buy-downs are used, meaning that debt service is reduced during the first to fifth year of the loan.

FNMA directives indicate that no more than three percentage points may be bought down, and that the interest rate may not be reduced below 12 percent for any loan to be purchased by FNMA. Also, FNMA will not purchase buy-down loans on which debt service changes more often than once in 12 months. Additional details of buy-down loans acceptable to FNMA may be obtained from FNMA regional offices.

In the immediate case, the Beyers need an $80,000 loan. With 15 percent interest and a 30-year term, the monthly debt service would be $1,011.55. With a buy-down of the interest rate to 12 percent (three points), monthly debt service to the Beyers would be $822.89 during the first three years. After three years, monthly debt service would increase to $1,011.55.

The difference of $188.66 per month for 36 months has a present value of $5,442, when discounted at 15 percent. This $5,442 is the cost of the buy-down to the seller. From the lender's viewpoint, either loan alternative is equally attractive. When used, a buyer and a seller are both satisfied with the arrangement because the seller disposes of a property and the buyer gets it. The seller should recognize that the transaction would be equally as attractive if the $5,442 discount were given directly to the buyer; that is, if the price were reduced by $5,442. If alternative financing is at all feasible, as in this case, a seller is not likely to agree to a buy down. William and Ellen Cellars say that they'll consider a buy-down only as a last resort.

Takeback of First by Seller.   A seller owning a property free and clear may accept or take back a first mortgage for part of the purchase price. This is most likely if no other financing is available or if no better investment opportunities are perceived by the seller. In this type of an "arm's length transaction," the terms of a seller first loan should be equivalent to those of an institutional first loan.

A seller accepting a lower interest rate might be wiser to lower the selling price and avoid the hassle of looking after the loan. For example, suppose the Cellars took back an $80,000 first loan at 13 percent for 30 years. Debt service would be $884.96—$126.60 per month less than the same loan at 15 percent. The present value of this difference for 30 years, discounted at 15 percent, is $10,012. Effectively, the Cellars would be equally well off to sell their house for $90,000 if they could reinvest the $90,000 elsewhere at 15 percent interest.

Upon inquiry to the Cellars, it is determined that they will not consider financing the entire transaction on a long-term basis. Therefore, this alternative must be dropped.

Summary of Alternatives.   A summary review of the alternatives for new financing gives the following results:

1. A new $80,000 ARM loan is not affordable. The maximum amount that might be obtained with $825 per month is $65,246. The Beyers drop the ARM loan from further consideration.
2. FNMA refinancing is dropped because FNMA does not hold the Cellars' loan. Also, in all likelihood, monthly debt service would be too high if it were available.
3. A new GPAM loan is barely affordable. Monthly debt service would begin at $825 in the first year, and increase to $1,125 in the sixth year. Worth further consideration.
4. A new SAM loan is more risky and less desirable than a new GPM loan to the Beyers. Therefore, drop from further consideration.

5. A new straight-term loan is not affordable. Drop from further consideration.
6. A new loan with a buy-down by the Cellars is feasible and acceptable to the Beyers. At this point the Cellars are not agreeable. This alternative is worth keeping as a last resort.
7. The Cellars will not consider providing long-term first financing. Drop from consideration.

Thus, the Beyers have the possibility of a GPAM loan and a seller buy-down. But they want to know their alternatives based on existing financing before making a decision.

Existing Financing Plus

The existing financing available on the home at 2001 Milky Way is a $50,000, 20-year loan at nine percent. Monthly debt service is $449.86, which rounds off to $450.

If the loan were taken over, the Beyers would need to borrow an additional $30,000. They would be able to pay $375 per month ($825 minus $450) for the additional financing.

The crucial issue with existing financing is whether the loan may be assumed. Many loan contracts contain a due-on-sale, or alienation, clause. Under this clause, a lender may require immediate payment of the entire debt if the pledged property is sold or conveyed. Alternatively, the lender may require an upward adjustment in the interest rate.

Considerable controversy and litigation surrounds the use of due-on-sale clauses. Lenders justify enforcement of a due-on-sale clause on the grounds that it is a part of the loan contract, and that the loan is personal and based on the credit reputation of the borrower. The main argument against enforcement of the clause is that enforcement acts as an unreasonable restraint of trade. The property continues to secure the loan and the original borrower remains liable on the note, even though the property is sold, unless released. Further, with the buyer assuming responsibility for payment of the loan, the lender is actually better off after the conveyance.

Lenders are increasingly including a clause in new loan contracts allowing them to adjust the interest rate to market upon alienation of the property. In time, this right of adjustment clause may do away with the controversy. For purpose of our case problem, the loan on 2001 Milky Way will be considered not to have an enforceable due-on-sale clause. That is, the $50,000 loan is considered to be assumable without an interest rate change. Supplemented financing may therefore be arranged.

Assumption Plus Junior Loans. As indicated, the Beyers need $30,000 in additional financing. They can afford $375 per month debt service for the financing.

The seller is very often requested to provide junior financing for a variety of reasons. First, the seller, in taking back a second loan, converts his or her equity into a loan, rather than receiving cash. Second, it is often easier for the seller to provide additional financing. Third, the seller may also want to provide the funds needed in order to postpone the payment of capital gains taxes. And last, and often the most important, the seller has a high incentive to extend the financing—to make the transaction take place. In summary, a seller can have much influence over the transaction and has much to gain by exerting that influence.

The resulting financial arrangement is the same, for all practical purposes, whether the financing is provided by a seller, a broker, a friend, a relative, or a disinterested third party. Junior financing is therefore first discussed here in general terms. This general discussion is immediately followed by several comments or cautions aimed specially at sellers.

A second mortgage typically contains the same clauses as a first mortgage, except for possible subordination and default in prior mortgage clauses (see Chap. 4). The property pledged as security is also the same. The first mortgage has priority of claim. The maturity or life of a second mortgage is usually shorter, however. Since there is somewhat higher risk, a second mortgage usually involves a higher interest rate than a first.

Helen Ardent believes the current market interest rate for a second loan is 18 percent per year or 1.5 percent per month. The typical term is seven years. A quick calculation shows that interest-only monthly debt service on $30,000 at 1.5 percent is $450, $75 more per month than the Beyers are prepared to pay.

An institution or other disinterested third party would not accept the loan at a lower interest rate. A friend or relative might make the loan at a lower rate as a favor. A seller might make the loan in order to secure the sale. For a seller, the reduced interest rate is a subsidy to the transaction. For example, the Cellars might agree to $375 per month (1.25 percent per month or 15 percent annually) with a ten-year balloon. In this case the subsidy would equal the present value of $75 per month for years discounted at 18 percent, or $4,162. The Cellars would be equally well off to sell for $96,000, except for differences due to income tax effects.

Several cautions apply to junior financing. The maximum loan-to-value ratio, from the seller's viewpoint, for the first and second loans combined should be no greater than for a new first loan, in this case 80 percent. To go to a higher LVR increases the risk of loss on foreclosure. A seller taking back a second loan must also police the loan, be concerned about nonpayment of debt service, and pay extra taxes on the higher price even though the loan is made at a discount.

Upon inquiry, the Cellars indicate that if they are to provide financing, it will be through a contract for deed arrangement only.

Contract for Deed. A contract for deed is also known as a land contract, a land sale contract, an installment land contract, or a contract for sale in escrow. Title remains with the seller until certain specified conditions are met, though a signed deed may be placed with the escrow agent. The seller therefore has less risk of loss than with the takeback of a second mortgage. A buyer under a loan contract is advised to ascertain that the seller has a valid legal claim to marketable title at the time the contract is made. If the seller has a loan against the property, the buyer is also advised to have the escrow agent make the debt service payments directly to the lender. Finally, the buyer is advised to have the contract recorded. A contract for deed is commonly used when a buyer does not have a large down payment or in order to preserve a favorable first mortgage.

The Beyers propose to pay $825 per month to the escrow agent, who in turn would pay the monthly debt service of $449.86 on the existing first loan of $50,000. Effectively, $375 per month is left for payments to the Cellars, who still have $30,000 of equity in the transaction. Amortization aside, payments of $375 per month would give a return of 1.25 percent per month or 15 percent per year. Helen Ardent believes the marginal rate for a $30,000 loan of this type would be 16.5 percent per year.

At 16.5 percent, monthly interest payments on the Cellars' equity on the land contract ($30,000) would amount to $412.50. No amortization of principal would take place during the seven-year term. Total debt service would be $862.36 ($449.86 plus $412.50). Based on her experience, Helen also believes that they would have to arrange new, permanent financing within seven years. The Beyers consider these terms within their capability, though it would be a stretch. They also want to compare these terms with their other alternatives. The Cellars would also have to be consulted about and agree to the specific terms.

Wraparound Mortgage (WAM) Loan. For our case problem, the wraparound mortgage loan would be for $80,000, which would be wrapped around the $50,000 first mortgage loan. The WAM lender might be the Cellars or an institutional lender other than the first mortgagee. The Beyers would make payments to the WAM lender, who in turn would pay the debt service of $449.86 to the lender holding the existing first mortgage. Because the WAM lender makes the payment on the first mortgage, default cannot occur on the first loan without the WAM lender's knowledge.

A wraparound mortgage is typically used when an owner or buyer considers it advantageous to preserve the first mortgage. In the immediate case, the incentive is to preserve the nine percent interest rate on the first loan. The interest rate on the WAM loan generally falls between the interest rate on the existing first loan and the market interest rate of a new loan. The WAM lender ends up with a higher than market rate on the additional monies advanced because of the leveraged position. In short, the first lender loses at the expense of the WAM lender and the borrower-owner. Let us now complete the example.

For simplicity, consider that the Cellars agree to a WAM loan of $80,000 at 13 percent to be amortized over 20 years. Twenty years is the same remaining term as for the first loan. Monthly debt service on the WAM loan would come to $937.26. The Cellars would pay $449.86 per month on the first loan and take the difference, $487.40, as debt service on the monies advanced for the WAM loan. In fact, the Cellars advanced only $30,000 of the $80,000 WAM loan. Therefore, they stand to get monthly debt service of $487.40 on a 20-year amortized amount of $30,000. The rate earned on this $30,000, the internal rate of return (IRR), calculates to 19.05 percent. In summary, the calculations go as follows:

	Dollar Amount	Monthly Debt Service
WAM Loan (13%, monthly, 20 years)	$80,000	$937.26
Less existing first loan (9%, monthly, 20 years)	− 50,000	− 449.86
Equals monies advanced and debt service received by WAM lender (X%, monthly, 20 years)	$30,000	$487.40
IRR earned on monies advanced	19.05%, compounded monthly.	

These WAM loan terms do not compare favorably with the land contract terms. The overall interest rate of 13 percent is higher and monthly debt service is greater. The WAM loan possibility is therefore rejected by the Beyers.

Rent with Option to Purchase. A potential buyer not having an adequate down payment or ability to meet monthly payments in a necessary loan may arrange to rent the desired property with the right to purchase later. In a buyer's market, the arrangement might be very loose and flexible, with only the price and the time limit stated. In a seller's market, the buyer might be asked to make a nonrefundable deposit of earnest money and to pay a higher rent than the market level to build an adequate down payment. Also, the price may be indexed to the price level in times of sharp inflation.

The situation of 2001 Milky Way represents a buyer's market. The monthly rent might therefore be set at $800 and the price fixed at $100,000 in a one-year contract. During the one year, the Beyers might improve their down payment position by $5,000 and improve their ability to cover debt service to $1,000 per month, or a combination of the two.

Renting with an option to buy represents a delayed purchase. The Beyers decide to use this alternative only if financing for an immediate purchase cannot be arranged.

Summary of Alternatives. A review of the alternatives for existing financing plus gives the following results:

1. Assumption of the existing first loan plus a second loan at a market rate of 18 percent results in a monthly debt service of $900, $75 higher than the Beyers can reasonably afford. Also, the Cellars indicated they would finance the transaction only through a contract for deed. Drop from consideration.

2. A contract for deed gives the seller more security than a second loan because title is retained. In turn, the interest rate would be slightly lower on the monies advanced. Monthly debt service of $862.50 would be required, including monthly interest of $412.50 to the Cellars on their $30,000 position in the land contract. This arrangement appears acceptable to both the Beyers and Cellars.

3. The WAM loan is rejected as an alternative by the Beyers because of its higher interest rate (13 percent) and high debt service ($937.26), when compared with the land contract.

4. Renting with an option to purchase for a year is considered an alternative of last resort by the Beyers. In effect, they prefer to buy now if at all possible.

COMPARING ALTERNATIVES AND MAKING A DECISION

Four alternatives stand out for the Beyers. Two involve new financing: a GPAM loan and a seller buy-down. The other two involve existing financing: contract for deed and rent with option to buy. The alternatives are summarized in Fig. 21–1.

Both options for new financing extend for 30 years and require higher interest rates than the land contract option. Both have lower initial debt service than the land contract for the first few years. The land contract financing seems likely to have a maximum duration of only 20 years, and it carries slightly more risk, in that title would be retained by the Cellars and refinancing of $30,000 would be required within seven years. Each of the alternatives is essentially within the FHLMC guidelines. The contract for deed arrangement is slightly more demanding for the first year or so, but overall it contains many advantages. The Beyers consider renting with an option to buy, an alternative to be tried if none of the other three works out.

The Beyers therefore rank the alternatives as follows:

1. Contract for deed
2. Seller buy-down
3. GPAM loan
4. Rent with option to buy

The Cellars consider the contract for deed alternative acceptable. Title is searched and found clear except for the existing loan. The land

FIGURE 21–1 Summary of Most Likely Financing Alternatives Open to Beyers for Purchase of Home

Items of Consideration	NEW FINANCING		EXISTING FINANCING PLUS	
	GPAM Loan	Seller Buy-Down	Contract for Deed	Rent with Option to Buy
Principal amount	$80,000	$80,000	$80,000, with underlying $50,000 first loan	
Monthly debt service (rent)	$825 increasing by steps to $1,175 in year 6	$822.89 for 3 years, increasing to $1,011.55	$862.36 ($449.86 + $412.50)	$800 for 1 year
Interest rate	15% and adjustable	12% for 3 years, then 15%	9% on first loan, 16.5% on seller's equity	
Duration	30 years	30 years	7 years on LC, 20 years on first loan	
Comment	Principal would increase to $87,715 at EOY5, assuming no change in interest rate	Buy-down of $5,442 required of seller; acceptable to Cellars only as last resort	Monthly debt service would be $37.36 higher than FHLMC guidelines in first year; refinancing required of Beyers within 7 years	Right to buy at $100,000 for 1 year while building equity and earning ability; offers greater flexibility

contract is drawn up and signed, and an escrow arrangement established. The Beyers are satisfied that they have obtained the best financing available under the circumstances because all alternatives were considered. The Cellars are satisfied because they disposed of their property, invested the money at the market rate, and deferred some taxes on the capital gain.

The escrow arrangement provides for the escrow agent to pay debt services for the first loan directly to the lender. This provision reduces administrative complexity and protects the Beyers from problems should the Cellars move to another section of the country.

OWNERSHIP FINANCING

An owner may refinance for several reasons—to obtain cash on good terms, to lower interest costs, to maintain leverage, to pyramid investments and build an estate, to spread risks, or to avoid taxes. The cash may be used to buy a car, to send a son or daughter to college, or to buy stocks. Maintaining leverage, pyramiding, spreading risk, lowering interest costs, and avoiding taxes may all be incorporated into a single strategy by a sophisticated investor. Let us look at two examples of an owner refinancing to gain advantage.

Refinancing a residence is a convenient way for many consumers to obtain cash. The interest rate is usually lower, the amount obtained is larger, and the term longer than with the typical consumer loan. Let us extend our Richard and Amy Beyers case.

Four years after buying 2001 Milky Way, Richard and Amy decide they want to buy a new car and a boat. The combined cost comes to $18,000. By this time, Amy is working full-time and their combined stabilized annual income is $70,000. The market value of their home has increased to $130,000. The balance of the nine percent first loan is $45,694, which is assumable. Above this, they owe William and Amy Cellars $30,000 for their interest in the land contract, which still has three years to run. Market interest rates have declined to 12 percent on new mortgage loans, with annual compounding. Richard and Amy decide that now is an excellent time to refinance their property.

Richard, being an accountant, makes some calculations to more clearly determine their alternatives. Twenty-five percent ($17,500) of their annual stabilized income may be devoted to total housing expenses (PIIT). Taxes and insurance amount to $3,100 annually, which leaves $14,400 per year ($1,200 per month) for debt service on any loan obtained.

The amount of $1,200 a month justifies a loan of $113,936 on a 25-year, 12 percent loan. With a $130,000 residence, $113,936 represents a market acceptable LVR of 87.6 percent. They owe $75,694 ($45,694 plus $30,000) on the house, meaning $38,242 could be obtained through refinancing.

Initially, Richard and Amy only wanted $18,000 in cash. Suddenly, they realize that by refinancing, they can buy a new car and a boat and have more than $20,000 left over for investing in stocks, bonds, or real estate. In addition, Richard and Amy realize they might better use a WAM loan rather than refinance with a new first loan. Investigation confirms their observation. A new WAM loan of $108,205 at 11 percent for 16 years can be arranged for the $1,200 per month debt service. This means they would have $5,731 less for investing: On the other hand, the debt service would only be required for 16 years rather than the 25 years with a new first loan. The alternative selected depends on whether or not a sufficiently attractive rate of return could be earned on the $5,731.

To Pyramid and Spread Risk

Sophisticated investors sometimes refinance rather than sell to retain control of high quality properties, to pyramid their investments, to take gains without paying taxes, and to spread risks. Let us look at another case—that of Joe King.

Joe King is an aggressive investor. Six years ago he began converting an old warehouse into small shops and food outlets. The property is located near the central business district of a city of nearly one million people in the Northeast. He had previously obtained an option to buy the warehouse in stages for $900,000. The shops and food outlets were exposed to an active market. Soon, large, well-established merchants rented space in the warehouse to the point where all the space has been absorbed. Joe financed the conversion in several phases. As a result, the financing on the entire project is a mix of many arrangements and terms. The property has an estimated market value of $18 million, $8 million of which represents debt financing.

Joe has an option to buy a machine shop and another warehouse nearby. He plans to convert the machine shop into an auto service center and the second warehouse into condominiums. Joe wants to extract money from the first warehouse development for personal needs, for his follow-up development, and for other investments.

Two alternatives appear likely for refinancing the original warehouse. The first would be to convert to a joint venture arrangement with an insurance company. The second would be to sell real estate mortgage bonds against the property.

Joint Venture. An inquiry to the investment manager of the Tower Insurance Company, Ed Maverick, produces a refinancing proposal for an 80 percent LVR, or a $14,400,000 loan on a straight-term mortgage. The interest rate would be fixed at 12 percent for six years, after which it would be renegotiable to the market rate every three years. The full duration of the loan would be 15 years. In addition, Tower Insurance Company (TIC) wants one-half of any increases in net operating income and one-half of any increases in value. Debt service on the $14,400,000 would come to $144,000 per month or $1,728,000 per year.

Mortgage Bonds. Initial investigation indicates that real estate bonds could indeed be sold against the warehouse and small pools of capital thereby tapped. The process would be to establish a mortgage trust through a local bank, which would hold title to the property and issue the bonds secured by the property. The bank trust officer suggests sale of 5,000 bonds in $1,000 denominations—a total of $5 million—and 1,000 bonds in $10,000 denominations to total $10 million. The bank would underwrite and sell the bonds, covering all costs involved, for a percent commission. Thus, Joe King would net $13,500,000. The interest rate on the bonds would be 15 percent, with annual payments over a 20-year amortization schedule. Annual debt service would be $2,396,422.

Decision Time. Joe King studies the alternatives and decides that a joint venture is the better choice. He believes that the TIC proposal is a first offer and better terms can be worked out. Negotiations with other insurance companies, as well as TIC, will therefore be made to get the best possible arrangement. Joe's reasoning is that more money and a lower interest rate are obtained, and some of his risk is also spread to the joint venture partner. In addition, he makes a contact for further financing that does not involve floating a bond issue. However, he gives up some control along with a portion of the equity position, but he obtains the use of more funds to continue his development and to make other investments.

DISPOSITION FINANCING

From a seller's standpoint, when does providing some financing make sense? What are the costs and risks involved? If disposition financing is to be provided, how can it be done most advantageously? These are important questions that an owner is advised to take into account prior to putting a property up for sale. Let us first look at a case against providing selling financing. Then we examine a situation in which seller financing makes sense and how it might best be done.

THE CASE AGAINST SELLER FINANCING

At least four major risks or concerns are involved in seller financing, whether recognized or not. These concerns parallel the risks faced by established lenders, in that the borrower and the property provide the main security for the loan. In addition, legal and administrative complexities are involved since individual owner-sellers are not set up for and are often inexperienced in originating and servicing loans.

Borrower Capability. Buyer-borrowers are the primary security for loans on one-family residences. Borrowers can default when two or more loans are involved as well as when only a first loan is used, and, upon default, the second lender must often make payments on the first loan to protect his or her interests. Of course, the seller-lender may foreclose, but the property is usually neglected during foreclosure. A seller may attempt to reduce these risks by requiring an acceptable credit report on the borrower prior to making the loan. Also, maintaining a borrower qualification based on FHLMC gross stabilized income guidelines as discussed in Chap. 17 reduces risk of default.

Loan-to-Value Ratio. The degree of risk in seller financing increases directly with the loan-to-value ratio. That is, the higher the LVR, the higher the risk. A high LVR means a low down payment. The same market forces that cause a borrower to default on debt service may also temporarily lower the value of the property and make it very difficult to sell. Also, there is a real possibility that the seller will lose money on the arrangement, even with foreclosure. Therefore, in addition to requiring a capable buyer-borrower, a seller is advised not to allow the LVR to exceed a reasonable level, most likely from 80 to 90 percent of market value.

Due-on-Sale Clause. Use of creative or seller financing often depends on the legality and enforceability of the due-on-sale, or alienation, clause. In some states, the clause is not enforceable even though it is included in a mortgage or trust deed. Obviously an enforceable clause completely kills secondary financing possibilities.

Laws and enforcement differ from state to state. Eleven states (Arizona, California, Colorado, Georgia, Illinois, Iowa, Michigan, Minnesota, New Mexico, South Carolina, and Washington) prohibit or limit alienation clauses. The answer to enforceability in a specific situation should come from a competent attorney, not a broker, a salesperson, or a friend.

Lenders sometimes allow assumptions of mortgages, when they are contested, even though the due-on-sale clause is enforceable, simply to maintain a favorable public image. In the process, the interest rate may be raised but not to the current market rate.

Administrative Complexity. The issues described above, and others, boil down to administrative complexities. The time and effort to properly qualify a buyer-borrower, to develop suitable documentation, and to service the loan can be high indeed for an individual. Tax complications are also incurred. With seller financing, an installment sale is created, thus interest earnings and capital gains must be calculated for each year of the arrangement. Further, creative financing often means higher sale prices and higher property taxes than were expected by the buyer, because the assessed value is based on the higher sale price. The higher sale price also means a higher sales commission to the broker. In addition, with default and foreclosure, legal problems need to be cleared up, and the property repossessed and sold again. High legal fees to clear up these problems often cut deeply into the seller's profits. In short, seller financing for an individual may be like flypaper—once involved or "stuck," it's hard to get it off your hands.

THE CASE FOR SELLER FINANCING

An owner, on the other hand, may find it highly advantageous to help finance the sale of a property. First, helping may make an impossible sale possible. Second, income taxes may be reduced. And third, the seller acquires an investment or an annuity.

Facilitate the Sale. In times of tight money or with a property in an uncertain location, a sale may be nearly impossible unless the seller helps with the financing. Using a second loan, a land contract, or a wraparound loan with an existing, low interest loan may mean the property can be afforded by many more buyers. Thus, the market is expanded and the chance of sale increased. Likewise, financing for a property in a blighted or slum area may not be available except from the seller. In a similar sense, seller assistance may be needed to sell vacant lots or raw land.

A reduced interest rate, which is typical of seller financing, constitutes the cost of providing financing for the transaction. This cost may be calculated very readily. Examples are given earlier in this chapter. For the Cellars, for instance, the cost of the buy-down mortgage was determined to be $5,442. And with the second loan, the calculated cost was $4,162. This cost is the present value of the difference in debt service due to the reduced interest rate. The current market rate for the type of loan involved is used in finding the present value of the difference in debt service. (See the examples mentioned above.) Before putting a property up for sale, a seller may increase the price by the expected cost of providing the financing.

Reduce Taxes. Capital gains on installment sales are not taxable until the money is actually received. Thus, money lent to a buyer-borrower is not taxable until payments are made. Thus, installment sales allow an owner to spread the receipt of capital gains and have them taxed at a lower rate. In addition, the receipt may be deferred until the owner-seller is in a lower tax bracket.

Acquire an Annuity. Selling converts a fixed asset into cash. The owner may really want an annuity. Providing the financing, as through an installment sale, converts the property into the investment-annuity, without the need to pay taxes in the process.

THE RIGHT WAY

A seller-lender can take several steps to reduce risk of default, illiquidity, and loss. The steps should be essentially the same as an established lender might take in originating a loan. The interests of a first and second lender are essentially the same, except for priority of claim.

Evaluate Security to Reduce Risk. The borrower and the property are the first line of defense against default, foreclosure, and loss. According to FHLMC guidelines, qualifying the buyer-borrower of a one-family residence is the first step. This means that no more than 25 percent of the borrower's stabilized gross income should go for housing expense and no more than 33 percent should go for installment payments, including housing expenses. A credit report should document the borrower's income, credit history, and credit worthiness. A seller-lender is also justified in asking the prospective buyer to complete the same FHLMC-FNMA loan application as required by established lenders.

The amount available for the seller's loan may be determined by deducting PIIT on the first loan and other housing expenses from the 25 percent of income available. Thus, for the Beyers, $450 monthly debt service on the first loan is deducted from the $825 available. This deduction leaves $375 per month available for the second loan.

In a comparable sense, when seller financing is being considered on an income property, total debt service on all loans should not exceed the NOI of the property being financed. Further, since the property is the primary security for the loan, the property management experience of the prospective borrower should evidence capability.

The property serves as security for the loan in case of default and foreclosure. Therefore, the LVR, including all loans, should not exceed 80 to 90 percent of market value, depending on how much risk the seller-lender is willing to accept. Market value should be determined by an independent appraisal. Note that the sale price being financed does not necessarily equal market value. In many cases, the cost of the financing is added to market value by sellers.

Document for Liquidity. Using the forms and underwriting criteria of FHLMC-FNMA reduces the risk of making a bad loan and improves the liquidity of the loan. Thus, the seller-lender of a single-family home is advised to require the FHLMC-FNMA appraisal form illustrated in Fig. 15–3. Likewise, the uniform FHLMC-FNMA mortgage forms, which are discussed in Chap. 4, are preferred to contracts taken from legal form books written for national circulation for the following reasons. The FHLMC-FNMA instruments are specific to each state. Also, they include all essential provisions, including penalties for prepayment or late payment, a due-on-sale clause, and impound or escrow accounts for taxes, insurance, and special assessments. Impounds may be adequately covered in the first mortgage or trust deed. A clause establishing the right to make payments on prior loans if the borrower defaults must be added to these standard instruments. Remember, time of recording is the main distinction between a first and second loan.

Standard documents are much more acceptable to mortgage loan investors and servicing agents than nonstandard documents. Standard documents are also more easily interpreted and administered. And the automatic inclusion of standard clauses more adequately protects the lender's position. In brief, standardized documentations greatly enhance saleability.

Incidentally, the many types of nonstandardized seller loans on paper are sometimes termed guerrilla financing. *Guerrilla loans* are originated by nontraditional lenders and are likely to turn up anywhere. According to *Business Week,* a large secondary market is developing to buy these homemade land contracts and second mortgages, often at a hefty discount.[2] The amount of the discount depends on the interest rate and the quality of the borrower, property, and the documentation. In turn, the buyers put together large packages of these guerrilla loans for marketing and resale to investors as pass-through securities. Transamerica Financial Corporation and Sears Roebuck and Co., through its PMI Insurance Co., are active in this area.

CREATIVE FINANCING: AN OVERVIEW

Creative financing, most likely to be used in times of economic stress and change, can be highly advantageous when properly done. The possibilities are limited only by the imagination of the parties involved. Arrangements should be carefully and completely thought through *before*

---

[2]July 13, 1981, p. 82.

the fact and then should be properly executed. Otherwise, the parties involved must live with a difficult or awkward situation or must pay dearly to set things straight.[3] With these words of caution, let us move on with our overview.

SOURCES OF MONEY

For the most part, the emphasis in this chapter is on seller financing. However, many other sources of money are possible. These sources may be tapped by direct involvement in the financing negotiations. Alternatively, paper may be created by a buyer-borrower and seller-lender and then sold to these sources. The sources are listed here according to their probable degree of concern or interest in the transaction and to the degree that they will be lenient in arranging terms. Sources of money having the most interest are listed first.

- Buyer's friends or relatives
- Broker or salesperson
- Buyer's employer
- Holder of existing financing
- Investors contacted through advertising
- Other brokers or salespeople
- Private, experienced investors
- Private loan companies

TECHNIQUES

The most commonly used techniques are examined in a case example discussed earlier. Let us look briefly at a few "far-out" techniques.

A company called Ticket Corporation in San Jose, California, arranges what is called tandem homebuying. An interested homebuyer, with a limited down payment (buyer-occupant), is matched with an interested investor able to make a large down payment (buyer-investor). The buyer-investor makes the down payment, say 20 percent of the purchase price. The buyer-occupant pays closing costs and fees, lives in the house, and makes the monthly loan payments. The buyer-investor therefore avoids carrying costs and management worries. The parties share in the appreciation upon resale. *Tandem homebuying* is therefore a specialized arrangement for partners to own housing for occupancy and capital gains benefits. The arrangement is somewhat similar to the SAM loan arrangement.

A fee may be split numerous ways to accommodate several distinct

---

[3]See "Creative Financing Can Give Headaches to Lenders and Sellers," *Wall Street Journal,* August 5, 1981, p. 1.

financing interests. Ownership of building and land may be split, for example, each to be financed separately. A short-term gap loan can be used to enable a developer to cover the difference between construction and permanent financing. Or a bridge loan can be used to enable a person to move from ownership of one property to another. Fee splitting is a legal process. The value of the interests, in the property, created depend on the financial or economic benefits to be received by each interest. This value determines the amount of money that may be borrowed against the interest in the property.

SUMMARY

According to a 1981 NAR survey, the main techniques of creative financing are (1) assumption of existing loans, (2) owner takeback of second loans, (3) land contracts, and (4) owner takeback of first loan. These techniques and others are covered in this chapter with TVM calculations taken into account. Of course, the feasibility of alternative techniques depends largely on the specific financial terms involved.

Four major risks or concerns are involved in providing seller financing. They are (1) borrower capability, (2) LVR, (3) due-on-sale clause, and (4) administrative complexities. On the other hand, sellers receive several benefits by providing financing, such as (1) sale is facilitated, (2) taxes are reduced, and (3) an investment may be acquired. Important steps in providing seller financing include (1) ascertain security (borrower and property) to reduce risks and (2) obtain proper documentation to enhance liquidity.

Numerous sources of money and techniques may be involved in creative financing, and there are many possibilities available to the ingenious individual.

KEY TERMS

Buy-Down	Owner Takeback of a	Tandem Homebuying
Guerrilla Financing	Mortgage	

QUESTIONS FOR REVIEW AND DISCUSSION

CASE STUDY

Michael and Merritt Chapman have an annual stabilized income of $40,000. They are both employed in secure jobs and are in their mid-twenties. They have no children but would like to start a family in about five years. They expect their income to increase about 10 percent per year, though some uncertainty exists about their life style after they start a family. They now wish to buy their first home.

Their only major financial obligation is a monthly car payment of $203 that will last for three years. They have saved $15,000 thus far toward a down payment, which is in a money market fund. If necessary, they believe they could borrow or get a gift letter from their parents for another $10,000. Real estate taxes and hazard insurance in their community typically run about 3 percent of market value. Mortgage interest rates are currently 12 percent, compounded monthly, with a 30-year term. Lenders make loans based on loan-to-value ratios of 75 to 90 percent.

Michael and Merritt have heard they should be able to afford a home costing 2.5 times their annual income, or $75,000. However, they have some doubts. They ask you to help them determine the approximate price level of housing they should consider, given their income and resources. Toward this end, you set out to calculate answers for the following questions, based on the FHLMC guidelines. See in particular Figs. 17–2 and 17–3.

1. How much can the Chapmans reasonably allocate to installment payments and housing expenses on an annual basis?

2. Figuring backward from the FHLMC guidelines for total installment payments, how much might the Chapmans commit for housing expenses?

3. Approximately how large a mortgage can they afford, taking property taxes and hazard insurance requirements into account? Assume they can pay from $700 to $800 per month for principal and interest.

4. At an 80 percent LVR, approximately how much they can pay for a house, making actual calculations for insurance and taxes at 3 percent of market value or purchase price?

CASE STUDY CONTINUED

The Chapmans locate the house they want. The asking price is $96,000. It has a $52,000 first loan on it carrying an interest rate of 10 percent that may be assumed. The remaining term is 21 years. The sellers indicate they will take back a second loan at 12 percent, compounded monthly, to be paid off within five years. In their excitement, the Chapmans make an offer of $91,000 with the condition that they pay interest only on a $30,000 second loan, which must be paid off within six years. The offer is accepted! Closing costs would be minimal ($2,000) in that the first loan can be easily assumed. Suddenly, the Chapmans are uncertain whether they are within their means and again turn to you to help them out.

5. How much debt service have they committed themselves to on a monthly and annual basis?

6. What total housing expenses are they committed to, if taxes and insurance work out to three percent of purchase price?

7. How much total closing cost must they pay?

8. What risks have they incurred?

9. In your judgment, are they in serious difficulty?

twenty-two

Calculations for Buying and Selling Existing Loans

Chapter 19, "Loan Negotiation Calculations," gives an explanation of basic time value of money calculations, including the development of loan amortization schedules. Methods of comparing financing are also discussed in that chapter. However, once a loan is originated, the situation changes and different types of TVM calculations may be necessary. In this chapter we take a look at these calculations as they are used to evaluate existing loans for buying and selling. Existing loans are sometimes bought locally, and the transaction may involve only one loan, or many loans may be sold in a package by a large primary lender to a secondary lender, for example. A primary lending institution may wish to obtain additional funds to extend new loans to local clientele or to balance its investment portfolio. The primary lender may also earn more fees servicing loans for secondary lenders in the process. At the same time, the buyer or secondary lender is seeking seasoned loans as investments and is very likely to be willing to pay the going service fee.

TVM calculations are used to determine the value of existing loans for purposes of buying and selling. In this chapter, we look at the calculations underlying this valuation process and at how the rate of return or yield to be earned from investing in a loan may be derived. Major topics covered in this chapter are as follows:

MORTGAGE LOAN DISCOUNTS AND PREMIUMS

To "discount" a statement or rumor made by a commonly known gossip or liar is to take the statement at less than face value. Merchants run sales at discounted prices, meaning reductions from regular or list prices. *Discounting* therefore means to buy or sell, or offer to buy or sell, at a price less than face value. A premium is the opposite of a discount; a premium means to buy or sell, or offer to buy or sell, at a price above face value.

A *mortgage discount* is an amount off or a reduction of the unamortized balance or face amount of a mortgage loan. A *mortgage premium* is an amount in addition to the unamortized balance at the time the loan is originated, a sale is made, or an offer to buy or sell is made.

Mortgage discounts and premiums are expressed in terms of dollars, percentages, or points. For example, a $10,000 loan that sells for $9,000 carries a discount of $1,000. A *dollar discount* is the amount off the balance or face amount of the loan.

$$\text{Dollar Discount} = \text{Loan Balance} - \text{Price or Market Value}$$

$$\text{Dollar Discount} = \$10,000 - \$9,000 = \$1,000$$

A *percent discount* is the amount of the dollar discount divided by the loan amount or face value. Each percent discount is termed a *point.*

$$\text{Percent Discount} = \frac{\text{Dollar Discount}}{\text{Current Loan Balance}}$$

$$\text{Percent Discount} = \frac{\$1,000}{\$10,000} = 10 \text{ percent} = 10 \text{ points}$$

In practice, points are compared and calculations are carried out to one one-hundredth (1/100) of a point or more. Quotations or comparisons between loans are therefore sometimes made in terms of 1/100 of a point, called *basis points.* Thus, a dollar discount of $2,010 off of a $20,000 loan would mean a discount of 10.05 percent. This discount would be 5 basis points greater than the 10 point discount on the $10,000 loan. In summary, 100 basis points off face value equals 1 percent or 1 discount point.

As mentioned, the market value of a loan may exceed the remaining loan balance, the difference giving rise to a premium. That is, a loan may sell for more than its face amount. A *dollar premium* is the amount in excess of the balance or face amount of the loan. A *percent premium* is the amount of the dollar premium divided by the loan balance or face value.

$$\text{Dollar Premium} = \text{Market Value} - \text{Unamortized Loan}$$
$$\text{of Loan} \qquad \text{Balance}$$

$$\text{Dollar Premium} = \$11,400 - \$10,000 = \$1,400$$

$$\text{Percent Premium} = \frac{\text{Dollar Premium}}{\text{Loan Balance}}$$

$$\text{Percent Premium} = \frac{\$1,400}{\$10,000} = 14 \text{ percent}$$

Mortgage discounts and premiums come about because the market interest rate differs from the contract or face interest rate on the loan. A person or institution in this situation has the option of making new loans at market interest rates or buying existing loans at prices that give an interest yield equal to that offered by the market. The following rules always apply:

1. When the market interest rate is higher than the face or contract interest rate, the market value of a loan is always less than the unamortized loan balance or face value, and the loan will sell at a discount.
2. When the market interest rate is lower than the contract rate, a loan will sell at a premium because the market value exceeds the face value.

DISCOUNT CALCULATIONS

Real estate loans sell for a discount when the market interest rate exceeds the contract interest rate, as mentioned above. The *market interest rate* is the interest rate at which new loans are being made at a given time. And, the market rate changes frequently in response to changing conditions in our money and capital markets. The *contract interest rate* is the interest rate negotiated in the loan being bought or sold at the time it was originated. The contract rate is also termed the *face rate of interest.*

The determination of the discount applicable to a given loan involves TVM calculations. Briefly, all future payments to be received on the loan are discounted to the present at both the market rate and the contract rate. The difference between the present values of the payments equals the dollar discount. Prepayment of the loan increases its present value in the market and reduces the dollar and percent discount. Let us look at some examples.

DISCOUNT WITHOUT PREPAYMENT

Assume a $100,000 loan with a contract interest rate of 10 percent and a life of 20 years. The monthly payments for principal and interest on the loan amounts to $965.00. At the end of year three, the primary lender, the Urbandale Savings and Loan Association, needs funds to service local demand for new loans. In the meantime, the market interest rate has increased to 12 percent. It is expected that the borrowers will make payments for the full 20 years of the loan; that is, they *will not* prepay. At what dollar and percent discount will the loan sell?

$$\text{Initial Principal} \times \text{PR} \, {}^{10\% \text{ mo.}}_{240 \text{ mos.}} = \text{Monthly DS}$$

$$\$100,000 \times .009650 = \$965.00$$

At the end of three years, monthly payments of $965 are expected for another 204 months or 17 years. The unamortized balance equals the present value of these payments, discounted at the face rate, 10 percent (see Fig. 22–1).

$$\text{Unamortized Balance} = \text{PV1/P} \, {}^{10\% \text{ mo.}}_{204 \text{ mos.}} \times \text{Monthly DS}$$

$$= 97.922998 \times \$965$$
$$= \$94,496 \text{ (rounded)}$$

Therefore, the face amount of the loan is $94,496.

However, the current market rate of interest is 12 percent. In turn, these same monthly payments of $965 must be discounted at 12 percent to determine the market value of the loan to a secondary lender.

FIGURE 22–1

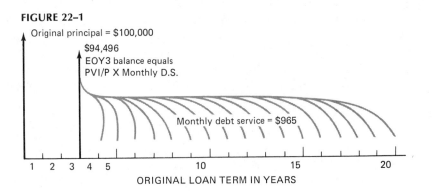

$$\text{Market Value of Loan} = \text{PV1/P} \, {}^{12\% \text{ mo.}}_{204 \text{ mos.}} \times \text{Monthly DS}$$

$$= 86.864698 \times \$965$$

$$= \$83,824$$

Thus, the market value of the loan is $83,824.

We can now determine the dollar discount applicable to the loan.

$$\text{Dollar Discount} = \text{Loan Balance} - \text{Price or Market Value}$$

$$= \$94,496 - \$83,824$$

$$= \$10,672$$

and the percent discount is calculated as follows:

$$\text{Percent Discount} = \frac{\$\text{Discount}}{\text{Loan Balance}} = \frac{\$10,672}{\$94,496}$$

$$= 11.29 \text{ percent}$$

Thus, the discount for the loan in the mortgage market is 11.29 percent.

DISCOUNT WITH PREPAYMENT

Mortgage loans are typically prepaid in from eight to twelve years after origination. Prepayment comes about because a borrower (1) inherits money or otherwise suddenly becomes wealthy, (2) refinances, (3) sells to a buyer who obtains new financing, or (4) defaults and the loan is foreclosed. The effect of prepayment is to increase the value of the loan or to decrease the amount of the warranted discount. With experience, participants in the secondary mortgage market take the chance of prepayment into account. Let us look at the calculation of the actual dollar and percent discounts.

Let us use the same loan as in the previous section, except that prepayment at the end of year ten is assumed. The time of possible sale by the savings and loan is still at the end of year three. The situation, therefore, appears as shown in Fig. 22–2.

To solve the problem, we must first find the amount to be prepaid at the end of year ten. This involves discounting the $965 for the last ten years at the contract rate. This amount is sometimes termed a balloon payment. A *balloon payment* is the last payment on an amortized loan, and it is much larger than the required periodic payments. The balloon payment and the required periodic payments are then discounted at the

FIGURE 22–2

Original principal = $100,000

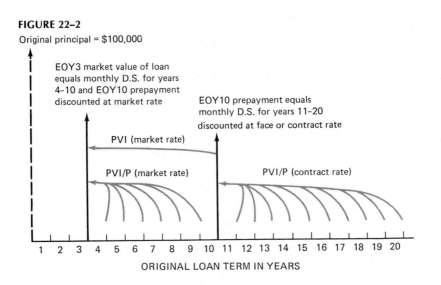

market rate back to the time the loan is being considered or offered for sale.

The amount of the prepayment calculates to $73,023.

$$\text{Prepayment, EOY10} = \text{Monthly DS} \times \text{PV1/P}^{10\% \text{ mo.}}_{120 \text{ mos.}}$$

$$= \$965 \times 75.671158$$

$$= \$73.023.$$

The $965 per month and the one-time prepayment of $73,023 must now be discounted for seven years at the market rate—12 percent.

FIGURE 22–3

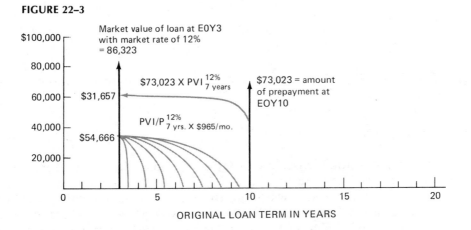

Present Value of
EOY10 Prepayment

$$= \text{Prepayment amount} \times \text{PV1}^{\,12\% \text{ mo.}}_{\,84 \text{ mos.}}$$

$$= \$73,023 \times .433515$$

$$= \$31,657$$

Present Value of Monthly
Debt Service
(years 4–10)

$$= \text{Monthly DS} \times \text{PV1/P}^{\,12\% \text{ mo.}}_{\,84 \text{ mos.}}$$

$$= \$965 \times 56.648449$$

$$= \$54,666$$

Indicated Market Value
of Loan (with Prepayment
Assumed at EOY10)

$$= \frac{\text{PV of}}{\text{prepayment}} + \frac{\text{PV of Monthly DS}}{\text{to prepayment}}$$

$$= \$31,657 + \$54,666$$

$$= \underline{\$86,323}$$

We are now able to determine the dollar and percent discounts applicable to the loan.

$$\text{Dollar Discount} = \text{Face Amount} - \text{Market Value}$$

$$= \$94,496 - \$86,323$$

$$= \$8,173$$

$$\text{Percent Discount} = \frac{\text{Dollar Discount}}{\text{Unamortized Balance or Face Amount}}$$

$$= \frac{\$8,173}{\$94,496}$$

$$= 8.65 \text{ percent}$$

Thus, the dollar discount equals $8,173, and the discount amounts to 8.65 percent.

ADDITIONAL CONSIDERATIONS

At this point, the Urbandale Savings and Loan knows reasonably well the amount of cash to be realized from sale of the subject loan. A secondary lender-investor would go through comparable calculations and arrive at a similar value. A transaction would result when they agreed on a price and probably a loan servicing arrangement. Upon getting the money, the Urbandale Savings and Loan would be in a position to make a new loan.

It should be recognized that the Urbandale Savings and Loan neither gains or loses in the transaction, insofar as rate of return realized. If the money were left in the subject loan, that is, if the loan were not sold, a 12 percent rate of return would still be realized, based on the market value of the loan at the end of year three. But, the Urbandale Savings and Loan does gain servicing income by selling the loan yet retaining the right to service it for the buyer.

It should also be recognized that these same techniques may be used to determine the market value of FHA, VA, and second mortgage loans, as well as amounts owned on land contracts. For that matter, this methodology is the same as that used to value bonds.

Finally, a note of distinction is warranted at this time. The discount on a mortgage loan differs from the discount rate used in TVM calculations. The discount applies to the principal amount of the loan. A discount rate is used to determine the principal amount, or the present value of the loan debt service. It is unfortunate the two terms are so similar and used in such close proximity to each other.

There is a rule of thumb to the effect that one point is the equivalent of one-eighth of a point in the yield or rate of return earned by a buyer-investor. This rule of thumb only applies when interest rates are around 6 to 7 percent and not when they are around 10 to 12 percent. In our examples, one point comes closer to equaling one-fifth of a percent in rate of return. Thus, without prepayment, an 11 percent discount raises the rate of return 2 percent—from 10 to 12 percent. The relationship actually changes depending on assumptions or circumstances.

PREMIUM CALCULATIONS

When the market interest rate falls below the contract interest rate, real estate loans sell for more than their face value—the difference is called *a premium.* The lower market rate increases the present value of future payments of debt service or principal prepayment over the contract loan balance.

The process of determining the premium is comparable to that for determining a discount. All future payments on the loan are discounted to the present at both the market rate and the contract rate. The difference between the present values of the payments equals the dollar premium, which is used to determine the percent premium.

PREMIUM WITHOUT PREPAYMENT

Again, let us begin with a 20-year $100,000 loan with a contract interest rate of 10 percent. Monthly debt service payments for principal and interest equal $965. The market interest rate is assumed to have declined to eight percent during the three years since the loan was originated. No prepayment is assumed. The unamortized balance at EOY3 remains at $94,496. The Urbandale Savings and Loan Association wants to know the probable dollar and percent premium to be realized if the loan were to be sold.

The $965 per month for the next 17 years, or 204 months, must first be discounted to the percent at the market rate (eight percent) to determine the market value of the loan.

$$\text{Indicated Market Value of Loan} = \text{PV1/P}\begin{smallmatrix}8\% \text{ mo.}\\204 \text{ mos.}\end{smallmatrix} \times \text{Monthly DS}$$

$$= 111.326724 \times \$965$$

$$= \$107,430$$

We can now determine the dollar premium applicable to the loan.

$$\text{Dollar Premium} = \text{Indicated Market Value} - \text{Loan Balance (EOY3)}$$

$$= \$107,430 - \$94,496$$

$$= \$12,934$$

In turn, the calculations indicate the loan would sell at a premium of 13.69 percent:

$$\text{Percent Premium} = \frac{\text{Dollar Premium}}{\text{Loan Balance or Face Amount}}$$

$$= \frac{\$12,934}{\$94,496}$$

$$= 13.69 \text{ percent}$$

PREMIUM WITH PREPAYMENT

Let us also see the calculation and the impact on the premium when prepayment of the loan is taken into account, assuming prepayment of the loan decreases its present value in the market and reduces the dollar and percent premium. We use the same loan but with prepayment considered to occur at the end of year ten. The amount of the EOY10 prepayment, as calculated earlier, is $73,023. The present value of $965 per month for seven years of the one-time payment of $73,023 must now be found, using the market discount rate of eight percent. The situation is illustrated in Fig. 22–4.

FIGURE 22–4

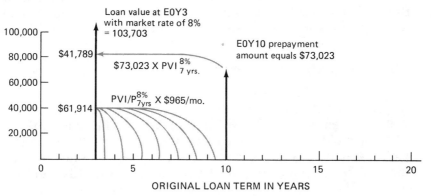

$$\text{PV of EOY10 Prepayment} = \text{Prepayment Amount} \times \text{PV1}^{8\% \text{ mo.}}_{84 \text{ mos.}}$$

$$= \$73,023 \times .572272$$

$$= \$41,789$$

$$\text{PV of Monthly DS (years 4–10)} = \text{Monthly DS} \times \text{PV1/P}^{8\% \text{ mo.}}_{84 \text{ mos.}}$$

$$= \$965 \times 64.159258$$

$$= \$61,914$$

$$\text{Indicated EOY3 Market Value of the Loan (assuming prepayment)} = \text{PV of EOY10 Prepayment} + \text{PV of Monthly DS (Years 4–10)}$$

$$= \$41,789 + \$61,914$$

$$= \$103,703$$

The dollar premium equals $9,207 ($103,703 − $94,496). In turn, a premium of 9.74 percent may be expected by the Urbandale Savings and Loan if the loan were sold in an eight percent market.

$$\text{Percent Premium} = \frac{\text{Dollar Premium}}{\text{Face Value}}$$

$$= \frac{\$9,207}{\$94,496}$$

$$= 9.74 \text{ percent}$$

The premium actually decreases with prepayment. This is because the higher contract rate applies to the last ten years of debt service, thereby giving the payments a lower present value at the EOY10.

DERIVING THE INTERNAL RATE OF RETURN

Buyers and sellers of loans often wish to determine the rate of return or yield implied in transactions in the market. The desire may be to compare the yield rates from one mortgage loan with those of another or the yield rates from mortgage loans with those of bonds or other investments. Let us look at the mechanics of deriving this yield rate, which technically is called the internal rate of return.

The *internal rate of return* (IRR) is that yield or discount rate that equates future cash flows to an initial cash investment. IRR is also the specific discount rate that gives a zero net present value to all cash flows. IRR is sometimes termed the *true rate of return* or the *equity rate of return.* To find the IRR, all future revenues and expenses connected with an investment must be estimated. IRR is the rate of return that makes the net present value of all receipts equal to the net present value of all outlays or expenses.

A computer or calculator is necessary to find an IRR, for all practical purposes. Even with a calculator, a trial-and-error process is involved. Examples are probably the best means of explaining the process. Note that the IRR derived from a given value or transaction depends on the assumptions involved. Thus, the IRR derived, assuming prepayments, differs from the IRR derived without this assumption.

IRR WITHOUT PREPAYMENT

Again, let us assume the $100,000, 10 percent, 20-year loan at EOY3. The unamortized balance is $94,496. The Urbandale Savings and Loan offers to sell the loan for $90,000 at the end of the third year. This price represents a dollar discount of $4,496 and a percent discount of 4.76. What rate of return would a buyer at this price realize, assuming no prepayment?

To begin with, any TVM calculation involves four items or variables: a payment, a value (often unknown), a time period, and a rate of return or interest. Typically, the payment is multiplied by the TVM factor to determine a value.

$$\text{Value} = \text{Payment} \times \text{TVM Factor} \, {}^{X\%}_{y} \text{ term}$$

If three of the four items are known, the fourth may be determined. In our example, the rate of return is unknown. Monthly payments of $965 are expected for the remaining 17 years of the loan. We know that monthly payment times PV1/P gives present value.

$$\text{Present Value} = \text{Monthly Payment} \times \text{PV1/P}\ _y^{X\%}\ \text{term}$$

With our data, the relationship becomes

$$\$90,000 = \$965 \times \text{PV1/P}\ _{204\ \text{mos.}}^{X\%}$$

Our earlier calculations show that the present value of $965 per month is $94,496 when discounted at 10 percent. Likewise, with a 12 percent discount rate the present value is $83,824. Thus, we have a value estimate on each side of the $90,000 target price. The 10 and 12 percent interest rates used involve a difference, or straddle, of 2 percent.

$$2\%\Big\langle\begin{array}{l}10\%\\X\%\\12\%\end{array}\quad\begin{array}{l}\$94,496\\\$90,000\\\$83,824\end{array}\Big\rangle\$4,496\ \Big\rangle\$10,672$$

The difference between $94,496 and $90,000 is $4,496, and the difference between our 10 percent value and our 12 percent value is $10,672 ($94,496 − $83,824). It follows that the rate of return earned with a purchase price of $90,000 is between 10 and 12 percent. We need to interpolate to get the exact rate of return.

$$\text{Indicated IRR} = 10\% + 2\%\left(\frac{\$\ 4,496}{\$10,672}\right)$$

$$= 10\% + 2\%\ (.4213)$$

$$= 10\% + .84\%$$

$$= 10.84\%$$

More refined calculations show that the internal rate of return is actually 10.8 percent. Some will say this same answer may be obtained by interpolating between TVM factors rather than dollar amounts, and that is correct. However, interpolating between factors will not work when prepayment is involved. Dollar amounts must be used.

IRR WITH PREPAYMENT

Let us now determine the IRR, assuming prepayment at EOY10 of the loan. Regardless of when prepayment occurs, the present value is $94,496 if the IRR is 10 percent. Hence, one side of our straddle is known.

We also know that the prepayment at EOY10 is $73,023, based on our previous calculations and discussion. Further, we previously determined the present value of prepayment and monthly debt service to be $86,323 when discounted at 12 percent. We therefore have the other side of our straddle as well.

Let us now calculate the IRR, assuming prepayment at EOY10.

$$
2\%
\begin{cases}
10\% & \$94,496 \\
X\% & \$90,000 \\
12\% & \$86,323
\end{cases}
\quad
\$4,496
\quad
\$8,173
$$

$$X\% = 10\% + 2\%\left(\frac{\$4,496}{\$8,173}\right)$$

$$= 10\% + 2\%(.5501)$$

$$= 10\% + 1.1$$

$$= 11.1\%$$

The IRR is approximately 11.1 percent under these circumstances.

SUMMARY

A mortgage loan discount occurs when the market interest rate exceeds the contract rate. A contract rate higher than the market rate results in a premium. A percentage discount or premium is calculated by dividing the dollar discount or premium by the unamortized balance of the loan.

The calculation of a loan discount or premium involves obtaining the present value of all expected payments at both the market and contract rates, assuming prepayment acts to lower the premium or discount expected on the loan.

If a loan discount or premium is known, the yield rate or internal rate of return to be realized by purchase of the loan may be determined. IRR is that rate of return that makes the present value of all cash inflows and outflows connected with an investment equal to zero.

KEY TERMS

Balloon Payment	Dollar Premium	Percent Discount
Basis Point	Face Rate of Interest	Percent Premium
Contract Interest Rate	Internal Rate of Return (IRR)	Point
Discount		Premium
Dollar Discount	Market Interest Rate	

1. Under what conditions might a loan sell for a premium in the secondary mortgage market? For a discount?

2. Does prepayment raise or lower the amount of a discount for a loan? Explain.

3. Distinguish between a discount rate as used in TVM calculations and the percentage discount at which a loan might sell. Are the two related in any way? Explain.

4. What is the internal rate of return or IRR?

5. A $20,000 loan is sold for $19,250.
   a. Was a discount or premium realized in the sale?
   b. How much is the dollar discount or premium?
   c. What is the percentage discount or premium?
   d. How many basis points are involved?

6. Distinguish between the market interest rate and the contract interest rate.

7. The Uniontown Federal Savings and Loan Association just made a $200,000 loan for 25 years at a contract interest rate of 12 percent, compounded monthly, based on a loan commitment extended eight months ago. The current market rate is 14 percent.
   a. Assuming payments being made to maturity (no prepayments), what dollar and percent discounts might be expected if the loan were sold?
   b. Assuming prepayment at the end of year ten, what dollar and percent discounts might be expected?
   c. Why the difference between the two discounts, if any?
   d. Why might a lender sell a loan such as this immediately after it is originated?

8. A $40,000 loan was made *four years ago* by the Third National Bank of Arkansas. The terms were for 12 percent, compounded monthly, with full amortization over 25 years. The current market interest rate is 10 percent. The bank now wants to sell the loan.
   a. What dollar premium is to be expected? (Remember that the loan is four years old.)
   b. What percent premium might be expected?

9. The Standard Life Insurance Company bought the loan in question 7 above for $184,304.

a. What internal rate of return is to be realized by the insurance company, assuming the loan is paid off as agreed? (13.2%)

b. If the loan were prepaid, would the yield (IRR) earned by the insurance company increase or decrease? Explain.

c. Calculate the IRR assuming prepayment at the EOY8 to verify your insight in answering part b of this question.

10. What is the IRR to a buyer of the $40,000 loan of question 8, assuming purchase for $42,000 and prepayment at the end of year 12 of the loan?

11. Match the following terms and definitions:

a. Internal Rate of Return _____

b. Basis Point _____

c. Premium _____

d. Discount _____

e. Contract Interest Rate _____

1. The interest rate being agreed to in loans now being originated.

2. One one-hundredth of a percent.

3. The interest rate agreed to in a specific loan.

4. Amount or percent in excess of face value.

5. The yield rate that discounts future payments exactly to the amount invested in a loan.

6. Amount or percent off face value.

twenty-three

Federal Credit Agencies and Mortgage-Backed Securities in the Secondary Mortgage Market

The secondary mortgage market is usually defined as the market in which existing mortgages are traded. Two types of transactions are involved. The first is the buying and selling of mortgage loans and/or mortgage loan participations. The second is the formation of pools of mortgages and the issuing of securities that are backed by the mortgages in the pools.

The secondary market performs a number of functions. It transfers funds from capital surplus areas to capital deficit areas and reduces regional differences in mortgage interest rates. It increases the liquidity of mortgages and thereby makes mortgages more desirable investments. It enables investors who lack the facilities to originate and/or service mortgage loans to invest in mortgages through payment of origination and service fees to primary lenders. The development of mortgage-backed securities is yet another way to attract funds to real estate from investors who prefer more liquid and easily managed investments.

The volume of secondary mortgage market transactions in one- to four-family home mortgages alone totaled about $70 billion in both 1979 and 1980. Additional secondary mortgage activity takes place with multifamily, commercial, and farm mortgages. The major buyers and sellers of one- to four-family house mortgages may be classified into one of four major categories. These categories are (1) the big four private institutional lenders, (2) mortgage companies, (3) federal credit agencies, and (4) mortgage pools. The big four (CBs, S&Ls, MSBs, and LICs) accounted for about one-quarter of the purchases and about one-third of the sales. The combined group is therefore a net seller; they sell more than they buy, even though life insurance companies and mutual savings banks are net purchasers. Mortgage companies accounted for less than 10 percent of the purchases and well over 50 percent of the sales. Federal credit agencies and mortgage pools accounted for about 10 percent of the sales and over 60 percent of the purchases.

The big four institutional lenders and mortgage companies are basically primary lenders and were therefore discussed in Chaps. 10 and 11. In this chapter our emphasis is on secondary lenders. Our attention is therefore mainly on the Federal National Mortgage Association (FNMA), the Government National Mortgage Association (GNMA), the Federal Home Loan Mortgage Corporation (FHLMC), and investors in mortgage-backed securities. These are the major net purchasers in the secondary mortgage market.

Figure 23–1 shows the mortgage holdings of FNMA, FHLMC, and GNMA at the end of 1980 and their purchases and sales during 1980. The mortgage holdings of FNMA dwarf those of FHLMC and GNMA; but FNMA's mortage purchases were only about twice those of FHLMC and four times those of GNMA. The considerably lower mortgage holdings of FHLMC and GNMA are due to their policy of disposing of mortgages that they purchase, when feasible. Note that the sales by FHLMC and GNMA vastly exceed those of FNMA.

Mortgage pools account for even a greater volume than the combined purchases of FNMA, FHLMC, and GNMA. GNMA guaranteed, mortgage-backed securities totaling about $20.6 billion were issued during 1980, and securities amounting to nearly $94 billion were outstanding at the end of 1980. The FHLMC issued $2.5 billion in mortgage-backed securities during 1980 and, at the end of 1980, outstanding securities amounted to over $15 billion. FmHA also issues mortgage-

FIGURE 23–1 FNMA, FHLMC, and GNMA Mortgage Holdings at the End of 1980 and Purchases and Sales during 1980

(In Millions)

Holdings	FNMA	FHLMC	GNMA
One- to Four-Family	$51,775	$3,873	$ 704
Multifamily	5,552	1,195	3,938
Total	$57,327	$5,068	$4,642
Purchases	$ 8,100	$3,722	$1,996[1]
Sales	$ 0	$2,526	$1,492

[1]Fiscal year ending September 30, 1980.

SOURCES: *Federal Reserve Bulletin,* June 1981, pp. A38–39; and *GNMA Annual Report,* 1979.

backed securities and, at the end of 1979, it had outstanding securities totaling more than $31.5 billion. Commercial banks, savings and loan associations, and mortgage companies also issue mortgage-backed securities, but these securities are not guaranteed or insured by government agencies.

In this chapter the secondary mortgage market activities of FNMA, GNMA, and FHLMC are first discussed. Then the nature and development of mortgage-backed securities are examined.

FEDERAL NATIONAL MORTGAGE ASSOCIATION

The Federal National Mortgage Association, nicknamed *Fannie Mae,* is the largest single purchaser of residential mortgages in the secondary mortgage market. FNMA is a federally sponsored corporation, which was at one time a government agency. In 1968 it became a federally chartered, shareholder-owned, and privately managed corporation.

Even though FNMA is a profit-oriented corporation, with its shares listed on the New York Stock Exchange, it retains many ties to the federal government. The President of the United States appoints five of the 15 members of FNMA's board of directors. The Secretary of the Treasury has the authority to purchase FNMA securities in order to provide emergency support. The Secretary of HUD has the authority to set FNMA's debt limit and debt-to-capital ratio. The Secretary of HUD may also require FNMA to participate in specific programs designed to provide adequate housing for low- and moderate-income families, if such programs do not unreasonably endanger FNMA's profit positions.

SOURCES OF FUNDS

FNMA's quasi-government status qualifies its bonds and notes as government securities for some regulated institutions. FNMA's principal sources of income are commitment fees and the interest on its mortgage holdings. FNMA's principal expenses are the interest on its borrowed funds, administrative costs, and mortgage servicing fees. FNMA's principal source of funds is bonds. Most of its bonds are debentures that do not pledge any specific assets as security. A small portion of its bonds are mortgage-backed bonds that are guaranteed by GNMA. Short-term notes are the second largest source of funds. Sales of common stock and retained earnings provide additional sources of funds.

TYPES OF LOANS PURCHASED

FNMA purchases a number of different types of residential mortgages and participations. FHA insured, VA guaranteed, and conventional one-to four-family mortgage loans accounted for over 99.9 percent of its purchases in 1979. Conventional home mortgage loans represented approximately one-half of FNMA's purchases in 1979. FNMA also purchases FHA insured multifamily mortgages, construction loan participations, and participations in pools of urban and rural residential mortgages.

The mortgage loans must meet various standards to be eligible for purchase by FNMA. The maximum dollar amount of an eligible FHA insured single-family mortgage is identical to the limit under Section 203(b), which, at this writing, is $67,500 in standard cost areas. VA guaranteed loans eligible for FNMA purchase may not exceed 75 percent of the purchase price or reasonable value of the subject property, whichever is less. Given a $27,500 guarantee, $110,000 becomes the maximum for a VA guaranteed loan. A VA loan must also be accompanied by an independent appraisal.

The maximum for a conventional single-family mortgage is $98,500, with higher limits in Alaska and Hawaii. The loan-to-value ratio can be as high as 95 percent if the mortgage is privately insured. The FNMA-FHLMC standardized mortgages and notes are the most readily accepted instruments for conventional loans. An independent appraisal must accompany each loan. Conventional loans must be fully amortizing and have escrows for real estate taxes and insurance. The borrower in a single-family loan must be the owner-occupant. Borrowers on two-to four-unit properties need not be owner-occupants. FNMA requires conventional mortgage loans to have been originated within one year of time of purchase by FNMA.

APPROVED SELLERS

Any organization desiring to sell loans to FNMA must apply to FNMA and meet certain net worth and other requirements. Under the FHA-VA program, an approved seller must be an organization whose principal purpose is either the origination or purchase of mortgage loans. If the seller desires to sell FHA mortgages, the seller must be an FHA approved mortgagee. If the seller desires to sell VA mortgages, the seller must be classified as a supervised lender by VA, an approved mortgagee by FHA, or otherwise approved by FNMA. Under the conventional loan program, the seller's principal business must be the origination of mortgage loans. The seller is responsible for underwriting the mortgage loans sold to FNMA and for meeting FNMA underwriting standards. The seller of home mortgage loans must be qualified and willing to service the loans or to arrange for a qualified third party to service the loans. FNMA pays the servicers of home mortgages an annual servicing fee of three-eighths of one percent on the unpaid balance of each loan.

In 1980 FNMA initiated a home seller loan program. The program allows homeowners who finance the sale of a home by taking back a first (purchase money mortgage) loan to sell the mortgage to FNMA, and thereby convert it into cash. The home seller must use the services of an FNMA approved lender in selling the loan to FNMA. The standard FNMA mortgage, note, and appraisal forms must be used in structuring or documenting the loans. The FNMA approved lender must agree to service the loan.

COMMITMENTS AND FREE MARKET SYSTEM

FNMA sells commitments to purchase whole mortgage loans and loan participations. The party purchasing the commitment assures itself of being able to sell the loans to FNMA. FNMA currently offers both optional delivery and mandatory delivery commitments. Under the *mandatory delivery commitment,* the potential seller must sell the loans to FNMA. Under the *optional delivery commitment,* the potential seller does not have to sell the loans to FNMA. When loans are sold to FNMA, the seller must purchase FNMA stock equal to one-fourth of one percent of the unpaid balance of the mortgages purchased.

FNMA charges a nonrefundable fee for its commitments. A one-half of one percent fee is charged for one- and two-month mandatory delivery commitments for single-family mortgage loans. The fee for the four-month optional delivery commitment is two percent of the amount of the commitment. FNMA temporarily suspended its twelve-month commitment program in 1981.

The one-, two-, and four-month commitments are issued under what is called the *free market system* (FMS). The FMS means that commitments are awarded on the basis of competitive bids at auctions. FNMA holds three separate auctions biweekly. The auctions are for (1) FHA and VA mortgages, (2) conventional mortgages, and (3) FHA insured graduated payment mortgages. No bidder-seller at the auction may make both a competitive bid and a noncompetitive bid.

A *competitive bid* specifies the yield that the bidder is willing to pay FNMA for the funds received from the sale of the mortgages. An offering fee of one-hundredth of one percent must be paid on competitive bids. An individual or institution is limited to five separate bids at any given biweekly auction. There is no limit on the total amount of mortgages offered by a single competitive bidder at a biweekly auction.

A potential seller may choose to make a noncompetitive bid rather than a competitive bid. A *noncompetitive bid* is a bid in which the potential seller agrees to accept the weighted average yield of the competitive bids accepted at the auction. A maximum of $500,000 in mortgage loans may be offered under a noncompetitive bid. FNMA reserves a portion of its total commitments at each auction for noncompetitive bidders in order to allow small sellers to obtain commitments.

At the auction the potential sellers submit their bids, and FNMA accepts a portion of the offerings and makes commitments to the highest competitive bidders. The *noncompetitive bidders* are given priority at the auction.

FNMA MORTGAGE SALES

FNMA sells as well as buys residential loans. When mortgage investors have excess funds, FNMA is willing to sell mortgages on an auction basis. It accepts the purchase offers that provide the lowest yields to the buyers. This results in FNMA realizing the highest price for the mortgage loans that are sold. In recent years, FNMA purchases have greatly exceeded its sales of mortgage loans. In the early 1970s, FNMA disposed of some of its mortgage holdings by selling GNMA guaranteed bonds backed by the mortgage loans.

FEDERAL HOME LOAN MORTGAGE CORPORATION

The Federal Home Loan Mortgage Corporation (FHLMC) is the second largest single purchaser of residential mortgages in the secondary mortgage market. FHLMC was founded in 1970 and is owned by the Federal Home Loan Banks. FHLMC's board of directors is composed of members of the Federal Home Loan Bank Board (FHLBB), and is chaired by the chairman of the FHLBB.

SOURCES OF FUNDS

FHLMC's principal source of funds for the purchase of mortgages is the sale of mortgage-backed securities such as mortgage participation certificates and guaranteed mortgage certificates. FHLMC may also raise funds by borrowing from the Federal Home Loan Bank.

TYPES OF LOANS PURCHASED

FHLMC was founded primarily to provide a secondary mortgage market for conventional residential mortgages, but it may also purchase FHA insured and VA guaranteed mortgages. In its early years, FHLMC purchased a large volume of FHA and VA mortgages, but this activity has gradually eased off in recent years. FHLMC did not purchase any FHA or VA mortgages in 1979. Only FHLMC's conventional mortgage loan purchases are discussed here.

FHLMC purchases both conventional whole mortgage loans and conventional mortgage participations secured by both one- to four-family and multifamily properties. Under the participation program

FHLMC purchases a specified percentage of each mortgage loan in a group of loans. The percentage ranges from 50 to 95 percent. Home mortgage loans and participations in home loans have accounted for approximately three-fourths of FHLMC's purchases in recent years. Multi-family loans and participations accounted for the remainder.

The whole mortgage loans and the loans in groups under the participations programs must meet various standards to be eligible for purchase. The standards for purchases are very similar to those maintained by FNMA. The maximum for a conventional single-family mortgage is $98,500; it is higher in Alaska and Hawaii. The loan-to-value ratio may be as high as 95 percent if the mortgage is privately insured. The FNMA-FHLMC standardized note and mortgage instruments must be used. And the loans must be fully amortizing. The borrower in a single-family loan must be the owner-occupant. FHLMC requires the conventional mortgages to have been originated within one year of time of purchase by FHLMC.

APPROVED SELLERS

Any organization desiring to sell mortgages to FHLMC must be approved by FHLMC. Members of the Federal Home Loan Bank System and/or Federal Savings and Loan Insurance Corporation are primarily savings and loans and some mutual savings banks, and they are automatically eligible to obtain approved seller status. Mortgage companies are also eligible for the approved seller status. Those institutions who are not members of the FHLBS or FSLIC are classified as nonmember sellers.

Any seller must be engaged in the origination of mortgages and servicing of mortgages and must be approved by FHLMC. The seller is responsible for underwriting the mortgage loans sold to FHLMC and for meeting FHLMC underwriting standards. The seller is also responsible for servicing the loans, but may arrange for another FHLMC approved seller to do the actual servicing. FHLMC allows the seller to retain three-eighths of one percent for servicing home loans, one-fourth of one percent for multifamily loans of $750,000 or less, and one-eighth of one percent for multifamily loans of more than $750,000.

HOME LOAN PURCHASE PROGRAMS

FHLMC also uses an auction system to sell commitments to purchase in its home mortgage loan and home loan participation programs. FHLMC holds weekly auctions for its immediate delivery program and monthly auctions for its forward commitment program. A *forward commitment* is one which is made before the loans offered have been originated. FHLMC accepts competitive and noncompetitive bids. Competitive bidders are limited to five separate bids at a given auction. There is a limit of $3,000,000 for total offerings by a competitive bidder and $500,000 for a noncompetitive bidder in a given weekly immediate delivery auction. Bids for forward commitments are limited to $5,000,000.

FHLMC accepts a portion of the competitive bids. It normally accepts all noncompetitive bids. The yield on noncompetitive bids is determined by the weighted average of the competitive bids. Members of the FHLBS pay no fee for an immediate delivery commitment, but nonmembers pay a fee of one-half of one percent. Both members and nonmembers must pay a one percent fee for a forward commitment.

The immediate delivery program makes delivery of the mortgages mandatory within 60 days after the acceptance of the bid by FHLMC. A *mandatory delivery commitment* means that the successful bidder must deliver the mortgages. Delivery under the eight-month forward commitment program is optional. Of course, FHLMC can choose to reject delivery of the mortgages under any of its programs if the mortgages do not meet the prescribed standards.

MULTIFAMILY LOAN PURCHASE PROGRAMS

FHLMC has an immediate delivery program and prior approval program for multifamily mortgage loans and participation. The prior approval program is used for loans that have not yet been closed. The prior purchase commitment from FHLMC gives a lender a market for a loan before it is originated. Under the prior approval program, both members and nonmembers pay a small offering fee and a two percent commitment fee. The two percent fee is refundable when the loan is fully funded. Under the immediate delivery program, members of the FHLBS pay no fee, and nonmembers of a fee of one-half of one percent.

FHLMC does not use the auction system to sell commitments in its multifamily mortgage loan and participation programs; rather it specifies the required yield.

The immediate delivery program makes delivery mandatory within 60 days after acceptance of the offer by FHLMC. Under the prior approval program, the prospective seller has ten days in which to accept FHLMC's specified yield. If the seller accepts FHLMC's offer, delivery is mandatory within 60 days of the acceptance.

FHLMC MORTGAGE SALES

FHLMC usually issues mortgage-backed securities rather than sell mortgage loans directly. FHLMC issues mortgage participation certificates, guaranteed mortgage certificates, and GNMA mortgage-backed securities, all of which are discussed later in the chapter.

The Government National Mortgage Association (GNMA) was established in 1968. GNMA is owned by the U.S. Government and is an agency within the Department of Housing and Urban Development (HUD). The Secretary of HUD is responsible for the operation of GNMA. GNMA operates two major programs: the mortgage purchase program and the mortgage-backed securities program. The mortgage-backed securities program is discussed later in this chapter.

Under its mortgage purchase program, GNMA purchases mortgages bearing below-market interest rates. GNMA purchases these mortgages to assist in the financing of housing for low-income families and to counter declines in mortgage lending and housing construction.

SOURCES OF FUNDS

GNMA finances a portion of its mortgage purchases by selling mortgages and occasionally by issuing mortgage-backed securities. The remainder of its funds are obtained by borrowing from the U.S. Treasury. Mortgages are often sold at a discount, and assistance from the U.S. Treasury is needed to absorb the losses incurred thereby. The U.S. Treasury also provides funds to support increases in GNMA mortgage holdings.

TYPES OF PROGRAMS

The special assistance function of GNMA involves over 20 purchase commitment programs for various types of FHA insured and VA guaranteed residential mortgage loans. About one-half of these programs involve loans to finance subsidized housing for low- and moderate-income families. Some involve loans to finance housing in Indian lands and Guam or to finance experimental housing. A few programs are designed specifically to provide below-market interest rate loans to stimulate residential construction.

GNMA offers commitments for both single-family and multifamily mortgage loans. The purchase commitments for single-family mortgages are usually forward commitments for one year. The commitments for multifamily mortgages are typically for two or three years. Delivery under forward commitments is optional. Most of GNMA's commitment and purchase activity involves mortgage loans for the construction or rehabilitation of multifamily properties that serve low- and moderate-income families.

GNMA also has two special emergency assistance programs for home mortgage loans that are activated only by the declaration of an emergency in the home construction and leaving markets. One provides for the purchase of FHA insured and VA guaranteed home mortgages The second provides for the purchase of insured conventional home mortgage loans, and it allows 10 percent of the purchases to be secured by existing single-family structures.

The commitment and purchase fees charged by GNMA vary among the different programs, and they are similar to those charged by FNMA. The sellers of single-family home loans are responsible for the servicing of loans sold to GNMA. GNMA contracts with FNMA and FHLMC for the servicing of multifamily loans.

THE TANDEM PLAN

In 1970 GNMA arranged to issue forward commitments to purchase mortgages and to transfer the commitments to FNMA, which is termed the *tandem plan*. The plan worked as follows. A lending institution obtains a commitment from GNMA to purchase a below-market interest rate mortgage at par or close to par. For example, assume the amount of the mortgage loan to be $1,000,000, which would be discounted to $900,000 to yield the market interest rate. The lender would be unwilling to make the loan if the $100,000 discount would have to be absorbed. GNMA extends the commitment to purchase the mortgage for $1,000,000, with the expectation of transferring it to FNMA for $900,000. GNMA purchases the mortgage for $1,000,000. GNMA then sells the mortgage to FNMA for $900,000 and absorbs the $100,000 discount.

The object of the GNMA tandem plan, or any GNMA purchase and sale program, is to reduce government outlays involved in subsidizing below-market interest rate mortgage loans. In the example cited above, GNMA spends $100,000 in absorbing the discount rather than the $1,000,000 which would be necessary to purchase and hold the mortgage. The procedure allows GNMA to subsidize a larger number of mortgage loans within a given budget.

In addition to GNMA tandem agreements with FNMA and FHLMC, GNMA purchases mortgages under the commitments and holds public auctions to sell the mortgages. Private investors such as mortgage companies purchase the mortgages and use most of them as security for mortgage-backed securities.

MORTGAGE-BACKED SECURITIES

Mortgage-backed securities accounted for only a small portion of secondary mortgage market purchases in 1970. But by the late 1970s they accounted for a greater volume of mortgage purchases than FNMA, FHLMC, and GNMA combined.

Mortgage-backed securities are certificates backed by specific mortgages and are issued by the holder of the mortgages. Securities issued by government agencies, government sponsored agencies, and private organizations whose assets consist primarily of mortgage loans are excluded unless specific pools of mortgage loans are placed in trust or are allocated as collateral for the certificates issued. Some state governments have issued mortgage-backed securities secured by specific mortgage pools, but these represent a relatively small dollar total.

There are two general types of mortgage backed securities. The *bond type* pays interest on a quarterly, semiannual, or annual basis, and the principal is usually paid on the maturity date of the bond. The *pass-through type* pays both interest and principal on a monthly basis. The payments on mortgage-backed securities may be guaranteed by the issuer or by a third party. Alternatively the pool of mortgages itself may be insured by a private mortgage insurer.

Figure 23–2 shows the outstanding principal balance of GNMA guaranteed, FHLMC, and FmHA mortgage-backed securities at the end of 1980. Private issues of mortgage-backed securities bring the total of mortgage-backed securities to over $145 billion at the end of 1980. GNMA guaranteed mortgage-backed securities accounted for nearly two-thirds of the total.

Mortgage-backed securities give the mortgage market improved access to the general capital markets, and they attract some investors that would normally invest only a small portion of their funds in mortgages, if any. FHLMC and FmHA mortgage-backed securities are issued by these respective agencies. GNMA guaranteed pass-through certificates and private issue pass-through certificates without a GNMA guarantee are issued primarily by mortgage companies, savings and loan associations, and commercial banks.

Mortgage-backed securities are discussed in more detail as follows: (1) GNMA guaranteed, (2) FHLMC issued, (3) FmHA issued, and (4) privately issued without a GNMA guarantee.

FIGURE 23–2 Outstanding Principal Balances of GNMA Guaranteed, FHLMC, and FmHA Mortgage-Backed Securities at the End of 1980

(In Millions)

	GNMA	FHLMC	FmHA
One- to Four-Family	$91,602	$13,471	$16,683
Multifamily	2,272	3,383	2,612
Commercial	—	—	5,271
Farm	—	—	6,964
Total	$93,874	$16,854	$31,530

SOURCE: Federal Reserve Bulletin, June 1981, p. A39.

GNMA guaranteed securities are backed by pools of FHA and VA insured or guaranteed mortgage loans. Pools containing single-family, multifamily, construction, or mobile home loans are eligible for the GNMA guarantee. Over 90 percent of GNMA guarantees involve pools of single-family mortgages. The securities may be bond type, serial notes, or pass-through type. FNMA and FHLMC have been the only issuers of GNMA guaranteed bond type securities. Only a small volume of serial type securities have been issued.

Our discussion is limited to GNMA guaranteed pass-through certificates secured by pools of single-family mortgage loans. These loans are currently secured by either level payment or graduated payment mortgage loans.

Types of Guarantees. There are three types of GNMA pass-through guarantees. The *straight pass-through* guarantees that the monthly payments of principal and interest will be passed on to the certificate holder as they are collected. The *partially modified pass-through* guarantees that monthly interest will be paid to the certificate holder even if payments are not collected. The *fully modified pass-through* guarantees that both the monthly interest and principal will be paid to the certificate holder even if payments are not collected. The bulk of GNMA mortgage-backed securities involves fully modified pass-through certificates.

If the issuer of the securities fails to pay as promised, GNMA pays the certificate holders. GNMA then takes action to collect from the issuer. This GNMA guarantee makes the securities high quality investments.

Issuers. Issuers of GNMA mortgage-backed securities must be FHA approved lenders, must be FNMA approved servicers, and must meet GNMA net worth requirements. While GNMA itself has issued GNMA guaranteed mortgage-backed securities, the principal issuers are mortgage companies, savings and loan associations, and commercial banks.

The Mortgage Pool. After an issuer's application is approved, the issuer has one year in which to assemble a pool of mortgages. In the case of single-family mortgages, the mortgages must have been insured or guaranteed within one year of the date of the GNMA guaranteed commitment, and the pool must contain mortgages totaling at least $1 million. Each mortgage in the pool must secure the same type of property such as single-family properties, and each mortgage must bear the same interest rate. The maturities of the loans are expected to be similar. When the pool is formed, a custodian such as the trust department of a commercial bank is appointed to act in the interest of the security holders. After the custodian verifies the documents and arrangements, the securities are issued.

Sale and Purchasers.   Nearly $25 billion in GNMA mortgage-backed securities were issued in 1979, and over $24 billion of the total represented issues secured by single-family mortgages. The securities are either sold by the issuer or by GNMA security dealers. The minimum amount of any single pass-through certificate is $25,000.

At the end of 1979, depository institutions held the following percentages of GNMA guaranteed securities: S&Ls, 15 percent; mutual savings banks, 10 percent; commercial banks, 6 percent; and credit unions, 2 percent. Retirement and pension funds held 10 percent in their own names and perhaps one-half of the 37 percent held in the names of nominees (parties other than the actual owners). Mortgage companies and security brokers and dealers held 7 percent, but their holdings primarily represent their inventory. The remaining 13 percent was held by insurance companies, state and local governments, trust funds, and others.

Fees.   The issuer pays a small application fee for the application for the guarantee. The interest rate on the GNMA guaranteed single-family pass-through certificates is one-half percent below the interest rate on the mortgages in the pool. The servicer of the loans receives the one-half percent, but the servicer must pay six one-hundredths of one percent to GNMA. The servicer retains 44 one-hundredths of one percent for servicing the loan.

The issuer also may have to pay the custodian and the GNMA security dealer if one was used to market the securities.

FHLMC MORTGAGE-BACKED SECURITIES

The FHLMC issues mortgage-backed securities to finance its purchases in the secondary mortgage market. It occasionally issues GNMA guaranteed mortgage securities to dispose of its FHA and VA loan holdings. FHLMC developed its own securities to dispose of its conventional mortgage holdings. FHLMC issued about $3.8 billion in mortgage participation certificates and $750 million in guaranteed mortgage certificates during 1979. In 1980, while no guaranteed mortgage certificates were issued, FHLMC issued over $2.5 billion in mortgage participation certificates.

Mortgage Participation Certificates.   FHLMC modeled its mortgage *participation certificate* (PC) after the GNMA guaranteed pass-through certificate. FHLMC's first issue of PCs was made in September 1971—about one and one-half years after the first issue of GNMA guaranteed pass-through certificates. FHLMC, as the issuer of PCs, guarantees monthly payments of interest and principal to investors.

The FHLMC sells its PCs through security dealers. While depository institutions are major purchasers, up to one-half of the PCs are purchased by pension funds, state and local retirement funds, bank trust departments, and other nontraditional mortgage investors.

PCs are sold under a number of programs in which FHLMC establishes the desired yield and offers the PCs for sale. One program calls for the purchaser to receive delivery of PCs within 7 to 29 days. If the purchaser agrees instead to take delivery after 29 days through 150 days, FHLMC pays a commitment fee to the purchaser.

Guaranteed Mortgage Certificates. FHLMC issued the first guaranteed mortgage certificate (GMC) in February 1975. A GMC is a bond like security. A GMC represents an ownership share in a large pool of residential mortgages. The GMC pays interest semiannually and principal payments annually. FHLMC agrees to repurchase the unpaid principal at par, normally at the end of 15 years if the holder elects to sell. GMCs are sold through security dealers. Pension funds, insurance companies, and bank trust departments are the major purchasers.

FmHA MORTGAGE-BACKED SECURITIES

The Farmers Home Administration finances much of its mortgage lending by selling mortgage-backed securities. FmHA made its first issue of Farm Home Insured Notes in July 1970 and its first issue of certificates of beneficial ownership in the Farmers Home Insured Note Trust in December 1973. From July 1970 through April 1974 the notes and certificates of beneficial ownership were sold to the investing public through security dealers. After April 1974, all new issues have been sold to the Federal Financing Bank, a government agency.

PRIVATE ISSUE MORTGAGE-BACKED SECURITIES

Privately issued mortgage-backed securities refer to those without guarantees or sponsorship in some form from governmental agencies. The two major types of privately issued mortgage-backed securities are mortgage-backed bonds and pass-through certificates.

Private mortgage-backed bonds and pass-through certificates are a significant alternative source of funds for institutional lenders. FNMA, FHLMC, and GNMA purchase whole loans and loan participations in the secondary market, but with minor exceptions they do not purchase mortgage loans which have been outstanding for more than 12 months.

Only FHA and VA loans are eligible to secure GNMA mortgage-backed securities, and the loans must have been originated within one year after GNMA accepts the issuer's application. Private mortgage-backed securities allow issuers to use conventional mortgage loans and seasoned FHA insured and VA guaranteed loans as security. They thereby increase the liquidity of the lender's mortgage loan holdings.

Mortgage-Backed Bonds. The first issue of private mortgage-backed bonds was issued by MGIC Mortgage Corporation in November 1973. The FHLBB announced its regulations for mortgage-backed bonds issued by federally chartered savings and loan associations and FSLIC insured S&Ls in 1975. The FHLBB requires S&L mortgage-backed bonds to have at least a five-year maturity, and the principal balance of the mortgage pool must exceed the outstanding principal of the bonds by at least 35 percent. Most private mortgage-backed bonds are issued by savings and loan associations, and over one billion dollars of these bonds were issued in 1977. Mortgage-backed bonds provide a way to use seasoned mortgage loans with interest rates below current market rates in order to raise funds.

Private Pass-Through Certificates. The issuance of private pass-through certificates constitutes a sale of assets. The mortgages are typically transferred to a trust, and the trust issues the certificates. The institution establishing the trust maintains the servicing. The purchaser of a pass-through certificate receives a monthly payment of interest and principal. The pass-through certificate may be backed by a pool of FHA insured, VA guaranteed, or conventional mortgage loans.

The conventional loans may be uninsured or insured. The individual mortgage loans are normally covered by private mortgage insurance if the loan-to-value ratio exceeds 80 percent. In addition the mortgage pool itself is usually insured by a private mortgage insurance company. The private mortgage insurance on the pool covers losses occasioned by default in payment on any mortgage loan in an amount equal to five percent of the adjusted aggregate principal balances of the mortgage loans in the pool. The pool insurance fee is typically one-eighth of one percent on the unpaid balance of each mortgage loan in the pool until its maturity.

Privately issued conventional pass-through mortgage certificates, commonly called *Connie Macs,* can be either public issues or private placements. Underwriting costs typically require that public issues of private pass-throughs total at least $50 million per issue. A subsidiary of MGIC Investment Corporation assists small issuers to combine their offerings to make the issuance of pass-through certificates financially feasible. In addition, there are a number of privately placed issues of conventional pass-through certificates. Standard and Poors developed a rating system for issues of private mortgage pass-through certificates in December 1977. A favorable rating makes them eligible investments for pension funds, insurance companies, bank trust funds, and many other regulated investors.

The Bank of America made the first offering of Connie Macs in September 1977. About $200 million in Connie Macs were issued in 1977 and about $800 million per year were offered in 1978, 1979, and 1980. Over $3 billion in Connie Macs had been issued by mid-1981.[1] The investing public is becoming more familiar with Connie Macs. And organizations to assist depository institutions and mortgage companies in issuing Connie Macs are gaining experience and acceptance. Connie Macs consequently have the potential to be more important than GNMA guaranteed pass-through certificates. Also, during 1981, both FNMA and FHLMC were in the process of initiating programs to guarantee the interest and principal payments on conventional mortgage-backed securities issued by mortgage companies and institutional lenders.

SUMMARY

The FNMA is the largest single purchaser of residential mortgages in the secondary mortgage market. FNMA purchases FHA insured, VA guaranteed, and conventional mortgages. The FHLMC is the second largest purchaser of residential mortgages, and it primarily purchases conventional mortgages. GNMA, carrying out its special assistance function, purchases primarily FHA insured residential loans bearing below-market interest rates. The principal goal of GNMA's special assistance function is to promote the construction of housing for low- and moderate-income families.

By the start of the 1980s, mortgage pools securing mortgage-backed securities accounted for more than twice the dollar volume of mortgages held by FNMA, FHLMC, and GNMA combined. FHLMC and FmHA issue and insure or guarantee their own mortgage-backed securities. GNMA guaranteed pass-through certificates are issued primarily by mortgage companies, commercial banks, and S&Ls, and they are the most common types of mortgage-backed security. Privately issued conventional pass-through certificates without a GNMA guarantee became significant in the late 1970s and promise to increase in importance during the 1980s.

---

[1]William B. Ross, "Finding New Markets for Mortgages," *Mortgage Banking,* 41, no. 12 (September 1981), 20.

KEY TERMS

Bond Type Security

Competitive Bid

Connie Macs

FHLMC

FmHA

FmHA Mortgage-Backed
Security

FNMA

Forward Commitment

Free Market System

Fully Modified Pass-
Through Guarantee

GNMA

GNMA Guaranteed
Mortgage-Backed
Security

GNMA Guaranteed Pass-
Through Certificate

Guaranteed Mortgage
Certificate (GMC)

Mandatory Delivery
Commitment

Mortgage-Backed Security

Mortgage Participation
Certificate (PC)

Noncompetitive Bid

Optional Delivery
Commitment

Participation Certificate
(PC)

Pass-Through Type Security

Private Mortgage-Backed
Bonds

Private Pass-Through
Certificate

Tandem Plan

QUESTIONS FOR REVIEW AND DISCUSSION

1. Fannie Mae is the largest single purchaser of residential mortgages in the secondary mortgage market. Explain how FNMA obtains funds for all its purchases.

2. FNMA makes two types of commitments to buy loans (1) the optional delivery and (2) mandatory delivery under its free market system—explain each type of commitment. Explain how the free market system works.

3. What is the main function of the FHLMC? Where does the FHLMC get funds to carry out its functions?

4. What does GNMA do, that is, what is its function? How does Ginnie Mae get its funds?

5. What is the tandem plan? Explain.

6. What is a mortgage-backed security? How does the mortgage-backed security system work?

7. What types of mortgages qualify as to support a mortgage-backed security?

8. Match the following key terms and definitions:

   a. Free-Market
   System _____

   1. A requirement that mortgaged loans be delivered.

b. Tandem Plan   _____

c. Mortgage-Backed
   Security   _____

d. Pass-Through Type
   Security   _____

e. Forward
   Commitment   _____

f. Noncompetitive
   Bid   _____

2. Awarding of commitments on the basis of competitive bids at auctions.

3. An offering at weighted average of competitive bids.

4. GNMA commitment to purchase mortgage loans for subsequent resale to FNMA.

5. Certificates backed by specific mortgage loans and issued by the holder of the loans.

6. Interest and principal paid monthly.

7. An agreement to buy a mortgage loan.

APPENDICES

Glossary

Abstract and Opinion of Title. A condensed history of the property's ownership (abstract) and a lawyer's opinion of the significance of any defects in the title (opinion of title).

Abstract of Title. A digest of conveyances, transfers, wills, and other legal proceedings pertinent to the title of a property, such as liens, charges, or encumbrances.

Acceleration Clause. A provision in a mortgage loan contract, land contract, or trust deed giving the lender the right to declare the entire remaining principal balance due and immediately payable when the borrower violates one of the covenants in the contract.

Acknowledgment. A formal declaration made before a public officer such as a notary public signifying that the document is being signed voluntarily.

Actual Notice. The party has actual knowledge of the event. The buyer and seller have actual knowledge of the sale.

Adjustable Mortgage Loan (AML). A type of variable-rate loan that national banks are allowed to originate.

Adjustable-Rate Mortgage Loan (ARM). A type of variable-rate loan that federally chartered savings and loan associations are allowed to originate.

Alligator. A property that has a negative cash flow and must be "fed" cash in order for the owner to continue to hold the property.

Amortization. The systematic repayment of borrowed money or the systematic recovery of the original investment.

Annual Loan Constant. The ratio of the annual debt service to the amount borrowed. If the monthly debt service payment is $100, the total of the payments for the year is $1,200. If the amount of the loan is $10,000, the annual loan constant is 12 percent.

Annual Percentage Rate (APR). A measure of the effective interest rate. The Truth in Lending Act requires disclosure of the APR to the borrower.

Appraisal. An estimate or opinion of value of a property, or some interest therein, rendered by a person skilled in property analysis and valuation.

Appraisal Process. An orderly, well-conceived set of procedures for valuing property.

Appraised Value. The worth of a property as estimated by a qualified appraiser.

Assignee. The party receiving the rights of another party in an existing contractual agreement.

Assignment of Lease. Transfers the lessee's entire interest under the lease to another party.

Assignment of Mortgage. The transfer of a mortgage note and the lender's rights under the mortgage to another party.

Assignment of Rents. The owner transfers the right to collect the rents to the lender. Usually the lender can collect the rents after default by the owner-borrower.

Assignor. The party transferring his or her rights in an existing contractual agreement to another party.

Assumption of Mortgage. The purchaser agrees to become personally liable for the payment of the mortgage debt to the lender. The original borrower is not automatically released from his or her obligation to the lender.

Balloon Loan. A term or partially amortizing loan that requires the entire or a large portion of the principal to be paid at the end of the term.

Balloon Payment. A relatively large payment at the end of the term to pay off the unamortized principal of a loan.

Basis Point. One-hundredth of one percent. There are 100 basis points in one percent. Do not confuse a basis point with a point, which is one percent.

Basket Clause. A clause in regulations that allows a financial institution to invest a small portion of its funds without regard to other regulations.

Basket Loan. Some institutions such as life insurance companies and mutual savings banks are allowed to invest a small portion of their assets without regard to other regulations. This is called the leeway or basket provisions, and loans made under this provision are called basket loans.

Bearer Note. A note payable to the party having possession of the note rather than to a specified party.

Below-Market Interest Rate Mortgage Loan (BMIR). The interest rate charged is subsidized, such as in the case of mortgage loans subsidized by the issuance of securities exempt from federal income taxes.

Beneficiary. A party who receives the benefits of the acts of another. The beneficiary of a trust deed is the lender or subsequent holder of the note.

Blanket Mortgage. A mortgage that pledges two or more parcels of real estate as security for the debt.

Bond Type Security. They pay interest periodically, such as quarterly or semi-annually. The principal payment is made at the maturity of the security.

Borrower Analysis. An examination of the loan applicant's assets, income, expense-to-income ratio, and willingness to pay.

Borrower's Right to Reinstate. A right given in a loan contract that allows the borrower to correct breaches of the contract.

Borrower Risk. The lender's risk that the borrower either will not have the funds necessary to repay the loan or will not be willing to repay the loan.

Borrowing Short Term and Lending Long Term. A situation in which a lender makes long-term loans such as mortgage loans and raises funds on a short-term basis. If the lender makes long-term fixed interest rate loans and the cost of its funds rises, the lender may experience substantial losses.

BOY. Beginning of the year, such as BOY1—beginning of year one. A designation of time for time value of money purposes.

Breakeven Occupancy Ratio. Total of operating expenses including collection losses and debt service divided by gross scheduled income. It specifies the level of occupancy necessary to cover the debt service and operating expenses.

Bridge Loan. A loan for the period of time between the purchase of a new home and the sale of the old home.

Budget Mortgage Loan. The loan requires the borrower to make monthly payments covering interest, principal, and one-twelfth of the annual haz-

ard insurance premium and/or one-twelfth of the annual real estate taxes.

Build-to-Suit Lease. If the tenant signs a long-term lease, an investor will acquire the land and erect improvements to meet the needs of the tenant.

Business Risk. The risk of default or the variability of the return derived from the business. In mortgage lending, the risk is that the mortgage loan will yield less than the expected rate of return.

Buy-Build-Sell Leaseback. The firm buys the land, erects a building, and on completion sells it to an investor and immediately leases it back.

Buy-Down Loan. A loan in which someone other than the borrower, such as the seller, contributes cash to the borrower's mortgage payments during the early years of the loan.

Capital Market. The market in which intermediate- and long-terms loans, bonds, and stocks are originated and traded.

Capitalization. Conversion or discounting of expected future income payments into a lump-sum present value.

Capitalization Rate. Ratio of income to value; a combination of discount rate and a capital recovery rate. When divided into income, for example, from a property, a present or capitalized value for the property results.

Certificate of Deposit (CD). An intermediate-term (two- to ten-year) savings instrument that earns a higher rate of interest than a passbook account at a bank or savings and loan association.

Certificate of Reasonable Value (CRV). The statement of the value of the property as determined by the Veterans Administration.

Chattel Mortgage. A mortgage that offers personal property as security for the debt.

Closed Loan. A term loan that is unexpired and not in default.

Closing Statement. See *Settlement Statement.*

Cognovit Provision. See *Waiver of Defense Clause.*

Collateral. The property pledged as the security for a loan.

Collection Function. The function of mortgage loan servicing that consists of the collection of past due accounts.

Commercial Bank. A financial intermediary that was originally organized to finance business and agriculture. Although they make mortgage loans, they emphasize short- to intermediate-term loans. A substantial portion of their funds is obtained from demand deposits.

Commitment. A pledge or a promise to do or to refrain from doing something.

Community Reinvestment Act (CRA). A federal law requiring regulated financial institutions to serve the convenience and needs of the communities in which they operate.

Compound Interest. Interest collected on the original deposit and any future deposits plus that collected on the accumulated or accrued interest.

Competitive Bid. The bid specifies the yield that the bidder is willing to pay a purchaser, such as FNMA, for the funds received from the sale of the mortgages.

Comptroller of the Currency. The individual in charge of the regulation of national banks.

Condominium. Fee ownership of a unit of space in developed realty plus an undivided interest in common areas owned jointly with other condominium owners in the development.

Conforming Mortgage Loan. A loan that conforms to established standards, such as those set by FHLMC and FNMA.

Connie Mac. Privately issued mortgage-backed security that is secured by conventional mortgage loans and is not guaranteed by any governmental agency.

Construction Loan. A short-term loan to finance the construction or development of realty.

Constructive Notice. Notice given to third parties by recording the document in the public records.

Contract Interest Rate. The agreed rate of interest specified on the note or loan. Also known as the nominal interest rate or face rate of interest.

Contract Rent. The amount of money paid for the use of space or realty based on the existing lease agreement or contract.

Conventional Mortgage Loan. A loan that is not insured, guaranteed, or granted by a government or government agency.

Convertible Mortgage. The borrower makes interest payments in cash but the principal is repaid by giving the lender an increasing equity interest in the property.

Cooperative. Ownership of a membership certificate or stock in a corporation or trust that carries the right to occupy a specific unit of space under a proprietary lease. The cooperative owns the entire property.

Corporation. An entity or organization, created by operation of law, with rights of doing business essentially the same as those of an individual. The entity has continuous existence regardless of that of its owners, and it limits the liability of owners to the amount invested in the organization.

The entity ceases to exist only if dissolved according to proper legal process.

Cost Approach to Value. An appraisal procedure using depreciated replacement costs of improvements and fixtures plus land value as a basis for estimating the market value of the subject property. Also known as the summation approach.

Covenant. A promise.

Creative Financing. There is no clear agreement on the definition. It is essentially any situation in which the financing includes financing above and beyond a single new mortgage loan from a third party and the purchaser's equity payment. A broader definition is any financing other than a single, new, level payment, fixed interest, first mortgage loan from a third party.

Credit Financing. Refers to the lender making a loan to help to finance a property.

Credit Loan. In relation to financing the leased fee, the long-term lease with an organization having a high credit rating is considered to be the primary security for the loan.

Credit Report. A report describing the credit history of an individual or business.

Credit Union. A financial intermediary that accepts funds from and makes loans to its members. The members must have a common bond such as a common employer. They emphasize consumer lending.

Credit Worthy. The credit worthy individual has consistently met financial commitments or obligations in a satisfactory manner and it is probable that he or she will continue to do such.

Curable Depreciation. Describes physical deterioration or functionally obsolete items that add more to value if corrected than the cost of correction.

Current Ratio. Calculated by dividing current assets by current liabilities. It indicates the ability to meet short-term obligations.

Debt Financing. Refers to the owner's use of borrowed funds to finance the property.

Debt Service. The periodic payment on a loan that usually includes both interest and principal repayment.

Debt Service Coverage Ratio (DSC). Net operating income divided by debt service.

Deed in Lieu of Foreclosure. An owner-borrower conveyance of the equity interest to a lender when in default to avoid foreclosure costs and procedures when the equity is less than costs of foreclosure.

Deed of Reconveyance. A deed from the trustee returning title to the owner-borrower-trustor to clear a trust deed. It is the equivalent of a mortgage release or satisfaction piece. Also known as reconveyance deed, release deed, or deed of release.

Deed of Release. See *Deed of Reconveyance.*

Deed of Trust. See *Trust Deed.*

Default. Failure to fulfill or live up to the terms of an agreement or contract; for example, in a mortgage loan contract, most often the failure to make the scheduled periodic payments to service the loan.

Default in Prior Mortgage Clause. A provision in a junior mortgage that allows the junior mortgage holder to correct the borrower's breach of the terms of a prior mortgage.

Default Ratio. The debt service divided by the net operating income of an income property. The higher the ratio, the higher the probability of default, all other things being equal.

Defeasance Clause. A mortgage provision returning clear title to the borrower-mortgagor after all terms of the loan, including repayment, have been met.

Deficiency Judgment. A judicial decree in favor of the lender for that portion of a mortgage debt that remains unsatisfied after default, foreclosure, and sale of the property pledged as security.

Demand Loan. A short-term loan that has no specified maturity date or that is callable before the specified maturity date. It is payable on demand by the lender.

Depreciation. A loss or decline in the utility contained in an asset, resulting in loss in value.

DIDMC Act of 1980. The Depository Institutions Deregulation and Monetary Control Act of 1980. It expanded the consumer installment-lending authority for S&Ls, provided for the phase-out of interest rate ceilings on deposits, and placed reserve requirements on transaction accounts in all depository institutions.

Discount. To reduce the value of a future payment or series of future payments, for example, to make an adjustment for the difference in time of receipt and the rate of discounting. The amount below the face value of, for instance, a mortgage loan. The opposite of a premium.

Discount Rate. The percentage used in time value of money calculations to find the present value of a future payment. The percentage charge for funds borrowed from a Federal Reserve bank.

Disintermediation. The process of savers withdrawing money from financial institutions and investing the money directly in the financial markets.

Diversification. To make varied. Diversification can serve to reduce the risk associated with a loan portfolio. Types of diversification include the area of lending, type of property, the group of borrowers, and the time of lending.

Dollar Discount. The dollar amount deducted from the loan balance or face amount of the loan.

Dollar Premium. The dollar amount of the market value of the loan in excess of the outstanding principal balance of the loan.

Due-on-Sale Clause. A provision in a mortgage that makes the outstanding loan balance and accrued interest due when the borrower sells his or her interest in the property securing the debt. Also known as an alienation clause.

Duration. The duration of a loan is the life or contract period of a loan. The time over which a loan is to be repaid.

Economic Depreciation. Diminished utility and value of a site or property because external factors and environment unfavorably affect its income or potential income. Also known as economic, environmental, and locational obsolescence.

Effective Gross Income. Revenues actually collected in operating an income property; gross scheduled income less allowances for vacancies and uncollectible rents.

Effective Interest Rate. The rate of interest received by the lender-investor or paid by the borrower.

End Loan. The long-term loan whose proceeds are used to pay off the interim loans created during the development process.

EOY. End of the year, for instance, EOY1—end of year one. A designation of time for time value of money purposes.

Equal Credit Opportunity Act (ECOA). A federal law forbidding discrimination in the granting of credit because of race, color, religion, national origin, age, sex, marital status, or the fact that all or part of the applicant's income is derived from a public assistance program.

Equal Principal Reduction Loan. A loan that provides for equal principal payments plus interest on the declining principal balance. The total debt service payment decreases with each payment.

Equitable Mortgage. A document that does not meet the state statutory requirements for a regular mortgage, but the court declares it to be a financing arrangement and treats it as a mortgage.

Equitable Right of Redemption. A borrower's right to recover a mortgaged property prior to foreclosure upon payment of debt, interest, and other costs of the lender. Also known as the equity of redemption.

Equitable Title. The right to legal title on the performance of specified acts. The purchaser has equitable title when he or she signs the real estate sales contract.

Equity. The owner's interest in the property. The disposition value of a property less any transaction costs and any liens or encumbrances against the property.

Equity Financing. Refers to the use of the owner's or buyer's funds to finance the property. In the case of 100 percent equity financing, the owner does not use any borrowed funds.

Equity Kicker. The lender receives an equity interest in the pledged property. Also see *Kicker.*

Equity of Redemption. See *Equitable Right of Redemption.*

Equity Participation Mortgage. A mortgage agreement that allows the lender to receive a portion of the equity in the pledged property in an addition to interest.

Escalator Clause. A provision that allows the lender to increase the interest rate and/or the payments on the debt after the occurrence of some specified event.

Escalator Lease. An agreement basing the rental payments on changes in costs or the movements in a specified index. Also known as an index lease.

Escrow Account. See *Impound Account.*

Escrow for Deed. The deed is deposited with a third party, an escrow agent, to be held until the terms of the real estate sales contract are fulfilled.

Estoppel Certificate. A written statement that, when signed and given to another party, legally prevents the person signing from subsequently saying that the facts are different from those set forth.

Excess Reserves. The amount of reserves that an institution has in excess of the amount of reserves required by the Federal Reserve System or other regulator.

Exculpatory Clause. A provision such as that in a mortgage loan agreement holding the borrower blameless in default and thereby limiting the borrower's personal liability. See *Sole Security Clause.*

Expense-to-Income Ratio. A ratio calculated by dividing expenses by income. Home buyers usually have to conform to a specified expense-to-income ratio to qualify for a mortgage loan.

Extension. The continuation of a contract or agreement. For example, the lender postpones the maturity date of the debt.

Face Rate of Interest. See *Contract Interest Rate.*

Fair Credit Reporting Act. A federal law requiring that information in credit reports be accurate and relevant.

Fannie Mae. See *Federal National Mortgage Association.*

Farmers Home Administration (FmHA). An agency within the U.S. Department of Agriculture that engages in a number of activities including the insurance or guarantee of mortgage loans on rural housing units.

Federal Deposit Insurance Corporation (FDIC). Insures deposits in commercial banks and many mutual savings banks.

Federal Home Loan Bank System (FHLBS). It is comprised of Federal Home Loan Banks, FSLIC, FHLMC, and member institutions, which are primarily savings and loan associations. It regulates its members and provides loans to member institutions.

Federal Home Loan Mortgage Corporation (FHLMC). Provides a secondary mortgage market and issues mortgage-backed securities. It is part of the FHLBS. It is also known as Freddie Mac and the Mortgage Corporation.

Federal Housing Administration (FHA). It insures mortgage loans made by approved lenders to qualified borrowers. It specifies minimum property standards to protect the borrower employing an FHA insured loan.

Federal Land Banks (FLBs). Part of the Cooperative Farm Credit System, which is administered by the Farm Credit Administration. They are the leading lender on farm property. The loans are originated by Federal Land Bank associations.

Federally Chartered. The charter authorizing the operation of the organization is granted by the federal government or an agency of the federal government.

Federal National Mortgage Association (FNMA). Provides a secondary mortgage market for residential mortgage loans. Also known as Fannie Mae.

Federal Reserve System. It is under the control of the Board of Governors of the Federal Reserve System, who are directed to use monetary policy to achieve economic goals. They establish the reserve requirements for transaction accounts at all depository institutions.

Federal Savings and Loan Insurance Corporation (FSLIC). It insures the deposits at most savings and loan associations and some mutual savings banks. Also known as Freddie Slic.

FHA. See *Federal Housing Administration.*

FHA Conditional Commitment. A commitment for mortgage insurance made by FHA after receiving the appraisal and determining that the property meets or will meet minimum property standards. The insurance is conditional on the approval of the borrower.

FHA Firm Commitment. A commitment for mortgage insurance made by FHA after both the property and the borrower have met the specified standards.

FHA Mortgage Loan. A mortgage loan insured by the Federal Housing Administration.

FHLMC. See *Federal Home Loan Mortgage Corporation.*

Fiduciary. A party occupying a position of trust and confidence to handle a financial transaction for another in good faith.

Finance Company. Finance companies include sales finance companies, consumer finance companies, and commercial finance companies. A finance company raises most of its funds by borrowing and invests its funds in business loans and/or consumer loans. They are significant sources of second mortgage loans.

Financial Intermediary. An institution that receives funds from parties that have excess funds and channels the funds to parties willing to pay for the use of additional funds.

Financial Markets. The markets in which all types of loans and equity interests are originated and traded.

Financial Risk. The risk that is added by the use of borrowed funds in the business. In mortgage lending it is the risk that the cost of funds will approach or exceed the yield from the mortgage portfolio. This leads to losses and possible insolvency.

First Mortgage. A mortgage that has first claim on the proceeds from the sale of the pledged property. It has priority over all other mortgages on the property.

Fiscal Policy. Adjustments in the government's expenditures and taxes to achieve an acceptable balance in the nation's economic goals of full employment, economic growth, and price stability.

Fixed-Rate Mortgage Loan (FRM). A mortgage loan in which the interest rate is held constant through the life of the loan.

Flexible Loan Insurance Program Mortgage Loan. See *FLIP Mortgage Loan.*

Flexible Payment Mortgage Loan (FPM). A loan in which there is a variation within the payment schedule. The loan could provide for interest-only payments in the early years and payments of both interest and principal thereafter.

FLIP Mortgage Loan. The flexible loan insurance program mortgage loan employs a pledged savings account. The lender receives level debt service payments, but the borrower makes increasing out-of-pocket debt service payments. The difference between the payment received by the lender and the out-of-pocket payment made by the borrower represents withdrawals from the pledged savings account.

Flood Insurance.   Provides protection against losses due to flood damage. It is offered by private insurance companies and subsidized by the federal government.

Floor-to-Ceiling Loan.   A loan agreement that specifies some minimum amount that will be advanced on completion and a maximum that will be advanced if the project meets a specified occupancy ratio.

FmHA.   See *Farmers Home Administration.*

FmHA Mortgage-Backed Securities.   The Farmers Home Administration places its mortgage holdings in mortgage pools and issues mortgage-backed securities.

FmHA Mortgage Loan.   A mortgage loan insured or guaranteed by the Farmers Home Administration.

FNMA.   See *Federal National Mortgage Association.*

Forbearance by Lender.   If the lender does not take action when the borrower defaults on a covenant, it is forbearance on the part of the lender.

Foreclosure.   A legal process initiated by the mortgagee or other lien creditor that specifies the time period in which the equitable redemption must be exercised. If the property is not redeemed within the specified period, it is usually sold to satisfy the mortgagee's claim.

Foreclosure and Public Sale.   A legal proceeding in which the defaulted property is sold at a public sale after termination of the equitable right of redemption in order to satisfy the mortgagee's claim.

Foreclosure by Entry.   A method of foreclosure employed in some New England states in which the lender takes possession either peacefully without court action or with a writ of entry.

Forfeiture Clause.   A provision in a land contract that allows the seller to keep the buyer's payments as liquidated damages when the buyer defaults on the terms of the contract. Also known as a liquidated damages clause.

Forward Commitment.   The party making the commitment issues it prior to the existence of the mortgage loan. The lender receiving the commitment originates the mortgage loan only after it has a commitment from another party to purchase the mortgage loan.

Freddie Mac.   See *Federal Home Loan Mortgage Corporation.*

Free Market System (FMS).   The commitments to purchase mortgages are awarded on the basis of competitive bids at auctions. FNMA employs the FMS.

FSLIC.   See *Federal Savings and Loan Insurance Corporation.*

Fully Amortizing Loan.   A loan in which the periodic payments of interest and principal throughout the term pay off the entire debt. There is no balloon payment.

Fully Modified Pass-Through Guarantee.   The party guaranteeing the mortgage-backed securities guarantees that the security holder will receive all interest and principal payments even if the issuer is not able to collect such.

Functional Depreciation.   The loss in value because a property cannot render a service in a given use as well as a new property designed for the use. Also known as functional obsolescence.

Future Value (FV).   The value of a deposit or series of deposits invested at compound interest at some specified date in the future. For example, a deposit of $100 invested today at a 10 percent interest rate has a future value of $110 at the end of one year.

Gap Loan.   A short-term second mortgage loan used to finance the difference between the amount received from a permanent loan and the total amount required to pay off the construction loan.

General Partnership.   All partners are general partners, and they all share in the management responsibilities and have unlimited liability in the event of losses.

Gift Letter.   A letter stating that the funds given to an individual are actually a gift and do not have to be repaid.

GI Guaranteed Mortgage Loan.   See *VA Guaranteed Mortgage Loan.*

Ginnie Mae.   See *Government National Mortgage Association.*

GNMA.   See *Government National Mortgage Association.*

GNMA Guaranteed Mortgage-Backed Securities.   Securities backed by pools of FHA insured or VA guaranteed mortgages and GNMA's guarantee of interest and/or principal payments to the security holders. They are either pass-through certificates or bond type securities.

GNMA Guaranteed Pass-Through Certificates.   Pass-through securities, also known as Ginnie Maes, that are backed by pools of FHA insured and VA guaranteed mortgage loans. GNMA guarantees that the security holders will receive interest and/or principal. Mortgage companies are the major issuers.

Government National Mortgage Association (GNMA).   An agency within HUD that provides a secondary mortgage market for specified types of mortgages, guarantees mortgage-backed securities, and administers a portfolio of mortgages. Also known as Ginnie Mae.

GPAM.   See *Graduated Payment Adjustable Mortgage Loan.*

Graduated Payment Adjustable Mortgage Loan (GPAM). A loan that combines the features of a graduated payment loan and an adjustable interest rate loan.

Graduated Payment Mortgage Loan. A loan in which the debt service payments begin at a low level and increase at a certain rate each year until they reach a predetermined level.

Gross Lease. A lease in which the tenant pays a stated rental and the lessor is responsible for the payment of real estate taxes, insurance, and maintenance costs.

Gross Scheduled Income. The potential income for the property if all space was rented out and all rentals collected. Also known as potential gross income.

Ground Lease. A lease giving use and occupancy of a vacant site or unimproved land. The tenant often has the right to erect improvements on the land. Also applies to a lease of improved property when the tenant intends to remove the existing improvements and erect new improvements.

Guaranteed Mortgage Certificate (GMC). Mortgage-backed securities issued by FHLMC. As the issuer, FHLMC pays interest semiannually and principal annually. FHLMC also agrees to repurchase the unpaid principal at par, normally at the end of 15 years.

Guerrilla Financing. Land contracts and first and junior mortgage loans originated by the seller.

Hard Money. Cash.

Hazard Insurance. A contract in which an insurer promises to compensate the insured party for losses on a specific property caused by specified hazards such as fire and wind.

Home Improvement Loan. A loan whose proceeds are used to finance home improvements such as remodeling the kitchen.

Home Mortgage Disclosure Act. A federal law requiring lenders to disclose the geographic distribution of their one- to four-family residential lending activities by zip codes or census tract numbers.

Housing Finance Agency. An agency of a state or local government that assists in the provision of mortgage loans. This can be by insurance, direct loans, or purchases in the secondary market.

HUD. The Department of Housing and Urban Development has a wide range of duties including the provision of adequate housing for low- and moderate-income households and community development grants. It supervises FHA, GNMA, and some aspects of FNMA activities.

Hypothecate. To pledge specific property as security for a debt or obligation without surrendering possession of the property.

Impound Account. An account established with another party to set aside funds for future needs such as the payment of real estate taxes or insurance premiums.

Income Approach to Value. An appraisal procedure using capitalization of the expected future income or utility (amenities) as a basis for estimating the market value of the subject property.

Income Participation Loan. A loan agreement that allows the lender to collect a base interest rate plus a share in the income generated by the project financed by the loan.

Incurable Depreciation. Physical deterioration, economic depreciation, or functionally obsolete items that would cost more to correct than the correction would add to value.

Individual Loan Risk. The risk that a given mortgage loan will result in a default and that the lender will realize a loss of principal and/or interest.

Insured Conventional Mortgage Loan. A conventional mortgage loan insured by a private mortgage insurance company.

Interest. The rent or price paid for the use of money; usually calculated as a percent per month or year of the amount borrowed.

Interest Due in Advance. Interest accruing, calculated, and payable at the beginning of each period. Also known as prepaid interest.

Interest in Arrears. Interest accruing, calculated, and payable at the end of each period.

Interest Rate Risk. The risk that interest rates will rise and cause a decline in the market value of the investment such as the portfolio of mortgage loans.

Interim Loan. A relatively short term-loan such as a construction loan. It is to be replaced by other financing.

Intermediate Theory. A theory of mortgage law that falls between the title theory and the lien theory.

Intermediation. The process of individuals and others placing their excess funds in financial institutions who transfer the use of the funds to parties needing and willing to pay for the use of those funds.

Internal Rate of Return (IRR). The yield or discount rate that equates the present value of future cash flows to the initial cash investment in the project. Sometimes known as the true rate of return or the equity rate of return.

Joint Venture. A combining of personal and financial abilities of two or more parties in a specific project. Also see *Syndicate*.

Judgment Lien. A court decree of indebtedness to another that fixes the amount of the debt. The lien is usually a general lien, but it could be a specific lien relating to a given parcel of real estate.

Junior Mortgage. Any mortgage other than a first mortgage or any mortgage that has lesser priority than another mortgage.

Kicker. Any benefit to the lender above ordinary interest, for example, a portion of any increased income, a share of any appreciation in value, or an equity interest in the pledged property.

Land Acquisition Loan. A loan used to acquire land.

Land Contract. A written agreement for the purchase of and payment for real property over an extended period of time, with recorded title remaining in the seller until the terms of the agreement are satisfied. Also known as contract for deed, installment sales contract, and land sale contract.

Land Development Loan. A loan that is used to finance the installation of utilities, streets, and other site improvements.

Landlord. See *Lessor*.

Late Payment Penalty Clause. A provision in a note that allows the lender to charge a late payment penalty if the past due payment is received after a specified time period.

Lease. An agreement giving possession and use of property in return for a specified rent payment.

Leased Fee. The landlord's rights in the leased property. Also known as a leased fee estate.

Leased Fee Mortgage. A mortgage that pledges the landlord's interest in the property as security for the debt.

Leasehold. The tenant's rights in the leased property. Also known as a leasehold estate.

Leasehold Mortgage. A mortgage that pledges the tenant's interest in a leasehold as security for the debt.

Leeway Clause. See *Basket Clause*.

Lessee. A person to whom property is rented under a lease. Also known as the tenant.

Lessor. The one who owns the right to use and occupy a property, which is transferred to another (a lessee) under a lease agreement. When real estate is involved the lessor is also known as the landlord.

Level Payment Loan. A loan that requires equal periodic debt service payments throughout the life of the loan.

Leverage. Use of other people's funds such as borrowed funds to increase the rate of return on the owner's investment. It is sometimes known as trading on the equity. Also see *Negative Leverage.*

Leveraged Sale-Leaseback. A sale and leaseback in which the purchaser borrows a substantial portion of the funds necessary to buy the property.

Lien. A claim, enforceable by law, to have a debt or charge satisfied out of the property belonging to the debtor.

Lien Theory. The theory of mortgage law that views a mortgage as merely a lien against the pledged property.

Life Insurance Company (LIC). A financial intermediary founded to offer financial protection for the beneficiaries of insurance policies.

Limited Partnership. A partnership arrangement whereby some members, termed limited or silent partners, are exempt by law from liability in excess of their contribution. Silent partners cannot participate in management under penalty of losing their limited liability status. The managing partners are termed operating or general partners.

Liquid Assets. Cash or assets that can be converted into cash quickly with little loss in value.

Liquidated Damages Clause. A clause in a contract that establishes a predetermined amount that will be paid to the injured party if the contract is breached. Also known as a forfeiture clause.

Liquidity. Relative ease or difficulty of converting an asset into cash at close to the market value of the investment; the higher the ease, the greater the liquidity.

Liquidity Risk. The risk of being unable to sell an asset such as a mortgage loan at a price near the last transaction price or near its long term or market value.

Lis Pendens. Notice of a suit pending.

Loan Application. Usually a written document stating the amount of loan and terms requested, identifying the property pledged, if any, and furnishing information about the characteristics of the prospective borrowers.

Loan Commitment. A pledge or promise, usually in writing, made by a lender to make a loan at a future date subject to the compliance with specified conditions.

Loan Correspondent. A party such as a mortgage banker that negotiates or originates loans for other lenders or investors. The correspondent often retains servicing of the loan.

Loan Discount. An amount deducted from the face amount of the loan or from the principal balance due. A loan discount raises the effective interest rate earned by the lender or purchaser of the loan.

Loan Interview. A meeting between the prospective borrower and lender in which the lender explains its general underwriting guidelines.

Loan Origination. The process in which the lender brings about a mortgage loan agreement with the borrower.

Loan Rating Grid. A document listing the various factors affecting the risks associated with the loan on the vertical axis and either comments or gives numerical ratings for the factors on the horizontal axis. The ratings can be totaled to assess the total risks.

Loan Servicing. The collection of loan payments, bookkeeping, preparation of real estate tax and insurance records, follow-up on delinquent loans, and other duties involved with seeing that the borrower complies with the terms of the loan agreement. It may also include foreclosure action.

Loan Terms Analysis. An examination of the amount of the loan requested, the loan-to-value ratio, the requested term, interest rate, and requested repayment pattern.

Loan-to-Value Ratio (LVR). The proportion of property's market value financed by a loan, expressed as a percentage.

Loan Underwriting. The process of examining the risks inherent in a given loan application and of deciding whether to accept or reject the requested loan. The underwriter analyzes the terms, the property, and the borrower characteristics.

Management Agreement. In relation to mortgage loans, it refers to an agreement between the borrower and lender to employ a competent manager for the property in order to avoid the necessity of a foreclosure.

Mandatory Delivery Commitment. The party making the commitment to buy the mortgage loans requires the successful bidder to deliver the mortgage loans.

Market Approach to Value. An appraisal procedure using the sale prices of properties similar to the subject property as a basis for estimating the market value of the subject property. Also known as direct sales comparison approach to value.

Market Interest Rate. The rate of interest currently demanded by lenders and investors in the market, or the rate currently paid for new loans.

Market Price. The amount actually paid or payable in a buy-sell agreement. It may be above, equal to, or below market value.

Market Rent. The amount of money that space or realty would bring if it was being rented today for its highest and best use. Also known as economic rent.

Market Value.   The price at which a property will sell, assuming a knowledge-able buyer and seller both operating with reasonable knowledge and without undue pressure. Also known as fair market value.

Maturity.   The due date or the time at which the debt, such as a mortgage note, becomes due and must be paid in full.

Mechanic's Lien.   A statutory lien in favor of those who performed work or furnished materials for the improvement of realty.

Mobile Home Loan.   A loan agreement in which a mobile home is offered as security for the debt.

Monetary Policy.   Adjustments in the nation's money supply to achieve an acceptable balance in the nation's economic goals of full employment, economic growth, and price stability.

Money Market.   The markets in which funds are borrowed or lent for short periods of less than one year.

Money Market Certificate (MMC).   A short-term (182-day) savings instrument that carries an interest rate based on the average yield of U.S. Government six-month Treasury bills in the most recent auction.

Monthly Draw Method.   In large projects it takes an extended period of time to complete a given stage of completion, therefore the advances on a construction loan are made on a monthly basis if adequate progress is being made.

Moral Suasion.   Efforts by political leaders to restrict or ease credit without direct regulation, for instance, by persuading bankers to hold to or change certain policies. It is also used in such cases as appeals by government for increased saving and the acceptance of lower wages to fight inflation.

Moratorium.   In a relation to a loan, the lender waives the principal payment and/or interest payment for some reasonable period of time.

Mortgage.   A pledge of property, usually real property, as security for a debt or obligation.

Mortgage Adjustments.   Changes in the terms of the loan agreement that are usually made to avoid the necessity of foreclosure.

Mortgage-Backed Securities.   The securities are secured by a pool of mortgage loans.

Mortgage Banker.   An organization that uses its own funds to originate mortgage loans with the expectation of selling the mortgage loans and retaining the right to service them for a fee.

Mortgage Broker. A person or organization who, for a fee, obtains mortgage money for a potential borrower or who finds a willing borrower for a potential lender.

Mortgage Clause. In a land contract, the clause allows the seller to obtain a mortgage loan on the property after the land contract is signed.

Mortgage Company. A company whose major activity is mortgage banking. It often engages in mortgage brokerage and sideline activities such as development.

Mortgagee. The lender in a mortgage loan agreement in whose favor the property is pledged as security.

Mortgagee in Possession. The lender obtains possession but not ownership of the pledged property after default by the borrower.

Mortgagee in Possession Clause. A provision that allows the lender to request possession of the property when foreclosure action is initiated.

Mortgagee's Title Insurance Policy. Compensates the lender for losses due to defects in the borrower's title.

Mortgage for Future Advances. An open-end mortgage such as one for a construction loan in which a number of advances are secured by the mortgage.

Mortgage Loan Servicing. See *Loan Servicing.*

Mortgage Market. The markets in which mortgage loans are originated and traded.

Mortgage Note. A promissory note that is secured by a mortgage.

Mortgage Participation Certificates (PCs). Mortgage-backed pass-through certificates issued by FHLMC. As the issuer, FHLMC guarantees the monthly payments of interest and principal to the certificate holders.

Mortgagor. The borrower in a mortgage loan agreement who pledges the property as security.

Motivation. The desire, drive, incentive, or impulse that drives a person to some act or goal. Motivation for a loan is a factor that the lender considers in the loan underwriting decision process.

Mutual Organization. An organization that is owned by its members. In the case of a mutual financial organization, it is owned by the depositors who expect to earn interest on their deposits. Profits are retained by the mutual organization.

Mutual Savings Bank (MSB). A financial intermediary that was founded to accept the funds of small savers. They invest a substantial portion of their funds in residential mortgage loans. They are found primarily in the Northeast. Also known as savings banks.

National Bank. A commercial bank that is federally chartered.

Negative Leverage. If the cost of funds obtained from others exceeds the rate of return on the property, the owner's rate of return may be sharply reduced.

Net Lease. A lease in which the tenant pays a stated rental and some or all of the cost of ownership such as real estate taxes, insurance, and maintenance. Also see *Triple Net Lease*.

Net Operating Income (NOI). Earnings of an income property after operating and maintenance expenses are deducted but before interest and depreciation deductions are deducted.

Nominal Interest Rate. The interest rate that is specified on the face of an agreement. See *Contract Interest Rate*.

Noncompetitive Bid. The bid specifies the dollar amount of mortgage loans that the party desires to sell but not the yield. The yield received by the purchaser is dictated by the purchaser. The yield may be the weighted average yield of competitive bids accepted.

Noninsured Pension Fund. A private pension fund that is not administered by a life insurance company. A majority are administered by the trust department of commercial banks.

Nonliquid Assets. Assets that cannot be converted into cash quickly or those that can be converted into cash quickly only if the seller is willing to absorb a substantial loss in value.

Novation. When the purchaser signs the mortgage note and assumes the debt, the original borrower is released from any obligation to pay the debt.

NOW Account. Negotiable order of withdrawal accounts offered by mutual savings banks and savings and loan associations: They are the equivalent of interest-bearing checking accounts.

Obligee. The party that is to receive payment under the terms of the promissory note.

Obligor. The borrower who promises to pay the debt evidenced by a promissory note.

Occupancy Ratio. The percentage of space occupied. It can be measured by dividing the rental due under the leases by the gross scheduled income. Or it can be measured in physical terms.

Open-End Mortgage. A mortgage contract that allows the borrower to obtain additional funds under the same mortgage.

Open Loan. A term mortgage loan that is past due and on which the lender has not declared a default; thus it becomes a demand loan.

Open-Market Operations. The buying and selling of monetary instruments by the Federal Reserve to regulate the money supply and influence interest rates.

Operating Ratio. For an income property, operating expenses divided by gross scheduled income. It is sometimes referred to as the operating expense ratio and is calculated by dividing operating expenses by effective gross income.

Option. An agreement in which one party holds open an offer usually for a specified period of time.

Optional Delivery Commitment. The party making the commitment to buy the mortgage loan gives the potential seller the option not to sell the loan.

Optionee. The party for whom the offer is held open, such as the potential buyer in an option to purchase.

Optionor. The party making the promise to hold open an offer, such as the potential seller in an option to purchase.

Option to Purchase. An agreement whereby an owner agrees to sell a property at a stipulated price to a potential buyer usually within a specified length of time. The buyer is not required to exercise the option.

Option to Sell. An agreement whereby a party agrees to buy a property at a stipulated price from a potential seller usually within a specified length of time. The seller is not required to exercise the option.

Origination. See *Loan Origination.*

Owner Rent Clause. A provision that allows the lender or receiver to charge the owner reasonable rent for occupancy of the property after foreclosure action is begun.

Owner Takeback of a Mortgage. The seller accepts a mortgage as partial payment for the property rather than demanding that the buyer pay the entire purchase price in cash at the time of the sale.

Owner's Title Insurance Policy. Compensates the owner for losses due to defects in title.

Package Mortgage. A mortgage that offers both real property and personal property as security for the debt.

Partial Release Clause. A provision in a blanket mortgage that requires the lender to release a given parcel of real estate on the payment of a specified portion of the debt.

Partially Amortizing Loan. A loan calling for systematic repayment of a portion of the principal throughout the life of the loan with a balloon payment at the end of the term.

Participation Mortgage. A mortgage loan in which two or more persons or institutions are lenders.

Pass-Through Type Securities. The issuer of this type of mortgage-backed securities promises to distribute the mortgage payments received from the mortgagors to the holders of the securities. The security holders normally receive interest and principal payments monthly.

Pension Fund. Funds that are accumulated during the employment years of individuals in order to provide those individuals with retirement income.

Percent Discount. The dollar amount deducted from the loan balance or face amount divided by the loan balance or face amount. The dollar discount stated as a percentage.

Percent Premium. The dollar amount of the premium divided by the outstanding principal balance of the loan. The premium is stated as a percentage.

Percentage Lease. An agreement basing the rental payment on a percentage of sales or income generated by the property. Often it provides for a fixed rental plus a percentage.

Permanent Loan. A long-term loan. The term is often used in relation to the long-term loan whose proceeds are used to pay off the construction loan.

Permanent Take-Out Commitment. The lender's promise to provide a long-term loan for the purpose of paying off the construction loan.

Physical Depreciation. A loss in value because of physical deterioration or impairment brought about by use in service, acts of God, or actions of the elements. Also known as physical deterioration.

Piggyback Mortgage. A type of privately insured participation mortgage loan. One lender is given a priority interest in the lien on the property. The other lender is given a priority claim on the proceeds from the private mortgage insurance policy.

PITI. Acronym for payments to a lender that cover principal, interest, taxes, and insurance on the property. Also known as PIIT.

Pledged Savings Account Mortgage Loan (PAL). A savings account used as additional security for a loan or used as a source of part of the debt service payments.

Point. Discount or premium made on the origination or the sale of a mortgage loan. Each point equals one percent of the loan amount.

Policy Loan. A loan made by a life insurance company to one of its policyholders. The loan is secured by the cash surrender value of the policy, and it normally carries a low interest rate.

Policy Reserves. Funds set aside and invested by insurance companies to meet future or contingent liabilities.

Pooling Effect. Assuming that there is less than perfect correlation between the risks associated with various investments as the number of investments in the portfolio increases, the total portfolio risk tends to decrease. Also known as the law of large numbers.

Portfolio. All the investments held by one individual or institution. A mortgage loan portfolio is all the mortgages held by an investor.

Portfolio Risk. The risk of receiving less than the expected rate or return on the portfolio. Mortgage loan portfolio risks include administrative, business, financial, interest rate, liquidity, and purchasing power risks.

Power of Sale. The right of a trustee to sell property in default on a trust deed loan without court proceedings. In some states the mortgagee can exercise the power of sale in a mortgage.

Premium. Amount above face value of a mortgage loan, for example; the opposite of a discount.

Prepayment Clause. A provision in the loan contract setting forth the conditions under which the loan can be prepaid.

Prepayment Penalty. A charge made by the lender if the borrower pays the debt before it is due.

Prepayment Privilege. The right of the borrower to pay the debt ahead of schedule.

Present Value. The current monetary value of future benefits or income; the discounted value of future payments.

PR Factor. Principal recovery factor. A time value of money multiplier to convert a current, lump-sum principal value, such as a mortgage loan, into a series of equal, periodic payments sufficient for amortization over the loan period or term. Also known as the installment to amortize one factor.

Primary Lender. A lender that originates loans.

Principal. Either the original amount of a loan or the remaining balance of a loan. The capital amount of a loan or investment that must be covered over the term of the loan or investment before any interest or profit can be earned.

Private Mortgage-Backed Bonds. Bond type mortgage-backed securities that are issued without any governmental guarantees.

Private Mortgage Insurance. Insurance issued by a private company that compensates the lender for any loss on a loan up to a specified percentage of the amount of the loan.

Private Pass-Through Certificates. Mortgage-backed pass-through certificates issued without guarantees or sponsorship in some form from governmental agencies. Both the mortgages in the pool and the mortgage pools are usually covered by private mortgage insurance.

Pro Forma Operating Statement. Shows the estimated income and expenses for a subject property for a specified future period.

Promissory Note. Statement, signed by the debtor or borrower, acknowledging a debt and the terms under which the debt is to be repaid.

Property Analysis. An examination of the appraisal report and the probable market value of the property in the early years of the loan.

Property Risk. The risk that the value of the property will be insufficient to pay the lender's claim when the lender must take action to collect the debt.

Proration. A division or distribution of proportionate shares of income or expenses, such as the division of real estate taxes between the buyer and seller at a title closing.

Prudent Man Rule. The legal expectation that an investment administrator or trustee handle funds entrusted to him or her in the same rational and careful manner that a prudent man would exercise in investing his own funds.

Public Trustee. A trustee that holds a government position such as a county clerk.

Purchase Money Mortgage (PMM). In the usual sense, a mortgage given by the purchaser to the seller as part of the purchaser's consideration for the property. In a broad sense, a mortgage given to a secure a loan to purchase the property pledged as security.

Purchasing Power Risk. The risk that the general price level will rise and the dollars received in the future will purchase less.

PV1 Factor. Present value of one. A time value of money multiplier used to convert a single payment in the future into a current lump-sum value.

PV1/P Factor. Present value of one per period factor. A time value of money multiplier used to convert a series of equal or level payments to be received in the future into a current lump-sum value.

Pyramiding. The process of continually using real property, or other assets, already owned to serve as collateral in acquiring additional property and thereby to expand one's holdings.

Real Estate Investment Trust (REIT). An organization that invests in real estate equities and/or mortgages and qualifies for special tax treatment. If it meets the basic requirements including the distribution of at least 90 percent of its earnings, it does not pay federal income tax on the earnings that it distributes to the investors.

Real Estate Mortgage. A mortgage that offers real property as security for the debt.

Real Estate Settlement Procedures Act (RESPA). A federal law requiring disclosure of settlement costs and the use of uniform settlement statements and having other provisions such as the prohibition of kickbacks.

Recasting. Keeping the same loan but changing some of the terms of the loan agreement such as the interest rate, debt service payments, or the amortization period.

Receiver. Usually a disinterested third party appointed by a court to preserve and manage the property in the best interests of both the borrower and lender.

Receiver Clause. A provision that allows the lender to request the appointment of a receiver to protect the lender's interest after default by the borrower.

Reconveyance Deed. See *Deed of Reconveyance.*

Redlining. The practice of imposing unjustifiably higher standards or terms for mortgage-lending activity in certain areas within a community.

Refinance. Obtaining a new and usually larger loan against a property with new terms.

Regulation B. The Federal Reserve Board regulation that implements the Equal Credit Opportunity Act.

Regulation X. The Federal Reserve Board regulation that implements the Real Estate Settlement Procedures Act (RESPA).

Regulation Z. The Federal Reserve Board regulation that implements the Truth in Lending Act, which requires disclosure of the annual percentage rate (APR) on the loan.

Release Deed. See *Deed of Reconveyance.*

Release of Mortgage. An instrument releasing part or all of the mortgaged property from the mortgage lien.

Renegotiable-Rate Mortgage (RRM). A loan in which the lender and borrower renegotiate the interest rate at stated intervals such as every three or five years.

Request for Reconveyance. After the trustor-borrower pays the debt, he or she asks the lender to send a request for reconveyance to the trustee that directs the trustee to issue a deed of reconveyance.

Required Rate of Return (RRR). The rate of return demanded by an investor. The rate of return on the investment includes compensation for deferred consumption, management, servicing, and accepting risks including the purchasing power risk. The required rate of return also provides for recovery of the original investment.

Rescission. The act of rescinding or canceling a contract. The seller recovers full title and the buyer receives the return of all payments minus costs and the fair rental value of the property.

Reserve Requirements. The level of monetary reserves required of financial institutions. Raising the reserve requirements tightens the money supply, and vice versa.

Return-on-Total-Assets Ratio. Net income plus interest divided by total assets. Also can be calculated by dividing net operating income before interest plus total income taxes by total operating assets. It is the measure of the earning power of the asset or assets.

Reverse Annuity Mortgage Loan (RAM). The borrower obtains a loan for a specified sum and the borrower usually receives monthly payments from the lender rather than a lump-sum amount.

Right of First Refusal. A provision that gives the lessee the right to purchase the property on the terms offered to any neutral third party if the lessor decides to sell the property.

Sale-Condo-Back. The owner sells the property to an investor and receives a deed to a condominium unit on the property as part of the purchase price.

Sale-Contract-Back. The owner sells the property to an investor and immediately enters a land contract agreement to buy the property back.

Sale in One Parcel Clause. A provision in a blanket mortgage that allows the lender to request that all the parcels be sold as a unit rather than separately, in the event of default.

Sale-Leaseback. The owner of the property sells it to an investor and immediately leases it from the investor.

SAM Loan. See *Shared Appreciation Mortgage Loan.*

Satisfaction Piece. An instrument acknowledging payment in full of the debt, which discharges the lien.

Savings and Loan Association (S&L). A financial intermediary founded to accept savings and to emphasize home mortgage loans. Known by a number of other names including building and loan association, homestead association, and co-operative banks.

Secondary Lender. An investor that purchases existing loans or that originates loans through primary lenders.

Secondary Mortgage Market. The markets in which existing mortgage loans are bought and sold.

Second Mortgage. A mortgage that has second claim on the proceeds from the sale of the pledged property.

Section 203(b). The standard mortgage loan insured by FHA. It is a nonsubsidized loan program.

Section 245/203. A graduated payment mortgage loan insured by FHA that otherwise meets the provisions of 203(b). It is a nonsubsidized loan program.

Security Deed. A deed that secures the payment of a specific debt and grants the lender the power of attorney to sell the property on default.

Seizin. Possession of realty by the owner or title holder, who has the right to sell or convey it to another.

Senior Mortgage. A first mortgage or any mortgage having priority over another mortgage depending on the context in which the term is used.

Service Corporations. Subsidiaries of savings and loan associations that are allowed to engage in activities that are otherwise forbidden to savings and loan associations.

Servicing. See *Loan Servicing.*

Settlement Statement. A financial summary of the charges and credits to the buyer and seller, including the amount due from the buyer and the amount due to the seller. Also known as a closing statement.

Shared Appreciation Mortgage Loan (SAM). A home loan agreement in which the lenders accept a lower interest rate and receive a portion of the increase in the value of the property over a specified time period.

Soft Money. Something of value other than cash. Developers and promoters may offer their services as their contribution to a project. The credit offered by the seller and secured by a purchase money mortgage is another example of soft money.

Soldiers and Sailors Relief Act. A federal law that protects borrowers who suffer a reduction in the ability to make mortgage payments due to being drafted into the armed services.

Sole Security Clause. A provision that in event of default the lender can only take action against the pledged property. The borrower is not personally liable for the payment of the debt.

Specific Performance. A remedy, under court order, compelling the defendant to fulfill the terms of an agreement or contract.

Stable Monthly Gross Income. Defined by the FHLMC as the borrower's gross monthly income from primary base earnings plus recognizable secondary income.

Stage of Completion Method. The system under which the proceeds of a construction loan are advanced in accordance with the progress made in erecting the structure such as when the foundation is in place.

Standby Commitment. A lender's promise to make a loan if the prospective borrower requests the loan. The prospective borrower is not obligated to borrow from the lender making the commitment.

State and Local Government Retirement Fund. A pension fund created to benefit the employees of either a state government or a local government such as a city.

State Chartered. The charter authorizing the operation of the organization is granted by a state government or an agency of a state government.

Statutory Redemption. The statutory right of redemption is a state law. It gives the right to recover property within a specified time period after the mortgage foreclosure sale by payment of the price plus back interest and foreclosure costs.

Stock Organization. An organization that is owned by the common stockholders. Normally the stockholders expect to earn a profit on their investment.

Strict Foreclosure. A legal proceeding in which the lender receives possession and clear title to the defaulted property on termination of the equitable right of redemption. There is no need for a foreclosure sale.

Subchapter S Corporation. A corporation that can elect to be taxed as a partnership for federal income tax purposes. Also known as a tax-option corporation.

Subject Property. The property under study, as in a feasibility analysis, an appraisal, or a loan application.

Subject to Mortgage. The purchaser recognizes the existence of the mortgage debt but does not become personally liable for the payment of the debt to the lender.

Sublease. Transfers a portion of the lessee's interests under the lease to another party.

Subordinated Fee Leasehold Mortgage. The leased fee is subordinated to the leasehold mortgage, which gives the leasehold mortgage first priority.

Subordination Agreement. A provision in a mortgage, lease, or other contract stipulating that a claim arranged at a later time is to have priority. Alternatively, the provision may be that a substitute mortgage, lease, etc., is to have priority on one's prior claims.

Subrogation Provision. A clause that provides for substitution of a third party in the place of a creditor. The third party takes over the creditor position. For example, if an insurance company pays one party for damage caused by another party, the insurance company has the right to sue the other party to collect the amount paid to the first party.

Substitute Trustee Clause. A provision in a trust deed agreement that allows the lender to appoint a substitute trustee.

Sue on the Note. The method of collecting the past due debt by bringing action under the note rather than by a foreclosure sale of the pledged property.

Supplemental Payment PAL Mortgage Loan. It operates in the same manner as a FLIP Mortgage Loan. See *FLIP Mortgage Loan.*

Sweat Equity. Equity in the property created by the individual's effort rather than by monetary payments.

Syndicate. A combining of personal and financial abilities of two or more parties to conduct business and to make investments; as a group, the parties are able to accomplish ends that each alone could not undertake and complete.

Take-Out Commitment. See *Permanent Take-Out Commitment.*

Take-Over Clause. A provision in a construction or development loan that gives the lender the right to complete the improvements if the borrower defaults.

Tandem Plan. GNMA purchases below-market interest rate mortgages at close to par and sells them at a discount. GNMA absorbs the loss. This reduces the funds needed by GNMA to subsidize the loans.

Tax Function. The function of mortgage loan servicing that consists of seeing that the real estate taxes and special assessments on the pledged properties are paid on schedule.

Tax-Option Corporation. See *Subchapter S Corporation.*

Tenant. See *Lessee.*

Term. The life or contract period of an agreement, such as the period of occupancy under a lease or the time period over which a loan is to be repaid.

Term Loan. A loan in which the entire loan balance is due in a single payment at the end of the term. Also known as a straight-term loan.

Time Value of Money (TVM). The relating of payments and value at different times by compounding or discounting at a certain interest rate or discount rate.

Title Insurance. Protection against financial loss due to defects in the title of real property that existed prior to the time of the purchase of policy and that were not excepted in the policy.

Title Theory. The theory of mortgage law that views a mortgage as a transfer of title to the lender and gives the lender the right to possession on default.

Torrens System. A method of land title registration in which clear title is established with a governmental authority, which subsequently issues title certificates to owners as evidence of their claims.

Transaction Account. A demand deposit (checking account), NOW account, or any other account in a depository institution that can be legally withdrawn on demand.

Trust. A fiduciary arrangement whereby property is turned over to an individual or institution (a trustee) to be held and administered for the profit and/or advantage of another person, termed a beneficiary.

Trust Deed. A legal instrument conveying title or an interest in realty to a third party (trustee) to be held as security for a debt owed a lender-beneficiary. Also referred to as a deed of trust or a trust deed in the nature of a mortgage.

Trustee. The person or institution holding title to the pledged property under a trust deed or deed in trust.

Trustee's Deed. A deed given by a trustee such as at a sale held by the trustee to enforce the terms of a note.

Trustor. The party placing property into a trust. The person establishing a trust, such as the owner-borrower transferring title to a trustee through a trust deed.

Truth in Lending Act. A federal law requiring disclosure of the terms of the loan such as the interest rate (APR), finance charges, the due date of payments, prepayment penalties, and late payment charges. Also known as Title I of the Consumer Credit Protection Act.

TVM. See *Time Value of Money.*

Underwriter. A party who examines the risks and decides whether or not to accept the risks associated with the project such as making a loan or issuing an insurance policy.

Underwriting. The process of examining the risks associated with a project such as a loan request and deciding whether or not the benefits derived from the project outweigh the risks.

Usury. Charging more than the legal rate of interest for a loan or credit.

Usury Law. A law that establishes a maximum allowable interest rate than can legally be charged by a lender.

Vacancy and Credit Losses (V&CL). The money not collected due to the failure to rent the space and/or the failure to collect the rental due.

VA Direct Mortgage Loan. A mortgage loan granted by the Veterans Administration.

VA Guaranteed Mortgage Loan.   A mortgage loan guaranteed by the Veterans Administration. Also known as a GI guaranteed loan.

VA Loan.   A loan insured, guaranteed, or granted by the Veterans Administration. Also known as a GI loan.

Variable-Rate Mortgage Loan (VRM).   A loan in which the interest rate fluctuates directly with an index over which the lender has no control.

Vendee.   The purchaser.

Vendor.   The seller.

Veterans Administration (VA).   A federal government agency that provides benefits for veterans. It makes direct loans and insures or guarantees mortgage loans.

Waiver of Defense Clause.   A provision that gives up the borrower's right to notice before the lender can obtain a judgment for payment of the debt. Also known as a cognovit provision.

Waiver of Homestead Exemption.   The borrower gives up the right to protect the homestead or a portion of its value from the Lender's claim in the event of default.

Warehouse Loan.   A short-term loan secured by a group of mortgage loans. Commercial banks made such loans to mortgage bankers. Mortgage bankers use such loans to finance their inventory holdings until the mortgages are sold to a permanent investor.

Willingness to Pay.   Refers to the question whether or not the individual would meet his or her obligations if adequate funds were available. It is judged by the individual's attitude and past credit history.

Wraparound Mortgage (WAM).   A refinancing mortgage in which the new lender assumes responsibility for the debt service payments on the existing mortgage loan.

Yield.   Rate of return or amount of return expected or earned on an investment.

Time Value of Money Tables

TABLE 1   PV1: Present Value Tables (Computed Annually)

YEAR	8%	9%	10%	11%	12%	13%	14%	15%	16%	17%	18%	19%	20%	22%	24%	26%	28%	30%	35%
1	.9259	.9174	.9091	.9009	.8929	.8850	.8772	.8696	.8621	.8547	.8475	.8403	.8333	.8197	.8065	.7937	.7813	.7692	.7407
2	.8573	.8417	.8264	.8116	.7972	.7831	.7695	.7561	.7432	.7305	.7182	.7062	.6944	.6719	.6504	.6299	.6107	.5917	.5487
3	.7938	.7722	.7513	.7312	.7118	.6931	.6750	.6575	.6407	.6244	.6086	.5934	.5787	.5507	.5245	.4999	.4768	.4552	.4064
4	.7350	.7084	.6830	.6587	.6355	.6133	.5921	.5718	.5523	.5337	.5158	.4987	.4823	.4514	.4230	.3968	.3725	.3501	.3011
5	.6806	.6499	.6209	.5925	.5674	.5428	.5194	.4972	.4761	.4561	.4371	.4190	.4019	.3700	.3411	.3149	.2910	.2693	.2230
6	.6302	.5963	.5645	.5346	.5066	.4803	.4556	.4323	.4104	.3898	.3704	.3521	.3349	.3033	.2751	.2499	.2274	.2072	.1652
7	.5835	.5470	.5132	.4817	.4523	.4251	.3996	.3759	.3538	.3332	.3139	.2959	.2791	.2486	.2218	.1983	.1776	.1594	.1224
8	.5403	.5019	.4665	.4339	.4039	.3762	.3506	.3269	.3050	.2848	.2660	.2487	.2326	.2038	.1789	.1574	.1388	.1226	.0906
9	.5002	.4604	.4241	.3909	.3606	.3329	.3075	.2843	.2630	.2434	.2255	.2090	.1938	.1670	.1443	.1249	.1084	.0943	.0671
10	.4632	.4224	.3855	.3522	.3220	.2946	.2697	.2472	.2267	.2080	.1911	.1756	.1615	.1369	.1164	.0992	.0847	.0725	.0497
11	.4289	.3875	.3505	.3173	.2875	.2607	.2366	.2149	.1954	.1778	.1619	.1476	.1346	.1122	.0938	.0787	.0662	.0558	.0368
12	.3971	.3555	.3186	.2858	.2567	.2307	.2076	.1869	.1685	.1520	.1372	.1240	.1122	.0920	.0757	.0625	.0517	.0429	.0273
13	.3677	.3262	.2897	.2575	.2292	.2042	.1821	.1625	.1452	.1299	.1163	.1042	.0935	.0754	.0610	.0496	.0404	.0330	.0202
14	.3405	.2992	.2633	.2320	.2046	.1807	.1597	.1413	.1252	.1110	.0985	.0876	.0779	.0618	.0492	.0393	.0316	.0254	.0150
15	.3152	.2745	.2394	.2090	.1827	.1599	.1401	.1229	.1079	.0949	.0835	.0736	.0649	.0507	.0397	.0312	.0247	.0195	.0111
16	.2919	.2519	.2176	.1883	.1631	.1415	.1229	.1069	.0930	.0811	.0708	.0618	.0541	.0415	.0320	.0248	.0193	.0150	.0082
17	.2703	.2311	.1978	.1696	.1456	.1252	.1078	.0929	.0802	.0693	.0600	.0520	.0451	.0340	.0258	.0197	.0150	.0116	.0061
18	.2502	.2120	.1799	.1528	.1300	.1108	.0946	.0808	.0691	.0592	.0508	.0437	.0376	.0279	.0208	.0156	.0118	.0089	.0045
19	.2317	.1945	.1635	.1377	.1161	.0981	.0829	.0703	.0596	.0506	.0431	.0367	.0313	.0229	.0168	.0124	.0092	.0068	.0033
20	.2145	.1784	.1486	.1240	.1037	.0868	.0728	.0611	.0514	.0433	.0365	.0308	.0261	.0187	.0135	.0098	.0072	.0053	.0025
21	.1987	.1637	.1351	.1117	.0926	.0768	.0638	.0531	.0443	.0370	.0309	.0259	.0217	.0154	.0109	.0078	.0056	.0040	.0018
22	.1839	.1502	.1228	.1007	.0826	.0680	.0560	.0462	.0382	.0316	.0262	.0218	.0181	.0126	.0088	.0062	.0044	.0031	.0014
23	.1703	.1378	.1117	.0907	.0738	.0601	.0491	.0402	.0329	.0270	.0222	.0183	.0151	.0103	.0071	.0049	.0034	.0024	.0010
24	.1577	.1264	.1015	.0817	.0659	.0532	.0431	.0349	.0284	.0231	.0188	.0154	.0126	.0085	.0057	.0039	.0027	.0018	.0007
25	.1460	.1160	.0923	.0736	.0588	.0471	.0378	.0304	.0245	.0197	.0160	.0129	.0105	.0069	.0046	.0031	.0021	.0014	.0006
26	.1352	.1064	.0839	.0663	.0525	.0417	.0331	.0264	.0211	.0169	.0135	.0109	.0087	.0057	.0037	.0025	.0016	.0011	.0004
27	.1252	.0976	.0763	.0597	.0469	.0369	.0291	.0230	.0182	.0144	.0115	.0091	.0073	.0047	.0030	.0020	.0013	.0008	.0003
28	.1159	.0895	.0693	.0538	.0419	.0326	.0255	.0200	.0157	.0123	.0097	.0077	.0061	.0038	.0024	.0015	.0010	.0006	.0002
29	.1073	.0822	.0630	.0485	.0374	.0289	.0224	.0174	.0135	.0105	.0082	.0064	.0051	.0031	.0019	.0012	.0008	.0005	.0002
30	.0994	.0754	.0573	.0437	.0334	.0256	.0196	.0151	.0116	.0090	.0070	.0054	.0042	.0026	.0016	.0010	.0006	.0004	.0001

TABLE 2 PV1/P: Present Value Tables (Computed Annually)

YEAR	8%	9%	10%	11%	12%	13%	14%	15%	16%	17%	18%	19%	20%	22%	24%	26%	28%	30%	35%
1	0.9259	0.9174	0.9091	0.9009	0.8929	0.8850	0.8772	0.8696	0.8621	0.8547	0.8475	0.8403	0.8333	0.8197	0.8065	0.7937	0.7813	0.7692	0.7407
2	1.7833	1.7591	1.7355	1.7125	1.6901	1.6681	1.6467	1.6257	1.6052	1.5852	1.5656	1.5465	1.5278	1.4915	1.4568	1.4235	1.3916	1.3609	1.2894
3	2.5771	2.5313	2.4869	2.4437	2.4018	2.3612	2.3216	2.2832	2.2459	2.2096	2.1743	2.1399	2.1065	2.0422	1.9813	1.9234	1.8684	1.8161	1.6959
4	3.3121	3.2397	3.1699	3.1024	3.0373	2.9745	2.9137	2.8550	2.7982	2.7432	2.6901	2.6386	2.5887	2.4936	2.4043	2.3202	2.2410	2.1662	1.9969
5	3.9927	3.8897	3.7908	3.6959	3.6048	3.5172	3.4331	3.3522	3.2743	3.1993	3.1272	3.0576	2.9906	2.8636	2.7454	2.6351	2.5320	2.4356	2.2200
6	4.6229	4.4859	4.3553	4.2305	4.1114	3.9976	3.8887	3.7845	3.6847	3.5892	3.4976	3.4098	3.3255	3.1669	3.0205	2.8850	2.7594	2.6427	2.3852
7	5.2064	5.0330	4.8684	4.7122	4.5638	4.4226	4.2883	4.1604	4.0386	3.9224	3.8115	3.7057	3.6046	3.4155	3.2423	3.0833	2.9370	2.8021	2.5075
8	5.7466	5.5348	5.3349	5.1461	4.9676	4.7988	4.6389	4.4873	4.3436	4.2072	4.0776	3.9544	3.8372	3.6193	3.4212	3.2407	3.0758	2.9247	2.5982
9	6.2469	5.9952	5.7590	5.5370	5.3283	5.1317	4.9464	4.7716	4.6066	4.4506	4.3030	4.1633	4.0310	3.7863	3.5655	3.3657	3.1842	3.0190	2.6653
10	6.7101	6.4177	6.1446	5.8892	5.6502	5.4262	5.2161	5.0188	4.8332	4.6586	4.4941	4.3389	4.1925	3.9232	3.6819	3.4648	3.2689	3.0915	2.7150
11	7.1390	6.8052	6.4951	6.2065	5.9377	5.6869	5.4527	5.2337	5.0286	4.8364	4.6560	4.4865	4.3271	4.0354	3.7757	3.5435	3.3351	3.1473	2.7519
12	7.5361	7.1607	6.8137	6.4924	6.1944	5.9176	5.6603	5.4206	5.1971	4.9884	4.7932	4.6105	4.4392	4.1274	3.8514	3.6060	3.3868	3.1903	2.7792
13	7.9038	7.4869	7.1034	6.7499	6.4235	6.1218	5.8424	5.5831	5.3423	5.1183	4.9095	4.7147	4.5327	4.2028	3.9124	3.6555	3.4272	3.2233	2.7994
14	8.2442	7.7862	7.3667	6.9819	6.6282	6.3025	6.0021	5.7245	5.4675	5.2293	5.0081	4.8023	4.6106	4.2646	3.9616	3.6949	3.4587	3.2487	2.8144
15	8.5595	8.0607	7.6061	7.1909	6.8109	6.4624	6.1422	5.8474	5.5755	5.3242	5.0916	4.8759	4.6755	4.3152	4.0012	3.7261	3.4834	3.2682	2.8255
16	8.8514	8.3126	7.8237	7.3791	6.9740	6.6039	6.2651	5.9542	5.6685	5.4053	5.1624	4.9377	4.7296	4.3567	4.0333	3.7509	3.5026	3.2832	2.8337
17	9.1216	8.5436	8.0216	7.5488	7.1196	6.7291	6.3729	6.0472	5.7487	5.4746	5.2223	4.9897	4.7746	4.3908	4.0591	3.7705	3.5177	3.2948	2.8398
18	9.3719	8.7556	8.2014	7.7016	7.2497	6.8399	6.4674	6.1280	5.8178	5.5339	5.2732	5.0333	4.8122	4.4187	4.0799	3.7861	3.5294	3.3037	2.8443
19	9.6036	8.9501	8.3649	7.8393	7.3658	6.9380	6.5504	6.1982	5.8775	5.5845	5.3162	5.0700	4.8435	4.4415	4.0967	3.7985	3.5386	3.3105	2.8476
20	9.8181	9.1285	8.5136	7.9633	7.4694	7.0248	6.6231	6.2593	5.9288	5.6278	5.3527	5.1009	4.8696	4.4603	4.1103	3.8083	3.5458	3.3158	2.8501
21	10.0168	9.2922	8.6487	8.0751	7.5620	7.1016	6.6870	6.3125	5.9731	5.6648	5.3837	5.1268	4.8913	4.4756	4.1212	3.8161	3.5514	3.3198	2.8519
22	10.2007	9.4424	8.7715	8.1757	7.6446	7.1695	6.7429	6.3587	6.0113	5.6964	5.4099	5.1486	4.9094	4.4882	4.1300	3.8223	3.5558	3.3230	2.8533
23	10.3711	9.5802	8.8832	8.2664	7.7184	7.2297	6.7921	6.3988	6.0442	5.7234	5.4321	5.1668	4.9245	4.4985	4.1371	3.8273	3.5592	3.3254	2.8543
24	10.5288	9.7066	8.9847	8.3481	7.7843	7.2829	6.8351	6.4338	6.0726	5.7469	5.4509	5.1822	4.9371	4.5070	4.1428	3.8312	3.5619	3.3272	2.8550
25	10.6748	9.8226	9.0770	8.4217	7.8431	7.3300	6.8729	6.4641	6.0971	5.7662	5.4669	5.1951	4.9476	4.5139	4.1474	3.8342	3.5640	3.3286	2.8556
26	10.8100	9.9290	9.1609	8.4881	7.8957	7.3717	6.9061	6.4906	6.1182	5.7831	5.4804	5.2060	4.9563	4.5196	4.1511	3.8367	3.5656	3.3297	2.8560
27	10.9352	10.0266	9.2372	8.5478	7.9426	7.4086	6.9352	6.5135	6.1364	5.7975	5.4919	5.2151	4.9636	4.5243	4.1542	3.8387	3.5669	3.3305	2.8563
28	11.0511	10.1161	9.3066	8.6016	7.9844	7.4412	6.9607	6.5335	6.1520	5.8099	5.5016	5.2228	4.9697	4.5281	4.1566	3.8402	3.5679	3.3312	2.8565
29	11.1584	10.1983	9.3696	8.6501	8.0218	7.4701	6.9830	6.5509	6.1656	5.8204	5.5098	5.2292	4.9747	4.5312	4.1585	3.8414	3.5687	3.3317	2.8567
30	11.2578	10.2737	9.4269	8.6938	8.0552	7.4957	7.0027	6.5660	6.1772	5.8294	5.5168	5.2347	4.9789	4.5338	4.1601	3.8424	3.5693	3.3321	2.8568

TABLE 3   Time Value of Money Computed at 6% Monthly

```
                                          MONTHLY                                    6.00%
                               TIME VALUE OF MONEY TABLES
              EFFECTIVE RATE=    0.500%                        BASE=  1.00500
```

	1 FV1 FUTURE VALUE OF ONE	2 FV1/P FUTURE VALUE OF ONE PER PERIOD	3 SF SINKING FUND	4 PV1 PRESENT VALUE OF ONE	5 PV1/P PRESENT VALUE OF ONE PER PERIOD	6 PR PRINCIPAL RECOVERY
MONTH						
1	1.005000	1.000000	1.000000	0.995025	0.995025	1.005000
2	1.010025	2.005000	0.498753	0.990075	1.985099	0.503753
3	1.015075	3.015025	0.331672	0.985149	2.970248	0.336672
4	1.020151	4.030100	0.248133	0.980248	3.950496	0.253133
5	1.025251	5.050251	0.198010	0.975371	4.925866	0.203010
6	1.030378	6.075502	0.164595	0.970518	5.896384	0.169595
7	1.035529	7.105879	0.140729	0.965690	6.862074	0.145729
8	1.040707	8.141409	0.122829	0.960885	7.822959	0.127829
9	1.045911	9.182116	0.108907	0.956105	8.779064	0.113907
10	1.051140	10.228026	0.097771	0.951348	9.730412	0.102771
11	1.056396	11.279167	0.088659	0.946615	10.677027	0.093659
12	1.061678	12.335562	0.081066	0.941905	11.618932	0.086066

YEARS							MONTH
1	1.061678	12.335562	0.081066	0.941905	11.618932	0.086066	12
2	1.127160	25.431955	0.039321	0.887186	22.562866	0.044321	24
3	1.196681	39.336105	0.025422	0.835645	32.871016	0.030422	36
4	1.270489	54.097832	0.018485	0.787098	42.580318	0.023485	48
5	1.348850	69.770031	0.014333	0.741372	51.725561	0.019333	60
6	1.432044	86.408856	0.011573	0.698302	60.339514	0.016573	72
7	1.520370	104.073927	0.009609	0.657735	68.453042	0.014609	84
8	1.614143	122.828542	0.008141	0.619524	76.095218	0.013141	96
9	1.713699	142.739900	0.007006	0.583533	83.293424	0.012006	108
10	1.819397	163.879347	0.006102	0.549633	90.073453	0.011102	120
11	1.931613	186.322629	0.005367	0.517702	96.459599	0.010367	132
12	2.050751	210.150163	0.004759	0.487626	102.474743	0.009759	144
13	2.177237	235.447328	0.004247	0.459298	108.140440	0.009247	156
14	2.311524	262.304766	0.003812	0.432615	113.476990	0.008812	168
15	2.454094	290.818712	0.003439	0.407482	118.503515	0.008439	180
16	2.605457	321.091337	0.003114	0.383810	123.238025	0.008114	192
17	2.766156	353.231110	0.002831	0.361513	127.697486	0.007831	204
18	2.936766	387.353194	0.002582	0.340511	131.897876	0.007582	216
19	3.117899	423.579854	0.002361	0.320729	135.854246	0.007361	228
20	3.310204	462.040895	0.002164	0.302096	139.580772	0.007164	240
21	3.514371	502.874129	0.001989	0.284546	143.090806	0.006989	252
22	3.731129	546.225867	0.001831	0.268015	146.396927	0.006831	264
23	3.961257	592.251446	0.001688	0.252445	149.510979	0.006688	276
24	4.205579	641.115782	0.001560	0.237779	152.444121	0.006560	288
25	4.464970	692.993962	0.001443	0.223966	155.206864	0.006443	300
26	4.740359	748.071876	0.001337	0.210954	157.809106	0.006337	312
27	5.032734	806.546875	0.001240	0.198699	160.260172	0.006240	324
28	5.343142	868.628484	0.001151	0.187156	162.568844	0.006151	336
29	5.672696	934.539150	0.001070	0.176283	164.743394	0.006070	348
30	6.022575	1004.515042	0.000996	0.166042	166.791614	0.005996	360
31	6.394034	1078.806895	0.000927	0.156396	168.720844	0.005927	372
32	6.788405	1157.680906	0.000864	0.147310	170.537996	0.005864	384
33	7.207098	1241.419693	0.000806	0.138752	172.249581	0.005806	396
34	7.651617	1330.323306	0.000752	0.130691	173.861732	0.005752	408
35	8.123551	1424.710299	0.000702	0.123099	175.380226	0.005702	420
36	8.624594	1524.918875	0.000656	0.115947	176.810504	0.005656	432
37	9.156540	1631.308097	0.000613	0.109212	178.157690	0.005613	444
38	9.721296	1744.259173	0.000573	0.102867	179.426611	0.005573	456
39	10.320884	1864.176824	0.000536	0.096891	180.621815	0.005536	468
40	10.957454	1991.490734	0.000502	0.091262	181.747584	0.005502	480

TABLE 4 Time Value of Money Computed at 8% Monthly

MONTHLY
TIME VALUE OF MONEY TABLES

EFFECTIVE RATE=   0.667%   BASE=   1.00667

	1 EV1 FUTURE VALUE OF ONE	2 EV1/P FUTURE VALUE OF ONE PER PERIOD	3 SE SINKING FUND	4 PV1 PRESENT VALUE OF ONE	5 PV1/P PRESENT VALUE OF ONE PER PERIOD	6 PR PRINCIPAL RECOVERY
MONTH						
1	1.006667	1.000000	1.000000	0.993377	0.993377	1.006667
2	1.013378	2.006667	0.498339	0.986799	1.980176	0.505006
3	1.020134	3.020044	0.331121	0.980264	2.960440	0.337788
4	1.026935	4.040178	0.247514	0.973772	3.934212	0.254181
5	1.033781	5.067113	0.197351	0.967323	4.901535	0.204018
6	1.040673	6.100893	0.163910	0.960917	5.862452	0.170577
7	1.047610	7.141566	0.140025	0.954553	6.817005	0.146692
8	1.054595	8.189176	0.122112	0.948232	7.765237	0.128779
9	1.061625	9.243771	0.108181	0.941952	8.707189	0.114848
10	1.068703	10.305396	0.097037	0.935714	9.642903	0.103703
11	1.075827	11.374099	0.087919	0.929517	10.572420	0.094586
12	1.083000	12.449926	0.080322	0.923361	11.495782	0.086988

YEARS							**MONTH**
1	1.083000	12.449926	0.080322	0.923361	11.495782	0.086988	12
2	1.172888	25.933190	0.038561	0.852596	22.110544	0.045227	24
3	1.270237	40.535558	0.024670	0.787255	31.911806	0.031336	36
4	1.375666	56.349915	0.017746	0.726921	40.961913	0.024413	48
5	1.489846	73.476856	0.013610	0.671210	49.318433	0.020276	60
6	1.613502	92.025325	0.010867	0.619770	57.034522	0.017533	72
7	1.747422	112.113308	0.008920	0.572272	64.159261	0.015586	84
8	1.892457	133.868583	0.007470	0.528414	70.737970	0.014137	96
9	2.049530	157.429535	0.006352	0.487917	76.812497	0.013019	108
10	2.219640	182.946035	0.005466	0.450523	82.421481	0.012133	120
11	2.403869	210.580392	0.004749	0.415996	87.600600	0.011415	132
12	2.603389	240.508387	0.004158	0.384115	92.382800	0.010825	144
13	2.819469	272.920390	0.003664	0.354677	96.798498	0.010331	156
14	3.053484	308.022574	0.003247	0.327495	100.875784	0.009913	168
15	3.306921	346.038222	0.002890	0.302396	104.640592	0.009557	180
16	3.581394	387.209149	0.002583	0.279221	108.116871	0.009249	192
17	3.878648	431.797244	0.002316	0.257822	111.326733	0.008983	204
18	4.200574	480.086128	0.002083	0.238063	114.290596	0.008750	216
19	4.549220	532.382966	0.001878	0.219818	117.027313	0.008545	228
20	4.926803	589.020416	0.001698	0.202971	119.554292	0.008364	240
21	5.335725	650.358746	0.001538	0.187416	121.887606	0.008204	252
22	5.778588	716.788127	0.001395	0.173053	124.042099	0.008062	264
23	6.258207	788.731114	0.001268	0.159790	126.031475	0.007935	276
24	6.777636	866.645333	0.001154	0.147544	127.868388	0.007821	288
25	7.340176	951.026395	0.001051	0.136237	129.564523	0.007718	300
26	7.949407	1042.411042	0.000959	0.125796	131.130668	0.007626	312
27	8.609204	1141.380571	0.000876	0.116155	132.576786	0.007543	324
28	9.323763	1248.564521	0.000801	0.107253	133.912076	0.007468	336
29	10.097631	1364.644687	0.000733	0.099033	135.145031	0.007399	348
30	10.935730	1490.359449	0.000671	0.091443	136.283494	0.007338	360
31	11.843390	1626.508474	0.000615	0.084435	137.334707	0.007281	372
32	12.826385	1773.957801	0.000564	0.077964	138.305357	0.007230	384
33	13.890969	1933.645350	0.000517	0.071989	139.201617	0.007184	396
34	15.043913	2106.586886	0.000475	0.066472	140.029190	0.007141	408
35	16.292550	2293.882485	0.000436	0.061378	140.793338	0.007103	420
36	17.644824	2496.723526	0.000401	0.056674	141.498923	0.007067	432
37	19.109335	2716.400273	0.000368	0.052330	142.150433	0.007035	444
38	20.695401	2954.310082	0.000338	0.048320	142.752013	0.007005	456
39	22.413109	3211.966288	0.000311	0.044617	143.307488	0.006978	468
40	24.273386	3491.007831	0.000286	0.041197	143.820392	0.006953	480

TABLE 5 Time Value of Money Computed at 9% Monthly

MONTHLY
TIME VALUE OF MONEY TABLES

EFFECTIVE RATE= 0.750%   BASE= 1.00750

	1 EV1 FUTURE VALUE OF ONE	2 EV1/P FUTURE VALUE OF ONE PER PERIOD	3 SE SINKING FUND	4 PV1 PRESENT VALUE OF ONE	5 PV1/P PRESENT VALUE OF ONE PER PERIOD	6 PR PRINCIPAL RECOVERY
MONTH						
1	1.007500	1.000000	1.000000	0.992556	0.992556	1.007500
2	1.015056	2.007500	0.498132	0.985167	1.977723	0.505632
3	1.022669	3.022556	0.330846	0.977833	2.955556	0.338346
4	1.030339	4.045225	0.247205	0.970554	3.926110	0.254705
5	1.038067	5.075565	0.197022	0.963329	4.889440	0.204522
6	1.045852	6.113631	0.163569	0.956158	5.845598	0.171069
7	1.053696	7.159484	0.139675	0.949040	6.794638	0.147175
8	1.061599	8.213180	0.121756	0.941975	7.736613	0.129256
9	1.069561	9.274779	0.107819	0.934963	8.671576	0.115319
10	1.077583	10.344339	0.096671	0.928003	9.599580	0.104171
11	1.085664	11.421922	0.087551	0.921095	10.520675	0.095051
12	1.093807	12.507586	0.079951	0.914238	11.434913	0.087451
YEARS						**MONTH**
1	1.093807	12.507586	0.079951	0.914238	11.434913	0.087451	12
2	1.196414	26.188471	0.038185	0.835831	21.889146	0.045685	24
3	1.308045	41.152716	0.024300	0.764149	31.446805	0.031800	36
4	1.431405	57.520711	0.017385	0.698614	40.184782	0.024885	48
5	1.565681	75.424137	0.013258	0.638700	48.173374	0.020758	60
6	1.712553	95.007028	0.010526	0.583924	55.476849	0.018026	72
7	1.873202	116.426928	0.008589	0.533845	62.153965	0.016089	84
8	2.048921	139.856164	0.007150	0.488062	68.258439	0.014650	96
9	2.241124	165.483223	0.006043	0.446205	73.839382	0.013543	108
10	2.451357	193.514277	0.005168	0.407937	78.941693	0.012668	120
11	2.681311	224.174837	0.004461	0.372952	83.606420	0.011961	132
12	2.932837	257.711570	0.003880	0.340967	87.871092	0.011380	144
13	3.207957	294.394279	0.003397	0.311725	91.770018	0.010897	156
14	3.508886	334.518079	0.002989	0.284991	95.334564	0.010489	168
15	3.838043	378.405769	0.002643	0.260549	98.593409	0.010143	180
16	4.198078	426.410427	0.002345	0.238204	101.572769	0.009845	192
17	4.591887	478.918252	0.002088	0.217775	104.296613	0.009588	204
18	5.022638	536.351674	0.001864	0.199099	106.786856	0.009364	216
19	5.493796	599.172747	0.001669	0.182024	109.063531	0.009169	228
20	6.009152	667.886870	0.001497	0.166413	111.144954	0.008997	240
21	6.572851	743.046852	0.001346	0.152141	113.047870	0.008846	252
22	7.189430	825.257358	0.001212	0.139093	114.787589	0.008712	264
23	7.863848	915.179777	0.001093	0.127164	116.378106	0.008593	276
24	8.601532	1013.537539	0.000987	0.116258	117.832218	0.008487	288
25	9.408415	1121.121937	0.000892	0.106288	119.161622	0.008392	300
26	10.290989	1238.798495	0.000807	0.097172	120.377014	0.008307	312
27	11.256354	1367.513924	0.000731	0.088839	121.488172	0.008231	324
28	12.312278	1508.303750	0.000663	0.081220	122.504035	0.008163	336
29	13.467255	1662.300631	0.000602	0.074254	123.432776	0.008102	348
30	14.730576	1830.743483	0.000546	0.067886	124.281866	0.008046	360
31	16.112406	2014.987436	0.000496	0.062064	125.058136	0.007996	372
32	17.623861	2216.514743	0.000451	0.056741	125.767832	0.007951	384
33	19.277100	2436.946701	0.000410	0.051875	126.416664	0.007910	396
34	21.085425	2678.056697	0.000373	0.047426	127.009850	0.007873	408
35	23.063384	2941.784474	0.000340	0.043359	127.552164	0.007840	420
36	25.226888	3230.251735	0.000310	0.039640	128.047967	0.007810	432
37	27.593344	3545.779215	0.000282	0.036241	128.501250	0.007782	444
38	30.181790	3890.905350	0.000257	0.033133	128.915659	0.007757	456
39	33.013050	4268.406696	0.000234	0.030291	129.294526	0.007734	468
40	36.109902	4681.320273	0.000214	0.027693	129.640902	0.007714	480

TABLE 6   Time Value of Money Computed at 10% Monthly

| | MONTHLY
TIME VALUE OF MONEY TABLES | | | | 10.00% |

EFFECTIVE RATE=   0.833%   BASE=   1.00833

	1 FV1 FUTURE VALUE OF ONE	2 FV1/P FUTURE VALUE OF ONE PER PERIOD	3 SF SINKING FUND	4 PV1 PRESENT VALUE OF ONE	5 PV1/P PRESENT VALUE OF ONE PER PERIOD	6 PR PRINCIPAL RECOVERY
MONTH						
1	1.008333	1.000000	1.000000	0.991736	0.991736	1.008333
2	1.016736	2.008333	0.497925	0.983539	1.975275	0.506259
3	1.025209	3.025069	0.330571	0.975411	2.950686	0.338904
4	1.033752	4.050278	0.246897	0.967350	3.918036	0.255230
5	1.042367	5.084031	0.196694	0.959355	4.877391	0.205028
6	1.051053	6.126398	0.163228	0.951427	5.828817	0.171561
7	1.059812	7.177451	0.139325	0.943563	6.772381	0.147659
8	1.068644	8.237263	0.121400	0.935765	7.708146	0.129733
9	1.077549	9.305907	0.107459	0.928032	8.636178	0.115792
10	1.086529	10.383456	0.096307	0.920362	9.556540	0.104640
11	1.095583	11.469985	0.087184	0.912756	10.469296	0.095517
12	1.104713	12.565568	0.079583	0.905212	11.374508	0.087916
YEARS						MONTH
1	1.104713	12.565568	0.079583	0.905212	11.374508	0.087916	12
2	1.220391	26.446915	0.037812	0.819410	21.670855	0.046145	24
3	1.348182	41.781821	0.023934	0.741740	30.991236	0.032267	36
4	1.489354	58.722492	0.017029	0.671432	39.428160	0.025363	48
5	1.645309	77.437072	0.012914	0.607789	47.065369	0.021247	60
6	1.817594	98.111314	0.010193	0.550178	53.978665	0.018526	72
7	2.007920	120.950418	0.008268	0.498028	60.236667	0.016601	84
8	2.218176	146.181076	0.006841	0.450821	65.901488	0.015174	96
9	2.450448	174.053713	0.005745	0.408089	71.029355	0.014079	108
10	2.707041	204.844979	0.004882	0.369407	75.671163	0.013215	120
11	2.990504	238.860493	0.004187	0.334392	79.872986	0.012520	132
12	3.303649	276.437876	0.003617	0.302696	83.676528	0.011951	144
13	3.649584	317.950102	0.003145	0.274004	87.119542	0.011478	156
14	4.031743	363.809201	0.002749	0.248032	90.236201	0.011082	168
15	4.453920	414.470346	0.002413	0.224521	93.057439	0.010746	180
16	4.920303	470.436376	0.002126	0.203240	95.611259	0.010459	192
17	5.435523	532.262780	0.001879	0.183975	97.923008	0.010212	204
18	6.004693	600.563216	0.001665	0.166536	100.015633	0.009998	216
19	6.633463	676.015601	0.001479	0.150751	101.909902	0.009813	228
20	7.328074	759.368836	0.001317	0.136462	103.624619	0.009650	240
21	8.095419	851.450244	0.001174	0.123527	105.176801	0.009508	252
22	8.943115	953.173779	0.001049	0.111818	106.581856	0.009382	264
23	9.879576	1065.549097	0.000938	0.101219	107.853730	0.009272	276
24	10.914097	1189.691580	0.000841	0.091625	109.005045	0.009174	288
25	12.056945	1326.833403	0.000754	0.082940	110.047230	0.009087	300
26	13.319465	1478.335767	0.000676	0.075078	110.990629	0.009010	312
27	14.714187	1645.702407	0.000608	0.067962	111.844605	0.008941	324
28	16.254954	1830.594523	0.000546	0.061520	112.617635	0.008880	336
29	17.957060	2034.847258	0.000491	0.055688	113.317392	0.008825	348
30	19.837399	2260.487925	0.000442	0.050410	113.950820	0.008776	360
31	21.914634	2509.756117	0.000398	0.045632	114.524207	0.008732	372
32	24.209383	2785.125947	0.000359	0.041306	115.043244	0.008692	384
33	26.744422	3089.330596	0.000324	0.037391	115.513083	0.008657	396
34	29.544912	3425.389447	0.000292	0.033847	115.938387	0.008625	408
35	32.638650	3796.638052	0.000263	0.030639	116.323377	0.008597	420
36	36.056344	4206.761236	0.000238	0.027734	116.671876	0.008571	432
37	39.831914	4659.829677	0.000215	0.025105	116.987340	0.008548	444
38	44.002836	5160.340305	0.000194	0.022726	117.272903	0.008527	456
39	48.610508	5713.260935	0.000175	0.020572	117.531398	0.008508	468
40	53.700663	6324.079581	0.000158	0.018622	117.765391	0.008491	480

TABLE 7 Time Value of Money Computed at 11% Monthly

MONTHLY
TIME VALUE OF MONEY TABLES
11.00%

EFFECTIVE RATE= 0.917%   BASE= 1.00917

	1 EV1 FUTURE VALUE OF ONE	2 EV1/P FUTURE VALUE OF ONE PER PERIOD	3 SF SINKING FUND	4 PV1 PRESENT VALUE OF ONE	5 PV1/P PRESENT VALUE OF ONE PER PERIOD	6 PR PRINCIPAL RECOVERY	
MONTH							
1	1.009167	1.000000	1.000000	0.990917	0.990917	1.009167	
2	1.018417	2.009167	0.497719	0.981916	1.972832	0.506885	
3	1.027753	3.027584	0.330296	0.972997	2.945829	0.339463	
4	1.037174	4.055337	0.246589	0.964158	3.909987	0.255755	
5	1.046681	5.092511	0.196367	0.955401	4.865388	0.205533	
6	1.056276	6.139192	0.162888	0.946722	5.812110	0.172055	
7	1.065958	7.195468	0.138976	0.938123	6.750233	0.148143	
8	1.075730	8.261427	0.121044	0.929602	7.679835	0.130211	
9	1.085591	9.337156	0.107099	0.921158	8.600992	0.116266	
10	1.095542	10.422747	0.095944	0.912790	9.513783	0.105111	
11	1.105584	11.518289	0.086818	0.904499	10.418282	0.095985	
12	1.115719	12.623873	0.079215	0.896283	11.314565	0.088382	
YEARS							MONTH
1	1.115719	12.623873	0.079215	0.896283	11.314565	0.088382	12
2	1.244829	26.708566	0.037441	0.803323	21.455619	0.046608	24
3	1.388879	42.423123	0.023572	0.720005	30.544874	0.032739	36
4	1.549598	59.956151	0.016679	0.645329	38.691421	0.025846	48
5	1.728916	79.518080	0.012576	0.578397	45.993034	0.021742	60
6	1.928994	101.343692	0.009867	0.518408	52.537346	0.019034	72
7	2.152204	125.694940	0.007956	0.464640	58.402903	0.017122	84
8	2.401254	152.864085	0.006542	0.416449	63.660103	0.015708	96
9	2.679124	183.177212	0.005459	0.373256	68.372043	0.014626	108
10	2.989150	216.998139	0.004608	0.334543	72.595275	0.013775	120
11	3.335051	254.732784	0.003926	0.299846	76.380487	0.013092	132
12	3.720979	296.834038	0.003369	0.268747	79.773109	0.012536	144
13	4.151566	343.807200	0.002909	0.240873	82.813859	0.012075	156
14	4.631980	396.216042	0.002524	0.215890	85.539231	0.011691	168
15	5.167988	454.689575	0.002199	0.193499	87.981937	0.011366	180
16	5.766021	519.929596	0.001923	0.173430	90.171293	0.011090	192
17	6.433259	592.719117	0.001687	0.155442	92.133576	0.010854	204
18	7.177708	673.931757	0.001484	0.139320	93.892337	0.010650	216
19	8.008304	764.542228	0.001308	0.124870	95.468685	0.010475	228
20	8.935015	865.638038	0.001155	0.111919	96.881539	0.010322	240
21	9.968965	978.432537	0.001022	0.100311	98.147856	0.010189	252
22	11.122562	1104.279485	0.000906	0.089907	99.282835	0.010072	264
23	12.409652	1244.689295	0.000803	0.080582	100.300098	0.009970	276
24	13.845682	1401.347165	0.000714	0.072225	101.211853	0.009880	288
25	15.447889	1576.133301	0.000634	0.064734	102.029044	0.009801	300
26	17.235500	1771.145485	0.000565	0.058020	102.761478	0.009731	312
27	19.229972	1988.724252	0.000503	0.052002	103.417947	0.009670	324
28	21.455242	2231.480981	0.000448	0.046609	104.006328	0.009615	336
29	23.938018	2502.329236	0.000400	0.041775	104.533685	0.009566	348
30	26.708098	2804.519736	0.000357	0.037442	105.006346	0.009523	360
31	29.798728	3141.679369	0.000318	0.033558	105.429984	0.009485	372
32	33.247002	3517.854723	0.000284	0.030078	105.809684	0.009451	384
33	37.094306	3937.560650	0.000254	0.026958	106.150002	0.009421	396
34	41.386816	4405.834459	0.000227	0.024162	106.455024	0.009394	408
35	46.176050	4928.296368	0.000203	0.021656	106.728409	0.009370	420
36	51.519489	5511.216962	0.000181	0.019410	106.973440	0.009348	432
37	57.481264	6161.592447	0.000162	0.017397	107.193057	0.009329	444
38	64.132929	6887.228628	0.000145	0.015593	107.389897	0.009312	456
39	71.554317	7696.834582	0.000130	0.013975	107.566320	0.009297	468
40	79.834499	8600.127195	0.000116	0.012526	107.724446	0.009283	480

TABLE 8 Time Value of Money Computed at 12% Monthly

12.00%

MONTHLY

12.00%

TIME VALUE OF MONEY TABLES

EFFECTIVE RATE= 1.000%   BASE= 1.01000

	1 EV1 FUTURE VALUE OF ONE	2 EV1/P FUTURE VALUE OF ONE PER PERIOD	3 SF SINKING FUND	4 PV1 PRESENT VALUE OF ONE	5 PV1/P PRESENT VALUE OF ONE PER PERIOD	6 PR PRINCIPAL RECOVERY
MONTH						
1	1.010000	1.000000	1.000000	0.990099	0.990099	1.010000
2	1.020100	2.010000	0.497512	0.980296	1.970395	0.507512
3	1.030301	3.030100	0.330022	0.970590	2.940985	0.340022
4	1.040604	4.060401	0.246281	0.960980	3.901966	0.256281
5	1.051010	5.101005	0.196040	0.951466	4.853431	0.206040
6	1.061520	6.152015	0.162548	0.942045	5.795476	0.172548
7	1.072135	7.213535	0.138628	0.932718	6.728195	0.148628
8	1.082857	8.285671	0.120690	0.923483	7.651678	0.130690
9	1.093685	9.368527	0.106740	0.914340	8.566018	0.116740
10	1.104622	10.462213	0.095582	0.905287	9.471305	0.105582
11	1.115668	11.566835	0.086454	0.896324	10.367628	0.096454
12	1.126825	12.682503	0.078849	0.887449	11.255077	0.088849

YEARS							**MONTH**
1	1.126825	12.682503	0.078849	0.887449	11.255077	0.088849	12
2	1.269735	26.973465	0.037073	0.787566	21.243387	0.047073	24
3	1.430769	43.076878	0.023214	0.698925	30.107505	0.033214	36
4	1.612226	61.222608	0.016334	0.620260	37.973959	0.026334	48
5	1.816697	81.669670	0.012244	0.550450	44.955038	0.022244	60
6	2.047099	104.709931	0.009550	0.488496	51.150391	0.019550	72
7	2.306723	130.672274	0.007653	0.433515	56.648453	0.017653	84
8	2.599273	159.927293	0.006253	0.384723	61.527703	0.016253	96
9	2.928926	192.892579	0.005184	0.341422	65.857790	0.015184	108
10	3.300387	230.038689	0.004347	0.302995	69.700522	0.014347	120
11	3.718959	271.895856	0.003678	0.268892	73.110752	0.013678	132
12	4.190616	319.061559	0.003134	0.238628	76.137157	0.013134	144
13	4.722091	372.209054	0.002687	0.211771	78.822939	0.012687	156
14	5.320970	432.096982	0.002314	0.187936	81.206434	0.012314	168
15	5.995802	499.580198	0.002002	0.166783	83.321664	0.012002	180
16	6.756220	575.621974	0.001737	0.148012	85.198824	0.011737	192
17	7.613078	661.307751	0.001512	0.131353	86.864707	0.011512	204
18	8.578606	757.860630	0.001320	0.116570	88.343095	0.011320	216
19	9.666588	866.658830	0.001154	0.103449	89.655089	0.011154	228
20	10.892554	989.255365	0.001011	0.091806	90.819416	0.011011	240
21	12.274002	1127.400210	0.000887	0.081473	91.852698	0.010887	252
22	13.830653	1283.065279	0.000779	0.072303	92.769683	0.010779	264
23	15.584726	1458.472574	0.000686	0.064165	93.583461	0.010686	276
24	17.561259	1656.125935	0.000604	0.056944	94.305647	0.010604	288
25	19.788466	1878.846626	0.000532	0.050534	94.946551	0.010532	300
26	22.298139	2129.813909	0.000470	0.044847	95.515321	0.010470	312
27	25.126101	2412.610125	0.000414	0.039799	96.020075	0.010414	324
28	28.312720	2731.271980	0.000366	0.035320	96.468019	0.010366	336
29	31.903481	3090.348134	0.000324	0.031345	96.865546	0.010324	348
30	35.949641	3494.964133	0.000286	0.027817	97.218331	0.010286	360
31	40.508956	3950.895567	0.000253	0.024686	97.531410	0.010253	372
32	45.646505	4464.650520	0.000224	0.021907	97.809252	0.010224	384
33	51.435625	5043.562459	0.000198	0.019442	98.055822	0.010198	396
34	57.958949	5695.894923	0.000176	0.017254	98.274641	0.010176	408
35	65.309595	6430.959471	0.000155	0.015312	98.468831	0.010155	420
36	73.592486	7259.248603	0.000138	0.013588	98.641166	0.010138	432
37	82.925855	8192.585509	0.000122	0.012059	98.794103	0.010122	444
38	93.442929	9244.292939	0.000108	0.010702	98.929828	0.010108	456
39	105.293832	10429.383172	0.000096	0.009497	99.050277	0.010096	468
40	118.647725	11764.772510	0.000085	0.008428	99.157169	0.010085	480

TABLE 9 Time Value of Money Computed at 13% Monthly

13.00%			MONTHLY TIME VALUE OF MONEY TABLES			13.00%
	EFFECTIVE RATE= 1.083%			BASE= 1.01083		

	1 EV1 FUTURE VALUE OF ONE	2 EV1/P FUTURE VALUE OF ONE PER PERIOD	3 SF SINKING FUND	4 PV1 PRESENT VALUE OF ONE	5 PV1/P PRESENT VALUE OF ONE PER PERIOD	6 PR PRINCIPAL RECOVERY
MONTH						
1	1.010833	1.000000	1.000000	0.989283	0.989283	1.010833
2	1.021784	2.010833	0.497306	0.978680	1.967963	0.508140
3	1.032853	3.032617	0.329748	0.968192	2.936155	0.340581
4	1.044043	4.065471	0.245974	0.957815	3.893970	0.256807
5	1.055353	5.109513	0.195713	0.947550	4.841520	0.206547
6	1.066786	6.164866	0.162210	0.937395	5.778915	0.173043
7	1.078343	7.231652	0.138281	0.927349	6.706264	0.149114
8	1.090025	8.309995	0.120337	0.917410	7.623674	0.131170
9	1.101834	9.400020	0.106383	0.907578	8.531253	0.117216
10	1.113770	10.501854	0.095221	0.897851	9.429104	0.106055
11	1.125836	11.615624	0.086091	0.888229	10.317333	0.096924
12	1.138032	12.741460	0.078484	0.878710	11.196042	0.089317

YEARS							**MONTH**
1	1.138032	12.741460	0.078484	0.878710	11.196042	0.089317	12
2	1.295118	27.241655	0.036708	0.772130	21.034112	0.047542	24
3	1.473886	43.743348	0.022861	0.678478	29.678917	0.033694	36
4	1.677330	62.522811	0.015994	0.596185	37.275190	0.026827	48
5	1.908857	83.894449	0.011920	0.523874	43.950107	0.022753	60
6	2.172341	108.216068	0.009241	0.460333	49.815421	0.020074	72
7	2.472194	135.894861	0.007359	0.404499	54.969328	0.018192	84
8	2.813437	167.394225	0.005974	0.355437	59.498115	0.016807	96
9	3.201783	203.241525	0.004920	0.312326	63.477604	0.015754	108
10	3.643733	244.036917	0.004098	0.274444	66.974419	0.014931	120
11	4.146687	290.463399	0.003443	0.241156	70.047103	0.014276	132
12	4.719064	343.298242	0.002913	0.211906	72.747100	0.013746	144
13	5.370448	403.426010	0.002479	0.186204	75.119613	0.013312	156
14	6.111745	471.853363	0.002119	0.163619	77.204363	0.012953	168
15	6.955364	549.725914	0.001819	0.143774	79.036253	0.012652	180
16	7.915430	638.347406	0.001567	0.126336	80.645952	0.012400	192
17	9.008017	739.201542	0.001353	0.111012	82.060410	0.012186	204
18	10.251416	853.976825	0.001171	0.097548	83.303307	0.012004	216
19	11.666444	984.594826	0.001016	0.085716	84.395453	0.011849	228
20	13.276792	1133.242353	0.000882	0.075319	85.355132	0.011716	240
21	15.109421	1302.408067	0.000768	0.066184	86.198412	0.011601	252
22	17.195012	1494.924144	0.000669	0.058156	86.939409	0.011502	264
23	19.568482	1714.013694	0.000583	0.051103	87.590531	0.011417	276
24	22.269568	1963.344717	0.000509	0.044904	88.162677	0.011343	288
25	25.343491	2247.091520	0.000445	0.039458	88.665428	0.011278	300
26	28.841716	2570.004599	0.000389	0.034672	89.107200	0.011222	312
27	32.822810	2937.490172	0.000340	0.030467	89.495389	0.011174	324
28	37.353424	3355.700690	0.000298	0.026771	89.836495	0.011131	336
29	42.509410	3831.637843	0.000261	0.023524	90.136227	0.011094	348
30	48.377089	4373.269783	0.000229	0.020671	90.399605	0.011062	360
31	55.054699	4989.664524	0.000200	0.018164	90.631038	0.011034	372
32	62.654036	5691.141761	0.000176	0.015961	90.834400	0.011009	384
33	71.302328	6489.445641	0.000154	0.014025	91.013097	0.010987	396
34	81.144365	7397.941387	0.000135	0.012324	91.170119	0.010969	408
35	92.344923	8431.839055	0.000119	0.010829	91.308095	0.010952	420
36	105.091522	9608.448184	0.000104	0.009516	91.429337	0.010937	432
37	119.597566	10947.467591	0.000091	0.008361	91.535873	0.010925	444
38	136.105914	12471.315170	0.000080	0.007347	91.629487	0.010914	456
39	154.892951	14205.503212	0.000070	0.006456	91.711747	0.010904	468
40	176.273210	16179.065533	0.000062	0.005673	91.784030	0.010895	480

TABLE 10 Time Value of Money Computed at 14% Monthly

```
                                         MONTHLY                          14.00%
                               TIME VALUE OF MONEY TABLES
            EFFECTIVE RATE=   1.167%                      BASE=  1.01167
```

	1 FV1 FUTURE VALUE OF ONE	2 FV1/P FUTURE VALUE OF ONE PER PERIOD	3 SF SINKING FUND	4 PV1 PRESENT VALUE OF ONE	5 PV1/P PRESENT VALUE OF ONE PER PERIOD	6 PR PRINCIPAL RECOVERY
MONTH						
1	1.011667	1.000000	1.000000	0.988468	0.988468	1.011667
2	1.023469	2.011667	0.497100	0.977069	1.965537	0.508767
3	1.035410	3.035136	0.329475	0.965801	2.931338	0.341141
4	1.047490	4.070546	0.245667	0.954663	3.886001	0.257334
5	1.059710	5.118036	0.195387	0.943654	4.829655	0.207054
6	1.072074	6.177746	0.161871	0.932772	5.762427	0.173538
7	1.084581	7.249820	0.137934	0.922015	6.684442	0.149601
8	1.097235	8.334401	0.119985	0.911382	7.595824	0.131651
9	1.110036	9.431636	0.106026	0.900872	8.496696	0.117693
10	1.122986	10.541672	0.094862	0.890483	9.387178	0.106528
11	1.136088	11.664658	0.085729	0.880214	10.267392	0.097396
12	1.149342	12.800745	0.078120	0.870063	11.137455	0.089787
YEARS						**MONTH**
1	1.149342	12.800745	0.078120	0.870063	11.137455	0.089787	12
2	1.320987	27.513180	0.036346	0.757010	20.827743	0.048013	24
3	1.518266	44.422800	0.022511	0.658646	29.258904	0.034178	36
4	1.745007	63.857736	0.015660	0.573040	36.594546	0.027326	48
5	2.005610	86.195125	0.011602	0.498601	42.977016	0.023268	60
6	2.305132	111.868425	0.008939	0.433815	48.530168	0.020606	72
7	2.649385	141.375828	0.007073	0.377446	53.361760	0.018740	84
8	3.045049	175.289927	0.005705	0.328402	57.565549	0.017372	96
9	3.499803	214.268826	0.004667	0.285730	61.223111	0.016334	108
10	4.022471	259.068912	0.003860	0.248603	64.405420	0.015527	120
11	4.623195	310.559534	0.003220	0.216301	67.174230	0.014887	132
12	5.313632	369.739871	0.002705	0.188195	69.583269	0.014371	144
13	6.107180	437.758033	0.002284	0.163742	71.679284	0.013951	156
14	7.019239	515.934780	0.001938	0.142466	73.502950	0.013605	168
15	8.067507	605.786272	0.001651	0.123954	75.089654	0.013317	180
16	9.272324	709.056369	0.001410	0.107848	76.470187	0.013077	192
17	10.657072	827.749031	0.001208	0.093834	77.671337	0.012875	204
18	12.248621	964.167496	0.001037	0.081642	78.716413	0.012704	216
19	14.077855	1120.958972	0.000892	0.071034	79.625696	0.012559	228
20	16.180270	1301.166005	0.000769	0.061804	80.416829	0.012435	240
21	18.596664	1508.285522	0.000663	0.053773	81.105164	0.012330	252
22	21.373928	1746.336688	0.000573	0.046786	81.704060	0.012239	264
23	24.565954	2019.938898	0.000495	0.040707	82.225136	0.012162	276
24	28.234683	2334.401417	0.000428	0.035417	82.678506	0.012095	288
25	32.451308	2695.826407	0.000371	0.030815	83.072966	0.012038	300
26	37.297652	3111.227338	0.000321	0.026811	83.416171	0.011988	312
27	42.867759	3588.665088	0.000279	0.023328	83.714781	0.011945	324
28	49.269718	4137.404359	0.000242	0.020296	83.974591	0.011908	336
29	56.627757	4768.093467	0.000210	0.017659	84.200641	0.011876	348
30	65.084661	5492.970967	0.000182	0.015365	84.397320	0.011849	360
31	74.804537	6326.103143	0.000158	0.013368	84.568442	0.011825	372
32	85.975998	7283.656968	0.000137	0.011631	84.717330	0.011804	384
33	98.815828	8384.213825	0.000119	0.010120	84.846871	0.011786	396
34	113.573184	9649.130077	0.000104	0.008805	84.959580	0.011770	408
35	130.534434	11102.951488	0.000090	0.007661	85.057645	0.011757	420
36	150.028711	12773.889538	0.000078	0.006665	85.142966	0.011745	432
37	172.434303	14694.368868	0.000068	0.005799	85.217202	0.011735	444
38	198.185992	16901.656478	0.000059	0.005046	85.281792	0.011726	456
39	227.783490	19438.584899	0.000051	0.004390	85.337989	0.011718	468
40	261.801139	22354.383358	0.000045	0.003820	85.386683	0.011711	480

TABLE 11 Time Value of Money Computed at 15% Monthly

```
                                      MONTHLY                              15.00%
                          TIME VALUE OF MONEY TABLES
            EFFECTIVE RATE=   1.250%                      BASE=  1.01250
```

	1 EV1 FUTURE VALUE OF ONE	2 EV1/P FUTURE VALUE OF ONE PER PERIOD	3 SE SINKING FUND	4 PV1 PRESENT VALUE OF ONE	5 PV1/P PRESENT VALUE OF ONE PER PERIOD	6 PR PRINCIPAL RECOVERY
MONTH						
1	1.012500	1.000000	1.000000	0.987654	0.987654	1.012500
2	1.025156	2.012500	0.496894	0.975461	1.963115	0.509394
3	1.037971	3.037656	0.329201	0.963418	2.926534	0.341701
4	1.050945	4.075627	0.245361	0.951524	3.878058	0.257861
5	1.064082	5.126572	0.195062	0.939777	4.817835	0.207562
6	1.077383	6.190654	0.161534	0.928175	5.746010	0.174034
7	1.090850	7.268038	0.137589	0.916716	6.662726	0.150089
8	1.104486	8.358888	0.119633	0.905398	7.568124	0.132133
9	1.118292	9.463374	0.105671	0.894221	8.462345	0.118171
10	1.132271	10.581666	0.094503	0.883181	9.345526	0.107003
11	1.146424	11.713937	0.085368	0.872277	10.217803	0.097868
12	1.160755	12.860361	0.077758	0.861509	11.079312	0.090258

YEARS							MONTH
1	1.160755	12.860361	0.077758	0.861509	11.079312	0.090258	12
2	1.347351	27.788084	0.035987	0.742197	20.624235	0.048487	24
3	1.563944	45.115505	0.022165	0.639409	28.847267	0.034665	36
4	1.815355	65.228388	0.015331	0.550856	35.931481	0.027831	48
5	2.107181	88.574508	0.011290	0.474568	42.034592	0.023790	60
6	2.445920	115.673621	0.008645	0.408844	47.292474	0.021145	72
7	2.839113	147.129040	0.006797	0.352223	51.822185	0.019297	84
8	3.295513	183.641059	0.005445	0.303443	55.724570	0.017945	96
9	3.825282	226.022551	0.004424	0.261419	59.086509	0.016924	108
10	4.440213	275.217058	0.003633	0.225214	61.982847	0.016133	120
11	5.153998	332.319805	0.003009	0.194024	64.478068	0.015509	132
12	5.982526	398.602077	0.002509	0.167153	66.627722	0.015009	144
13	6.944244	475.539523	0.002103	0.144004	68.479668	0.014603	156
14	8.060563	564.845011	0.001770	0.124061	70.075134	0.014270	168
15	9.356334	668.506759	0.001496	0.106879	71.449643	0.013996	180
16	10.860408	788.832603	0.001268	0.092078	72.633794	0.013768	192
17	12.606267	928.501369	0.001077	0.079326	73.653950	0.013577	204
18	14.632781	1090.622520	0.000917	0.068340	74.532823	0.013417	216
19	16.985067	1278.805378	0.000782	0.058875	75.289980	0.013282	228
20	19.715494	1497.239481	0.000668	0.050722	75.942278	0.013168	240
21	22.884848	1750.787854	0.000571	0.043697	76.504237	0.013071	252
22	26.563691	2045.095272	0.000489	0.037645	76.988370	0.012989	264
23	30.833434	2386.713938	0.000419	0.032432	77.405455	0.012919	276
24	35.790617	2783.249347	0.000359	0.027940	77.764777	0.012859	288
25	41.544120	3243.529615	0.000308	0.024071	78.074336	0.012808	300
26	48.222525	3777.802015	0.000265	0.020737	78.341024	0.012765	312
27	55.974514	4397.961118	0.000227	0.017865	78.570778	0.012727	324
28	64.972677	5117.813598	0.000195	0.015391	78.768713	0.012695	336
29	75.417320	5953.385616	0.000168	0.013260	78.939236	0.012668	348
30	87.540995	6923.279611	0.000144	0.011423	79.086142	0.012644	360
31	101.613606	8049.088447	0.000124	0.009841	79.212704	0.012624	372
32	117.948452	9355.876140	0.000107	0.008478	79.321738	0.012607	384
33	136.909199	10872.735858	0.000092	0.007304	79.415671	0.012592	396
34	158.917970	12633.437629	0.000079	0.006293	79.496596	0.012579	408
35	184.464752	14677.180163	0.000068	0.005421	79.566313	0.012568	420
36	214.118294	17049.463544	0.000059	0.004670	79.626375	0.012559	432
37	248.538777	19803.102194	0.000050	0.004024	79.678119	0.012550	444
38	288.492509	22999.400699	0.000043	0.003466	79.722696	0.012543	456
39	334.868983	26709.518627	0.000037	0.002986	79.761101	0.012537	468
40	388.700685	31016.054774	0.000032	0.002573	79.794186	0.012532	480

TABLE 12   Time Value of Money Computed at 16% Monthly

16.00%   MONTHLY   16.00%
                                        TIME VALUE OF MONEY TABLES
                    EFFECTIVE RATE=   1.333%   BASE=   1.01333

	1 FV1 FUTURE VALUE OF ONE	2 FV1/P FUTURE VALUE OF ONE PER PERIOD	3 SF SINKING FUND	4 PV1 PRESENT VALUE OF ONE	5 PV1/P PRESENT VALUE OF ONE PER PERIOD	6 PR PRINCIPAL RECOVERY
MONTH						
1	1.013333	1.000000	1.000000	0.986842	0.986842	1.013333
2	1.026844	2.013333	0.496689	0.973857	1.960699	0.510022
3	1.040536	3.040178	0.328928	0.961043	2.921743	0.342261
4	1.054410	4.080713	0.245055	0.948398	3.870141	0.258389
5	1.068468	5.135123	0.194737	0.935919	4.806060	0.208071
6	1.082715	6.203591	0.161197	0.923604	5.729665	0.174530
7	1.097151	7.286306	0.137244	0.911452	6.641116	0.150577
8	1.111779	8.383457	0.119283	0.899459	7.540575	0.132616
9	1.126603	9.495236	0.105316	0.887624	8.428199	0.118649
10	1.141625	10.621839	0.094146	0.875945	9.304144	0.107479
11	1.156846	11.763464	0.085009	0.864419	10.168563	0.098342
12	1.172271	12.920310	0.077398	0.853045	11.021609	0.090731

YEARS						MONTH
1	1.172271	12.920310	0.077398	0.853045	11.021609	0.090731	12
2	1.374219	28.066412	0.035630	0.727686	20.423539	0.048963	24
3	1.610957	45.821745	0.021824	0.620749	28.443811	0.035157	36
4	1.888477	66.635803	0.015007	0.529527	35.285465	0.028340	48
5	2.213807	91.035516	0.010985	0.451711	41.121706	0.024318	60
6	2.595181	119.638587	0.008359	0.385330	46.100283	0.021692	72
7	3.042255	153.169132	0.006529	0.328704	50.347235	0.019862	84
8	3.566347	192.476010	0.005195	0.280399	53.970077	0.018529	96
9	4.180724	238.554316	0.004192	0.239193	57.060524	0.017525	108
10	4.900941	292.570569	0.003418	0.204042	59.696816	0.016751	120
11	5.745230	355.892244	0.002810	0.174057	61.945692	0.016143	132
12	6.734965	430.122395	0.002325	0.148479	63.864085	0.015658	144
13	7.895203	517.140233	0.001934	0.126659	65.500561	0.015267	156
14	9.255316	619.148703	0.001615	0.108046	66.896549	0.014948	168
15	10.849737	738.730255	0.001354	0.092168	68.087390	0.014687	180
16	12.718830	878.912215	0.001138	0.078624	69.103231	0.014471	192
17	14.909912	1043.243434	0.000959	0.067069	69.969789	0.014292	204
18	17.478455	1235.884123	0.000809	0.057213	70.709003	0.014142	216
19	20.489482	1461.711177	0.000684	0.048806	71.339585	0.014017	228
20	24.019222	1726.441638	0.000579	0.041633	71.877501	0.013913	240
21	28.157032	2036.777427	0.000491	0.035515	72.336367	0.013824	252
22	33.007667	2400.575011	0.000417	0.030296	72.727801	0.013750	264
23	38.693924	2827.044294	0.000354	0.025844	73.061711	0.013687	276
24	45.355757	3326.981781	0.000301	0.022046	73.346552	0.013634	288
25	53.173919	3913.043898	0.000256	0.018806	73.589534	0.013589	300
26	62.334232	4600.067404	0.000217	0.016043	73.796809	0.013551	312
27	73.072600	5405.444997	0.000185	0.013685	73.973623	0.013518	324
28	85.660875	6349.565632	0.000157	0.011674	74.124454	0.013491	336
29	100.417742	7456.330682	0.000134	0.009958	74.253120	0.013467	348
30	117.716787	8753.759030	0.000114	0.008495	74.362878	0.013448	360
31	137.995952	10274.696396	0.000097	0.007247	74.456506	0.013431	372
32	161.768625	12057.646856	0.000083	0.006182	74.536375	0.013416	384
33	189.636635	14147.747615	0.000071	0.005273	74.604507	0.013404	396
34	222.305489	16597.911700	0.000060	0.004498	74.662626	0.013394	408
35	260.602233	19470.167508	0.000051	0.003837	74.712205	0.013385	420
36	305.496388	22837.229116	0.000044	0.003273	74.754998	0.013377	432
37	358.124495	26784.337116	0.000037	0.002792	74.790576	0.013371	444
38	419.818887	31411.416562	0.000032	0.002382	74.821352	0.013365	456
39	492.141422	36835.606677	0.000027	0.002032	74.847605	0.013360	468
40	576.923018	43194.226353	0.000023	0.001733	74.870000	0.013356	480

TABLE 13 Time Value of Money Computed at 17% Monthly

```
17.00%                                    MONTHLY                         17.00%
                                  TIME VALUE OF MONEY TABLES
              EFFECTIVE RATE=   1.417%                      BASE=   1.01417
```

	1 FV1 FUTURE VALUE OF ONE	2 FV1/P FUTURE VALUE OF ONE PER PERIOD	3 SF SINKING FUND	4 PV1 PRESENT VALUE OF ONE	5 PV1/P PRESENT VALUE OF ONE PER PERIOD	6 PR PRINCIPAL RECOVERY	
MONTH							
1	1.014167	1.000000	1.000000	0.986031	0.986031	1.014167	
2	1.028534	2.014167	0.496483	0.972258	1.958289	0.510650	
3	1.043105	3.042701	0.328655	0.958676	2.916965	0.342822	
4	1.057882	4.085806	0.244750	0.945285	3.862250	0.258916	
5	1.072869	5.143688	0.194413	0.932080	4.794330	0.208580	
6	1.088068	6.216557	0.160861	0.919060	5.713391	0.175027	
7	1.103482	7.304625	0.136900	0.906222	6.619613	0.151066	
8	1.119115	8.408107	0.118933	0.893563	7.513176	0.133100	
9	1.134969	9.527222	0.104962	0.881081	8.394257	0.119129	
10	1.151048	10.662191	0.093789	0.868774	9.263031	0.107956	
11	1.167354	11.813238	0.084651	0.856638	10.119669	0.098817	
12	1.183892	12.980593	0.077038	0.844672	10.964341	0.091205	
YEARS							MONTH
1	1.183892	12.980593	0.077038	0.844672	10.964341	0.091205	12
2	1.401600	28.348209	0.035276	0.713471	20.225611	0.049442	24
3	1.659342	46.541802	0.021486	0.602648	28.048345	0.035653	36
4	1.964482	68.081048	0.014688	0.509040	34.655988	0.028855	48
5	2.325733	93.581182	0.010686	0.429972	40.237278	0.024853	60
6	2.753417	123.770579	0.008079	0.363185	44.951636	0.022246	72
7	3.255747	159.511558	0.006269	0.306772	48.933722	0.020436	84
8	3.859188	201.825006	0.004955	0.259122	52.297278	0.019121	96
9	4.568860	251.919548	0.003970	0.218873	55.138379	0.018136	108
10	5.409036	311.226062	0.003213	0.184876	57.538177	0.017380	120
11	6.403713	381.438553	0.002622	0.156159	59.565218	0.016788	132
12	7.581303	464.562540	0.002153	0.131903	61.277403	0.016319	144
13	8.975441	562.972341	0.001776	0.111415	62.723638	0.015943	156
14	10.625951	679.478890	0.001472	0.094109	63.945231	0.015638	168
15	12.579975	817.410030	0.001223	0.079491	64.977077	0.015390	180
16	14.893329	980.705566	0.001020	0.067144	65.848648	0.015186	192
17	17.632089	1174.029800	0.000852	0.056715	66.584839	0.015018	204
18	20.874484	1402.904761	0.000713	0.047905	67.206679	0.014879	216
19	24.713129	1673.867935	0.000597	0.040464	67.731930	0.014764	228
20	29.257669	1994.658995	0.000501	0.034179	68.175595	0.014668	240
21	34.637912	2374.440878	0.000421	0.028870	68.550346	0.014588	252
22	41.007538	2824.061507	0.000354	0.024386	68.866887	0.014521	264
23	48.548485	3356.363651	0.000298	0.020598	69.134261	0.014465	276
24	57.476150	3986.551756	0.000251	0.017399	69.360104	0.014418	288
25	68.045538	4732.626240	0.000211	0.014696	69.550868	0.014378	300
26	80.558550	5615.897651	0.000178	0.012413	69.712000	0.014345	312
27	95.372601	6661.595368	0.000150	0.010485	69.848104	0.014317	324
28	112.910833	7899.588246	0.000127	0.008857	69.963067	0.014293	336
29	133.674202	9365.237774	0.000107	0.007481	70.060174	0.014273	348
30	158.255782	11100.408126	0.000090	0.006319	70.142196	0.014257	360
31	187.357711	13154.661953	0.000076	0.005337	70.211479	0.014243	372
32	221.811244	15586.676066	0.000064	0.004508	70.270000	0.014231	384
33	262.600497	18465.917458	0.000054	0.003808	70.319431	0.014221	396
34	310.890557	21874.627526	0.000046	0.003217	70.361184	0.014212	408
35	368.060758	25910.171179	0.000039	0.002717	70.396451	0.014205	420
36	435.744387	30687.817929	0.000033	0.002295	70.426241	0.014199	432
37	515.873821	36344.034396	0.000028	0.001938	70.451403	0.014194	444
38	610.738749	43040.382285	0.000023	0.001637	70.472657	0.014190	456
39	723.048553	50968.133160	0.000020	0.001383	70.490609	0.014186	468
40	856.011201	60353.731845	0.000017	0.001168	70.505773	0.014183	480

TABLE 14   Time Value of Money Computed at 18% Monthly

18.00%				MONTHLY		18.00%
				TIME VALUE OF MONEY TABLES		
	EFFECTIVE RATE=	1.500%			BASE= 1.01500	

	1	2	3	4	5	6
	EV1	EV1/P	SE	PV1	PV1/P	PR
	FUTURE VALUE	FUTURE VALUE	SINKING	PRESENT VALUE	PRESENT VALUE	PRINCIPAL
	OF ONE	OF ONE	FUND	OF ONE	OF ONE	RECOVERY
		PER PERIOD			PER PERIOD	
MONTH						
1	1.015000	1.000000	1.000000	0.985222	0.985222	1.015000
2	1.030225	2.015000	0.496278	0.970662	1.955883	0.511278
3	1.045678	3.045225	0.328383	0.956317	2.912200	0.343383
4	1.061364	4.090903	0.244445	0.942184	3.854385	0.259445
5	1.077284	5.152267	0.194089	0.928260	4.782645	0.209089
6	1.093443	6.229551	0.160525	0.914542	5.697187	0.175525
7	1.109845	7.322994	0.136556	0.901027	6.598214	0.151556
8	1.126493	8.432839	0.118584	0.887711	7.485925	0.133584
9	1.143390	9.559332	0.104610	0.874592	8.360517	0.119610
10	1.160541	10.702722	0.093434	0.861667	9.222185	0.108434
11	1.177949	11.863262	0.084294	0.848933	10.071118	0.099294
12	1.195618	13.041211	0.076680	0.836387	10.907505	0.091680
YEARS						MONTH
1	1.195618	13.041211	0.076680	0.836387	10.907505	0.091680	12
2	1.429503	28.633521	0.034924	0.699544	20.030405	0.049924	24
3	1.709140	47.275969	0.021152	0.585090	27.660684	0.036152	36
4	2.043478	69.565219	0.014375	0.489362	34.042554	0.029375	48
5	2.443220	96.214652	0.010393	0.409296	39.380269	0.025393	60
6	2.921158	128.077197	0.007808	0.342330	43.844667	0.022808	72
7	3.492590	166.172636	0.006018	0.286321	47.578633	0.021018	84
8	4.175804	211.720235	0.004723	0.239475	50.701675	0.019723	96
9	4.992667	266.177771	0.003757	0.200294	53.313749	0.018757	108
10	5.969323	331.288191	0.003019	0.167523	55.498454	0.018019	120
11	7.137031	409.135393	0.002444	0.140114	57.325714	0.017444	132
12	8.533164	502.210922	0.001991	0.117190	58.854011	0.016991	144
13	10.202406	613.493716	0.001630	0.098016	60.132260	0.016630	156
14	12.198182	746.545446	0.001340	0.081979	61.201371	0.016340	168
15	14.584368	905.624513	0.001104	0.068567	62.095562	0.016104	180
16	17.437335	1095.822335	0.000913	0.057348	62.843452	0.015913	192
17	20.848395	1323.226308	0.000756	0.047965	63.468978	0.015756	204
18	24.926719	1595.114630	0.000627	0.040118	63.992160	0.015627	216
19	29.802839	1920.189249	0.000521	0.033554	64.429743	0.015521	228
20	35.632816	2308.854370	0.000433	0.028064	64.795732	0.015433	240
21	42.603242	2773.549452	0.000361	0.023472	65.101841	0.015361	252
22	50.937210	3329.147335	0.000300	0.019632	65.357866	0.015300	264
23	60.901454	3993.430261	0.000250	0.016420	65.572002	0.015250	276
24	72.814885	4787.658998	0.000209	0.013733	65.751103	0.015209	288
25	87.058800	5737.253308	0.000174	0.011486	65.900901	0.015174	300
26	104.089083	6872.605521	0.000146	0.009607	66.026190	0.015146	312
27	124.450799	8230.053258	0.000122	0.008035	66.130980	0.015122	324
28	148.795637	9853.042439	0.000101	0.006721	66.218625	0.015101	336
29	177.902767	11793.517795	0.000085	0.005621	66.291930	0.015085	348
30	212.703781	14113.585393	0.000071	0.004701	66.353242	0.015071	360
31	254.312506	16887.500372	0.000059	0.003932	66.404522	0.015059	372
32	304.060653	20204.043526	0.000049	0.003289	66.447412	0.015049	384
33	363.540442	24169.362788	0.000041	0.002751	66.483285	0.015041	396
34	434.655558	28910.370554	0.000035	0.002301	66.513289	0.015035	408
35	519.682084	34578.805589	0.000029	0.001924	66.538383	0.015029	420
36	621.341343	41356.089521	0.000024	0.001609	66.559372	0.015024	432
37	742.887000	49459.133344	0.000020	0.001346	66.576927	0.015020	444
38	888.209197	59147.279782	0.000017	0.001126	66.591609	0.015017	456
39	1061.959056	70730.603711	0.000014	0.000942	66.603890	0.015014	468
40	1269.697544	84579.836287	0.000012	0.000788	66.614161	0.015012	480

TABLE 15 Time Value of Money Computed at 19% Monthly

19.00%　　　　　　　　　　　　　　　　MONTHLY　　　　　　　　　　　　　　19.00%

TIME VALUE OF MONEY TABLES

EFFECTIVE RATE=　1.583%　　　　　　　　　　BASE=　1.01583

	1 EV1 FUTURE VALUE OF ONE	2 EV1/P FUTURE VALUE OF ONE PER PERIOD	3 SF SINKING FUND	4 PV1 PRESENT VALUE OF ONE	5 PV1/P PRESENT VALUE OF ONE PER PERIOD	6 PR PRINCIPAL RECOVERY
MONTH						
1	1.015833	1.000000	1.000000	0.984413	0.984413	1.015833
2	1.031917	2.015833	0.496073	0.969070	1.953483	0.511906
3	1.048256	3.047751	0.328111	0.953965	2.907449	0.343944
4	1.064853	4.096007	0.244140	0.939096	3.846545	0.259974
5	1.081714	5.160860	0.193766	0.924459	4.771004	0.209599
6	1.098841	6.242574	0.160190	0.910050	5.681054	0.176024
7	1.116239	7.341415	0.136214	0.895865	6.576920	0.152047
8	1.133913	8.457654	0.118236	0.881902	7.458822	0.134069
9	1.151866	9.591566	0.104258	0.868156	8.326978	0.120092
10	1.170104	10.743433	0.093080	0.854625	9.181602	0.108913
11	1.188631	11.913537	0.083938	0.841304	10.022906	0.099771
12	1.207451	13.102168	0.076323	0.828191	10.851097	0.092157
YEARS						**MONTH**
1	1.207451	13.102168	0.076323	0.828191	10.851097	0.092157	12
2	1.457938	28.922394	0.034575	0.685900	19.837878	0.050409	24
3	1.760389	48.024542	0.020823	0.568056	27.280649	0.036656	36
4	2.125583	71.089450	0.014067	0.470459	33.444684	0.029900	48
5	2.566537	98.939196	0.010107	0.389630	38.549682	0.025941	60
6	3.098968	132.566399	0.007543	0.322688	42.777596	0.023377	72
7	3.741852	173.169599	0.005775	0.267247	46.279115	0.021608	84
8	4.518103	222.155973	0.004501	0.221332	49.179042	0.020334	96
9	5.455388	281.392918	0.003554	0.183305	51.580735	0.019387	108
10	6.587114	352.870328	0.002834	0.151812	53.569796	0.018667	120
11	7.953617	439.175798	0.002277	0.125729	55.217118	0.018110	132
12	9.603603	543.385424	0.001840	0.104128	56.581415	0.017674	144
13	11.595879	669.213441	0.001494	0.086238	57.711314	0.017328	156
14	14.001456	821.144606	0.001218	0.071421	58.647086	0.017051	168
15	16.906072	1004.594042	0.000995	0.059150	59.422084	0.016829	180
16	20.413254	1226.100247	0.000816	0.048988	60.063930	0.016649	192
17	24.648004	1493.558135	0.000670	0.040571	60.595501	0.016503	204
18	29.761257	1816.500430	0.000551	0.033601	61.035743	0.016384	216
19	35.935259	2206.437425	0.000453	0.027828	61.400348	0.016287	228
20	43.390065	2677.267240	0.000374	0.023047	61.702310	0.016207	240
21	52.391377	3245.771169	0.000308	0.019087	61.952393	0.016141	252
22	63.260020	3932.211806	0.000254	0.015808	62.159509	0.016088	264
23	76.383375	4761.055238	0.000210	0.013092	62.331041	0.016043	276
24	92.229182	5761.843068	0.000174	0.010843	62.473102	0.016007	288
25	111.362218	6970.245332	0.000143	0.008980	62.590755	0.015977	300
26	134.464421	8429.331851	0.000119	0.007437	62.688195	0.015952	312
27	162.359199	10191.107326	0.000098	0.006159	62.768894	0.015931	324
28	196.040777	12318.364881	0.000081	0.005101	62.835728	0.015915	336
29	236.709632	14886.924139	0.000067	0.004225	62.891079	0.015901	348
30	285.815282	17988.333579	0.000056	0.003499	62.936920	0.015889	360
31	345.107947	21733.133503	0.000046	0.002898	62.974886	0.015879	372
32	416.700935	26254.755909	0.000038	0.002400	63.006328	0.015871	384
33	503.145960	31714.481694	0.000032	0.001987	63.032369	0.015865	396
34	607.524092	38306.784745	0.000026	0.001646	63.053935	0.015859	408
35	733.555571	46266.667644	0.000022	0.001363	63.071796	0.015855	420
36	885.732406	55877.836195	0.000018	0.001129	63.086589	0.015851	432
37	1069.478478	67482.851256	0.000015	0.000935	63.098840	0.015848	444
38	1291.342856	81495.338274	0.000012	0.000774	63.108986	0.015846	456
39	1559.233220	98414.729710	0.000010	0.000641	63.117389	0.015843	468
40	1882.697708	118844.065787	0.000008	0.000531	63.124348	0.015842	480

TABLE 16 Time Value of Money Computed at 20% Monthly

MONTHLY
TIME VALUE OF MONEY TABLES

EFFECTIVE RATE= 1.667%   BASE= 1.01667

	1 FV1 FUTURE VALUE OF ONE	2 FV1/P FUTURE VALUE OF ONE PER PERIOD	3 SF SINKING FUND	4 PV1 PRESENT VALUE OF ONE	5 PV1/P PRESENT VALUE OF ONE PER PERIOD	6 PR PRINCIPAL RECOVERY
MONTH						
1	1.016667	1.000000	1.000000	0.983607	0.983607	1.016667
2	1.033611	2.016667	0.495868	0.967482	1.951088	0.512534
3	1.050838	3.050278	0.327839	0.951622	2.902710	0.344506
4	1.068352	4.101116	0.243836	0.936021	3.838731	0.260503
5	1.086158	5.169468	0.193444	0.920677	4.759408	0.210110
6	1.104260	6.255625	0.159856	0.905583	5.664991	0.176523
7	1.122665	7.359886	0.135872	0.890738	6.555729	0.152538
8	1.141376	8.482551	0.117889	0.876136	7.431865	0.134556
9	1.160399	9.623926	0.103908	0.861773	8.293637	0.120574
10	1.179739	10.784325	0.092727	0.847645	9.141283	0.109394
11	1.199401	11.964064	0.083584	0.833749	9.975032	0.100250
12	1.219391	13.163465	0.075968	0.820081	10.795113	0.092635

YEARS							**MONTH**
1	1.219391	13.163465	0.075968	0.820081	10.795113	0.092635	12
2	1.486915	29.214877	0.034229	0.672534	19.647986	0.050896	24
3	1.813130	48.787826	0.020497	0.551532	26.908062	0.037164	36
4	2.210915	72.654905	0.013764	0.452301	32.861916	0.030430	48
5	2.695970	101.758208	0.009827	0.370924	37.744561	0.026494	60
6	3.287442	137.246517	0.007286	0.304188	41.748727	0.023953	72
7	4.008677	180.520645	0.005540	0.249459	45.032470	0.022206	84
8	4.888145	233.288730	0.004287	0.204577	47.725406	0.020953	96
9	5.960561	297.633662	0.003360	0.167769	49.933833	0.020027	108
10	7.268255	376.095300	0.002659	0.137585	51.744924	0.019326	120
11	8.862845	471.770720	0.002120	0.112831	53.230165	0.018786	132
12	10.807275	588.436476	0.001699	0.092530	54.448184	0.018366	144
13	13.178294	730.697658	0.001369	0.075882	55.447059	0.018035	156
14	16.069495	904.169675	0.001106	0.062230	56.266217	0.017773	168
15	19.594998	1115.699905	0.000896	0.051033	56.937994	0.017563	180
16	23.893966	1373.637983	0.000728	0.041852	57.488906	0.017395	192
17	29.136090	1688.165376	0.000592	0.034322	57.940698	0.017259	204
18	35.528288	2071.697274	0.000483	0.028147	58.311205	0.017149	216
19	43.322878	2539.372652	0.000394	0.023082	58.615050	0.017060	228
20	52.827531	3109.651838	0.000322	0.018930	58.864229	0.016988	240
21	64.417420	3805.045193	0.000263	0.015524	59.068575	0.016929	252
22	78.550028	4653.001652	0.000215	0.012731	59.236156	0.016882	264
23	95.783203	5686.992197	0.000176	0.010440	59.373585	0.016843	276
24	116.797184	6947.831050	0.000144	0.008562	59.486289	0.016811	288
25	142.421445	8485.286707	0.000118	0.007021	59.578715	0.016785	300
26	173.667440	10360.046428	0.000097	0.005758	59.654512	0.016763	312
27	211.768529	12646.111719	0.000079	0.004722	59.716672	0.016746	324
28	258.228656	15433.719354	0.000065	0.003873	59.767648	0.016731	336
29	314.881721	18832.903252	0.000053	0.003176	59.809452	0.016720	348
30	383.963963	22977.837794	0.000044	0.002604	59.843735	0.016710	360
31	468.202234	28032.134021	0.000036	0.002136	59.871850	0.016702	372
32	570.921630	34195.297782	0.000029	0.001752	59.894907	0.016696	384
33	696.176745	41710.604726	0.000024	0.001436	59.913815	0.016691	396
34	848.911717	50874.703014	0.000020	0.001178	59.929321	0.016686	408
35	1035.155379	62049.322767	0.000016	0.000966	59.942038	0.016683	420
36	1262.259241	75675.554472	0.000013	0.000792	59.952466	0.016680	432
37	1539.187666	92291.259933	0.000011	0.000650	59.961018	0.016678	444
38	1876.871717	112552.303043	0.000009	0.000533	59.968032	0.016676	456
39	2288.640640	137258.438381	0.000007	0.000437	59.973784	0.016674	468
40	2790.747993	167384.879555	0.000006	0.000358	59.978500	0.016673	480

TABLE 17 Time Value of Money Computed at 30% Monthly

            MONTHLY

TIME VALUE OF MONEY TABLES

EFFECTIVE RATE= 2.500%   BASE= 1.02500

	1 EV1 FUTURE VALUE OF ONE	2 EV1/P FUTURE VALUE OF ONE PER PERIOD	3 SF SINKING FUND	4 PV1 PRESENT VALUE OF ONE	5 PV1/P PRESENT VALUE OF ONE PER PERIOD	6 PR PRINCIPAL RECOVERY	
MONTH							
1	1.02500	1.00000	1.00000	0.975610	0.975610	1.025000	
2	1.05062	2.02500	0.493827	0.951814	1.927424	0.518827	
3	1.07689	3.07562	0.325137	0.928599	2.856024	0.350137	
4	1.10381	4.15252	0.240818	0.905951	3.761974	0.265818	
5	1.13141	5.25633	0.190247	0.883854	4.645828	0.215247	
6	1.15969	6.38774	0.156550	0.862297	5.508125	0.181550	
7	1.18869	7.54743	0.132495	0.841265	6.349391	0.157495	
8	1.21840	8.73612	0.114467	0.820747	7.170137	0.139467	
9	1.24886	9.95452	0.100457	0.800728	7.970866	0.125457	
10	1.28008	11.20338	0.089259	0.781198	8.752064	0.114259	
11	1.31209	12.48347	0.080106	0.762145	9.514209	0.105106	
12	1.34489	13.79555	0.072487	0.743556	10.257765	0.097487	

YEARS							**MONTH**
1	1.34489	13.79555	0.072487	0.743556	10.257765	0.097487	12
2	1.80873	32.34904	0.030913	0.552875	17.884986	0.055913	24
3	2.43254	57.30141	0.017452	0.411094	23.556251	0.042452	36
4	3.27149	90.85958	0.011006	0.305671	27.773154	0.036006	48
5	4.39979	135.99159	0.007353	0.227284	30.908656	0.032353	60
6	5.91723	196.68912	0.005084	0.168998	33.240078	0.030084	72
7	7.95801	278.32056	0.003593	0.125659	34.973620	0.028593	84
8	10.70264	388.10576	0.002577	0.093435	36.262606	0.027577	96
9	14.39387	535.75465	0.001867	0.069474	37.221039	0.026867	108
10	19.35815	734.32599	0.001362	0.051658	37.933687	0.026362	120
11	26.03456	1001.38237	0.000999	0.038410	38.463581	0.025999	132
12	35.01359	1360.54352	0.000735	0.028560	38.857586	0.025735	144
13	47.08938	1843.57532	0.000542	0.021236	39.150552	0.025542	156
14	63.32999	2493.19940	0.000401	0.015790	39.368388	0.025401	168
15	85.17179	3366.87157	0.000297	0.011741	39.530361	0.025297	180
16	114.54659	4541.86350	0.000220	0.008730	39.650797	0.025220	192
17	154.05243	6122.09701	0.000163	0.006491	39.740348	0.025163	204
18	207.18339	8247.33540	0.000121	0.004827	39.806934	0.025121	216
19	278.63862	11105.54477	0.000090	0.003589	39.856445	0.025090	228
20	374.73796	14949.51860	0.000067	0.002669	39.893259	0.025067	240
21	503.98090	20119.23605	0.000050	0.001984	39.920632	0.025050	252
22	677.79828	27071.93126	0.000037	0.001475	39.940985	0.025037	264
23	911.56333	36422.53336	0.000027	0.001097	39.956119	0.025027	276
24	1225.95134	48998.05362	0.000020	0.000816	39.967372	0.025020	288
25	1648.76826	65910.73027	0.000015	0.000607	39.975739	0.025015	300
26	2217.41000	88656.40010	0.000011	0.000451	39.981961	0.025011	312
27	2982.16993	119246.79724	0.000008	0.000335	39.986587	0.025008	324
28	4010.68701	160387.48049	0.000006	0.000249	39.990027	0.025006	336
29	5393.92814	215717.12561	0.000005	0.000185	39.992584	0.025005	348
30	7254.23367	290129.34698	0.000003	0.000138	39.994486	0.025003	360
31	9756.13780	390205.51190	0.000003	0.000102	39.995900	0.025003	372
32	13120.92069	524796.82767	0.000002	0.000076	39.996951	0.025002	384
33	17646.17960	705807.18408	0.000001	0.000057	39.997733	0.025001	396
34	23732.14974	949245.98949	0.000001	0.000042	39.998315	0.025001	408
35	31917.10296	1276644.11828	0.000001	0.000031	39.998747	0.025001	420
36	42924.95507	1716958.20277	0.000001	0.000023	39.999068	0.025001	432
37	57729.29235	2309131.69416	0.000000	0.000017	39.999307	0.025000	444
38	77639.48012	3105539.20474	0.000000	0.000013	39.999485	0.025000	456
39	104416.46913	4176618.76527	0.000000	0.000010	39.999617	0.025000	468
40	140428.54240	5617101.69610	0.000000	0.000007	39.999715	0.025000	480

TABLE 18   Time Value of Money Computed at 40% Monthly

```
                                        MONTHLY
                              TIME VALUE OF MONEY TABLES
              EFFECTIVE RATE=    3.333%                    BASE=   1.03333
```

	1 FV1 FUTURE VALUE OF ONE	2 FV1/P FUTURE VALUE OF ONE PER PERIOD	3 SF SINKING FUND	4 PV1 PRESENT VALUE OF ONE	5 PV1/P PRESENT VALUE OF ONE PER PERIOD	6 PR PRINCIPAL RECOVERY
MONTH						
1	1.03333	1.00000	1.000000	0.967742	0.967742	1.033333
2	1.06778	2.03333	0.491803	0.936524	1.904266	0.525137
3	1.10337	3.10111	0.322465	0.906314	2.810580	0.355798
4	1.14015	4.20448	0.237841	0.877078	3.687658	0.271175
5	1.17815	5.34463	0.187104	0.848785	4.536444	0.220437
6	1.21743	6.52279	0.153309	0.821405	5.357849	0.186642
7	1.25801	7.74021	0.129195	0.794908	6.152757	0.162529
8	1.29994	8.99822	0.111133	0.769266	6.922023	0.144466
9	1.34327	10.29816	0.097105	0.744451	7.666474	0.130438
10	1.38805	11.64143	0.085900	0.720436	8.386910	0.119233
11	1.43432	13.02948	0.076749	0.697196	9.084106	0.110082
12	1.48213	14.46379	0.069138	0.674706	9.758813	0.102471
YEARS						MONTH
1	1.48213	14.46379	0.069138	0.674706	9.758813	0.102471	12
2	2.19670	35.90097	0.027854	0.455229	16.343144	0.061188	24
3	3.25579	67.67357	0.014777	0.307146	20.785634	0.048110	36
4	4.82549	114.76459	0.008713	0.207233	23.783010	0.042047	48
5	7.15198	184.55943	0.005418	0.139821	25.805358	0.038752	60
6	10.60014	288.00421	0.003472	0.094338	27.169849	0.036806	72
7	15.71075	441.32246	0.002266	0.063651	28.090479	0.035599	84
8	23.28532	668.55951	0.001496	0.042946	28.711634	0.034829	96
9	34.51179	1005.35356	0.000995	0.028976	29.130732	0.034328	108
10	51.15083	1504.52493	0.000665	0.019550	29.413499	0.033998	120
11	75.81200	2244.36005	0.000446	0.013191	29.604284	0.033779	132
12	112.36298	3340.88927	0.000299	0.008900	29.733008	0.033633	144
13	166.53614	4966.08429	0.000201	0.006005	29.819859	0.033535	156
14	246.82763	7374.82887	0.000136	0.004051	29.878458	0.033469	168
15	365.82977	10944.89301	0.000091	0.002734	29.917995	0.033425	180
16	542.20599	16236.17966	0.000062	0.001844	29.944670	0.033395	192
17	803.61786	24078.53576	0.000042	0.001244	29.962669	0.033375	204
18	1191.06332	35701.89947	0.000028	0.000840	29.974812	0.033361	216
19	1765.30649	52929.19473	0.000019	0.000566	29.983006	0.033352	228
20	2616.40751	78462.22538	0.000013	0.000382	29.988534	0.033346	240
21	3877.84688	116305.40647	0.000009	0.000258	29.992264	0.033342	252
22	5747.45959	172393.78762	0.000006	0.000174	29.994780	0.033339	264
23	8518.46210	255523.86308	0.000004	0.000117	29.996478	0.033337	276
24	12625.43833	378733.15000	0.000003	0.000079	29.997624	0.033336	288
25	18712.49660	561344.89792	0.000002	0.000053	29.998397	0.033335	300
26	27734.28689	831998.60684	0.000001	0.000036	29.998918	0.033335	312
27	41105.72128	1233141.63835	0.000001	0.000024	29.999270	0.033334	324
28	60923.87838	1827686.35149	0.000001	0.000016	29.999508	0.033334	336
29	90296.89400	2708876.82012	0.000000	0.000011	29.999668	0.033334	348
30	133831.41854	4014912.55610	0.000000	0.000007	29.999776	0.033334	360
31	198355.09056	5950622.71684	0.000000	0.000005	29.999849	0.033334	372
32	293987.33408	8819590.02237	0.000000	0.000003	29.999898	0.033333	384
33	435726.41546	13071762.46384	0.000000	0.000002	29.999931	0.033333	396
34	645801.66260	19374019.87792	0.000000	0.000002	29.999954	0.033333	408
35	957159.75120	28714762.53596	0.000000	0.000001	29.999969	0.033333	420
36	1418631.82208	42558924.66248	0.000000	0.000001	29.999979	0.033333	432
37	2102591.80258	63077724.07727	0.000000	0.000000	29.999986	0.033333	444
38	3116307.30753	93489180.22585	0.000000	0.000000	29.999990	0.033333	456
39	4618761.16575	138562804.97262	0.000000	0.000000	29.999994	0.033333	468
40	6845588.27315	205367618.19456	0.000000	0.000000	29.999996	0.033333	480

TABLE 19 Time Value of Money Computed at 50% Monthly

MONTHLY
TIME VALUE OF MONEY TABLES

EFFECTIVE RATE= 4.167%   BASE= 1.04167

	1 FV1 FUTURE VALUE OF ONE	2 FV1/P FUTURE VALUE OF ONE PER PERIOD	3 SF SINKING FUND	4 PV1 PRESENT VALUE OF ONE	5 PV1/P PRESENT VALUE OF ONE PER PERIOD	6 PR PRINCIPAL RECOVERY
MONTH						
1	1.0417	1.0000	1.000000	0.960000	0.960000	1.041667
2	1.0851	2.0417	0.489796	0.921600	1.881600	0.531463
3	1.1303	3.1267	0.319822	0.884736	2.766336	0.361489
4	1.1774	4.2570	0.234906	0.849347	3.615683	0.276573
5	1.2264	5.4344	0.184013	0.815373	4.431055	0.225680
6	1.2775	6.6608	0.150132	0.782758	5.213813	0.191798
7	1.3308	7.9384	0.125971	0.751447	5.965261	0.167637
8	1.3862	9.2691	0.107885	0.721390	6.686650	0.149552
9	1.4440	10.6553	0.093850	0.692534	7.379184	0.135516
10	1.5041	12.0993	0.082649	0.664833	8.044017	0.124316
11	1.5668	13.6034	0.073511	0.638239	8.682256	0.115177
12	1.6321	15.1703	0.065918	0.612710	9.294966	0.107585

YEARS							MONTH
1	1.6321	15.1703	0.065918	0.612710	9.294966	0.107585	12
2	2.6637	39.9296	0.025044	0.375413	14.990082	0.066711	24
3	4.3475	80.3390	0.012447	0.230019	18.479535	0.054114	36
4	7.0955	146.2911	0.006836	0.140935	20.617557	0.048502	48
5	11.5805	253.9312	0.003938	0.086352	21.927544	0.045605	60
6	18.9004	429.6098	0.002328	0.052909	22.730186	0.043994	72
7	30.8472	716.3340	0.001396	0.032418	23.221973	0.043063	84
8	50.3456	1184.2947	0.000844	0.019863	23.523295	0.042511	96
9	82.1688	1948.0507	0.000513	0.012170	23.707918	0.042180	108
10	134.1072	3194.5724	0.000313	0.007457	23.821039	0.041980	120
11	218.8755	5229.0131	0.000191	0.004569	23.890349	0.041858	132
12	357.2255	8549.4118	0.000117	0.002799	23.932816	0.041784	144
13	583.0256	13968.6151	0.000072	0.001715	23.958835	0.041738	156
14	951.5527	22813.2650	0.000044	0.001051	23.974778	0.041711	168
15	1553.0236	37248.5662	0.000027	0.000644	23.984546	0.041694	180
16	2534.6807	60808.3366	0.000016	0.000395	23.990531	0.041683	192
17	4136.8375	99260.0996	0.000010	0.000242	23.994198	0.041677	204
18	6751.7082	162016.9965	0.000006	0.000148	23.996445	0.041673	216
19	11013.4233	264442.1596	0.000004	0.000091	23.997822	0.041670	228
20	17984.7361	431609.6673	0.000002	0.000056	23.998666	0.041669	240
21	29352.7823	704442.7760	0.000001	0.000034	23.999182	0.041668	252
22	47906.5038	1149732.0917	0.000001	0.000021	23.999499	0.041668	264
23	78187.9238	1876486.1714	0.000001	0.000013	23.999693	0.041667	276
24	127610.0517	3062617.2407	0.000000	0.000008	23.999812	0.041667	288
25	208271.6166	4998494.7996	0.000000	0.000005	23.999885	0.041667	300
26	339918.8835	8158029.2051	0.000000	0.000003	23.999929	0.041667	312
27	554779.6154	13314686.7705	0.000000	0.000002	23.999957	0.041667	324
28	905452.5553	21730837.3274	0.000000	0.000001	23.999973	0.041667	336
29	1477783.8030	35466787.2714	0.000000	0.000001	23.999984	0.041667	348
30	2411882.2743	57885150.5825	0.000000	0.000000	23.999990	0.041667	360
31	3936418.9087	94474029.8077	0.000000	0.000000	23.999994	0.041667	372
32	6424606.2048	154190524.9140	0.000000	0.000000	23.999996	0.041667	384
33	10485562.0918	251653466.2039	0.000000	0.000000	23.999998	0.041667	396
34	17113424.3684	410722160.8411	0.000000	0.000000	23.999999	0.041667	408
35	27930719.5024	670337244.0582	0.000000	0.000000	23.999999	0.041667	420
36	45585563.4226	1094053498.1434	0.000000	0.000000	23.999999	0.041667	432
37	74399930.5990	1785598310.3750	0.000000	0.000000	24.000000	0.041667	444
38	121427690.2356	2914264540.9333	0.000000	0.000000	24.000000	0.041667	456
39	198181420.7346	4756354073.6300	0.000000	0.000000	24.000000	0.041667	468
40	323450733.9356	7762817591.8946	0.000000	0.000000	24.000000	0.041667	480

Bibliography

BOOKS

BERGFIELD, PHILIP B. *Principles of Real Estate Law.* New York: McGraw-Hill, 1979. A well-written discussion of real estate law. Chapters 15 and 16 cover mortgages, deeds of trust, and installment contracts.

BOYKIN, JAMES H. *Financing Real Estate.* Lexington, Mass.: Lexington Books, 1979. A comprehensive book on real estate finance. It is particularly good on mortgage banking and the major institutional lenders.

BRITTON, JAMES A., AND LEWIS O. KERWOOD, eds. *Financing Income-Producing Real Estate.* New York: McGraw-Hill, 1977. Covers all aspects of financing income-producing properties and has 11 case studies on various types of properties.

BRUEGGEMAN, WILLIAM B., AND LEO D. STONE. *Real Estate Finance* (7th ed.). Homewood, Ill.: Richard D. Irwin, 1981. A comprehensive discussion of real estate finance with considerable attention given to the mathematics of finance and investment decision making.

CASE, FREDERICK E., AND JOHN M. CLAPP. *Real Estate Financing.* New York: John Wiley, 1978. A relatively comprehensive discussion of real estate finance that emphasizes the risk-taking and decision-making aspects.

DENNIS, MARSHALL. *Fundamentals of Mortgage Lending.* Englewood Cliffs, N.J.: Prentice-Hall, 1978. Provides case studies showing the necessary documentation for VA guaranteed, FHA insured, and conventional residential mortgage loans.

DOUGALL, HERBERT E., AND JACK E. GAUMNITZ. *Capital Markets and Institutions* (4th ed.), Prentice-Hall Foundations of Finance Series. Englewood Cliffs, N.J.: Prentice-Hall, 1980. A short, descriptive, and informative book about capital markets and financial institutions.

FRENCH, WILLIAM B., AND HAROLD F. LUSK. *Law of the Real Estate Business* (4th ed.). Homewood, Ill.: Richard D. Irwin, 1979. An easy-to-read book with a very good treatment of deeds of trust and land contracts.

KRATOVIL, ROBERT. *Modern Mortgage Law and Practice.* Englewood Cliffs, N.J.: Prentice-Hall, 1972. Covers more technical aspects of mortgage law.

——, *Modern Real Estate Documentation.* Englewood Cliffs, N.J.: Prentice-Hall, 1975. Discusses clauses in various documents. Chapter 25 discusses the clauses in mortgages and trust deeds in large-scale transactions.

——, and RAYMOND J. WERNER. *Real Estate Law* (7th ed.). Englewood Cliffs, N.J.: Prentice-Hall, 1979. Easy to read and understand and contains many case examples. Chapters 19 through 21 pertain to mortgage law.

MAISEL, SHERMAN J. *Financing Real Estate: Principles and Practices.* New York: McGraw-Hill, 1965. Although the book is dated, it contains the best treatment of the lending decision and the management of portfolio risks.

REILLY, JOHN W. *The Language of Real Estate.* Chicago: Real Estate Education Co., 1977. A well-written and extensive dictionary of real estate terms. It also contains a large number of forms used in real estate.

RING, ALFRED A., AND JEROME DASSO. *Real Estate: Principles and Practices* (9th ed.). Englewood Cliffs, N.J.: Prentice-Hall, 1981. A comprehensive book on real estate principles that emphasizes analysis for real estate decision making.

SELDIN, MAURY, ed. *The Real Estate Handbook.* Homewood, Ill.: Dow Jones-Irwin, 1980. Extensive coverage of major real estate topics. Chapter 5 is devoted to land contracts. Chapters 6 and 36 through 54 are devoted to real estate finance.

SHENKEL, WILLIAM M. *Modern Real Estate Appraisal.* New York: McGraw-Hill, 1978. Provides a good discussion of appraisal principles and techniques and their application.

THYGERSON, KENNETH J., AND DENNIS J. JACOBE. *Mortgage Portfolio Management.* Chicago: United States League of Savings Associations, 1978. Discusses portfolio management in both the primary and secondary mortgage markets. Explains the use of the GNMA futures market.

Underwriting Guidelines: Home Mortgages. Washington, D.C.: Federal Loan Mortgage Corporation, 1979. Describes the home mortgage loan guidelines for "investment quality conventional mortgage loans."

ARTICLES

ANGELL, ROBERT J., AND BRUCE N. WARDREP. "Evaluating the Shared Appreciation Mortgage," *Mortgage Banker,* April 1980. Shows the effective rate of return and cost for a SAM loan under various assumptions.

BEERS, RICHARD M. "Shorter Mortgage Terms Are Better for Home Buyers," *Real Estate Review,* Fall 1981. Argues that with higher interest rates the borrower should select a shorter amortization term for the loan.

BERANEK, WILLIAM, AND ALEX O. WILLIAMS. "Controlling Risk in Mortgage Portfolios," *Mortgage Banking,* October 1981. Applies modern portfolio theory to the management of a mortgage portfolio.

"Buydowns Take Off," *Seller Servicer,* October 1981. Explains the mechanics of a buydown mortgage loan.

GARRIGAN, RICHARD T. "Refinancing with a Wrap Around Loan," *Real Estate Today,* June 1981. Explains the mechanics of a wrap around mortgage loan.

HENDERSHOTT, PATRIC H., AND KEVIN E. VILLANI. "Secondary Mortgage Markets and the Cost of Mortgage Funds," *AREUEA Journal,* Spring 1980. Discusses the secondary mortgage market and argues that it has increased interregional flow of mortgage funds and decreased the differential between mortgage interest rates relative to other market interest rates.

HU, JOSEPH. "In Search of the Ideal Mortgage," *Seller Servicer,* April–June 1981. A fine discussion of graduated payment mortgage loans and the adjustable-rate GPM loan.

IEZMAN, STANLEY L. "The Shared Appreciation Mortgage and the Shared Equity Program," *Real Estate Review,* Fall 1981. Compares the SAM loan and the shared equity program. In a shared equity program, an investor makes a portion of the down payment and pays part of the monthly payment.

McTERNAN, JAMES P., AND REID NAGLE. "The GPM/VRM: A Mortgage for Inflationary Times," *Mortgage Banking,* October 1981. Argues that a GPM loan with a variable interest rate meets the needs of both the borrower and lender during periods of double digit inflation.

MITCHELL, MAXINE, AND AMY ROSS. "The Boom in Residential Second Mortgage Lending," *Mortgage Banker,* September 1980. Discusses the increased use of second mortgage financing.

PREISS, ALVIN. "The 'Mortgage-in-Law': Imaginative Financing," *Mortgage Banking,* July 1981. Explains how developers have made loans to the purchasers of homes owned by parties desiring to buy dwelling units from the developer.

ROSS, WILLIAM B. "Finding New Markets for Mortgages," *Mortgage Banking,* September 1981. Discusses conventional mortgage-backed securities as a source of mortgage funds.

SALKIN, MICHAEL S. "Adjustable-Rate Mortgages: The National Scene," *Mortgage Banking,* November 1981. Discusses the regulations for ARMs for national banks and federally chartered S&Ls and the types of ARMs eligible for purchase by FNMA and FHLMC.

SANDERS, BARRETT. "Due-on-Sale: The National Picture," *Mortgage Banking,* October 1981. Discusses the current status of the enforceability of the due-on-sale clause in various states.

STAFFORD, JOHN. "For Portfolio Lenders, the Key to the New Loan Is Cost of Funds Pricing," *Savings & Loan News,* July 1981. Argues that lenders can best maintain their spread by using adjustable-rate mortgage loans and linking the rate to their cost of funds.

STEPHENS, ROGER B. "Second Mortgage Conduits: Link to the Capital Markets," *Mortgage Banker,* June 1981. Discusses second mortgage pass-through certificates.

PERIODICALS

Federal Reserve Bulletin. Washington, D.C.: Board of Governors of the Federal Reserve System. A convenient source of the volume of mortgage debt outstanding and the yields in the secondary mortgage market. Published monthly.

Federal Home Loan Bank Board Journal. Washington, D.C.: U.S. Government Printing Office. Contains articles on real estate finance and statistical data relating to S&Ls. Published monthly.

Life Insurance Fact Book. Washington, D.C.: American Council of Life Insurance. Includes data about the mortgage-lending activities of life insurance companies. Published annually.

Mortgage Banking, formerly the *Mortgage Banker.* Washington, D.C.: Mortgage Bankers Association of America. Contains articles on real estate finance and data on the activities of mortgage companies. Published monthly.

National Fact Book of Mutual Savings Banking. New York: National Association of Mutual Savings Banks. Primarily a statistical presentation of the activities of mutual savings banks and the mortgage market. Published annually.

Savings & Loans News. Chicago: U.S. League of Savings Associations. Contains news items and articles about the operation of S&Ls and real estate finance. Published monthly.

Savings and Loan Sourcebook. Chicago: U.S. League of Savings Associations. Contains data about the mortgage market and savings and loan associations. Published annually.

Answers
to Questions
and Problems

CHAPTER ONE: INTRODUCTION AND OVERVIEW

1. *Reasons to understand the financing of real estate?*

   (a) To better arrange to finance personal housing.

   (b) To improve investment performance—buy on better terms, balance return and risk, improve salability on disposition.

   (c) As possible employment as loan officer.

   (d) To earn higher fees or profits for high quality professional performance as real estate practitioner—appraiser, broker, counselor, builder, developer.

2. *Real estate ownership or decision making cycle?*
   Series of decisions required of equity investor in owning real estate:

   (a) Acquisition.

   (b) Administration.

   (c) Disposition.

   Place of real estate finance in cycle:

   Ownership must be financed by either equity or debt. Knowledge of real estate finance particularly important in acquisition and disposition, either because of *need* or *leverage*.

3. *Steps in the decision making process?*
   (a) Recognize problem or decision making situation.
   (b) Collect data.
   (c) Identify problem.
   (d) Pose alternatives.

4. *Steps in administrative process?*
   (a) Decision to achieve objective.
   (b) Organize resources.
   (c) Exert leadership.
   (d) Control operations.
   (e) Periodic reevaluation.

5. *Four major divisions of this book?*
   (a) Instruments and law, or techniques.
   (b) Primary institutions and sources of funds.
   (c) Financing negotiations and calculations.
   (d) Secondary institutions and sources of funds.

6. *Meaning and implication of leverage?*

   Positive financial leverage (PFL) is borrowing money at an agreed interest rate or cost to acquire an investment which earns at a higher rate, or to "leverage" up the rate of return. Negative financial leverage (NFL) occurs when the cost of money exceeds the rate of return. Operating on other people's money is another way of indicating leverage. See Figures 1–2, 1–3, and 1–4 for example. Leverage is a key ingredient of successful investing.

7. *Match key terms and definitions?*
   (a) 4   (b) 8   (c) 9   (d) 1   (e) 7   (f) 5   (g) 3

CHAPTER TWO: MORTGAGE BASICS

1. *Changes in mortgage financing? Desirable?*
   From Chapter One, two basic principles are established:

   • Borrower retained possession even though property pledged.
   • Repay by "law day" or lose property.

   But, many *desirable* refinements, including development of key concepts, for fairer treatment of parties.

   (a) Defeasance clause.
   (b) Equitable right of redemption.
   (c) Foreclosure suit or order.
   (d) Strict foreclosure.
   (e) Foreclosure by public sale.
   (f) Statutory right of redemption.

2. *Distinguish between lien, title, and intermediate theory of mortgage law as to rights of mortgages and mortgagors?*

Lien Theory	Intermediate	Title Theory
Mortgagor (borrower) retains title upon pledging and retaining possession on default.	Mortgage written as lien; title transfer on default.	Mortgagee (lender) receives title on pledge; gets possession on default, including right to collect rent.

3. *Equitable mortgage? Difference from regular mortgage? Recognized from document?*

Equitable mortgage created when document in mortgaging process is faulty or events constructively imply a mortgage was intended. Differs because technically, the property was not pledged as security. The existence of an equitable mortgage is based on a decision by a court of law, and not on documents involved.

4. *Seven essential elements of a valid mortgage or bond? Discuss.*

(a) Written instrument.

(b) Obligor (borrower) and obligee (lender) with contractual capacity.

(c) Borrower's explicit promise to pay a specific sum.

(d) Terms of payment.

(e) Default clause, with reference to mortgage covenants.

(f) Proper execution.

(g) Voluntary delivery and acceptance.

See chapter, and business law texts, for discussion details.

5. *Purpose of note or bond?*

Evidence of debt makes borrower personally liable.

6. *Eight essential elements of a mortgage? Discuss.*

(a) Written instrument.

(b) Parties with contractual capacity.

(c) Interest in property that may be pledged as security.

(d) Offer of the interest as security.

(e) Adequate property description.

(f) Mortgagor's covenants.

(g) Proper execution.

(h) Voluntary delivery and acceptance.

See chapter for discussion details.

7. *Purpose of a mortgage?*

To pledge or promise property interest as security for a debt.

8. *Implications of mortgage as to transferability of pledged property?*

Title may be transferred, unless clause specifically prohibits. Transfer may be free and clear, subject to the mortgage, or based on grantee's assuming the mortgage.

9. *Termination of mortgage?*

   (a) Payment of debt with mortgage release on satisfaction piece as required by defeasance clause.

   (b) Voluntary release by lender without repayment.

   (c) Foreclosure proceedings.

   (d) Deed in lieu of foreclosure (from borrower to lender).

   (e) Merger of lender's and borrower's interests.

   (f) Statute of limitations invalidates.

10. *Match key terms and definitions:*

   (a) 5   (b) 3   (c) 4   (d) 6   (e) 7   (f) 2

CHAPTER THREE: MORTGAGE TYPES

1. *Conventional mortgage? Why so called?*
   A conventional mortgage loan is one not insured or guaranteed by the government. In the 1930s when FHA and VA loans were introduced, the borrower had option of a government backed or a conventional (traditional) mortgage.

2. Main differences between conventional, FHA, and VA?

Conventional	FHA	VA
No automatic backing, though lender-borrower may agree that private mortgage insurance to be used; borrower pays insurance premium.	Lender insured against loss by FHA; borrower pays insurance premium.	Lender guaranteed against loss by federal government. Available only to veterans or dependents of veterans.
Dominant method of financing; no upper limit on amount.	Upper limit on amount of insurance.	Upper limit on amount guaranteed. Down payment may not be required.

3. *Interrelationships: Construction, permanent, and gap loans?*

Construction	Gap	Permanent
Finance costs of building and improvements. Usually short terms, to be repaid from proceeds of permanent loan. Commitments for permanent loan usually required before obtained.	Short term second loan when payment loan is "floor to ceiling" or not all paid out until required occupancy achieved.	Long term, end, 15–30 years typical.

4. *Is a wraparound loan a junior mortgage? Explain.*
   Yes, a WAM loan is a special form of second or junior financing. The loan is for the amount of a first loan plus any amounts advanced by the second (WAM)

lender. All debt service is paid WAM lender, who in turn makes payments to first lender. See chapter for example.

5. *Distinguish between the following loan payment patterns.*

   (a) Demand: Typically a short term loan, often without a specific maturity date, and often debt service interest only. Frequently used for interim financing.

   (b) RRM: Long term financing with interest rate and debt service periodically renegotiated, like every 3–5 years. Most likely to be used on income or commercial property loans.

   (c) VRM: Financing in which interest rate (and possibly debt service or term) is periodically adjusted in accordance with a neutral index of interest rates. Adjustments may be up or down. Used in times of fluctuating interest rates.

   (d) Term: Financing with interest only debt service and a "balloon" repayment of principal at the end of the loan period. Used to minimize debt service and maintain leverage.

6. *Distinguish between the following "security" mortgage types.*

   (a) Blanket: one loan, several properties pledged. Results when land subdivided.

   (b) Chattel: loan secured by personal property, as when a car, boat, or refrigerator is pledged.

   (c) Package: real estate loan that includes items often considered personal property (stove, refrigerator, etc.) as security. First time homebuyers often use to get lower interest rates and longer repayment period in buying household furniture.

   (d) Leasehold: Tenant's interest in leases pledged as security. Used to finance construction when ground is rented.

7. *What is a purchase money mortgage? What special characteristics?*
   Conventional loan from seller to buyer. Has first priority automatically against any claims from buyer's actions unless subordinated. No deficiency judgment in foreclosure.

8. *Advantages and disadvantages of an adjustable rate loan (VRM, RRM)?*

Borrower	Lender	General Public
ADVANTAGE		
Money obtained even though interest rates increasing.	Interest rate kept at market.	Flow of funds into real estate loans maintained even though interest rate increasing.
DISADVANTAGE		
Interest rate may increase	Interest rate may decrease.	

9. *Age group most likely to benefit?*

   (a) GPM Loan: young people (and first time homebuyers)

   (b) RAM Loan: elderly

   (c) Budget Loan: young (and low income)

10. *Matching terms and definitions.*

    (a) 7   (b) 5   (c) 6   (d) 2   (e) 3   (f) 8

CHAPTER 4: MORTGAGE CLAUSES

1. *Note separate from mortgage. Why?*

    The note evidences the debt and makes it the borrower's personal obligation. The mortgage references the note only and therefore may be recorded without disclosing the specific details of the loan arrangements.

2. *Why include acceleration and prepayment clauses in note?*

    The note is the borrower's personal obligation; the acceleration makes it possible to sue for immediate payment of entire debt upon default, even if forebearance practiced by lender. Prepayment clause specifies when and if loan may be paid off early; without clause, borrower may not prepay without lender's consent.

3. *Importance of covenant of seizen.*

    Covenant makes borrower liable for any liens or claims that have priority to mortgage; reduces risk to lender.

4. *Purpose of following uniform clauses.*

    (a) Application of Payments: clarifies priority of claims on payments; avoids misunderstanding.

    (b) Hazard Insurance: protects lender against losses from fire, smoke, hail, flood, or earthquake.

    (c) Preservation of Property: protects lender against loss because of deterioration or demolition by borrower.

    (d) Forebearance: lender does not lose right of action because of nonuse.

    (e) Property Transfer/Loan Assumption: alienation or due-on-sale clause gives lender right to renegotiate loan if property transferred; therefore, control over who borrower is to be.

5. *Purpose of following clauses in mortgage?*

    (a) Power of Sale: allows foreclosure without court proceedings; reduces cost, shortens time of foreclosure.

    (b) Receiver: speeds process of appointing a receiver to look after lender's interests.

    (c) Owner Rent: allows rent to be charged owner-borrower for occupancy after foreclosure suit is initiated.

6. *Who benefits from following clauses? Explain.*

    (a) Subordination: borrower; allows refinancing by substitution of one first loan with another.

    (b) Default in Prior Mortgage: subordinate lender; may protect interest by meeting borrower's obligations.

    (c) Exculpatory: borrower; not held personally liable in default on loan.

(d) Subrogation: lender; may act to protect self if borrower fails to act.

(e) Alienation or Due-on-Sale: lender; greater control of loan terms.

7. *Three most important clauses? (Opinion)*

(a) Borrower: borrower's copy, prepayment privilege, right to reinstate, defeasance, subordination.

(b) Lender: pledge of property, default, subrogation, acceleration, due-on-sale.

(c) Junior Lender: pledge of property, default in prior mortgage, subordination.

8. *Match key terms and definitions.*

| (a) 3 | (b) 5 | (c) 7 | (d) 6 | (e) 1 | (f) 2 |

CHAPTER 5: MORTGAGE DEFAULT AND ITS IMPLICATIONS

1. *Five adjustments to default by borrower? Explain each briefly.*

(a) Extension: give borrower more time to meet obligation; delay maturity date.

(b) Recast: changing loan terms to better suit borrower's situation.

(c) Management Agreement: property operation taken over by manager.

(d) Deed-in-Lieu-of-Foreclosure: voluntary conveyance of title from borrower to lender to minimize expenses clearing the default.

(e) Voluntary Sale: property sold by borrower to meet mortgage obligation; most likely used when value exceeds loan by large margin.

2. *Alternatives of lender to recover money, on default? Explain.*

(a) Foreclosure and Sale: exercise terms of mortgage.

(b) Sue on Note: suing on note, as when value of pledged property is inadequate to cover lender's claims and borrower has other assets.

3. *Three ways to protect lender's interest pending foreclosure? Explain.*

(a) Mortgagee in Possession: lender takes possession of property with or without borrower's cooperation.

(b) Appointment of Receiver: a third party is appointed by the court to look after property.

(c) Possession under Assignment of Rents: rents paid directly to lender, upon default.

4. *Basic rule of priority of interests in realty?*

"First in time is first in line" of priority of claim, with exceptions based on taxes, mechanics liens, and subordination clauses. See text for full explanation.

5. *Strict foreclosure? What alternatives?*

Mortgagee perfects title for self without sale; process terminates rights of borrower and others claiming through borrower. Alternatives are (1) foreclosure and judicial sale, (2) foreclosure by power of sale, and (3) foreclosure by entry.

6. *Value of deficiency judgment to lender-mortgagee?*

At least six states prohibit deficiency judgments and eight limit the amount of judgments. FHA prohibits. VA discourages. Trend is toward limitation. They are seldom used or enforced anyway, so the value is small in most cases.

7. *Distinguish between equitable and statutory rights of redemption.*

Equitable right of redemption is based in common law and may be exercised up to the time specified in the foreclosure decree or up to the sale of the pledged property. Statutory right of redemption may be exercised after foreclosure or sale for a specified time.

8. *Benefits of using private mortgage insurance, FHA insurance, or a VA guarantee, from lender's viewpoint.*

Main benefit is limiting losses in foreclosure. Extent of protection varies among them.

9. *Distribution of foreclosure sale proceeds?*

Expenses of sale paid first. Lender's claim for expenses, interest, and principal are second. Lesser claims are paid third, as of junior lien holders. Residual funds are paid to the borrower, if any.

10. *Match key terms and definitions.*

(a) 3   (b) 5   (c) 4   (d) 1   (e) 6   (f) 2

CHAPTER 6: TRUST DEED FINANCING

1. *In trust deed financing, who is trustee? Beneficiary? Trustor?*

Trustee: neutral third party, holds title.
Beneficiary: lender.
Trustor: borrower, conveys legal title to trustee but retains equitable title.

2. *Advantages and disadvantages of trust deed financing.*

Borrower	Lender
ADVANTAGES	
Easier to obtain money, at lower cost.	Power of sale, quicker satisfaction on default, and less expensive.
	Retains good will by use of trustee.
	Statutory right of redemption avoided or downgraded.
	Hides lender identity.
DISADVANTAGES	
Administrative cost of third party; delays.	Possible loss of deficiency judgment.
Faster foreclosure action, particularly with power of sale, included.	
Faster loss of property in default.	

3. *Trust deed versus mortgage financing?*

• Trust deed equivalent for each type of mortgage, as FHA, VA, blanket, junior, etc.

- Title transferred to neutral third party; faster action at lower cost likely with trust deed.
- Power of sale more likely included with trust deed.

4. *When is trust deed more appropriate than mortgage?*

   A trust deed is clearly preferred when borrowing large amounts of money against a large property. Trustee can represent and act for the many bond holders, whose identity need not be disclosed.

5. *How is a trust deed foreclosed?*

   Exercise of power of sale is the most likely action to be used following default without appropriate adjustment. Specific state laws may modify. The trustee administers the foreclosure process.

6. *Match key terms and definitions.*

   (a) 3   (b) 5   (c) 1   (d) 4   (e) 2

CHAPTER 7: LAND CONTRACT AND OPTION FINANCING

1. *What is a land contract?*

   Written sales agreement for deed or title to real estate, with title remaining with seller but occupancy usually given buyer.

2. *Conditions under which land contract is commonly used?*

   Land contract is often used where conventional financing is unavailable, is extremely expensive, or to defer taxes. Specifically, often used with raw land, vacant lots, substandard properties, or properties in blighted areas. In deferring taxes, land contract allows gains to be received over two or more years.

3. *Other common names for land contract?*

   - contract for deed
   - land sale contract
   - installment land contract
   - installment sales contract

4. *Rights and duties of parties in land contract?*

Vendor	Vendee
Retains legal title	Obtains equitable title and general possession and use
Receives payments	Makes payments and maintains property
May borrow against property	May sell interest
May assign interest	
Must deliver deed and marketable title	

5. *Identify and explain three critical interests of buyer in land contract.*

   (a) Ascertain that seller has marketable title or can obtain marketable title. No point in making payments for several years and then not being able to get marketable title.

   (b) Have deed delivered into escrow. Makes it possible to obtain deed and title even though seller dies, is disabled, or simply becomes stubborn.

(c) May also want to have payments made into escrow if claims against property, as a mortgage. Escrow agent would see that periodic payments are made.

(d) Include clause that seller can't refinance above his or her equity in property. Problems may result if seller refinances with buyer's equity.

6. *Seller refinancing of pledged property?*
    See item (d) in 5. above.

7. *Difference between financing with land contract and purchase money mortgage.*
    Both involve seller financing and usually installment payments. Main difference, with PMM, title conveyed to buyer and foreclosure must be initiated to recover property and clear title. With LC, contract may simply be rescinded or declared forfeit.

8. *What is an option? How used?*
    An agreement to hold an offer open. Most usually, an option to purchase is used in real estate. An option to purchase means the buyer may acquire the property at a stated price to the buyer for a certain time; the buyer may exercise the option or not.
    An option is commonly used to control land for development pending feasibility analysis; it may be combined with a lease; or, an option may be used to assemble several parcels of land for plottage value.

9. *Match key terms and definitions.*

    (a) 6   (b) 3   (c) 1   (d) 5   (e) 2   (f) 7

CHAPTER 8: LEASE FINANCING

1. *Define and distinguish between following types of leases.*
    (See chapter and glossary for definitions and explanations.)

2. *Explain use of a lease as a financing technique.*
    Leasing realty or equipment is roughly equivalent to using 100% debt financing with a straight term loan. Rental payments must be adequate to meet debt service on any loans taken out by the owner-lessor as well as to give the owner-lessor a return on his or her equity investment.

3. *Distinguish between short and long term leases.*
    Distinction is relative and arbitrary, depending on context. Nonresidential leases are not long term unless for ten years or longer, and sometimes 21 years or longer. Possibly a better distinction is that tenant is responsible for management, maintenance and operation of the property with a long term lease.

4. *Significance of following lease clauses?*

    (a) Assignment of Leasehold: retains control for owner-lessor in long term leases; tenant may assign or sublet only with owner's approval.

    (b) Security Deposit: required in short term leases to insure maintenance and clean-up of property upon termination.

(c) Option to renew: requires communication between lessor-lessee concerning intent to renew, notice to prevent renewal, and rental upon renewal.

(d) Subordination: stipulates priority of leasehold and leased fee relative to financing and refinancing of the interest.

5. *Mortgaging of leasehold? Value of leasehold?*

A leasehold has value because the parcel or space provides a flow of benefits with a value in the market that exceeds the rental payments. The value is the capitalized worth of the net difference. In turn, the leasehold's value may be pledged as security for a loan, to be repaid from the net difference. See text for example.

6. *Explain the sale and leaseback arrangement.*

Selling a property and simultaneously leasing it back from the buyer-investor. Often used where original owner has used up tax benefits of ownership or wishes to release monies for growth or a higher rate of return. In effect, the seller uses to leverage the rate of return earned on his or her monies.

7. *Advantages and disadvantages of sale-leaseback financing to lessee.*

Advantages	Disadvantages
100% financing.	Value appreciation of property foregone.
Leveraged use of funds.	May be forced to relocate, lease not extended.
Rental payments tax deductible.	Absorbs increased taxes, insurance, and operating cost on net lease.
More freedom to relocate.	Committed to rental contract and payments, even if property no longer useful.

8. *Advantages and disadvantages of sale-leaseback financing to lessor.*

Advantages	Disadvantages
Higher yield on lease than on mortgage.	Higher LVR; greater chance of default.
Value appreciation on property.	Property may decline in value.
Large, long term investment.	
Faster repossession than with mortgage.	

9. *Match key terms and definitions.*

(a) 8   (b) 4   (c) 1   (d) 6   (e) 5   (f) 7   (g) 2   (h) 3

CHAPTER 9: MORTGAGE MARKET OVERVIEW

1. *Primary Lender? Secondary Lender?*

Primary Lender: originates and services loans.

Secondary Lender: buys loans from or originates loans through primary lenders; also, usually depends on primary lenders to service the loans.

2. *Distinguish between financial, money, and capital markets? Which involves mortgage market?*

Financial markets are where *all types* of loans are originated and exchanged. Money markets involve short duration loans (less than one year) whereas capital markets provide loans for longer than one year. Long term real estate loans (mortgage loans) are part of capital markets.

3. *Financial intermediation and disintermediation? Significance?*

Intermediation is channeling money from savers to borrowers through financial institutions. Disintermediation is withdrawal of monies from intermediaries for direct investments. Less money goes into mortgage loans with disintermediation.

4. *Main mortgage loan borrowers?*

- Households
- Builders and developers
- Businesses (including farms)
- Investors in commercial and income properties

5. *Main mortgage loan lenders and their relative importance? Main originators?*

Holders (Fig. 9-5)	Originators
1. S & Ls	1. S&Ls
2. CBs	2. Mortgage Bankers
3. Federal & Related Agencies	3. CBs
4. Individuals & others	
5. LICs	
6. MSBs	

6. *Nature and significance of DIDMCA of 1980? Impact on real estate?*

Gives a "level playing field" for all financial institutions, meaning they all will operate on the same rules. Deregulates interest rate limitations on time deposits. Also gives the Fed much more control over the reserve requirements of thrift institutions. Will probably mean that funds for real estate will increasingly have to come from other than thrift institutions. See text for more discussion.

7 *Match key terms and definitions.*

(a) 6　　(b) 3　　(c) 4　　(d) 2　　(e) 1　　(f) 5　　(g) 7

CHAPTER 10: PRIVATE DEPOSITORY LENDERS

1. *Distinguish between Certificate of Deposit and Money Market Certificate.*

CD is intermediate term savings instrument (two to ten years) that earns at a higher rate than an MMC. MMC is a short term (182 day) savings instrument that earns at an average yield of six-month, U.S. Treasury bills established in most recent auction.

2. *Compare S & L lending authority to actual performance.*

	AUTHORITY		PERFORMANCE	
	1 Family Res.	Commercial Investment	1 Family Res.	Commercial Investment
Property type financed	no limit	20% max	83%	17%
Loan to Value Ratio	90–95%		76%	
Loan Duration	40 years	30 years	28 years	

3. *Why aren't there more MSBs in the South and West? How liberal are MSBs in lending activities?*

CBs moved into accepting savings deposits during expansion to the South and West. MSB appear to be somewhat more liberal as to property type finance; 35% commercial investment. At the same time, MSBs have a slightly lower LVR.

4. *Four top types of asset investments of CBs?*

Rank	Asset Type	Percentage
1.	Commercial industrial loans	20%
2.	Securities	19%
3.	Mortgage loans	16%
4.	Cash	11%
5.	Consumer installment	10%

Real estate is important, but not as much so as short term loans and securities. CBs are important because of their dominance as a financial institution, and overall are the second largest private lenders on real estate. See text.

5. *Modus operandi of credit unions?*

CUs are mutual organizations that accept savings from and extend loans to their members. Most members of any single CU work for the same employer. Installment credit loans emphasized as for cars, boats, mobile homes, and home improvement. DIDMCA may result in CUs broadening their scale of activities with time.

6. *Match key terms and definitions.*

(a) 4   (b) 1   (c) 2   (d) 6   (e) 3

CHAPTER 11: PRIVATE, NONDEPOSITORY LENDERS

1. *Regulation of life insurance companies? Effect of regulation on LIC investing?*

Mainly state regulation. Not many limitations on investing. Geographical limitation is U.S., and sometimes Canada. Lending policies of individual companies tend to be more restrictive than regulation.

2. *Main source of funds for LICs? Influence on investment policies?*

Policy reserves made up over 80% of LIC funds. In any given year, funds available for investment come from net premium income, pension fund contributions, loan repayments, maturing securities, and other investment income.

Long term investments emphasized because contractual obligations are long term.

3. *What is a basket clause? Significance?*
    Basket or leeway clause means LIC may invest small portion of their funds without regard to regulations. Means LICs may go into income or equity participation loans, into joint ventures, as high LVR loans.

4. *LICs prefer large loans on projects. Rationale?*
    Loans on large multi-family and commercial properties preferred. Generally higher interest rates, also lower servicing costs in that a large loan generally requires little more servicing than a small loan.

5. *Loan correspondent? Function of correspondent?*
    Loan correspondent originates and often services loans for investors, as LICs. Mortgage bankers and brokers are main categories of correspondents. Therefore, correspondent is representative or agent of lender-investor.

6. *Mortgage company? Function and operation?*
    Mortgage companies originate, sell, and service loans, and are mainly mortgage bankers. Important source of loans for secondary lenders. Improve efficiency of mortgage market by originating loans in areas of capital shortages for lenders in areas with capital surplus.

7. *Mortgage companies have less regulation. Why? What restrictions?*
    Mortgage companies have little regulation because they are not fiduciaries for depositors, policyholders, or pensioners. Main limitations are requirements of investors for whom they originate loans.

8. *Significance of pension funds as real estate lenders? Outlook?*
    Pension funds, with only one percent of their assets in mortgage loans, are not significant as real estate lenders. In that pension funds have long term contractual obligations, real estate should be a desirable investment for them.

9. *Three basic types of REITs? Significance as lenders in real estate? Outlook?*
    Main types of REITs are equity, mortgage, and mixed or hybrid. REITs have been major sources of funds for construction and multi-family residential properties. Have often borrowed short and lent long, resulting eventually in profit squeeze. Outlook is uncertain, though equity REITs should be able to become dominant if quality properties are developed and the property is administered.

10. *Major categories of individual real estate lenders? Similarity in motivation and operation?*
    Individuals are significant lenders on one-to-four family residential properties and farms. Main categories are property sellers, relatives and close associates, and wealthy, individual investors, with respective motivations being easier sale of property, assistance to a friend or relative, and higher rates of return.

11. *Match following key terms and definitions.*

| (a) 4 | (b) 7 | (c) 1 | (d) 6 | (e) 5 | (f) 2 |

CHAPTER 12: GOVERNMENT AND RELATED AGENCIES

1. *Distinguish between fiscal and monetary policy, and implications of each for real estate finance?*

    Fiscal Policy: taxation and government spending strategies to achieve economic goals.

    Monetary Policy: managing money supply and interest rate to achieve economic goals. Rising or high interest rate (limited money supply) directly affects real estate financial activity. Government expenditures balanced by tax receipts have little or no direct impact on real estate finance. Deficit financing with borrowing in financial markets also is likely to affect finance markets, interest rates, and real estate finance.

2. *Fed's use of open market operations to change money supply and interest rates?*

    Purchases of government securities act to increase reserves of financial institutions thereby increasing money supply and lower interest rate. Sale of securities requires buyers to pay cash to Fed, decreasing money reserves and money supply, and more than likely, increasing interest rates.

3. *Federal agencies insuring savings deposits? Merging likely?*

    • FDIC–for commercial and mutual savings bonus.
    • FSLIC–for federal S & Ls and some MSBs.
    • NCUSIF– for credit unions.

    Merging likely in long run but not in short run. S & Ls appear more nearly insolvent because of their high proportion of asset holdings made up of mortgage loans. Commercial banks not likely to allow FDIC insurance reserves to be used to bail out S & Ls and MSBs.

4. *Down payment for residence with market value of $72,000 assuming a FHA 203(b) loan were obtained?*

    Assuming residence is FHA approved, down payment is three percent of first $25,000 of value and five percent over $25,000 of value. Maximum loan on a one-family property is $67,500.

3% × $25,000	$750
5% × 47,000 ($72,000–25,000)	2350
Total	$3100

    Loan required $72,000 − 3,100 = $68,900, which exceeds the maximum loan. Thus, down payment equals $72,000 − 67,500 = $4,500.

5. *FHA conditional versus firm commitment for loan insurance?*

    Conditional commitment is for loan based on property acceptable to FHA but buyer unknown. Buyer-borrower subject to approval later. Upon approval of both property and borrower, commitment is *firm,* meaning the loan would be insured, at borrower's and lender's option, and upon payment of insurance premiums.

6. *FHA income and expense criteria for qualifying borrowers?*

   • Basic standard is that housing costs must not exceed 35% of effective income (projected average for next five years) on a monthly basis.
   • Total fixed obligations should not exceed 50% of effective income, also on a monthly basis.

7. *Match key terms and definitions.*

   (a) 3   (b) 4   (c) 7   (d) 6   (e) 2   (f) 5

CHAPTER 13: EQUITY FUNDING AND PLANNING

1. *Three important reasons for equity planning and funding?*
   Equity financing is a prerequisite to arranging debt financing. If equity financing cannot be arranged, debt financing cannot be obtained. Equity position is necessary to see to management and maintenance of the property; and failure to plan may mean the loss of the equity position. Finally, at the proper time, disposition on dissolution must be arranged.

2. *Steps in the real estate financing process, in sequence.*
   See Figure 13–1. Steps are purchase contract, lender analysis, loan processing (application, borrower analyses, property analysis, financing terms, and lender commitments), and close of financing.

3. *Three phases of equity planning? At least two functions or activities in each phase?*
   Equity planning has three phases: (1) acquisition, (2) administration, and (3) disposition. In phase one, title is cleared and financing arranged. Phase two requires meeting debt service, administering the investment, keeping operating costs under control, and leverage maintained. In phase three, dissolution continuation of the investment must be arranged.

4. *Four alternative arrangements for equity funding, and conditions of use?*

Arrangement	Condition of Use
1. Personal resources	Mainly for individual investor.
2. Partnership	Venture too large to be handled individually.
3. Corporation	High risk venture; many investors needed.
4. REIT	Large investment requiring many investors; easy pass-through of benefits.
5. Syndicate/Joint Venture	Often limited partnership, to enable several to join together to invest.
6. Condominium/Cooperative	Joining together of many owners for investment, usually for personal use.
7. Long term lease	Share equity funding with a landowner.

5. *Match of key terms and definitions.*

   (a) 4   (b) 7   (c) 5   (d) 1   (e) 2   (f) 3

CHAPTER 14: LOAN UNDERWRITING AND SETTLEMENT PROCEDURES

1. *Essential purpose of a loan interview?*

    Enable loan officer to explain general underwriting policies and procedures for his or her institution and to obtain information about applicant and property. In net, the purpose is to make a preliminary decision as to whether a loan arrangement is feasible and probable for both parties.

2. *Advantage of FHLMC–FNMA loan application forms? To lender?*

    Use of FHLMC–FNMA documents make loan more easily negotiable in the secondary mortgage market. Also improves chances that all pertinent data is collected. For lender and borrower, FHLMC–FNMA guidelines improve chances that, if loan is made, it will work out successfully for both parties.

3. *Underwriter? What information is evaluated?*

    An underwriter analyzes the risks and benefits toward making a decision about a loan. In broad terms, the underwriter evaluates the terms of the loan relative to the potential borrower's capability and the property's value.

4. *FHLMC guidelines regarding expense to income ratios of potential borrowers? Purpose of guidelines?*

    FHLMC has two general expenses-income ratio requirements to keep borrowers from overcommitting themselves:

    • Monthly housing expense should not exceed 25–28% of borrower's stable gross monthly income.
    • Total monthly debt or installment payments should not exceed 33–36% of borrower's stable gross monthly income.

5. *What is "willingness to pay"? How judged? Why important?*

    "Willingness to pay" is a combination of attitude and history toward use of credit. Attitude must be positive that debt will be paid. History is person's credit-performance history showing that past credit obligations have been met. "Willingness to pay" is important because it is an important indicator of motivation to pay.

6. *Evidence of valid title in obtaining a loan? Lender preference?*

    Evidence of valid title may be shown by (1) abstract and opinion of title, (2) owner's certificate, and (3) title insurance policy. Lenders generally prefer title insurance because losses to policy holders are guaranteed or protected against rather than involving a distant lawsuit.

7. *RESPA? Purpose of RESPA procedures?*

    RESPA means Real Estate Settlement Procedures Act. Purpose is to give a full accounting of calculations and payments for buyer and seller. The lender is responsible for proper preparation of a RESPA statement.

8. *Match key terms and definitions.*

    (a) 3   (b) 4   (c) 2   (d) 8   (e) 1   (f) 7

CHAPTER 15: PROPERTY ANALYSIS

1. *Two reasons for a value estimate in real estate financing process?*
   Most lenders limited by regulation or policy to a maximum LVR ratio in originating loans. The LVR is based on market value or purchase price, whichever is lower. Lenders also want a value estimate to ascertain that the LVR is not likely to increase during the life of the loan.

2. *Two reasons for use of a FHLMC–FNMA standard appraisal form to document value?*
   Data may be collected or read and interpreted more quickly with a standard form. Further, the form acts as a checklist to insure against omitting information. The standard form also facilitates understanding and review by underwriters and secondary lenders, should the loan be offered for sale.

3. *Two alternative definitions of market value?*
   "Most probable selling price" is one definition. Also, "the highest price in terms of money which a property will bring if exposed for sale on the open market, with a reasonable time to find a purchaser, buying with full knowledge of all uses to which it is adapted and for which it is capable of being used." Or, "the price at which a property will sell, assuming a knowledgeable buyer and seller both operating with reasonable knowledge and without undue pressure." *See Figure 15–2 for a definition used by FNMA–FHLMC.*

4. *Main data required of lender on form 70?*
   Borrower, property location, and property rights to be appraised, date of sale. Lender also lists the sale price, real estate taxes, loan charges to be paid by seller, and concession in price.

5. *Main sections of Form 70 pertaining to data about subject property?*
   Neighborhood; site; improvements; interior finish and equipment; property rating; the valuation sections—cost, direct sales comparison, and income approaches—all implicitly pertain to the subject property.

6. *Which of three approaches is ordinarily most important in finding value of subject?*
   The market data or direct sales comparison approach is ordinarily most relied on if adequate data is available. The cost and income approaches serve as checks.

7. *Match the key terms and definitions.*
   (a) 6   (b) 5   (c) 2   (d) 8   (e) 4

CHAPTER 16: LENDER CONSIDERATIONS AND ANALYSIS

1. *Describe/discuss lender concerns in the following areas:*
   (a) Level of economic activity   Impact property values. Also, decline in economic activity leads to unemploy-

ment and reduced property incomes; therefore defaults on loans.

(b) Level of real estate activity — Demand for loans high with strong activity. More conservative policies during slow activity.

(c) Interest rates — Affect availability and cost of money; also value of existing loans in portfolio and possible disintermediation.

(d) Value of dollar — Affects rate of return required on loans to make up for loss of purchasing power during inflation. Indirectly, spread between cost of money and rate earned on money by lender affected.

(e) Government policies — Both fiscal and monetary policy affect lenders. Deficit spending, for example, drives interest rates up. Also, lenders subject to regulation by governmental agencies.

2. *Distinguish between and explain individual loan risks and portfolio risks.*

   - *Individual loan risk* is chance that default will occur and a loss result from a specific loan. Borrower and value of pledged property both important as protection.
   - *Portfolio risk* is chance of loss on all loans held. Portfolio risk breaks down to administrative, business, financial, interest rate, liquidity, and purchasing power risk.

3. *Lender decision costs?*

   Origination, servicing, and default and foreclosure costs. Also termed administrative costs.

4. *Lender diversification to avoid business risk? Residual risks that can't be avoided? Explain.*

   Lending over *wide geographic area,* on many *types of property,* to many different *types of borrowers* with adequate *time distribution.* Residual risk, as from a major depression or prolonged inflation, may partially be offset with loan insurance or increased use of flexible interest rate loans.

5. *Lender protection against purchasing power and liquidity risks?*

   Protection against purchasing power risk may be obtained by adjusting interest rate to take account of expected inflation, using flexible interest rates, or equity participations. Liquidity risk is best offset by clear, accurate forecasting of needs and by keeping portion of funds in short term investments, as treasury bills. Also, by occasional borrowing.

6. *Most difficult loan servicing function?*

   Collection of past due payments, making adjustments, and/or initiating foreclosure proceedings, if necessary.

7. *Match key terms and definitions.*

   (a) 6   (b) 5   (c) 7   (d) 2   (e) 4   (f) 1   (g) 3

1. *Items making up annual stabilized income according to FHLMC guidelines?*

    Income from a job is the most basic input into annual stabilized income. Other ingredients include income from retirement funds, trusts, overtime earnings, bonuses, commissions, dividends, interest, and net rents. Income from alimony, child support, or welfare may also be included. Source, amount, and certainty of receipt are all important considerations.

2. *Items making up housing expenses?*

    Rent, loan debt service, hazard insurance, property taxes, and mortgage insurance. Also, homeowner association dues, ground rents, and utility payments may be included.

3. *Willingness to pay? How determined?*

    Willingness to pay involves both credit worthiness and motivation or attitude. A person's credit history is important in determining, as documented by credit reports and references. That is, individuals who have met their financial obligations in the past are considered credit worthy and motivated.

4. *Borrower's personal risks and their implications?*

    Inability to pay because of loss of income, sickness, death, or separation and divorce are all personal risks of borrowers. Failure to pay on a loan will almost certainly lead to default and foreclosure.

5. *Criteria in evaluating a corporate loan applicant?*

    Financial statements provide the basis of evaluating a business firm. Net worth and the current ratio must be acceptable, as well as a demonstrated profitable use of assets, evidence by the return on total assets ratio.

6. *Matching key terms and definitions.*

    (a) 7   (b) 6   (c) 4   (d) 3   (e) 2

CHAPTER 18: LOAN REPAYMENT PATTERNS

1. *Two basic motivations for borrowing against real estate? Associated risks?*

    Need and leverage. Financial risk is undertaken when borrowing, which must be weighed against the financial advantage of leverage gained in borrowing.

2. *Basic motivations of lenders? Main risks?*

    Lenders seek profit by placing money to earn a higher rate of return than it costs. Many lenders borrow short and lend long, causing risks of withdrawal of funds or rising interest rates when loans are locked in at a specified rate.

3. *Benefits and risks of straight term loan from borrower's viewpoint? From lender's viewpoint?*

    Borrower: Debt service smaller; doesn't contain capital repayment. Therefore higher cash flow to borrower-investor. Leverage is maintained at higher level than with amortizing loan also. Risk increase at time of refinancing; interest rates may have increased or funds may not be available.

Lender: Value of property may decrease, reducing level of protection against loss.

4. *Benefits and risks of a fully amortizing, fixed rate loan from borrower's standpoint? Lender's?*

BORROWER's	LENDER'S
Advantages	Advantages or Benefits
Payments cover principal and interest and sometimes taxes and insurance. Equity built up through time, as loan is paid off; no need to refinance then.	Advantages include that loan may be paid off while property value increases, giving greater protection against loss. Maturities of loans in portfolio spread out over longer time, giving greater chance to place money as it comes in. Stability of operations.
Risk or Disadvantage	Risk or Disadvantage
Borrower locked in at high interest rate on long term loan if rates fall.	Property may fall in value faster than loan is amortized, meaning greater risk of loss. Income may fall resulting in nonpayment of debt service.

5. *Risks increased or decreased with adjustable interest rates on fully amortizing loans?*

Borrower	Lender
Chance for negative amortization, higher interest rates, higher debt service, longer life. Of course, all contribute eventually to higher risk of default.	Risk of being locked in on FRM reduced, risk of default increased with higher interest rates.

6. *VRM risks versus RRM risks?*

Risks are highly similar for both.

- Risk of default increased if income goes down or debt service increases too rapidly.
- Borrower's equity would decrease if value declined too rapidly, lessening amount of security.

7. *Compare GPAM, RRM, and SAM as to repayment period, risk, and other characteristics.*

Repayment Period	Risk	Other
GPAM and RRM		
Repayment could be extended if rate increases too quickly.	Increasing LVR possibly greater chance of loss.	
SAM		
Stable; FRM likely, no change in length.	Lender risks lower return if appreciation not adequate. Rapid value increase means borrower paid too high a rate of interest.	Might serve where no other loan suitable.

8. *Mechanics of income and/or equity participation loans? Who benefits? Who risks?*

In a fixed interest rate below market, lender gets share of income and/or value appreciation. Lender benefits if value and/or income goes up rapidly.

Slow increase means borrower is main beneficiary. Both benefit in sense that deal works out. Both risk chance of some loss for greater potential gain.

9. *Matching key terms and definitions.*

(a) 4   (b) 5   (c) 2   (d) 6   (e) 1

CHAPTER 19: LOAN NEGOTIATION CALCULATIONS

1. *Money received in future has less value than money in hand?*

   (a) Current consumption preferred over future consumption.

   (b) Investors allocate money to alternative opportunities to get highest rate of return on a risk adjusted basis.

   (c) Inflation requires a premium rate of return to maintain purchasing power.

   (d) Risk of loss on delaying receipt calls for a payment.

   (e) In net, reality is that money cannot be borrowed without paying interest.

2. *Three year CD purchased for $2,000 to earn nine percent, compounded annually. Amount to be received at EOY3:*

   $2,000 \times (1.09)^3 = \$2,000 \times 1.29503 = \$2,590.06$

3. *Sell three year CD at EOY1.*

   $\$2,590.06 \times PV1\,^{9\%}_{2\,yrs.} = \$2,590.06 \times .84168 = \$2,180.$
   Yes. $2,000 \times 1.09 = \$2,180 = \$2,000$ at 9% for one year or EOY1.

4. *Loan amount for John & Linda Hunter? Under FHLMC guidelines?*

Maximum to housing expenses (28% × $36,000)	$10,080
Less taxes & hazard insurance	840
Available for loan debt service or $770/mo.	$ 9,240/yr.
Loan amount (20 year, 10%, monthly payment)	$79,791

5. *Maximum value property Hunters might buy.*
   Effectively, Hunters can borrow $80,000. The amount of money they have available for down payment and closing cost determine property they can afford. Thus, with $5,000 for closing costs and $20,000 down, they could buy a $100,000 property. They would need at least 10% down without arranging for mortgage insurance.

6. *Hunters set maximum of 25% of income to debt service, with 80 LVR. What size loan? What value home?*

   Loan: $750/mo. $\times PV1/P\,^{12\%,\,mo.}_{25\,yr.} = \$750 \times 94.94655 = \$71,210.$

   Value: $71,210 ÷ .80 = $89,012.

7. *What size loan for Hunters at 15%? Price or value?*

   Loan: $750/mo $\times PV1/P\,^{15\%,\,mo.}_{25\,yr.} = \$750 \times 78.07434 = \$58,556.$

   Value: $58,556 ÷ .80 = $73,195.

8. *$75,000. 20 years. 12%. Monthly. What monthly debt service?*

   $75,000 \times \text{PR factor}\ ^{12\%,\ \text{mo.}}_{20\ \text{yr.}} = \$75,000 \times .011011 = \$825.82.$

9. *Property taxes $2,100. Hazard insurance $312. Total monthly PITI for Hunters?*

Monthly taxes + insurance ($2,100 + $312) ÷ 12	$ 201
Monthly debt service (from eight above)	$ 825.82
Total monthly PITI	$1,026.82

10. *Match key terms and definitions.*

    (a) 4   (b) 6   (c) 5   (d) 1   (e) 2

CHAPTER 20: RESIDENTIAL INCOME PROPERTY FINANCING

1. *Greater emphasis on property than borrower in income property underwriting?*

   Property is primary security for loan under an exculpatory or sole security clause which is generally included in such agreements.

2. *Four dominant numbers of an annual operating statement?*

   > GROSS SCHEDULED INCOME
   > Less   VACANCY AND CREDIT LOSSES
   > Equals   EFFECTIVE GROSS INCOME (EGI)
   > Less   TOTAL OPERATING EXPENSES
   > Equals   NET OPERATING INCOME

3. *Sections of FNMA/FHLMC standard appraisal form for residential income property? Source of and nature of content of each?*
   (See Appraisal Report division of Chapter 20).

4. *Purposes of loan underwriting analysis?*

   • Estimate risks associated with loan under consideration.
   • Estimate proper amount of financing for loan understudy.
   • Determine optimal financing to balance lender's risk and return.

   Ultimately, the concern is the ability of the borrower and the property to repay the loan and/or protect against loss.

5. *Four key financial ratios used in income property loan underwriting?*

   (a) Loan to Value Ratio $= \dfrac{\text{Initial Loan Amount}}{\text{Market Value (or Purchase Price)}}$

   (b) Operating Ratio $= \dfrac{\text{Total Annual Operating Expenses}}{\text{Gross Annual Scheduled Income}}$

   (c) Debt Service Coverage Ratio $= \dfrac{\text{Net (Annual) Operating Income}}{\text{Annual Debt Service}}$

   (d) Break-even Occupancy Ratio (BO Ratio) $= \dfrac{\text{Total Annual Expenses + Annual Debt Service (V \& CL + Operating)}}{\text{Gross Annual Scheduled Income}}$

6. *Calculations of four ratios?*

    (a) LVR $\qquad = \dfrac{\$672,000}{\$940,000} = .7149$ or 71.5%

    (b) Operating Ratio $\qquad = \dfrac{\$42,000}{\$130,000} = .3231$ or 32.3%

    (c) DSC Ratio $\qquad = \dfrac{\$88,000}{\$88,000} = .99099$ or 99.1%

    (d) BO Ratio $\qquad = \dfrac{\$42,000 \ + 88,800 = \$130,000}{\$130,000}$

$$= 1.0062 \text{ or } 100.6\%$$

7. *Analyze the ratios calculated in 6 from underwriter's perspective? Loan accept-able? Restructure?*

    A 71.5% LVR would generally be quite acceptable for residential income property. However, with an operating ratio of 32.3%, it appears that not a large enough portion of Gross Scheduled Income is allocated to operating expenses. Alternatively, NOI is too high. If market rents are realistic, the value of the property appears overstated.

    Both the DSC ratio (99.1) and the BO ratio (100.6%) strongly indicate that the financing costs are too much for the property to carry. The property is an "alligator" to begin with. And with the operating ratio indicating that expenses are understated, the proposed loan is extremely risky and should not be under-taken.

    Adjustments/restructuring?

    With 40% operating ratio and gross annual income taken as realistic, NOI looks more like $78,000. Capitalizing $78,000 at 9.36% ($88,000 ÷ 940,000 = 9.36%) gives a revised market value of $833,333. In turn, a $600,000 loan would mean a 72% LVR, quite acceptable. The loan might then be set up at 12% with amortization scheduled over 30 years by monthly payments and a balloon at EOY15. Flexible interest rates might also be introduced. Debt service would then be $6,171.68 per month or $74,060 per year. DSC ratio would then be $78,000 ÷ $74,060 or 1.0532, and BO ratio would be 96.97% [$52,000 + $74,060) ÷ $130,000]. These ratios would be marginally acceptable. But, adjustments along these lines would have to be worked out with the borrower-applicant for the loan to be acceptable to a lender.

8. *Matching key terms and definitions.*

    (a) 4   (b) 5   (c) 2   (d) 6   (e) 1

CHAPTER 21: CREATIVE FINANCING

1. *Allocation for installment payments?*
    $40,000 × 33% = $13,200.
    Allocation for housing expense?
    $40,000 × 25% = $10,000

2. *How much for housing expense, figuring from allocation for installment payments?*

	Annual	Monthly
Annual stabilized income	$40,000	$3,333
Times 33% equals allocation for installment	$13,200	$1,100
Less continuing obligations: car	−2,436	−203
Amount available for housing expense	$10,764	$897

3. *How large a loan can Chapman's afford? (Ballpark figure)*

Amount available for housing expense is $10,764/yr. or $897/mo. Maximum loan supported with $897 and disregarding taxes and insurance would be $87,205. Taxes and insurance on an $87,205 property would be $2,616/yr. or $218/monthly. Monthly debt service of $679 ($897 − 218) would support a 30 year, 12% loan of $66,011. The $15,000 saved for a down payment has not yet been taken into account. But, roughly a loan from $70,000 to $80,000 seems feasible.

4. *At 80% LVR, what price house can be afforded?*

Amount available for housing expense must cover all debt service, PITI. Thus, on an annual basis, the following relationship applies:

$$\text{Amount for housing expense} = (80\% \text{ LVR})\,(\text{Market Value})\,(12 \times \text{PR}_{30 \text{ yr.}}^{12\% \text{ mo.}}) + 3\% \text{ MV}$$

(for loan payments)   (for taxes and insurance)

$$\begin{aligned}
\$10,764 &= .80 \text{ MV} (12 \times .010286) + .03 \text{ MV} \\
&= (.80 \text{ MV})(.123434) + .03 \text{ MV} \\
&= .098747 \text{ MV} + .03 \text{ MV} \\
\$10,764 &= .128747 \text{ MV} \\
\$83,606 &= \text{MV}
\end{aligned}$$

5. *How much debt service commitment, on monthly and annual basis?*

	Monthly	Annual
1st $52,000, 21 years, 10% monthly	$494.41	$5,932.92
2nd $30,000, interest only, 1%/mo. (6 yr. term)	300.00	3,600.00
Total Debt Service	$794.41	$9,532.92

6. *Total housing expense commitment?*

	Monthly	Annual
Total debt service	$794.41	$9,533
Insurance and taxes (3% of $91,000)	227.50	2,730
	$1,021.91	$12,263

7. *Closing cost commitment?*

Purchase price	$91,000
Less loans	82,000
Equals down payment required	$9,000
Plus other closing costs	2,000
Total cash required for closing	$11,000

8. *Risks incurred by Chapmans?*

The Chapmans could only afford $10,764 in the first year for housing expenses according to the FHLMC guidelines. Yet, they committed to $12,263; the difference is $1,499. The excess over the 25% of income ($10,000) is $2,263. Their income is expected to go up 10% per year ($4,000 and $4,400 in the next two years). Thus, in two years they should be able to afford $12,100 for housing expense, which is in line with their commitment. At the same time, they now have $4,000 in savings for emergencies or contingencies.

Their second big risk is the $30,000 note due in six years, at the time they expect to have children. They need to refinance in three to five years in such a way that they will be able to afford their housing after starting their family. A sharp increase in interest rates might make this extremely difficult.

9. *Are the Chapmans in serious difficulty?*

Probably not! They are near their limits of their financial capability, like most families buying their first house. At the same time they have savings in reserves and possible loans from friends and relatives. Few families acquire homes without risk. If economic times worked against them, Merritt Chapman might have to work longer than planned, however.

CHAPTER 22: CALCULATIONS FOR BUYING AND SELLING EXISTING LOANS

1. *Conditions under which a loan sells at a premium? Discount?*

A loan sells at a premium when the current market interest rate is below the contract or face interest rate of a loan. This is because the lower the interest rate, the greater the present value of a stream of payment. A loan sells at a discount when the market rate exceeds the contract rate.

2. *Does prepayment raise or lower the discount on a loan? Explain.*

Expected prepayment lowers the amount of a discount. Prepayment means that payments are discounted at the lower face rate for a portion of the loan period, raising their present value. Determining the market value of the loan then involves finding the present value of the debt service plus the present value of the prepayment, both discounted at the higher market rate.

3. *Distinguish between discount rate and percent loan discount. Relationship between two?*

The discount rate is the opposite of the compound interest rate to calculate future value. The percent discount on a loan means the market value is less than the face value because the market interest rate is higher than the contract interest rate. Both involve TVM considerations and both mean a reduction in value.

4. *What is the internal rate of return?*

IRR is the rate of return or discount that makes the present value of all payments including initial cash outlay equal to zero. Alternatively, IRR is the rate that makes the discounted value of all future receipts exactly equal to the initial investment at time zero.

5. *A $20,000 loan is sold for $19,250.*

    (a) *Discount or premium?*   Discount

    (b) *What dollar discount*
       or premium? $750 = $20,000 − $19,250.

    (c) *What percentage discount*
       or premium?   % Discount $= \dfrac{\$ \text{Discount}}{\text{Face Value}} = \dfrac{\$750}{20,000} = 3.75\%$

    (d) *How many basis points?*   One percent equals 100 basis points, so
                                       375 basis points involved.

6. *Market vs. contract interest rate?*

    Market rate is rate at which loans are currently being made. Contract rate is rate agreed to when loan was initiated, which presumably was the market rate at that time.

7. *Uniontown Federal S & L $200,000. 25 years. 12% monthly.*
Loan commitment 8 months ago. Current market rate is 14%.

    (Slight variation in answers to be expected depending on TVM factors used and number of decimal places carried.)

    (a) *$ and % discount, w/o prepayment*

    Market value = $174,989

    % Discount $= \dfrac{\$ \text{Discount}}{\text{Face Value}} = \dfrac{\$25,011}{\$200,000} = \underline{12.51\%}$

    (b) *Prepayments, EOY 10. What $ and % Discount?*

    Market value = $135,667 + $43,633   = $179,300

    % Discount $= \dfrac{\$ \text{Discount}}{\text{Face Value}} = \dfrac{\$20,700}{\$200,000} = \underline{10.35\%}$

    (c) *Difference in discounts?* $4,311 or 2.16%.
       Difference is due to prepayment assumption.

    (d) To gain liquidity to make new loans and to build revenues from loan servicing. Loan may have been originated for immediate resale based on commitment obtained eight months earlier.

8. *Third National Bank of Arkansas. $40,000. 12% monthly. 25 years. Four years ago. Current rate is 10% monthly.*

    (a) *What dollar premium?* Loan has 21 years to maturity. Assuming no prepayment, market value is $421.29 debt service discounted over 21 years at 10%, or $44,310.
       $ premium $44,310 − $38,697 = $5,613.

    (b) *Percent premium?* $\dfrac{\$\ 5,613}{\$38,697} = 14.51\%$

9. *Standard LIC buys loan in question 7 for $184,304.*

   (a) *What IRR, assuming no prepayment.*
   $$\$184{,}304 = \$2{,}106.45 \times \text{PV1/P}^{\,x\% \text{ mo.}}_{25 \text{ years}}$$

   $$\text{PV1/P}^{\,x\% \text{ mo.}}_{24 \text{ yr.}} = 87{,}495.075 \times \% = \underline{13.2}$$

   (b) *Prepayment increase or decrease rate of return?*
   Increase. Debt service would be discounted at lower rate for portion of the contract term.

   (c) *IRR with prepayment at EOY8.*
   $$\$184{,}305 = (\$2{,}106.45 \times \text{PV1/P}^{\,x\% \text{ mo.}}_{8 \text{ yr.}}) + (\$182{,}976 \times \text{PV1}^{\,x\% \text{ mo.}}_{8 \text{ yr.}})$$

   $$x\% = \underline{\underline{13.66\%}} \text{ (by calculator)}$$

By interpolation:

Target

12%	$200,000
$x\%$	184,304
14%	181,349

$$x\% = 12\% + 2\% \left(\frac{15{,}696}{18{,}651}\right)$$

$$= 12\% + 2\% \, (.84155)$$
$$= 13.68\%$$

10. *IRR? $40,000 loan purchased at $42,000, assuming prepayment EOY12.*
    IRR = $\underline{11.2\%}$

11. *Match key terms and definitions.*

    (a) 5   (b) 2   (c) 4   (d) 6   (e) 3

CHAPTER 23: FEDERAL CREDIT AGENCIES AND MORTGAGE-BACKED SECURITIES IN THE SECONDARY MORTGAGE MARKET

1. *FNMA obtains funds?*
   Mainly sale of bonds and short term notes. Also, common stock. FNMA earns income from commitment fees and interest on mortgage loans held.

2. *FNMA commitments?*

   (a) *Optional delivery* (four months, with delivery at option of seller).
   (b) *Mandatory delivery* (delivery is required).
   The commitments are issued under the free market system, meaning competitive bids at an auction.

3. *Main function of FHLMC? Source of funds?*
   Provide secondary mortgage market for conventional residential mortgages by sale of mortgage backed securities, such as mortgage participation certifi-

cates and guaranteed mortgage certificates. May also borrow from Federal Home Loan Banks.

4. *What does GNMA do? Function? Source of funds?*

GNMA operates the mortgage purchase program and the mortgage backed securities program. GNMA guarantees payment on mortgage backed securities issued by others; also GNMA issues mortgage backed securities and sells mortgages to obtain funds. May also borrow from the U. S. Treasury. GNMA also has a special assistance function, as loans to finance subsidized housing for low and moderate income families and for minorities. Also, at times, to stimulate residential construction.

5. *Tandem plan?*

Tandem plan is purchase of BMIR loans by GNMA at or close to par for resale to FNMA at market value. Discount or difference between the two amounts is absorbed by GNMA. Allows more financing than if GNMA bought and held the mortgages.

6. *Mortgage-backed security? How does system work?*

Mortgage-backed securities are certificates backed by specific mortgage loans issued by holders of the loans. In effect, ownership of the loans is sold along with an agreement by the holder to service the loans and to pass along income as it is received.

Mortgage-backed securities therefore convert mortgage loans into a general type security that may be owned without demand to look after the loan and that may be bought and sold in our financial markets.

7. *What mortgage loans qualify as support for a mortgage-backed security?*

FHA insured, VA guaranteed, and conventional loans may all be used to support a mortgage-backed security. The conventional loans may be insured or uninsured. The securities may be guaranteed by GNMA, issued by FHLMC or FmHA, and by private underwriters. The loans in a pool supporting a security must be relatively homogeneous as to property pledged as security, maturity, and interest rate. Thus, a pool may be made up of loans on single family properties at 12-½% interest with from 22 to 23 years to maturity.

8. *Match key terms and definitions.*

(a) 2   (b) 4   (c) 5   (d) 6   (e) 7   (f) 3

Index

Balloon payment, 388
Basket clause, 187
Basket mortgage loan, 52
Blanket mortgage loan, 48
Borrower's right to reinstate
    clause, 72
Breakeven occupancy ratio, 356–
    57
Budget mortgage loan, 47
Buy-down mortgage loan, 52,
    366–67, 372

C

Chattel mortgage loan, 47, 49
Civil Rights Act of 1968, 254
Cognovit provision, 74
Commercial bank (CB), 150, 152,
    164, 170, 175–80, 182, 184,
    189, 192–93, 204, 209, 400
  lending policies, 177–80
  regulation of, 175–79, 311–12
Community Reinvestment Act
    (CRA), 254
Comptroller of the Currency,
    175, 177, 254, 311
Construction mortgage loan,
    37–9, 76, 89, 168, 174, 178–
    80, 187, 190, 194, 256, 283
Consumer Checking Account
    Equity Act, 160
Consumer Credit Protection Act,
    254
Consumer Price Index, 168
Conventional mortgage loan;
    30–2, 157, 169, 173, 187,
    193, 209–10, 239–40, 297,
    337, 402, 404
Convertible mortgage loan, 50
Cooperative Farm Credit System,
    205–206
Covenant of seizin, 66
Credit financing, 9
Credit loan, 133
Credit report, 241, 293, 294–95

Credit union, 150, 154, 160–61,
    164, 180–82

D

Debt financing, 222–30, 303–18,
    341–58
  calculation, 335–36
  defined, 9
Debt, net public and private, 3,
    147
Debt service calculations, 392–93
Debt service coverage ratio, 355–
    56
Debt-to-capital ratio, 401
Deed in lieu of foreclosure, 26,
    86
Deed of trust: *see* FNMA-FHLMC
    uniform instruments, deed
    of trust; Trust deed
Default: *see* Foreclosure;
    Mortgage procedures,
    default
Default in prior mortgage
    clause, 76
Defeasance clause, 18, 20, 74
Deficiency judgment, 25, 94–5,
    114, 124, 280
Demand mortgage loan, 42
Department of Agriculture, 205,
    207
Department of Housing and
    Urban Development
    (HUD), 33, 107, 149, 154,
    200, 205, 209, 216, 258, 401
  settlement statement, 247,
    248–49, 250, 257
Deposit insurance, 203–204
Depository institutions, 161,
    164–82, 276, 278, 281, 285
  characteristics, 182
  regulation of, 159–61
Depository Institutions
    Deregulation Act (DIDA),
    160

Mortgage loans (*cont.*)

graduated payment (GPM), 45–6, 169, 174, 179, 216–17, 282, 362, 365–66

income participation: *see* Mortgage loans, equity participation

junior, 40, 57, 75–6, 169, 179, 281

land acquisition, 37

land development, 37, 76, 168

leasehold, 48–9, 133–34, 137–38, 169, 174, 179, 187, 230

open-end, 51–2, 89

package, 47–8

partially amortizing, 43, 168, 304, 312, 315–17

participation, 49–50, 210

permanent, 39

pledged savings account (PAL), 45–6, 48

purchase money (PMM), 32, 89, 123–35

real estate, 20–2, 47

regular, 20

renegotiable-rate (RRM), 3, 169, 174, 179, 238, 285, 312, 362, 365

reverse annuity (RAM), 51

senior, 40

shared appreciation (SAM), 50–1, 282, 284, 315–16, 362, 366

straight-term, 42, 306–308, 313, 366

tandem, 380

VA: see Veterans Administration, mortgage loans

variable-rate (VRM), 3, 30, 46, 57, 169, 174, 179, 238, 275, 280, 282, 284–85, 311, 362, 365

warehouse, 190

wraparound (WAM), 41, 370–71

Mortgage market:

defined, 146

participants, 148–49, 150–54

secondary, 399–413

Mortgage note: *see* FNMA-FHLMC uniform instruments

Mortgage procedures, 20–6

assignment, 25

assumption, 25

default, 59, 81–99, 133

(*See also* Foreclosure)

foreclosure: *see* Foreclosure

recording, 23–4, 242–43

servicing, 192

termination, 26

transfer, 24–5

Mortgage Subsidy Bond and Interest Exclusion Tax Act of 1980, 219

Mutual savings bank (MSB), 150–52, 155, 160–61, 164, 170–76, 182, 189, 191, 400

history, 170–71

lending policies, 172–75

organization, 171

regulation of, 171

Mutual Savings Central Fund of Massachusetts, Inc., 171

N

National Association of Realtors, 361–62

National Credit Union Administration, 180

National Credit Union Share Insurance Fund (NCUSIF), 180, 203–204

National Flood Insurance Act, 257–58

Negotiated order of withdrawal account (NOW), 159–60, 166, 172, 202

Net operating income (NOI), 305, 317–18, 352, 378

Senior mortgage loan, 40
Service corporation, 170
Settlement statement: *see*
    Department of Housing
    and Urban Development,
    settlement statement
Shared appreciation mortgage
    loan (SAM), 50–51, 282,
    248, 315–16, 362, 366
Small Business Administration,
    95, 168
Soldiers and Sailors Civil Relief
    Act, 98–9
Sole security clause, 77
Standard and Poors, 413–14
Statutory redemption laws, 19,
    95–6
Straight-term mortgage loan, 42,
    306–308, 313, 366
Subchapter S corporation, 228–29
Subordination clause, 76
Subrogation of rights provision,
    69
Substitute trustee clause, 112
Syndicate: *see* Equity financing,
    syndicate

T

Take-over clause, 77
Tandem mortgage loan, 380
Tandem plan: *see* Government
    National Mortgage
    Association, tandem plan
Tax-exempt organization, 140
Time value of money factor
    (TVM), 303, 321–23, 384–96,
    451–70
Title theory of mortgage law, 19,
    87
Torrens certificate, 244
Torrens system, 244
Trust deed, 21, 30, 74, 81, 102–14,
    304, 369, 376
    defined, 10

Trust deed (*cont.*)
    FHA, 107
    foreclosure, 113–14
    use, 104–106
    (*See also* FNMA-FHLMC
    uniform instruments, deed
    of trust)
Truth in Lending Act (TIL), 161,
    224, 234, 254–56

U

Underwriter, 223–50, 260–71,
    352–53
    defined, 233
Underwriting, 233–50, 277,
    352–55, 358, 379
    defined, 233
    Federal Home Loan Mortgage
    Corporation (FHLMC)
    guidelines, 290–301, 363,
    372, 378
Uniform Commercial Code, 47
Uniform instruments: *see*
    FNMA-FHLMC uniform
    instruments
Usury laws, 258

V

Variable-rate mortgage loan
    (VRM), 3, 30, 46, 57, 169,
    174, 179, 238, 275, 280, 282,
    284–85, 311, 362, 365
Veterans Administration (VA),
    34–5, 95–6, 98, 137, 168,
    173, 178, 181, 190, 210–12, 233
    history, 210–11
    mobile home loans, 49
    mortgage loans, 2–3, 30–1,
    34–5, 56, 60, 71, 82, 84, 95,
    156–57, 168, 170, 173, 175,
    178–79, 181, 189–91,
    208–12, 227, 258, 285,
    337–38, 401, 404, 413

W